# Lost Londons

*Lost Londons* is a major new study of the transformation of early modern London. By focusing on policing, prosecution, and the language and perceptions of the authorities and the underclasses, Paul Griffiths explores the swift growth of London and the changes to its cultures, communities, and environments. Through a series of thematic chapters he maps problem areas and people; reconstructs the atmosphere of the streets; and traces the development of policing in the city. The book provides the first full study of petty crime before 1660, analysing worlds and words of crime, criminal rings and cultures, and tracking changing meanings of crime to reveal new emphases on environmental crimes and crimes committed by women. It also examines the key roles of Bridewell prison, hospitals, medical provision, and penal practices, shedding new light on investigation, detection, surveillance, and public prosecution. Viewed through this unique account, the city will never look the same again.

PAUL GRIFFITHS is Associate Professor of Early Modern British Cultural and Social History at the History Department, Iowa State University. His previous publications include *Youth and Authority: Formative Experiences in England, 1560–1640* (1996), winner of the Royal Historical Society's Whitfield Prize, and, as co-editor, *Penal Practice and Culture, 1500–1900: Punishing the English* (2004).

*Cambridge Social and Cultural Histories*

Series editors:
Margot C. Finn, *University of Warwick*
Colin Jones, *University of Warwick*
Keith Wrightson, *Yale University*

New cultural histories have recently expanded the parameters (and enriched the methodologies) of social history. Cambridge Social and Cultural Histories recognizes the plurality of current approaches to social and cultural history as distinctive points of entry into a common explanatory project. Open to innovative and interdisciplinary work, regardless of its chronological or geographical location, the series encompasses a broad range of histories of social relationships and of the cultures that inform them and lend them meaning. Historical anthropology, historical sociology, comparative history, gender history, and historicist literary studies – among other subjects – all fall within the remit of Cambridge Social and Cultural Histories.

Titles in the series include:

1. Margot C. Finn *The Character of Credit: Personal Debt in English Culture, 1740–1914*
2. M. J. D. Roberts *Making English Morals: Voluntary Association and Moral Reform in England, 1787–1886*
3. Karen Harvey *Reading Sex in the Eighteenth Century: Bodies and Gender in English Erotic Culture*
4. Phil Withington *The Politics of Commonwealth: Citizens and Freemen in Early Modern England*
5. Mark S. Dawson *Gentility and the Comic Theatre of Late Stuart London*
6. Julie-Marie Strange *Death, Grief and Poverty in Britain, 1870–1914*
7. Sujit Sivasundaram *Nature and the Godly Empire: Science and Evangelical Mission in the Pacific, 1795–1850*
8. Rod Edmond *Leprosy and Empire: A Medical and Cultural History*
9. Susan K. Morrissey *Suicide and the Body Politic in Imperial Russia*
10. Carolyn Steedman *Master and Servant: Love and Labour in the English Industrial Age*
11. Joseph Clarke *Commemorating the Dead in Revolutionary France: Revolution and Remembrance, 1789–1799*

# Lost Londons

*Change, Crime, and Control in the Capital City, 1550–1660*

Paul Griffiths
*Iowa State University*

CAMBRIDGE UNIVERSITY PRESS
Cambridge, New York, Melbourne, Madrid, Cape Town, Singapore, São Paulo

Cambridge University Press
The Edinburgh Building, Cambridge CB2 8RU, UK

Published in the United States of America by Cambridge University Press, New York

www.cambridge.org
Information on this title: www.cambridge.org/9780521885249

© Paul Griffiths 2008

This publication is in copyright. Subject to statutory exception
and to the provisions of relevant collective licensing agreements,
no reproduction of any part may take place without
the written permission of Cambridge University Press.

First published 2008

Printed in the United Kingdom at the University Press, Cambridge

*A catalogue record for this publication is available from the British Library*

*Library of Congress Cataloguing in Publication data*
Griffiths, Paul, 1960–
Lost London: change, crime, and control in the capital city, 1550–1660/ Paul Griffiths.
p. cm. – (Cambridge social and cultural histories)
Includes bibliographical references and index.
ISBN 978-0-521-88524-9
1. Crime – England – London – History – 16th century.  2. Crime – England – London – History – 17th century.  3. Law enforcement – England – London – History – 16th century.  4. Law enforcement – England – London – History – 17th century.  I. Title.
HV6950.L7G85   2008
364.942109′031–dc22
                                                              2007051671

ISBN 978-0-521-88524-9 hardback

Cambridge University Press has no responsibility for the persistence or
accuracy of URLs for external or third-party internet websites referred to
in this book, and does not guarantee that any content on such
websites is, or will remain, accurate or appropriate.

For Bob Scribner (1941–1998)

I touched all sides, and nobody knew where I belonged.
> Saul Bellow, *The Adventures of Augie March* (1995), pp. 132–3.

Yet there is a sure and necessary empowerment in naming things. Words – and numbers too – may be weightless, as insubstantial as light, yet they are terribly powerful: they can start a war, order the strip-mining of a mountain, or trigger the secretion of endorphins. And names allow us to possess our environment and manipulate it in scaffolds of thought and design.
> David G. Campbell, *A Land of Ghosts: The Braided Lives of People and the Forest in Far Western Amazonia* (Boston and New York, 2005), pp. 144–5.

'People don't like to have their categories threatened', says Taylor. 'They like to think, "That's a moth" and "That's a fly". Fixed categories. They don't like to think of lots of hybridizing and change all the time'.
> Jonathan Weiner, *The Beak of the Finch: A Story of Evolution in Our Time* (New York, 1994), p. 257.

This city can be known only by an activity of the ethnographic kind: you must orient yourself in it not by book, by address, but by walking, by sight, by habit, by experience; here every discovery is intense and fragile, it can be repeated or recovered only by memory of the trace it has left in you: to visit a place for the first time is thereby to begin to write it: the address not being written, it must establish its own writing.
> Roland Barthes, *Empire of Signs*, trans. Richard Howard (New York, 1982), p. 36.

In the anonymous city, in the close quarters of the slum, the overriding interest is law and order, stability.
> Suketa Mehta, *Maximum City: Bombay Lost and Found* (New York, 2004), p. 64.

# Contents

*Maps and tables*     *page* ix
*Abbreviations*     xi
*Preface*     xiii

Introduction: Rhetorics and records     1

**Part I    Change**     25

1   Troubled times     27
2   Mapping troubles     67
3   Streets     98

**Part II    Crime**     135

4   Crime: worlds     137
5   Crime: words     179

**Part III    Control**     211

6   Court days     213
7   Bodies     253
8   Policing: people and policy     291
9   Policing: night battles     332

| 10 | Policing: process and prosecution | 361 |
| 11 | Policing: knowledge | 400 |
|  | Conclusion | 433 |
|  | *Appendix* | 438 |
|  | *Bibliography* | 475 |
|  | *Index* | 514 |

# Maps and tables

| | | |
|---|---|---|
| Map 1 | London's wards | *page* 443 |
| Map 2 | Locations of arrests by 'public' officers by ward, 1604–1658 | 444 |
| Map 3 | Locations of arrests of vagrants by ward, 1604–1658 | 445 |
| Map 4 | Locations of arrests of thieves by ward, 1604–1658 | 446 |
| Map 5 | Locations of arrests of nightwalkers and people walking late by ward, 1604–1658 | 447 |
| Map 6 | Locations of arrests of beggars by ward, 1604–1658 | 448 |
| Table 1a | Household offences prosecuted at Bridewell, 1605–1657 | 449 |
| Table 1b | Hospital offences prosecuted at Bridewell, 1605–1657 | 450 |
| Table 2a | Sexual offences prosecuted at Bridewell, 1605–1657 | 451 |
| Table 2b | Alehouse disorders prosecuted at Bridewell, 1605–1657 | 452 |
| Table 2c | Religious offences prosecuted at Bridewell, 1605–1657 | 452 |
| Table 3a | Violence and abuse cases prosecuted at Bridewell, 1605–1657 | 453 |
| Table 3b | Lifestyle and character offences prosecuted at Bridewell, 1605–1657 | 454 |
| Table 3c | Officer abuse and political offences prosecuted at Bridewell, 1605–1657 | 455 |
| Table 4a | Illicit movement prosecuted at Bridewell, 1605–1657 | 456 |
| Table 4b | Traffic and street-selling offences prosecuted at Bridewell, 1605–1657 | 457 |
| Table 5a | Theft and cozening prosecuted at Bridewell, 1605–1657 | 458 |
| Table 6a | Number of prosecuted offences in overall categories, 1605–1657 | 459 |

| | | |
|---|---|---|
| Table 7a | Labels recorded in Bridewell's courtbooks by gender, 1559–1657 | 460 |
| Table 7b | Labels recorded in Bridewell's courtbooks by individual volume | 465 |
| Table 7c | Selected labels revealing rising female labelling | 466 |
| Table 8a | Bridewell committals by categories, 1559–1658 | 467 |
| Table 8b | Leading sources of Bridewell committals, percentage changes | 468 |
| Table 8c | Committals to Bridewell by 'public' officers, 1559–1658 | 469 |
| Table 8d | All sources of Bridewell committals, 1604–1658 | 470 |
| Table 9a | Offences of Bridewell prisoners ordered to be transported, 1604–1658 | 472 |
| Table 9b | Destinations of Bridewell prisoners ordered to be transported | 473 |
| Table 9c | Offences of Bridewell prisoners pressed into armies, 1604–1658 | 474 |

# Abbreviations

| | |
|---|---|
| APC | J. R. Dasent *et al* eds., *Acts of the Privy Council*, 46 vols. (1890–1964) |
| BHC | Bridewell and Bethlem Hospital Courtbooks |
| BL | British Library, London |
| BRHA | Bethlem Royal Hospital Archives and Museum |
| CLRO | Corporation of London Record Office |
| CSPV | Calendar of State Papers Venetian |
| CQSF | City of London Quarter Sessions Files |
| GCL | Goldsmiths' Company Library |
| GL | Guildhall Library, London |
| HOL | House of Lords Record Office |
| Jour | Journal of London Common Council |
| LMA | London Metropolitan Archives |
| MP | House of Lords Main Papers |
| TNA | National Archives |
| NOTTRO | Nottinghamshire Record Office |
| Rep | Repertory of the London Court of Aldermen |
| SBHA | St Bartholomew's Hospital Archive, London |
| SCH | Stationers' Company Hall |
| SP | State Papers Domestic |
| SRPC | J. F. Larkin, ed., *Stuart Royal Proclamations, Volume II: Proclamations of King Charles I, 1625–1646* (Oxford, 1983) |
| SRPJ | J. F. Larkin and P. L. Hughes, eds., *Stuart Royal Proclamations, Volume 1: Royal Proclamations of King James I, 1603–25* (Oxford, 1973) |
| STAC | Star Chamber |
| TRP | P. L. Hughes and J. F. Larkin, eds., *Tudor Royal Proclamations, Volume 3, The Later Tudors, 1588–1603* (New Haven and London, 1969) |
| TT | Thomason Tracts |
| WAC | Westminster Archives Centre |

# Preface

Cities were moods, emotional states, for the most part collective distortions, where human beings thrived and suffered, where they invested their souls in pains and pleasures, taking these pleasures and pains as proofs of reality. (Saul Bellow, *The Dean's December* (1998), p. 285).

I want to think of London four centuries or so ago as a city to imagine or perceive. A city that existed in the mind, as well as in wood or brick. One where perceptions of its current state made all the difference for which policy to follow or crime to track down. And a city packed with people who we should evaluate on their own terms, their own senses of what London meant for them, because when all is said and done it was these perceptions that led to each one of the policies and prosecutions that we can count and measure today.

Bellow writes of any city in plurals, as 'moods', 'states', or 'distortions'. Sixteenth- and seventeenth-century London, too, was a city of pluralities and multiplicities. It was a city marked by difference, needless to say: differing experiences, impressions, standards of living, hopes, and failures. There is no such thing as a single London, except for what it meant to each one of the many thousands who traipsed along its streets each day of the week. Of course London was a physical city, a known space to walk or ride around, but it was also a city to see, take in, perceive, and police if anything was to be done about the growing numbers of vagrants streaming in through its seven gates. In this book London is a city imagined as well as experienced, imagined in mental maps that helped people to get from one place to another, in terms of bright or gloomy impressions of civic prestige and authority, or in more pathological terms as a condition: stable, healthy, unsteady, stormy, or in a mess. There are many more perceptions in the chapters that follow, but for now I want to spell out the significances of images of civic 'fame' and the condition of the city. When I speak of 'Lost Londons' or losing London I am thinking of a train of thought that claimed loudly and clearly that London was suffering a slump in prestige and power in the midst of a population boom and migrant influx that gathered pace from about the middle of the sixteenth century. Lost Londons because the city had to be constantly reimagined as one change followed quickly on the heels of another. These same conditions led to perceptions that London was living through 'extraordinary' troubled times with one crime-wave after another, all the more interesting because they were expressed in terms of first-hand observation, immediacy, or 'experience'. The ties between rhetorics and perceptions of declining civic 'fame' and London's troubles are in many ways the crux of this book. I see them tellingly revealed in thinking about crime and criminal cultures, anti-foreigner (migrant) points of view, the City's crusade to spruce up its 'filthy' and tatty parts, the need for a bridewell to come down hard on the shifty poor, and frequent efforts to improve policing. The meanings (and perceptions) of decline and crime/crime control were more or less synonymous at times. In this book, therefore, I explore law and order to learn more about larger London, the city that was growing and changing quickly, with too many negative side-effects, magistrates thought at the time.

*Lost Londons* is divided into three unequal sections: three chapters on change, two more on crime, and six on control. The first five cover London's troubles. The second six look at the other side of the coin: steps to keep on top of London's mass and mess. The opening chapters look at London's troubles, streets, geographies, and environments at length, and offer new ideas about conditions and cultures there. London's growth and resulting problems are charted in perceptions first of all, before a more empirical examination of troubles that derived directly from quick growth – building without permission, for example, lodging inmates with no roots in London, vagrants and drifting 'big bellied women', and abandoning small children – that all peaked around 1625. I turn next to mapping troubles for better senses of the breeding grounds of crime. The streets are a common thread between growth that was evident up and down their length and breadth and rising crime that left magistrates sometimes holding their hands up in the air in despair. Visuality and visibility were significant for conceptions of crime and the city, and Chapter 3 is about the hustle and bustle on the streets which was the most public sign of both: traffic speeding along all day, beggars pestering passers-by, vagrants walking up and down, unsettled and unwanted, and women (mostly) selling anything from fish to pans all through the city, breaking laws, but needing money to get by. All this activity is a sign of a bigger and busier city, and of vagrant and begging cultures that took root steadily. Next in line is a thick analysis and description of the worlds and words of crime (Chapters 4–5), mixing and mingling vagrants, thieves, prostitutes, and others who caught the eye of magistrates. Chapter 4 for the first time turns to widespread archival sources for the full century after 1550 to think once more about the case for criminal underworlds existing in London at this time. Its companion chapter digs deep into labelling languages and processes to track changing meanings of crime from 1560 on. These meanings took a different course after 1600: one new path tilted towards crimes directly related to speedy growth; another, less predictable, was the much greater female involvement in London's troubles.

Policing and prosecution are the leading subjects of the second half of this book. If they got caught and were unlucky enough to end up in court, most vagrants and thieves spent some time in Bridewell, London's main lock-up for petty criminals that took in its first prisoners in 1555. To help us better situate this new prison in London, I spend time in Chapter 6 thinking about attitudes towards it in a range of constituencies from polished legalese to street talk, partly to pick up more about what Londoners thought about crackdowns on crime. A variety of attitudes from warm support to intense legal scepticism are considered not alone but with reference to Bridewell's process and regime (also weighed up with regard to other courts and hospitals/prisons). The next chapter examines the treatment of bodies in Bridewell: looking at cleanliness, sanitation, medical care, bodily discipline, examining bodies for evidence, and punishment. Bridewell also had a policing role, in a minor way with its own beadles, but more importantly with its tight ties to existing policing when it first opened, and later on as it became more heavily involved in attempts to improve policing. The final four chapters cover policing the fast growing city, looking in turn at the men who held office and policies that poured out from the Guildhall (Chapter 8), trouble and policing after dark (Chapter 9), processes of arrest and prosecution (Chapter 10), and some ways in which magistrates made highly effective use of surveillance and records to keep tabs on London's escalating social ills (Chapter 11). My main aim in these last four chapters is to show policing *in action*, with the practical purpose of watching strategies develop over time. I do not dwell for long on the backgrounds of officers or a piece-by-piece institutional inquiry, but seek to get out onto the streets and into courtbooks to show that London would have been in far worse shape without policing that was surprisingly capable and quick-witted. This is first and foremost a book on crime and control, then, but always with larger London in mind. London's growth and changes are the background canvas for each piece of policy and each one of the 40,000 or so crimes that are the mainstay of this book.

I began work on *Lost Londons* not long after I became a research fellow at Clare College, Cambridge, in Autumn 1991. Clare was a perfect place to get cracking on it, and I will always be grateful to Clare's master and fellows for giving me a golden opportunity to do so. One of them, in particular, has been (and still is) critical to the development of my thinking on change, crime, and control in early modern England. Bob Scribner is sadly no longer with us, but he first helped me to get my foot in the door at Clare and later, in one sparkling conversation after another that continued up until his last Winter, kept changing my ideas with little gems of wisdom, always making his most forceful points in his softest voice. I dedicate this book to Bob's inspiring memory with deep thanks and happy memories. Roger Schofield has also given me all kinds of help from the time since we first met at Clare. Keith Wrightson supervised my 1992 Cambridge PhD thesis which was published as *Youth and Authority: Formative Experiences in England, 1560–1640* (Oxford, 1996), the time when I first thought long and hard about issues at the core of this book, and Keith has given me more guidance about them than he can ever imagine. No mention of the friends/scholars who have helped me the most over the last two decades or so could ever be complete without Ian Archer, John Beattie, Ian Gentles, Martin Ingram, Mark Jenner, Dave Postles, Dave Rollison, Jim Sharpe, and Andy Wood.

Money matters, too, and I have been lucky enough to get support to help research and write *Lost Londons* from Clare College (Cambridge), the British Academy, the University of Leicester, Iowa State University College of Liberal Arts and Science, the Office of the Vice President for Research and Economic Development, and Arts and Humanities Centre, the National Endowment of the Humanities, and the National Humanities Centre (NHC) in North Carolina, where I had the best part of a year to do nothing else except write in excellent company and with the sort of support that gives no excuse for not finishing something. The 2002–3 NHC fellows were a great bunch, but I would like to give special thanks to Ed Craun, Andy Delbanco, Ginger Frost, David Porter, Joanne Rappaport, Moshe Sluhovsky, and Harriet Ritvo, and our warm little group in the Renaissance seminar. The NHC staff were first-rate, just like the staff of the various archives I have worked in. I cannot be the only London historian who misses the old Corporation of London Record Office (CLRO) now that it too is a thing of the past, not least because Vivienne Aldous, Sophie Bridges, Hugo Deadman, Larry Francis, Philip Gale, Tim Harvey, Elizabeth Scudder, and Jim Sewell, did so much to help my research tick along. I think that I spent more time in the CLRO than any other archive, but the Guildhall Library, Manuscripts Division, was not far behind, and the same thanks for the same amount of help go to the people who have worked there ever since I first dropped in to read something in 1988. Thanks, too, to the staff at my other main ports-of-call: the London

Metropolitan Archives, Westminster Archive Centre, St Bartholomew's Hospital Archive, the Bethlem Royal Hospital Archives and Museum, the old Public Record Office (now The National Archives), British Library, and Cambridge University Rare Books Reading Room and Manuscripts Room (and especially Godfrey Waller). My warm thanks also to all who listened and offered suggestions when various versions of some chapters were presented at seminars and conferences in Boston, Brisbane, Cardiff, Cambridge, Durham, Flagstaff, Guelph, Leicester, London, the National Humanities Centre, New Orleans, Oxford, San Marino, Toronto, Victoria (British Columbia), and York. I hope that I haven't missed out anyone who gave references and suggestions, or just sat down to chat one day about something in this book: Kevin Amidon, Ian Archer, Phil Baker, John Beattie, Peter Borsay, Bernard Capp, David Cressy, Simon Devereaux, Adam Fox, Malcolm Gaskill, Laura Gowing, Vanessa Harding, Tim Harris, Cynthia Herrup, Steve Hindle, Tim Hitchcock, Martin Ingram, Mark Jenner, Peter King, Randall McGowen, John Morrill, John Monroe, Maggie Pelling, Dave Postles, Dave Rollison, Ulinka Rublack, Alan Stewart, Bob Tittler, Phil Withington, and Andy Wood have all made *Lost Londons* a better book. Ian Gentles, Mark Jenner, and Andrejs Plakans all read draft chapters, and I am deeply grateful to them, and even more so to Ian Archer, Moshe Sluhovsky, and Keith Wrightson, who slogged through the whole thing for me.

# Introduction: Rhetorics and records

## Lost Londons

'The world is sare chaunged', William Bullein wrote with wonder from London in 1564. 'She is growne so great, I am almost afraide to meddle with her', Donald Lupton wrote in 1632.[1] London's size and shape changed speedily, and people felt that they were losing the city that they once knew. The population inside and outside the walls nearly quadrupled between 1500–1600, reaching roughly 200,000, and it almost doubled over the next five decades to around 375,000. The city spilled over its walls, numbers on the eastern edges soared more than fourfold in the seventeenth century (90,000), and sixfold in the West End in 1600–40 (18,500). Deaths outnumbered births and London would have shrunk without migrants. Our best estimate is that somewhere in the region of 5,600 were needed each year around 1650 to keep growth on track. Maybe one-in-six of the English spent time in London, hoping to strike it lucky.[2]

---

[1] William Bullein *A Dialogue Both Pleasaunte and Piety-Full Against the Fever Pestilence* (1564), p. 7; Donald Lupton, *London and the Country Carbonadoed and Quartered Into Severall Characters*, 1632, The English Experience, 879 (Amsterdam and Norwood, NJ, 1977), p. 1.

[2] Roger Finlay, *Population and Metropolis: The Demography of London, 1580–1650* (Cambridge, 1981), chap. 3; Vanessa Harding, 'The population of London, 1550–1700: a review of the published evidence', *London Journal*, 15 (1990), 111–28; Steve Rappaport, *Worlds Within Worlds: Structures of Life in Sixteenth-Century London* (Cambridge, 1989), chap. 3; M. J. Power, 'The east London working community in the seventeenth century', in Penelope J. Corfield and Derek Keene, eds., *Work in Towns, 850–1850* (Leicester, 1990), pp. 103–20; Norman G. Brett-James, *The Growth of Stuart London* (1935), chaps 6–7; Jeremy Boulton, 'The poor among the rich: paupers and the parish in the West End, 1600–1724', in Paul Griffiths and Mark S. R. Jenner eds., *Londinopolis: Essays in the Cultural and Social History of Early Modern London* (Manchester, 2000), pp. 197–225, esp. pp. 200–1; E. A. Wrigley, 'A simple model of London's importance in changing English society and economy, 1650–1750', *Past and Present*, 37 (1967), 44–70. This, of course, was not the first time that London experienced dramatic growth. See Derek Keene, 'Material London in time and space', in Lena Cowen Orlin, ed., *Material London, ca. 1600* (Philadelphia, PA, 2000), pp. 55–74, esp. p. 58.

My title – *Lost Londons* – expresses in a couple of words the sense of loss as 'sare' growth changed familiar environments and cultures for ever.[3] Lupton 'quartered' London in the same year (1632) that aldermen looked to Whitehall for help when it became clear that the City freedom, once 'of very great esteem is [now] grown to be of little worth', cheapened by 'the extraordinary enlargement of the suburbs', 'multitudes' of new buildings 'on every side', and 'great numbers' of 'foreigners' from other counties and countries who settled outside the walls with the same 'benefits' as freemen, but without serving a single day as an apprentice.[4] By the second quarter of the seventeenth century City leaders felt that there was now nothing that they could do to stop growth. Too much had changed. Familiar things once taken for granted had now gone: skies now shrouded in smog, long-term job security for men with seven-year apprenticeships under their belts, or simply shopping in busy markets without nervous over-the-shoulder glances at huddles of thieves. London spilled over its walls, consuming green fields, and despite scores of City laws and orders, vagrants flooded in. London was so daunting that awestruck Lupton was 'almost afraide' to put pen to paper. The very sight of London would frighten me if my wife and friend did not live there, one man mused at around the same time.[5]

A sense of loss was widespread in print and policy. London changed so suddenly that nostalgia was a leading note in Stow's *Survey of London* (1598).[6] The past can seem sunnier, though Stow wrote with real feeling for a city now gone before epidemics of builders, inmates, and vagrants. Like others he looked back longingly to a time when care and community meant more. His judgment was not always sound, but fear of the new was common enough with aldermen who wrote policies not books.[7] Loss and regret led to action, and for a long while aldermen believed that they could reverse change. Stow's lost London was depicted as 'changeless' for four centuries before religious reform. His *Survey* was a leading work in 'a stabilizing urban consciousness' that put faith in permanence, sameness, and civic values in an otherwise

---

[3] This sense of loss is also vividly evoked in Ian Munro, *The Figure of the Crowd in Early Modern London: the City and its Double* (Basingstoke, 2005), pp. 27–9.
[4] TNA PC2/42/305–6.  [5] TNA SP16/423/19.
[6] Ian Archer, 'The nostalgia of John Stow', in David L. Smith, Richard Strier, and David Bevington, eds., *The Theatrical City: Culture, Theatre, and Politics in London, 1576–1649* (Cambridge, 1995), pp. 17–34; Patrick Collinson, 'John Stow and nostalgic antiquarianism', in J. F. Merritt, ed., *Imagining Early Modern London: Perceptions and Portrayals of the City from Stow to Strype, 1598–1720* (Cambridge, 2001), pp. 27–51.
[7] See below, pp. 27–47.

Introduction 3

changing world.[8] Nearly all things are in place. Wards are described one-by-one and Stow sings the praises of pillars of communities, landmarks, churches, or guilds. His London was walkable, and readers followed him along patternless small streets and main roads to track down monuments and stories.[9] All in all, his *Survey* was a picture of stability, and its steadiness and textbook account of authority were reassurances. Nostalgia was not just warmth for something lost, however. One of Stow's later editors said that he 'had a mighty concern for the reputation of the city', and that he was 'uneasy at some things in his time that abated it'.[10]

After Stow, Anthony Munday brought the *Survey* up to date – in 1618 and again in 1633 – and it remained a tribute to London's grand past and present, much like his eight scripts for mayors' parades.[11] It would have pleased Stow that three decades after his death institutions that he had thought of as civic bedrocks – guilds and parishes – forked out large sums for Munday's edition of his *Survey*. Stow had himself become a piece of nostalgia by now; he was 'old Stow'.[12] London was dramatized and described more often around 1600. Some writing adapted stresses and strains for the stage in crime scenes or pauper characters. Jonson wrote about 'sucking shifters' who plotted crime all day long. Scenes were set in Bridewell and Bethlem, symbols of rising crime and disorientation.[13]

---

[8] J. F. Merritt, 'Introduction: perceptions and portrayals of London, 1598–1720', in Merritt, ed., *Imagining Early Modern London*, pp. 1–24; James Knowles, 'The spectacle of the realm: civic consciousness, rhetoric and ritual in early modern London', in J. R. Mulryne and Margaret Shewring, eds., *Theatre and Government under the Stuarts* (Cambridge, 1993), pp. 157–89.

[9] Cynthia Wall, *The Literary and Cultural Spaces of Restoration London* (Cambridge, 1998), pp. 99, 101. Cf. Andrew McRae, '"On the famous voyage": Ben Jonson and civic space', in Andrew Gordon and Bernhard Klein eds., *Literature, Mapping and the Politics of Space in Early Modern Britain* (Cambridge, 2001), pp. 181–203, esp. p. 183.

[10] John Strype, *A Survey of the Cities of London and Westminster: Containing the Original, Antiquity, Increase, Modern Estate and Government of Those Cities, Written at First in the Year MDXCVIII by John Stow ... Corrected, Improved, and Very Much Enlarged: and the Survey and History Brought Down from the Year 1633*, 5 books in 2 vols. (1720), vol. I, p. xvii.

[11] J. F. Merritt, 'The reshaping of Stow's *Survey*: Munday, Strype, and the Protestant City', in Merritt, ed., *Imagining Early Modern London*, pp. 52–88, esp. p. 64.

[12] GL MSS 4383/1, fo. 191; 4071/2, fo. 39; 3907/1, 1618–19; 1002/1, fo. 431v; 959/1, fo. 137; GCL company minute books P, fo. 162; R2, fo. 21. See also Ian Archer, 'The arts and acts of memorialization in early modern London', in Merritt, ed., *Imagining Early Modern London*, pp. 89–113, esp. p. 92.

[13] Anne Barton, 'London comedy and the ethos of the city', *London Journal*, 4 (1978), 158–80; Lawrence Manley, *Literature and Culture in Early Modern London* (Cambridge, 1995), chaps 3 and 6–8; John Twyning, *London Dispossessed: Literature and Social Space in the Early Modern City* (Basingstoke, 1998), pp. 6, 28, 54; William C. Carroll, *Fat King, Lean Beggar: Representations of Poverty in the Age of Shakespeare* (Ithaca, NY, 1996), chap. 3; Carol Thomas Neely, *Distracted Subjects: Madness and Gender in Shakespeare and Early Modern Culture* (Ithaca, NY, 2004), chaps. 5–6.

4     Lost Londons

Rogue literature kept thieves and vagrants in the limelight. Dekker promised to bring 'notorious villanies' 'to light' and to name criminal 'tribes' 'over and over again' until people knew them off by heart. 'Read and learn, read and loathe', he told his readers.[14] These 'new fictions of urban settlement' helped people cope with unsettling change through descriptions in plays, comic spoofs, or pamphlet-journalism.[15] Like maps, literature made London seem negotiable. Stow's *Survey* was a portable prose map, and streets were 'uttered' more often in the *Cries* (1599) and *Cryes of London* (1614). Only a smallish number of city maps were drawn at this time, though there was a need for more as built-up areas mushroomed.[16] As with literature, maps 'laid a lucid order' over a city that was anything but still. They offered comfort, putting things in place, and trying to make change appear familiar all at once.[17]

Another form of 'corporate continuity' was the spate of printed histories of guilds that drew stable images of society and economy. Guilds funded them, as well as portraits of their great and good members, all part of what Archer calls 'the arts and acts of memorialization'.[18] There was more memorializing of this sort in civic bodies around 1600, as people turned to history for examples of confident and solid societies. The city's first 'remambrancer' – Thomas Norton – got the post in 1571. As with the Dick Whittington story that was more widely circulated at this

---

[14] Twyning, *London Dispossessed*, pp. 66–7, 63. See also Linda Woodbridge, *Vagrancy, Homelessness, and English Renaissance Literature* (Urbana and Chicago, IL, 2001); Gamini Salgado, *The Elizabethan Underworld* (Stroud, 1977); Manley, *Literature and Culture*, pp. 341–55; John L. McMullan, *The Canting Crew: London's Criminal Underworld, 1550–1750* (New Brunswick, NJ, 1984); G. M. Spraggs, 'Rogues and vagabonds in English literature, 1552–1642', unpublished PhD thesis, University of Cambridge (1980).

[15] Eric Wilson, 'Plagues, fairs, and street cries: sounding out society and space in early modern London', *Modern Language Studies*, 25, (1995), 1–42; McRae, '"On the famous voyage"', p. 182; Knowles, 'Spectacle of the realm', p. 162; Manley, *Literature and Culture*, pp. 130, 126, 77; Jean E. Howard, *Theater of a City: the Places of London Comedy, 1598–1642* (Philadelphia, PA, 2007), pp. 4–14.

[16] Sean Shesgreen, *Images of the Outcast: the Urban Poor in the Cries of London* (New Brunswick, NJ, 2002), esp. chaps 1–2; Wilson, 'Plagues, fairs, and street cries', 30; Andrew Gordon, 'Performing London: the map and the city in ceremony', in Gordon and Klein, eds., *Literature, Mapping and the Politics of Space*, pp. 69–88; Wall, *Literary and Cultural Spaces of Restoration London*, pp. 78, 86.

[17] Cynthia Wall, '"At Sheakespear's-Head, over-against Catharine-Street in the Strand": forms of address in London streets', in Tim Hitchcock and Heather Shore, eds., *The Streets of London from the Great Fire to the Great Stink* (2003), pp. 10–26, esp. p. 13; Wall, *Literary and Cultural Spaces of Restoration London*, p. 80. Cf. Helen Mills, 'Mapping the early modern city', *Urban History*, 23 (1996), 145–70; Rhonda Lemke Sanford, *Maps and Memory in Early Modern England: a Sense of Place* (Basingstoke, 2002).

[18] Ian Anders Gadd, 'Early modern printed histories of the London livery companies', in Gadd and Patrick Wallis, eds., *Guilds, Society, and Economy in London, 1450–1800* (2002), pp. 29–50, esp. p. 44.

Introduction 5

time, history strengthened spirits of citizenship and solidarity.[19] Civic funerals also became more impressive, with marches arranged according to status. Tomb inscriptions listed at length the worthy acts of good magistrates, and ministers also lauded charitable works in funeral sermons. Stow spoke proudly of London's charitable spirit, and others took turns after him at Spital sermons and other pulpits to praise a proud protestant city that rated greatness by giving. The more money citizens spend 'the more honour' they bring 'unto our citie', Richard Johnson bragged in 1607.[20]

Civic ceremonies also stressed both unity and continuities with an ordered past.[21] More money was spent on parades and more fulsome verses when the freedom was no longer the shining light of yesteryear that had made people feel proud and protected. Once a modest horseback parade, the mayor's autumn welcome into office developed into the highpoint of the civic year by 1600, with long processions of governors and guilds in rank order, highly crafted montages, dazzling colours, day-long dancing and music to keep crowds in high spirits, and leading dramatists vying to come up with scripts for pageants. All this effort and show to inflate civic 'fame' at a total cost often above £1,000 came at the same time that suburbs mushroomed. But the civic map of display was located within the walls. There was no wish to celebrate larger metropolitan identities incorporating the ribbon-developments that sapped specific senses of civic identity. This day, that City magistrates hoped would stick in minds all year long, looked backwards and forwards to present images of a prosperous and united city, in stark contrast to the dark forebodings of trouble and loss that reverberated throughout the rest of the year.[22] A more sprightly civic consciousness was also signified in

---

[19] LMA Rep. 17, fos. 101v-2; James Robertson, 'The adventures of Dick Whittington and the social construction of Elizabethan London', in Gadd and Wallis, eds., *Guilds, Society, and Economy in London*, pp. 51–66. On civic histories see Robert Tittler, *The Reformation and the Towns in England: Politics and Political Culture, c. 1540–1640* (Oxford, 1998), pp. 280–94.

[20] Richard Johnson, *The Pleasant Walkes of Moore-fields* (1607), fo. A4v.

[21] Knowles, 'Spectacle of the realm', p. 180. See also Manley, *Literature and Culture*, chap. 5; Michael Berlin, 'Civic ceremony in early modern London', *Urban History Yearbook*, 13 (1986), 15–27; Theodore B. Leinwald, 'London triumphing: the Jacobean Lord Mayor's show', *Clio*, 11 (1982), 137–53; Knowles, 'Spectacle of the realm', pp. 167, 171; Charles Phythian-Adams, 'Ceremony and the citizen: the communal year at Coventry, 1450–1550', in Peter Clark and Paul Slack, eds., *Crisis and Order in English Towns, 1500–1700* (Toronto, 1972), pp. 57–85; Mervyn James, 'Ritual, drama, and the social body in the late medieval English town', in his *Society, Politics, and Culture: Studies in Early Modern England* (Cambridge, 1986), pp. 16–47.

[22] Richard Mackenny, *Traders and Tradesmen* (Beckenham, 1987), pp. 155–65, 172; Munro, *Figure of the Crowd*, chap. 2; Manley, *Literature and Culture*, chap. 5; Berlin, 'Civic ceremony', 24–5; Knowles, 'Spectacle of the realm', pp. 173–4; William Hardin, 'Spectacular constructions: ceremonial representations of city and society in early

building schemes, improvements, and embellishments: 'incomparable paving' that flattened one thousand 'deformities in the streets', running water, trim landscaped walks, a stately new Exchange, grander churches, a spruced up cathedral (the crowning 'master-peece to all the rest'), and more besides.[23] Unlike 'dangerous growth', these works were civil, soothing, and moral. Smithfield was a 'civil walk'; Moorfields was 'most beautiful', healthy, and 'a continual comfort to behold', reflecting the 'noble' minds of citizens.[24]

The City often thought that its next-door neighbour in Whitehall did not do nearly enough to stop the slump in civic 'fame'. Strange, then, that it was now that London became a gleaming capital city.[25] The first Stuart monarchs had sky-high hopes, bragging that their 'imperial city' would some day soon become 'the greatest' Christian city in 1615, with all the brash self-confidence of an imperial throne.[26] New landscaped walks in London or a smarter cathedral lifted a bloated 'imperial ideal of metropolitan grandeur'. Slack comments that 'absolute power' made 'a bid to shape even the landscape' around this time. The Crown backed plans to

Stuart London', unpublished PhD thesis, University of North Carolina, Chapel Hill (1995); Gordon, 'Performing London'. Cf. Joseph P. Ward, *Metropolitan Communities: Trade Guilds, Identity, and Change in Early Modern London* (Stanford, CA, 1997).

[23] Roland Freart, *A Parallel of the Antient Architecture With the Modern*, trans. John Evelyn, 2nd edition (1707), epistle dedicatory, fo. 5r; James Howell, *Londinopolis: an Historical Discourse or Perlustration of the City of London, the Imperial Chamber and the Chief Emporium of Great Britain* (1657), p. 10; Knowles, 'Spectacle of the realm', pp. 176–7; Mark S. R. Jenner, 'Early modern English conceptions of "cleanliness" and "dirt" as reflected in the environmental regulation of London, c. 1530-c.1700', unpublished DPhil thesis, University of Oxford (1991); LMA Rep. 23, fos. 536v-7; Jour. 30, fos. 256–6v; J. F. Merritt, 'Puritans, Laudians, and the phenomenon of church building in Jacobean London', *Historical Journal*, 41 (1998), 935–60; Peter Lake, 'The Laudian style: order, uniformity, and the pursuit of the beauty of holiness in the 1630s', in Kenneth Fincham, ed., *The Early Stuart Church, 1603–42* (Basingstoke, 1993), pp. 161–85; TNA SP16/195/32; John King, *A Sermon at Paules Crosse on behalfe of Paules Church, March 26 1620* (1620), pp. 55–6. On 'urban renaissance' see Peter Borsay, *The English Urban Renaissance: Culture and Society in the Provincial Town, 1660–1770* (Oxford, 1989). See also Edmund Howes, *Annales, Or, A Generall Chronicle of England Begun by John Stow: Continued and Augmented With Matters Forraigne and Domestique, Ancient and Moderne, Unto the End of the Present Year, 1631* (1631), p. 1021; Knowles, 'Spectacle of the realm', pp. 161–2; Tittler, *Reformation and the Towns*, pp. 338–41.

[24] King, *Sermon at Paules Crosse*, p. 55; Howes, *Annales*, p. 1024; Johnson, *Pleasant Walkes of Moore-fields*, fos. A2r, A3r, B1r; Howell, *Londinopolis*, p. 301; LMA Jours. 27, fos. 364v, 396; 28, fos. 16v, 81; Reps. 27, fos. 142, 366; 29, fos. 13v-14; Letterbook V, fo. 291v; *The Letters of John Chamberlain*, ed. Norman Egbert McClure, 2 vols., The American Philosophical Society (Philadelphia, PA, 1939), vol. I, p. 235; Laura Williams, '"To recreate and refresh their dulled spirites in the sweet and wholesome ayre": green space and the growth of the city', in Merritt ed., *Imagining Early Modern London*, pp. 185–213, esp. pp. 191–2; Brett-James, *Growth of Stuart London*, pp. 455–7.

[25] J. C. Robertson, 'Stuart London and the idea of a royal capital city', *Renaissance Studies*, 15 (2001), 37–58.

[26] LMA Jour. 29, fos. 351–1v.

'beautify' the city, singling-out bringing 'the new streame unto the west parts', paving Smithfield, planting Moorfields, the new Royal Exchange, Sutton's hospital, and 'the reedifying of Algate, Hicks Hall', and 'like workes'.[27] Imperial London was toasted in shimmering prose. Munday called 'supreme' London Great Britain's 'royal chamber' and 'metropolis' beyond compare. Thomas Jackson wrote a sparkling sketch a decade earlier: 'opulent and famous and renowned' London was 'the chamber of our land and empresse of our island'. It was also an 'open haven for all merchandize and commerce', Munday said, and a 'store-house of peace and plenty'.[28]

Aldermen did not see much 'peace and plenty' in the city around them, though they could crow about grand buildings or ships stuffed with spices. But on their daily rounds they saw too many blankets of filth, dirt-coated vagrants, and eyesore slums. From a distance the Exchange gleamed in the sunlight, but close up they saw loose-tongued women selling their wares on its edges. Stow's changeless city had long since gone. Authors now wrote about the urban whirl, hoping to acclimatize people to what they now thought to be an unsafe larger London. True enough the City talked up trade or pet projects like the new river, and Londoners counted their blessings not to be living in a backwoods village (the slick urban polish/country bumpkin trope was secure by now). Like celebratory authors, they window dressed the city in imperial garb, but the City was also unsure about its new imperial airs and graces. This was Whitehall talk in the main, the grandiose image management of monarchs who wanted to outshine their rivals on mainland Europe with sparkling baroque courts and imperial razzmatazz. But this imperial façade slipped easily, and in the end the City came to the jaded conclusion

---

[27] SRPC (136), pp. 280–7; LMA Jour. 29, fos. 351–1v; Paul Slack, *From Reformation to Improvement: Public Welfare in Early Modern England* (Oxford, 1999), p. 69; LMA Jour. 29, fos. 351–1v. See also Kevin Sharpe, *The Personal Rule of Charles I* (New Haven, CT, and London, 1992), pp. 403–12; Manley, *Literature and Culture*, p. 496, and chap. 5; Malcolm Smuts, *Court Culture and the Origins of a Royalist Tradition in Early Stuart England* (Philadelphia, PA, 1987); J. Newman, 'Inigo Jones and the politics of architecture', in Kevin Sharpe and Peter Lake, eds., *Culture and Politics in Early Stuart England* (Basingstoke, 1994), pp. 231–45; Robertson, 'Stuart London'; Robertson., 'London 1580–1642: the view from Whitehall; the view from the Guildhall', unpublished PhD thesis, Washington University (1993). Robert Ashton comments that after 1603 the Crown tried to turn London into 'a more civilized urban environment worthy of a great capital city': *The City and the Court, 1603–1643* (Cambridge, 1979), p. 168.

[28] Anthony Munday, *The Survey of London Written in the Yeere 1598 by John Stow ... Since Then Continued and Much Enlarged ... by Anthony Munday* (1618), epistle dedicatory, p. 4; Thomas Jackson, *Londons New-Yeeres Gift, Or the Uncovering of the Foxe* (1609), fo. 8r.

that it could not now stop either 'dangerous growth' or the perceived slide in civic prestige.

### Rhetorics

This book is composed from rhetorics and records and not many, if any, should be taken at face value. I do not necessarily believe claims that the freedom's worth hit rock-bottom in 1632, or others that vagrants were falling on London like swarms of locusts. These were rhetorics and perceptions, calculated and strong enough, London's magistrates hoped, to make people believe what was being said and to act accordingly and quickly.

No magistrate worth his salt was ever satisfied with what he saw on the streets. His job was to squeeze more effort from people and keep officers on their toes. And so complaints poured out about bungling officers, crime-waves, or empty coffers. Policing was a shambles, magistrates said, to make people aware of the need to police better; resources were thin, they complained, prodding people to dig deeper into their pockets; and the freedom was of 'little worth' nowadays, they said, hoping that someone in Whitehall would at long last take action to stop suburban sprawl or protect jobs. Yet not one complaint would have been taken seriously or made any difference unless it had had some basis in day-to-day realities. Magistrates were not crying wolf all of the time. We know that London's growth led to more disorder, overcrowded areas, smog, and concern. Policing shows the double-edged nature of rhetoric: at once embellishment but also corresponding to some reality. Magistrates complained about amateurish officers all the time, and this is enough evidence of deep-rooted flaws for some scholars.[29] But this tedious critical chorus has all the appearance of routine calls to order to urge vigilance from officers, who were told to be 'continually' at 'constant stacons'.[30] Magistrates always see room for improvements. In fact there were second-rate officers, but this is not the full story, although it is the handiest one when a case was being made for improvements. There were also plenty of hard-working officers, as we will see.

Rhetorics often point in several directions at once. Tainted or otherwise, they matter less for the truths they might tell than for the extent to

---

[29] Steve Hindle, *The State and Social Change in Early Modern England, c.1550–1640* (Basingstoke, 2000), p. 173. Cf. J. M. Beattie, *Policing and Punishment in London, 1660–1750: Urban Crime and the Limits of Terror* (Oxford, 2001), p. 132; Ian W. Archer, *The Pursuit of Stability: Social Relations in Elizabethan London* (Cambridge, 1991), pp. 221–2.
[30] LMA Rep. 56, fo. 22v; Jour. 20, fo. 323; Rep. 40, fo. 72.

Introduction

which it is possible to recreate mind-sets embedded in crime clamp-downs, for example, or long-drawn-out efforts to 'sweeten' slums. We must put ourselves inside the minds of people sitting in the Guildhall if we want to understand how policies and plans began, and ask what they felt about the state of their city, always aware that anything they say might be tinged with exaggeration for effect. Such a perspective will give us a clearer idea of the responses of Londoners in terms of their perceptions of how change challenged the existing, perceived nature of the city and citizenship. This is how the City understood its own stresses and strains. Archer notices a 'sense of perceived crisis' in London towards 1600.[31] If Londoners felt that their city was in dire straits, then quite frankly it is of less importance what we say today about whether or not the city was stable all that time ago. What matters above all else is a perception and appearance of troubling flux, even if it turns out to be Guildhall hyperbole. Perceptions spawned policies and prosecutions, and each piece of rhetoric that we read in records today. City leaders did not sit around inventing ever more unlikely scenarios. They travelled deep into each quarter of the city and saw things with their own eyes. Information also poured into the Guildhall that provided sources for new understandings of London and its 'sare' growth. And the resulting rhetorics were what magistrates thought and felt at the time.

But they are also a confusing clutter. Ambiguities abound. There was even pride in growth/size: John Graunt was not the first to gloat that London was better than Paris or Amsterdam because it was bigger.[32] But long before he sang larger London's praises, magistrates in at the deep end feared growth because its exact extent was unknowable. It was simply 'extraordinary' or 'excessive', not something that was fully comprehended.[33] This not knowing led to panicky rhetoric and apparent incongruities as magistrates worked hard to steady the ship. London was at one and the same time a golden imperial city and a ghost of its former grand self; Europe's trading hub and an employment wasteland for citizens and a thieves' paradise. Which one of these standpoints is credible depends on who is speaking, at what time, and for what reason. The bright portrayal of the Renaissance city was royal rhetoric in the main. The City basked in this regal sun now and then, but aldermen thought that they had more than enough to cope with in their own back-yard. Uplifting civic rhetorics

[31] Archer, *Pursuit of Stability*, pp. 8–9.
[32] Paul Slack, 'Great and good towns', in Peter Clark, ed., *The Cambridge Urban History of Britain: Volume II, 1540–1840* (Cambridge, 2000), pp. 347–76; and 'Perceptions of the metropolis in seventeenth-century England', in Peter Burke, Brian Harrison, and Slack, eds., *Civil Histories: Essays Presented to Sir Keith Thomas* (Oxford, 2000), pp. 161–80.
[33] See below, pp. 36–40.

tended to share elevated senses of civic pride, settled government, and a sparkling past. London was also painted brightly or dimly in literature and letters with the same regard for purpose and accuracy. James Howell must have suspended smell when writing that Paris's streets were caked in an 'oily stain that can never be washed off', unlike London's, and could 'be smelt' ten miles away. But his spin-doctoring *Londinopolis* (1657) was written to drum up pride in the 'imperial chamber' or 'chief emporium of Great Britain'. Alexander Magno could write with gusto that 'London is a very beautiful city' in 1562, but he was scared stiff of stepping outside after dark.[34] The City, too, could slip from lofty grandeur to seedy crime in the short space of a few sentences of the same order/pronouncement, juxtaposing optimism and pessimism for effect.

The point, needless to say, is that, as John Lawrence said in 1624 with no hint of paradox, London had 'many things' worthy to be 'comend[ed]' and many blemishes.[35] Magistrates did not flit from one seemingly contradictory rhetoric to another without purpose. There was a grain of truth in each positive or negative note. Contrary rhetorics depended on each other and despite outer oppositions existed in what Slack calls 'productive counterpoint'.[36] Differing ideas of dilapidation and elegance were meant to persuade people of the need to improve the environment. Rhetorics of losing London could sit on the same page as others lauding London and no one would have been taken aback. All of these perceptions had validity and collectively created senses of change and novelty, but also of threat and anxiety. Regal/shabby or disorderly/orderly, London was neither one thing or the other. But like any city of similar size going through swift growth, London was always tense, and this was why many people looked back longingly with Stow to better times. Later on Londoners would glance back to these 'troubled' times that now looked like a bygone halcyon age: 'How this city flourished under James in wealth and riches', 'great ornament of public and private building', and rousing 'expressions' of glory, William Gough wrote with rose-tinted glasses in 1682, even thinking that the 'numerousness of inhabitants' was a blessing back then.[37] Such is the power of losing London: longing

---

[34] Howell, *Londinopolis*, p. 392; 'The London Journal of Alessandro Magno 1562', eds., Caroline Barron, Christopher Coleman, and Claire Gobb, *London Journal*, 9 (1983), 136–52, esp. 141, 148.

[35] John Lawrence, *A Golden Trumpet to Rowse up a Drowsie Magistrate: Or, a Patterne for a Governors Practise Drawne From Christs Comming to, Beholding of, and Weeping Over Hierusalem. As it was Sounded at Pauls Crosse the 11 of Aprill, 1624* (1624), pp. 100–1.

[36] Slack, 'Perceptions of the metropolis', p. 163.

[37] William Gough, *Londinium Triumphaus* (1682), p. 346. Almost three centuries later, John Timbs walked through the city and wrote *Walks and Talks about London* (1865), 'a nostalgic tour through a city in transition', Lynda Nead notes, 'Written at a time when

Introduction 11

for something sunnier that existed somewhere else back in time before the first rumblings of the storm began. What Londoners wanted was the stability performed in civic parades: a booming city without vagrants, that to all intents and purposes did not grow. But whipping up enthusiasm for a spirited civic identity was not nearly reassuring enough on its own. The counter-rhythms of celebration or jeremiad needed buttressing by a third rhetoric of magistracy and government that had institutional backbone and expression: rhetorics of administration, policing, regulation, classification, and surveillance, which in turn fed off dark discursive dirges of crime. These rhetorics and strategies are the main subjects of this book.

In terms of both rhetorics and records Bridewell prison looms large in what follows. It was an essential thread in civic rhetorics, along with other 'hospitals' (Christ's, St Thomas's, and St Bartholomew's), called 'one body' when St Bartholomew's was added to the 'union' in 1557 or the '4 hospitalls', each with something to give to the overall design of battling sickness, sin, and vagrancy.[38] This unity was sealed in outward show: governors from all hospitals sat together at showcase civic events like Spital sermons or the funerals of City bigwigs – in rows according to 'sorte and order' – and were expected to turn out at colleagues' funerals, no matter what the affiliation of the civic worthy in the coffin.[39] Bridewell was imagined in this collective form that exemplified the aspirations of this period – reformation, stability, and order – but also alone in terms of control, surveillance, and discipline.

Bridewell symbolizes a lost and new London. It was a royal palace in its first colours: 'the ancient mansion of many English kings'. 'Thus Fortune can tosse the world, a Princes Court / Is this a prison now?', a Bridewell master muses in Dekker's *Honest Whore, Part II* (1605). No one could have guessed that a glittering palace in its hey-day would one day become a showpiece house of correction. 'We thought it a pity that such a palace should be turned to such a mean purpose', Lupold von Wedel wrote in the mid-1580s. It was 'a place of entertainment for the worst of villains', William Fuller said when locked up there over a century later, 'I thought

---

most of the significant building works in the city were under way': *Victorian Babylon: People, Streets, and Images in Nineteenth-Century London* (New Haven, CT, and London, 2000), p. 58.

[38] GL MS 12806/1, fo. 8v; LMA Reps. 14, fo. 39; 30, fos. 18, 23v; 32, fo. 186. William Waddington referred later on to the 'relative policy of the hospitals connected together': *Considerations on the Original and Proper Objects of the Royal Hospital of Bridewell Addressed to the Governors* (1798), p. 14. 'A new [common] seale' was cut for the hospitals in 1561: LMA Rep. 14, fo. 532. See also Paul Griffiths, 'Building Bridewell: London's self-images, 1550–1640', in Norman L. Jones and Daniel Woolf, eds., *Local Identities in Late Medieval and Early Modern England* (Basingstoke, 2007), pp. 228–48.

[39] BHC 7, fo. 363; GL MSS 12806/2, fos. 26v, 27, 260v, 361v; 12806/3, fo. 264; 12806/4, fos. 87–8.

12   Lost Londons

Hell could not be worse'.[40] Bridewell's switch from palace to prison is a well-known story by now. This was a time of institutional flux: five 'hospitals' opened for the first time or were reopened on new footings in a short seven year span (1546–53). Orphans and urchins were sheltered and schooled in Christ's; Bethlem took in the insane; St Thomas's and St Bartholomew's cared for the sick; while Bridewell's particular province was to curb vagrancy and vice.[41] Bridewell began with growth. The City asked Edward VI for his father's palace in 1552, just as the population boom began to have serious effects. Already, Thomas Lever had preached chillingly at Paul's Cross about a plague of vagrants in 1550: 'It is to thy great shame before the world and utter damnation before God' that rogues abound, he scolded City magistrates.[42] Complaints about crippling poverty and thieving vagrants soared in years leading up to his blast. The common 'cry' in the mid-1540s was that the poor 'daylie increase in greate number then have bine in tymes paste'. Streets 'swarmed with beggars and rogues' with nothing to do and sick people with nowhere to go. To cap it all London was put on red alert in the 'comocon' time in 1549, when rebels plotted to storm the city from

---

[40] Thomas Dekker, *The Honest Whore, Part 1*, in T. Bowers, ed., *The Dramatic Works of Thomas Dekker*, 4 vols. (Cambridge, 1955–61), vol. II, 5:2. 15–16; Gloucester Ridley, *The Life of Dr Nicholas Ridley, Sometime Bishop of London Shewing the Plan and Progress of the Reformation* (1763), pp. 398–9; 'A journey through England and Scotland made by Lupold von Wedel in the years 1584 & 1585', ed., G. von Bulow, *Transactions of the Royal Historical Society*, new series, 9 (1895), 223–70, esp. 233; William Fuller, *Mr W. F's Trip to Bridewell With a True Account of His Barbarous Usage in the Pillory ... Written by His Own Hand* (1703), p. 8. See also Simon Thurley, *The Royal Palaces of Tudor England: Architecture and Court Life, 1460–1547* (New Haven, CT, and London, 1993); R. S. Mylne, 'Old Bridewell', *Transactions of the London and Middlesex Archaeological Society*, new series, 2 (1910–13), 86–110; L. W. Cowie, 'Bridewell', *History Today*, 23 (1973), 350–8; *The History of the Life of Thomas Ellwood*, ed., C. G. Crump (1900), p. 96.

[41] The fullest history of Bridewell is still E. G. O'Donoghue, *Bridewell Hospital, Palace, Prison, and School, From the Death of Elizabeth to Modern Times*, 2 vols. (1923, 1929). See also Christopher T. Daly, 'The hospitals of London: administration, refoundation, and benefaction, c.1500–1572', unpublished DPhil thesis, University of Oxford (1994), pp. 210–20; Paul Slack, 'Hospitals, workhouses and the relief of the poor in early modern London', in Ole Peter Grell and Andrew Cunningham, eds., *Health Care and Poor Relief in Protestant Europe, 1500–1700* (London, 1997), pp. 234–51; Joanna Innes, 'Prisons for the poor: English bridewells, 1555–1800', in Francis Snyder and Douglas Hay, eds., *Labour, Law, and Crime: a Historical Perspective* (Oxford, 1987), pp. 42–122, esp. pp. 49–61; A. L. Beier, 'Foucault *Redux*?: The roles of humanism, protestantism, and an urban elite in creating the London Bridewell, 1500–1560', *Criminal Justice History*, 17 (2002), 33–60; Beier, *Masterless Men: the Vagrancy Problem in England, 1560–1640* (1985), pp. 164–9; Archer, *Pursuit of Stability*, chap. 6. See also Anthony Munday, *A Briefe Chronicle of the Successe of Times from the Creation of the World to This Instant* (1611), pp. 521–2.

[42] Thomas Lever, *A Sermon Preached at Paul's Crosse the xiiii Daie of December* (1550), fos. Oiiir-v.

the east and west, and anxieties sharpened in times that we once called the 'Mid-Tudor' crisis.[43]

With four hospitals in place by 1552, the next need was for somewhere to take care of the 'third degree' of vagrant poor. The City looked longingly at empty Bridewell and after letters and meetings with royal officials, with Bishop Ridley leading a lobby of 'hot' protestants and humanists,[44] a royal charter was duly sealed in 1553.[45] The first prisoner was locked up two years later and rules and ordinances followed two years after that.[46] But the hospitals were quickly caught up in a backlash when Catholics took the country back in 1553. 'The change of religion almost overturned them', 'Dutie' said later in *John Howes' MS* (1582), 'for there was nothing but fly, fly or burn burn', and 'nothing else looked for but down with them, down with them'. But 'of all houses', he said, 'malice was most chiefly against Bridewell'. Like the others it was linked in catholic minds with loss of church lands and protestant bigotry, but Bridewell also intruded on jurisdictional patches thought to concern only church courts.[47] The writing on the wall looked bleak, but Queen Mary's death after barely five years on the throne 'ended all strife'. This was long enough to bring the mass back to Bridewell and elsewhere, but not to return wholesale to the days before the turn to 'heresy'. The hospitals survived more or less in one piece with endowments confirmed, but make

---

[43] SBHA Governors' Journal 3, n.p., front of book; LMA Letterbook R, fos. 13v, 22v, 36v, 64, 127v, 269v; *John Howes' MS, 1582, Being A Brief Note of the Order and Manner of the Proceedings in the First Erection of the Three Royal Hospitals of Christ, Bridewell, and St Thomas the Apostle*, ed., William Lampiere (1904), pp. 8, 55–6; GL MS 6, fos. 3–3v, 9v–10; Ridley, *Life of Dr Nicholas Ridley*, pp. 375–7; Lever, *Sermon Preached at Pauls Cross*, fos. Oiiir-v; Strype, *Survey*, V, pp. 174–5. See also Daly, 'Hospitals of London', pp. 60–1, 70, 72, 106–7, 120–3, 208–9; Paul Slack, 'Social policy and the constraints of government, 1547–1558', and Robert Tittler, 'The emergence of urban policy, 1536–58', both in Jennifer Loach and Tittler, eds., *The Mid-Tudor Polity, c.1540–1560* (Basingstoke, 1980), pp. 94–115, esp. pp. 74–93.

[44] Beier, 'Foucault *Redux*?', 45–50; *John Howes' MS, 1582*, p. 10.

[45] For the story of the City lobby and Bridewell's foundation see Richard Grafton, *A Chronicle at Large and Meere History of the Affayres of Englande* (1569), pp. 1322–3; Gilbert Burnet, *The History of the Reformation of the Church of England*, 1679, ed. N. Pocock (Oxford, 1865), pp. 367–8; *John Howes' MS*, pp. 8–11, 21, 23–5; Ridley, *Life of Dr Nicholas Ridley*, pp. 377–9; *A Treatise or Letter Written by Dr Ridley Instead of His Last Farewell to All His True and Faithfull Friends in God; With a Sharp Admonition Withal Unto the Papists*, in The Acts and Monuments of John Foxe, ed., S. R. Cattley, 8 vols. (1841), pp. 559–60; Strype, *Survey*, V, pp. 177–8; Dairmaid Macculloch, *The Boy King: Edward VI and the Protestant Reformation* (New York, 2001), p. 23.

[46] Orders for the 'good and politique governement of Chrysts, St Thomas and Brydewell' were also issued in 1556: LMA Letterbook S, fos. 68–9, 104v; Rep. 13ii, fos. 454, 544v.

[47] *John Howes' MS*, pp. 65, i, 11, 64–5, 71–2 (and 63–74); Daly, 'Hospitals of London', pp. 226–43. See also Susan Brigden, *London and the Reformation* (Oxford, 1989), pp. 622–4; Claire Schen, *Charity and Lay Piety in Reformation London, 1500–1620* (Aldershot, 2002), p. 94.

no mistake, 'Dutie' tells 'Dignitie' in *John Howes' MS*, 'yf Quene Marie had contynued longer they woulde have suprest [Bridewell] by one meane or other'.[48] Bridewell took its first batch of prisoners half-way through Mary's reign, and City records give details of a number sent there before her death: someone who cheated people with 'counterfeitte messages and tokens', a hard-nosed husband who 'crasely' abused his wife, a 'masterles man', a 'sturdy vacabonde', 'straunge beggers and idle persones', and a clothworker who jeered at a constable.[49]

The City gave its full backing to Bridewell, taking its side when church courts tried to claw back their 'lost' jurisdictions or if catholics vented their spleen, like the time in 1558 when a Paul's Cross preacher pitched in with a 'rasshe' 'reporte' that an apprentice had been flogged within an inch of his life in Bridewell.[50] This 'heroic' phase of protestantism that had more than its fair share of martyrs was key to establishing Bridewell as a shining civic emblem. Bridewell's beginnings were soaked with religious rhetoric and reasoning. It was opened in a 'charitable' and 'blessed' time by citizens 'imbued with godliness'. The hospitals were 'holy' and 'truly religious houses' and a 'blessed work of God', Bishop Ridley wrote in his final farewell to the city before his martyr's death.[51] Eulogizing began early in the 'dangerous days'. Thomas Mountain brazenly asked Bishop Gardiner if he could say how many 'notable things worthy of perpetual memory' were set up under Edward VI, and chiefly the 'fair hospitals': 'Are not all these good works, my Lord', he closed cannily.[52] Bridewell's stirring short history soon became civic godly propaganda. 'Look into London', Bishop Pilkington invited readers less than a decade after the first inmate walked in through the gate, 'and see what hospital was founded before the gospel time and the poor relieved, youth godly brought up, and the idle sent to work'. 'Popery would sometimes feed the hungry', he said dryly, 'but seldom correct the unprofitable'. God will bless London, John Howes said in a protestant flush in 1582, with

---

[48] *John Howes' MS*, pp. 73, 71.
[49] Ridley, *Life of Dr Nicholas Ridley*, pp. 398–9; LMA Rep. 13ii, fos. 415v, 451v, 516, 557, 531.
[50] LMA Reps. 13ii, fos. 456v, 457, 463, 478v, 509v, 569; 14, fos. 14, 24v, 29v.
[51] *John Howes' MS*, pp. 6, 42–3; Strype, *Survey*, V, p. 176; *Treatise or Letter Written by Dr Ridley*, pp. 559–60; Ridley, *Life of Dr Nicholas Ridley*, pp. 377–9, 375. The descriptions of the governors are in the 1557 Bridewell ordinances and the Declaration of the City of London, both of which can be found in *The Thirty-Second Report of the Charity Commissioners of England and Wales*, Per Acts 38 Geo. 3 c.91 and Geo. 3 c. 81, Part VI (1840), 219, xix, Part 1, pp. 390, 389 (hereafter *Charity Commissioners Report*). See also David J. Hickman, 'The religious allegiance of London's ruling elite, 1520–1603', unpublished PhD thesis, University of London (1995), pp. 154–60; O'Donoghue, *Bridewell Hospital*, vol. I, pp. 143–4.
[52] Mountain is quoted in Daly, 'Hospitals of London', pp. 243 and 313.

Introduction 15

hospitals now caring for the sick, mad, and bad.[53] This celebratory rhetoric continued into the next century and after. The 'citizen' in Richard Johnson's *Pleasant Walkes of Moore-fields* (1607) brags that London has three 'immortall comendations': the Orphan's Court, Christ's Hospital, and Bridewell, 'where vice is justly corrected'. Thomas Jackson paid tribute to the 'great bounty' of 'opulent, famous, and renowned' London in 1609, as seen in the comfort and care given in hospitals. Bridewell also earned a special place in Burnet's *History of the Reformation* (1679), who ranked its foundation among Europe's 'noblest' acts since Luther nailed up his ninety-five theses. Preaching in Bridewell chapel in 1694, Francis Atterbury reminded governors sitting listening that they must show themselves to be 'the true heirs' of famed Bridewell's 'founding fathers' 'piety and bounty'. If they failed to live up to their bright example, he admonished, 'these great buildings and endowments' will suddenly 'become a reproch rather than be an honor'.[54]

Bridewell launched a new word into penal rhetorics and quickly became synonymous with house of correction or prison, titles that merged in images of confinement and bodily discipline. Bridewell was a 'revolutionary', 'unique', and 'pioneering' prison, the first anywhere in Europe to twin hard work with custodial sentences.[55] The idea of Bridewell as a tough response to crime and joblessness soon became a blueprint for other cities, counties, and countries,[56] finding a place in

---

[53] James Pilkington, *The Burning of St Paul's Church: Confutation of an Addition* (1563), in *The Works of James Pilkington, B. D., Lord Bishop of Durham*, ed., J. Schofield, Parker Society (1842), pp. 610–11; *John Howes' MS*, p. 17.

[54] Johnson, *Pleasant Walkes of Moore-fields*, fo. B1v; Jackson, *Londons New-Yeeres Gift*, fo. 8r; Burnet, *History of the Reformation*, pp. 367–8; Francis Atterbury, *The Power of Charity to Cover Sin: A Sermon Preach'd Before the President and Governors of the Hospitals of Bridewell and Bethlem, in Bridewell Chapel, August 16 1694* (1708), p. 16.

[55] Beier, *Masterless Men*, p. 164; id., 'Foucault *Redux*?', 33; Slack, 'Hospitals, workhouses, and the relief of the poor', p. 237; Innes, 'Prisons for the poor', pp. 42, 53; Martin Ingram, 'Regulating sex in pre-Reformation London', in G. W. Bernard and S. J. Gunn, eds., *Authority and Consent in Tudor England: Essays Presented to C. S. L. Davies* (Aldershot, 2002), pp. 79–95, esp. p. 84; Julius R. Ruff, *Violence in Early Modern Europe, 1500–1800* (Cambridge, 2001), p. 112; Pieter Spierenburg, *The Prison Experience: Disciplinary Institutions and Their Inmates in Early Modern Europe* (New Brunswick, NJ, and London, 1991), pp. 23–5; Robert Jutte, *Poverty and Deviance in Early Modern Europe* (Cambridge, 1994), pp. 169–70, 172–3, 174.

[56] Spierenburg, *Prison Experience*, p. 24. Cf. Carol Kazmierczak Manzione, 'Sex in Tudor London: abusing their bodies with each other', in J. Murray and K. Eisenbichler, eds., *Desire and Discipline: Sex and Sexuality in the Premodern West* (Toronto, 1996), pp. 87–100, esp. p. 98. Even early American hospitals had roots in London's mid-sixteenth-century hospitals. See Morris J. Vogel, 'The transformation of the American hospital', in Norbert Finzsch and Robert Jutte, eds., *Institutions of Confinement: Hospitals, Asylums and Prisons in Western Europe and America, 1500–1950* (Cambridge, 1996), pp. 39–54, esp. pp. 41–2.

rhetorics and practices of magistracy and control until long after 1700 in places as far afield as Great Yarmouth, Northampton, Colchester, Dorchester, Norwich, Marlborough, Oxford, Salisbury, and next-door Westminster, and was used interchangeably with house of correction or another word for a lock-up.[57]

Bridewell also took a leading role in the drive to contain crime in London. It was the first port-of-call in a vagrant storm. Its links to policing run by wards, parishes, and the City are covered in the final four chapters (its place in tangled jurisdictions is covered in Chapter 7). Galloping vagrancy and vice were mainly in the minds of magistrates when Bridewell's indentures were sealed and its commission put down on paper. The commission (1555) made it clear that Bridewell's 'intent' was to get rid of 'the great number' of vagrants and 'valiant beggars'. Bridewell's role and powers were also spelled out in its charter and in a run of orders, starting with the 'Order of the Hospitals' (1556). Uniquely, it was in a position to prosecute and punish. It was the only prison in the land with its own formally constituted court of governors inside its walls, who had sweeping power and authority to 'searche, enquyre, and seke owt' all 'ydell ruffians and taverne haunters, vagabonds, beggars' and 'persons of yll name and fame' in London and built-up Middlesex, and bring them in for questioning and trial after, if the governors saw fit. 'For what offenders is that Bridewell chiefly reserved?', the gentleman asks in Johnson's *Pleasant Walkes of Moore-fields* (1607): 'for idle persons', the citizen answers, 'as vagabondes and for those that

---

[57] Essex Record Office, Colchester Branch D/B5/SB1/4, n.p., 17–3–1631; D/B5/SB4/3, fos. 10v, 22; Dorset Record Office DC/DOB/8/1, fos. 8v, 65, 90, 170v, 241, 328; Norwich and Norfolk Record Office Y/C/19/5, fos. 37v, 75v, 121; Norwich City Quarter Sessions Minute Books 1629–36, fos. 6v, 22v, 43v, 75; 1630–8, fos. 45, 78v, 114v; 1637–64, fos. 8v, 20, 44v; 1639–54, fos. 23, 54, 101, 132, 148v; Wiltshire Record Office G22/1/205/2, fos. 49v, 59v, 69v, 116, 164v; G23/1/3, fo. 156v; Northamptonshire Record Office Northamptonshire Quarter Sessions Minute Books 2, fo. 84; 3, fos. 117v, 184v; 4, fos. 75, 114v; Oxfordshire Record Office QS/C/A1/O1, fos. 149, 678; QS/C/A1/O2, fos. 32, 106v, 145, 178; C/FC/1/A1/O2, fos. 206v, 296v; C/FC/1/A1/O3, fos. 35, 134v; C/FC/1/A1/O4, fo. 224v; QSM1/1/ii, fos. 67, 73; QSM1/1/iv, fos. 4, 22; Suffolk Record Office, Ipswich Branch B/105/2/1, fo. 12; WAC F2002, fo. 231; F2003, fo. 340; E2416, fos. 18, 47, 96, 153, 182, 228. The Duke of Portland had a copy of Bridewell's royal letters patent in his Nottinghamshire residence: NOTTRO DD4P/68, fo. 23. St Margaret's Westminster officials 'transcribed' a series of 'presidents and orders' from 'Old Bridewell in London' when they were planning a new house of correction: WAC E13, 1622–3. See also LMA Rep. 18, fos. 56–6v; J. F. Merritt, *The Social World of Early Modern Westminster: Abbey, Court, and Community, 1525–1640* (Manchester, 2005), p. 284; *The Notebook of Robert Doughty, 1662–1665*, ed., James M. Rosenheim, Norfolk Record Society, 54 (1989), pp. 53, 30, 43, 47, 53, 60, 61. On a trip to Amsterdam in 1641, John Evelyn 'stepp'd in to see the Spin-house', 'which is a kind of Bridewell', he wrote, 'where incorrigible and lewd women are kept in discipline and labour': John Evelyn: *An Account of Architects and Architecture* (1707 edition), p. 42.

Introduction 17

are obstinate and will not live in the feare of God, but abuse their bodies with lewd vice, whoredome and such like'.[58] Key words to describe Bridewell's principal functions included 'training', 'reclaiming', 'chastizing', 'correcting', or 'reducing' pests through tough work. A portrait of the founder – Edward VI – was hung up next to the chapel pulpit with a short statement of purpose: Bridewell was 'a chastening' or 'chastising house of vagrant crimes'.[59] It was also called a 'house of correction', a 'place of confinement for harlots and villains', 'a house of occupations', a 'house of labour', and a 'school'. Revealingly, it was also called a prison. The porter was told to 'keepe this hospitall as a prison with the dores shut' in 1602. But Bridewell's most common title throughout its first century was 'hospital', an omnibus term that covered caring, teaching, and training, as well as tough work, sharp correction, and confinement.[60]

This word jumble must not muddle the fact that Bridewell was first and foremost a lock-up. But it served the City in more ways than one: granaries within its walls stored corn for the poor, lighters brought lime and sand to lime kilns, and wood, coal, and gunpowder were stockpiled in 'roomes'. There were many people to take care of in Bridewell. The end-of-year report for the twelve months up to March 1599 counted 2,043 'poor' who spent some time there, with 243 there at the time of the count. This total dropped to 1,952 in 1600, with 184 inmates 'kept continually' at work when the count was taken, but rose to 2,730 in 1601, with

---

[58] LMA Jour. 16, fos. 370v-1; *Charity Commissioners Report*, pp. 390, 389; *John Howes' MS*, pp. 56–60; GL MSS 6, fo. 6v; 9384; Johnson, *Pleasant Walkes of Moore-fields*, fo. B1v. Bridewell's indenture was sealed in 1553: LMA Rep. 13i, fo. 60; Letterbook R, fo. 256.

[59] White, *Short History of the Royal Hospitals*, p. 9; Ridley, *Life of Dr Nicholas Ridley*, pp. 379, 398–9; Grafton, *Chronicle*, p. 1321; *Howes' MS*, pp. 16–17; William Maitland, *History of London From Its Foundations by the Romans to the Present Time* (1739), p. 661; Munday, *Briefe Chronicle*, pp. 521–2; Waddington, *Considerations*, p. 29; Howell, *Londinopolis*, p. 311. Eighteenth-century opinion continued to list Bridewell's functions in terms of disciplining and correcting. See Robert Moss, *A Sermon Preach'd Before the Right Honourable the Lord Mayor of London, the Court of Aldermen, and the Governors of the Several Hospitals of the City, at the Parish Church of St Sepulchre ... in Easter Week* (1709), p. 15; Atterbury, *Power of Charity to Cover Sin*, p. 15; Strype, *Survey*, V, p. 191.

[60] BRHA BHC 4, fo. 327. Examples of other descriptive tags used here can be found in *Howes' MS*, pp. 16–17; BRHA BHC 4, fos. 18, 215v; 'A journey through England and Scotland made by Lupold von Wedel', 233; LMA Jours. 26, fo. 49; 30, fo. 43v; Rep. 44, fos. 194v, 197, 208, 212, 218; BHC 5, fo. 63v; Pilkington, *Burning of St. Paul's Church*, p. 611; *Treatise or Letter Written by Dr Ridley*, pp. 559–60. In the middle of a row about Bridewell's role three centuries later, a governor wrote that 'Prison objects and hospital objects have varied with the varying circumstances of the times, and ... varying condition of the poor': *A Letter to the President of the Royal Hospitals of Bridewell and Bethlem upon the Original Designs and Present Pursuits of one of these Ancient Foundations of Mercy .... From a Governor* (1830), pp. 12–13.

172 people locked up during the count.[61] Magistrates considered work to be the best panacea for the luckless, feckless, and rootless poor. Laziness was poisonous, and people with time on their hands could only be up to no good. 'Necessary bodely laboures' were good mental corrections that helped people to stand on their own two feet. Not long after Bridewell first opened, City committees met to plan 'profytable arts and occupacions' to keep inmates from 'idleness'. The City drew up lengthy orders for Bridewell in 1579: including clauses about 'good' work for inmates.[62] Bridewell's 'occupacons' included spinning, knitting, weaving, beating hemp, threading beads, and making buttons, gloves, nails, pins, points, shoes, hats, caps, cards, clothes, thread, wire, and tennis balls, amongst other things.[63] Work was long and hard, usually starting at the crack of dawn and lasting until deep into the evening, though Sunday was a day of rest.[64] Inmates also worked outside, like chain gangs: vagrants 'clensed' Smithfield pond in 1564; 'vagabonds' cleaned 'common sewers and ditches' in 1569, each one with 'a collar of iron about the neck' under the watchful eyes of beadles; twenty-four 'vacabonds' 'skowered' Tower Ditch in the same year; 'lusty idle men and able women' cleaned streets in 1631 and were warned not to 'mingle'; and 'vagabonds and masterlesse men' dredged soil and sand from the Thames in 1567, getting sixpence if there were two tides in a single day.[65]

As well as putting prisoners to work, qualified artmasters took charge of apprentices, rearing youngsters to be masters themselves one day.[66]

---

[61] BRHA BHC 4, fos. 76, 154, 227v.

[62] LMA Rep. 15, fos. 29v, 414, 430; Jour. 20, fo. 502. The Court of Aldermen ordered that 'felt, lynnen clothe and pynnes', as well as 'spynnynge wheles and all other necessarye toles and instruments' for the 'makyng of lynnen clothe' should be provided for Bridewell in 1562: LMA Rep. 15, fo. 115. See also Daly, 'Hospitals of London', p. 223.

[63] LMA Reps. 14, fo. 163; 15, fo. 115; 18, fo. 354v; 21, fo. 507v; 23, fos. 60v, 125, 241v, 327v, 578; 26(1), fo. 43v; 31(1), fo. 26v; 39, fos. 2–2v; Jour. 33, fo. 163v; BHC 2, fo. 216v; 3, fos. 382, 418v-19; 5, fos. 49, 222v; 6, fos. 85v, 108v; 7, fo. 206v; 8, fos. 35v, 107v, 279v, 325-5v; 9, fos. 430, 547, 618; BRHA BHC 4, fos. 32, 56, 115, 149, 201v, 288v, 325v, 443, 467v.

[64] Women worked until nine at night in 1632: BHC 7, fo. 298. There was also no work on other 'holy dayes', as well as 'dayes of publique fasting and thanksgiving' in the 1640s/50s. Inmates got two days off at Easter and Christmas in 1657: BHC 9, fos. 779, 811.

[65] LMA Rep. 15, fo. 364; GL MS 12806/2, fos. 39, 40; LMA Reps. 16, fos. 472v, 490; 45, fo. 234v; 16, fo. 153. See also LMA Reps. 16, fo. 138; 22, fos. 268v-9; 23, fos. 327v, 578; Letterbook V, fo. 79v; BHC 3, fos. 308, 423; 6, fos. 16, 387–7v; 7, fo. 128v.

[66] LMA Letterbook S, fo. 69; Waddington, *Considerations*, pp. 9–10, 16v; *The Humble Petition of Thomas Stanley . . . (On Behalf of Christs Hospital, St Thomas's Hospital, and Bridewell)* (1621?), n.p.; *John Howes' MS*, pp. 14, 16–17; Munday, *Briefe Chronicle*, p. 379. It seems that the first use of the term artmaster in surviving sources was in 1597, although there is a gap in Bridewell books from 1579–98. See Waddington, *Considerations*, pp. 18–19; J. G. White, *A Short History of the Royal Hospitals of Bridewell and Bethlem* (1899), pp. 7–8. Cf. Cowie, 'Bridewell', esp. 353–4.

Artmasters usually signed on for a term of seven years or so, but many chalked up at least a decade of service. They were expected to set shining examples and be solid citizens. Some had a certain number of inmates working with them: a pinmaker had charge of '40 vagrant boyes' in 1605; a glover had 'xxtie persons or more if nede be' under him in 1578.[67] Almost 100 apprentices were living and learning inside Bridewell in 1642. They were mostly the children of freemen with too many mouths to feed and not enough money to put their child in service, or young waifs found straggling on the streets: vagrants, beggars, and thieves among them, some just nine-years-old, and some 'poor' and 'fatherles', like 'little' Issac Marshal who was lucky enough to find an artmaster 'willing to take him in respect of his litlenes'.[68]

## Records

There are a million words and more in the nine surviving Bridewell courtbooks from before 1660, but they are broken records. The first surviving entry is from 1559, but there is not a single word from thirty-four of the next 100 years. The Elizabethan books leave us most in the dark: the first four cover 1559–62, 1574–9, and 1598–1604. The next six years are squashed into one book and the seven after are lost altogether. But records are unbroken from 1617 on, except for bouts of heavy plague; the court closed for four months in 1625 when the city was crushed by 'sickness'.[69] It was England's busiest judicial court, meeting twice weekly soon after it opened and three times in seven days in crunch times, notching up scores of sittings in plague-free years. The clerk's job was

---

[67] BHC 5, fo. 12v; 3, fo. 382.
[68] BRHA BHC 4, fos. 120, 125; LMA Jour. 26, fo. 312v; Rep. 21, fo. 507v; BHC 8, fos. 329, 44, 58v, 75, 122, 123v, 235, 263v, 274, 279, 287v, 288v, 304v, 355, 372, 372v, 383, 388. Parishes or families were expected to cover costs of placing children, but rates were so 'great' in 1600 that 'the pynner' complained of a 'want of boyes'. Bridewell (or the City) picked up more of the costs from then on. For later figures on numbers in Bridewell see Richard Willis, *A Sermon Preach'd Before the Right Honourable The Lord Mayor of London and the Honourable Court of Aldermen and Governours of the Several Hospitals of the City ... on Easter Tuesday, 1702* (1702), p. 18; Richard West, *A Sermon Preached Before the Right Honourable the Lord Mayor and the Honourable Court of Aldermen and Governors of the Several Hospitals of the City of London ... Being One of the Anniversary Spittal Sermons* (1711), p. 25; Maitland, *History of London*, p. 661; Faramerz Dabhoiwala, 'Summary justice in early modern London', *English Historical Review*, 121 (2006), 796–822. Work was backed up by religious guidance; a minister taught 'the word of God': BRHA BHC 4, fo. 406; BHC 7, fo. 350v; 9, fos. 204, 147, 171, 187. The bench looked for 'a fitt scholemaster' in 1632 to teach children to read and write: BHC 7, fo. 289v. A committee considered 'what roomes may bee fitt to place therein artists for keeping and educatinge girles within this hospitall in like manner as boyes' in 1652: BHC 9, fos. 580, 425.
[69] BHC 6, fo. 405.

made full time in 1577 as London grew and business boomed. The court met on Wednesday and Saturday in 1600, with two assistants from 1602 to wade through higher workloads more speedily. It sat on one day only three decades later, 'Wednesday weekly'. The day was moved to Friday soon after, back to Wednesday in 1641 (to 'suit better with the leasure of many of the governors'), and back to Friday again nine months later when governors were asked not to go to the Exchange 'about their own occacons' until the last case was over.[70]

Not only did the court fall back on weekly sittings, the number of cases in its books fell from the early 1630s on, and this had something to do with the more extensive use of summary justice around then (see Appendix Table 6a).[71] Bridewell's court single-handedly made the nature of summary justice in the city 'distinctive'.[72] It has also left us with a treasure-trove of sixty-six years of cases from its first century. No other court in London or anywhere else has left so many cases. My samples from these fat books for sources of committals, the geography of arrests, taking stock of changing meanings of crime, and, lastly, counting prosecution profiles, are 39,516, 16,320, 50,277, and 35,399 cases (respectively). Bridewell's books are thick but they do not cover everything. As well as missing years, even books stuffed with cases do not report their real scale, by as much as a factor of three Archer believes, noting disparities between the number of prisoners in a courtbook in one year (1600–1: 954 prisoners) and a count in Bridewell's end-of-year report (2,730). Dabhoiwala also notices the same shortfall over a longer timespan.[73] The entries in these books are all that we have, but we should always ask why an unknown number of cases did not make it into the

---

[70] BHC 1, fo. 158v; 3, fo. 211v; BRHA BHC 4, fo. 1; LMA Rep. 25, fo. 380; BRHA BHC 4, fo. 326; BHC 7, fo. 345; 8, fos. 327, 349v.

[71] Dabhoiwala, 'Summary justice', 798: 'Summary justice was particularly prominent in the capital: metropolitan justices appear to have relied upon it very heavily'. See also Paul Slack, 'Books of orders: the making of English social policy, 1577–1631', *Transactions of the Royal Historical Society*, 5th series, 30 (1980), 1–22; Henrik Langeluddecke, 'Law and order in seventeenth-century England: the organization of local administration during the personal rule of Charles I', *Law and History Review*, 15 (1997), 49–76; Anthony Fletcher, *Reform in the Provinces: the Government of Stuart England* (London and New Haven, CT, 1986), pp. 122–35.

[72] Dabhoiwala, 'Summary justice', 800.

[73] Ibid.; Archer, *Pursuit of Stability*, p. 238. Dabhoiwala concludes that the seventeenth-century books 'contain details of about a third of all committals' ('Summary justice', 806). Strangely, while Archer and Dabhoiwala both question what they see in the books, neither brings the same standards to bear on end-of-year counts, which they accept at face value, albeit Dabhoiwala notes difficulties in taking annual tallies from some sources ('Summary justice', esp. 804). It would be nice if we had more comparisons from the years before the full flowering of summary justice. For the earliest end-of-year counts reported in the books see BRHA BHC 4, fos. 76, 154, 227v, 322–3v.

Introduction 21

books. One possible answer is that not all referrals from elsewhere were jotted down by the clerk; another, that the bench took advantage of its wide-ranging discretionary powers to hear cases out of court; or that committals and discharges were not noted down outside court days.[74] The next question is whether or not what remains on the page is representative of the entire caseload. Archer urges caution: we know next to nothing about missing cases, so prosecution patterns from courtbooks cannot tell the whole story. Dabhoiwala, on the other hand, finds 'little reason to doubt their overall representativeness' in the time covered by this book.[75] I lean towards the view that the cross-section of cases in and out of the courtbooks is unlikely to be significantly different, except for the nagging concern that cases that ended up in court were often the results of targeted prosecution strategies. In either case, however, the message is the same: shifts in prosecution patterns resulted from perceptions and strategies.

But one thing is clear, even if they do not reveal the true scale of offending, London's mass and mess is written down in Bridewell's chock-full books. London was getting bigger not better, people thought, and the reasons are all in these books, which reveal London's growing pains in detail: vagrants, beggars, ballad-singers/sellers, pedlars, scroungers, thieves, tricksters, nips, nightwalkers, prostitutes, fishwives, inmates and their hawkish landlords, surly street porters, workshy dropouts, people with nothing to live on, all these and more metropolitan misfits fill Bridewell's pages. Each one is linked in some way to London's influx with a relation to two or more of the following: movement, streets, not being known, being lost, making ends meet, sinking. Physical and environmental scars also cover the books: dirt, smell, shabbiness, clamminess, sickness, rundown houses, dense alleys veering off at strange angles, hard-up migrants jammed into rooms like sardines. There are no better records to study petty crime before 1660. None so bulky that let us go so deep into street life or what it meant to be vagrant or pregnant with nowhere left to turn. There are vagrants on almost all pages,

---

[74] Archer, *Pursuit of Stability*, p. 238; Dabhoiwala, 'Summary justice', 801. Dabhoiwala, however, imposes a later reading on early Bridewell process. He thinks that the court 'met every two or three weeks' up until the second quarter of the eighteenth century. In fact, it met more often than this early on. This matters because he argues that disparities in counts of prisoners largely result from committals and discharges made when the court was not sitting ('Summary justice', 800). Nor is it clear that prisoners only turn up in the books if admissions or discharges occurred on court days. Early courtbooks often state that prisoners making their first appearance had been admitted earlier. Bridewell process changed continually.

[75] Archer, *Pursuit of Stability*, p. 238; Dabhoiwala, 'Summary justice', 807.

sometimes sixty or more on one leaf. Thieves turn up on most court days, some starving with nothing to live on at hunger's door except light fingers. Beggars abound. We read about startled people suddenly at sea in London, maybe fifty times the size of the town they now miss, or a thousand times bigger than the little village that now seems cozy and secure. There is real suffering, sickness, and hard luck in these books: child vagrants crawling under stalls for shelter after dark, vagrants huddling together for warmth, two boys were found huddled up in a hole one night in 1640.[76] Stories of suffering and loss, it is sometimes easy to forget that these are legal records and not the touching journals of some Tudor Mayhew. But entries get shorter as time passes. The Tudor books are a thick narrative mix with dazzling snapshots of London's slums and seedy sides. But much of this depth and texture is gone by the time we get deep into the Stuart books. So many people were coming to the court by then that they were listed one-by-one on the page to save space and time: name, address (if they had one), job (if lucky), and a single sentence about offence. Lines and lines of vagrants, but there still remained a concern for character and circumstance in Bridewell, as we will see later in Chapter 7.

I count and think with Bridewell's courtbooks, mixing archival number crunching with work on the roots and meanings of crime. Resulting timelines often move up and down – sometimes suddenly – in shifts embedded in cultures and conditions. This book is about these conditions and cultures. It is about the city, not Bridewell. Although the metropolis was Bridewell's patch, London's story cannot be told from the books of one court alone. True enough Bridewell opens up aspects of London life in vivid detail and colour, and we can lean on its records for crime figures that dwarf other judicial courts in terms of size and significance. But we also need to look at records from both sides of the walls. Quarter sessions books, rolls, and registers from the City and next-door Westminster and Middlesex, along with Westminster's Court of Burgesses, give us far better senses of suburban sprawl. And when we add church court stories to this bumper crop – from London Diocese/Archdeaconry deposition/correction books – long gone London is resuscitated for a while. The city inside the walls was jam-packed with 'little worlds' like parishes, and the only way to get to know them is to work with parish, ward, and guild materials and think small in terms of their successes and setbacks, but also tall for what these local stories tell us about larger London. I have worked with the accounts and/or vestry books of

---

[76] BHC 8, fo. 316.

almost half of London's 109 parishes (and a number from across the Westminster border), as well as a handful of surviving wardmote books covering decades before 1660 (and some more that start later) and enough guild records to give us a good feel for their part in trying to keep London safe in testing times with senses of identity that were something to be proud of.

I want to get deep into the minds of people on both sides of the law. All policies or prosecutions begin with perceptions, and can be traced back to an idea formulated one day in certain constructions of circumstances. Journals and Repertories of London's leading governing bodies – Common Council and Court of Aldermen – survive for the entire time span of this book, and with City Remembrancia books, Letterbooks, and Cashbooks give us wonderful windows on policies and perceptions through their meetings, think-tanks, and laws at the end of the line. And one advantage of recreating London from guild, ward, and parish materials is that we can reconstruct pipelines that made it possible for news, laws, or guidelines to travel quickly through the city, and to look at local circumstances that made Guildhall big-wigs think that it was high time to take action. The longest pipeline stretched west to Whitehall, keeping the City and Crown in touch with one another. We can follow both ends of this dialogue by reading City sources alongside Privy Council Registers, Crown proclamations, or various categories of State Papers. Another Whitehall source – Star Chamber – adds thick details about life and labour in London in cases that can run on for several hundred pages in stories that are never dull. Last but not least, House of Lords Main Papers add more background material on the state of the city. The last link of major significance for what follows is the one that joined London's hospitals in a system of referrals, advising, and sometimes pooling resources. Bridewell was one of five, and I have worked through the surviving journals and accounts from the other four – Christ's, St Bartholomew's, St Thomas's, and Bethlem (the last bound up in Bridewell books) – from the 1550s on. This small mountain of archives from the City, Crown, church courts, criminal courts, hospitals, parishes, prisons, and wards covers all points east, west, north, and south of the city, and not too many stones are left unturned (these manuscript sources are listed one-by-one in the bibliography at the end of this book).

★ ★ ★

The 'house' did not topple down until 1863 when Bridewell was demolished, leaving behind its plum riverside spot for developers and speculators. The last prisoner left in 1855, exactly three centuries after the first one walked in through the gate. Nothing remains now only the name in Bridewell Lane, Place, or Theatre, rhetoric in other words.[77] Nothing physical that is, except for records. And rhetorics are also still with us today in these books and records. It is now time to more closely relate these rhetorics of civic fame, citizenship, crime, growth, magistracy, and control to the scope and scale of London's troubles, and to see in what ways, if any, interpretations of crime and steps to improve policing were linked to senses of change and loss. The first chapter continues to look at London's 'sare' changes and perceptions of troubles, and one thing to take note of will be the near synchronicity between feelings that London's freedom had slumped to an all-time-low and accelerations in troubles after 1620, a time also when perceptions of crime altered significantly.

---

[77] Derek Gadd and Tony Dyson, 'Bridewell Palace: excavations at 9–11 Bridewell Place and 1–3 Tudor Street, City of London, 1978', *Post-Medieval Archaeology*, 15 (1981), 1–79, esp. 2.

*Part I*

Change

# 1 Troubled times

### 'Panic milieux'

Not one day goes by in any city of decent size without troubles – some slight, others more momentous – that *continually* shake its fabric and surface. Cities are never still, and they are never 'at rest'.[1] They grow, buzz, and change all the time, and keeping on top of trouble is always a round-the-clock concern. 'Disorder', one historian writes, 'was the natural enemy of urban life'.[2] Travellers are always trooping in and out of cities where they often have few or no roots. Some settle down somewhere and stay put long enough to become accepted and trusted by their new neighbours. Others are less lucky and struggle to stay above water. Many sink unless they can turn to makeshifts and crime to keep hunger at bay. This was how many thousands of people kept on top of things against the odds in sixteenth- and seventeenth-century London.

They arrived in droves, although migration did not mean the same for different classes, ages, genders, or races. Migrants came from all over the country and overseas. Many of them were down on their luck and hoped to scratch a living with a bit of work here and there. More fortunate were young men who came to London for a formal craft training to start working their way up the City ladder.[3] London was the 'head' and 'fountaine' of the land, authors gloated, pulling in people from far and wide. With so much movement in and out London set trends for other parts of the land to follow. 'We much imitate your fashions', Robert

---

[1] Spiro Kostof, *The City Shaped: Urban Patterns and Meanings through History* (Boston, 1991), p. 13.
[2] Christopher Friedrichs, *The Early Modern City, 1450–1750* (Harlow, 1995), pp. 245, 274, 323.
[3] Roger Finlay, *Population and Metropolis: The Demography of London, 1580–1650* (Cambridge, 1981), chaps. 5–7; Steve Rappaport, *Worlds Within Worlds: Structures of Life in Sixteenth-Century London* (Cambridge, 1989), chaps. 7–8.

Jenison said in 1630, 'good and evil'.[4] London was a magnet for migrants, for better or for worse. There was real suffering on the streets, and migrants glutted the workforce, depressing wages at the lower ends of job-markets and sending prices so high that guilds and others said that hard done by residents had less food to put on the table.[5]

Vagrants kept coming in flocks despite scores of laws and more policing. 'We cannot banish that pestilent canker by any degree', Robert Hitchcock groaned in 1580.[6] By now, and with more force as time passed, London's leaders *thought* that their city was on the brink of collapse. London had become what Roland Barthes calls 'a panic milieu'.[7] Barthes was commenting on Racine's Seraglio, and what he means by 'panic milieu' was somewhere or something 'subject to an external certitude that terrorizes it', but about which it knows almost nothing at first, not even what makes up this threat on its doorstep.[8] This state of not knowing and the speculations and anxieties that always follow describes the uneasy situation that City magistrates found themselves in four centuries or so ago. They did not call their plight a 'panic milieu', but they did say over and over again that their city was facing up to 'extraordinary' and 'infinite' difficulties that seemed far beyond their comprehension.

Strange, then, that some historians argue that early modern London was stable, blessed with 'fundamental stability' in a time of whirlwind growth.[9] London was like a 'helter-skelter' rushing to the plum position

---

[4] John Lawrence, *A Golden Trumpet to Rowse up a Drowsie Magistrate: Or, a Patterne for a Governors Practise Drawne From Christs Comming to, Beholding of, and Weeping Over Hierusalem. As it was Sounded at Pauls Crosse the 11 of Aprill, 1624* (1624), p. 38; Robert Jenison, *The Cities Safetie. Or a Fruitfull Treatise (and Usefull for These Dangerous Times)* (1630), epistle dedicatory. See also A. L. Beier, *Masterless Men: the Vagrancy Problem in England, 1560–1640* (1985), chap. 3; Peter Borsay, 'The London connection: cultural diffusion and the eighteenth-century provincial town', *London Journal*, 19 (1994), 21–35; Borsay, 'London, 1660–1800: a distinctive culture?', in Peter Clark and Raymond Gillespie, eds., *Two Capitals: London and Dublin, 1500–1840*, Proceedings of the British Academy, 107 (Oxford and London, 2001), pp. 167–84.

[5] Jeremy Boulton, 'Food prices and the standard of living in the "century of revolution", 1580–1700', *Economic History Review*, 53 (2000), 455–92.

[6] Robert Hitchcock, *Hitchcockes New Yeres Gift to Englande. A Pollitique Platt for the Honour of the Prince, the Greate Profite of the Publique State, Relief to the Poore, Preservation of the Riche, Reformation of Roges and Idle Persones, and the Wealthe of Thousandes that Knowes not Howe to Live* (1580), fo. A ir.

[7] Roland Barthes, *On Racine*, trans. Richard Howard (New York, 1981), p. 98.

[8] Ibid., quoting p. 98. Cf. Michel De Certeau, *The Practice of Everyday Life*, trans. Steven Randall (Berkeley, CA, 1984), p. 95.

[9] Ian W. Archer, *The Pursuit of Stability: Social Relations in Elizabethan London* (Cambridge, 1991), p. 9.

of Europe's largest city, but it was stable.[10] Stability is the keyword in work stretching back over more than twenty-five years – 'the politics of stability', 'change and stability', or 'the pursuit of stability'. Foster calls the last chapter of his 'portrait of the rulers' 'the triumph of stability', without the slightest nod at the 'hurly burly' of daily life. Stability was 'fundamental', 'pervasive', and in 'full flower' in the middle of a population boom. Later on, as the suburbs circled the city in a pincer-like movement, consuming and asphyxiating it in stark contemporary metaphors, London was by and large 'peaceful and harmonious'. True this was a testing time, but 'in some respects' it was a time of 'remarkable stability and continuity'.[11] Yet the very idea of a stable city is a paradox, something that is a wish rather than a reality. After all, it is the pace and perpetual flux of cities that makes them such exhilarating subjects for us.

It was a tough task to keep on top of swift changes. Archer argues that London's leaders 'pursued' stability from one day to the next. Stability was never inevitable but the outcome of nonstop policy-making and situations when citizens pulled together for London's benefit. Historians who lean towards a stable London dwell upon social structures, administration, and institutions, pinning interpretations on functions, smart policies, and common causes that linked citizens. The absence of deep-seated divisions among the top brass is a reason why the city stayed stable. Not even religious reformation caused cracks to appear. There was always enough middle ground to make sure that policies stayed on course. We now have a little library of work on structures of life and government, showing that the city *did work well* in even the worst of times. Office-holding reached far down social ladders to the lowliest householders, spreading common identities through participation and a stake in the parish, ward, and city. As many as one-in-ten householders held office at any one point in time. Another argument is that public welfare helped to keep London stable, placating paupers with

---

[10] Quoted in Lawrence Manley, *Literature and Culture in Early Modern London* (Cambridge, 1995), p. 427. Cf. Lien Bich Luu, '"Taking the bread out of our mouths": xenophobia in early modern London', *Immigrants & Minorities*, 19 (2000), 1–22, esp. 5: 'Massive immigration combined with high mortality rates in London produced high population turnover and a very unstable society'.

[11] F. F. Foster, *The Politics of Stability: a Portrait of the Rulers of Elizabethan London* (1977), p. 4; Archer, *Pursuit of Stability*, p. 9; Valerie Pearl, 'Change and stability in seventeenth-century London', in Jonathan Barry, ed., *The Tudor and Stuart Town: a Reader in English Urban History, 1530–1688* (Harlow, 1990), pp. 139–65, first published in *London Journal*, 5 (1979), 3–34; Rappaport, *Worlds Within Worlds*, p. 18; Vanessa Harding, *The Dead and the Living in Paris and London, 1500–1670* (Cambridge, 2002), p. 274. Even suburban fringes have been seen in better lights: Joseph P. Ward, *Metropolitan Communities: Trade Guilds, Identity, and Change in Early Modern London* (Stanford, CA, 1997); Ian W. Archer, 'The government of London, 1500–1650', *London Journal*, 26 (2001), 19–28, esp. 19.

decent hand-outs. There were also ties between citizenship, respectability, and hard graft in guilds that were as democratic as we could expect in this culture. Guilds provided a focus for belonging through 'brotherly' citizenship and recommended policies to tackle the glut of foreign workers. Other ties were clinched in vestries and wards where middling people rubbed shoulders with their neighbours to work for the good of the community. Neighbourliness is often said to have been a social glue that encouraged people living side-by-side to stick together through thick and thin. Neighbours were told to get along in Christian ethics and bad-tempered neighbours could suddenly find themselves frozen out from opportunities to work, socialize, or to ask for good turns. Even individual aspirations were directed towards the city's stability. Ambitious citizens, this argument runs, were comforted by the chance of moving through the ranks all the way up to the mayor's 'seat', like lucky Dick Whittington. Generations of citizens were raised on rags-to-riches stories in apprentice literatures that made a virtue of patiently waiting for the next chance to move upwards. The dream of ascent smoothed frustrations with the hope of a better office/rank in the not too distant future. 'The apprentice doth not think it much to wipe his master's shoes and sweep the gutters', James Howell mused, 'because he hopes one day to be an alderman'.[12]

---

[12] James Howell, *Familiar Letters or Epistolae Ho-Elianae*, 3 vols. (1903), vol. III, p. 136. The main works on social structure, institutions, and administration include Archer, *Pursuit of Stability*, esp. chaps 2–5; Archer, 'The arts and acts of memorialization in early modern London', in J. F. Merritt, ed., *Imagining Early Modern London: Perceptions and Portrayals of the City From Stow to Strype, 1598–1720* (Cambridge, 2001), pp. 89–113; Archer, 'Government of London'; M. Bembow, 'The Court of Aldermen and the Assizes: the policy of price control in Elizabethan London', *Guildhall Studies in London History*, 4 (1980), 93–118; Jeremy Boulton, *Neighbourhood and Society: a London Suburb in the Seventeenth Century* (Cambridge, 1987); Boulton, 'London, 1540–1700', in Peter Clark, ed., *The Cambridge Urban History of Britain: Volume II, 1540–1840* (Cambridge, 2000), pp. 315–46; Susan Brigden, *London and the Reformation* (Oxford, 1989); Harding, *The Dead and the Living*, chap. 9; Harding, 'Reformation and culture, 1540–1700', in Clark, ed., *Cambridge Urban History*, pp. 263–88; Harding, 'Controlling a complex metropolis, 1650–1750: politics, parishes, and powers', *London Journal*, 26 (2001), 29–37; R. W. Herlan, 'Social articulation and the configuration of parochial poverty in London on the eve of the Restoration', *Guildhall Studies in London History*, 2 (1976), 43–53; Herlan, 'Poor relief in the London parish of Antholin's Budge Row, 1638–1664', *Guildhall Studies in London History*, 2 (1977), 179–99; Herlan, 'Poor relief in the London parish of Dunstan in the West during the English Revolution', *Guildhall Studies in London History*, 2 (1977), 13–36; David Hickman, 'Religious belief and pious practice among London's Elizabethan elite', *Historical Journal*, 42 (1999), 941–60; R. G. Lang, 'Social origins and social aspirations of Jacobean London merchants', *Economic History Review*, 2nd series, 27 (1974), 28–47; A. E. McCampbell, 'The London parish and the London precinct, 1640–1660', *Guildhall Studies in London History*, 2 (1976), 107–24; Valerie Pearl, *London and the Outbreak of the Puritan Revolution: City Government and National Politics* (Oxford, 1961);

Troubled times 31

These explanations cannot cover everyone living and working in London in the sixteenth and seventeenth centuries. Office-holding and membership of civic bodies apply to male citizens only and leave out London's largest social groups – women and young people – as well as the 'infinite multitude' of rogues and foreigners. The stability story of Dick Whittington's waiting patiently in line for the next move up the ladder is a citizens' tale, and only people with claims through settlement could get long-term parish hand-outs. Recent estimates suggest that around three-quarters of resident adult men took the citizens' oath in 1550, a figure that fell to almost one-half nine decades later. Even so, barely *one-in-five* of all Londoners were citizens in 1550; a figure that slumped after that.[13] The citizens' story was a minority one. Most people had shallow roots in the city and no chance to climb social ladders. Family or trade ties could help some migrants to settle down, along with ready-made communities from their home counties or countries.[14] But many lacked a head start and life was a gamble of makeshifts and hardships. Focus on the 'structures of life' only gives us fleeting glimpses of these sides of the city and the good-for-nothings who lived rough in London, who were the main sources of trouble in the minds of magistrates.

This limited social focus has not gone unnoticed, but the leading line so far has been to show how pressured social structures held together. Magistrates teamed up with the right blend of clout and care, bridging gulfs between rich and poor with hand-outs and spreading civic duties far and wide. But arranged one after another like this, a list of 'working-parts' makes interpretations seem almost inevitable. Analysing functions like social mobility or office-holding leads like clockwork to the position that things ticked over smoothly, even more so when sources slant interpretations, like the guild records on which Rappaport pins so much or the

---

Pearl, 'Change and stability in seventeenth-century London'; Pearl, 'Social policy in early modern London', in H. Lloyd-Jones, B. Worden, and Pearl, eds., *History and Imagination: Essays in Honour of H. R. Trevor-Roper* (1979), pp. 115–31; Rappaport, *Worlds Within Worlds*, esp. chaps 2 and 5–8; Rappaport, 'Social structure and mobility in sixteenth-century London: part I', *London Journal*, 9 (1983), 107–35; Rappaport, 'Social structure and mobility in sixteenth-century London: part II', *London Journal*, 10 (1984), 107–34; Ward, *Metropolitan Communities*, esp. chaps 2 and 5–6.

[13] Rappaport, *Worlds Within Worlds*, pp. 52–3; Boulton, *Neighbourhood and Society*, pp. 151–4.

[14] Peter Clark, *British Clubs and Societies 1580–1800: the Origins of an Associational World* (Oxford, 2000), chap. 8; Clark, 'Migrants in the city: the process of social adaptation in English towns, 1500–1800', in Clark and David Souden, eds., *Migration and Society in Early Modern England* (1987), pp. 267–91; Vivien Brodsky, 'Mobility and marriage in pre-industrial England: a demographic and social structural analysis of marriage, 1570–1690, with particular reference to London and general reference to Middlesex, Kent, Essex, and Hertfordshire', unpublished PhD thesis, University of Cambridge (1978), esp. pp. 220–33.

churchwarden accounts used by Pearl.[15] These sources depict London's more stable sides, giving lop-sided views that lessen disagreement or dissatisfaction. We need more work on how people viewed offices. There was a sliding scale of satisfaction: shovelling muck and lighting lamps were lower down the pecking order than balancing parish accounts. Some work also exaggerates the unity of guilds and vestries.[16] But Archer for one notices deepening differentiation in guilds and vestries towards 1600 that was increasingly expressed in discriminatory vocabularies of 'sorts of people', and claims by the cream of the parish or guild to be the 'better sort', 'good men', or 'chiefest', to whom power belonged like a law of nature.[17] Archer has skillfully shown the growing distance between the haves and have-nots towards 1600, and the biting inequalities that caused some to complain bitterly about their hard luck.[18] London was fast becoming a city of difference not deference.

The opposite point of view to stability is that there was staggering strain and *real* crisis in London. Pearl calls this 'doom and gloom' and wonders why authors write bleakly about 'a totally dangerous, primitive but huge city'.[19] Pearl wrote this at the same time that Lee Beier, looking through a reverse lens, saw sprawling urban mess, like Calcutta's ghettos today. Another 'doom and gloom' historian – Peter Clark – writes that in London in 1595 it looked like 'the whole fabric of the urban community might be about to disintegrate'.[20] This could be another city altogether

---

[15] Cf. Archer, *Pursuit of Stability*, pp. 15–16.

[16] Most recently Ward, *Metropolitan Communities*.

[17] Archer, *Pursuit of Stability*, pp. 116–18 and 120–4. Typical examples of this discriminatory vocabulary are GL MSS 9236/1, account book, fo. 94, register of orders and decrees, fos. 76–7; 3016/1, fo. 45; 4415/1, fo. 88 (2nd pag. series); 3570/2, fo. 97; 4887/1, fos. 196, 214; 4216/1, fos. 62, 72; 959/1, fos. 58, 84v; SCH company minute book C, fo. 77; GCL company minute books P2, attached papers at end of book, fo. 10; T, fo. 17; E. Freshfield, ed., *Minutes of the Vestry Meeting and Other Records of the Parish of St Christopher le Stocks in the Parish of London* (1886), p. 23; Freshfield, ed., *The Vestry Minute Book of the Parish of St Margaret Lothbury in the City of London, 1571–1677* (1887), pp. 14, 24. Significances of this social vocabulary are discussed by Keith Wrightson, 'Estates, degrees, and sorts: changing perceptions of the social order in Tudor and Stuart England', in Penelope Corfield, ed., *Language, History, and Class* (Oxford, 1991), pp. 30–52; and '"Sorts of people" in Tudor and Stuart England', in Jonathan Barry and Christopher Brooks, eds., *The Middling Sort of People: Culture, Society and Politics in England, 1500–1800* (Basingstoke, 1994), pp. 28–51; Archer, *Pursuit of Stability*, p. 67; Sidney and Beatrice Webb, *English Local Government . . . the Parish and the County* (1906), pp. 40, 176.

[18] Archer, *Pursuit of Stability*, p. 9 and chaps 5–6.

[19] Pearl, 'Change and stability', pp. 140–1. Cf. Rappaport, *Worlds Within Worlds*, pp. 1–22.

[20] A. L. Beier, 'Social problems in Elizabethan London', in Barry, ed., *Tudor and Stuart Town*, pp. 121–38, quoting p. 138, first published in *Journal of Interdisciplinary History*, 9 (1978–9), 203–21; Peter Clark, 'A crisis contained? The condition of English towns in the 1590s', in Clark, ed., *The European Crisis of the 1590s* (1985), pp. 44–66.

from the one in Foster's or Pearl's pages. For a long time now we have talked about an end-of-century crisis in the 1590s when trade slumped, jobs disappeared, harvests failed, riots erupted, and sky-high inflation sucked up rock-bottom wages. London scraped through a mid-1590s crisis, in Archer's view, but at a heavy price.[21] This is still the leading position on London's troubles, but crisis is not a helpful term. Its copious use by historians implies some blessed interlude when things settled down for a while, suffering was over for the time being, and people could now breathe a collective sigh of relief.[22] If we think that London was hit by crisis in the 1590s, we will need fresh words for later decades like the 1620s or 1630s, when tensions were sharper and longer lasting, and living standards slumped to all-time lows for the lower classes.[23]

Stability and crisis are tricky terms, not always handled carefully. The opposites of stability, Rappaport writes, are 'anarchy', 'chaos', or 'rebellious' routs. London is either about to fall apart or it is calm.[24] It was not Europe's rowdiest city by this measure. Apart from the 1590s, when empty granaries led to 'broyles and tumults', it was largely untouched by food riots. But London had a long tradition of 'anti-alien' unrest, stretching back to 'Evil' May Day 1517 when lives were lost.[25] Another tradition, this time a festive one, led to large-scale riots on holidays like Shrove Tuesday, when Venice's ambassador spoke with concern about 'furious misrule and impetus': 'no proclamations, no authority [and] no force' could quell the 1617 brothel sackers.[26] 'Multitudes' also took to the streets for high-profile executions, like Strafford's gallows day (1641),

---

[21] Archer, *Pursuit of Stability*, pp. 9–14; Archer, 'The 1590s: apotheosis or nemesis of the Elizabethan regime?', in A. Briggs and D. Snowman, eds., *Fins de Siècle: How Centuries End, 1400–2000* (London and New Haven, CT, 1996), pp. 65–97; M. J. Power, 'London and the control of the "crisis" of the 1590s', *History*, 70 (1985), 371–85; Power, 'A "crisis" reconsidered: social and demographic dislocation in London in the 1590s', *London Journal*, 12 (1986), 134–45.

[22] Cf. Laura Gowing, *Domestic Dangers: Words, Women, and Sex in Early Modern London* (Oxford, 1996), pp. 28, 275, who questions a model of 'crisis' in gender relations in 1560–1640 because 'Gender is *always* in contest' and is a scene of 'perpetual conflict'.

[23] Boulton, 'Food prices and the standard of living', esp. 468.

[24] Rappaport, *Worlds Within Worlds*, pp. 18, 19.

[25] LMA Rep. 23, fos. 413, 414; Archer *Pursuit of Stability*, pp. 1–7; Andrew Pettigree, *Foreign Protestant Communities in Sixteenth-Century London* (Oxford, 1986), p. 292 and chap. 9; Roger Manning, *Village Revolts: Social Protest and Popular Disturbances in England, 1509–1640* (Oxford, 1988), chap. 8.

[26] CSPV 1617–19, p. 247; TNA SP14/90/135; Paul Griffiths, *Youth and Authority: Formative Experiences in England, 1560–1640* (Oxford, 1996), pp. 151–61; Keith Lindley, 'Riot prevention and control in early Stuart London', *Transactions of the Royal Historical Society*, 5th series, 33 (1983), 109–26. For crowd-control see LMA Jours. 22, fos. 56v, 366; 23, fo. 370; 24, fo. 274v; 25, fo. 322; 31, fo. 152; 36, fo. 224v; 37, fo. 268v; Reps. 38, fo. 61; 41, fo. 273v; 53, fo. 139v.

or funerals, like Buckingham's (1628), when it was said that they leaped with 'joy'.[27] These outbursts were linked by coherent political positions, including anti-alien feelings, anti-corruption, anti-Catholicism, and defending jobs. This politics also questioned political systems, as when crowds camped outside Parliament in the winter of 1641–2, or when Lambeth Palace was mobbed in 1640.[28]

So London was not without riots. But this was not the main meaning of instability at this time. Pearl or Rappaport do not imagine instability as small commonplace acts like picking pockets or creeping unseen into the city, even though this was a time when movement without a pass was more than enough to put people behind bars. Instability is all too often imagined in terms of cataclysms that shake systems; as riots, rebellions, or social chaos. This is not how London's leaders imagined instability four centuries ago. They certainly worried about rebellions and riots and kept granaries topped up to make sure that hunger would not lead to violence. But I cannot think of a single text from the leading records of City government that ever uses the languages of instability/stability to describe social order four centuries or so ago in quite the same way as historians use them today to make measurements on some sort of social strain gauge. Magistrates did not think in terms of chaos on one side and tranquility on the other. They never juxtaposed stability and instability like this. Yet we still ask how stable or unstable was London back then, and how severe was social strain. But contrasting peaks of stability/instability are not convincing descriptions of the state of the city. It is better to leave behind the habit of constantly opposing them and accept instead that no city in the grip of the sort of growth that London experienced after 1550 could ever avoid deep-rooted tensions and widespread disorder. But this is not the same thing as saying that London was tottering on the brink of 'disintegrat[ion]'. This debate about the nature of social relations and order in sixteenth- and seventeenth-century London now needs to be recast.

There was no overall model of stability to set against the continuous problems caused by rapid growth. Rather there was a 'daily' stress on

---

[27] CSPV 1628–9, p. 337; 1640–2, pp. 147–8, 151. Other serious disturbances included the murder of Dr Lambe in 1628 (CSPV 1628–9, p. 157), the aftermath of the Blackfriars roof collapse in 1623 (CSPV 1623–5, p. 189), and the Southwark riots in 1592 (LMA Remembrancia Book 1, fos. 341–2).
[28] TNA SP16/468/99–114; HOL MP 10–12–1641; 27-12-1641; 15-1-1642; CSPV 1640–2, pp. 80, 83, 97, 225, 271–2 (the 'December Days'); TNA SP16/453/43, 16/453/61–2; 16/454/39; 16/455/7–8; 16/455/102 (Lambeth riots). See also Tim Harris, *London Crowds in the Reign of Charles II: Propaganda and Politics from the Restoration until the Exclusion Crisis* (Cambridge, 1987).

process; on making policy, policing the streets, and on good working relations between the Guildhall and each guild, ward, and parish to try and keep on top of problems. For magistrates, vagrants, beggars, and thieves were the root cause of the city's disorders, not daring rebels or wild rioters. The results of vagrancy were among the city's most pressing concerns: dilapidation, disease, crushing poverty, or crime. Even Rappaport slips in a reference to 'daily crime and violence', but this is not his litmus test of instability.[29] It is better to stick to contemporary perceptions that brooded on crimes like vagrancy that were related to rapid growth. Meanings of crime followed suit in the seventeenth century when the courts were snowed under by such 'environmental' crimes.[30] London did not have a single stable day if we follow magistrates' perceptions. Vagrancy was a round-the-clock concern for one thing, and cutpurses and cutthroats walked the streets, as we shall see. Vagrants taunted and injured officers and mocked well-to-do passers-by. Not many days went by without some loud-mouthed or violent vagrant showing up in courtrooms, and there were more of these small street wars after 1600. This sense of continuous concern comes out strongly from the records of City government, and it meant that London's leaders were always on edge with predictably pessimistic perceptions that still matter greatly for us. We can chart London's size and shape statistically, but such quantification can lead to some inappropriate calculations and interpretations. Rappaport, for example, estimates that vagrants numbered less than one-fifth of 1 per cent of London's total population and concludes that they could not have been any sort of serious threat to the city's well-being.[31] But vagrants swarmed continually through London, or at least City magistrates *thought* that they did, saying over and over again that 'badde people' and vagrants 'dailie arrive', 'dailie swarme', and 'dailie haunte' all corners of the city. Their repetitive emphasis upon here and now – 'dailie' – and first-hand experience is as good a guide as we are ever likely to get to perceptions of threats that cannot be retrieved from cold numbers alone. Magistrates knew that vagrancy was on the rise. They saw it with their own eyes out on the streets and inside courtrooms. They watched the decay of some parts of their city with dismay. And a number of them were also victims of crime themselves, or knew someone who had lost something to a thief one day or been hounded on a street by aggressive beggars on another.

---

[29] Rappaport, *Worlds Within Worlds*, p. 18.  [30] See below, pp. 199–204.
[31] Rappaport, *Worlds Within Worlds*, p. 5.

### Here and now, in front of our eyes

'What London hath beene of auncient time, men may here see, as what it is now every man doth behold', Stow wrote, mixing past and present in verbal optics. 'It is impossible that our tongues should unfold so fully the enormities of this great cittie, as your eyes may discern them', John Lawrence said and saw in 1624.[32] This stress on seeing and present-day experience was stronger after 1600. 'Our eyes are on you', Stephen Denison told London in 1627.[33] People knew that London was growing even without exact mathematics. London 'thou art so thronged with multitudes of people, that they go in and out at thy gates by hundreds and thousands', Thomas Jackson marvelled in 1609. The city 'is growne very populous and inlarged over what in antient tyme it was', Common Council complained in 1644. 'It is grown at last too big for the kingdom', Peter Heylyn said in 1652.[34] Governors groaned about 'overpeopling' (1580), 'populousness' (1579), and 'an overflow of people' (1608). Aldermen said that 'the citty groweth dayly more populous' in 1609, and Common Council claimed that it was 'exceeding full' in 1627. John Jones called this the 'populous age'. The press of people was so great that it even seemed that houses might topple down. People meet 'in such shoales', Dekker wrote, 'that postes are set up of purpose to strengthen the houses, least with justling one another they should shoulder them downe'.[35] Growth was talked about all the time in the Guildhall, around vestry tables, and in alehouses and parlours. It was also apparent from headcounts, like the weekly totals of deaths at the foot of the *Bills of Mortality* that shaped understandings of the city for Londoners thumbing through their columns, along with the first demographers, chief among them John Graunt and William Petty. Working with the *Bills*, Petty reckoned that London's population had doubled in just four decades to

---

[32] Stow is quoted in Cynthia Wall, *The Literary and Cultural Spaces of Restoration London* (Cambridge, 1998), p. 99; Lawrence, *A Golden Trumpet*, p. 41.
[33] Stephen Denison, *The White Wolfe: Or, a Sermon Preached at Pauls Crosse, Feb. 11 ... 1627* (1627), epistle dedicatory. Cf. Manley, *Literature and Culture*, p. 165; David Harris Sacks, 'London's dominion: the metropolis, the market economy, and the state', in Lena Cowan Orlin, ed., *Material London, ca. 1600* (Philadelphia, PA, 2000), pp. 20–54, esp. p. 23.
[34] Thomas Jackson, *Londons New-Yeeres Gift, Or the Uncovering of the Foxe* (1609), fo. 15v; LMA Jour. 40, fo. 110; Peter Heylyn, *Cosmographie* (1652), p. 270. Cf. Paul Slack, 'Perceptions of the metropolis in seventeenth-century England', in Peter Burke, Brian Harrison, and Slack, eds., *Civil Histories: Essays presented to Sir Keith Thomas* (Oxford, 2000), pp. 161–80; Vanessa Harding, 'City, capital, and metropolis: the changing shape of seventeenth-century London', in Merritt, ed., *Imagining Early Modern London*, pp. 117–43, esp. p. 123.
[35] Thomas Dekker, *The Seven Deadly Sinnes of London*, 1606, in A. B. Grosart, ed., *Non-Dramatic Works of Thomas Dekker*, 5 vols. (1884–6), vol. II, p. 50.

Troubled times 37

about 670,000 in 1682.[36] But the costs of growth were well known to Londoners a full century before Petty started counting.

Growth had moral and political dimensions and was often imagined as grotesque. London, Roland Freart snapped, was 'a monstrous body'.[37] Multitudes of alehouses popped up, 'more frequented than the church', John Lawrence preached with sadness. Sin was a 'fashion' in London. 'You see how full it is of sinne?', George Webbe asked at Paul's Cross in 1609. 'Never were people so defiled with it as in our age', Webbe added. London was Sodom, Adam Hill said with sorrow, also at Paul's Cross in 1595.[38] The city can turn the tables, John Jones quipped, and send its 'strumpets, rogues, beggars, heretics, theeves, false witnesses, [and] gluttons' back home. But London was long past the point of no return by now.[39] It had taken no notice of warnings like plagues, floods, or earthquakes, as God, sick of the moral mess below, tossed lightning rods or whipped up waves to get people to change for the better.[40] Crime and sin cut deeply into the city's crust; even the stones were stained by the vice 'volcano'. 'O London if I should hold my peace, the very stones would speak against it', Webbe said again at Paul's Cross, mingling morals and the environment.[41] This was not good growth and it modified ideas of the city and crime, which were more often explained in terms of physical change after 1600. Worse still, population 'overflows' were not evenly spread. It was the 'meaner sort' who packed into the city without the

---

[36] J. C. Robertson, 'Reckoning with London: interpreting the *Bills of Mortality* before John Graunt', *Urban History*, 23 (1996), 325–50, esp. 338–9; William Petty, *Another Essay in Political Arithmetick Concerning the Growth of the City of London* (1683), fo. A2r and pp. 9–10, 26. See also Petty, *Five Essays in Political Arithmetick* (1687); John Graunt, *Natural and Political Observations ... Made Upon the Bills of Mortality* (1662). The best accounts of political arithmetic include Paul Slack, *From Reformation to Improvement: Public Welfare in Early Modern England* (Oxford, 1999), chap. 4; Slack, 'Government and information in seventeenth-century England', *Past and Present*, 184 (2004), 33–68; Barbara J. Shapiro, *A Culture of Fact: England, 1550–1720* (Ithaca, NY, 2000), chap. 3; Steven Shapin, *A Social History of Truth: Civility and Science in Seventeenth-Century England* (Chicago, IL, 1994), chap. 5.
[37] Roland Freart, *A Parallel of the Antient Architecture with the Modern*, trans. John Evelyn, 2nd edition (1707), epistle dedicatory, fo. 5v.
[38] Lawrence, *A Golden Trumpet*, p. 101; George Webbe, *Gods Controversie with England. Or a description of the Fearefull and Lamentable Estate which this land at this Present is in ... Preached at Pauls Crosse upon Trinitie Sunday ... 1609* (1609), pp. 114, 112; Adam Hill, *The Crie of England. A Sermon Preached at Paules Crosse, ... September 1593* (1595), pp. 3–4; John Jones, *The Arte and Science of Preserving Bodie and Soule in Healthe, Wisdome, and Catholike Religion* (1579), p. 40.
[39] Jones, *Arte and Science of Preserving Bodie and Soule*, p. 40.
[40] See Alexandra Walsham, *Providence in Early Modern England* (Oxford, 1999), chap. 3; Margaret Healy, *Fictions of Disease in Early Modern England: Bodies, Plagues, and Politics* (Basingstoke, 2001), chaps 2–3.
[41] Webbe, *God's Controversie With England*, p. 112.

comforting balance of more magistrates.[42] It was pointed out that parishes grew quickly but that the numbers of constables stayed the same. The weak spot a few years later was the lack of justices in 'populous' London.[43] Matching arguments were made for opening more bridewells in the London area. A single one in Bridewell's large patch could not cope with waves of wanderers and thieves, it was said in the case for a house of correction in Middlesex in 1614.[44] Steps were taken to speed up legal processes clogged by heavy caseloads. Special 'screening' sessions worked through the backlog of cases two days before gaol deliveries, binding over suspects until the next sessions. A special sessions dealt with rogues in 1595. The City carpenter carved a new desk for the Newgate clerk two decades later, 'for the easier drawing of indictments and more speedier dispatche of [sessions] busines'. But the pace was still too slow in the courtroom, and not long after the Old Bailey dock was 'enlardged' to cram in more prisoners.[45]

London seemed awash with intractable problems. Even past weather seemed better. Nobody could remember a winter so bitter as the one in 1607–8, when the city was blockaded and freezing.[46] This chill, like the downpour of vagrants (1607) or the number of inmates (1630–7), fishwives (1584), subdivided tenements (1637), printing presses in 'secret corners' (1583), or alehouses (1614, 1629) was 'excessive'.[47] London was 'exceedingly pestered' by beggars (1636), 'much pestered' by vagrants (1616), and more 'pestered' by 'loose and idle' vagrants and thieves than anywhere else (1580, 1614, and 1642). The streets were also 'pestered' by speedy traffic (1613) and smelly 'filth' (1619).[48] If this was not bad enough, vagrants 'swarmed' in 'great multitudes' (1557–1630), more so after 1600, but as long ago as 1523, spreading panic and plague. 'The swarme' of rogues was 'insufferable' in 1628. Soldiers and sailors also 'swarmed' in 1626, picketing for unpaid wages. They 'swarmed' like strangers, lodgers, carriers, fishwives, and unlicensed porters. Buildings

---

[42] SRPJ (87), p. 193.  [43] LMA Jour. 40, fos. 45v-6, 265–5v.
[44] APC 1613–14, pp. 597–9. St Margaret's parish Westminster had a functioning house of correction – 'the Rounde howse' – by the early 1570s; St Martin-in-the-Fields had a house of correction around 1604. St Margaret's built a new house of correction in Tothill Fields in the 1620s. See J. F. Merritt, *The Social World of Early Modern Westminster: Abbey, Court, and Community, 1525–1640* (Manchester, 2005), pp. 283–4.
[45] LMA Reps. 23, fo. 349v; 29, fo. 162; 33, fo. 148.
[46] CSPV 1607–10, p. 148.
[47] LMA Jour. 27 fo. 212v; APC 1613–14, p. 601; 1629–30, pp. 313–14; TNA PC2/47/ 405–6; SP12/161/1; SP16/356/52. See also LMA Jour. 20, fo. 502.
[48] LMA Remembrancia Book 8, fos. 101–2; Jours. 24, fo. 91v; 31, fo. 315; Rep. 34, fo. 121; GL MS 1509/7; LMA Remembrancia Book 1, fo. 18v; APC 1613–14, pp. 598–9, 238–9; 1619–21, p. 342; 1625–6, pp. 251–2; 1629–30, pp. 313–14; HOL MP 1-11-1641.

appeared in such 'multitudes' that the city was 'overgrowe[n]' in 1580. It was so big by 1621 that it was nothing but 'a vast receptacle of a disordered multitude of imperfect workmen and misgoverned people'.[49]

These were not the only words used to convey the dynamism and fears of growth. Vagrants begged 'continually' (1624) and 'robberies, burglaries, and pilferies' were 'continual' (1615).[50] Numbers of vagrants and timewasters were 'greate' (1551–1643), 'abundant' (1602), 'infinite' (1625), and 'extraordinary' (1639), as were sudden bursts of growth along the city's edges (1632). The king was 'offended'.[51] 'Strangers and foreigners' flocked in 'great' numbers (1636), as did speeding coaches (1636). Fishwives walked streets in 'greate and superfluous numbers' (1584). 'Their number is wonderfully increased', Common Council grumbled in 1590, along with 'great inconveniences'.[52] Alehouses 'abound[ed]' (1636), as did vagrants and rogues (1628). Beggars 'swarm[ed] and abound[ed]' (1625). Priests and jesuits 'abundantly swarme[d]' (1610). Traffic was 'continual' (1629). Cutpurses and 'harlots' streamed to plays in 'great' numbers (1593). The cost of sponging inmates was 'heavy' (1649), and the number of workers with no craft training was 'vast' (1635).[53] Counting was one response. The number of censuses rose after 1600 to get better senses of the dimensions of problems that all too often got lost in their own magnitude. 'People of mean condition' crammed into grubby alleys in 'unlimited' numbers (1636), and vagrants, catholics, 'aliens', 'lazy' hawkers selling shoddy goods, and banned buildings seemed 'infinite' or 'extraordinary' (1616–40).[54]

This language of scale also conveyed the sheer magnitude of growth with an urgent focus on the here and now. Theft, begging, vagrancy, nightwalking, street-selling, banned building, barred traders, sleazy plays, catholics, bad health, and 'filthy stinking things' were all 'dayly'

---

[49] LMA Jours. 12, fos. 239–9v; 20, fo. 120; 24, fo. 91v; 30, fo. 227v; 33, fo. 34; 36, fos. 203–3v; Reps. 13ii, fo. 531v; 27, fo. 367v; 33, fo. 88; 39, fos. 1v-2; 43, fos. 154v-5; Remembrancia Book 1, fo. 18v; GL MS 1175/1, fo. 42; 4415/1, fo. 45v; 4655/1, fo. 52; TNA PC2/42/305–6; HOL MP 12–3-1621; APC 1613–14, pp. 383–4; 1619–21, pp. 118; 1629–30, pp. 313–14; SRPC (85), pp. 185–6.

[50] LMA Rep. 38, fo. 114v; APC 1615–16, pp. 211–12.

[51] LMA Jours. 16, fo. 127; 23, fo. 74; 26, fos. 7v, 186v; 27, fos. 367v, 380, 422; Rep. 16, fo. 340; Remembrancia Book 8, fos. 117–18; Letterbook T, fo. 151v; GL MS 12806/2, fo. 29v TNA SP16/5/119; PC2/42/305–6.

[52] TNA PC2/46/133–4, 282; SP12/103/32; LMA Rep. 21, fo. 73; Jours. 22, fo. 378v; 24, fo. 91v; Rep. 21, fo. 73; SRPC (210), pp. 495–6.

[53] TNA SP16/320/75; LMA Reps. 43, fo. 266; 36, fo. 114; Remembrancia Book 1, fo. 325v; GL MS 4813/1, fo. 78; SRPJ (111), pp. 249–50; APC 1625–6, pp. 251–2; TNA PC2/44/584.

[54] TNA PC2/46/323–4; APC 1615–16, pp. 693–4; HOL MP 16–8-1641; TNA SP16/5/119; APC 1615–16, pp. 483–4; HOL MP 2–5-1621; SRPC (210), pp. 495–6.

blights. Constables claimed that they were 'dayly' sued for simply doing their duties, or hospitals worried about dwindling resources as paupers trooped 'dayly' to their doors.[55] Other troubles also rose 'dayly'.[56] On top of this, there was a gloomy sense that there was worse to come. Robbery had 'growne' to 'a height' in 1615, and to 'an unusual height' a decade later.[57] Magistrates were sure that troubles had soared 'of late'. Common Council complained that vagrants 'swarme[d]' through the city in 1623 'more then heretofore'. They swarmed 'at this present more frequent and in greater numbers than formerly' (1629); 'more than heretofore' (1570); 'and never at any time more than now' (1638).[58] Their numbers 'much more abounded' 'at this presente' (1608), 'of late years' (1597), 'this time' (1639), or 'nowadays' (1627), as well as thieves (1626), cheats (1604), catholics (1621), and divided dwellings and inmates (1614). 'Never at any time more than now' was a lament for lost Londons. 'A greater concourse of recusants than has usually been at other times' poured into London in 1628, while noblemen were building houses 'as frequently in every corner as at any time heretofore' in 1616.[59] Like vagrancy, 'forrein buying and selling' (1646), theft (1580 and 1627), inmates (1627 and 1635), or seedy alehouses (1614), were graver dangers 'of late'.[60] None of this was necessarily new jargon, but there was significantly more of it in the decades around 1600, and it also had seasonal or calendar rhythms. Experience taught Londoners that vagrant flocks grew with Christmas just around the corner. Vagrants also came in droves when Parliament was sitting, or when troops demobilized. Common Council worried about the 'great number of soldiers' streaming into the city from 'the Lowe Countreys' in 1609, 'and more [are] dayly expected', they added gloomily.[61]

---

[55] LMA Jours. 12, fos. 239–9v; 18, fos. 361–1v; 30, fo. 227v; 36, fos. 203–3v; Reps. 16, fo. 430; 21, fo. 53; 39, fos. 1v-2; Remembrancia Book 1, fos. 57, 325v; GL MSS 12806/1, fo. 41v; 12806/2, fo. 29v; 4415/1, fo. 45v; 3016/1, fos. 198–9, TNA PC2/42/305–6; SP16/270/51; CSPV 1628–9, p. 171; APC 1615/16, pp. 211–12; 1630–1, p. 260; LMA H1/ST/A1/3, fo. 123; H1/ST/A1/4, fo. 178.

[56] LMA Jours. 17, fos. 299v-300; 18, fos. 361–1v.

[57] APC 1615–16, pp. 211–12; LMA Jour. 33, fo. 162v.

[58] LMA Jours. 32, fo. 127v; 20, fo. 120; Remembrancia Book 8, fos. 113v-14; APC 1628–9, p. 397; 1630–1, p. 137.

[59] LMA Jours. 27, fo. 291v; 26, fo. 156; Remembrancia Book 8, fo. 118; Jour. 24, fo. 225v; APC 1627, pp. 125, 253; 1613–14, pp. 589–91; 1615–16, pp. 483–4; 1614–15, pp. 64–5; 1628–9, p. 397; LMA Letterbook T, fo. 151v; Jour. 18, fo. 139v; SRPJ (111), p. 247; GL MS4813/1, fo. 83v; TNA PC2/46/133–4.

[60] LMA Jours. 40, fos. 189v-90; Remembrancia Book 1, fo. 57; APC 1613–14, pp. 268, 393–2, 601; 1619–21, p. 353; 1626, pp. 371, 27, 127; 1630–1, p. 137; HOL MP 16-8-1641; GL MS 4352/1, fo. 69.

[61] LMA Jours. 31, fo. 315; 26, fo. 186v; 27, fo. 379v; 39, fos. 331v, 361v; 40, fos. 42, 55v.

Mention of the 'eye' is striking in government sources, adding immediacy for us. There was more eye-catching drama around 1600 (and more for ears to pick up), and more reason to use optical allusions to describe trouble. Early modern culture was sharply sensitive to optic order.[62] Sight (Opsis) was one of the characters in Thomas Heywood's civic pageant *Londini Speculum: or London's Mirror* (1637). To this we can add the all-seeing eye of a providential God who sent warnings when necessary.[63] Surveillance was stepped up from above and below. Not just God (and his church) but governments kept a closer eye on people through counting, registration, and labelling.[64] A much used word was 'observation', implying both seeing and commenting. 'Never' have so many vagrants 'pestered' people 'at any time more than now', privy councillors said in 1638, 'being in every mans observation that at this time there is such an extraordinary confluence of vagabonds and beggars', as if laws no longer mattered. A 'greater [than usual] swarm and concourse' of vagrants was 'observed' in 1626, and a 'greater freedom and access' of 'strangers' in 1613 (with no 'notice taken of their numbers'), a 'greater sort' of 'strangers' in the next decade, and many more paupers drifting across the city in the next one.[65]

Magistrates had plum positions from which to watch trouble grow; vagrants were banging on Whitehall's garden gates in 1625.[66] This is the eye in the sources that sees so much. 'We did plainly see before our eyes', royal ministers griped in 1615, that it is 'impossible' to stop building unless we can find a penalty that will match the crime. 'Nothing' is more of a 'scandal' to us, they said later on, than that 'the eyes of foreigners' living with us continually 'observe' how the 'principal' city of the land 'swarms and abounds' with ragged beggars. The mayor said in 1617 that he 'had seen' a line of 'strangers' with 'bags and baggage by his door', on their way to who knew where. In other views the king 'cast' an 'eye' over shabby St Paul's, noting what improvements still needed to be made to patch it up; while his 'board' saw 'the fruits' of the speedy implementation of the Book of Orders (1631); and officers were asked to 'see' all 'evils'

---

[62] See my 'Bodies and souls in Norwich: punishing petty crime, 1540–1700', in Simon Devereaux and Griffiths, eds. *Penal Practice and Culture, 1500–1900: Punishing the English* (Basingstoke, 2004), pp. 85–120; and 'Inhabitants', in Carole Rawcliffe and Richard Wilson, eds., *Norwich Since 1550* (2004), pp. 63–88. Cf. Lynda Nead, *Victorian Babylon: People, Streets, and Images in Nineteenth-Century London* (New Haven, CT, and London, 2000), pp. 14, 57–62. On sight and seeing more generally see Stuart Clark, *Vanities of the Eye: Vision in Early Modern European Culture* (Oxford, 2007).
[63] On providence see Walsham, *Providence in Early Modern England*.
[64] See below, chap. 11.
[65] LMA Remembrancia Book 8, fos. 113v-14; Jour. 39, fo. 122v; APC 1626, p. 371; LMA Remembrancia Book 8, fo. 118; APC 1613–14, p. 268; 1627, p. 127.
[66] APC 1625–6, p. 13.

ranging from banned buildings to vagrants.[67] 'Noticing', 'perceiving', or 'viewing' were among other words of watching and warning that appear in the sources. The rush of new building was 'notorious in the viewe of the whole kingdome', and something that was not to be expected in a 'well pollicied' city, the monarch's ministers blasted in 1608. With carelessness came more crime, everyone knew that.[68] People were asked to keep their eyes open. Watchmen were told to keep 'a vygylante eye' on people coming in and out of the gates (1549). Aldermen kept a 'vigilant eye' on youth in tense times in 1554 and 'the expellinge and abolishinge of vice and synne' (1566), and 'a special eye' on the state of the city in 1626. A 'vigilant eye' also kept a look-out for 'greate and outragyous' hose and breeches in 1560. While beadles kept a 'good eye' on fishwives in 1570. 'Espy' was another word in guides to wards and parishes.[69] Thomas Dekker told his fellow Londoners that 'good and perfect eye-sight' would root out wrongdoers. Other good uses of the 'eye' included putting proclamations in prominent places where people 'maye see' or plague bills on doors that could be 'plainly' seen. Badges and brands on bodies were also meant to be seen.[70] This was an optic order where the visual validation of order mattered, suspects were 'seen', public punishments stung more than whipping behind closed doors, and the languages of seeing blended sight and surveillance: the eye, observation, signs, view, and such like optic references.

Governors and the cream of society had first-hand experience of vagrants and the trouble that they could bring. Nobody needed to tell the Earl of Arundel that crime was on the rise in 1624 or Lady Slingsby six years later: Arundel was sailing along the river when Elizabeth Tribe hurled stones and tiles 'violently' at his boat as he was passing under the bridge; while two vagrants threw 'dirt and stones and other rubish' at Slingsby when she was shopping in a draper's shop in Cheapside.[71] With other titled victims, their senses of crime were sharpened by actual suffering and loss. Two velvet cushions were pinched from the Earl of Holland's coach when it was parked on a street; Lord Leicester lost two

---

[67] SRPJ (155), p. 247; APC 1625–6, pp. 251–2; GL MS 4665/1, fo. 52; TNA SP16/195/32; LMA Remembrancia Book 8, fos. 36v, 113v; APC 1615/16, pp. 483–4; 1614, p. 662; SRPJ (51), p. 111.
[68] SRPJ (87), pp. 193–4; LMA Jour. 37, fo. 231v; Remembrancia Book 8, fos. 38v-9; APC 1625–6, p. 13; TNA STAC8 30/17; SRPJ (78), p. 171.
[69] LMA Letterbooks R, fo. 22v; V, fo. 69v; Reps. 13i, fo. 120v; 14, fo. 332v; 17, fo. 39v; Jour. 20, fo. 323; APC 1626, p. 371.
[70] Dekker is quoted in John Twyning, *London Dispossessed: Literature and Social Space in the Early Modern City* (Basingstoke, 1998), p. 73; LMA Reps. 22, fo. 90v; 10, fos. 26, 135; APC 1630–1, p. 257.
[71] BHC 6, fo. 367; 7, fo. 186.

Troubled times 43

pricey silver saucers in a single day; while the Countess of Devonshire lost her best cloak. Monarchs also lost costly plate or jewels. The upper classes were also victims of violence and vandalism. Joan Sims got into trouble for trying to pull a gentleman off his horse. Other well-to-do folk were mocked on streets, and damage was greater if riff-raff laughed along. Two sailors ended up behind bars for 'veary lewde and slanderouse speaches against Sir Francyas Drake' in Armada year. Streets were chancy places when taunts were cracked, and experience taught that vagrants hung around in places where haughty noblemen passed 'most frequently'. Nathaniel Grace was locked up in 1632 after 'affronting and abusing' nobles on business at Westminster's courts.[72]

Magistrates also lost possessions. One sheriff lost the princely sum of £15 18s. Seeing crime or smarting after a loss made crime more immediate, giving personal edges to law-making and enforcement. Vagrant Elizabeth Smith was arrested for 'spitting into Mr Attorney [General's] coach' in 1635. Beggars hung on 'privie counsells coaches' and the lord chancellor's 'coachside'.[73] Policies were also affected by encounters with vagrants, thieves, and loudmouths. Grumbling about prices could turn into personal salvos: widow Agnes Young called the mayor a 'knave' guided by 'knaves' and wished that somebody would string him up on the gallows in 1596, when prices soared and wages hit rock bottom. Hard times spawned bitterness, as when Ginkins Roberts called City leaders 'rebels' in 1574, or when Elizabeth Bradley was whipped for 'wishinge my lorde maior to be in Hell' in 1573: he 'never did good', she said, and was the 'cause' why bread and coals were 'so deare that she could get none'. Mayors were called 'bankruptes', no better than 'the worst beadell', and swindlers who creamed money from the Court of Orphans for 'private profit'.[74] London's 'pilot and master' was mocked by 'sedicous' or 'saucy' sneers, and word circulated that a riot was being planned against him in 1567.[75] People also poked fun at the Court of Aldermen. Griffin Appryce

[72] LMA Jours. 16, fo. 341; 35, fos. 349 411; BHC 6, fo. 216v; 8, fos. 156v, 290v; 3, fo. 390v; LMA WJ/SR/NS/31/5; BHC 8, fo. 192; LMA Rep. 21, fos. 577v, 582; Jours. 26, fo. 186v; 32, fo. 127v; BHC 7, fo.306. See also LMA WJ/SR/NS/29/61, 29/88; 31/6; MJ/SR/518/4; MJ/SBR/2, fos. 103, 150, 267, 356, 438, 508; Reps. 11, fo. 39; 12, fo. 104; 32, fo. 262; 34, fo. 553; APC 1621–3, p. 13.
[73] BHC 8, fo. 294; 1, fo. 120v; 2, fo. 145; 3, fo. 70v; 6, fo. 437; 7, fos. 74v, 203; 8, fos. 117, 164, 46v.
[74] LMA Rep. 23, fo. 595; BHC 2, fo. 44; LMA Rep. 18, fo. 90v. See also BHC 6, fo. 196; LMA Reps. 18, fo. 98; 23, fos. 229v, 549; 34, fo. 229v; TNA STAC8 6/8; 32/18; and Ian Archer's accounts of protests against Mayor Spencer in 1595: *Pursuit of Stability*, pp. 1–2 and 5–6.
[75] James Howell, *Londinopolis: An Historical Discourse or Perlustration of the City of London, the Imperial Chamber and the Chief Emporium of Great Britain* (1657), p. 38. For words mocking the mayor see LMA Reps. 10, fo. 103; 11, fo. 329; 12, fos. 125, 371v, 521v;

was put in the pillory for calling it 'a cosoninge corte' in 1575; while a porter shouted that 'hee cared not a fart for the court of lord maior and aldermen' in 1623, 'and clapped his hand on his breeches'.[76] Aldermen were also taunted in public places like the Exchange or Cheapside. I wish 'all theyre hedds weare in a bagge', a waterman with a grudge jeered in 1581. A group of actors landed in trouble in 1639 for 'personat[ing]' aldermen and 'reflect[ing] upon the present government' in lines on 'a new duty upon wines': 'the aldermen, the aldermen, base drunken Scottish knave', one of them said on stage, 'I care not for the aldermen, I say the aldermen is a base drunken Scottish knave'.[77] The City was sensitive to public knocks to authority when swift change challenged the perceived nature of the city and the worth of citizenship. And on times too many for comfort someone ended up in court for speaking 'lewde, sedycyous, slaunderouse' or 'dyspytefull words' against the City or 'the hole number of the cytyzens'. Other malcontents threatened to burn the city down to the ground.[78]

The law was insulted in public over and over again. The judicial bench was lampooned and lambasted along streets in words that made magistrates blush and boil. 'Money justice', Cassandra Cliff snapped when she fell out with Justice Musklett in 1629. Thomas Rowe told Justice Herne that he was 'a turdy justice'. 'The devill shit justices', William Crutch reminded Justice Ward. Others mocked or ripped up warrants. 'A farte' for Justice Collyn's warrant, a spinster scoffed, I 'care not for it'.[79] Officers were also at risk when they enforced the law or distrained goods to cover unpaid fines. Kiss 'my tayle', a merchant's servant said, when a deputy came to search his master's house.[80] So many

---

13(ii), fo. 341v; 15, fo. 200v; 16, fos. 401, 526; 18, fo. 352; 23, fo. 589v; 28, fo. 284v; 30, fo. 282v; 33, fo. 387v; 34, fo. 207; 41, fo. 105v; 46, fo. 320; 55, fos. 197v-8; 59, fo. 93; CQSF 109/6; BHC 5, fo. 201v.

[76] LMA Reps. 19, fo. 3v; 37, fo. 200. See also LMA CQSF 110/indict. John Sinkin; Remembrancia Book 1, fo. 32v; Reps. 18, fo. 27; 28, fos. 63–3v; 30, fo. 346; 31(2), fo. 429v; 32, fo. 110; 33, fo. 194v; 34, fo. 304v; 39, fo. 196v; 50, fo. 60v; 51, fo. 223; 52, fo. 247.

[77] LMA Rep. 20, fo. 268; TNA SP16/429/51. See also LMA CQSF 106/35; 107/14; 125/99; Reps. 11, fo. 109; 12, fo. 288; 15, fo. 432v; 16, fo. 527; 17, fo. 464v; 20, fo. 441v; 21, fo. 281v; 23, fo. 554; 29, fo. 240v; 30, fo. 383v; 33, fo. 31v; 48, fo. 60v; 55, fo. 117; TNA SP16/423/85.

[78] For example, LMA Reps. 10, fo. 351; 12, fo. 405v; 18, fo. 2v; 22, fo. 133v; BHC 2, fos. 114, 120; 9, fo. 69; LMA MJ/SR/512/93. See also Bernard Capp, 'Arson, threats of arson, and incivility in early modern England', in Burke, Harrison, and Slack eds., *Civil Histories*, pp. 197–213.

[79] LMA MJ/SBR/5, fo. 108; MJ/SBR/6, fo. 358; MJ/SBR/1, fo. 139; MJ/SR/506/128. See also BHC 1, fo. 212v; 3, fo. 353v; 5, fo. 429; 6, fo. 242; 7, fo. 100v; BRHA BHC4, fo. 414; LMA CQSF 83/40; MJ/SR/804/128; MJ/SBR/1, fo. 517; MJ/SBR/5, fo. 465; MJ/SBR/6, fo. 628.

[80] LMA Rep. 15, fo. 275v. See also BHC 1, fo. 75; 2, fo. 228v; 3, fo. 23; 6, fo. 98v; 8, fo. 51; LMA Reps. 15, fo. 275v; 18, fo. 152.

words made crime-waves seem more apparent, and crime-waves, in turn, sharpened the sting of words, especially when the law was slapped in public, as when Alice Burwood squared up to Justice Snape: you are 'an asse and foole' and you should 'kisse' me where I 'shitt upon Saterday', she said, I will never be 'controlled' by 'a shitten breech justice'. Not even the highest officers in the land or men of God were immune. Brian Chadborne spat in a 'divines' face as he walked along a street and punched him.[81]

Words could fly at any time. No one knew who might be 'slapt' next.[82] These abuses added to an emphasis on *experience* in civic orders. 'Experience' taught that 'a great number of masterles men' hung around the city in 1601, 'liv[ing] upon stealth, pilfering, and lewd practises'; that some rowdy street-porters were vagrants on the run from the law (1617); that 'hard and continual labour' was a better deterrent than 'terror of death' (1621); or that building laws were scantly regarded (1619). Filth, crime, plague, and slums all taught through 'wofull experience'.[83] First-hand experience of crime as victims, bystanders, or judges shaped perceptions. A 'panic milieu' was likewise made more credible by 'experience'. This was why a cavalier poke at the law or trivial sounding piece of wit might lead to all sorts of trouble, even when a loudmouth spouted 'crackbrayned' gibberish.[84] Rumours were always 'blowne abroad' to all corners, and it was hard to keep track of their course once they were passed from person to person like wildfire. London was a chattering city. The 'city is full of a rumour', the Venetian ambassador noted in 1623.[85] A juicy rumour set tongues wagging and everyone liked tittle-tattle. Crown and City retaliated with words of their own that rubbished rumours, asking citizens to turn in 'rumor spreaders' and 'taletellers'. Grace Perryman landed in court in 1614 for 'careying of tales from neighbour to neighbour'. Officers were also asked to read proclamations throughout the city to put the record straight, and precepts were sent round to the wards to stop rumours in their tracks. It was hoped that the city would soon settle down once tensions cooled.[86]

As with the identities of people who broke the law, magistrates wanted to know about rumours 'blowne abroad'. Like incomplete identities, snatches of rumours spawned speculation. Magistrates felt more secure

---

[81] LMA MJ/SBR/6, fo. 346; BHC 7, fo. 282v.   [82] LMA WJ/SR/NS/35/39.
[83] APC 1601–4, pp. 27–8; LMA Jour. 30, fo. 227v; TNA SP14/119/78; APC 1619–21, pp. 22–3. See also LMA Jour. 11, fos. 346v-7; TNA SP/12/177/7; HOL MP 8–5–1621; APC 1615–16, pp. 483–4; SRPJ (51), pp. 111–12; (20), pp. 267–9.
[84] BHC 9, fo. 101.   [85] CSPV 1621–3, p. 691.
[86] WAC WCB2, fo. 8; LMA Reps. 20, fo. 139; 13ii, fo. 311; 15, fo. 418; 16, fos. 22, 340v; 18, fos. 15v, 71; TNA SP 12/140/18.

46    Change

with full stories, and rumours were always more numerous 'in time of troubles'.[87] Like thieves creeping through the city after dark, rumour-mongers spread poison 'devilishly' as people slept. Londoners woke up one morning to find rabble-rousing calls to stand up against 'aliens' scattered all over the city.[88] The rumour-mongers' 'black' had seditious tinges, magistrates said. They wanted to topple authority or humiliate social betters. Libels were slipped under magistrates' gates. A rumour snaking through the city in Winter 1567 'nourish[ed] dissention' and mocked the 'good credit and fame' of nobles. Contentious political events can be followed down the years in rumours: Queen Elizabeth's religious leaning, catholic plots, the botched Spanish match, Buckingham's wheeling and dealing, Laud's popery, or the Scottish war, all appeared in alternative news networks that gave many sides of the same story and became 'common talk' in pubs. The many 'misinformacons', 'false rumors and untrue aspersions' let loose to grow reminded people of 'dangerous' disorders all around them. Paul's Cross preachers were asked not to read out any 'bill' that was 'suddenly' slipped into their hands as they climbed into the pulpit in case it attacked authority.[89] Magistrates wanted to keep tight control of preachers and presses. Books also sowed sedition if they dodged the censor's veto and other red tape. It was uncomfortable listening for his company chiefs when a stationer who ran conventicles in his house told them 'that it was lawfull for all men to print lawful books'. A complaint that was heard more often as the political situation heated up around 1640 was that 'seditious and libelous books and pamphlets' streamed through the city like loose talk. Street sellers had 'bad' books in their packs, and there was a troubling number of printing presses shut away in 'secret corners', 'secret rooms', and 'dark cellars' pumping out these books.[90]

Odious print and speech created bad publicity, but *visual* impacts caused most fuss. Disorder was out in the open. Rumours were more than talk if they were nailed on posts or gates or scattered on streets. 'Many libells and noates' are stuck on posts and 'scattered' across the city, Common Council complained in 1640, and groups of 'disordered and tumultuous people' gathered to read, chat, and plot at posts. One libel

---

[87] LMA Jour. 33, fo. 268; HOL MP 25-11-1640.    [88] TNA SP12/281/7-8.
[89] LMA Reps. 20, fo. 133v; 21, fo. 317; 16, fo. 265v; Letterbook R, fos. 90, 158. See also TNA SP12/44/52, 12/71/16, 16/278/12, 16/423/55, 16/423/83; HOL MP 27-1-1629; CSPV 1623-5, p. 149, 1636-9, p. 376; LMA Reps. 20, fo. 133v; 21, fo. 317; 16, fo. 265v; Adam Fox, *Oral and Literate Culture in England, 1500–1700* (Oxford, 2000), chap. 7.
[90] TNA SP12/15/39; HOL MP 6-1-1642; TNA SP12/161/1. See also Dagmar Freist, *Governed by Opinion: Politics, Religion and the Dynamics of Communication in Stuart London, 1637–1645* (London and New York, 1997).

was 'fixed in public view' on a post near Billingsgate where 'most merchants' passed on their way to get coal. Other dangerous 'papers' were put on the Exchange's pillars.[91] The City's posts were meant for official orders only but some were pulled down. The 'vagabond' and 'verlet' George Taylor was dumped in Bridewell in 1560 after he 'pulled down the maiours proclamacons'. Others scribbled on posts and proclamations, or drew cartoons to alter meanings. A salter's apprentice was whipped in 1612 for 'very insolently and contemptuously' lampooning government and the mayor's 'authoritie' by drawing a 'picture of a gallous and a man hanging' on a proclamation that had been pinned up 'for the good of the citie', 'publickely upon a post at Queenehithe'. Some grocers went from post to post to rip off a proclamation that let apothecaries branch out on their own outside the Grocers' guild. While William Merrell plucked down 'orders made by the commissioners for annoyances' and set them on fire.[92] Other targets for acts against authority included civic landmarks like the arms of the City or a notable citizen. Police hunted high and low for the 'evell doers' who 'defaced Sir Thomas Greshams armes' that glittered on 'the west dore of his new works upon Cornhill' in 1569. Nobody could miss Cheapside Cross in the middle of London's main street, and it too was a tempting target for vandals, iconoclasts, and people messing about, like the chimney sweeps who threw stones at it in 1634. The conduit was another Cheapside civic crest and an eyesore when it was 'very fowle', not least because of people like Sara Guy who 'sundry tymes' 'beastlye' pissed in it. The conduits were meeting places for apprentices on the way to a punch-up or riot, and 'whooping and shouting' boys. Pickpockets also prowled around them, trying to catch waterbearers and others off guard.[93]

### Dangerous growth

Thoughts of trouble and decay did not go away. Growth showed no signs of slowing down, evident in slums and London's housing squeeze. Tatty buildings were blots on landscapes, but better buildings did not avoid damage. There were damage reports from the Exchange, and 'decayed' St Paul's, once London's 'grace and glory', became an eyesore. What

---

[91] TNA SP12/15/39; LMA Jour. 39, fo. 84v; TNA STAC8 41/12; LMA Rep. 34, fo. 195v. See also BHC 2, fo. 104v; LMA Reps. 15, fo. 129; 20, fo. 137; 21, fo. 407v; 22, fos. 97, 259v; 23, fos. 191v, 418; 28, fo. 105v; Jour. 40, fo. 69; TNA SP12/60/49, 16/72/45.

[92] BHC 1, fo. 75v; LMA Rep. 30, fo. 317; TNA STAC8 26/1; LMA MJ/SR/508a/12.

[93] LMA Reps. 16, fos. 447v, 448v, 456v; 22, fo. 387; 23, fo. 230; BHC 8, fo. 6; GL MS 12806/2, fo. 245v; BHC 8, fo. 410. See also LMA Remembrancia Book 1, fo. 103v; Rep. 17, fo. 22v.

little patience governors still had snapped when taxes to patch up the cathedral arrived in dribs and drabs.[94] St Paul's dominated London's silhouette, but a glut of low-grade buildings got more notice from magistrates. London was running out of space; even graveyards were jam-packed.[95] People moved east and west after 1600, but until then new houses were built on old foundations or sparse plots of empty land inside the walls. Landlords split tenements into box rooms to squeeze in lodgers, cramming the poor into 'small and straite roomes'.[96] 'The excesse of new buildings' had 'daylie more and more increased' the city in its 'vastness', a royal proclamation observed with some alarm in 1618. A decade earlier another royal command slammed the 'overflow of people'.[97]

Complaints about pauper lodging and new building picked up from about 1580. The City worried about 'overpeopling' and the 'multitude' that 'dyd soe overgrowe' in 1580, and the mayor fretted about 'inconveniences' that 'hath appeared verie great of newe buyldings'. New clauses warning tenants not to divide houses were added to City leases in 1581. The city was 'overlargely increased' in 1583, and orders to ban building had only had 'a slender effect'.[98] Crown and City had a common cause in making London splendid. A royal order of 1615 said that London would become a 'great' city if 'private building' was cut back. It was slipping behind 'other well pollicied cities' across the Channel. A shabby city was a badly run city; Freart called grand building an 'indication of a prudent government'.[99] A run of royal orders, starting in Elizabeth's reign but peaking in the next, set strict standards for building with steep fines for offenders. 'We have every week almost a new proclamation for buildings', one wit quipped in 1619.[100] The Crown wanted 'uniformity' in building that would 'grace' the city and make streets shine with 'honour, beauty, and lustre'. A hotchpotch of materials, measurements, or plans was a mark of mediocrity.[101] Crown orders produced building blueprints that were microscopic in their care for

[94] LMA Jour. 20, fo. 341; Remembrancia Book 8, fo. 36v; TNA SP16/195/32.
[95] Harding, *The Dead and the Living*, esp. chap. 3.  [96] SRPJ (25), pp. 47–8.
[97] SRPJ (175), pp. 398–400.
[98] LMA Rep. 20, fo. 136; Remembrancia Book 1, fo. 45v; Rep. 20, fo. 243; Remembrancia Book 1, fos. 248v, 261–1v.
[99] LMA Jour. 29, fos. 351–1v; SRPJ (87), pp. 193–4; Freart, *Parallel of the Antient Architecture With the Modern*, epistle dedicatory, fo. 5r.
[100] TNA SP14/107/43. See also T. G. Barnes, 'The prerogative court and environmental control of London building in the early seventeenth century', *California Law Review*, 58 (1970), 1332–63; and Brett-James, *Growth of Stuart London*, chaps 3–4.
[101] LMA Jours. 28, fos. 243–3v; 32, fo. 109v; 35, fos. 214–16v. See also my 'Politics made visible: order, residence, and uniformity in Cheapside, 1600–1645', in Paul Griffiths and Mark S. R. Jenner, eds., *Londinopolis: Essays in the Cultural and Social History of Early Modern London* (Manchester, 2000), pp. 176–96; Kevin Sharpe, *The Personal Rule of*

Troubled times 49

details, with exact dimensions for fronts, corners, windows, walls, cellars, ceilings, and chimneys. Londoners were also told to build with brick rather than inferior and more inflammable wood. The first Stuart king wanted to leave behind a city of 'bricke' rather than 'stickes' after his death, just like the first Roman emperor whose sparkling legacy to Rome was a city of marble. Brick was 'farre more durable [than wood], safe from fire, beautifull and magnificent'.[102]

Aldermen lobbied the Crown in person and in petitions for orders to ban buildings, split houses, and renting rooms cheaply,[103] and drafted Parliamentary bills at what might have been moments when building was getting out of hand. The recorder took three aldermen with him to Whitehall in 1593 to lobby for 'favours' to get a bill passed against inmates and unlawful building.[104] Two decades later a City committee met to draft 'a bill to be drawne and exhibited into the Parliament for suppressing of inmats and other grievances'. The bill did not make it into law, the same fate met by another one to end the 'odious and loathsome sinne of drunckenes'.[105] A bill 'for the ordering of manner of buildings and restraint of inmates and subdividing tenements' was sent to Parliament in 1621, and although it said that the number of new buildings was 'extraordinary', it also failed. One more followed two decades later when the City pushed for stronger laws against vagrants, but again it never became the law of the land, even though the spate of building was so bad that it spelled 'the utter undoinge and destrucon' of the city.[106] But traffic was not all one way. Privy councillors also put pressure on the City to take action. 'Hot' letters were sent to the City asking for a 'speedy

---

*Charles I* (New Haven, CT, and London, 1992), esp. pp. 407–12; J. Newman, 'Inigo Jones and the politics of architecture', in Kevin Sharpe and Peter Lake, eds., *Culture and Politics in Early Stuart England* (Basingstoke, 1994), pp. 231–45; Robert Tittler, *Architecture and Power: the Town Hall and the English Urban Community, c. 1500–1640* (Oxford, 1996), chaps 4–6; Peter Borsay, *The English Urban Renaissance: Culture and Society in the Provincial Town, 1660–1770* (Oxford, 1989), chaps 3–4 and 9–10; and Friedrichs, *Early Modern City*, esp. pp. 200–1.

[102] SRPJ (152), pp. 245–7; (51), pp. 111–12; (78), pp. 174–5; (204), pp. 487–8; SRPC (9), pp. 20–6; (136), pp. 280–7. On the superiority and splendour of building with brick see Howell, *Londinopolis*, p. 398. Evelyn called London a 'wooden city' in 1651; one where 'magistrates have no power or care to make' people 'build with uniformity' (*A Character of England*, in *Miscellaneous Writings of John Evelyn*, 1651, ed., William Upcott, 3rd edition (1825), pp. 156–7).

[103] LMA Reps. 27, fo. 218; 28, fo. 93v; 46, fo. 387v; 47, fo. 9; TNA SP16/325/2.

[104] LMA Rep. 23, fo. 31.

[105] LMA Rep. 31(2), fos. 296v-7, 302v. For attempts to turn houses into pubs see LMA Reps. 27, fos. 134v, 349; 28, fo. 308; 30, fos. 54v-5; 31(1), fos. 69, 162v; 31(2), fos. 249v-50, 429; 32, fos. 31v, 246, 253v; 33, fos. 72v, 226; 34, fos. 174v, 479v, 575v-6; 40, fo. 151v; 44, fo. 336v.

[106] LMA Jour. 31, fo. 290; HOL MP 15-5-1621; LMA Jour. 40, fos. 6, 33, 110.

course', and it set up think-tanks to guide strategies, to 'survey' banned building, to pressure the wards to step up surveillance, and to meet with justices in surrounding suburbs to co-ordinate strategies. Star Chamber also took a leading role in the drive to stop 'bad' building, putting out orders, advice, and warnings. The Court of Aldermen sat down to read all of the 'board's' letters and orders 'towching the new errecons, devidinq of houses and inmates' in 1614, and that would have been a fairly large pile by then.[107]

There was a rise in prosecutions for splitting tenements and 'bad' building towards 1600, and also in the number of orders to view or pull down buildings.[108] The situation was the same over the walls in built-up Middlesex and Westminster.[109] Some building to the west was on a grand scale as nobles and gentry attracted by London's nascent season built lush mansions in landscaped squares, so long as they followed royal regulations: the Earl of Leicester was told to build his new house in St Martin-in-the-Fields with 'brick and stone', with a 'forefront' of 'uniform sort and order as may best beautify the place'.[110] The City had mixed feelings about all this new building on its western doorstep, and lobbied the Crown to 'pray' for 'a stay' of building in Covent Garden in 1632, because it was felt that it would only cause 'great hurte and detriment'; the 'great increase of new building' in Lincoln's Inn Fields was also the object of concern that it caused too many smoke clouds.[111] The royal 'board' did take action against building 'abuses' outside Temple Bar, but the City was not always sure that it acted in its best interests, believing that royal willingness to let offenders compound weakened any deterrent effect; even privy councillors agreed that this had a 'contrary effect' in 1616.[112]

---

[107] LMA Rep. 32, fo. 7. See also LMA Jours. 26, fos. 12–12v; 27, fo. 30v; 30, fo. 158; 35, fo. 252; 37, fo. 338v; Reps. 33, fo. 82; 20, fo. 456v; 27, fo. 218; Remembrancia Book 8, fos. 87v-8; APC 1615–16, p. 460; 1617–19, pp. 209, 253–4, 283–4; 1619–21, pp. 20–1, 266; 1629–30, p. 339; TNA SP12/233/25.

[108] LMA Reps. 20, fo. 75; 21, fo. 466v; 22, fo. 362v; 23, fo. 477; 27, fos. 142v, 264; 28, fo. 301v; 29, fo. 279; 31(1), fo. 94; 32, fo. 262; 33, fo. 217; Jours. 19, fos. 16v-17; 21, fo. 299; 23, fo. 340v; BHC 8, fo. 147; GL MSS 942/1, fo. 91v; 577/1, fo. 45; 6522/1, fo. 132; TNA STAC8 30/17; SP12/150/45–45i, 12/140/87, 14/98/23, 16/193/76, 16/380/73, 16/296/29; APC 1615–16, p. 460; 1617–19, p. 245. Cf. Brett-James, *Growth of Stuart London*, pp. 80–4, 92–5, 106–7, 111–13.

[109] For example, LMA MJ/SBR/1, fos. 122, 264, 374, 406, 496, 640; MJ/SBR/2, fos. 7, 98, 345, 520; MJ/SBR/3, fos. 7. 535; MJ/SBR/5, fo. 499; MJ/SBR/6, fos. 203, 334, 523; MJ/SR/505/14, 506/5, 512/77, 521/143–5, 524/179; WAC WCB/1, fos. 39, 41, 103, 104, 125, 167, 201, 212, 287, 289; WCB/2, fos. 10, 11, 12, 69, 140, 161.

[110] TNA SP16/198/36.   [111] LMA Rep. 46, fo. 63v; HOL MP, 16-8-1641.

[112] APC 1615–16, pp. 434–5; 1614–15, pp. 123–4; CSPV 1617–19, p. 549. See also Chamberlain's comments on compounding in *The Letters of John Chamberlain*, ed. Norman Egbert McClure, 2 vols., The American Philosophical Society (Philadelphia, PA, 1939), vol. I, pp. 559, 601.

'Nowadays' men take 'intollerable liberty' to build and divide houses, the royal 'table' said in 1614. There were 'new beginnings and plots of whole streets' all over London's northern fringe two years later.[113] For a time it was felt that 'dangerous growth' could be controlled. The City could still do something: regulate building, chart its scale, and kick out hard-up migrants. London might even go back to its former comfortable shape and size. But the Crown put the blame for continuous troubles on slack magistrates and 'inferior officers like constables' for their lack of care, and blamed builders for their 'small regard', 'great boldnes', and 'covetous' craving for 'private benefitt'.[114] The Crown was never cold about London's troubles, but there were times when they clashed with the City over growth, as when the City begged Whitehall not to hand out building licences in 1634.[115] But London kept growing, and as with rundown streets, 'bad' building was a safety matter. Even the builders of West End mansions were ticked off now and then.[116] But most attention was given to congested hovels. Magistrates knew well from 'wofull experience' that the 'worse and basest sort' of 'rogish persons' crammed into such small spaces.[117] Numbers of 'dangerous' poor outstripped the controlling hand of 'government'. The City 'advysed' the Crown in 1580 'that the multitude' did 'soe overgrowe that theare was some feare and perill of theyre governance'. London in its 'vastness' was becoming ungovernable. The cry in 1607 was that 'the worst sort' had grown 'to so great numbers [as] are not well to be governed' by 'wonted officers and ordinarie jurisdiction'. In the next year it was that the 'overflow of people' of the 'meaner sort' can 'hardly be fed and susteyned or preserved in health or governed'.[118] The Crown just wanted its capital city to be 'safe and healthfull'.[119]

Like vagrants and grubby streets, packing inmates in 'petty and small' houses harmed the 'health and safety' of all Londoners. 'Meane and base people' crammed into stuffy rooms in slums and passed on germs to each other (and afterwards to innocent bystanders) by brushing against each other or sucking in the foul clammy air all around them. All 'strangers' were called 'comonlie unclene people' who never 'regard[ed] the good of

---

[113] APC 1613–14, p. 589; 1615–16, pp. 483–4.
[114] LMA Remembrancia Book 7, fos. 197–8; APC 1619–21, pp. 22–3, 483–4; SRPJ (87), pp. 193–4; TNA PC 2/43, fos. 81–2; SP16/372/12–13; SRPJ (255), pp. 597–8.
[115] LMA Remembrancia Book 8, fos. 59v-61.
[116] LMA Remembrancia Book 7, fos. 197–8.
[117] SRPJ (87), pp. 193–4; LMA Rep. 20, fo. 136; SRPJ (25), pp. 47–8; LMA Jour. 40, fo. 33.
[118] LMA Rep. 20, fo. 136; SRPJ, (175), pp. 398–400; (78), pp. 171–5; (87), pp. 193–4; TNA SP14/105/66.
[119] SRPJ (204), p. 485.

52    Change

this citty'.[120] Their hovels were health hazards whose 'meane' tenants were a real danger to citizens, never more so than when plague struck. Thomas Browne squashed two widows into a space big enough for only one of them, 'to the greate perill' of 'infectyng' citizens with 'pestilence and other contagious diseases'.[121] City plague orders tried to stop grubby paupers from bumping into citizens on the streets,[122] and people hanging clothes out to dry or 'ayre' when their touch might prove fatal. It was 'notoriously known by daily experience' that the 'sickness' grew through 'using and occupying of bedding, clothes, and garments'. While selling second-hand clothes and rags on streets was thought to be 'very dangerous for the increase of plague'.[123] Crowded rooms were also a greater health risk in times of plague; 'one of the chiefest occasions of the great plague and mortality', magistrates said in 1603, as London endured yet another awful 'infeccon'. Squashing 'twoe or three householdes in one' helped plague sweep quickly through the city.[124] Parishes and wards were the front lines of this inmate-war. William Shambrooke landed in trouble with many of his neighbours in Cornhill in 1586 after 'devid[ing]' his house 'into many howsholdes as inmats', who begged all day long and were thought to be very 'daungerous for infeccon and fyer'. John Passmore got in similar trouble two decades later for splitting his house along Harper Alley and stuffing 'many' paupers into 'litle romes', who lived 'sluttishly' in ways 'apt to breed infection'.[125] London's inmate problem was not a new one, but it is more visible in surviving sources after 1575 in both city and suburban parishes.[126] It was in 1580 that aldermen asked the recorder for a tighter definition of 'inmate': seeking 'his opynyon who [is] to be accompted' for one.[127] The word was an old

---

[120] LMA Jour. 35, fo. 252; Remembrancia Book 1, fo. 18v; Jour. 33, fo. 203v.
[121] LMA CQSF 113/interrog. Thomas Browne.
[122] For example, LMA Jours. 26, fo. 138; 31, fo. 143v; 33, fo. 146v; 35, fos. 169, 180v; Reps. 20, fos. 131, 191; 21, fo. 5; 29, fo. 215. For a few cases that emphasize the dangers of taking in inmates in time of plague see LMA MJ/SBR/4, fo. 374; WJ/SR/NS/38/151.
[123] LMA Jours. 11, fos. 346v-7; 20, fo. 428; 26, fo. 127; 35, fo. 349v; MJ/SBR/1, fo. 215; TNA PC 2/44, fo. 182; PC 2/46, fos. 148, 364; PC 2/47, fos. 24, 117, 270; BHC 6, fo. 400.
[124] SRPJ (25), pp. 47–8; LMA Letterbook T, fo. 199; WJ/SR/NS/46/19.
[125] GL MS 4069/1, fos. 42, 147v. See also GL MS 4069/1, fos. 67, 151, 154; LMA CQSF 114/interrog. John Henlyes.
[126] Archer, *Pursuit of Stability*, pp. 184–5. For early action against inmates see, for example, GL MS 1499; LMA Jours. 19, fos. 216v-17; 20, fo. 503; 21, fos. 58, 299; 22, fo. 411; 24, fo. 149v; 28, fos. 217–18; 33, fos. 146v, 203v; Reps. 16, fo. 40v; 17, fos. 18, 153, 452v; 18, fos. 7, 155v, 239v, 330; 19, fo. 251; 20, fos. 136v, 294v, 366v; 23, fo. 125; 27, fo. 88v; 28, fos. 29v, 314v; 30, fo. 41v.
[127] LMA Rep. 20, fo. 139.

Troubled times 53

one, but it now needed a new meaning as people from various backgrounds streamed into the city all at once.

Scares about barred building and inmates peaked around 1620 and after, and there is no better sign of this than the inmates who fill the pages of parish accounts and vestry books. The scale and scope of this campaign against inmates in parishes and wards was unprecedented in records stretching back to 1550 from when there are enough good runs of accounts for us to follow this rise with some precision in the amount of money, time, and trouble spent driving out inmates. We find payments for 'booke[s] of orders from the lords of the counsell', drafting 'answeres' to requests for information, copying precepts, 'rowles' for inmates, 'printed bills against inmates', counting inmates, food and drink at 'meeteings' about them, 'warning' inmates to get out of parishes, and for lists of presentments and indictments when they stayed put.[128] Some parishes held monthly meetings of 'the most and chiefest parishioners' after 1600 until, in the words of St Margaret New Fish Street vestry, 'we have purged the parish' of the 'danger' of inmates.[129] The piece of paper most prized by parishes was a landlord's pledge to cover the cost of his lodger's stay. Parishes often pressured pauper 'pensioners' who gave room and board to inmates. It was a 'common custom' in St Dionis Backchurch for 'pensioners' to 'take in inmates and lodgers' to get by, and they were told in 1654 and 1655 that they would lose a year's pension and pay a steep fine if they did not get rid of their lodgers.[130] Many parishes hired 'informers' and 'promoters' to track down inmates and take them to court, along with others whose job description was to 'remove' or to look 'to' inmates. Some of these inmate-'avoyders' built up long-running ties with parishes. Mr Mould can be followed in records for fifteen years 'removeinge' inmates from St John Walbrook (1617–32). He picked up £1 9s in 1630–1 for getting rid of inmates 'at iis vid a peece'; Goodman Mums crops up in St John Zachary in 1648 on the heels of inmates and again twelve years later; while Goodman Newice, Newce, or Nuce spent no less than a decade tracking down inmates in St Laurence Pountney (1619–28).[131]

---

[128] For example. GL MSS 942/1, fo. 143v; 878/1, fo. 246v; 577/1, fo. 143; 4385/1, fo. 99v; 1124/1, fo. 205; 7673/2, fo. 67v; 4241/1, fo. 508; 6574, fo. 165v; 4180/1, fo. 190; 4956/2, fo. 198v; 1432/3, fo. 171; 662/1, fo. 94v; 1431/2, fo. 85; 959/1, fo.247v; 819/1, fo. 99; 978/1, fo. 12v; 943/1, fo. 82v; 4216/1, fo. 99; 4813/1, fo. 146v; 1175/1, fo. 84v; 3908/1, fo. 85v.
[129] GL MSS 1175/1, fo. 42; 819/1, fo. 64.   [130] GL MS 4216/1, fos. 98, 99, 112, 121.
[131] GL MSS 577/1, fos. 39v, 52, 54, 54v, 56, 61v, 63v, 67, 69; 590/1, fos. 201, 228v; 3907/1, 1620–1, 1623–4, 1626–7, 1627–8.

54     Change

The other side of the coin is represented by greedy or needy people who brushed aside City orders. James Snape appeared at St Dunstan-in-the-West wardmote in four successive years from 1571 for 'devid[ing]' a house near Temple Bar into 'severall chambers and lodginges for gentlemen'. William Spaniard turned up each year from 1563 to 1578 for keeping 'evell rule' all night long and lodging 'suspect persons' in his cellar. And he was joined by Thomas Pitman, and after by his widow, for the last five years of his stay in the books.[132] Just one ward – Cornhill – has continuous coverage, starting in 1571, and we can plot a rise in the number of troublesome landlords and lodgers from then on, as cases came to the wardmote in nearly all years.[133] Some alleys had bad reputations, but many of these 'problem' landlords were not from the 'dregs' of society. Some were well off enough to own a clutch of houses, like Michael Leake, who rented rooms to 'very poore men' in 'dyvers houses within Creplegate', or John Hunter who 'let his tenements' in an alley in Portsoken to 'pore people' who went out begging all day.[134] The occupations of 'landlords of alleys' who signed bonds in 1569 to stop their tenants from falling on the parish looks like a cross-section of London's trades: four cooks, one mercer, five pewterers, three butchers, fourteen drapers, two carpenters, a single merchant, haberdasher, clothworker, grocer, and so on.[135] It was an uphill task to control inmates, but precepts kept coming from the Guildhall.[136] Magistrates also asked hospitals to clean their own back yards. Bridewell kept a close watch on its tenants, setting up counts and house-to-house inquiries for inmates. Prosecutions and expulsions peaked shortly after 1600 and again after 1625. St Bartholomew's ran a rule over its little next-door parish, and inmates also lurked in almshouses.[137] Guilds were also asked to take action against tenants or workers who lodged inmates. A Common Council order added compulsory clauses to guild leases in 1626, so that tenants

[132] GL MS 3018/1, fos. 23v, 25, 26v, 28v (Snape), 11v, 13, 14, 18v, 19, 27, 29, 30, 33v, 35v. See also ibid., fos. 67v, 74, 74v, 77, 86, 87, 92, 97, 97v, 98, 100, 103, 104v, 106.
[133] GL MS 4069/1, fos. 8v, 42, 67, 87, 116, 125v, 135, 145v, 147v, 151, 154, 160, 171, 179.
[134] LMA Reps. 18, fo. 167v; 19, fo. 38v. See also LMA Rep. 19, fo. 38.
[135] LMA Reps. 17, fos. 427v-8, 432, 444, 446, 448, 452v; 18, fo. 7.
[136] GL MSS 2968/1, fo. 425; 5090/2, fo. 85v; 878/1, fos. 239v, 246; 6836, fo. 61; 1002/1, fo. 520; 2088/1, 1599–1600; 4956/2, fo. 198v; 4570/2, fo. 318; 3556/2, 1658; 662/1, fo. 94v.
[137] BHC 5, fos. 119v, 126v, 152v, 162, 224, 240, 318, 339v, 323–3v, 398, 417; 7, fos. 299, 300–300v, 314; 8, fos. 5v, 107v, 112, 162v, 172v, 200, 202v, 240v, 246v, 256, 317, 349v, 353v; 9, fos. 219, 440, 758, 873; LMA Rep. 27, fo. 345v. For other hospitals see GL MS 12806/2, fos. 42, 81; 12806/4, fo. 52; SBHA Governors' Journals 2, fo. 136v; 3, fo. 120; 4, fos. 67, 95, 101, 149; 5, fo. 154; LMA H1/ST/AS1/1, fo. 42; H1/ST/AS1/4, fos. 27, 41v, 86, 101, 124; Rep. 46, fos. 297v-8.

would know that they would be prosecuted if they split their houses.[138] Money was never far from the thoughts of parishes with thin resources; inmates were 'intollerable burdens'. One parish asked for a count of inmates in 1650 that 'lye so heavy'.[139] They *deprived* citizens. There was less food to go around and more mouths to feed. A 1641 draft bill for stopping the building blitz said that the city was running short of food, fuel, water, and any trust or belief that it could be 'governed' at all with so many floods of migrants 'of desperate fortunes and smale ability' from the 'meaner sort'.[140]

Another floating population who often appear after 1600 were vagrant 'big bellied' women. We know next to nothing about them, not even their names. Once spotted, they were shunted away, and identified by their bodies and babies.[141] They were poor and single in the main, some were scared servants made pregnant by their masters and now looking for a place to stay after being turned out-of-doors. Their sad stories are of a cold London where hard-hearted men treated maids like goods, and left them to get by in parishes that saw them in terms of pounds, shillings, and pence. Women like Ellen Bedford, who spent two decades in service with Richard Crutchely of St Martin-in-the-Fields, until he kicked her out as she was 'great with child' in 1637. She then 'wandered up and down' in a tizzy for a week, not knowing what to do, before crossing into London for a month to find a warm resting place, getting more nervous as her 'time' drew nearer. At last, knowing that there was not a minute to lose, she went back to Crutchley's house, a sad figure shuffling along his street whom he had hoped to never see again, and, thinking only of himself, he got his sister to smuggle her into a friend's house in next-door St Margaret's, where she gave birth less than a day later. When the case came to court, the parishes were at loggerheads about the cost and care of Bedford and her baby.[142] Drifting women were outside rituals of birthing rooms that

---

[138] LMA Jour. 33, fo. 203v; Rep. 29, fos. 20–0v; GL MS 5770/1, fo. 393; GCL company minute book T, fo. 117v.
[139] GL MS 4813/1, fos. 74v, 78.
[140] LMA Jour. 40, fo. 33; Rep. 20, fo. 136; SRPJ (175), pp. 398–400; TNA SP12/268/102.
[141] LMA MJ/SBR/7, fo. 43.
[142] LMA WJ/SR/NS/48/38. See also Griffiths, *Youth and Authority*, pp. 273–87; David Postles, 'Surviving lone motherhood in early modern England', *The Seventeenth Century*, 21 (2006), 160–83; Bernard Capp *When Gossips Meet: Women, Family, and Neighbourhood in Early Modern England* (Oxford, 2003), pp. 146–8; Tim Meldrum, 'London domestic servants from depositional evidence, 1660–1750: servant-employer sexuality in the patriarchal household', in Tim Hitchcock, Peter King, and Pamela Sharpe, eds., *Chronicling Poverty: the Voices and Strategies of the English Poor, 1640–1840* (Basingstoke, 1997), pp. 47–69.

were meant for married women with roots in parishes.[143] Vagrant women usually gave birth outside rather than inside, seeking shelter if it could be found next to walls or in porches. 'Big bellied' vagrants had no stake in the community and could not build legitimate households that were the sources of 'honest' parishes. Pregnant and alone they were inevitably immoral in many minds. The physical signs of pregnancy in their single-state marked them out as 'lewd', unlike wives who 'searched' them and led them out of parishes and off relief rolls. Motherhood gave older women authority, and there must have been some antagonism towards pregnant drifters: some people landed in trouble for 'beating', 'kickinge', or 'hurtinge' them.[144]

The first mention of action against 'great bellied' women in parishes nearly always comes from around 1600, often five or six decades after accounts start to survive.[145] There were more 'great bellied' women seeking shelter then, and the number of attempts to put them out of parishes also shoots up. They were a familiar sight after 1600, ambling awkwardly and alone, often in pain, asking for money or directions to get somewhere.[146] 'Big bellied' women could not easily escape notice. Some were shunted between parishes in turf-wars to cut costs,[147] although many left with money in their pockets, never less than sixpence, and nearly always a shilling or more: five shillings was given 'to a woeman that would a ben delivered of a child in Bowyers Hall'.[148] There was always concern when 'big bellied' women were spotted on streets. A 'poore woman great with child' was given 2/6d by a parish not to leave

---

[143] Laura Gowing, *Common Bodies: Women, Touch, and Power in Seventeenth-Century England* (London and New Haven, CT, 2003), p. 159.

[144] GL MS 1176/1, 1595; Gowing, *Common Bodies*, p. 51; LMA MJ/SBR/1, fos. 221, 432, 576, 633; MJ/SBR/2, fos. 170, 205, 217, 477; MJ/SBR/6, fo. 398.

[145] The first mention in St James Garlickhithe was in 1623 (accounts survive from 1555). In St Mary Magdalene Milk Street, St Martin Orgar, St Mary Woolnoth, St Stephen Walbrook, St Alphage London Wall, St Margaret Pattens, and St Laurence Pountney it was 1606, 1627, 1635, 1623, 1607, 1638, and 1591 respectively (accounts survive from 1518, 1471, 1539, 1549, 1580, 1558, and 1530 respectively). See GL MSS 4180/1, fo. 224; 2596/1, fo. 234v; 959/1, fo. 170; 1002/1, fo. 505; 593/2, fos. 144–4v; 1432/1, fo. 89v; 4570/2, fo. 326; 3907/1, 1590–1.

[146] For example, GL MSS 4524/1, fos. 52, 161, 239; 524/1, fo. 42v; 4383/1, fos. 271, 350, 441; 2968/2, fo. 316v; 559/1, fos. 29, 62; 1176/1, 1600, 1620, 1629, 1640; 4423/1, fos. 67v, 180v; 577/1, fos. 56, 102v, 125, 146v; 951/1, fo. 135; 590/1, fos. 80, 165v, 213; 1046/1, fos. 75, 188v, 264; 4457/2, fos. 98, 152, 213v, 281, 323v; 2596/2, fos. 43, 100, 120, 156; 818/1, fos. 31v, 118v, 199, 239; 4051/1, fos. 53, 75, 135; 6574, fos. 16, 188; 1002/1, fo. 516; 4180/1, fos. 194, 232v.

[147] GL MSS 878/1, fo. 239; 7673/2, fo. 52; 1432/3, fo. 89v; 818/1, fo. 146; 524/1, fo. 42v.

[148] GL MS 1432/4, 1648–9. See also GL MSS 1568, fos. 402, 650, 693, 699, 706, 715; 4071/2, fos. 138, 150, 166v, 170v, 176v, 199, 208, 229; 1124/1, fos. 158, 161v, 167v, 168, 171; 4409/1, fos. 40, 144, 144v, 147; 818/1, fos. 59, 104, 165v; 524/1, fo. 34v.

Troubled times 57

her child there. Another paid watchmen 2/7d 'for watching' a woman all night long who sat down at 'parrishioners doores'.[149] Some 'big bellied' women were removed in the nick of time. Goodman Lowde picked up sixpence for getting a woman out of one parish who was 'redie to lye downe'; while St Sepulchre (Middlesex branch) paid one shilling to shift a woman 'that was going to cry out'. Women who were 'redie to be delivered' or 'brought to bedd' were snatched from doorsteps, church doors, cloister doors, from 'under' church walls, or next to the cage. A beadle was paid five shillings in 1617 for getting rid of a woman who 'was in labour' at a Cheapside door.[150] Some women were so sick, weary, and dizzy that the only way that they could be moved was on a coach or chair. St Benet Gracechurch gave three shillings to a pair of porters who carried 'a poore woman bigg with child' at a door to 'Ratcliffe in a chear'. Another parish spent three shillings to hire a coach to take a poor milkwoman 'ready to bee delivered from Snow Hill to Islington'. All Hallows the Great forked out three shillings to replace a chair that got 'lost' when two porters took a woman back across the river to Newington in 1642.[151] Some women tried to sneak back into parishes, and they had probably made plans to give birth there. An officer got two shillings for taking the same 'great bellied' woman out of a parish 'twice in one day'. Guards were sometimes posted at parish borders to stop women getting back in again. Three 'poore men' each got tenpence from St Michael Crooked Lane in 1624 for 'kepeing owt' a 'woeman great with child' who slipped into the parish around midnight, taking advantage of the dark. Another parish spent 1/6d on look-outs when 'a great bellied woman' was seen hanging around its edges, scouting for chances to sneak in.[152] Parishes also got tip-offs if a 'great bellied woman' was heading their way. Moorfields keepers were given 2/6d by a parish in 1623 'for bringing word of divers women in laboure', whom they had spotted walking across the fields.[153]

All local officers helped to track down 'big bellied' women. Neighbours also gave helping hands, but it was often women of the parish who

---

[149] GL MSS 4051/1, fo. 127; 1181/1, fo. 176.
[150] GL MSS 2596/2, fos. 25, 40v; 9080/8, 1662. See also GL MSS 4071/2, fos. 56, 136v, 158, 212; 818/1, fos. 27v, 73v, 80v, 212v; 4051/1, fo. 61; 4383/1, fo. 254; 5018/1, fo. 57; 2895/2, 1619–20, 1631–2, 1637–8, 1640–1; 645/2, fo. 56; 4409/1, fos. 21v, 147, 278; 1181/1, fo. 209.
[151] GL MSS 1568, fo. 576; 3146/1, fo. 146v; 818/1, fo. 146. See also GL MSS 593/4, 1656–7; 4071/2, fo. 158; 593/4, 1657–8.
[152] GL MS 3907/1, 1634–5; 1181/1, fo. 89; 4385/1, fo. 240v. See also GL MSS 1303/1, 1650–1, 1651–2; 577/1, fo. 97v; 4524/1, fo. 128; 1176/1, 1610; 7673/2, fo. 52; 4570/2, fo. 332; 1432/3, fos. 104, 107v; 524/1, fo. 35; 6544/1, fo. 38.
[153] GL MS 4457/2, fo. 222v.

'carryed' or 'conveyed' 'wayward' 'big bellied' women somewhere else in support of male-made authority. They acted alone at times, although they also worked side-by-side with officers to stop a costly birth on parish ground. St Stephen Coleman Street put a small team together in 1621 made up of a constable, 'severall watchmen and two women' to get a woman who was 'ready to be delivered' safely away from Moorfields. A pair of porters and 'ii weomen' shared 1/6d after they spared another parish from looking after 'a poore woman in travel of a child'.[154] Something else that leaps out of the records is how many of these women were said to be 'poore'. Two 'poore women' shared a shilling when they helped lead 'a poore woman' out of a parish who was 'ready to be delivered'. While four 'poore parishioners' divided fifteenpence after getting 'a poore woman ready to be brought to bed' out of another parish in 1603.[155] This was the poor leading the poor, and doubtless most of these escorts were mothers and members of childbirth rings, and this gave them some status and authority in local circles.[156] There is a strong likelihood that many women who took part in these evictions were in effect 'carers', who stayed by the side of 'big bellied' women and comforted them until they were safely over the border. One parish paid for 'woemens helpe' to get 'a pore woman in labor' off their patch.[157] Midwives are mentioned in some accounts. A midwife and 'two poore women' were given eight shillings in 1630 for taking 'a woman redy to be delivered in the street' out of a parish.[158] Widows and goodwives turn up more than once. But more often than not records refer to 'ye women' or 'other wemen' with nothing else noted, like the '3 women' who were paid eight shillings in 1647 'to gett a woman in labour out of the parish' of

---

[154] Ibid., fo. 212v; GL MS 4409/1, fo. 112. See also GL MSS 577/1, fo. 105v; 4457/2, fos. 76, 212; 645/2, fo. 59; 4180/2, fo. 52v; 3556/2, 1659. Cf. Gowing, *Common Bodies*, pp. 41–51; Gowing, 'Ordering the body: illegitimacy and female authority in seventeenth-century England', in Michael J. Braddick and John Walter, eds., *Negotiating Power in Early Modern Society: Order, Hierarchy, and Subordination in Britain and Ireland* (Cambridge, 2001), pp. 43–62; and Capp, *When Gossips Meet*, esp. chap. 7.

[155] GL MSS 4409/1, fo. 198; 4457/2, fo. 76. See also GL MSS 577/1, fo. 105v; 1568, fo. 569; 645/2, fo. 56; 1432/4, 1654–5.

[156] Gowing, *Common Bodies*, pp. 46, 70–3. On childbirth see Adrian Wilson, 'The ceremony of childbirth and its interpretation', in Valerie Fildes, ed., *Women as Mothers in Pre-Industrial England* (1990), pp. 68–107; Laura Gowing, 'Secret births and infanticide in seventeenth-century England', *Past and Present*, 156 (1997), 87–115; Gowing, 'Ordering the body', pp. 148–61; Patricia Crawford, 'The construction and experience of maternity in seventeenth-century England', in her *Blood, Bodies, and Families in Early Modern England* (Harlow, 2004), pp. 79–112.

[157] GL MS 1303/1, 1627. See also GL MSS 2088/1, 1616–17; 1568, fo. 569; 4409/1, fos. 198, 224; 4409/2, 1663–4; 1432/4, 1654–5.

[158] GL MS 645/2, fo. 56. See also GL MSS 4051/1, fo. 135; 577/1, fo. 105v; 1568, fo. 514; 4432/1, fo. 185.

St Martin Orgar.[159] This scene seems like a mobile childbed as women-only support-groups guided a 'big bellied' woman through the streets, always alert in case she began to give birth there and then. As many as six 'poore women' shared eighteenpence on one occasion for walking with a woman 'yt was ready to be delivered' to the edge of St Stephen Coleman Street parish.[160]

Another aspect of this 'problem' that made it more troubling was its apparent organization, including go-betweens who helped 'big bellied' women get from one place to shelter elsewhere. Alice Harris, who was grabbed on the bridge in Spring 1633, was 'accused usually to carry women great with child from one place to another to be brought to bed in other parishes then where they dwell'. She was spotted taking a woman 'in a cheare to beg', and took a share of the spoils. A note was made in Bridewell's book in 1624 that Alice Williams 'maketh [a] common course' of 'bringinge women into parishes who are delivered of children in the streets'. Widow Susan Gardener of Westminster was prosecuted in 1636 for bringing 'whores' into her parish where they gave birth to 'bastards'.[161] In some cases guides were heading for particular places. Elizabeth Gibbs landed in trouble in 1630 'for bringeing a woman' who was 'greate wth childe' to Widow Evans's house in an alley off Whitecross Street. One parish 'laid out' two shillings in 1636 to put a woman in prison, 'who brought [another] woman to lye in' there. At other times guides looked out for hideaways where a 'great bellied' woman could give birth. Christian Pellam, 'a comon nightwalker' with a long criminal record, was brought back to Bridewell in 1637 for 'leading a woman ready to be delivered of a bastard child from one parish to another'.[162] Some pregnant wanderers had a safe shelter to go to, someone who was known to provide a childbed for a fee. There was a network of midwives that made public knowledge about practices, people, and contacts.[163] It is likely that some women who took in pregnant women were midwives at the more murky end of the trade. Alehouses and other cheap boarding-places also appear in records. A woman was sent to Bridewell in 1600 for 'keeping whores and lewd women in childbed'. A Wapping man – Simon Veasey – took 'lewde women' 'great with childe' to Joanne Pinckerney's house in 1610, 'contractinge with her for their aboade'. It was noted that

---

[159] GL MSS 2895/2, 1632–3; 959/1, fos. 179v, 204v.   [160] GL MS 4457/2, fo. 76.
[161] BHC 7, fo. 324; 6, fo. 355; LMA WJ/SR/NS/46/136.
[162] LMA MJ/SBR/1, fo. 47; GL MS 4385/1, fo. 200v; BHC 8, fo. 123v. See also LMA MJ/SBR/2, fo. 479; MJ/SBR/5, fo. 197; WJ/SR/NS/39/86; BHC 6, fos. 279, 415; 7, fos. 22v, 362v; 8, fo. 334v.
[163] Doreen Evenden, *The Midwives of Seventeenth-Century London* (Cambridge, 2000), p. 13. See also Gowing, *Common Bodies*, pp. 156–7.

60     Change

Veasey was always 'p[res]nte at the birthe'. William Webb got into trouble three decades later for giving room and board to a woman 'who was delivered of a bastard child in his house'. The court was tipped off that he 'usually received money of weomen greate with child of bastardes' to cook up false paternity accusations. A married couple in Westminster also ended up in court for 'sufferinge young women' to 'lodge' in their house and 'to be brought to bed there'. They owned up that there were two women staying with them at that moment: one 'in childbed', they said, and another who was making a return visit after giving birth to a 'bastard' there 'before'.[164]

Apart from Simon Veasey, all the 'leaders' of 'big bellied' women I have come across were other women. A woman 'with child' had a better chance to walk through the streets with other women without attracting attention in a society where women gathered around pregnant friends with handy help. But more men crop up offering beds to 'big bellied' women, though the margin is not great. Thirty-five men (56.45 per cent) and twenty-seven women appear in my records: two women were said to be widows, five more were wives, and there was a single spinster. Four married couples also appear and there is a good chance that many 'stand-alone' men were husbands who were given all the legal blame.[165] The men were a mixed bag: a chimney-sweep, clothworker, falconer, feltmaker, chandler, tinker, and trussmaker. 'Big bellied' boarders offered landlords/ladies a chance to earn money on the side. Many of them did so more than once and their offences are listed in plurals of 'diverse women' or 'lightwomen'. Anne Bagley, who lived with her husband (a yeoman) along St John Street, was said to be 'a comon harborer of greate bellied women'.[166] It was a risky business that turned a parish against one of its own. But men and women were prepared to throw caution to the wind for money in hard times. And as the number of tramping pregnant women continued to climb after 1600, so did the number of Londoners who gave them a helping hand at a price.

What became of new-borns is rarely known. Some were put out to nurse. Some mothers tried their luck living in London with their child

---

[164] BRHA BHC 4, fo. 155v; LMA MJ/SBR/1, fo. 220; MJ/SBR/6, fo. 598; WAC WCB/1, fo. 118. Maurice Prince was called 'a comon receiver and lodger of infected persons and young women to lodge and lye in his house' (WAC WCB/1, fo. 210).
[165] For some other cases see BHC 2, fos. 154, 208; 3, fos. 27, 346; 8, fo. 59; BRHA BHC 4, fos. 7, 155v, 258v, 415; GL MSS 1046/1, fo. 172v; 4457/2, fo. 145v; 4241/1, fo. 352; LMA CQSF 90/20; MJ/SBR/1, fos. 144, 567; MJ/SBR/2, fos. 40, 318, 467, 522; MJ/SBR/4, fos. 143, 258, 545, 707; MJ/SBR/5, fos. 161, 417, 520; MJ/SBR/7, fo. 44; WJ/SR/NS/34/66, 37/102, 40/150, 43/37–8, 46/150, 47/110; WAC WCB/1, fos. 15, 144, 195; WCB/2, fos. 77, 101–2, 109, 162.
[166] LMA MJ/SBR/1, fos. 47, 108, 578.

Troubled times 61

again, perhaps with the help of friends, family, or parish hand-outs. Some fathers covered the costs of births and sometimes gave something for keep of the child they did not want. One father came from Hampshire to haggle with his daughter's master after he made her pregnant. They first 'resolve[d]' that she should go back home, but another plan was hatched when the carrier did not turn up, and she was sent to lodge with a friend in Westminster – for 'sixpence a weeke' – and gave birth soon after.[167] Other children disappeared. Agnes Hancock said that she never kept track of children born in her house. Elizabeth Marshal (alias Burde), who lived next to the Smithfield pens, made money by boarding 'lewd women', and two or more had been 'brought to bed' there and 'the children made away'. More is known about Thomas Merrick of Charterhouse Lane, who was in trouble in 1612 after word spread that he buried children 'delivered' by 'whores' he 'harbored in his house' in dunghills. Another child died it was said 'by the mothers default'.[168] New-borns were also left on porches, steps, or at hospital gates for others to care for. Landlords/ladies also ditched children. John Burkill got in trouble in 1634 'for suffering a bastard child to be borne' and 'creesened' in his Whitechapel house and later leaving it on the other side of the city in St Dunstan-in-the-West. Alice Easton, who lodged 'women wth childe', said that she had nothing to do with 'the layeing of a yonge sucklinge child' near Paul's Wharf in 1609, but 'officers of Lambeth Marshe' where she lived knew better: they told Bridewell's bench that she 'tould pore women that att any time for xs she could helpe them away with a child that should be kepte better than they coulde keepe yt and by men of good ability'.[169]

Abandoned children first turn up in long-running parish accounts after 1600, when the number of foundling baptisms also rose.[170] The big leap in Bridewell cases came after 1620: forty-one in 1618–27 and 123 over

---

[167] LMA WJ/SR/NS/35/1.
[168] LMA MJ/SRB/1, fo. 220; BRHA BHC 4, fo. 63; LMA MJ/SBR/1, fos. 478, 480; BHC 8, fo. 45v.
[169] LMA WJ/SR/NS/40/78; BHC 5, fo. 373v. See also Valerie Fildes, 'Maternal feelings re-assessed: child abandonment and neglect in London and Westminster, 1550–1800', in Fildes, ed., *Women as Mothers*, pp. 139–78; Claire Schen, *Charity and Lay Piety in Reformation London, 1500–1620* (Aldershot, 2002), pp. 181–2, 230–1; Tanya Evans, *'Unfortunate Objects': Lone Mothers in Eighteenth-Century London* (Basingstoke, 2005), pp. 129–37.
[170] The first mention in St Stephen Walbrook was 1584, Mary Magdalene Milk Street 1585, St Mary Aldermanbury 1586, St James Garlickhithe 1586, St Peter Westcheap 1587–8, St Mary Woolnoth 1587–8, St Olave Jewry 1597, St Lawrence Pountney 1602–3, St Martin Orgar 1607, and St Margaret Pattens 1627. See GL MSS 593/2, fo. 72; 2596/1, fo. 178v; 3556/1, fo. 184; 4180/1, fo. 70; 645/1, fo. 124; 1002/1, fo. 288v; 4409/1, fo. 29v; 3907/1, 1602–3; 959/1, fo. 105; 4570/2, fo. 275. On foundlings

the next fifteen years.[171] This 'problem' had grown greatly 'of late' in 1614 and in 1624, by-laws said. One parish griped that 'ye charge of ye foundlings' is 'so great' in 1631. Numbers of orphans and street-strays admitted to Christ's Hospital also rose after 1620: 1619/78, 1624/113, 1633/179, 1639/179, 1649/152.[172] Cost and care were the main matters. Parishes spent money to track down 'unnatural' mothers, and to stop them leaving children. St Stephen Walbrook splashed out 15/4d on Anne Walker's room and board 'for 23 weekes att 8d per weeke to keepe her from laying her child'. This charity could make a difference. Elizabeth Butler told Joanne Loader that she could not bring herself to 'lye' her child 'at the Three Cranes in the Vintrey' because the 'parishe had bine good to her' in the past.[173] 'Lewde disposed woemen more unnaturall and unkinde then brute beasts', was how one by-law described women who had 'forsaken the frutes of their bodies' near wells or open cellars without 'eny maner of comfort', never once looking back as their child started to cry.[174] Only a few children died after they were found, while others were already dead on a step in one case, and in a church and on Blackfriars stairs leading down to the river in others.[175] Most mothers did not dump children at the first chance in dingy corners or wasteland. They left them where they could be seen: on steps in almost half of my cases (156/325). Mary Carthis put a 'bastard child' in a basket for Ann Cope to 'leave at a mans door' in 1637, though she left it in Hyde Park.[176] Hard-up mothers had high hopes that their child would be better looked after, and some left notes with their child.[177] The step of a nice-looking house

see Richard Adair, *Courtship, Illegitimacy, and Marriage in Early Modern England* (Manchester, 1996), pp. 204–5, Table 7.6 and Figure 7.2. Foundlings and other abandoned children were one concern at the opening of Christ's Hospital. See Carol Kazmierczak Manzione, *Christ's Hospital of London, 1552–1598: 'A Passing Deed of Pity'* (Selinsgrove, 1995), pp. 138–42.

[171] The sources for these figures are BHC 6–8. Abandoned children were also noted in Common Council Journals, and the number of these reports also rose in the 1630s: see LMA Jours. 37, fos. 125, 173; 38, fos. 40, 54v, 101, 172, 236, 249v, 299; 39, fos. 52, 81, 86, 134.

[172] LMA Jours. 29, fo. 177; 32, fo. 318; GL MSS 4383/1, fo. 317; 12806/3, fos. 209–10v, 432–5; 12806/4, fos. 9–13, 312–15, 568–72. The number of foundling baptisms in Bills of Mortality rose after 1620: Fildes, 'Maternal feelings re-assessed', p. 143.

[173] GL MS 593/4, 1657; BRHA BHC 4, fo. 122v.

[174] LMA Jour. 26, fo. 289. See also LMA Letterbook K, fo. 81v.

[175] GL MSS 4051/1, fo. 29; 590/1, fos. 110, 180v; 4423/1, fos. 34, 34v; 2999/1, 1669–70; LMA CQSF 116/27–8.

[176] LMA WJ/SR/NS/47/206. My cases come from parish accounts, vestry books, quarter sessions records, and Bridewell and Christ's. See also Fildes, 'Maternal feelings re-assessed', pp. 151–8.

[177] BRHA BHC 4, fo. 315. See also Fildes, 'Maternal feelings re-assessed', pp. 152–7.

Troubled times 63

offered a glimmer of hope. 'Thou foole yt wilbe kepte better then thou arte able to keepe yt', Joanne Loader snapped at Elizabeth Butler when she told her that she wanted to go back to get her child, even though they were now 'a good waye from yt'. Parishes helped out women like Butler. Anne Wilkinson was punished for leaving her child but was also given 2/6d to help her get back home. Other mothers got helping hands after taking children back and this was the cheapest outcome for parishes in the long run.[178] One parish spent £4 1s 4d over ten months to look after a child who had been left on a deputy's doorstep. Like 'big bellied' women, some foundlings became victims of tugs-of-war between parishes anxious to scrimp and save on costs.[179]

There was a good reason why London's elite knew about the spate of left children as some woke up one day to find one on their step: including Sir John Spencer, Sir Martin Lumley, and Sir Baptist Hicks. One 'vagrant begginge woman' left her child 'att the lord maiors dore' in 1603; Joanne Bell left hers at the Earl of Arundel's gate.[180] Magistrates and the well-to-do stood out because of their wealth, and mothers or their friends knew where they lived. Joan Wylye admitted that she 'layd a yonge childe' at 'a mans dore' on Cheapside in 1562. She did so, she said, with the 'councell' of Elizabeth Welch, who 'said unto her ley yt at some riche mans dore and yt will be better kepte than thowe canste kepe yt'. The doorsteps of ward deputies were also singled out, along with those of doctors, ministers, and captains and colonels: Colonel Blundell had three children laid at different times at his door.[181] Other men were given the title 'Mr', and many of them were overseers, constables, churchwardens, clerks, or others of local note in positions to help a child who suddenly appeared from nowhere one day.[182]

---

[178] BRHA BHC 4, fo. 122v; GL MS 12806/2, fo. 38. For some other hand-outs see GL MSS 4524/1, fo. 159v; 4383/1, fo. 448; 2968/3, fo. 176; 951/1, fo. 181; 4071/2, fo. 153v; 3907/1, 1608–9, 1630–1; 593/4, 1640; 2596/1, fo. 234; 2596/2, fo. 50; 4570/2, fos. 289, 322; 818/1, fo. 191.

[179] GL MS 4423/1, fo. 87; 524/1, fo. 56.

[180] GL MSS 6386, fo. 57; 645/2, fo. 81; 2596/2, fo. 15v; 4423/1, fo. 64v; 1046/1, fo. 10; 2596/1, fo. 214; 5090/2, fos. 100v, 167v, 223; 2895/2, 1660–1; 4409/2, 1660–1; BRHA BHC 4, fo. 414v; BHC 3, fo. 291.

[181] BHC 1, fo. 207v; GL MSS 4524/1, fo. 255v; 4423/1, fo. 87; 577/1, fo. 103v; 2596/2, fo. 131; BRHA BHC 4, fos. 80v, 243v; GL MSS 2596/2, fo. 103; 6836, fo. 279; 2895/2, 1652–3; 2593/1, 1623, fo.5; 6574, fo. 58.

[182] For example, GL MSS 3146/1, fo. 81v; 1176/1, 1603; 2593/1, 1590–1; 6836, fo. 202; 951/1, fo. 182; 4385/1, fo. 140; 1046/1, fo. 161v; 1303/1, 1642; 5090/2, fo. 262; 1124/1, fo. 137; 1568, fo. 705; 2895/2, 1659–60; 1016/1, fo. 202; 645/2, fo. 50; 4180/2, fo. 70; 593/2, fo. 137v; 4409/2, 1662–3; 593/4, 1642–3; 2596/2, fo. 106; 4956/3, fo. 237; 4051/1, fo. 157; 1181/1, fo. 173; 9080/4, 1655; 2999/1, 1634–5. Only one woman is named in records that I have seen, a child was left on Mistress Offler's step in St Mary Woolnoth parish: GL MS 1002/1, fo. 288v.

Thirty-four children were left in churches on benches, porches, or steps. Twenty-nine more were put on stalls and others in busy places like an Inn of Court, the Exchange, a company hall, or a hospital. Christ Hospital's porter was taken to task in 1625 for opening a gate at the crack of dawn without a beadle 'at hand' to stop a woman slipping in and leaving a child 'next to the cloisters'. Beadles took turns to go up and down 'the walke' from Christ's to St Bartholomew's Hospital in 1615 to see that no children were left there.[183] Another child turned up in a coach. All we know in nearly 100 other cases is that children were left in a street, alley, court, or yard. Nothing is said about a step or stall.[184] But here too there was an expectation that they would be found quickly in busy alleys or yards like Charterhouse Yard or Harper Alley in Cornhill. Mothers also picked streets that were crowded by day and watched over at night – Fleet Street, Bishopgate Street, Lombard Street, Cheapside – or landmarks, like the 'condyt in Cornehill', under Cornhill arch, Birchin Lane corner, Temple gates, or 'over againste the greate conduit in Cheapeside'.[185] Don't leave your child in Christchurch, Joanne Loader told Elizabeth Butler, 'butt in some place of more resort of people', and Butler followed her advice and left her child on Mr Davye's stall along Birchin Lane.[186]

Loader was what Christ's bench called 'counsell givers' to leave children in streets. It turned out that she was a midwife, and the only one with Butler when she gave birth at a 'longe privyhouse' near the 'Thamessyde'.[187] These 'counsell givers' knew London better and could pinpoint the best spots to leave children. Ursula Robinson was whipped in 1603 'for receyving women and layinge bastards at mens doors'. James Marshall (alias Muskott) also appeared there in the same year 'for councelling' a woman 'to leave her child'.[188] People were 'hired' to leave children somewhere or to lead mothers to a good spot. A woman who crossed the river to leave 'a bastard childe' in St Sepulchre said that she had been 'hired to dyspose of the child'. Elizabeth Needham spent 2/6d to hire a woman to leave her child in Christchurch, 'in her presence'.

---

[183] GL MS 12806/3, fo. 555; SBHA Governors' Journal 4, fo. 74v.
[184] Fifty-nine children were found on the streets, seventeen in alleys, thirteen in courts, and nine in yards.
[185] GL MSS 4071/2, fos. 180, 199, 207v, 213v; 9080/1B, 1647–8; 9080/4, 1655, 9080/5, 1655; 4423/1, fo. 187; 2999/1, 1653–4, 1638–9, 1640–1; 4051/1, fo. 53; 6574, fo. 14v; 2596/2, fos. 15v, 50; 4071/1, fo. 133v; 2999/1, 1660–1; 1240/1, fo. 24v; BRHA BHC 4, fos. 308, 380v, 397.
[186] BRHA BHC 4, fo. 125v.   [187] GL MS 12806/2, fo. 117v.
[188] BRHA BHC 4, fos. 375, 376, 414v. Robinson 'perswaded' Alice Avery to leave her child at a door, and Avery said that her child 'is now kept at a tailor's house who is being paid for looking after' it.

Troubled times 65

While an Irishwoman said it was 'true' that she 'did cause one to laie a childe in Xptes Hospitall and that the childe is hers'.[189] Illegitimacy rates rose after 1600, not by much but enough to add to the rise in child abandonment that is evident in parish records.[190] Information is not always at hand, but nearly all of these children were illegitimate, and the number of mothers who were vulnerable maidservants was high.[191] The rise in abandonment was yet another sign of speedy growth: more children, cost, and rootlessness. And yet another problem of the streets that peaked in the 1620s/30s.

Abandoned children were another growing pain. But there were also opportunities for the poor in 'dangerous' growth. Paupers poured into London and others made money lodging inmates, leading 'big bellied' women, letting rooms for births, and laying children on steps. There were opportunities, but not of the Dick Whittington sort. They were make-shifts not mayoralties, but they helped people to get by. London's leaders thought differently about these money-making schemes. For them they were tumours, sucking life from the city. It should be clear by now that I would like to move debate about the state of the city away from a starting position of how fraught social structures weathered severe strains more or less intact. Administration and civic bonds will feature in what follows. Well-run government is a key part of the story. I also give much prominence to the uphill struggle to tackle growth. We have not looked enough so far at the combined contributions of policy, police, and prosecution. Only Archer has given significant space to crime-fighting, but his work still sticks to the stability/instability conundrum and comes down on the side of stability. We need to be more nuanced than this and accept that there was always a jumpy balance between keeping order and heavy crime that could tip one way or another, that was viewed negatively by London's leaders. Their perceptions grew darker over time. They are our best guide to whether or not the city was stable, if that stays on our agenda. They also suggest that there was a crunch time after 1620 when vagrant floods

---

[189] LMA CQSF 106/6; BHC 8, fo. 111; BRHA BHC 4, fo. 315. See also BRHA BHC 4, fos. 46v, 51, 125, 281v, 425; LMA MJ/SBR/2, fo. 337; MJ/SBR/5, fo. 110.
[190] Adair says that 'a reasonable guess' is that under a quarter of foundlings were 'illegitimate before the Civil War'. He largely bases this argument on intervals between abandonment and birth, believing that illegitimates were abandoned straight after birth. I would expect a rise in illegitimacy to trigger more abandonment. See Adair, *Courtship, Illegitimacy, and Marriage*, p. 213; and Fildes, 'Maternal feelings re-assessed', p. 149, Table 6.4. Adrian Wilson believes that the proportion of illegitimates in totals of foundlings was higher: 'Illegitimacy and its implications in mid-eighteenth-century London: the evidence of the foundling hospital', *Continuity and Change*, 4, (1989), 103–64.
[191] Griffiths, *Youth and Authority*, pp. 271–4.

seemed to overwhelm the city. Numbers of inmates, 'big bellied' vagrants, and abandoned children also seemed to soar at the same time. This same chronology recurs in changing perceptions of 'environmental' and gendered crime, as we will shortly see. Crimes and troubles have chronologies and histories, and also geographies. Time and space were always on the minds of London's leaders. The city was a patchwork of neighbourhoods, some safer, others more dangerous. London had a fair share of crime hot beds and red light belts, and we can map crime as well as follow it through time, something that the next chapter tries to do.

# 2 Mapping troubles

### 'Little worlds'

Trying to say something definitive about this metropolitan maze is like trying to square a circle. 'There are so many little worlds in her', Donald Lupton marvelled in 1632. There were twenty-six wards, 109 parishes, and a mesh of criss-crossing jurisdictions. Wards were split into about 242 precincts, many of which crossed parish lines, blurring borders still further. 'Many little worlds', indeed, and many were just small specks on maps but with their own sights, sounds, stench, and stories to tell. London has not one history or even a dozen histories, but hundreds of histories of places, peoples, and cultures. Not one was hermetically sealed from the rest or forked off in one direction on its own. They all crossed constantly like London's streets and jurisdictional patches. These 'little worlds' and histories are set in London and they all have something to say about living in the city, but they are not histories *of* London.[1]

London's quick growth modified mental and physical landscapes and how people experienced the city. These human responses are swamped by growth, and people living 400 years ago can easily get lost in population counts.[2] Londoners made their own environments but each self was affected in some way by place, people, landscape, and living standards. Each Londoner carved out his or her experience and niche in the city, making it their own. Not one London, but around 200,000 Londons by 1600, all making it certain that the city could never be fixed in a single place or mind. Women, for example, were freer and more able to shirk patriarchal rules and roles in cities. Single women sometimes moved in

---

[1] Donald Lupton, *London and the Country Carbonadoed and Quartered Into Severall Characters*, 1632, The English Experience, 879 (Amsterdam and Norwood, NJ, 1977), p. 1; LMA COL/WD/03/044. Cf. Mark S. R. Jenner and Paul Griffiths, 'Introduction', in Jenner and Griffiths, eds., *Londinopolis: Essays in the Cultural and Social History of Early Modern London* (Manchester, 2000), pp. 1–23.

[2] Margaret Pelling, 'Skirting the city? Disease, social change, and divided households in the seventeenth century', in Griffiths and Jenner, eds., *Londinopolis*, pp. 154–75, esp. p. 155.

with kin and friends, but once in London they tended to drift more often than men from service to service, and this left them open to all the insinuations that went hand-in-hand with not being under the thumb of a father, husband, or master.[3] Away from parents for the first time, the city was doubtless dazzling for many of them with a wider pool of jobs and people to meet. Although they commonly lived with their master/employer, city women had a larger say in shaping their own lives. They married later than women who still lived at home, in London or anywhere else, and usually after a few years of working for wages, more often than not in victualling or vending trades.[4] Women married a little later in life in London, but higher mortality rates meant that more of them lived longer than their husbands. Not many widows stayed single for very long, however, and as many as one-quarter of tradesmen, who were often on the young side, tied the knot with a widow. Often older than their second (or third) husband with a workshop to bring to the marriage, the scales of patriarchy did not always lean towards men in these households as moralists asked, and the predatory widow was a stock caricature on the stage and in cheap print.[5]

But London was not an idyll for women, no matter what people said at the time. They could not skip from job to job or have fun at the drop of a hat. Women may have seemed to get the upper hand too often, but that

[3] Paul Griffiths, 'Masterless young people in Norwich, 1560–1645', in Griffiths, Adam Fox, and Steve Hindle, eds., *The Experience of Authority in Early Modern England* (Basingstoke, 1996), pp. 146–86; P. J. P. Goldberg, *Women, Work, and Life-Cycle in a Medieval Economy: Women in York and Yorkshire, c.1300–1520* (Oxford, 1992), pp. 299–300; Marjorie Keniston McIntosh, *Controlling Misbehaviour in England, 1370–1600* (Cambridge, 1998), pp. 110–11, 159; Amy M. Froide, 'Marital status as a category of difference: singlewomen and widows in early modern England', and Ruth Mazo Karras, 'Sex and the singlewoman', both in Judith M. Bennett and Froide, eds., *Singlewomen in the European Past, 1250–1800* (Philadelphia, PA, 1999), pp. 236–69 and 127–44; Ruth Mazo Karras, *Common Women: Prostitution and Sexuality in Medieval England* (Oxford, 1996), pp. 52, 112–13, 135; Sharon Farmer, *Surviving Poverty in Medieval Paris: Gender, Ideology, and the Daily Lives of the Poor* (Ithaca, NY, 2002), pp. 113–17, 157; Ulinka Rublack, *The Crimes of Women in Early Modern Germany* (Oxford, 1999), pp. 152–4.

[4] Laura Gowing, '"The freedom of the streets": women and social space, 1560–1640', in Griffiths and Jenner, eds., *Londinopolis*, pp. 130–51; esp. pp. 132–3; Vivien Brodsky, 'Singlewomen in the London marriage market', in R. B. Outhwaite, ed., *Marriage and Society: Studies in the Social History of Marriage* (1981), pp. 81–100; Ian W. Archer, 'Material Londoners?', in Lena Cowen Orlin, ed., *Material London, ca. 1600* (Philadelphia, PA, 2000), pp. 174–92, esp. pp. 184–5.

[5] Vivien Brodsky, 'Widows in late Elizabethan London: economic opportunity and family orientations', in Lloyd Bonfield, Richard Smith, and Keith Wrightson, eds., *The World We Have Gained: Histories of Population and Social Structure. Essays Presented to Peter Laslett on his Seventieth Birthday* (Oxford, 1986), pp. 122–54; Jeremy Boulton, *Neighbourhood and Society: a London Suburb in the Seventeenth Century* (Cambridge, 1987), esp. pp. 127–9; Barbara J. Todd, 'The remarrying widow: a stereotype reconsidered', in Mary Prior, ed., *Women in English Society, 1500–1800* (1985), pp. 54–92.

was frequently the projection of male fears and fantasies. Judicial records are cold reminders of the precarious position of maids. Some masters saw their maids as pieces of property and treated them with arrogance and aggression: 'Thowe art my servant and I may doe with thee what I please', Robert Parker told Alice Ashemore in 1605, in the course of sexual abuse that lasted for over a year. Without friends, the top priority for newly arrived women was to get a job and somewhere to live, but many fell prey to streetwise sharks on the look-out for potential prostitutes and cheap labour. Katherine Fuller got in trouble for taking 'countrie wenches from the carriers', who she then dressed up in 'gentlemens apparell' and put to work in her 'notorious bawdie house' in Clerkenwell.[6] The pull of domestic service kept pushing up the number of single women, and London's population was younger than most other places with a sex ratio that tipped towards men around 1600, but swung the other way as time passed. Significantly, the ratio of female vagrants kept rising each decade. Just over one-quarter of vagrants brought to Bridewell were women around 1600 (28.6 per cent), a figure that climbed to four-tenths in the 1630s, and higher still over the next two decades (43.5 per cent).[7] More women came to the city over time and specific brands of metropolitan femininity were made (and remade) by women themselves and by magistrates who, it appeared, were always lit by deep anxieties about women at large in London with little restraint. There were strong and clear feminine slants to urban disorders.

So many migrants made the city somewhat faceless, letting people sink into crowds and back streets. Anonymity always troubled London's rulers who wanted to find out as much as possible about people in their midst. Population surges could certainly increase anonymity and alienation, turning London into a city of passing strangers, short-lived relationships, and loneliness. People could steer clear of others if they needed to or find a handy place to hide. London's 'largeness' offers 'conveniency for any

---

[6] BHC 5, fo. 23v; LMA MJ/SR/510/33. See also Paul Griffiths, *Youth and Authority: Formative Experiences in England, 1560–1640* (Oxford, 1996), pp. 267–87; Tim Meldrum, 'London domestic servants from depositional evidence, 1660–1750: servant-employer sexuality in the patriarchal household', in Tim Hitchcock, Peter King, and Pamela Sharpe, eds., *Chronicling Poverty: the Voices and Strategies of the English Poor, 1640–1840* (Basingstoke, 1997), pp. 47–69.

[7] Roger Finlay, *Population and Metropolis: the Demography of London, 1580–1650* (Cambridge, 1981), pp. 140–2. Cf. D. V. Glass, 'Notes on the demography of London at the end of the seventeenth century', in Glass and R. Revelle, eds., *Population and Social Change* (1972), pp. 275–85; David Souden, 'Migrants and the population structure of late seventeenth-century provincial cities and market towns', in Peter Clark, ed., *The Transformation of English Provincial Towns, 1660–1800* (1984), pp. 133–68; Griffiths, 'Masterless young people', p. 153. Vagrancy profiles are taken from BHC 4–9.

concealment', Lattroon said in Richard Head's *The English Rogue* (1672). It was not 'a greenwood forest', as McMullan calls it (Henry Fielding also called London 'a vast wood or forest'),[8] but it had many winding alleys and nooks and crannies. People could always disappear in public squares or fields for a while. William Wilson ran away from his master in 1601 'and lay in the fields' until he was turned over to the authorities.[9] The city must have seemed chilly and daunting to newcomers. A young apprentice, many miles from home, probably felt homesick, and may not have ventured far from his master's house at first, and then only gingerly. The city was scary and exciting, but it is easy enough to exaggerate its anonymity. Neighbourhoods there and on its outskirts were not always aloof, and neighbourliness was a social force that could pull people together.[10] The rate of population turnover was less than might be expected, and many families stayed in the same house for a long while. Over four-tenths of witnesses at London's church courts between 1600 and 1640 had lived in the same house for a decade or more, and a near matching residential pattern has been found across the river in Southwark.[11]

Some newcomers may have had trouble settling in, but many people lived cheek-by-jowl, backing onto each other in cramped alleys, for example, with small spaces to get into yards or hang clothes out to dry. The press of people was greatest inside the walls where ninety-five houses were squashed into a single acre in the most crowded parishes. Spaces

---

[8] Lattroon is quoted in Cynthia Wall, *The Literary and Cultural Spaces of Restoration London* (Cambridge, 1998), p. 136; John L. McMullan, *The Canting Crew: London's Criminal Underworld, 1550–1700* (New Brunswick, NJ, 1984), p. 15; Fielding is quoted in Hal Gladfelder, *Criminality and Narrative in Eighteenth-Century England: Beyond the Law* (Baltimore, MD, 2001), p. 164.

[9] BRHA BHC 4, fo. 253v.

[10] Patricia Fumerton, 'London's vagrant economy: making space for "low" subjectivity', in Orlin, ed., *Material London*, pp. 206–25, esp. p. 209; Fumerton, *Unsettled: the Culture of Mobility and the Working Poor in Early Modern England* (Chicago, IL, 2006), esp. chap. 2. Arguments against exaggerating urban anonymity include Boulton, *Neighbourhood and Society*; Ian W. Archer, *The Pursuit of Stability: Social Relations in Elizabethan London* (Cambridge, 1991), p. 76; Archer, 'The charity of early modern Londoners', *Transactions of the Royal Historical Society*, 6th series, 12 ((2002), 223–44; esp. 242–3; J. F. Merritt, 'Introduction: perceptions and portrayals of London, 1598–1720', in Merritt, ed., *Imagining Early Modern London: Perceptions and Portrayals of the City from Stow to Strype, 1598–1720* (Cambridge, 2001), pp. 1–24, esp. pp. 11–13; David Garrioch, *Neighbourhood and Community in Paris, 1740–1790* (Cambridge, 1986), p. 257; R. A. Houston, *Social Change in the Age of Enlightenment: Edinburgh, 1660–1760* (Oxford, 1997), pp. 147, 230; P. Griffiths, J. Landers, M. Pelling, and R. Tyson, 'Population and disease, estrangement and belonging 1540–1700', in Peter Clark, ed., *The Cambridge Urban History of Britain: Volume II, 1540–1840* (Cambridge, 2000), pp. 195–233, esp. pp. 222–32.

[11] Gowing, *Domestic Dangers*, p. 18; Boulton, *Neighbourhood and Society*, pp. 110, 116–17, 120–38, 217; Finlay, *Population and Metropolis*, pp. 45–8.

over the walls were also filling up, though the crush was less severe in ribbon developments, with averages of about fifteen houses standing on each acre. But there was little breathing space in many older quarters, even the Guildhall was hemmed in by houses until the Great Fire (1666) cleared land and slums in one go.[12] With houses leaning over narrow streets towards each other, thin walls, windows so close that people could peer next door without straining their necks, and overcrowding, it is little wonder that historians comment on a lack of privacy. With so much to see, neighbourly chitchat kept lives in public view.[13] We need only open a book of depositions on cases relating to sex and slander to drop in on neighbours chattering, backbiting, and snooping. Yet it is easy to assume that proximity meant little privacy or endless tittle-tattle. 'Private' was an insinuation or allegation: to be tucked away in a room in 'private' or in some 'private corner' was evidence enough to land people in court. Some people also guarded their privacy with indignant care, and snooping around peoples' conversations and windows caused trouble. There was a clear idea of eavesdropping, and many taletellers and nosy-parkers ended up in court.[14] Privacy mattered, especially in a society with strong leanings towards oligarchy and secrecy. But the anonymity/neighbourliness dichotomy is not always helpful, as each one was more relevant for particular groups. Neighbourliness will not matter much for people who had not long arrived in London and had no history in any one of the city's communities or neighbourhoods.

Migration altered London's face. There were more slums, but more than anything else there was the 'unspeakable increase of people'. People, crime, smog, stench, and traffic merged in perceptions of the 'unsavourie', 'fumy', 'smutty', or 'mistie' city.[15] This was the city that the

---

[12] Finlay, *Population and Metropolis*, pp. 168–72; Brett-James, *Growth of Stuart London*, p. 43.

[13] Gowing, *Domestic Dangers*, pp. 70–2, 98–9, 269–70; Lena Cowen Orlin, 'Boundary disputes in early modern London', in Orlin, ed., *Material London, ca. 1600* (Philadelphia, PA, 2000), pp. 345–76, p. 367; Adam Fox, *Oral and Literate Culture in England, 1500–1700* (Oxford, 2000), p. 342; Diane Shaw, 'The construction of the private in medieval London', *Journal of Medieval and Early Modern Studies*, 26 (1996), 447–66.

[14] Cf. Gowing, '"Freedom of the streets"', p. 134; Linda Pollock, 'Living on the stage of the world: the concept of privacy among the elite of early modern England', in Adrian Wilson, ed., *Rethinking Social History: English Society and its Interpretation, 1570–1920* (Manchester, 1993), pp. 78–96.

[15] Edmund Howes, *Annales, Or, A Generall Chronicle of England Begun by John Stow: Continued and Augmented With Matters Forraigne and Domestique, Ancient and Moderne, Unto the End of the Present Year, 1631* (1631), p. 996; James Howell, *Familiar Letters or Epistolae Ho-Elianae*, 3 vols. (1903), vol. I, 244; *The Life and Letters of Sir Henry Wotton*, ed., Logan Persall Smith, 2 vols. (Oxford, 1907), vol. II, p. 355; *The Letters of John Chamberlain*, ed., Norman Egbert McClure, 2 vols., The American Philosophical Society (Philadelphia, PA, 1939), vol. II, p. 24.

migrants made according to the authorities, and it was dangerous and contaminating. Nowhere was immune from growth and its showers of germs, crooks, and beggars, but some areas had more unsavoury characters. The city's edges contained 'swamps' where many migrants made their homes, and this is supported by patterns of vagrancy and residence. Foreigners settled close to the walls in the eastern wards, around the bridge, or in Farringdon Within to the west. They also put down roots in Southwark and outside the walls in the sprawling ward of Farringdon Without or Whitechapel or East Smithfield.[16] Crossing the Channel from the Low Countries and France in the main, they brought new skills and cultures. They also made their own 'little worlds', and many citizens felt that they cared little for their second country. 'Strangers' always stay in their own 'companies or societies', citizens moaned, and they never go to our churches, trade with us, marry our children, wear clothes like us, or even bother to take the time to learn our language.[17]

There were other antagonisms between Londoners and 'strangers', but this sense of snooty distancing shattered the city into 'little worlds'. As a seaport and trade hub with ship crews putting up in port for short stays, London had always had ethnic mixes. But the influx of religious refugees fleeing Catholic rulers to worship in safety was sufficient to alter the character of communities. Nor were they the only migrants or visitors from overseas. Quite apart from foreign ambassadors and their trains, there was a little league of nations in parish account books logging charity to 'foreigners'. 'Grecons', 'Grecians', or 'poore Greeks' appear more than anyone else, one of them was given six shillings.[18] Hand-outs were also given to 'a Portugall', three 'Bohemia men', 'poore' Armenians, 'foure turkes undon by sea', 'a Transilvanian', homeless Frenchmen, Dutch stragglers, 'a scholler of the Pallatinat Christianus' (who got 3/4d), and to stateless 'poore barbaryans'. Patrick Wildiung, 'a hungarian undon by

---

[16] LMA Remembrancia Book 7, fos. 715–8; Andrew Pettigree, *Foreign Protestant Communities in Sixteenth-Century London* (Oxford, 1986), pp. 82–3; Charles Littleton, 'Social interactions of aliens in late Elizabethan London: evidence from the 1593 return and the French Church consistory "actes"', and Lien Bich Luu, 'Assimilation or segregation: colonies of alien craftsmen in Elizabethan London', both in *Proceedings of the Huguenot Society of Great Britain and Ireland*, 26 (1995), 147–59, 160–72.

[17] TNA SP12/81/29; Luu, 'Assimilation or segregation', 160, 168–9; Luu, 'Natural-born versus stranger-born subjects: aliens and their status in Elizabethan London', in Nigel Goose and Luu, eds., *Immigrants in Tudor and Early Stuart England* (Brighton and Portland, OR, 2005), pp. 57–75.

[18] GL MSS 9235/2, fo. 236v; 2968/2, fos. 201v, 299; 4423/1, fo. 81; 4385/1, fo. 138v. Cf. Claire Schen, 'Greeks and "Grecians" in London: the "other" strangers', in Charles Littleton and Randolph Vigne, eds., *From Strangers to Citizens: the Integration of Immigrant Communities in Britain, Ireland, and Colonial America* (Brighton and Portland, OR, 2001), pp. 268–75.

Mapping troubles 73

sea', got two shillings in 1616.[19] Closer to home, helping hands were given to 'a poore man of the Isle of Wight undone by fire', Scottish travellers, and to scores of Irish vagrants, like 'Finniene Cartinian', who got two shillings in 1594.[20] Help was also given to refugees fleeing religious repression and others set free by pirates or Turks after months or more in captivity. 'A stranger of Gallatia' received two shillings towards his ransom 'out of the turks slavery'. Foreigners who turned their backs on 'false religions' also got help. John Martin, a 'Spaniard being turned to the truth', left a parish with 2/6d in 1627, and a pair of 'Turkes turned christians' each got a shilling.[21] Although many foreigners were on their way somewhere else, others stayed put in the city, making it their home. And although London was not exactly a multi-cultural hive, it was possible to bump into people of different races and colours all the time.

For the first time around 1600 London's records begin to mention 'blackamore' workers or servants who seemed to be settled in the city. The number of 'imported blacks' was rising at this time as West African trade grew along with the greedy demand for slaves in the Spanish New World.[22] The Privy Council sent letters to mayors of leading cities in 1596 pointing out 'that there are of late divers blackamores brought into this realm', adding to the large number of this 'kind of people' already living in the land. Mindful of the 'great [population] increase' and dwindling resources, royal ministers gave orders that 'blackamores' 'should be sent forth of the land'. But little had changed five years later when central authorities made a deal with a Lubeck merchant to ship 'negroes and blackamores' back home.[23] 'Blackamores' were born and buried in London and were looked after if poverty or pain laid them low. Parish accounts list payments for taking 'blackamores' to one of the hospitals, taking care of a 'blackamore child' who was left on a doorstep in St Benet Fink parish, giving other 'blackamore' children food and board, buying a shroud for Mary Blackamore, and burying others.[24] The earliest mention of 'blackamores' in my sources is from 1577 when Peter Perringie

---

[19] GL MSS 9235/2, fo. 245v; 951/1, fo. 108; 4409/1, fo. 170; 2895/2, 1624–5; 2593/1, 1616, fo. 8; 4956/2, fo. 247; 2596/2, fo. 15; 2968/2, fo. 196v; 5714/1, fo. 78; 4071/1, fo. 130; 4071/2, fo. 37v; 1181/1, fo. 6; 4956/3, fo. 100.
[20] GL MSS 577/1, fo. 2; 5714/1, fo. 4; 2895/1, fo. 251v; 951/1, fos. 111, 143v, 153; 4423/1, fo. 72; 4385/1, fo. 231v; 4457/2, fos. 346–6v; 5714/1, fos. 135v, 162v-4; 4241/1, fo. 378.
[21] GL MSS 4409/1, fo. 216; 6574, fo. 101v; 4071/2, fo. 37v; 4956/2, fo. 323; 4457/2, fo. 267; 4383/1, fo. 161; 4071/2, fo. 80; 1432/3, fo. 165v.
[22] James Walvin, *Black and White: the Negro and English Society 1555–1945* (1973), p. 7.
[23] APC 1596–7, p. 16; TRP (804), p. 221.
[24] GL MSS 1303/1, 1662; 4524/1, fo. 96; 959/1, fo. 221; 593/2, fo. 106; 9237, fos. 40v, 57, 75v.

('blackamore') admitted a charge of fornication. Another 'blackamore' got in trouble for the same crime a year later. Others ended up in court for scoffing at masters or mistresses, living vagrantly, or harming others: Peter Cavandigoe was whipped for 'breaking a boyes leg with a broome staffe' in 1628. 'Morely a negroe' was put to work in Bridewell after admitting that a boarder in her master's house was the father of her child; a hatmaker's apprentice also ended up there for 'the abhominyable synne of whoredome' with a 'blackamore' who served in his master's household in 1603; while Mary Dane, 'a negro' or 'negar', was locked up three years earlier at the 'request' of her master who also paid all her bills.

Some 'blackamores' made return trips to Bridewell, like 'Hamey', a 'vagrant blackamor', who was locked up until he could 'be sent beyond seas [back] into his owne countrey'.[25] Others were victims of crime, like Helenor Myou who lost a set of 'bandes, a pillober, and other goodes' in 1612.[26] There are few biographical scraps to work with, apart from these short administrative entries, although names can tell us something. English sounding names such as Mary Peter – 'a [vagrant] blackamore woman' – might suggest marriage with a Londoner or an adopted name. Bridewell's court often made up names for people who would not give one when asked, and ethnicity was often worked into surnames. Katherine Moore and Mary Blackamore also appear in records with similar significances. Others had Portuguese/Spanish sounding names, like Peter Cavandigoe the 'blackamore'. There are fewer than twenty 'negros' or 'blackamores' in the sources I have examined, but they come from all age-groups and cover the major moments of the life course: birth, marriage, and death. Some of them seem settled long enough to get parish hand-outs. But others were put back on ships as soon as possible to go back to their 'owne countrey'. By 1650, several generations of blacks had got off ships at London's waterfront and quite a few of them stayed in the city. As with all 'aliens', however, attitudes towards Africans were mixed. But there was an exoticism that was enough to make African servants a mark of fashion in plush homes and even at the royal court.[27]

Irish vagrants also troubled the peace and purse. London's mayor gladly updated royal ministers with the good news that around fifty Irish beggars had been rounded up in a single busy day in 1583 and were now safely under lock and key. Most of them are 'very savage and

---

[25] BHC 3, fos. 218, 261v; 5, fos. 94v, 337v; 6, fos. 103v, 127, 205v; 7, fos. 65v, 271v, 375; BRHA BHC 4, fos. 96, 144, 344.
[26] LMA MJ/SBR/1, fos. 479, 498.
[27] Walvin, *Black and White*, pp. 7, 9, who also discusses attitudes to Africans in chaps 1–3.

nasty', he added, confirming the validity of existing opinions. Some Irish wanderers had been in England for a good while, but others had not long got off the boat: the shortest recorded stay in the city was four months and the longest was five years.[28] Anthony Hill was given nearly £30 for escorting 'the yrysshe beggynge people' to Bristol in 1585, and another pack of 'yrsshe beggars' made the same trip west a couple of years later.[29] No year was ever free of Irish vagrants, but they were more noticed around 1630. A band of Irish beggars were said to be moving through Essex in 1629 *en route* to London, and the Crown issued orders 'for the speedy sending away of the Irish beggers' in the same year. Other orders were passed not long after to get rid of the Irish, but a couple of years later 'greater numbers' of 'loose Irish people' than 'usual' were reported to be camped in London.[30] The Irish also loomed large in the imagination after the Irish Rebellion (1641), when surveillance was stepped up in the city (and elsewhere), and parishes gave hand-outs to 'distressed' and 'poore [Irish] protestants' who had 'lost all by the rebells': 'Irish papist vagrant[s]' ended up behind bars.[31] Irish vagrants often travelled in small groups or pairs, and were less likely to travel alone than vagrants who started their trips in England. Entire Irish families took to the road at times, but there were also split families at large seeking relief, mostly mothers with children in tow looking for charity. Family ties were still important, however; three brothers were rounded up in one swoop in 1630. Gender ties also offered some sort of companionship. Irish women and 'wenches' travelled together now and then. A 'cople of Irish women' were given fourpence by St Katherine Creechurch parish.[32] We are rarely told why vagrants left Ireland in the first place, although we can assume that most of them were looking for work or had heard that the city across the sea was a good place to get charity. Begging, working, and walking is how many Irish vagrants far from home got from one day to the next, though there were also Irish cutpurses, pickpockets, and thieves active in the city.[33]

Even if an Irish community did not put down firm roots in London at this time, the Irish presence registered in perceptions and policies. 'The Irish' was a much used collective description. 'The Irish people in

---

[28] TNA SP12/164/80-80i.  [29] LMA Rep. 21, fos. 119v, 140v, 429v, 454v.
[30] TNA SP16/139/1; SRPC (114), pp. 233-5; LMA Jours. 35, fo. 484; 39, fo. 132; APC 1629-30, pp. 313-14; TNA SP16/467/90.
[31] HOL MP 13-11-1641; GL MSS 7673/2, fo. 19v; 4071/2, fo. 135; 4241/1, fo. 385; 7674, fos. 37, 39, 42; 2088/1, 1642-3; BHC 9, fos. 101, 113.
[32] GL MS 4524/1, fos. 203, 204; BHC 7, fo. 163v; GL MSS 7706, fo. 11; 4457/2, fo. 222v; 4383/1, fo. 424; BHC 7, fo. 284; BRHA BHC 4, fos. 14v, 369, 399, 432v, 438, 467.
[33] For example, BHC 7, fos. 102v, 126; 8, fo. 358.

Moorfields' came to the notice of a parish in 1587 after 'a lewd and unnatural englishwoman' left her six-week-old 'manchild' with them. A poor minister 'had his house fired by the wild Irishe'.[34] As with other nationalities passing through – but in larger numbers – the Irish made Londoners aware of other worlds than their own, even if they did call them 'wild'. Continual growth meant that Lupton's 'little worlds' became more various as time passed. London was indeed 'sare changed', with still more changes to come.[35] London, Lupton said, should be 'carbonadoed'. There were scores of 'little Londons' inside the minds of all Londoners, each one rooted in highly individual experiences and perceptions of the city's places, spaces, and buildings. London was drawn on paper, but the city was much more commonly imagined in mental maps inside heads that helped Londoners to get from one place to another, or to form opinions about the character of particular places.

### Mental maps

These mental or 'verbal maps' gave information about London's changing contours and landmarks, with handy hints about good places to shop or walk, for example, or the location of a constable's house if something went wrong and help was needed.[36] They also warned people to tread carefully in some places and to avoid others at all costs. Streets were signless, and without A-Z pocket guides or street maps the city could not be taken in at a glance. Nobody could ever know each nook or cranny, even more so when growth was so swift or when the Great Fire made the city seem suddenly strange in 1666.[37] This not knowing stiffened panic about London's growth. There are hints, however, that Stow's *Survey* (1598) was used as a work of reference and updated from time to time by its owners if something new caught their eye on their travels. The *Bills of Mortality* also helped people to map the city through better understandings of the sites and routes of disease, and they gave London dimensions, mapping its outer limits. Street maps were produced in bulk later on in

---

[34] GL MSS 12806/2, fo. 388v; 4409/1, fo. 205.
[35] William Bullein *A Dialogue Both Pleasaunte and Pietifull Against the Fever Pestilence* (1564), p. 7.
[36] Quoting Daniel Lord Smail, *Imaginary Cartographies: Possession and Identity in Late Medieval Marseille* (Ithaca, NY, 1999), p. 6.
[37] Vanessa Harding, 'City, capital, and metropolis: the changing shape of seventeenth-century London', in Merritt, ed., *Imagining Early Modern London*, pp. 117–43, 140; Wall, *Literary and Cultural Spaces of Restoration London*, esp. pp. 3, 36, 71, 73, 94–5, 104, 116, 122.

the century and, along with street directories, they helped people to fill in their mental maps with more standard guides to the city.[38]

Until then, however, people got to know the city by walking, looking, or asking for directions. They drew maps in their heads from memories that were theirs alone. The points on a midwife's map, for example, were not the same as those on maps made by merchants or pimps.[39] Nor were itineraries followed by street sellers, civic ceremonies, or marshals on patrol the same, though they criss-crossed. A point on a map did not mean the same for all people, although landmarks like alehouses, hospitals, churches, or conduits helped them to get around.[40] People were also coupled with places, as when the house of some city notable acted as a signpost, or if areas took on the character of their residents. Some streets were still identified with workers who had once settled there, and a few occupational clusters remained.[41] Work was mapped, along with crime. Crime pamphlets and trial reports listed trouble spots, a geography that was dispersed far and wide by word of mouth, giving ammunition to name-callers. One Newgate woman called another 'St Katherine's whore'. Mary Sad called Margaret Eddis 'hospital whore', mixing morals with places linked to seedy sex or pox. Anne Webb screamed at a neighbour in 1592: 'thow Hackney queane, thow Hackney jade, comon ridden jade, codpeace queane, thow monster'. Go to 'Codpeece Row', she snapped. There was a 'Codpiece Row' in Whitechapel, a 'Whore Alley' in Moorfields, a 'Scolding Alley' in St Peter Westcheap parish, and a 'Thieveing Lane' in Westminster.[42] Turnmill Street on the corner of present-day Farringdon tube station was widely known to be London's

---

[38] Merritt, 'Introduction', pp. 7, 23; J. C. Robertson, 'Reckoning with London: interpreting the *Bills of Mortality* before John Graunt', *Urban History*, 23 (1996), 325–50, esp. 340, 343, 345; Paul Slack, 'Perceptions of the metropolis in seventeenth-century England', in Peter Burke, Brian Harrison, and Slack, eds., *Civil Histories: Essays Presented to Sir Keith Thomas* (Oxford, 2000), pp. 161–80, esp. pp. 170–2.

[39] Doreen Evenden, *Midwives of Seventeenth-Century London*, pp. 91–3. For one man's mental map see Vanessa Harding, 'Mortality and the mental map of London: Richard Smyth's Obituary', in Robin Myers and Michael Harris, eds., *Medicine, Mortality, and the Book Trade* (Folkstone and Newcastle, DE, 1998), pp. 49–71.

[40] Cf. Smail, *Imaginary Cartographies*, pp. 13–14, 93–4, 142–60.

[41] M. J. Power, 'The social topography of Restoration London', in A. L. Beier and Roger Finlay, eds., *London 1500–1700: the Making of the Metropolis* (Harlow, 1986), pp. 199–223, esp. pp. 218–19; Power, 'Shadwell: the development of a London suburban community in the seventeenth century', *London Journal*, 4 (1978), 29–46, esp. 36; Boulton, *Neighbourhood and Society*, p. 132; Griffiths *et al.*, 'Population and disease, estrangement and belonging 1540–1700', p. 226; Smail, *Imaginary Cartographies*, pp. 141–2, 171–87.

[42] Gladfelder, *Criminality and Narrative*, p. 22; Gowing, '"Freedom of the streets"', p. 145; GL MS 9057/1, fo. 12; LMA D/L/C/214, fos. 407, 412; WJ/SR/NS/37/172; BRHA BHC 4, fos. 40, 101v; GL MS 645/2, fo. 90v.

seediest spot. Mud stuck with a Turnmill missile. Anne Cave was called 'a Turnebull streete whore'. Elizabeth Walsh snapped at Mary Peters: 'Thou art a base queane and a strumpett, get thee out of my house into Turnbull Streete'. These were cutting terms because Turnmill street *was* lined with brothels and 'suspect' houses where nightwalkers 'intice[d]' 'passengers', thieves found safe-houses, and 'secret' printing presses pumped out pamphlets. Patience ran thin in 1624 when the Middlesex justices slammed the 'many lewd and loose persons' living along Turnmill Street, who:

> keepe comon and notorious brothell howses and harboure and entertaine divers impudent and infamous queanes and whores whoe take noe other course of life to maintaine themselves but by prostituting theire bodies unto the beastly lust of loose and dissolute persons as frequent the said brothill howses, and by allureing and inticeing of such as passé by to committ the detestable sinne of whoredome and fornicacon.

Pockey Faced Dall also kept a house there in 1633. In Lo Barry's play *Ram Alley* (1633), a prostitute slated her foe, Captain Face, by calling him a 'swaggering cheating Turne-bull-streete roague'. Scorning someone's morals with place-names with dubious associations was a standard line of attack in street slanging matches as well as on the stage. Dekker did it all the time, and so did others after him, including later authors of Restoration comedy.[43]

Only a loose sense of place was enough to cause harm, as an Aldgate carpenter found to his cost when 'chardged with haunting places commonly defamed for incontinency'. But most mental maps singled out seedy places, like London's suburbs.[44] Everybody knew about the 'sinful' suburbs or 'suburbe stewes' ringing the city. 'Why do you suffer stews and brothel-houses to live at your elbowes?', John Lawrence asked in 1624, or

---

[43] BHC 7, fo. 74v; Walsh is quoted by Gowing, *Domestic Dangers*, p. 100, as is Margaret Wild, who told Susan Lark's daughter that 'Turnebull Streete is more fitt for hir to live in then amongst honest people': TNA STAC8 203/20; 249/18; BHC 3, fo. 68; 7, fo. 269v; BRHA BHC 4, fos. 430, 434; LMA MJ/SR/522/2, 523/97, 806/201; MJ/SBR/1, fo. 323; MJ/SBR/2, fo. 428; MJ/SBR/4, fos. 84–5; MJ/SBR/5, fo. 80; Dagmar Freist, *Governed by Opinion: Politics, Religion and the Dynamics of Communication in Stuart London, 1637–1645* (London and New York, 1997), p. 62; David Turner, *Fashioning Adultery: Gender, Sex, and Civility in England, 1660–1740* (Cambridge, 2002), pp. 96–7, 105–6. The prostitute is quoted in Bryan Reynolds, *Becoming Criminal: Transversal Performance and Cultural Dissidence in Early Modern England* (Baltimore, MD, 2002), p. 109. See also BRHA BHC 4, fos. 428v-30v, 434–4v, 439, 461, 474v (Turnmill Street suspects). Cf. images of Holywell Street in Victorian London: Lynda Nead, *Victorian Babylon: People, Streets, and Images in Nineteenth-Century London* (New Haven, CT, and London, 2000), pp. 161–89.

[44] LMA CQSF 130/25; Gowing, '"Freedom of the streets"', pp. 145–6; Reynolds, *Becoming Criminal*, p. 108; McMullan, *Canting Crew*, chap. 4.

'next door to magistrates', Thomas Nashe asked a little earlier. Suburbs are 'darke dennes for adulterers, murderers, and every mischief worker', Henry Chettle said in 1592, 'daily experience before magistrates confirmes this for truth'.[45] Arrests show that major red-light areas were located over the walls and river, with the seediest patches in Clerkenwell, St Katherine's, Shoreditch, Stepney, Whitechapel, and Wapping to the east, where sailors spent shore-leaves with money to spend.[46] Speaking in Parliament in 1601, Sir Stephen Soame said that London's edges were 'the very sink of sin, the nurcery of naughty and lewde people, the harbour of rogues, theeves and beggars, and maintainers of idle persons', where thieves flee to hide after they rob our shops and houses, he added. The suburbs need a good 'polish', Roland Freart chipped in, ever mindful of their ugly 'deformity' and 'ingovernable enormities'.[47] To make matters worse, 'the suburbs are grown far bigger', City leaders said, when they lobbied the Crown to reverse the fortunes of London's freedom in 1632. The suburbs, James Howell noted in 1657, 'are much larger than the body of the City', no good thing, many people thought.[48]

A number of historians also see the suburbs as hotbeds of 'deviance, marginality, and crime' and home to a restless 'rough and lawless population', ringing the city in ominous ever-growing circles.[49] Suffocating, squashing, and consuming were contemporary metaphors for London's enclosure. Howell was concerned that the city would be sucked up. One day soon, he wrote, it would be a small swamped nucleus. This sense of loss led to metaphors of battered bodies, broken bowels, and damaged

---

[45] Thomas Dekker, *The Wonderful Year* (1600), fo. Di; George Webbe, *Gods Controversie with England. Or a description of the Fearefull and Lamentable Estate which this land at this Present is in ... Preached at Pauls Crosse upon Trinitie Sunday ...* 1609 (1609), p. 112; Thomas Nashe is quoted in John Twyning, *London Dispossessed: Literature and Social Space in the Early Modern City* (Basingstoke, 1998), p. 58; Lawrence, *Golden Trumpet to Rowse up a Drowsie Magistrate*, p. 101; Henry Chettle, *Kind-Hartes Dreame* (1592), fos. Fir-v.

[46] Archer, *Pursuit of Stability*, pp. 211–12. For other cases see BRHA BHC 4, fos. 72, 311v, 439, 524; LMA MJ/SBR/1, fos. 97, 186, 275, 398, 498, 632; MJ/SBR/2, fos. 95, 132, 318, 356; MJ/SBR/3, fos. 28, 94; GL MSS 9064/14, fo. 189; 9064/15, fos. 88v, 169; 9064/16, fo. 53; 9064/20, fos. 81v, 172; 9064/21, fos. 52v, 139. Cf. Lynda Ann Price, 'Parish constables: a study of administration and peacekeeping, Middlesex, 1603–1625', unpublished PhD thesis, University of London (1991), pp. 12–20.

[47] Soame is quoted in Margaret Healy, *Fictions of Disease in Early Modern England: Bodies, Plagues and Politics* (Basingstoke, 2001), p. 93; Roland Freart *A Parallel of the Antient Architecture With the Modern*, trans. John Evelyn, 2nd edition (1707), epistle dedicatory, fo. 5v.

[48] TNA PC2/42/305–6; Howell is quoted in Lawrence Manley, ed., *London in the Age of Shakespeare: an Anthology* (University Park, PA, and London, 1986), p. 47.

[49] McMullan, *Canting Crew*, pp. 55, 79. Cf. Healy, *Fictions of Disease*, p. 93.

insides. The suburbs were an 'infection', shooting germs into the city, and letting thousands of unwelcome people slip through the gates, like phantoms.[50] Central and civic leaders found it hard to co-ordinate strategies when authority was split between counties, boroughs, and parishes. True enough Southwark and Westminster vestries worked hard to meet local needs. But even after the setting up of the Westminster Court of Burgesses in 1585, suburbs lacked the more cohesive and solid administrative structures that made implementing policy a smoother process inside the walls.[51] Suburban government was always a bone of contention. Flocks of newcomers settled in the suburbs after 1600 instead of making the short hop into the city. Population soared outside the walls, a mixed blessing, as the number of divided dwellings also boomed, along with disease, disorder, and work at sweatshop rates.[52] Londoners preferred to imagine their city without the vice-monsters on its edges. When they thought about the city before 1660 they nearly always had in mind the square mile within the walls. Ward's case that a guild-rooted metropolitan community/identity steered London through stormy growth is not convincing. 'Ideologically', he writes, no reason existed to stop the city from pulling the suburbs into a metropolitan-wide 'embrace'. The much lamented depreciation of the City's ancient privileges was reason enough. In citizens' minds London's suburbs fragmented the city's once secure and cohesive identity and created one crime-wave after another. Rather than create metropolitan-wide communities, magistrates and authors worked hard to disentangle London from its troublesome suburbs. It was also becoming harder to think of them as somewhere to rest, stretch, exercise, and breathe better air. Citizens needed to travel further for fresh air and some peace and quiet, far beyond the suburbs.[53]

[50] Twyning, *London Dispossessed*, pp. 70, 72, 73; Thomas Dekker, *Lanthorne and Candlelight*, 1608, The English Experience, 585 (Amsterdam and New York, 1973), fo. G6v.
[51] Vanessa Harding, *The Dead and the Living in Paris and London, 1500–1670* (Cambridge, 2002), p. 33; Ian W. Archer, "The government of London, 1500–1650', *London Journal*, 26 (2001), 19–28, esp. 25–6; Jeremy Boulton, 'The poor among the rich: paupers and the parish in the West End, 1600–1724', in Griffiths and Jenner, eds., *Londinopolis*, pp. 197–225; Boulton, *Neighbourhood and Society*. chaps 8–10. On the establishment of Westminster's Court of Burgesses see J. F. Merritt, *The Social World of Early Modern Westminster: Abbey, Court, and Community, 1525–1640* (Manchester, 2005), chap. 7.
[52] Robertson, 'Reckoning with London', 349; Healy, *Fictions of Disease*, pp. 92–3; Boulton, 'Poor among the rich'; Harding, 'City, capital, and metropolis', pp. 131–3; Harding, *The Dead and the Living*, p. 27; Valerie Pearl, *London and the Outbreak of the Puritan Revolution: City, Government and National Politics, 1625–1643* (Oxford, 1961), pp. 15–16.
[53] Joseph P. Ward, *Metropolitan Communities: Trade Guilds, Identity, and Change in Early Modern London* (Stanford, CA, 1997), p. 26; Robertson, 'Reckoning with London', 349; Laura Williams, '"To recreate and refresh their dulled spirites in the sweet and wholesome ayre": green space and the growth of the city', in Merritt, ed., *Imagining Early Modern London*, pp. 185–213, esp. pp. 186–7, 203, 212–13; Pelling, 'Skirting the city'.

Mapping troubles 81

The liberties located both inside and outside the walls also hampered government. Often originating as church liberties, they acquired squalid reputations as hideaways for criminal riff-raff, who thought that they were safe from the City's jurisdiction in these independent islands. This is enough for some scholars to see liberties in lawless lights as bandit zones. McMullan calls the Alsatia slum in the Whitefriars a no-go area for officers.[54] 'Credible information' was given to Middlesex justices in 1618 about a hideaway called 'the Barmoodes' on Milford Lane, where a motley crew of thieves, murderers, and other outlaws 'had gotten harbour and as it were taken sanctuarye'. It was said that no officer would dare go there because he would never leave in one piece. The idea of 'privileged places' where bankrupts and outlaws could find sanctuary was widely believed.[55] But it was the royal Tower liberty that created the most trouble for the City.[56] There was much anger when Tower officers dug up the markstone that signified London's limits, one man rushed to raise the alarm shouting 'Deputy Vinton they are carrying away my lord mayor's stone'. There were also tussles over parish perambulations along the Tower/City border,[57] and equally grating were tit-for-tat arrests when one side arrested the other's officers for straying onto their turf.[58] People blocked arrests at other times when City officers chased suspects onto privileged ground. On the run from sheriff's officers in 1582, Christopher Jones got trapped in 'ye lane leadynge from Pawles Churche to Ivye Lane', but got a helping hand from a cathedral bailiff who was defending 'Pawles' exempt status. The mayor caused 'great heat' in St Paul's or one of the Inns of Court if he walked 'with his sword upp' rather than down, as a mark of respect in other jurisdictions. Inns of Court were also out of bounds to City officers, who could not come in through the gate unless they had permission to enter. Staple Inn asked officers serving warrants for 'ordinary actions' or 'personal causes' on one of its 'gents' to first go to the principal or his deputy to let them know of it. One officer – appropriately named Henry Bath – dived into Lincoln's Inn

---

[54] Pearl, *London and the Outbreak of the Puritan Revolution*, pp. 23–6; McMullan, *Canting Crew*, pp. 19–20, 53–4, 59–60, and chap. 4.
[55] LMA MJ/SBR/3, fo. 61; TNA STAC8 153/6. See also Price, 'Parish constables', pp. 129–32.
[56] LMA Reps. 15, fos. 204, 482v; 16, fos. 157, 201, 207v; 17, fo. 333v; 18, fo. 160v; 19, fos. 285, 332, 422v-3; 20, fo. 101v; 21, fos. 52, 59; 23, fos. 413, 545; Remembrancia Book 1, fos. 41, 101v, 189–9v, 192–2v, 236v-8; TNA SP12/157/22–4; 12/175/177.
[57] APC 1615–16, pp. 81–2, 252–3; 1626, pp. 355–6; 1630–1, p. 347; TNA SP14/13/58; 14/35/62; 14/116/7; 16/38/4; 16/39/5; 16/191/68.
[58] LMA Reps. 19, fo. 222; 21, fo. 446; Remembrancia Book 1, fos. 187–7v; APC 1613–14, pp. 131–4; 1615–16, pp. 305–6; 1623–5, pp. 402, 413–15; TNA SP12/160/36; 14/74/32; STAC8 187/1.

on the heels of a student and ended up soaking wet after some 'gentlemen of the Inn' doused him under a pump for an hour and cut his hair, 'close all one side to his great disgrace'. Another officer who chased an offender into the same Inn waving a warrant was 'shaved' by thirty 'gents'.[59]

Liberties were irritating anomalies but the City was steadily gaining an upper hand over them as time passed. City committees sat down with legal counsel to run through the 'cities tytle' or 'right of jurisdicon' in the 'Whyte and Blackefryers' and elsewhere, often turning to lord chief justices for advice. A string of legislation after 1600, along with the chance to prune the liberties' rights when a new City charter was drafted in 1608, tightened checks on 'pretended exempt places'. The liberties did loom large in contemporary minds as dens of disorder, but they were often only niggling nuisances, rather than criminal headquarters or 'enduring protectorates' in McMullan's words.[60]

### Crime maps

We can also draw our own crime maps from courtbooks. There are 16,320 cases in Bridewell's books covering the period 1604–58, when a note was made of either the location of an arrest or the patch of an arresting officer.[61] A thorny question is how we should best use these cases: as registers and geographies of arrests or crime? We cannot always be sure, except in cases where suspects were caught red-handed. There were times when officers chased suspects into next-door wards or parishes. But most mapped arrests were for crimes that did not depend on a crime-scene, as theft would have done. They were victimless character-faults or suspicious acts in the main. Vagrancy, nightwalking, and begging made up three-quarters of all cases. While pilfering, picking pockets, and cutting purses were a little under one-tenth of total cases written down in Bridewell's courtbooks. Nonetheless, whether we are looking at arrest- or crime-scenes, each one has something to tell us about topographies of disorder and law enforcement in London.

But these are also crime maps drawn from Bridewell's courtbooks and Bridewell's location and function as a prison for vagrants, thieves, or

---

[59] LMA Rep. 20, fo. 320; TNA STAC8 49/6; SP16/148/9; STAC8 33/9. See also LMA Rep. 16, fos. 137v, 261.

[60] LMA Reps. 18, fo. 289; 19, fos. 403, 404, 409v, 411, 415, 421; 20, fos. 19–19v, 23v, 24, 47, 74, 92v, 145, 158v, 172; 23, fos. 291, 314; 25, fo. 24; Remembrancia Book 1, fo. 18v; Archer, 'Government of London', 22; Pearl, *London and the Outbreak of the Puritan Revolution*, pp. 30–1; McMullan, *Canting Crew*, p. 53, and quoting p. 75.

[61] There are 47 cases from 1574–6, 1,546 from 1604–10, and 14,774 from between 1617–58.

Mapping troubles 83

anyone else who did not fit in with the City's moral ethos of hard-working households, must have a bearing on what we see. Looming high over the Thames, on the site where the Unilever building now nestles next to Blackfriars bridge, it was impossible to miss from passing boats. It sat stinking, some said, in a Blackfriars bog just before it was handed over to the City. People waded through 'filthy ditches' and 'stinking lanes' to get to it from Fleet Street.[62] Bridewell's shabby environs and its position on the spot where the dirty Fleet River poured into the Thames seem suitable settings for a 'house' in which to lock up London's 'filthie' flotsam. Bridewell was located a little over London's west walls in the Blackfriars, walls that aldermen said were 'marvously broken down' in 1624, because of barges that 'choked' Bridewell's dock.[63] Bridewell was also sandwiched between the smelly Fleet River and Salisbury House to the west, the grand home of a privy councillor with a prolific attendance record at the royal 'board' in the time of Charles I's 'personal rule' – the Earl of Dorset – who grumbled about dirty rags hanging down from Bridewell's windows, chickens and dogs leaping out from them into his trim gardens, and prisoners peeping and pissing out of windows.[64] Lord Buckhurst complained to aldermen about the stinking smell from Bridewell's 'pryvey howse and vaulte' in 1593. It was so bad, he told them, that he could no longer stretch his legs and enjoy his 'walke'. He was back in the Court of Aldermen with more complaints two years later, this time about the sickly stench from 'burnyng of lyme at Brydewell'.[65] The Fleet Ditch, running along Bridewell's east side, was said to be very dirty, 'dangerous, infectious, and noisome', and even poets and playwrights wrote about its reeking stench.[66] Bridewell's riverside wharf needed patching up from time to time. St Bride's raker got in trouble in

---

[62] *John Howes' MS, 1582, Being A Brief Note of the Order and Manner of the Proceedings in the First Erection of the Three Royal Hospitals of Christ, Bridewell, and St Thomas the Apostle*, ed. William Lampiere (1904), pp. 54–5; GL MS 6, fo. 4v. The City ordered a large 'dongehill' near Bridewell to be 'taken awaye' in 1549: LMA Rep. 12, fo. 37.
[63] LMA Remembrancia Book 8, fos. 21–1v; Reps. 34, fo. 530v; 37, fo. 123; 38, fos. 162v-3.
[64] BHC 8, fos. 213v, 329v, 334v-5; 9, fo. 632. Dorset and Bridewell also squabbled about lands. See, for example, BHC 5, fo. 417v. For more on Dorset's political career see David L. Smith, 'The 4th earl of Dorset and the politics of the sixteen-twenties', *Historical Research*, 65 (1992), 37–53; Smith, 'The fourth earl of Dorset and the personal rule of Charles I', *Journal of British Studies*, 30 (1991), 257–87.
[65] LMA Rep. 23, fos. 90v, 102, 352v, 353v.
[66] TNA SP12/177/7; LMA Jour. 27, fos. 78v-9; Reps. 15, fo. 427v; 27, fos. 165–5v. Alexander Pope and Ben Jonson, amongst others, wrote about Fleet Ditch's muck and stench. See Wall, *Literary and Cultural Spaces of Restoration London*, p. 128; Andrew McRae, '"On the famous voyage": Ben Jonson and civic space', in Andrew Gordon and Bernhard Klein, eds., *Literature, Mapping and the Politics of Space in Early Modern Britain* (Cambridge, 2001), pp. 181–203, esp. p. 192.

1629 for dumping dung into the dock. Bridewell Bridge straddling the Fleet River was also in a shoddy state in 1646: 'broken and ruinous' and about to fall down.[67] Bridewell was also in a very busy spot. Carts sped along the long lean lane that led down to the dock. Traffic clogged 'narrow' Bride/Bridewell Lane at peak times. 'The continuall passage of horses, carts, and carriages' blocked pathways, 'pulled upp' pavements, knocked into shops, stalls, and walls, scared shoppers and residents, and led to more than a few accidents and injuries. 'Heavy carryages' loaded with 'long timber' 'weare and break the stret there', Bridewell's bench noted in 1634, a familiar complaint by now. The pavement was cracked all the way from the prison gate to the riverside seven years later.[68] The prison was attached to Bridewell precinct: defined in 1618 as 'all inhabitinge within the gates of this hospitall from the carpenters yard' to 'the gates of the same', and stretching from 'the channell in the streete before the [yard] downe all the wharfes and places to the ryver of Thames'. The precinct population was a mixed bag of workers, widows, and other women, so hard-up in 1644 that they could not find their share of the minister's wages, and they also got top-ups through renting rooms to inmates new to the London area. Next-door St Bride's parish, whose church backed on to Bridewell with a little lane running in between, was a poor parish that was often forced to scrape by with hand-outs from other better-off parishes in tough times.[69]

Significantly, Bridewell was also located in a crime hot-spot – Farringdon Without ward. The busiest east–west street – Fleet Street – cut through the city just one block to the north of Bridewell, and the endless flows of travellers and vagrants along this main east–west route kept officers busy both day and night. London's most notorious female thief – Moll Cutpurse/Mary Frith – lived nearby in St Dunstan-in-the-West for the last half of her long life (d. 1659). There was also a 'publique playhouse' in the Blackfriars that caused crime, traffic jams, injuries, and quarrels, aldermen said in

---

[67] BHC 5, fo. 178v; LMA Reps. 18, fo. 368; 29, fo. 277; 47, fos. 171–1v, 198–8v; BHC 6, fo. 269v; 7, fo. 113v; 9, fo. 282; LMA Rep. 13(2), fo. 383v; 34, fo. 530v.
[68] LMA Rep. 43, fo. 266; BHC 8, fo. 7v; 7, fos. 50, 152; 8, fo. 3; 6. fo. 259v; 8, fo. 327; LMA Rep. 30, fo. 156.
[69] BHC 6, fo. 33; 9, fos. 82, 165–6, 369v. For St Bride's ranking see Archer, *Pursuit of Stability*, pp. 150–4. Bridewell fell out with the parish and Farringdon Without ward now and then, blocking the parish perambulation from marching through its grounds in 1627. There were also some jurisdictional spats over the precinct, tithes, pressing soldiers, and watching/warding. But prison, precinct, parish, and ward got along most of the time. Bridewell let the wardmote inquest meet in its great hall, though for a fee, forty shillings in 1645. See BHC 5, fo. 182v; 6, fos. 17, 33; LMA Reps. 22, fo. 220v; 31(2), fo. 420; BHC 5, fo. 242; 9, fo. 165; BRHA BHC 4, fo. 6; GL MS 33063/1, Ann/1645.

1619.[70] Indeed, it would be something of a shock if an area as busy as this one did not figure highly in the arrests that are logged in Bridewell's courtbooks and the statistics that they generate. But there remains a risk, however, that mapping trouble from Bridewell's archive alone will give us bogus results that lean too far to the west of the city. And sure enough nearly one-fifth of all suspects in my 'place sample' were brought to Bridewell from off neighbouring Fleet Street. All-in-all, nearly four-tenths of them were picked up in Farringdon Without ward, at locations all the way from the riverside right round the walls to Aldersgate and up to the edges of built-up Middlesex (see Appendix Map 2). This might be a misleading westerly preponderance, except for the fact that Farringdon Without was the one ward in the city that was most often singled out as *the* troublespot in London. It was a sprawling ward, and only next-door Farringdon Within had more 'divisions and precincts': seventeen, two more than its neighbour.[71] Farringdon Without also had six more constables than any other ward in 1613. 'It appears to us to be very spatious and full of daungerous persons', Common Council noted with alarm six years later. Special sessions were sometimes set up for 'Faringdon Extra', and 'special' care was taken with the ward's watches. The 'landlords of all alleyes' there were called before aldermen in 1573, and special checks on beggars were ordered in the same year when St Sepulchre parish (which was within the ward) was identified as their pet patch. St Sepulchre was filled to the brim with sleazy alleys and poor families, someone said four decades later.[72] Farringdon Without had long been the most trouble-prone ward. No other ward had as many brothels on the eve of the Reformation or three centuries later. Nor did any other have as many prostitutes who dipped into their clients' pockets in the eighteenth century, or as much graffiti scratched on walls. This was also the ward with the highest number of 'irregular' healers (equal with Bridge ward), and it was also a hotbed of radical preaching. London had branched out to all points of the compass by 1800, but the most notorious criminal zones were still said to be in the same places over the western walls as three centuries earlier.[73]

---

[70] For Moll Cutpurse see Gustav Ungerer, 'Mary Frith, alias Moll Cutpurse, in life and literature', *Shakespeare Studies*, 18 (2000), 42–84; *Oxford Dictionary of National Biography*, n.v. Moll Cutpurse; LMA Rep. 34, fo. 38v.
[71] LMA COL/WD/03/044.
[72] LMA Jours. 26, fo. 70; 29, fo. 120v; 31, fos. 318–18v, 352v; Reps. 14, fo. 509; 15, fo. 30; 17, fos. 423, 425; TNA STAC8 160/16. Brett-James wrote that St Sepulchre was 'infamous for filth, crime, and plague' (*Growth of Stuart London*, p. 215).
[73] Frank Rexroth, *Deviance and Power in Late Medieval London* (Cambridge, 2007), pp. 45–6; Mazo Karras, *Common Women*, pp. 75–6; J. M. Beattie, *Policing and Punishment in London 1660–1750: Urban Crime and the Limits of Terror* (Oxford, 2001), p. 140; Tony Henderson, *Disorderly Women in Eighteenth-Century London: Prostitution and Control in the Metropolis, 1730–1830* (Harlow, 1999), pp. 64–5, 67, 68, 75; Lisa Forman Cody,

Perhaps it was Bridewell's location that made London's leaders lobby the Crown so hard for its palace in the first place. A handy foothold in the most trouble-prone ward would give a huge helping hand to law and order drives. Farringdon Without headed all categories of offences reported in Bridewell's courtbooks when the location of an arrest was jotted down (see Appendix Maps 2–6): its highest share was for nightwalking (49.63 per cent), and its lowest for vagrants (33.33 per cent). Farringdon Without contained Holborn and Smithfield on the edges of Middlesex's red light belt, home to raucous Bartholomew Fair that drew hordes of thieves and vagrants. Cutpurses and pickpockets were festive hazards and magistrates locked up 'known' thieves in the days leading up to the fair in late August as a safety measure 'untill after the fayre be past'.[74] But purses still went missing and vagrants hung around: one bunch was arrested around midnight in the middle of a game of cards. Three drunk women were dragged to Bridewell for 'singeinge bawdie songs' in the fair in 1609. 'Lewd' John Page, 'who had a pardon condicionally', was taken to Newgate in 1634 for lounging around the fair. Jigging, jeering, 'flouting and mocking' were all part of the fun of the fair, although things could quickly turn nasty, as when a sailor pulled out a knife and lunged at his enemy. There were also odd sights, like the woman caught leading an ape dressed as a child. The Fair was 'troublesome', Christ's Hospital board said, and a time when all of their hospital children should stay safely away from the giant 'concourse'. A 'good and substantiall double watch' was added to regular watches on each day of the Fair to stop things from getting out of hand. St Sepulchre parish gave a shilling each to four warders to walk through the crowds, and also posted officers around the Fair's rails to stop dangerous 'trespasses' on its grounds.[75]

---

'"Every lane teems with instruction, and every alley is big with erudition": graffiti in eighteenth-century London', Deidre Palk, 'Private crime in public and private places: pickpockets and shoplifters in London, 1780–1823', and Heather Shore, 'Mean streets: criminality, immorality and the street in early nineteenth-century London', all in Tim Hitchcock and Shore, eds., *The Streets of London from the Great Fire to the Great Stink* (2003), pp. 82–100, 135–50, 151–64 esp. pp. 87–8, 142, 153–4; Freist, *Governed by Opinion*, p. 123; Margaret Pelling, 'Defensive tactics: networking by female medical practitioners in early modern London', in Alexandra Shepard and Phil Withington, eds., *Communities in Early Modern England: Networks, Place, Rhetoric* (Manchester, 2000), pp. 38–53, esp. p. 44; Paul S. Seaver, *The Puritan Lectureships: the Politics of Religious Dissent, 1560–1662* (Stanford, CA, 1970), pp. 113, 144, 175, 233–7, 248ff.

[74] GL MS 12806/2, fo. 390; LMA Jours. 20. fo. 423v; 30, fo. 228; 31, fo. 343; 32, fo. 73; 36, fo. 286; Rep. 18, fo. 413v; GL MS 3146/1, fos. 112v, 123v, 50v, 58v, 71v, 93, 111, 138v; BHC 5, fo. 375v; 6, fos. 245v, 47, 292v; 8, fo. 304v.

[75] BHC 1, fo. 99; 7, fos. 39v, 342, 344v; 8, fos. 194, 308, 404; 9, fo. 672; 3, fo. 339; 5, fos. 284, 378; 7, fos. 39v, 85v; 8, fo. 194; GL MS 12806/2, fo. 94; LMA H1/ST/A1/3, fo. 106v; BRHA BHC 4, fo. 105. For some theft arrests in the Fair see BHC 1, fo. 99; 5, fo. 375v; 6, fos. 245v, 292v; 7, fos. 39v, 342v, 344v; 8, fos. 194, 308, 404; 9, fo. 672.

Next-door Farringdon Within over the west walls was ranked second in the table of arrests by ward (see Appendix Map 2). Exactly 15 per cent of offenders were taken to Bridewell from this ward. Farringdon Within was also ranked second in every category of offence (see Appendix Maps 3–6): nightwalking was its lowest share (13.38 per cent), and theft was its highest (18.31 per cent). It pushed eastwards from Newgate to Cheapside with forks to the north and south around St Paul's, and it also curled south around the walls to a small riverside stretch. Its hub was Newgate Market. The two main east–west routes through London cut through it, and the flow of people was constant from sunrise to sunset. Nearly 55 per cent of all Bridewell arrests with a location noted were made in the Farringdon wards. Again, geography might produce a lop-sided westward slant; it was convenient to shuttle suspects to Bridewell from nearby. Yet suspects ended up there from all wards and from across the river. The trek from London's most easterly edge to Bridewell was not far, even on foot. Officers could choose between taking vagrants there for the night or to one of the compters (the sheriffs' lock-up) in the Poultry – handily placed in the heart of the city – or Wood Street, round the corner from the Guildhall. The route from London's east end to Bridewell passed both compters, and it may have been less trouble to drop off suspects in one of their 'hoales' rather than push on the extra half-mile or so to Bridewell, especially if it was getting late. Not one admission book survives for either compter before 1660, however, although both Bridewell and Court of Aldermen records sometimes note committals to either one of them. The profile of these prisoners was not unlike those in Bridewell's charge-sheets (some were actually on their way there): a mixed bag of vagrants, rogues, thieves, people walking late, nightwalkers, sex-offenders, women who abandoned children, tricksters with false dice, wife-beaters, and others like the 'comon and abhomhynable harlot of her bodie' Flouncing Bess, or Margaret Jones who was moved to Bridewell from a compter in 1575, because 'she fayned herselfe madd' and 'wolde not be quiet'.[76] Without

---

[76] For example, BHC 1, fos. 3v-4, 94; 2, fos. 24–4v, 130, 230v; 3, fos. 49v-50, 331v, 402; 6, fos. 39, 252; 8, fos. 8v, 84v, 281, 340; 9, fos. 348, 586; GL MS 9064/20, fo. 140v; LMA Jours. 26, fos. 179, 240v, 393; 27, fos. 19, 168v; 29, fos. 109v, 394; 33, fo. 140; 34, fos. 102v, 261; 35, fos. 101, 504; Reps. 11, fos. 354v, 451, 12, fo. 423; 13i, fo. 144; 19, fo. 442; 22, fo. 130v; 33, fos. 182v-3; 40, fo. 184v; GL MSS 2895/2, 1637–8; 6574/1, fo. 4v; 818/1, fo. 155v. In *The House of Correction: Or, Certayne Satyricall Epigrams* (1619), I. H. describes how two men who lost their way ended up in the compter: 'Two friends that had not met a long time since / Together supt: But at their parting thence, / Tom Swore hee'd have Kit home: But all in vayne, / Kit swore as fast hee'd have Tom backe agayne, / In kindnesse thus they strive and strivinge goe / from home to home: nor could they end . . . / But too and fro, walking through many a street: / It now being late, the constable they meete / He gave command his belmen quickly staid them, / And took them thence and in the Compter laid them.'

more concrete data, however, the compters remain 'dark places' with unknown implications for crime maps. That said, however, Bridewell could take more prisoners and it had its own courtroom, which meant that suspects could be more speedily taken from the start of the criminal process to its finish.

A Bridge watchman became mixed up in a taxing Star Chamber case in 1615, when he was accused of dragging people to Bridewell on no charge or cause. The watchman said in his defence that he had been only doing his duty, that he was standing at St Magnus Corner keeping a look-out for suspicious stragglers one night when he spotted the plaintiffs walking past him three or four times. They were unable to give good enough answers when he questioned them, and so he took them to Bridewell, being 'the usual place [he said] to which constables do ordinarily commit idle and vagrant persons'.[77] The compters were nearer to St Magnus corner than Bridewell. It was only a short walk to the Poultry. The watchman may have preferred to hug the river and follow Thames Street before forking north to Ludgate, rather than cut through the city along Cheapside, a route that would have taken him past Wood Street. But Bridewell was his prison of choice. In fact, Bridge ranked third in the count of arrests by ward (see Appendix Map 2): a little more than 6 per cent of suspects were picked up there. Next in line was Cheap (5.87 per cent), and Bridge and Cheap also swapped third and fourth position in all categories of offending apart from walking late. Cheap was followed by Castle Baynard (3.46 per cent), Queenhithe (3.37 per cent), Cripplegate (3.26 per cent), and Bread Street (3.09 per cent). Portsoken had fewest arrests (0.11 per cent), with Bassishaw (0.13 per cent), Broad Street (0.43 per cent), Dowgate (0.60 per cent), and Lime Street (0.62 per cent), a little ahead on the ladder.

But patterns were not always inevitable. Some eastern wards had moderately high levels of arrests that topped others to their west. Bishopgate ranked ninth in the table of arrests by ward, for example (2.91 per cent), Langbourn tenth (2.83 per cent), with Billingsgate one place behind (2.04 per cent), while Tower ranked fourteenth (1.39 per cent). Both Bishopgate and Billingsgate had markets, and Billingsgate was on the river's edge, close to the bridge, with busy Thames Street running through it, in much the same way that Bishopgate Street sliced through the more northerly ward. Langbourn's hub was a busy crossroads where three main streets ran into each other: Gracechurch, Fenchurch, and Lombard Streets. On top of this, major markets attracted crowds on both Langbourn's western and eastern borders: Leadenhall and the Stocks. These essential routes and

---

[77] TNA STAC8 100/10.

bustling markets explain the high rankings of Billingsgate for arresting people caught walking late (eighth), Bishopgate for picking up night-walkers and thieves (sixth and fifth), and Langbourn for bringing beggars and thieves to Bridewell (tenth and seventh).

Equally unpredictably, some wards that were closer to Bridewell than those mentioned in the last paragraph sent fewer suspects there in seemingly reverse patterns: Bassishaw ranked twenty-fourth on the table of arrests by ward, Vintry was four places higher, Cordwainer was another four places higher in sixteenth position, and Aldersgate ranked higher still in fifteenth position. All of these wards were a shorter walk from Bridewell, but none of them had markets, although Vintry was on the riverside, and Aldersgate was split by a busy street and was next to more troublesome Smithfield (Aldersgate was ranked fifteenth in arrests of people walking late and eleventh for thieves). We can usually point to a market or to main roads when arrest rates were high overall or for a particular offence. Cheap ward was only once ranked lower than fourth (walking late), and this amount of trouble was due to its position in the city centre with the Stock's Market on its east edges and Cheapside slicing it in two. Wards with high begging levels relative to their overall standing had busy crossroads or junctions. Next-door neighbours Broad Street and Coleman Street had junctions where Lothbury crossed main streets: Threadneedle and Coleman Streets. While Cordwainer's northernmost border was a small section of Cheapside with busy Watling Street to the south. Well-travelled routes also cut through wards with fairly high shares of people walking after dark. Candlewick Street was the hub of the ward that took its name; Thames Street ran along the length of the riverside wards of Dowgate and Queenhithe. While Walbrook not only had Stocks Market in its north-west corner, but a major three-way confluence at the side of the market where Cornhill and Lombard and Threadneedle Streets streamed into the Poultry, and a junction where Candlewick Street joined London Stone to the south. Wards with markets could expect spurts of theft whenever shopping was brisk. Lime Street, for example, had Leadenhall Market in its west wing and its highest ranking in arrest tables was, as we might expect, for beggars, thieves, and vagrants.

Markets, main roads, crossroads, and riverside locations cannot explain everything that we map and see in the Bridewell courtbooks. But there is more than enough evidence in records and perceptions of the time to show that they did make a difference. Thieves scouted around markets, looking for chances to pounce when careless shoppers left their purses hanging out of their pockets, or if a stall owner turned away from his stall, if only for a minute. The Bridewell court said that Christopher Lusher was 'a dayly pickepockett in the marketts', and shipped him to

Virginia in 1635. Katherine Waller was 'noted' to be a 'market pickepocket' three years later. While others, like Elizabeth Carie in 1639, were said to be 'comon pickepockett[s] and haunter[s] of markets and publique meetings'. Thieves toured markets, sometimes alone, but often in pairs or small gangs, jostling shoppers and causing distractions to get a good shot at a pocket.[78] Books went missing from stalls, along with lace, gloves, handkerchiefs, and other fancy goods. Most people who grabbed something from stalls needed meat and meal to keep going. Meal was stolen more than anything else. Meal sacks were sliced open or grabbed from markets or busy quaysides. Pepys sniffily watched a 'silly' 'jade' swipe mutton from a stall in Leadenhall Market. But not all meal thefts were simply to keep hunger at bay. The 'picksacke', Issac Triffe, was locked up for selling stolen meal in 1601. Swindlers grabbed chances to pass 'counterfeite' coins with so much money changing hands in market-time.[79] A market-day was a busy but also dicey day. Beggars liked crowds, and counted on shoppers to hand over a few pennies.[80]

It is small wonder that Bridge ward ranked third on the table of arrests. It was on the riverside and the bridge after which it was named brought heavy traffic to and from the south side of the river. Houses and shops lined both sides of the bridge, offering golden opportunities for thieves. The 'notorious vagrant pilferer', Thomas Holcroft, was locked up in 1620 for 'frequenting' the bridge 'daily'. Pickpockets, cutpurses, and thieves were all caught there, like Edward Dye who was 'taken on the bridge' in 1605, 'cutting things from behinde horsemen that passé that waie'.[81] The stream of people also offered surefire markets for people selling bread, apples, and other food. Guards were also posted at each end of the bridge to stop vagrants and beggars crossing to the other riverbank. Beadles watched at the bridge in shifts to send vagrants and beggars back to Southwark in 1563. One of the first actions taken when riots ripped through Lambeth in 1640 was to put a strong watch at the bridge.

---

[78] BHC 8, fos. 60, 175v, 227v; 1, fo. 91. See also BHC 1, fos. 10, 205; 2, fo. 41v; 3, fos. 140v, 167v; 5, fos. 345v, 406; 6, fos. 2v, 60, 149v, 207v, 280, 306, 335v, 336v, 375, 384, 393; 7, fos. 55, 84, 102, 113, 138, 179v, 187, 211v, 224v, 311v; 8, fos. 160–0v, 183, 210, 226v, 264, 284v, 410; 9, fo. 18; LMA CQSF 98/recog., Susannah Cobb; WJ/SR/NS/34/125; MJ/SBR/4, fo. 431.

[79] The *Diary of Samuel Pepys*, eds., Robert Latham and William Matthews, 11 vols. (1970–83), vol. IX, p. 285; BHC 1, fo. 205; 5, fos. 396v, 406; 6, fos. 60, 128, 139, 185, 232v, 241, 241v, 280, 306, 317, 324v, 375, 384, 384v, 386; 7, fos. 55, 187, 224v, 253, 305v, 308; 8, fos. 160, 160v, 210, 284v, 328, 410; BRHA BHC 4, fos. 37, 56, 117v, 181v, 249, 277v; LMA CQSF 109/17.

[80] BHC 5, fo. 381v; 6, fos. 63, 117, 119v, 125v, 133, 204, 291, 325v, 369, 383v; 7, fos. 106v, 111v, 179v, 195v, 248v, 309; 8, fos. 318v, 344, 361.

[81] BHC 6, fo. 209; 5, fo. 77v. See also BHC 2, fos. 94, 95, 181v; 6, fos. 2, 21, 27v, 69, 380v; 7, fos. 155v, 302; 8, fo. 69; 9, fo. 456; LMA Jour. 36, fo. 59v; CQSF 71/20, 71/102.

Officers were asked to check that the bridge gates were shut tightly at night. But despite these precautions vagrants sneaked across the bridge. Alice Prest was spotted by the watch one morning, 'having three severall mornings beene taken cominge over the bridge with linen on her apron'. She said that she was crossing the river to wash clothes, but it was known that she had once had the pox, and officers decided that she was a 'lewd wench' and took her to court. On most days pregnant women, sick paupers, abandoned children, vagrants, or nightwalkers were taken back across the bridge to Southwark.[82] As one of London's most public places, government proclamations were posted on the bridge, and traitors' heads were pinned on spikes on top of the gates as a blunt warning to anyone passing-by to take note and behave better.

The riverside had weak spots all along the shore where people slipped through watches. Gates were put up 'for the sauffegarde of the river' in 1538, and more were made 'in tymes of great daunger', like 1642, when 'substantiall gates' sealed off landing places at Queenhithe ('lawless' watermen bragged 'that they may do what they list now it is Parliament time'). Watches kept a 'special eye' on 'the Theamyssyde' and at gates and landing places.[83] Boats and barges brought supplies, but some had less welcome cargoes. Warders 'daylie' checked water traffic from Gravesend and Grays when loads were dropped off at Billingsgate to see if any vagrants were on board. Watermen were told not to take vagrants across the river, but many did so for a few pennies. Some offenders also made a getaway across the river. A Southwark waterman got into trouble 'for receavinge a woman into his boate knowing her to have killed a man'. Rumours, papists, and germs also travelled over the water.[84] But without the river London's commerce could never have grown so great, so quickly. River traffic was brisk and it picked up quickly as trade thrived, choking the river, some concerned observers said.[85] There were accidents. Boats bumped into each other and some unlucky people drowned. A waterman was locked up in Bridewell in 1643 'for endangeringe many mens and womens lives on the Thames'.[86]

---

[82] LMA CQSF 115/5; 116/94–5; Reps. 33, fo. 66v; 16, fo. 483; 17, fo. 378v; 23, fo. 517v; GL MS 12806/2, fo. 16; LMA Remembrancia Book 8, fo. 26; Jour. 21, fo. 536; BHC 7, fo. 141v; BRHA BHC 4, fo. 186; GL MSS 878/1, fo. 328; 4071/1, 1598–9; 4071/2, fos. 60v, 136v; 1303/1, 1632, 1696; 1568, fo. 556; 4956/3, fos. 93, 118. See also LMA CQSF 108/20; BHC 8, fo. 69.
[83] LMA Reps. 10, fos. 126, 135; 56, fo. 9; 12, fos. 149–9v; 16, fo. 450; 48, fos. 54v-5.
[84] LMA Reps. 16, fo. 449v; 17, fos. 378v, 401; 18, fos. 127–7v; 19, fo. 193v; 20, fo. 137; 30, fo. 294v; Jour. 20, fo. 500v; CQSF 79/28, 32; MJ/SBR/1, fo. 498; WJ/SR/NS/33/105–6; BHC 6, fo. 419; APC 1629–30, p. 385.
[85] APC 1616–17, pp. 105–6.
[86] GL MSS 878/1, fo. 268v; 5714/1, fos. 32v, 73; 2088/1, fos. 4, 8, 1612–13; 2991/1, 1635–6; 2089/1, 1639–40; BHC 9, fo. 31.

92     Change

Like the river, fields ringing London seemed wide and open, even though chunks of green disappeared as the city grew. Fields were still large enough to shelter seedy sex, and insults took on board this idea. 'Go into the fields and play the whore with the boys', George Harwood jeered at Margaret Ellis. This vocabulary of green vulgarity included 'hedgeharlot', 'hedgewhore', and 'hedgehaunter'. 'Stragglyng naughty packs' and 'idle loyteringe drabbes' were all caught in fields. Mary Lister was called 'a common harlot and ronner in the fields' in 1561. 'Harlots and rogues' were also taken together suspiciously in fields. The cutpurse Richard Browne was 'sometymes' picked up with 'whores' in fields in 1575.[87] It was common knowledge that fields were a place to go for sex. Portugal's ambassador was tipped off that his servants 'associate[d] themselves with lewd women in fields' in 1641.[88] Fields also offered shelter for runaway servants and hiding places for thieves to stash stolen goods. Watches at the 'end of streets towards the fields' were asked to keep a sharp look-out for drifters who 'live upon stealth' and pilfering. Fields were often searched after a spate of 'burglaries and pilferies', but they also gave opportunities for thieves, who sometimes swiped washing that was drying on hedges and gardens, or grabbed the chance to milk a cow that was feeding on the grass. Joan Helliker was brought to Bridewell in 1603 'for stealinge milke' from a cow in Islington Fields.[89]

These understandings of London's fields lasted long after Moorfields was spruced up with landscaped walks and smart shrubbery after 1600. Walls and rails marked out Moorfields walks for 'pleasure' and 'recreaccon'. The walks are 'sweet and delightful', Richard Johnson gushed in 1607, the air is 'sweet' to stroll in, and trees 'yeelde' much 'delight' to my eyes. Moorfields was also a 'continual comfort' for James Howell, and Pepys went there 'for a little ayre'.[90] But like the river, fields brought both profit and pain. Vagrants dropped dead in them and mothers gave birth,

---

[87] Gowing, '"Freedom of the streets"', pp. 144–5; Williams, '"To recreate and refresh their dulled spirites"', p. 212; BHC 3, fos. 317v, 338, 378, 379, 392v; 1, fos. 83, 140v, 145v, 151, 204v, 214v, 217v; BRHA BHC 4, fos. 165, 438; BHC 2, fo. 95v; WAC F301/14. See also Henry Goodcole, *Heaven's Speedie Hue and Cry Sent After Lust and Murder Manifested upon the Suddaine Apprehending of Thomas Sherwood and Elizabeth Evans* (1635), pp. 8–9.

[88] BHC 3, fos. 146v, 304v, 405v; 8, fo. 5; BRHA BHC 4, fos. 30v, 33, 82, 152, 286v, 291, 368v, 421, 421v; HOL MP, 2–8–1641.

[89] BRHA BHC 4, fos. 253v, 396v, 10, 26, 373v; APC 1601–4, pp. 27–8; SRPJ (161), pp. 360–2.

[90] LMA Rep.27, fo. 142; Jours. 27, fos. 364v, 396; 28, fos. 16v, 81; 30, fos. 256–6v; Richard Johnson, *The Pleasant Walkes of Moore-fields* (1607), fos. A3v, A2r; James Howell, *Londinopolis: An Historical Discourse or Perlustration of the City of London, the Imperial Chamber and the Chief Emporium of Great Britain* (1657), p. 301; Pepys, *Diary*, vol. IX, 14–3–1668.

Mapping troubles 93

leaving unlucky parishes to pick up the costs.[91] Moorfields was guarded by warders; a pair of stocks was also handily placed there. But they could not stamp out all of the trouble. Thieves swiped 'rayle posts' and 'iron from the rayles'. Nightwalkers met in shadows. Warders and others were beaten and 'abused'. While people still dumped 'filthy and noisome things' in ditches and 'ease[d] their bodies' in fields.[92] Fields also meant different things for different people. Alessandro Magno saw 'men and women gather to meet and play' on Sundays at Moorfields in 1562. Men shot guns and arrows after church, and bowls was a popular field-sport. But rough games could turn nasty and some football matches with hundreds on each side turned into pitched battles. People also settled scores in fields. After a hotly contested Chancery suit, Sir Henry Brittain warned his rival 'that the fields were very near'.[93] Trained bands drilled on fields and were put on red alert in festive seasons when they became battlefields.[94] Fields were places of fun and fear. People stretched their legs on landscaped walks, admired greenery and shrubbery, and played, while others swapped blows. The dual character of fields was clear when women hung out clothes to dry, although warders told them to stop draping clothes over walls or rails in 1609. Hawks snooped around as clothes dried in the sun. One pimp's 'chefe brokinge' was to 'go to fields among those women that are dryinge clothes' to 'trye them by gevinge them a quart of wyne or som other thinge whether they be for hym'.[95]

## Composite spaces

No part of the city was left untouched by unrest. Not even its heart escaped lightly. The din was so loud in a brothel next to the Guildhall one night that it was said 'that my lord mayor heard the noyse' and could not get to sleep. Humphrey Pugh was picked up begging in and around

---

[91] GL MS 4457/2, fos. 169v, 212, 212v, 222v; LMA MJ/SBR/1, fos. 94, 524, 532; GL MSS 2968/1, fos. 351, 361; 4457/2, fos. 98, 102; WAC F301/15; 309/14; 310/21; 311/10.
[92] BHC 6, fos. 314, 408; 9, fos. 76, 128; 8, fo. 94v; LMA Rep. 47, fo. 46; Jour. 27, fo. 31.
[93] 'The London Journal of Alessandro Magno 1562', eds. Caroline Barron, Christopher Coleman, and Claire Gobb, *London Journal*, 9 (1983), 136–52, 141; Gowing, '"Freedom of the streets"', p. 144; BRHA BHC 4, fo. 402v; LMA MJ/SBR/2, fos. 140, 440; MJ/SBR/5, fo. 96; MJ/SBR/7, fo. 162; TNA STAC8 243/23; 85/3.
[94] LMA Reps. 13ii, fos. 131, 133v; 27, fos 173v, 175v; Jour. 20, fo. 388. See also Keith Lindley, 'Riot prevention and control in early Stuart London', *Transactions of the Royal Historical Society*, 5th series, 33 (1983), 109–26; Griffiths, *Youth and Authority*, pp. 151–61. An innholder 'much abuse[d] and disturbe[d]' Captain Bradley's band as they mustered in fields on May Day 1640, 'riding amongst them with his horse and stricking some of them': LMA Rep. 54, fo. 169.
[95] LMA Rep. 29, fo. 14; BHC 3, fo. 110. See also TNA STAC8, 126/10; BRHA BHC 4, fo. 29v; Johnson, *Pleasant Walkes of Moore-fields*, fos. A3v, A4v.

the Guildhall in 1653.[96] Few places where the cream of society gathered were trouble free. Thieves and beggars were sent to prison from the Temple, and vagrants also milled around the royal court. Twenty-two were 'taken' in one swoop 'loitering' outside the court at Greenwich in 1634. While so many vagrants 'pestered' Whitehall's gates in 1625 that nobody could go in or out, 'without great molestation'. 'Very greate troupes' of 'theeves, whores, and cutpurses' even crammed into the small space 'betweene Newgate and the sessions hall' in 1609 when trials were in full swing, showing support for friends in the dock, but also looking out for open pockets or loose purses.[97] A tailor was grabbed cutting purses in the Star Chamber in 1614, and Andrew Lee was caught cutting purses in 'the Excheq[ue]r Chamber'.[98] The Exchange, Temple, Court, and law courts were mainly male spaces and authority landmarks. But they also showed off the ambivalence of public places. Vagrants buzzed around them and women dropped in just as often, working, walking, and raising suspicions.[99]

Trouble brewed at meeting places like the Exchange, where merchants and seekers of foreign information/intelligence caught up on the latest news. It was a second home for well-heeled merchants, but also a place of contrasts where trade talk often mingled with 'lewd' words, like the time when 'Kicko an Indian' mocked his master 'before the marchaunts'.[100] Beggars hung hopefully around the Exchange by day, thieves clipped lace and gold and silver buttons from merchants' coats when they were not looking, and pickpockets pounced when merchants got lost in talk. Even corpses were found on the Exchange, and some women gave birth in this commercial hub. Other women blocked walkways day and night, sitting selling.[101] A few women left children on the Exchange, and a quite different commerce went on there: 'whores and other disordered persons' met at 'unlawfull houres', along with nightwalkers and other 'comon

---

[96] BHC 3, fo. 120; 9, fo. 620.
[97] BHC 6, fos. 202v, 237v; 7, fos. 335, 338; 8, fos. 157v, 2v; APC 1625–6, p. 13; SRPJ (23), pp. 44–5; (179), p. 408; BHC 6, fos. 355v, 360v; LMA Jour. 27, fo. 330.
[98] LMA MJ/SBR/2, fo. 41; MJ/SBR/5, fo. 375.
[99] Cf. Gowing, '"Freedom of the streets"'.
[100] BHC 7, fo. 245v. See also LMA CQSF 106/35; Reps. 21, fo. 579; 23, fo. 91; BHC 8, fo. 201; Linda Woodbridge, 'The peddler and the pawn: why did Tudor England consider peddlers to be rogues?', in Craig Dionne and Steve Mentz, eds., *Rogues and Early Modern English Culture* (Ann Arbor, MI, 2004), pp. 143–70. See also Jean E. Howard, *Theater of a City: the Places of London Comedy, 1598–1642* (Philadelphia, PA, 2007), chap. 1.
[101] BHC 6, fos. 272, 363; 8, fos. 215v, 284; 7, fos. 23, 332; 8, fo. 201; GL MSS 4383/1, fos. 291, 304; 4071/2, fos. 14v, 71, 94, 115v, 124 125; BHC 6, fo. 272; 8, fos. 149v, 194; 9, fo. 511.

haunters of the Exchange'.[102] A 'greate number' of children and 'yonge roges' fooled around there on Sundays and 'holy daies', 'showtinge and hallowinge' so loudly that worshippers in a nearby church could not follow the sermon. Aldermen banned 'boyes' from the Exchange in 1585 to stifle 'noyses', but nearby parishes were still paying for warrants 'to cleare the Exchange' five decades later.[103]

Not even sacred spaces were exempt from London's troubles. Jeremy Farrer was found 'abusing himselfe on the fast day in St Faith's church' in 'a sodomiticall manner' in 1628, and he owned up to having done the same 'in other churches for the space of a yeare'. A 'yonge infant' with a broken neck was found one day in a church pew.[104] Thieves mingled with worshippers in church pews, breaking the eighth commandment constantly. Andrew Jones 'haunted churches at lecture times to pilfer'. Mary Badham was 'taken in the act' of cutting purses in William Gouge's church as he boomed from the pulpit, while Henry Huff picked 'a preacher's pockett' in church. One parish paid tenpence 'for an iron plate for the poore mens boxe to keepe it from pyckinge'. Others had to replace stolen service books.[105] Nor was St Paul's safe from thieves, like the 'helper of cosenors', Richard Wilson: he 'goeth like an agent', someone said, and links up with thieves 'at Powles and other places wher sermons are made'. The Spital was one such 'place', and four pickpockets were taken there in the middle of one sermon. A pickpocket was also 'taken' in Westminster Abbey with his hand deep in a pocket.[106]

Churches ought to have been trouble-free places where people spoke only when spoken to by a minister and then with respect. Imagine the palaver in their main sabbath-day rival, then, as alehouses sprouted up all over London, some licensed, many not, and too many for comfort in

---

[102] GL MS 4069/1, fos. 21v, 26v, 29, 31, 33, 38, 40, 42; BHC 2, fo. 38v; 8, fos. 104v, 149; 9, fo. 511; LMA Rep. 20, fo. 375.

[103] GL MS 4069/1, fos. 14–14v, 15v, 19, 21; LMA Rep. 20, fo. 414; GL MSS 4383/1, fos. 303, 314, 362v, 371; 4423/1, fo. 143; 4071/2, fo. 86v. See also Ian W. Archer, 'Material Londoners?', in Orlin, ed., *Material London*, pp. 174–92, esp. p. 186; Archer, 'Social networks in Restoration London: the evidence of Samuel Pepy's diary', in Alexandra Shepard and Phil Withington, eds., *Communities in Early Modern England: Networks, Place, Rhetoric*, (Manchester, 2000), pp. 76–94, esp. pp. 80–1; Hitchcock, 'Publicity of poverty', p. 169; Henderson, *Disorderly Women*, p. 161; Gowing, '"Freedom of the streets"'. p. 143; Fox, *Oral and Literate Culture*, p. 346.

[104] BHC 7, fo. 67; LMA Jour. 18, fo. 64v.

[105] BHC 6, fo. 90v; 7, fo. 309v; 6, fo. 359v; GL MS 4071/1, fo. 127v. See also BHC 1, fo. 41; 2, fo. 16; 6, fos. 36v, 394; 7, fos. 102, 194, 306; 8, fos. 8v, 227v, 397; 9, fos. 30, 254; BRHA BHC 4, fo. 369; WAC F2002, fo. 225; F2003, fo. 314; GL MS 1124/1, fo. 148v; LMA WJ/SR/NS/30/59.

[106] BHC 3, fo. 273; 6, fo. 422v; 7, fo. 120; LMA WJ/SR/NS/42/99. See also BHC 6, fo. 23; 7, fos. 38, 102, 194, 227, 247, 273; 8, fo. 222v; 9, fo. 511.

dingy corners. Governors argued that one way to stamp out crime was to close down backstreet pubs where thieves traded loot and drank long into the night, planning robberies. They tried to trim their number to a 'reasonable proporcon'. Their 'excessive number and disorder' was a lament of the times.[107] One group of toughs sat around a table in one to plan an attack on rate collectors. Alehouses were also magnets for vice workers, who slipped upstairs with clients. Common councillors said that there would have been fewer 'harlots', 'bastards', or diseases if alehouses were kept in line.[108] Many alehouses were amphibious sites where labouring scruffs bumped into people from better backgrounds. Not many pub regulars were born with silver spoons in their mouths, but there were enough heavy drinking well-to-do patrons, fops, and rakes for us to rule out calling London's many alehouses one-class societies.[109]

This was even truer of playhouses, where London's high society could look down on the hoi-polloi below from the galleries ringing the stage.[110] One of London's three playhouses was a stone's throw away from Bridewell in the Blackfriars, and when it was first mooted as a suitable site for plays there were immediate protests that it would become a magnet for vagrants and other 'lewd people' in no time. It did not take long for playhouses to pick up a bad press. Magistrates complained that 'great numbers' of 'harlots, cutpurses, cuseners, pilferers' and other 'lyke' 'light and lewd' crooks and suspicious people flocked to playhouses in 1593. Cutpurses worked stealthily through the crowds who stayed behind for 'jigges, rymes, and daunces' after the end of the play at the Fortune playhouse on Goulding Lane in 1612. A number of Bridewell 'gessts' had reputations for being playhouse pilferers. A marshal gave evidence at Bridewell that John Maryne and Owen Cannon always 'follow[ed] plays to pick pocketts and cut purses' in 1628. Theatre pits were also good

---

[107] For example, LMA Jour. 20, fo. 502; Reps. 11, fo. 384v; 14, fo. 316v; 17, fo. 213v; 19, fos. 245, 502v; 22, fo. 134v; TNA SP16/226/77, 16/244/11, 16/250/22, 16/282/12, 16/420/4.

[108] TNA STAC8 160/16; LMA Jour. 20, fo. 502.

[109] For alehouses see Peter Clark, *The English Alehouse: A Social History, 1200–1830* (1983); Alan Jay Epstein, 'The social function of the alehouse in early modern London', upublished PhD thesis, New York University (1976); Judith Hunter, 'English inns, taverns, alehouses, and brandy shops: the legislative framework, 1495–1797', in Beat A. Kumin and Ann B. Lusty, eds., *The World of the Tavern: Public Houses in Early Modern Europe* (Aldershot, 2002), pp. 65–82.

[110] Andrew Gurr, *Playgoing in Shakespeare's London*, 2nd edition (Cambridge, 1996); Paul Whitfield White and Suzanne R. Westfall, eds., *Shakespeare and Theatrical Patronage in Early Modern England* (Cambridge, 2002); Anthony B. Dawson and Paul Yachnin, *The Culture of Playgoing in Shakespeare's England* (Cambridge, 2001); Charles Whitney, '"Usually in the werking daies": playgoing, journeymen, apprentices, and servants in guild records, 1582–92', *Shakespeare Quarterly*, 50 (1999), 433–58.

places for prostitutes to tout for clients, and regular 'riotts' added much more spice to the drama on the stage.[111]

I have only looked at some of the more trouble-prone spots in mapping troubles so far. It might seem that there were few calm places, but streets, markets, fields, and the Exchange also had sober sides when shop-talk or rest focused minds. London is better thought of in terms of overlapping areas and cultures. Boundaries were inevitably blurred with so many sudden changes as more people crammed into a city that was becoming starved of space. Thieves walked the same spaces as 'honest' citizens, 'regular' and 'irregular' trade went on side by side. A receiver of stolen goods who was in league with cutpurses lived in 'a sellar under a barbor' next door to St Thomas's Hospital. Cutpurse gangs met at a barn next door to the Bishop of Carlisle's house to split loot and meet 'whores'.[112] Magistrates appreciated the dual character of churches or markets, never without the potential for trouble but necessary at the same time. Some streets were singled out with bad names, but more generically streets embodied these troubled times like nothing else. Londoners could almost calculate growth by looking at choked streets. Street-traffic and street-life are the subjects of the next chapter, that will tell us more about London's hodgepodge geography, the strategies through which thieves, vagrants, and beggars kept above the hunger line and one step ahead of the authorities, and remind us once more that things took a decided turn for the worst after 1620 in magistrates' minds.

---

[111] TNA SP12/260/16; LMA Remembrancia Book 1, fo. 325v; MJ/SBR/1, fo. 559; BHC 7, fo. 75v; 6, fo. 389; LMA MJ/SBR/4, fo. 396. See also Ian Munro, *The Figure of the Crowd in Early Modern London: the City and its Double* (Basingstoke, 2005), pp. 41–4, 118–22; Price, 'Parish Constables', p. 19; McMullan, *Canting Crew*, pp. 137–8.

[112] BHC 2, fo. 95; BHC 3, fo. 3. On this question of 'overlapping areas' for later periods see Vic Gatrell, *City of Laughter: Sex and Satire in Eighteenth-Century London* (New York, 2006), Part 1; and John Barrell, *The Spirit of Despotism: Invasions of Privacy in the 1790s* (Oxford, 2006), chap. 1.

# 3 Streets

**Traffic jams**

The world runs on wheels, Thomas Dekker noted dryly in 1606. People ransacked their memories for a time when traffic was thicker, without luck. Thomas Procter thought that streets were to blame for 'the dayly continuall great griefe and heartbreaking of man and beast'. 'The greate streete called Cheapside' was clogged up by carriages, coaches, and carts, Common Council complained in 1657. Venice's ambassador had a long delay there one day when his coach was hemmed in by twenty carts. No place seemed safe from 'the continuall passage of horses, carts, and carriages'.[1] This hustle and bustle grew with London. Pickpockets brushed against shoppers on Cheapside; the conduit was a good place to catch people unawares. Women sold 'garden' goods there, blocking pavements. 'A world of knaves and cheaters passes' Cheapside cross 'each day', Henry Peacham said in 1641, 'herbwomen on one side and costermongers and tripe-wives on the other'. One 'herbwyfe' who stood selling close to the cross was locked in the stocks for a couple of hours in 1605 for tossing 'beane, shales, and other things' at the emperor's ambassador as he walked along Cheapside.[2]

Crowded streets led to calls to 'demynissh' the number of 'carres' in 1573, 1580, and 1582. 'The oversight' of 'carts and carres' was put in the hands of Christ's Hospital board in 1582, and one of their first steps was to pick officers to 'take up disordered cars' and make sure that carmen served seven-year-long apprenticeships. But not a single cart was taken

---

[1] Thomas Procter, *A Worthy Worke Profitable to this Kingdom Concerning the Mending of all High-waies, as Also for Waters and Ironworkes* (1607), fo. A3v; LMA Jour. 41, fo. 161v; CSPV 1615–17, p. 908; GL MS 4097/1, fo. 111; LMA Reps. 45, fos. 81v-2; 36, fo. 114; 43, fo. 266; Jour. 36, fo. 197v; TNA PC2/43/267–8.

[2] BHC 2, fo. 95; 7, fo. 231; 8, fos. 174v, 187, 410; LMA Jour. 41, fo. 161; Rep. 45, fo. 529v; Henry Peacham, *A Discourse Between the Crosse in Cheap and Charring Crosse* (1641), p. 1; LMA Rep. 27, fo. 55. For Cheapside, see my 'Politics made visible: order, residence, and uniformity in Cheapside, 1600–45', in Griffiths and Jenner, eds., *Londinopolis*, pp. 176–96.

off the streets, and their number was still 'excessive' in 1596 (a plan to cut this number by five did not get off the ground). There were 400 'lawfull' 'carres' and carts around 1600 with special 'marks' on their side to help spot 'foreign carts'. The limit was bumped up two decades later, mainly, it was said, to keep up with brisker trade.[3] A new menace was added to traffic jams not long after, when hackney coaches rushed up and down looking for custom from the 1630s on. John Taylor called them 'impudent' and 'sawcie intruder[s]'. Their nick-name was 'hell-carts', John Evelyn noted in 1651. Moves to cut their numbers started almost at once.[4]

Numbers was not the only focus for road-safety lobbies, however. Traffic was noisy and people lost lives, limbs, and loads through the 'promiscuous use' of coaches along the streets. Bystanders were 'sometimes crushed' by speeding traffic, the Privy Council noted with alarm, asking London's leaders to take action straight away. Dodging traffic became a necessary skill for getting around the city in one piece. Carmen caused 'dayly hurt', magistrates complained in 1610, and eight years later accidents and injuries had grown to 'excesse'. Thomas Lewis was punished in 1640 'for rydinge a galloppe in his cart along St John Streete', forcing shoppers to run for cover. One carman whose cart clipped a child on Creed Lane tried to put the blame on his parents, claiming that they should have 'look[ed] better to him'; carts travel along that street all day long, he said, as if this was reason enough to get soft treatment at the hands of the court. One voice after another scolded drivers for 'carelesnes'. Many left 'carres' standing in the street with no one to look after them. One driver was put on trial for 'letting his cart stand in the streete without a guide' and killing a woman after it rolled down a slope.[5] Grumbling about 'extraordinary

---

[3] LMA Letterbook K, fo. 160v; TNA STAC8, 81/38; LMA Reps. 17, fo. 286v; 20, fos. 121, 320v, 342v; 23, fo. 352; Jours. 30, fos. 358v-9; 36, fo. 277v; GL MSS 12806/2, fo. 307; 12806/3, fos. 24v-5v, 35v, 47v; APC 1613–14, pp. 238–9. The Woodmongers' Company also ran a rule over traffic.

[4] Taylor is quoted in Mark Jenner, 'Circulation and disorder: London streets and hackney coaches, c. 1640-c.1740', in Tim Hitchcock and Heather Shore, eds., *The Streets of London From the Great Fire to the Great Stink* (2003), pp. 40–53, at p. 40; Evelyn, *Character of England*, p. 150; SRPC (210), pp. 495–6; TNA SP16/40/64–5; LMA Remembrancia Book 7, fo. 181; TNA SP/16/307/121. See also Emily Cockayne, *Hubbub: Filth, Noise, and Stench in England* (New Haven, CT, and London, 2007), 169–73.

[5] TNA SP/16/307/121; SRPC (210), pp. 495–6; LMA Rep. 34, fos 591v-2 CQSF 112/34. See also LMA Jour. 41, fos. 104–4v; Rep. 29, fo. 247; CQSF 125/35, 130/53; MJ/SBR/1, fo. 615; MJ/SBR/2, fo. 319; MJ/SBR/5, fos. 65, 353; MJ/SBR/6, fo. 607; MJ/SBR/7, fo. 82; WJ/SR/NS/32/87, 37/170, 44/68; TNA STAC8, 81/38; BHC 6, fo. 289; 9, fo. 783; GL MSS 942/1, fo. 91v; 1124/1, fo. 167; 645/2, fo. 100; Jenner, 'Circulation and disorder', p. 46; Emily Jane Cockayne, 'A cultural history of sound in England 1560–1760', unpublished PhD thesis, University of Cambridge (2000), pp. 251–2.

carting' soared as time passed: the upper limit was lifted to 300 in 1654, and by 100 more eight years later.[6]

More traffic and trade went hand-in-hand, of course, but not without costs. Magistrates called streets eyesores not worthy of a glittering city. They were lined with filth and the stench was 'noisome' in hotter summer weather, although winter snow melted over dirt to make streets mucky and slippery.[7] Thoughtless householders dumped 'loads of noisome soil' and ashes on streets, and lazy rakers and scavengers, who were stock characters in City complaints, added to the rubbish heap by dodging duties. Loose animals also soiled streets, hogs more than most if complaints are right. Dead hogs, dogs, and cats littered Water Lane next to Fleet Street in 1595.[8] Growth and grime were twins. Not many months passed without griping about soot, soil, or dung spread across streets like skin, or spilling into 'canals' (channels) on their edges. Complaints about sub-standard street-cleaning rose after 1600, with more orders to sweep streets and pick up rubbish.[9] Particular places were sometimes singled-out for being 'very foul', like 'the backside of the Cockpit playhouse in Lincolns Inne Fields', or the ground around Charing Cross.[10] Householders were asked to keep pavements spick and span, but some of them ended up in court for letting dirt pile up outside their door.[11] Uneven paving was another blemish. People lost their footing and tripped up and water did not run straight into roadside canals but formed stinking puddles. Parishes organized 'views' of streets and pavements from time to time to draw up lists of 'deformities'. St Dunstan-in-the-West paid for a 'dynner' each time their 'aunciients' walked through the parish to check over streets and pavements with the alderman and others.[12] Judging by account rolls, parishes spent most money on paving

---

[6] GL MS 4097/1, fos. 35, 54, 125, 132v, 148v, 154, 165v; Jenner, 'Circulation and disorder', p. 41.
[7] APC 1619–21, pp. 21–3; LMA Jour. 31, fo. 273.
[8] LMA Jours. 23, fo. 403v; 36, fo. 20v.
[9] Mark S. R. Jenner, 'Early modern English conceptions of "cleanliness" and "dirt" as reflected in the environmental regulation of London, c.1530–c.1700', unpublished DPhil thesis, University of Oxford (1991), Table 3:1, and chap. 3. For Guildhall orders see LMA Reps. 14, fo. 88; 20, fo. 84v; 21, fo. 63v; Jours. 13, fo. 469v; 14, fo. 254; 16, fo. 389; 18, fo. 323; 19, fo. 243v; 20, fo. 485; 21, fos. 41, 199v, 430v; 22, fo. 48; 23, fo. 130; GL MS 6552/1, fos. 153v, 161v, 175v, 205v, 236v, 248.
[10] TNA SP14/120/49; 16/214/85; 16/257/130; 16/310/20; LMA Jours. 20, fo. 126v; 11, fos. 204v-5; 29, fo. 329v; 32, fo. 251; 34, fos. 297, 311; 35, fos. 20v, 239; 37, fos. 30–0v; 41, fos. 111v-12v, 113, 113v, 117v, 118, 119–20v, 121, 121v, 123–5; GL MS 1264/1, fos. 57–7v; TNA PC2/42/28, 51.
[11] TNA SP16/424/124; LMA MJ/SBR/5, fos. 538–9; GL MS 4072/1, fo. 43; LMA Jours. 20(2), fo. 436v; 23, fo. 268v.
[12] LMA Jours. 33, fos. 129, 304; 34, fo. 73; 35, fo. 59v; GL MS 2968/2, fos. 39, 157.

around churches, and somewhat less on areas near vestry-houses, wells, stocks, or alleys. St Mary Woolnoth spent 7/6d for 'paving 30 yards in the streete before the church' in 1625.[13] There were also plans in hand to make things better. In 1634 the king urged the City to put in place Daniel Nys's plan to 'beautify' streets 'by raising them to a convenient height and evenness and decency', and cleaning them day and night with 'pipes of lead'. Nys met with a City committee but his plan never got off the ground.[14]

Dirty streets reminded people of risky growth and vagrant floods. Each day is 'a foggy day', Evelyn said, after seeing the city smothered in smog for so long.[15] Foul air hovered over vagrants, an atmospheric outpouring of smells and harmful miasmas. Like vagrants, dirty streets spread plague. An order from around 1520 noted that 'filthy stinking things' tossed in streets hurt 'bodily health' and spread 'diseases daily'.[16] But complaints continued. The 'dirt and rubbish' piled up from Westminster to Temple Bar bred 'infection' in 1635 and set people fretting as this stretch of road was used by the upper crust and high-ranking royal officials, but was also a tramping route for vagrants.[17] Filth was more than a matter of hygiene and health. Street-cleaning and order went hand-in-hand in couplings of crime and cleanliness in by-laws. Vagrants not thieves were the real root of crime perceptions around 1600, unlike one century later, Beattie notes, when theft headed concerns.[18] Vagrants were imagined in terms of growth, shabbiness, sickness, and intuitive crime. The courts were swamped by crimes directly related to the speedy growth of the city after 1600. By then, crime was said to be both the cause and consequence of urban sprawl and squalour, something clearly seen on London's streets.

---

[13] GL MS 1002/1, fo. 463. See also GL MSS 6552/1, fo. 238v; 577/1, fo. 78; 6836, fo. 93; 951/1, fo. 69; 4385/1, fo. 225v; 590/1, fos. 77v, 310v; 1046/1, fo. 94v; 4457/2, fos. 14v, 212; 5714/1, fos. 25, 174v; 7673/1, fo. 64v; 4071/2, fo. 116; 5018/1, fo. 77v; 4241/1, fo. 379; 1568, fo. 137; 1016/1, fo. 135; 1002/1, fo. 523v; 645/1, fo. 72v; 4180/1, fo. 174v; 4570/2, fo. 193.

[14] LMA Remembrancia Book 7, fos. 135–6; Rep. 48, fo. 418; Remembrancia Book 8, fo. 80.

[15] Evelyn, *A Character of England*, p. 157.

[16] LMA Jour. 11, fos. 348–8v.

[17] TNA SP16/305/4. See also TNA SP16/420/27, 16/424/70.

[18] See Mary Douglas, *Purity and Danger: an Analysis of the Concepts of Pollution and Taboo* (1966); Jenner, 'Early modern conceptions of "cleanliness" and "dirt"', introduction; J. M. Beattie, *Policing and Punishment in London 1660–1750: Urban Crime and the Limits of Terror* (Oxford, 2001). For examples of by-laws see LMA Jours. 14, fo. 232v; 15, fo. 33; 16, fo. 353v; 17, fos. 40v, 313v; 18, fos. 2, 342v; 19, fo. 247; 20, fo. 18; 20(2), fo. 364; 23, fo. 123.

## Vagrant floods

The streets were the most public and visible sign of London's condition.[19] If anything the press of people was even more apparent than speeding traffic. The 'extraordinary' and 'infinite' number of vagrants at large was a theme of the times. Vagrants have long been seen as archetypal figures of pain or fear in what we once called Tawney's century. They came from all over the country, with concentrations from counties ringing the city and numbers dropping the nearer we get to one of the coasts.[20] Many were looking for jobs because work was scarce back home. Some said that they were on the road on business. Richard Thorpe walked from Kent to buy drugs for his physician father, he said. Others claimed that they were chasing legal matters. One had a 'hearinge in the Exchequer'; another said that he 'came up' 'for a writt'. William Overall came from Essex 'to bring a letter to Mr Woodall of the Prerogative Office'. Other stories seem half-baked. John Baker, who was caught in 1637 with a woman 'with her coats up', said that he came from the 'countrey' to 'solicitte suits of lawe'. The courts also heard many hard-luck stories. John Snow, who made the short trip across the river from Kent Street, said that his mother 'turned him out of dores and bed him goe seeke his fortune'.[21]

Some vagrants were passing through *en route* to somewhere else, although London was journey's end for most with hope in their hearts but little else to fall back on. Some did not have time to join the job-hunt before becoming another vagrant statistic. Their first London bed was in Bridewell. Ellen Hall was locked up 'the first night she came to London out of Hampshire' in 1637. I got here 'last Wednesday', another fed-up vagrant said a little while earlier. Many 'latelie' landed migrants were sitting ducks and it did not take long for them to fall into the clutches of the law: one day, two days, one week, eight days, nine days, ten days, and two weeks were the short tastes of freedom for vagrants mentioned in courtbooks. Some skipped around the city for longer: six weeks, eleven weeks, three months, six months, Shropshire native Margaret Lee 'had lyved looslie about London this quarter of a yeare', she said

---

[19] Cf. Lynda Nead, *Victorian Babylon: People, Streets, and Images in Nineteenth-Century London* (New Haven, CT, and London, 2000), p. 16.
[20] Bridewell's court surveyed the homes of vagrants one day in January 1601 with these results: Berkshire (1), Buckinghamshire (1), Cambridgeshire (1), Derbyshire (1), Devon (1), Essex (2), Ireland (1), Kent (2), Northamptonshire (1), Richmondshire (1), Shropshire (1), Somerset (1), Suffolk (1), Surrey (1), Warwickshire (1), Worcestershire (1), Yorkshire (3) (BRHA BHC 4, fos 225v-8).
[21] BHC 6, fo. 375; 8, fo. 221v; 7, fos. 27v, 39v; 8, fo. 237v; 6, fo. 242.

in 1608.[22] But there were also long-stay vagrants who had found somewhere to live in London's basement boarding culture. Yorkshireman and 'notorious theefe' Dennis Bourne managed to find cheap lodgings in Chick Lane, and he admitted that he had lived in London for four years. Richard Whetstone had scratched out a living in Westminster for four years when he landed in the vagrant bin in 1614.[23] Other vagrants seemed to hang around the city forever. Thomas Savage – alias Bonner – is 'often here', Bridewell's clerk wrote wearily in 1578, and this time, to add insult to injury, the neck collar pinned on him by the court for a public notice of his roguish reputation had been 'knocked off' by a Tower Hill smithy. Veteran vagrants like Thomas Hopkins and Alice Gilbert – alias Hilarde – who had both been 'burned in the eares' were London's bad apples.[24] Other vagrants left home on seasonal sorties, coming and going with harvests, and other times when work was more abundant for a time. John Perkins got into trouble 'for running into mens houses with a pronge and truncheon to their great terror' in 1641, and he said that he had a home in Cambridge but 'came to work here this harvest'.[25]

And still they kept coming: children, grown-ups, gypsies, street-sellers, sailors, soldiers, ballad-singers. Most wanted work, wages, and help, quickly. Demobbed sailors headed to London from the coast to get back-pay. Soldiers back from the wars made the same tired trek, scavenging, stealing, scrounging. The number of hangings always went up when soldiers left ships, unpaid and unhappy.[26] Imagine the alarm in London's high offices as news spread of another 'troop' of starving sailors or soldiers on the road from the south coast. A Hampshire sheriff sent word of a mob of 300 sailors who had not long left Portsmouth docks after a year at sea without pay in 1626. The Duke of Buckingham added to the tension, bringing word of a spate of 'insolencies and disorders' on roads leading to London. They 'lock together in companies', another anxious account

---

[22] BHC 8, fo. 104; 7, fo. 23v; 5, fo. 280v. See also BHC 2, fos. 225v-8; 3, fo. 140v; 5, fo. 441v; 6, fos. 32v, 98v, 100, 112, 120, 133, 148, 157v, 203, 242, 258v, 268, 278v, 354v, 375, 408, 435; 7, fos. 23, 31, 56v, 62, 96, 101; 8, fos. 104, 210, 230v, 342v; BRHA BHC 4, fos. 244, 313v, 384v, 454.

[23] BHC 6, fo. 328v; WAC WCB/2, fo. 73.

[24] BHC 3, fos. 350v, 359, 392v. Hopkins 'denied' that he 'ever was burned in the eare', but the court noted that 'his eare sheweth that he hath'.

[25] BHC 8, fo. 337v.

[26] CSPV 1610, p. 778. See also Douglas Hay, 'War, dearth, and theft in the eighteenth century: the record of the English courts', *Past and Present*, 95 (1992), 117–60; Nicholas Rogers, 'The politics of war and dearth, 1756–1757', in his *Crowds, Culture, and Politics in Georgian Britain* (Oxford, 1998), pp. 58–84; P. G. Lawson, 'Property crime and hard times in England, 1559–1624', *Law and History Review*, 4 (1986), 95–127.

said as the 'crew' got nearer.[27] Hungry angry out-of-work soldiers and sailors milled around the city, refusing to go home until the pay-day they had pinned their hopes on. They camped in fields, muttered in alehouses, ganged up on streets, hounded royal revenue officials, and begged for food.[28] Letters raced between Whitehall and the Guildhall. Watches were doubled until tense temperatures fell; trained bands were put on red alert; and martial order was imposed when things got out of hand. There were 'swarmes' of soldiers and sailors loose in London in November 1626. They say that they will die rather than starve one day longer, Venice's ambassador wrote in reports filed for his masters back home, and they also put a price on the Duke of Buckingham's head, he added. Sailors in bands three or four hundred strong poured through the city in 1628, stealing food, committing 'many excesses'.[29] Many soldiers and sailors got caught in Bridewell's net. Others ended up in Middlesex courts, including a 'company of sailors' who ran riot in Turnmill Street, and another gang of hard-up sailors who blocked the Countess of Bridgewater's coach in Clerkenwell and beat up her coachman in 1628.[30] There was more brouhaha in the Civil War crisis, as we might expect. 'Reformadoes and soldiers' stormed through the city and blockaded Parliament. Other soldiers broke into houses or attacked 'whores' at doors, lit fires in 'Paules', and started pitched battles with constables and watchmen. General Fairfax himself was called on one time in 1649 to get rowdy soldiers to calm down.[31]

The vagrant drifting life was the reverse side of stable settled lifestyles. Not all vagrants were anti-authority rabble-rousers as blanket condemnations would have it. But there were scores of street skirmishes when vagrants took on officers, baiting and beating them, getting the upper hand now and again. They took sides, nicely demonstrated when vagrants ripped vagrancy laws off posts. Vagrants also walked through streets making proclamations of their own, in parodies of proper performances. Jasper Smith, whose 'common course of livinge' was with 'lewde dronken vagrants', walked up and down shouting 'scandalous proclamacons in the

---

[27] TNA SP16/31/112; APC 1626, p. 307; SRPC (54), pp. 109–10.
[28] For example, BHC 8, fos. 57v, 59v, 61, 67, 98v, 103v, 105, 105v, 111v.
[29] LMA Jour. 34, fo. 16v; CSPV 1626–8, pp. 125, 55, 606–7; 1628–9, p. 23; TNA SP16/53/9; 16/485/10; HOL MP 5 October 1641, 1 November 1641, 4 November 1641.
[30] LMA MJ/SBR/4, fos. 626, 649. See also LMA Rep. 12, fo. 258v; Jour. 34, fo. 76. Examples from one Bridewell book include BRHA BHC 4, fos. 275, 339v, 341, 342v, 357, 358v, 360, 361, 361v, 364v, 365v, 371, 375v, 397v, 398. A big fear was that soldiers and sailors would link up with rowdy groups, like apprentices: see Griffiths, *Youth and Authority*, p. 160.
[31] LMA Jours. 39, fo. 237v; 40, fos. 226, 227, 228–8v, 231v–2v, 273–3v; Rep. 59, fos. 322v, 339v, 343.

streets' in 1619. Robert Griffin was 'well' whipped in 1598 for 'cursinge the magistrats for executing her m[ajes]ties lawe touching the Acte of Parliamente for the punishing of rogues'. He also crossed swords with a deputy who was 'setting up a post by the conduite in Cheape'. Some vagrants followed seditious styles. 'Lewde' Edward Mopine told the mayor that 'it was a good dede to knock out the braynes of those that apprehended rogues'. Vagrant Josiah Haddington carried a 'greate batt' with him at all times to 'strike at officers'. 'Comon roge' William Jackson shouted that he 'trusted' to see constables and citizens 'pluckt out of their houses by the eares' in 1577.[32] Attitudes were miles apart here. The sight of someone rich with airs and graces strolling on streets could set off fireworks. Vagrant father and son Walter and William Styles were caught 'abusing men and women of good creditt on the bridge in worde and deed' in 1621. When 'honest gents' walked past vagrant John Davies he would fall down and roll in dirt to 'spoyle' their trim clothes, shouting and spitting. Another 'lewde unruly vagrant' – John Street – was caught spitting 'in mens faces' in 1618.[33] Sometimes contrasts between the haves and the have-nots were too painful to bear any longer. Nor should we rule out class bitterness as inequality had a real sting. But there were also real differences of opinion when starving vagrants with no money in their pockets pinched food. This was the only option left for most of them, who put themselves first in a straight struggle to survive. Theft will be looked at in deeper depth in the next chapter; begging comes under the spotlight in the next section. For now the counter-cultural 'wordes and deedes' by enough vagrants can stand as signs of deep divisions in these troubled times.

There was no such thing as a typical vagrant experience, no matter how many times by-laws described vagrants as a single body. It only takes a few pages in a courtbook to separate suffering from streetwise sharpness or bad luck from arty counterfeiting and slick tricks. Straggling children with no one to turn to filled streets according to magistrates, squeezing under stalls with a little pile of straw for a pillow, if lucky. 'Poore boyes and children' 'lye nightlye in the streets', aldermen said in 1593. 'Boyes and gerles [lye] in the streats everie night very pittyfully', Cornhill wardmote said with real concern in 1574, and starving children still slept in streets there two decades later. Seven 'vagrant girls' huddled under a single stall in Cheap one night in 1640. Three 'vagrant boyes' were 'taken sleeping' on top of a stall in 1631.[34] Their ages struck anyone with a heart.

---

[32] BRHA BHC 4, fo. 24v; BHC 6, fos. 127, 296; 7, fo. 59v; 3, fo. 262v; BRHA BHC 4, fo. 24v.
[33] BHC 6, fos. 258v, 152v, 46v.
[34] LMA Rep. 23, fo. 14; GL MS 4069/1, fos. 14v, 67; BHC 8, fo. 298; 7, fo. 249v. See also BHC 8, fos. 149v, 407; LMA Rep. 22, fos. 210v, 335v; GL MSS 12806/3, fo. 321; 3146/1,

Something had gone wrong: harrowing family breakdown, children suddenly orphaned with not even a neighbour to lend a hand, a socialization string snapped. Sad bad-luck stories were written down in the red-tape formulas of Christ's Hospital books. Children 'without comfort' on chilly streets were given new chances there. Orphans found support and sympathy after time alone in a cold place. The average age of children given a fresh start in Christ's from parishes or streets was a little more than five-and-a-half years.[35] Carriers were often blamed for dumping children. Christ's board blasted carriers 'whiche daylye bringe children to the city and leave them in the streetes' in 1556. They were threatened with prison in 1579 if they carried children to London over land or water and left them to fend for themselves.[36] Carriers came from all over with commercial cargos and people, some so young that the trip looks like staged abandonment. Eight-year-old William Candy was found crying in Christ's cloisters in 1595 after he was dropped off by a Daventry carrier. A 'welche caryer' – Howell Aproberte – brought 'smale children' from Wales in 1561 and left 'them in the streates unprovided', before going back for his next batch. Agnes Goodwin (aged twelve) was 'taken up in the streets' with 'a very sore head' in 1586 after a little time in London. She had been ditched by the Portsmouth carrier, her uncle's last act for her. These lost children all too easily fell into the clutches of preying bawds or thieves looking for nimble youngsters to squeeze into houses. Carriers took risks. They could be tracked down, as most of them stayed at the same inn to tout custom, accommodation arrangements made public in John Taylor's *The Carriers Cosmographie* (1637). It was known that the Portsmouth carrier who dumped Agnes Goodwin, for example, always stayed in the same Southwark alehouse each week.[37]

Irish vagrants tried their luck in the city, as well as continental migrants and thieves who crossed the water having heard of rich pickings in London. One 'old' Frenchman run aground in London said that he 'landed in England by foule wether'.[38] 'Egyptians' were caught roaming, stealing, selling, scrounging, and simply surviving. Two male 'gypsies' ended up in Bridewell in 1654, along with a pair of female gipsies soon

---

fo. 47; 4956/3, fo. 45; 4071/1, fo. 153; 12806/2, fo. 385v; Rice Bush, *The Poor Mans Friend, or Narrative of What Progresse Many Worthy Citizens of London Have Made in that Godly Work of Providing for the Poor* (1649), pp. 2, 13.

[35] GL MS 1280/1, fos. 18v, 19v, 22. The average age figure is taken from the age at admission of 1,465 children in GL MSS 12806/1–2.

[36] GL MS 12806/1, fo. 4; LMA Jour. 20, fo. 500v; Rep. 19, fo. 502v.

[37] GL MS 12806/3, fo. 16; BHC 1, fo. 183v; GL MS 12806/2, fo. 376v; John Taylor, *The Carriers Cosmographie. Or a Briefe Relation of the Innes, Ordinaries, Hoste[l]ries, and Other Lodgings in and Neere London* (1637). See also BHC 2, fo. 18; 3, fo. 334v; 5, fos. 61v, 77, 107v, 127v, 279v; 7, fo. 285; BRHA BHC 4, fos. 30, 217.

[38] BHC 6, fo. 437.

after.[39] London was a job-feast, people from the provinces thought. Its chaos or spell was a drug for some. But opportunity alone was enough to keep up vagrant floods. Hard-up people needed to make shift, on or off poor rolls.[40] Street-sellers hawked goods up and down. Other people sold their skills, or, if necessary, themselves. Vagrants could put on a good show; remember that players and minstrels are on the list of vagrant-types in legislation. A vagrant juggler thrilled crowds with 'tricks by sleight of hand' in 1619. A bagpipe player with 'no good accompt of his living' was trapped in Bridewell's net in 1634. A 'musicioner' agreed to 'goe for a souldier' in 1637. A beggar sang 'bawdy songs' loud enough for a marshal to hear. A spicey or jokey ballad stopped people in their tracks. 'Ballet singers' popped up on corners and streets in beggars operas that troubled governors; drawing the lottery of crowds for one thing. Watchmen swooped on a 'ballad singer' in 1617 'singing ballads in streets and gathering a tumult about him'. Other vagrant 'ballett singers' walked 'up and downe the streets' singing at the tops of their voices. 'Idle' William Clapham was grabbed singing 'songes and ballads at folks dores' in 1618, for a fee maybe.[41] Vagrants were also caught selling songs. Margaret Lee, who came from Shropshire to find her husband, 'lyved looslie' in London for three months in 1608, selling ballads to buy a new waistcoat. 'Idle' James Gittens was picked up singing and selling ballads 'in the streets and draw[ing] much people together whereby much hurt is done'. Last but not least, fortune-tellers added to this street jamboree, promising people that they could see deep into their futures.[42] The carpenter John Munch also looked far ahead in 'fabulous dreames', he said, that let him 'provosie of matters of state': he is 'a playne dunsticall cuntrye[man]', Bridewell's clerk wrote snootily. Thomas Daunce – another bumbling 'countryman' – rushed to London with 'a messauge' for the privy council 'from God the father', informing the central government 'that our saviour wilbe in Pawls on Whitson Monday'.[43]

Some vagrants were noisy, making music, singing, shouting. Some were 'silly' and 'sad', London's walking wounded, spouting strange

---

[39] BHC 9, fos. 637, 677; LMA MJ/SBR/7, fo. 127.
[40] Steve Hindle, *On the Parish? The Micro-Politics of Poor Relief in Rural England, c.1550–1750* (Oxford, 2004), chap. 1.
[41] Peter Roberts, 'Elizabethan players and minstrels and the legislation of 1572 against retainers and vagabonds', in Anthony Fletcher and Roberts, eds., *Religion, Culture, and Society in Early Modern Britain: Essays in Honour of Patrick Collinson* (Cambridge, 1994), pp. 29–55; BHC 6, fo. 100v; 8, fos. 2v, 146v; 9, fo. 52; 8, fo. 147; 6, fos. 418, 38v. See also LMA MJ/SBR/6, fo. 12; CQSF 93/2; BHC 6, fos. 243, 337, 410; 7, fos. 77v, 100v, 166v, 271v, 298; 8, fos. 43, 45, 61, 80v, 94v, 184v, 226v, 228, 410; 9, fos. 332, 341, 645.
[42] BHC 5, fo. 280v; 6, fo. 65; 7, fo. 303v; 8, fo. 384v; BRHA BHC 4, fos. 19v, 54v, 79.
[43] BHC 5, fo. 87; 7, fo. 127.

talk. Anthony Speerne caused a fuss when he walked up and down crying 'woe to Rome, woe to Rome' in 1623, and he was back in town spouting gibberish two years later. William Lene thought 'folishely' and 'fondly' that he was 'fedd by angels' in 1575. A 'rouging' tailor called himself 'the quenes fole'.[44] Other sad-seeming vagrants were more pitiful than strange. John Williams was called 'an unlovely vagrant'. Martha Davis was 'harborles'. A parish gave a shilling to 'a poore woman in misery'. Another gave 2/6d 'to a poore man that carryeth his head in his bosome'. Robert Wilbrome was 'a broken man'. Vagrant Elizabeth Johns tried to drown herself and her 'prettie young childe' in 1622. Thomas Hayes was found cowering 'under a painthouse bleating like a calf' at night in 1637. Other vagrants 'cryed out' in misery in ditches or churchyards, or crumpled at gates or doors, knocking for help that never came. They slumped on streets, some so hungry that they had little strength left. Homeless and helpless, this was the true sorrow of the streets. One 'vagrant and wicked liver' had 'noe leggs'. John Batris was taken 'tumbling' in dirt in 1640, 'miserable poore and naked'. Other 'poore and naked' vagrants stumbled along, even in frosty winter, and on one occasion 'three forren naked vagrants' caused tongues to wag on the longest night of the year, as people wondered how they coped in the cold. With energy all gone, some vagrants fell asleep on streets, with stone for cushions.[45] Three women were 'taken lyeing altogether in strawe in the street' with nine other vagrants in 1640. The Fleet Street watch came across three out-of-work women sheltering in a shed in 1642. Any place would do for warmth or a hiding place from passing policemen. Seven 'comon rogues' – all women – were pulled from 'the Fleete privie' one night in 1579. Other 'street people' sought shelter in stables, markethouses, haylofts, 'haymows', and 'holes'. A group of 'rogues and vagabonds' camped on Tower Hill in 1586 and burned straw all night long 'to warm themselves'.[46]

Others vagrants were 'simple', 'silly', or 'folishe', words not without sympathy. Drifting Robert Stonehill was called 'a silly ideot boy'. Rebecca Hawkins was dubbed 'a cilly weake wench'. There could be sympathy too in harsh sounding titles like 'crased' in 'witts' or 'crackt

---

[44] BHC 6, fo. 322v; 7, fo. 39; 2, fo. 123v; 3, fo. 408v; 7, fo. 282v.
[45] BRHA BHC 4, fo. 358v; GL MSS 3146/1, fo. 70; 577/1, fo. 58; 6574, fo. 110; BHC 6, fos. 431v, 282v; BHC 8, fo. 121; GL MSS 4423/1, fo. 155; 2968/2, fo. 294; 4409/1, fo. 204v; 878/1; fo. 322v; 4069/1, fo. 67; WAC F301/14; BHC 6, fos. 23, 371; 7, fo. 99v; 8, fos. 122v, 318v.
[46] BHC 8, fos. 286, 405; 3, fo. 368v; 7, fos. 79v, 121; 8, fos 2v, 3, 316; TNA SP12/187/20; GL MS 4241/1, fos. 239, 244. See also GL MSS 1002/1, fo. 316; 2088/1, 1583–4, 1612–13; 3018/1, fos. 23v, 25, 26v, 28v, 32, 33v; BHC 8, fos. 195, 375.

brayned'. Most of these dim-wits were given help to get home if they had one.[47] Other vagrants were sick in body not mind. They hobbled along streets, one cursing and coughing, worrying people rushing past him to avoid infection; another with an eye infection walked gingerly, holding onto his helper for dear life. Others were victims of speeding traffic or other accidents. A 'poore man' got help after he was struck by a thunderbolt. In other cases vagrants were laid low with falling sickness, 'dead palsey', or the king's evil. Women were treated more kindly if they had 'a wolfe' in their arms or breasts (cancerous growths or sores). A 'poore woman' with 'a mole' got sixpence from one parish. Another street sound was the tapping sticks of blind vagrants. 'A poor man with bleare blind eyes' had sixpence from a parish. The ranks of the vagrant poor included many with sore legs and heads. Lame tramps struggled to reach wherever it was they were heading.[48] For some it was too late. They had put up with too much and there was nothing left now except to give in to the hard city. Vagrants dropped dead on streets, cold and lonely deaths, and turn up in parish papers with no name or passport to tie them somewhere. Vagrant bodies were found slouched on streets, under stalls, in markets, on wharfs, docks, and doorsteps, in churchyards or porches. St Michael Cornhill paid 4/2d to bury 'a poor man that dyed in the pulpett' in 1584. Another parish covered the costs of burying 'a pore woman' who 'dyed in the comon pryvie'; a second vagrant woman 'died in the house of office' a little later.[49] But lives also began on streets in chilling conditions. Women with no help at hand gave birth in the only place that was left to them on 'open' streets or in alleys, entries, doorsteps, markets, conduits, fields, or church pews, porches, and yards. Mary Cowper gave birth to twins on a street side in 1601. One wandering woman delivered her child herself at 'Mr Alderman Gore's warehouse dore as she passed alonge'. Another panic-stricken vagrant gave birth in a 'colehole' in St Helen Bishopgate in 1644. A child born in a 'common pryvie' in

---

[47] BHC 6, fo. 439v; BRHA BHC 4, fo. 405; BHC 9, fos. 534, 824; 6, fos. 120, 160; 8, fos. 14v, 175; 9, fo. 664.
[48] BHC 6, fo. 394v; GL MSS 6574, fo. 101; 4180/2, fo. 71v; BRHA BHC 4, fo. 388; BHC 5, fo. 182; 6, fos. 277, 435; 7, fo. 98v; GL MSS 3146/1, fo. 13; 4524/1, fo. 200; 942/1, fo. 31v; 577/1, fo. 46v; 4409/1, fo. 151v; 593/2, fo. 149; 4051/1, fo. 43; 4385/1, fo. 188; 3907/1, 1641–2; 645/2, fo. 39; 4956/2, fo. 321v; 1181/1, fo. 175. My thanks to Mark Jenner for the help with 'wolfe'.
[49] GL MSS 4071/1, fo. 122v; 2088/1, fos. 40, 1609–10. See also GL MSS 645/2, fo. 56; 3146/1, fo. 113; 4383/1, fo. 377; 2968/1, fo. 355v; 5090/2, fo. 223; 5714/1, fo. 214v; 4071/2, fo. 30v; 2088/1, 1630–1; 4241/1, fo. 230; 1568, fo. 534; 6574, fo. 162; 3907/1, 1630–1; 4180/1, fo. 224; 4180/2, fo. 174; 593/2, fo. 149; 4409/2, 1651–2; 2596/1, fo. 193v; 4956/2, fo. 189v; 1279/2, fo. 173; 959/1, fo. 215; 818/1, fo. 147; 524/1, fos. 10, 15, 45v; WAC F308; F309/15; F310.

110    Change

St Andrew-by-the-Wardrobe in 1600 soon lost the struggle for survival. Many other street-births met the same sad swift end. A child not yet one day old became one more sorry street statistic.[50]

Not all vagrants ended up down and out, stuck on their own with no one to turn to. We have already seen gloomy groups huddled in sheds, stalls, or 'comon privies'. These were chance meetings in the main, people running into each other by cold circumstance. Nine vagrants – seven women and two men – bedded down in a cellar for the night in 1579. A bunch of 'vagrant girls' 'broke into an empty house' next to the Custom House in 1630, and 'made a fire' for warmth, jeopardizing nearby houses, neighbours said. Two women were taken sleeping on the stones in 'Paules Churchyard' in 1627. There was comfort in company, even if only for a short while it was better than being alone.[51] A gang of ten vagrants, all 'comon frequenters of Paulls', lingered there in 1619, casual comrades in alms and living roughly. Most of them were stringing along for the confidence that can come from belonging to a group of like-minded people in tight spots. But many ties were short lived, not even days old, though useful nonetheless for short spells until something else came along. But there were longer-lasting leagues of thieves, vagrants, and beggars, as we shall soon see. Vagrants also had regular haunts, like the group of ten who pestered 'Pawles'. Other 'Powles customers' included a vagrant 'comon gamester' who clowned around and drew 'lewde company to him' in 1622.[52] Vagrants also 'hanckered about' the royal court in largish groups hoping to scrounge something from well-to-do courtiers: five at one time, six at another, and twenty-two who were 'taken loitering at his ma[jes]ties court at Greenwich' one day in 1634. Vagrants knew where to go to find crowds massing in markets, busy junctions, or watering holes.[53] Makeshift lodgings or fleeting friendships do not sound like the sort of thing people had in mind when they first took to the road. But some were resilient and resourceful. We even get nice snapshots of vagrants having fire-side chats, sitting down and sharing their road stories. One group is seen talking long into the night and playing cards; another tucked into a meal of mutton. We even have a

---

[50] GL MSS 4071/1, 1600–1; 4385/1, fo. 134; 6386, fo. 192; 2088/1, 1599. See also BRHA BHC 4, fo. 398v; GL MSS 4071/1, fo. 105; 2968/2, fo. 331v; 942/1, fo. 115; 951/1, fo. 40; 4385/1, fo. 250v; 5090/2, fo. 205v; 5714/1, fo. 37; 1002/1, fo. 515v; 645/2, fo. 90v; 4956/2, fo. 353v; 2956/2, fo. 160v; 1432/3, fo. 127; 524/1, fo. 72; 559/1, fo. 9; 1046/1, fo. 116v; 818/1, fo. 19.
[51] BHC 3, fo. 362; 7, fos. 168v, 31v; 8, fo. 47v; 1, fo. 172v; 3, fos. 359, 392v; 6, fo. 293v; 7, fos. 47v, 57v, 62; 8, fo. 119v; BRHA BHC 4, fo. 21v.
[52] BHC 6, fo. 291v; 3, fos. 8v, 369, 425v; BRHA BHC 4, fo. 360.
[53] BHC 5, fo. 419; 6, fos. 355v, 360v; 8, fo. 2v.

vagrant wedding party. Agnes Artors and Richard Salisbury (two 'old [Bridewell] gests') got married in St Sepulchre church in 1562, and afterwards went to John Hall's house in Turnagain Lane to drink and dance. The bench counted at least five 'vacabonds and harlotts of this house' at the celebration, and Hall was later warned and 'well whipped' for giving room and board to 'vile and naughtie vacabonds'.[54]

There was a world of difference between lonely lost vagrants and others with enough experience to survive on streets. A broken window or rickety door was all some needed to take over cellars for a night or more. An empty barn was a godsend on a cold windy night. One group set up house in a long barn in St Clement Danes near to 'a dangerous pit' that caused stomach-churning stench, fed-up residents said, and no one can walk by there 'either early or late' without 'danger of ryfling', they added.[55] Like thieves, clued-up vagrants could count on safe-houses where they could get bed and board. The same streets or sites crop up in north-west suburbs: Cow Cross, Clerkenwell, St John Street, and Turnmill Street, naturally. There are countless 'comon receivers', 'harborers', and 'hosts' in courtbooks, renting rooms to vagrants. Many ran alehouses and some had ties to crime rings, lining pockets with their shares. Magistrates nearly always pinpointed alehouses and low-grade boarding houses when sending out 'searchers' to round up vagrants and other shifty riff-raff. Quite typical was 'hoste' John Cotton 'who keepeyth petye hostrye', aldermen heard in 1559, and took in vagrants and other 'idle and suspecte persons' for a fee. A Chick Lane cobbler was brought to book for giving 'masterless' men and beggars a bed 'for a penny a night'. Andrew Packwood, who lived along shady Cock and Key Alley, was warned by his wardmote to stop giving vagrants shelter for a few years in a row. Like other 'hostes' he was not from the dregs of society. Barber-surgeons, cobblers, cutlers, and others from middle-ranking trades boosted their earnings with cheap rents for several years or longer.[56]

Vagrants did not lack helping hands. There were always Londoners ready to top-up their livings by dipping into 'black economies'. Once they had spent time in the city's 'black belts' vagrants soon found out where to go for forged passports, safe shelter, or to fence loot. Their first defence was always a passport giving them the right to be on the road. A vagrant by

---

[54] BHC 5, fo. 228; 6, fos. 27v, 29v; 7, fo. 105; 1, fos. 192–3.
[55] TNA STAC8 212/3.
[56] LMA Rep. 14, fo. 267; MJ/SR/806/205; BHC 1, fo. 197; GL MS 3018/1, fos. 64v, 11v. See also WAC WCB/1, fo. 292; WCB/2, fos. 28, 173. BHC 1, fos. 8v-9; 3, fo. 291v; LMA MJ/SR/505a/27, 514/5, 519/56, 521/114; 806/80, 806/206, 806/207, 806/215, 806/221; WJ/SR/NS/44/143; Reps 13ii, fo. 402v; 14, fo. 150; 16, fos. 449v, 450, 455; 19, fo. 59; GL MS 12806/1, fos. 36v, 39.

definition did not have one, and a cottage industry filled this gap, pumping out fake travel permits. Many forgers were based in the city, as we might expect, giving vagrants cover to walk there or to leave for good. Michael Rogers was charged with 'foregeing' passports 'in the name of certen men of worship' in 1570. A group of 'false pasport' 'makers' were 'whipped at a cartes arse' in 1578. The 'counterfeyter' John Mason was taken with 'seaven seales' in his pockets in 1623. Thomas Gunwell was also locked up a week later for making 'counterfeit passes for anyone yt will give him money'.[57] Vagrants took risks in turning to neighbourhood forgers or someone on the road. A Kent tinker 'counterfeyted' passports for vagrants under two justices' hands in 1598 for 'two potts' of beer; the same going rate for an Oxford 'scoller' who made 'divers false pasports' for John Evans in 1578. A Sandwich forger gave another London-bound job-seeker a false passport and asked for 'one of his shoes of his feet'. Other fake passports were D-I-Y efforts, made at home or on the road. I made my own passport, vagrant Richard Nicholl said in 1604, and 'had the seale from a soldier'. The fact that magistrates spotted fake signatures or handwriting on passports from neighbouring counties (and further away) says something about the scale of this racket in phony passports, and also about the knowledge from experience that helped them to catch vagrants and their sidekick forgers.[58] As with beggars, as we shall soon see, London was flooded with false papers.

## Buzzing beggars

Hard-up Londoners begged in home patches even after begging was banned by statute in 1601. Not many people took notice of this ban, however, as plaintive pleas for alms still touched people enough for them to reach into their purses for pennies that could make all the difference. 'Indiscreete and wastful giving' was a 'vice' of the 'better sort', Robert Allen said disapprovingly a year before the begging ban. Do not even give crumbs to 'roguish, vagabonde, and idle persons', he lectured his mainly 'middling' hearers and readers.[59] But beggars still haunted the streets of

---

[57] BHC 3, fo. 319v; 6, fos. 343, 344.
[58] LMA Rep. 17, fo. 18v; BRHA BHC 4, fos. 47, 209, 451; BHC 3, fos. 327, 425v. See also LMA Reps. 14, fo. 367v; 15, fo. 364; 16, fos. 175–5v, 307; 17, fos. 10, 234v; Letterbook V, fo. 144v; BHC 2, fos. 14, 34, 57v; 5, fo. 164v; 6, fos. 337, 338, 341v; 7, fo. 246; BRHA BHC 4, fos. 358v, 407.
[59] Robert Allen, *A Treatise of Christian Beneficience* (1600), pp. 67, 35. Cf. A. W., *A Fruitfull and Godly Sermon, Preached at Paules Crosse* (1592), fo. C2v; Robert Fealty, *The Tree of Life Springing Out of the Grave*, in his *Clavis Mystica: a Key Opening Divers Difficult and Mysterious Texts of Holy Scripture, Handled in Seventy Sermons* (1636), p. 178. See also Hindle, *On the Parish?*, pp. 66–76.

the city, especially those of better-off parishes. From the poorer parts of Smithfield, Blackfriars, Whitefriars, St Giles-in-the-Field, St Giles Cripplegate, St Botolph Bishopgate, St Sepulchre, or from run-down riverside homes in Queenhithe, Dowgate, or near Custom House Quay, pauper processions headed for the city centre where wealth walked.[60] They also slipped into the city from built-up Middlesex and eastern slums in shabby Stepney, Whitechapel, and Ratcliffe.[61] But the biggest influx came from south of the river. Southern beggars sneaked over the bridge or boarded boats to beg in the wealthier city districts with reputations for giving generously. The river, we know, was a weak spot, lined with landing places that could not all be covered at once. Aware of the porous waterside, aldermen posted guards at strategic spots along the bank and each end of the bridge. Guards were placed deep in Southwark in 1569 to stop 'stout beggars' from reaching the river. Watermen were banned from bringing beggars 'over the water' time and again, but they shrugged off warnings so often that their wardens were told to force them to toe the line. Watermen found it hard to turn their backs on money, however. William Shereman (waterman) was taken to task in 1577 for bringing 'roges by water'. John Burchall also ended up in court half-a-century later for bringing 'roges over the water' from the south.[62]

Most beggars who gave an address or last living place came from the London area. Beggars hopped into the city from nearby Lambeth, Islington, Hampstead, or Highgate, or further afield from Harrow-on-the-Hill, Kingston, Croydon, or Gravesend, all within walking distance or a short boat trip.[63] Others took to the road for two or three days from one of the counties ringing London or walked west from East Anglia or north from the south coast.[64] Midland migrants came south in heavy numbers for London largesse, along with others who made the longer trip from Welsh border counties.[65] West Country beggars added their accents to this beggars' brew, and they made some of the longest trips from inside the country, as well as northerners hoping to hit the jackpot in distant

---

[60] For example, BHC 6, fos. 68v, 281v, 295v, 399; 8, fos. 102, 147; 9, fos. 94, 334, 550, 554, 606, 611, 619, 620, 637, 680, 768, 804, 813; BRHA BHC 4, fos. 137, 138v, 139v.
[61] For example, BHC 5, fo. 353; 6, fo. 250; 7, fo. 67; 8, fos. 56v, 60, 213v; 9, fos. 554, 603, 680, 813; BRHA BHC 4, fo. 138v.
[62] GL MS 12806/2, fos. 16, 37; LMA Reps. 16, fo. 483; 17, fos. 378v, 401; 18, fos. 127–7v; 23, fo. 517v; 30, fo. 294v; 19, fo. 193v; BHC 6, fo. 419.
[63] For example, BHC 6, fos. 16, 94, 279, 387v; 8, fos. 74v, 99v, 362; 9, fos. 407, 494, 516, 680. Cf. Tim Hitchcock, *Down and Out in Eighteenth-Century London* (2004), pp. 6–7.
[64] For example, BHC 8, fos. 52, 61v, 108v, 111, 111v; 9, fos. 254v, 274v, 382v, 406, 497, 506, 554, 643, 654, 680; BRHA BHC 4, fos. 137, 139v.
[65] For example, BHC 6, fo. 291; 8, fos. 49v, 68, 71v, 73, 108v, 110, 334v; 9, fos. 147, 322, 391, 414, 515, 643, 654, 768; BRHA BHC 4, fo. 138v.

114    Change

London from as far away as Cumberland.[66] The Irish had a special place in London's growth, coming over the sea in droves and putting down ethnic roots eventually despite campaigns to drive them back over the sea. Irish beggars rubbed shoulders with Welsh and Scottish drifters who hoped to find something more secure than a begging pan. And London's cosmopolitan sheen was confirmed somewhat by foreign beggars, who washed up in the city from nearby France, as well as far-flung Turkey.[67]

Unlike two centuries later when London's beggars 'were predominantly women', more men were picked up begging over Bridewell's first century.[68] A little over six-in-ten beggars were men then (1,343/2,174: 61.8 per cent). If any comment was passed on their ages it was usually to call attention to youth or old age, with sympathetic subtexts that needy people unable to work full-time had more reason to beg in uncertain times (after 1601) when even legal experts still thought that licensed begging was still lawful.[69] Begging was in legal limbo but parishes still gave handouts to deserving cases, like 'distressed' ministers fallen on hard times or soldiers trying to get home; one lost a hand after fighting in Bohemia, another was missing both hands. One parish gave hand-outs to wayfarers laid low by 'great losse and misfortunes by fyer, sea, sicknesse, and other calamities'. Another gave Matthew Howard 1/6d to help him cope with a '1200li [loss] by shipwarack'.[70] Parishes did not bend rules for healthy household heads, however. Beggar Robert Butler turned out to be 'an householder in Ould Street' in 1608 with 'a wife and manie children', and a walking mockery of conventional standards, the court thought, because he had 'a reasonable estate yett beggs up and downe the towne'. Well-to-do beggars mocked good-natured givers with nerve and cheek. 'Notorious' Andrew Ratcliffe, who took 'no warning', had 'a great estate in Cumberland', but lived in London 'upon begging'. Bridewell's court heard that 'old beggar' John Hammond 'hath xxxli per annum land in Somersetshre', and had as much as 21/6d in his pockets at the time of his arrest in 1643.[71]

---

[66] For example, BHC 6, fos. 233, 266v, 279, 331v, 386, 387v; 8, fo. 60v; 9, fos. 94, 322, 428, 619, 645; BRHA BHC 4, fo. 138v.
[67] BHC 6, fos. 95v, 291, 377v; 7, fos. 37, 56, 66v, 92v, 100v, 101, 101v, 107, 374; 8, fos. 59v, 70; 9, fo. 603. BRHA BHC 4, fos. 137, 138v.
[68] Quoting Hitchcock, *Down and Out in Eighteenth-Century London*, p. 4.
[69] My thanks to Steve Hindle for help on this point.
[70] GL MSS 2968/2, fo. 162v; 818/1, fo. 143v; 4524/1, fos. 188v, 190, 191, 197v, 219v, 232v, 239, 248v, 254; 1124/1, fo. 144v; 4241/1, fo. 325; 2895/1, fos. 240v, 272; 6574, fo. 80; 4180/2, fos. 71–2; 4409/1, fos. 138, 144v, 145, 156v; 2968/2, fos. 134v, 174v, 201v, 202, 213v, 215, 232v, 339v-40; 590/1, fo. 137v; 4071/2, fo. 117v; 4383/1, fos. 4, 6, 31, 109, 152, 200, 419.
[71] BHC 5, fo. 243; 6, fo. 279; 8, fo. 82. See also BHC 6, fos. 19, 35v, 250, 286, 287; 8, fo. 102.

There are many 'colde', 'ould', or 'poore' boys or girls in Bridewell's beggar rolls. One 'poore ould woman', who had 'dwelt xxviiity yeares in Southwarke', begged, she said, to pay legal bills.[72] Many walked up and down rather than stay in the same spot and risk catching an officer's eye once too often. They were rarely pictures of health and were often pitied for this. But healthy beggars scorned laws and christian compassion, and their clean bill of health was used against them. Nicholas Johnson got an extra lashing in 1574 for being in 'lusty' physical condition. Westminster beggar Catherine Dunn was in double trouble in 1615: she was 'a lusty strong woman' with 'other means' of living.[73] On the other side were the begging blind, lame, or 'sickley', like blind Dominic Chamberlain, who had 'a pencon att Salisbury and will not stay there [magistrates moaned] but beggeth here', or the old blind man who was put in Bridewell in 1632 with a boy who led him along streets. St Bartholomew's board banned their house 'poore' from begging outside in 1556 and again a century later. One of 'Bart's' 'poore', 'saughsie' John Green, was warned that he would end up in Bridewell if he ever begged again. Blind William Mitchell, 'one of the poore of the locke in Southwerk', had a weekly shilling bait to drop 'the trade of beggyng' to 'live well and honestly' in a 'lawfull occupacon'.[74]

Begging was a full-time trade for some. Salisbury-born Chamberlain had 'continued a begger many yeares'. 'Dangerous' William Wiles from St Giles-in-the-Fields was a five-year veteran of the begging 'game'. Francis Dale begged 'continually', as did Rebecca Aden with her 'young child sucking upon her'. Thomas Harris drifted 'from place to place', aldermen heard in 1551, 'lyvynge onely by begginge'. Seeking pity, Winifred Rowse said that she 'cannot worke but liveth by begginge'. William Morley came clean in 1651: I 'must begge or steale', he said.[75] Beggars could make decent livings. The 'notorious begger', Edward Todd, had a 'good store of gold and money found about him'. John Appleby had seventeen shillings and a shiny gold ring in his pockets when 'taken begging' in 1577. Irishman Lawrence Donache had 'xxis xd about him' after a hard day's begging in 1578. Another beggar had 'gotten much' with his outspread arms. Some beggars fell out when they

---

[72] BHC 5, fo. 387. See also BHC 5, fos. 330v, 394v; 6, fos. 42v, 100, 156v, 195v, 291, 353, 433; 7, fos. 40v, 61, 75v, 112v, 147, 219v, 248, 297v, 319, 334, 334v; 8, fos. 45, 94, 115, 233, 325.
[73] GL MS 12806/2, fo. 112; WAC WCB/2, fo. 137.
[74] BHC 7, fos. 37v, 45v, 257; SBHA Governors' Journals 1, fo. 153; 5, fo. 88v; 1, fo. 186v; 2, fo. 132. For some other blind beggars see BHC 6, fos. 61v, 105, 282v, 387v; 7, fo. 67.
[75] BHC 6, fos. 437, 202v; 9, fo. 637; 8, fo. 122v; 9, fo. 420; LMA Rep. 12, fo. 444v; BHC 6, fo. 279; 9, fo. 494.

split pickings. Three 'lewde unruly' women came to blows over their shares in 1618.[76]

We imagine beggars in rags, leaning on crutches, hollow-eyed, crying children in tow. This was also a stereotype when artists drew abject beggars.[77] Many beggars fitted this picture, down on their luck, lives and clothes in tatters. They were not hard to spot, plodding along streets. But begging was also a craft with narrative skills and tones of its own. Londoners expected beggars to be pitiful and feeble. Smart beggars dressed down to fit the figure, hoping to catch citizens' eyes or ears with verbal and visual urging, using their bodies as resources, hobbling on one leg, holding out twisted arms, rubbing sores, empty sleeves dangling where an arm once hung, spinning stories in croaky tones that spoke suffering. Rags helped; tears too. Tatty rags were beggars' trademarks, signifying suffering. Sad looks spoke sorrow. There was an art to the right tone. Some heart-tugging pleas helped waverers in two minds to reach for purses. But not too much and not loudly. Insistence could backfire, and it was better not to try too hard for only pennies. A softer lower tone with shades of suffering opened purses. It was also a smart move to think ahead and give thanks as there was a good chance that people would walk back the same way again. A 'God bless you' as a coin fell into a stretched palm made both sides feel good about themselves. Flattery was fine, but it was clever not to overdo it. Begging and sugar-coated speech did not go together too well, somehow. But a joke lifted someone's spirits with cash to spare, although tomfoolery could get awkwardly out of hand. There were fine lines between importuning and intimidation or chitchat and cheek.

Not all of this supplicant drama was real, needless to say. Much of it was street theatre in rags. Not all beggars had to swallow their pride to go cap in hand, however. Some sharp-witted ones knew how to cash in on crowds, falling back on street lore or plain common sense. They crowded around coaches they found standing still in streets or 'hung' on others trying to push through traffic at a snail's pace, often in groups for stiffer intimidation. William Hartley was 'taken begging at a coach door with a great cudgell in his hand'. Others overstepped the mark by pulling people from coaches. The 'incestuous beggar' and 'comon follower of coaches', Thomas Oliver, pulled a 'gentlewoman out of a coache'. Meredith Merrick was stopped in the nick of time in 1627, 'ready to pull gentlemen out of coaches'. Phillipa Nelson aimed high in 1610, clinging to 'the privie counsells coachs' and hanging on the 'lord chancellors coachside'. One 'comon begger' 'followed' the lord chief justice up and down streets and

---

[76] BHC 6, fo. 427; 3, fos. 190v, 349; 6, fos. 269v, 48.
[77] Cf. Hitchcock, *Down and Out in Eighteenth-Century London*, chaps 3 and 5.

would not leave him alone but hassled and haraunged him. Wiliam Charnley also set his sights on plum pickings; he was jailed for 'begging and disturbing the Spanish Ambassadour in his house with contynuall lowd begging'.[78]

Churches also peppered beggars' maps. A parish gave a shilling 'to a poore man' with 'a lycence to begg' just before the begging ban; another gave '3 beggers' in 'great need' sixpence five decades later.[79] Beggars lined up as church congregations streamed out, forming churchyard choruses, jostling for coins. The Sunday crush was so great in one parish that it spent sixteenpence to hire 'one in Bowyers Hall to kepe beggers out of ye church'. John Bull walked through St Sepulchre's streets in 1596 to catch vagrants before they got to church. St Peter Cornhill vestry plotted a 'course' to stop 'beggars standing at church doors on Sundays'. The 'disorderly carriage' of beggars in St Martin-in-the-Fields was too much to bear in 1659, and beadles were posted to stop the 'poore' pressing on officers as they stood 'collecting' at the church doors. Not even guards helped in the long run, however, and constables were told to 'take care' to set 'stricte warde' on Sunday in the church and nearby lanes in 1663 to ward off beggars, who were 'great enemyes to our impotent poor'.[80] Well-off people gave money to the poor at their funerals, drawing needy flocks scrambling for coins. St Botolph Aldgate's churchyard door was 'broken' by a stampede of 'poore people' at one funeral in 1609.[81] Beggars also buzzed around St Paul's. A warder got sixpence weekly to round up beggars 'dayle frequenting and annoying' the cathedral in 1559, and the number of 'bedells of beggars' was topped up shortly after, 'specyally to loke' to 'Powles roges'. But the cathedral remained a beggar-puller. The 'lower church' was a 'daily receptacle for roges and beggers', vergers said in 1598, and 'religious mynded people' could not stand this affront any longer. In spite of everything, they were seething a few years later when 'obstinate' paupers still 'daily begg[ed] in the church'.[82]

---

[78] BHC 8, fo. 248; 5, fo. 84; 7, fo. 45v; 5, fo. 419v; 6, fo. 115v; LMA MJ/SBR/6, fo. 318. See also BHC 5, fo. 434v; 6, fos. 219v, 230v, 257, 257v, 265, 265v, 279v, 292v, 414v, 426v; 7, fo. 98.

[79] GL MSS 2088/1, 1597–8; 1124/1, fo. 167v. See also GL MS 4241/1, fo. 482.

[80] GL MSS 1432/3, fo. 45; 4072/1, fo. 287; 12806/1, fo. 18v; 12806/3, fo. 28; WAC F2003, fos. 213, 309, 314. See also GL MSS 4251/1, fos. 34, 189, 211; 1124/1, fo. 167v; 1176/1, 1656; 878/1, fo. 334v; 577/1, fo. 76; 9235/2, fo. 199v; 12806/3, fo. 28; WAC F2002, fo. 225; BHC 3, fo. 364; 8, fo. 122v; LMA Reps. 18, fo. 13v; 40, fo. 71v; Jour. 32, fos. 127v, 192v.

[81] GL MS 9235/2, fo. 199v.

[82] GL MS 12806/1, fo. 22v; LMA Rep. 16, fo. 450; GL MS 25175, fos. 41, 47. See also LMA Rep. 17, fo. 392v; GL MSS 12806/1, fo. 26; 25175, fo. 3; SBHA Governors' Journal 2, fo. 194v; BHC 5, fo. 133v; 6, fos. 61v, 153, 291v; 7, fos. 3v, 47v, 57v, 62, 312; 8, fo. 220; BRHA BHC 4, fos. 49, 79v, 239, 360, 394.

118    Change

Better beggars learned that one good way to squeeze sympathy was to beg with children by their side, looking lost and lonely. This beggars' drama depicted dire domestic scenes of mothers clinging to children. Some families did end up falling back on charity: a husband and wife begged with their three children in 1622.[83] But there was also a trade in children. Millicent Parker was whipped 'for borrowing a child to beg' in 1598. Anne Wray landed in trouble 'for borrowing two children' to 'make herselfe the better color to beg'. Anne Palmer ended up spending a few days behind bars in 1632 for 'taking anothers child to be a pretence to color her begging'. Anne Greene stole 'yonge children from theire friends to beg with them'. One 'little boy' was 'stollen from Woolwich by a beggar' he said in 1622. Anne Kenny tried to cash in after a begging spree in 1628, 'offering to sell a childe which was stollen'. Some people supplied stolen children to beggars. Margaret Jones was 'accused to be a carrier [of children] to beggers' in 1627.[84] Other pressure was put on children to dress up in beggars' rags to bump up takings. Vagrant Elizabeth Greene 'intised a litell [five-year-old] child' to beg. 'Vyle and nawghtie' heavy-drinking Joan Hippie 'starved her owne childe' to get more money and pity in 1562.[85]

Young beggars also got tips from older hands. Katherine Vaughan said that two goodwives living in Long Lane 'taught her to fayne herself dom' to beg better. 'Lewd' Joan Phillips coached fourteen-year-old Edward Pewter 'to fayne himselfe to be bothe deffe and dombe' and took his takings, 'some daye xxid, some daye is iiiid, some daye xiid'. Elizabeth Brolvin was 'a comon noryssher and brynger up of girls in begyng'. Mabel Copinger was whipped 'for bringing up of a chyld to go a beggyng'. Older bullies forced children to go out on the streets to beg for them. The 'comon taker up of children', John Hore, made at least three court appearances for forced begging in 1575, once before aldermen who sentenced him to stand on the Cheapside pillory for three long hours. He 'dothe comonlie take uppe children' to 'begge for him', Bridewell's bench heard, and one of his boys was in such poor shape that he was sent to a hospital straight away 'to be healed', and of the 'litle gerles' he kept 'to begg', the board heard, one had 'a sore head' and rotting feet, and another 'made as though hir backe was broken'. He had only one boy in his stable late in 1575 – Alice Jones had recently run from him 'when she grew to

---

[83] BHC 6, fo. 287.
[84] BRHA BHC 4, fo. 1v; BHC 7, fos. 22, 282v; 3, fo. 368v; 6, fo. 283v; 7, fos. 70, 52v. See also BHC 1, fos. 113v, 120; 2, fo. 253v; 3, fos. 243, 395v, 434; 5, fo. 59v; 6, fos. 268, 337v, 349, 432; 7, fo. 223; 8, fo. 35; GL MSS 12806/1, fo. 28; 12806/2, fo. 123; LMA Rep. 21, fo. 427v.
[85] BRHA BHC 4, fo. 14v; BHC 1, fo. 191v; 7, fo. 127.

bignes' – and he sent him 'daily abegging', getting 'some day 12d, some day 16d, and some day 20d'. Two men were stopped in the street in 1649 'carrying a lame woman on a hand barrowe and begginge with her'.[86] Other 'notorious counterfeit crank' beggars put on acts, faking lost limbs, disabilities, and sickness to get sympathy. One 'counterfeyted lamenes in his armes to color his begginge'; another 'counterfeited the losse' of an arm. Rice Bush heard about a beggar who conned people into believing that 'his heels grew to his buttockes'. Patrick Russell 'counterfeited himself to be lame', leaning heavily on a crutch, although he soon got muscle back in his legs when it was taken away from him.[87] Other bogus beggers and 'counterfeit criples' faked 'falling sicknesse' or 'the palsey'. George Croft 'counterfeited the fallyng sycknes' in 1559, but suddenly seemed 'upright and perfit whole' when a whip was dangled in front of him. Still others put on acts of suffering, bleating meekly like lambs in one case. 'Lewd' Monger Stephenson made 'much noyse in the night to mete people to compassion and pittie', but once he got money he skipped off to the nearest alehouse to smoke tobacco and drink beer. Bartholomew Symons's trick to coax hand-outs was to 'lie under a stall and counterfeite as yf he were givinge up the gost', when in fact aldermen heard that he was 'verie lustie and full of vilanie'. While 'idyll' William Hodges made 'mocke falsehood and dysymulacon' on doorsteps and stalls, 'crying out piteously as though he had byn verye sycke', although he was 'in good helthe' all the time.[88]

The body was a box of tricks. 'Comon beggar' Margaret Darby 'made herselfe a greate belly with clothes' to get pity. Elizabeth Leman stuffed 'a bundle of raggs' under her top 'to make shew of her great bely'.[89] Beggars appeared helpless, shivering naked in bitter weather. John Howell 'had good apparel' but 'went naked to deceyve people and gett money'. John Haines went 'naked begging' in chilly wintry weather, selling his clothes, 'thinking thereby to be pityed'.[90] Chattering teeth in winter's deep freeze was like the patter of insanity to warmly clothed citizens counting their blessings. Some beggars faked insanity, like Edgar dressing down as Tom-a-Bedlam in *King Lear*. People begged with false claims to

---

[86] BHC 2, fo. 29; 1, fos. 89, 52, 130v-1; 9, fo. 410. For Hore see BHC 2, fos. 93, 123v; LMA Rep. 18, fo. 378v. See also BRHA BHC 4, fo. 467.

[87] BRHA BHC 4, fo. 296v; BHC 5, fos. 378, 388v; 1, fo. 211v; Bush, *Poor Man's Friend*, p. 10. See also LMA Rep. 12, fos. 78, 171; BHC 2 fo. 56v; 5, fos. 120v, 126, 158v; 6, fos. 240, 270, 434v; 9, fos. 38, 240, 436, 458, 645.

[88] BHC 1, fo. 26; LMA Reps. 16, fo. 153; 11, fo. 394v; 20, fo. 152v; BHC 6, fo. 34v; 5, fo. 432v; LMA Rep. 13, fo. 16v; BHC 1, fo. 80v; 2, fos. 72, 113; 6, fo. 346v.

[89] BHC 7, fos. 49v, 95v. See also BHC 1, fos. 35v, 41v; 6, fo. 405v; 7, fo. 254; GL MSS 5090/2, fo. 291; 4071/2, fos. 199, 199v, 229; 5018/1, fo. 22v; 4180/2, fo. 81v.

[90] BHC 3, fo. 359; 7, fo. 97.

120  Change

Bethlem licenses. Shrewsbury-born Nicholas Richardson begged for five months with a 'false licence fayning to have bene in Bedlem'. Roguish Edward Griffin said there were 'xx persons in Kent' who 'beg for Bedlem' with fake licenses in 1579, naming three, including Humphrey Griffen, who 'stuttereth' to melt hearts. John Dawson cadged coins with a fake 'priviledge to begge with a bell' from Highgate hospital in 1629.[91] Other beggars acted dumb, pointing to pretend useless mouths, making noises that formed no words. The career beggar William Worrall, with fifteen years of begging behind him, was 'well whipped' in 1561 for 'faining' to be 'borne dumb' so that 'people should have more pitie on him'; he slipped in word of 'dangers' he had faced 'in the princes affaires' in a last-ditch effort to avoid the whip.[92]

Other beggars made up pathos-packed stories or faked identities that pitched courts into identity puzzles that were trouble to unravel. George Fisher begged 'under color' of a phony story of 'losse by fire' at Coleraine in 1624. 'Marvelously dissemblyng' Sybil Steyre (alias Okeley) cooked up a story that her husband had been 'borned for religion at Canterburye in Queene Maryes tyme', losing a house and two acres of good land, and she was now left alone with no money and eight children to care for.[93] Other actor beggars took the parts of more sympathetic characters to win over kind spirits. 'Comon begger' Elizabeth Barker got 'much money' in 1622 posing as a hard-up minister's wife with no home to go to. William Thompson and Daniel Venables went begging 'in manner of maymed soldiers' in 1602, spinning stories that they had just got back from the wars with wounds and other losses.[94] All this scripted story-telling, sharp-witted trickery, teaching cheating skills, role-playing, and handy begging lore, is more than enough evidence to suggest that there was some team-work and shared skills in begging worlds. Two boy beggars – Alexander Folfare and James Denny – lived cheaply with one James in Westminster in Spring 1575, who 'alwaies [had] halfe of their gaynes'; their best pay-day to date, they said, was 'iis viiid at one tyme on the backsyde of Powles'. Some beggars worked in groups of three and four or more, and others were also rounded-up in largish packs, nine in a single case from 1630.[95]

[91] BHC 7, fos. 50, 107v; LMA Rep. 15, fo. 154v; BHC 2, fo. 35v; 3, fos. 354v, 384; 7, fo. 129.
[92] BHC 1, fo. 183. See also BHC 1, fo. 89; 2, fo. 257; 6, fo. 205; 9, fo. 497.
[93] BHC 6, fo. 377v; 1, fo. 66.
[94] BHC 6, fo. 269v; BRHA BHC 4, fo. 338v. See also LMA MJ/SBR/4, fo. 598; BHC 7, fo. 309; 8, fo. 96; 9, fo. 620; LMA Rep. 21, fo. 53v; TNA SP12/261/70.
[95] BHC 2, fo. 83; 7, fo. 189v.

Some of the best windows on these begging ties come from production lines in fake licences. Beggars flooded London with false papers: 'false passes', 'false letters of testimoniall to begge', 'counterfete lycenses', and 'counterfeit breifes'. Forgers stockpiled out-of-date licences, and it was simple to scratch one clean and fill in new names and dates. John Pickering's fake licence was made by a Long Lane scrivenor from an old one he got from a Northumberland man, who told him to see a gardener in the same lane 'to help him to one that would make a copy and amend the date if near expired'. John Steele got a 'false licence to begg' from a Shoreditch forger who charged 2/6d, writing a typical hard-luck story of hardship after a house burned down. A more standard fee was six or sevenpence. Seals could cost more. A 'comon' beggar 'for Bedlam', Edward Griffin, spent fourteenpence for a seal from a Chelmsford pauper. A 'free' goldsmith, Christopher Bowsell, used university and 'my lord mayors' seals on false permits. Scrivenors with workshops in Foster Lane, Long Lane, King Street, and Turnmill Street had sidelines in forgery, together with scholars like John Tankerd – 'a scholler of Oxforde' – who pumped out licences for London-bound beggars. 'Scholars' Thomas Evans and John Williamson stood in shame on the pillory in 1576 'for forgeing a licence to begge'. Alehouse-keepers with hands in crime-rings complemented country 'counterfeiters' from Norfolk, Somerset, Wiltshire, and elsewhere, who were always ready to make up a licence on the spot and a story of some tragedy striking out of the blue.[96]

Not all beggars knew that there was a script to follow to get a beggars' mint. Anne Taylor did not have the beggars' knack: 'if she asked [for] money and have anything given her then she is good', magistrates heard in 1628, but 'if not shee throweth durte into their faces'. Katherine Bowen 'abused' people who did 'not give her anything when she asketh', throwing dirt and screaming insults. Mary Wray 'threw stones at a silkmans wives head in Cheapside' when she 'would not give her what she would have'.[97] The grotesque contrast was too much for some, sinking to rock bottom as well-dressed strangers with a square meal inside them brushed

---

[96] GL MS 12806/2, fo. 150v; BRHA BHC 4, fo. 355; BHC 2, fo. 35v; 3, fo. 418v; 1, fos. 185v-6; 3, fo. 82. Griffin's forger may have been William Hodgson of Waltham Cross who was prosecuted not long after Griffin for being 'a comon maker of false licenses for beggers': BHC 3, fo. 368v. See also BHC 1, fo. 189; 3, fos. 9v, 174, 379v; 6, fos. 228, 341v; 9, fo. 235; LMA MJ/SBR/2, fo. 431; MJ/SBR/3, fo. 94; MJ/SBR/5, fo. 327; MJ/SR/ 515/64, 66; Reps. 12, fo. 450v; 15, fo. 482; 16, fo. 462; 17, fo. 338; 19, fo. 349; 21, fo. 447; BHC 1, fo. 79; 2, fo. 83; 3, fos. 167v, 231v, 236v, 291, 297, 364, 436; 5, fos. 53, 59v, 83; 6, fos. 283, 338v, 341v; BRHA BHC 4, fo. 357v.

[97] BHC 7, fos. 80, 45v, 41.

past. Brought down to earth with a bitter bump, they let curses fly like bullets. 'If she prevaile not to get what she would', Bridewell's board heard about 'vagrant beggar' Margaret Palmer, she rattled off 'imprecacons and cursings against people that refuse to give unto her'. Loutish Thomas Dowell was picked up in 1605 'for outragious begginge in the streets': 'yf people would not releve him when he cryed out and called for relief', he 'wold curse and sware' and one time bashed a constable 'in the face with one of his patens'. 'Comon beggar' Richard Camel 'will take no warninge', a marshal said in 1621, 'but if people give him not he curseth' them. James Fea 'cursed' a Bridewell governor who walked past him seven years later.[98] Other bitter beggars 'railed' or 'roared', like 'notable' Margaret Purvis, who carried 'a childe up and downe the streets to beg [magistrates heard] and unlesse she may have what she tell shee rayleth and offereth to leave her childe' on the street. Officers tipped off Bridewell's bench that 'vagrant beggar' Margaret Robinson 'rayleth' each time 'people will not give her food'. Thomas Derborne, who was called 'an ordinary beggar' in 1639, lost his temper at the drop of a hat, and was constantly caught 'railinge on men that will give him nothing'.[99] A group of five 'daungerous' 'frenchmen' took matters into their own hands in 1642 by storming 'into mens houses', and they will 'not bee denyed', witnesses said, 'to the terror of people'. 'Stubborne' Thomas Barnfield said with menace that 'he would have reliefe where he begged whether they would or noe'.[100]

Violence was the next step after threats or if words could not soothe a beggar's bile. It was not a good idea to box someone's ears on streets, but some beggars could not control their temper. Common Council complained in 1628 that 'slack' officers took no action against 'sturdy beggars' armed with truncheons who 'used insolent behaviour' if any 'refused to give them almes'. 'Dangerous' Andrew Abraham begged with two knives in 1643. 'A crewe' of 'valiant beggars' were caught standing 'in the highway with weapons'.[101] Hard-done-by beggars thumped people who turned a blind eye. Philip Edwards was locked up in 1657 for 'strikeing John Rawlins because hee would not give him a penny'. William Gittoe also begged 'outragiouslye' in 1578, lunging at a 'gent' who walked past him hurriedly. Other beggars squared up to officers. Nicholas Briggs stood his ground at Bridewell in 1618, shouting that 'he will begg in London whosoever say nay'. Vagrant Margaret Hopkins bragged that

---

[98] Ibid, fo. 45v; BHC 6, fo. 233v; 7, fo. 60. See also BHC 6, fo. 105v; 8, fo. 220; 9, fo. 626.
[99] BHC 6, fos. 167, 191; 8, fo. 245v. See also BHC 3, fo. 305v; 6, fo. 286; 7, fo. 57v.
[100] BHC 8, fo. 410; 7, fo. 260.
[101] LMA Jour. 34, fo. 248v; BHC 9, fo. 46; 1, fos. 115, 118.

'she will begge whatsoever any officer shall saye to the contrary'.[102] Many gritty beggars turned their backs on authority. Katherine Wilson 'reviled' 'officers and others in a beastly and unseemely manner' when they tried to stop her begging in 1632, and rounded on one officer, threatening 'to make his gutts fall about his heeles'. 'A Spitle beggar' – Thomas Havering – 'broke a beadles head with his bell' in 1608 when he stopped him on the street. Aptly named Martha Justice told the mayor to his face that she 'wished' his 'neck broken' in 1620 when, not for the first time, she was caught begging along streets.[103] Women were in the thick of these street struggles, jumping into spats with the law as gamely as men, matching them word for word, making stronger perceptions of female offending that would soon become embedded in policies and prosecutions.

### Street sellers

Sellers were another street species whose numbers grew with the city. Unlike beggars they were mostly women, or at least this was the thinking in the Guildhall, one more reason why 'loose' walking became a female crime for the most part. Men 'cried' work and wares also. Christopher Bullyvant was caught 'goinge upp and downe the towne with hoops and cryinge work' in 1607. Coopers and tinkers were warned not to 'cry and carry' work. Thomas Skinner was caught 'cryinge for tinckers and bellowesmenders worke'.[104] Like women, men walked all over the city selling and touting. Vagrant Oliver Ridley was said to be 'a goer about with aquavita and girthes'. An Irish boy attracted attention 'cryeing matches' in 1639. John Andrews was heard 'cryinge frying panns, kettles, bellowes, and trayes' a little later. Other men were caught 'cryeing' pots, glasses, marrow bones, 'buying and crying hot iron' and 'old yron', and selling apples on the bridge.[105] Others were stopped on streets hawking and haggling, women as well as men. Hucksters are not named all that often, but more of them were men, like Ezekiel Gilman who troubled Cornhill ward in 1633 with his trade in woollen yarn. The same could be said

---

[102] BHC 9, fo. 626; 3, fo. 296v; 2, fo. 102v; 6, fos. 33, 64; See also BHC 5, fo. 54.
[103] BHC 7, fo. 276v; 5, fo. 261; 6, fo. 196. See also BHC 6, fos. 34, 105, 227v, 311v; 8, fo. 294.
[104] BHC 5, fos. 197, 182v; 8, fo. 181; LMA CQSF 90/6. See also LMA CQSF 90/4, 90/18, 125/18.
[105] BHC 5, fo. 397; 8, fo. 251; LMA MJ/SR/806/102. See also BHC 5, fo. 338v; 6, fo. 128; 7, fo. 387v; LMA MJ/SR/517/58, 61; MJ/SBR/1, fos. 364, 589, 596; WJ/SR/NS/29/45; Rep. 33, fo. 66v.

about petty chapmen.[106] 'Pore raggatherers' also toured the city looking for second-hand tatty clothing and bedding to sell on for a pittance or to use themselves after a clean-up. Again, both men and women rummaged for rags. Clare Cawsey was warned in 1605 to stop rooting round for rags and shreds and other 'like things which shalbe gathered or racked'. William Frank was given a lease at Bridewell in 1604 to gather 'raggs, shredes, and cuttinges of paper and other things'.[107]

The gender of sellers was the crux of the matter. Women with things to sell walked up and down main or 'menes' streets, as Cornhill ward complained when presenting 'women sellers of yarne' in 1585 who 'hinder[ed] passage in the menes high strete'.[108] There was nothing new about female street-sellers, but signs are that people thought there were more of them. 'Nowe of late years there be two sorts of people' growing each day who 'greatlie hinder ordinarie' shopkeepers, Common Council said in 1602: one was the old thorn 'forryners', the second was 'for the most parte women' selling on streets. They fused with 'big bellied' vagrants, abandoned children, and more feminized crime labels in a perception of urban women as too big for their boots.[109] 'Fishwife' was not far behind a Turnmill Street address in implying immorality. Fishwives were characterized as sour-minded, sour-mouthed, and flirtatious. Lupton listed heavy drinking 'fisher-women' in his London 'characters', who trawled for trade on 'Turnebull Street' if they did not sell enough fish, and 'when they hath done their faire', he said, 'they meet in mirth, singing, dancing', and 'use scolding'.[110] No other street-sellers came close to their questionable reputations. Four middle-aged women kept 'wenches to carrye fishe about the city' and forestall markets in 1601. Joanne Proctor and Jane Wilkinson (alias Griffin) ran a small-scale trade with three 'wenches and mayds to crye fishe'. Dames hired servants to walk all day long with fish. 'Idle' 'very yong' Alice Taylor was found 'sellinge fishe at Billingsgate' in 1628; 'her dame' was in prison for forestalling markets. Another Alice Taylor was arrested five years later for selling fish on streets to 'enhance' prices 'to the hinderance of the

---

[106] LMA WJ/SR/NS/38/23; MJ/SBR/3, fo. 46; GL MS 4069/1, fo. 205; LMA WJ/SR/NS/34/29. See also BRHA BHC 4, fos. 312, 313; LMA MJ/SBR/2, fo. 106; WJ/SR/NS/32/65, 32/70, 32/93, 29/60; Reps. 14, fo. 125v; 31(2), fo. 386.
[107] BHC 5, fo. 18; BRHA BHC 4, fo. 459v. See also BHC 5, fo. 106v; BRHA BHC 4, fos. 241, 400.
[108] GL MS 4069/1, fo. 40.
[109] LMA Jour. 27, fo. 205. See also LMA Rep. 15, fo. 239v; Jour. 27, fo. 205.
[110] Donald Lupton, *London and the Country Carbonadoed and Quartered Into Severall Characters*, 1632, The English Experience, 879 (Amsterdam and Norwood, NJ, 1977), pp. 92–3.

poore'; her dame was 'an applewoman'.[111] The few fishwives who gave addresses lived in cheap lodgings in poor quarters. Isabel Wetton sold fish by day and 'lay' at Goodwife Tuck's house in Golding Lane, paying sixpence each week for her room and board.[112]

Fishwives joined with others to conjure images in magistrates' minds of streets no longer paved with gold, but jam packed with women, reshaping street life.[113] Evidence for this was in the glossary of names jotted down in laws, parish papers, police casebooks and guidelines, or by trade lobbies: a legion of brushwenches, basketwomen, applewomen, tripe-wives, fishwives, coffeewomen, herbwomen, oysterwenches and yarnwives who hogged the City books around 1600. And their visibility made them more dangerous, turning 'menes' streets into mobile markets run by women and wenches, like vagrant Katherine Lee who 'crieth buttons about the streets', or the women standing selling yarn and blocking traffic in the merchant haunt of Cornhill. Catherine Lloyd was taken to task 'for selling from house to house after the maner of a hagler' in 1634. Elyn Kyne appeared in court in 1560 for 'gadding about the streets' selling brushes 'by way of hawkyng'.[114] Some sellers were picked up in pairs or larger groups. The mayor sent five 'fishewomen' for a short spell in Bridewell in 1607.[115] They bunched at busy crossroads, well-situated 'corners', or other plum selling points. 'Fishewomen' grouped on a 'corner neare Smythfield' and were 'warned not to stand there any more' in 1628. Women 'standinge in Fleete Streete with apples and fruite' got short shrift at quarter sessions in 1617. 'Herbe and fruit sellers' caused pile-ups on already clogged Cheapside in 1657, and fruitsellers were moved on from St Bartholomew's gates more than once.[116] Other popular selling spots included churches. Nor was this always against the law, so long as

---

[111] BRHA BHC 4, fos. 240, 242; BHC 7, fos. 77v, 344v. See also LMA Rep. 14, fos. 119, 127v; BHC 7, fo. 239; 8, fo. 243; BRHA BHC 4, fos. 11, 119v, 267, 267v, 366v, 378, 389, 418v.

[112] BRHA BHC 4, fo. 80v. See also BHC 5, fo. 163.

[113] Cf. Gowing, '"The freedom of the streets"', in Griffiths and Jenner, eds., *Londinopolis*, pp. 130–51, who has a few paragraphs on street selling.

[114] BHC 6, fo. 280v; GL MS 4069/1, fo. 51v; LMA WJ/SR/NS/40/91; BHC 1, fo. 113v. See also GL MSS 1432/4, 1666–7; 4069/1, fos. 42, 44, 49, 50, 60, 62v, 65, 67, 85; BHC 5, fo. 164; LMA WJ/SR/NS/35/57; Rep. 14, fo. 125v; CQSF 122/1, 122/8, 122/10; BRHA BHC 4, fo. 403v.

[115] BHC 5, fo. 163v.

[116] BHC 7, fo. 78v; LMA CQSF 76/36; Jour. 41, fos. 161–1v; SBHA Governors' Journals 2, fo. 60v; 5, fo. 61v. Anne Laurence was licensed at the 'pleasure of the governors to sell apples at Smithfield gates' in 1657, so long as she took up 'noe more roome than 9 foot in length from the gate on the east side towards the shopp of Mr Knight' and '2 foot in breadth', and always paid her quarterly rent on time (SBHA Governors' Journal 5, fo. 184).

sellers had the parish's permission to sit or stand somewhere safe and left no mess behind them at the end of the day. St Botolph-without-Aldgate warned 'fruiterers, herbwomen, or any others' selling anything under the church wall, not to dump 'their forms, baskets, boards, or anything else' in the churchyard or porch. 'Yerbwifes' had a prime spot on 'grounde underneathe the churchyarde of Gracechurche corner'. Shoppers could buy 'household stuff' at 'the churchyard wall' in St Margaret New Fish Street, meat tongues at St Clement Eastcheap's church door, and various wares along the churchyard wall in St Margaret's Westminster. An applewoman petitioned vestrymen in St Dunstan-in-the-West for a place to 'stand and sell fruit at the churchyard wall against Clifford Inn Lane' in 1647.[117]

Street-sellers mingled with merchants, knowing that these monied men were pillars of buying and selling, and that good openings would always be near at hand on their trading days. Cornhill has left us the only wardmote book with long-running entries before 1640, but even if others survived today none would say as much about street-selling because London's merchant hive, the Royal Exchange, stood in this ward and its edges were lush pastures for sellers. Some sneaked onto the Exchange floor to sell some staples of the merchants' daily diet: news. Goodwives Gaines, Geary, White, and Crouch were ordered to stay away from the Exchange in 1660, where they 'dayly cryed' and sold 'printed papers, books, and pamfletts'. Gaines and Geary were back on the Exchange's grounds two years later with their book packs, and Geary clearly took ward warnings lightly as her name again appears on its list of pests in 1663.[118] Hawkers, regrators, and forestallers also appear on earlier lists. Hawkers floated around the Exchange selling linen and poultry in 1599. 'Great abuses and annoyances' blocked the south gate – 'especially at Exchange time' – in 1621 when 'ratcatchers' and 'sellers of birds, dogs, plants, [and] trees' would not budge from their prime positions near this commercial citadel.[119] Fruitsellers got more flak from authorities than any other hawker. 'Certen women maidens' sitting selling 'orreneges, apples, and other things att the Exchange gate' in 1590 were roundly slammed for 'cursinge and swearinge' to the 'great grief' of people living nearby and others passing by.[120]

Ward orders flowed over the next decade to plug crude mouths and clear walkways, with little success, it seems. 'Maidens' would not leave

---

[117] GL MS 9236/1, fo. 43; LMA Rep. 13ii, fo. 471; GL MSS 568, fo. 160; 1175/1, fo. 18v; 978/1, fos. 19, 21; WAC E2413, fo. 18v; GL MS 3016/1, fos. 301, 337, 433.
[118] GL MS 4069/2, fos. 281, 287v, 290.
[119] GL MS 4069/1, fos. 85, 157, 49, 67, 83, 160, 170v.   [120] Ibid., fo. 51v.

the Exchange, despite warnings from the wardmote, and 'women' were still sitting at the gates selling oranges, lemons, mangy poultry, 'and other things' all the way through the 1590s. 'Burders' also ended up on the ward's wrong side for selling birds at the front gate in 1596 and afterwards. Yarnwomen also grabbed plum spots on the 'Exchange side'.[121] 1610 was a low point when many 'idle' fruitsellers flocked to the Exchange and the busy street outside was said to be 'obstructed with baskets', so that coaches and carts had to steer around the sitting sellers, who stayed long into the night, 'intice[ing] apprentices and servants to wast ther moneyes unduly', and talking and brawling so late and loud that people living nearby could not sleep. A 'generall meetinge' in the 'Queste house' tried to push through a ban on women selling fruit 'before th'Exchange' in the next year when a widow and two 'goodwives' were singled out for selling fruit at the south gate. Cases continued regardless, and the wardmote complained that 'sellers of fruit' still 'pestered the street' in 1613. John Powell's wife (her first name was not noted) was taken to task for selling fruit and getting in the way of 'gentry merchants' two years in a row, and warned by the ward that next time there would be no more half-measures. Thirteen years later, the ward was still wearily noting 'great abuses' by fruit- and bird-sellers sitting in front of the Exchange, 'disturbing' merchants and others going in and out. Nothing could stop this booming street trade, not least because it had the double boon of cheaper goods for shoppers and bread money for some of London's poorest people.[122]

Steps to limit street selling accelerated towards 1600. Aldermen leaned towards putting caps on who could sell and where from the start and not on stamping out selling altogether. But they could not let sellers swamp streets or markets. The steadier course was to keep a lid on selling by fixing it in time, size, and space, giving herbwives, for example, particular patches in markets with set days and times to stand and sell from a single spot. Aldermen drew up 'orders for reformacon' of market 'disorders' in 1588. 'Hearbewyves' were told not to sell 'hearbes or flowers' on sabbath or 'comon markett dayes savynge onlye in the markett tymes', and only then in Newgate Market. Hucksters were given a patch in Cheap Market. Timetables limited trade to market hours.[123] Butter-sellers stood in one place in Leadenhall Market in 1615: 'close to the bench on the east side of Leadenhall gate downe to the gate of Mr Bells house'. 'Hearbewomen' lining pavements in Cheapside Market were told to stay put in Broad

---

[121] Ibid., fos. 21v, 26v, 29, 31, 33, 38, 40, 42, 48v, 51v, 54, 56, 60, 62v, 67, 71v, 83, 116, 159, 182, 196, 218, 219.
[122] Ibid., fos. 118v, 127, 125v, 128v, 135, 218, 219.   [123] LMA Rep. 21, fos. 542–4.

128  Change

Street in 1631.[124] If rules had been followed, markets would have been trim tableaus of segregated strips, like fields after enclosure. The image is a tidy one, but the reality was usually messy. 'Greate abuses' spoiled market protocol in 1636 when 'regrators, hucksters, [and] haglers' crowded into 'the moste parte' of markets, blocking 'country people' who had little chance to sell fresh produce, hidden behind 'hucksters', fanning out in all directions. Officers were asked to see that markets were 'cleered' no later than 2 p.m. 'Otemele wives' stayed late in Cornhill market in 1597. Herbwomen also caused trouble over the west walls in Westminster Market in 1614, barging in on the best 'standings', not giving any ground to 'country people', who went home with half-full carts. Not even the threat of six hours sitting in shame in the stocks could make them move. They were back one year later, shutting out 'country' traders from their 'rooms', jostling, shouting, laughing.[125]

Magistrates let women sell on the move with limits on licences to tell 'irregulars' apart. The same 1588 order that put herbwives and hucksters in their place, made fishwives 'goe up and downe' the 'common streets' to 'crye' fish, cockles, mussels, and oysters. Hugh Alley and his team got a mayor's warrant to 'move' fishwives from 'comon sittings in Cheapside' in 1601, and got a reward from grateful fishmongers.[126] There were moves to curb fish-selling from the 1550s on, with laws, counts, prunings, badging drives, and age and character controls (fishwives should have had husbands and spotless characters). Magistrates requested higher standards of policing and caps on the numbers of fishwives in wards: 120 were 'tollerated' in the whole city in 1590, in 'proporcons' ranging from two in five wards (including Bridge Within) to thirty-six in the largest ward, Farringdon Without. Laws were read out loud at busy docks and quays and other 'apte places', to make sure that the message got round.[127]

---

[124] LMA Reps. 32, fos. 58v-9; 45, fo. 529v.
[125] LMA Jours. 37, fo. 142; 40, fo. 98; GL MS 4069/1, fo. 71v; WAC WCB/2, fos. 57, 123.
[126] LMA Rep. 21, fos. 542–4; GL MS 5770/1, fo. 289. For Hugh Alley see Ian Archer, Caroline Barron, and Vanessa Harding, eds., *Hugh Alley's Caveat: the Markets of London in 1598*, London Topographical Society, 137 (1988). For more on marketing food in sixteenth- and seventeenth-century London see F. J. Fisher, 'The development of the London food market, 1560–1640', *Economic History Review*, 5 (1934–5), 46–64; Sara Pennell, 'The material culture of food in early modern England, c.1650–1750', unpublished DPhil thesis, University of Oxford (1997).
[127] LMA Reps. 14, fos. 460, 469, 469v, 473v; 15, fos. 94v, 239v, 500, 503v; 21, fos. 53, 544; 22, fos. 164v, 172, 176v, 345; 16, fo. 333v; Letterbook V, fo. 161. Only three fishwives were 'tollerated' in Billingsgate, home of their main market. Fourteen were 'allowed' over the river in Bridge Without. The upper ceiling had been two in 1568, and only one fishwife was licensed and badged to sell fish in sprawling Farringdon Without and in Southwark. See also GL MS 4069/1, fos. 9, 61v; LMA CLRO/05/389/001, 1624, 1634.

Aldermen knew that their fishwife 'problem' had been growing for some time. 'A very great number' of women flock to Billingsgate to 'engrosse' fish fresh from boats, they grumbled in 1561, and 'carrye' their ill gotten fish to 'sell to theire moste advauntage'. And now, they said, getting angrier with each clause, women are 'too proud' to serve as servants without wage hikes. Magistrates wanted ceilings on numbers with 'especiall' badges for authorized sellers.[128] But the big bump in numbers of 'tollerated' fishwives, from under fifty in 1568 to 120 two decades later (with badges 'especyallye devysed'), reveals a resigned acceptance that fishwives would never fade away, as street trading was so bound up now in London's economy and household budgeting.

1584 was a crunch year in the anti-fishwife drive, as aldermen protested about 'a great number of lewd and evyll disposed women', who committed 'horryble abuses' night and day to God's 'great offence', breaking laws 'under pretence of buyinge fyshe and frute at Billinsgate' to sell 'abroade'. Bridewell officials were told to question all fishwives and to devise a plan to cut their 'superfluous number'. Bridewell's board was given more clout later on, when 'thappointment, nominacon, and government' of fishwives was put in their hands. Marriage was a safety net, and aldermen asked governors to make sure that fishwives were no younger than thirty, from stable households with 'good name and fame', who sold 'sweete' fish 'wholesome for mans bodye', and not near landing places or markets but 'abroad according to old custome', wearing metal badges.[129] Their number was topped up to 160 in 1596 – another token of their vital value – and Bridewell minted metal badges displaying the City's arms along with the year and 'two lres for the name' of each seller. But there was no magic wand to stamp out the 'fishwife problem', not even a clutch of Common Council Acts. The waterbailiff was asked to put fish forestallers in prison in 1605. Two years later 'fower yeomen of the watersyde' gave advice to a City committee set up to 'devyse some good course' to stop 'fishewomen' hanging round Billingsgate dockside. A little later another working group was asked to think one more time about the 'fitt' 'nomber of fyshewyves' for the city and each ward. 1607 was another busy year in the fishwife saga. The working group set up a large-scale census to give shape and size to the 'fishwife problem'. Wards were told to round up 'women or maids' selling fish on streets to count

---

[128] LMA Letterbook T, fo. 32. Aldermen added their usual refrain that the 'fishwife problem' had mushroomed in 'late yeres' in 1561. They were asked to order each ward beadle to 'call before hym the fyshwyves' in the ward to find out if 'they have their badges or not', and to bar them from selling on the streets 'unles they have ther badge': LMA Rep. 17, fo. 39v. See also LMA Reps. 19, fo. 153; 20, fo. 322v.
[129] LMA Rep. 21, fos. 73, 115.

them and give a breakdown of their status – 'maids, wives or widdows' – 'their behaviors, qualities, yeares, condicons', how long they had lived there, and, lastly, if they were married to freemen or foreigners.[130]

1612 was another crunch year. For a long time now magistrates had fretted over fish-sellers 'manie' 'abuses'. Yet another Common Council Act was pieced together, not unlike earlier ones, with clauses limiting fish-selling to wives and widows of gleaming 'honest name' (aged thirty or older) married to citizens or 'auncient dwellers' with first-rate credentials; fishwives shelled out sixpence for a tin badge from Bridewell to pin on in 'open shewe or sight'; their names were logged in a special book kept up-to-date by Bridewell clerks; and there was the standard rundown of selling spots and times, although it was more exact this time. The Act was read out to ward and parish officers shortly after, who were told to bring women who 'cried fishe' to Bridewell to check that their names appeared on lists of licensed sellers with tin badges 'to weare for the manifestation of their allowance'.[131] But again this hard work led to disappointment for aldermen and a couldn't-care-less bravura for fishwives. The recycling of clauses from one Act to the next suggests that nothing altered for the good, from the alderman's perspective that is. It was old wine in new bottles, and not long after the 1612 Act the number of fishwives without badges was on the rise. The message did not sink in, and not many 'irregular' fishwives turned over new leaves. They cause 'exceeding greate harm to this citty', common councillors with experience of sellers in their home wards complained in 1615, as had their predecessors over two generations.[132] And a decade or so later we start to see home-grown 'auncient poore fishewifes' lobbying aldermen to take action against 'forraine fishwifes' who 'buy upp all the fishe' at Billingsgate before anyone else could get a look-in, running selling rings that 'imploy[ed] aboute two hundred wenches'. They sound like a guild with long tradition on its side, moaning about 'forrainers' with no craft training muscling in on their trade from suburban hideaways. Licensed fishwives had apparently come of age with a little clout and a finely tuned sense of how to get something done in the Guildhall. Three years later it was the turn of 'poore milke-women', their blood boiling because 'yong maydes and wenches' bought up milk bright and early and sold it on streets for a nice windfall.[133]

---

[130] LMA Reps. 23, fo. 514v; 27, fo. 10; 28, fos 124v, 159; Jour. 27, fo. 205. See also LMA Reps. 21, fo. 148; 22, fo. 52v; 30, fos 175, 310v.
[131] LMA Jour. 28, fos. 300–301v, 303v. This 1612 Act banned selling on any 'vessell' on the Thames 'or at Billinsgate', or 'any standing place between [the] Thames and Little Eastcheap or between the river and street from Little Eastcheap' towards 'the end of Tower Streete or betweene the river and Tower Streete or betweene St Magnus Corner and the Tower'.
[132] LMA Jour. 29, fo. 187.  [133] LMA Reps. 42, fo. 214v; 45, fos. 296v-7.

The anti-street-selling drive was coloured by gender from the first. In 1618 aldermen asked Billingsgate beadles to set up a cucking stool on the dockside to give wet warnings to 'wenches, yonge girles, [and] hearbewyves' who dashed there first thing in the morning to snap up fish.[134] The anti-street-selling rant mainly targeted rambling women. A law to stop 'fruiterers, milkewoman [and] hearbwomen' selling in streets on the sabbath at dusk and after was sent round to wards in 1638 and again two years later. This did not stop Anne Holloway from 'carrying mackerill' one Sunday in 1639. Sunday selling had long been the focus of laws, like one in 1561 to ban 'hearbwyfes' peddling herbs and flowers on sacred Sundays. A damp squib this one, as another with similar wording was passed two decades later. And three decades after, one parish spent fourpence for a copy of the latest 'precept concerninge hearbwyfes and milkmaydes for prophaning the saboth dayes'. But the brisk Sunday trade in flowers, food, and drink in this eager shopping city was routine by now for people who worked all week long. They could pick up food for the week or material for a suit in one of Sunday's street bazaars. Mary Stevens was warned for 'crying silke in the streets' on one sabbath day in 1629.[135]

Street selling had never been imagined as an economic problem alone. It was also about larger London. Many sellers were rounded-up as vagrants, like Faith Bird, 'a vagrant wench', who was 'taken in the streets gathering raggs' in 1632, or three 'fyshwyves' servants who were in trouble in 1609 after 'goeing up and downe with fysh'.[136] Trouble followed 'gadders' like shadows. Numbers of 'loose' beggars will shoot up, magistrates said in 1615, unless we crack down on fish-, onion-, and saltsellers. There was no time to lose, but the same lament had rung loud four years earlier and aldermen would hear it again and again in years to come.[137] They were not spinning yarns. Street-sellers never lacked opportunities to pinch purses or anything else exposed on crowded streets. Ellen Chambers stole things 'under color of butter selling' in 1627. Rag gatherers had bad reputations for spying out opportunities as they went from door to door. A pair of 'comon vagrants' were picked up in Newgate Market for pilfering 'under color of gathering rags'. Sellers stole,

---

[134] LMA Rep. 34, fo. 10.
[135] LMA Jours. 38, fos. 172–2v; 39, fo. 50v; BHC 8, fo. 242v; LMA Reps. 14, fo. 511; 20, fo. 348v; GL MS 6836, fo. 80v; BHC 7, fo. 133. See also LMA Rep. 35, fo. 240v; BHC 6, fo. 421; 9, fo. 342. For shopping see Linda Levy Peck, *Consuming Splendor: Society and Culture in Seventeenth-Century England* (Cambridge, 2005), chap.1.
[136] BHC 7, fo. 286; 5, fo. 351. See also BHC 5, fo. 128; 6, fos. 231, 254v, 298, 399; 7, fo. 303; 8, fos. 121, 145; BRHA BHC 4, fos. 141v, 383, 382.
[137] LMA Jours. 29, fo. 187; 28, fo. 250; BHC 5, fo. 251v; 7, fo. 109; GL MS 4069/1, fo. 83.

132     Change

magistrates said, and also received stolen goods, nudging others to steal for them. Six guilds clubbed together in 1586 to ask aldermen to take action against 'lewdlye disposed' 'forreynors', who under cover of selling 'olde yron, leadd, tynne, brasse, mayle, harneys, swordes, daggers, hearre, [and] woole', go round houses coaxing servants to steal from their masters, lurking in the wings like 'comon receivers' as their cronies went to work. Only freemen should 'goe hawkinge', the six guilds said.[138] Sellers also conned customers into buying fake things. There were scores of double-dealers like Elizabeth White, who for the last year, Bridewell's court heard in 1602, had gone up and down fobbing off phony 'latten' rings, scooping 'xiid, xvid and xviiid' for each imitation. There was also a brisk trade in fake calico with petty chapmen in the driving seat. One 'vagrant fellowe' – Thomas Horley – was caught selling 'callico to defraud men as a petie chapman' in 1604. Christopher William also ended up in Bridewell in the same year after cozening people who gave him money for poor quality calico on good faith.[139]

'Lewd' epithets soon flowed when magistrates imagined women running freely through streets. Agnes Volmer was caught 'ronnyng about with brusshes' in 1560. 'She seemeth also to be a naughty pack', magistrates added, and sure enough she was caught two years later, still selling brushes. The Billingsgate 'comon harlott', Joanne Horsey, was brought back to Bridewell 'for her evell lyfe' in 1575 after she was caught 'whorlinge mens fishe'. 'Lewd' fishwives were also packed off to hospitals to get rid of 'foule diseases'. Others were caught in compromising situations in the middle of sex, after sex, or about to start sex. A drunk apple-wife was 'taken' with a man under a stall at night in 1627, but suspicion was the only thing laid at her door.[140] Sellers sold long into the night, often only to make more money, but raising suspicions all the same. Margaret Sadler was 'taken' 'sucpiciouslie' in 1635, and said 'she sate late to sell her apples'. A constable said that 'iii vagrant wenches' caught out late in 1603 'loyter and nightwalke' under 'cullor of beinge fishwives'. Susan Slugger, another Southwark 'fishwoman', was 'taken' 'lying under a stall' near midnight in 1628.[141] Enough sellers liked drinking late to bring alcohol into the equation between selling and sex. 'Oysterwoman' Alice Price was

---

[138] BHC 6, fo. 441; 5, fo. 278v; LMA Rep. 21, fo. 274v. See also BHC 6, fos. 40, 141; 7, fo. 35; 9, fo. 3.
[139] BRHA BHC 4, fos. 321v, 441v, 444. See also Ibid., fo. 447.
[140] BHC 1, fos. 81v, 202; 2, fo. 117; BRHA BHC 4, fo. 230; BHC 7, fos. 44, 44v. See also BHC 1, fo. 81v; 2, fos. 163–3v; 5, fo. 101v; 7, fos. 151, 329; BRHA BHC 4, fos. 345, 449.
[141] BHC 8, fo. 63; BRHA BHC 4, fo. 416; BHC 7, fo. 97. See also BHC 5, fos. 101v, 108v; 6, fos. 321v, 350, 392; 8, fo. 46v; BRHA BHC 4, fo. 88.

known in her neighbourhood as a 'notorious drunkard', 'comon whore', husband-basher, and for staying out until midnight with 'broome men'. Violence followed heavy drinking like clockwork, and more than enough street-sellers lashed out to make this stereotype stick. Two 'scoulding' 'fishewomen' were 'taken' with a third woman scuffling on a street in 1628, 'pulling one another by the haire of the head', shrieking blasphemies, and roughing up 'the lord maiors officers'. Simon Bell, who 'hawkes ducks', officers said in 1606, 'slaundered' a Bridewell governor in court, scoffing that he 'compacted with a queane'.[142]

Like vagrants, street-sellers' mixed morals and dirty bodies came under a stronger lens when plague hit hard. Streets were darker and deadlier in time of plague, but they were also surprisingly full on 'dread' days.[143] John Elliott had a plan in 1636 to curb the 'unlimited number of people of mean condition' from alleys and other 'dangerous places for infection', who poured onto streets to sell fruit. His tone was little different from a panicky petition to privy councillors a decade earlier that pointed with horror to the 'infinite number of idle and lazy people' streaming onto streets to sell fruit 'from places of most danger [for spreading plague] as alleys and private corners'. Cornhill ward was warned to stop 'vagrant weoman' thought to come from 'visited' houses who sold apples there in 1581.[144] Sticky summer heat spoiled food in another link between high temperatures and plague peaks. Common councillors thought that rancid oysters left too long in the sun were 'very daungerous' in 'this tyme of the heate of somer and increase of infection'.[145] Likewise, cast-off clothes caked in stains and crawling with lice were deadlier in plague seasons. William Mitchell was told 'not to crie' 'ould doubletts' during the 'infeccon' in 1606. 'Cryers and carryers' of bedding and old clothes were told to stay home when plague hit again two years later. Fear raced when 'idle and loyteringe women and boyes' 'dailie' picked up 'raggs, marrow bones, [and] old shoes' that were 'caste out of mens howses' as plague roared through London in 1603. People watched with horror as rubbish pickers washed rags and bones in 'comon sewers' and hung them 'openlie to drye'. 'Poor people' slipped out of 'visited' houses with rags to sell in 1636, trailing 'soil carts to the common quay and other moorings', 'infecting' the air each step of the way.[146]

---

[142] BRHA BHC 4, fo. 147v; BHC 7, fo. 93; 5, fo. 116; 7, fo. 93; BRHA BHC 4, fo. 312.
[143] *London College of Physicians. Certain Necessary Directions, As Well for Cure of the Plague as for Preventing the Infection* (1636), unpag.
[144] TNA PC2/46, fos. 323–4; SP16/5/119; GL MS 4069/1, fo. 33.
[145] LMA Jour. 27, fo. 76v.
[146] BHC 5, fo. 125v; LMA Jours. 27, fo. 275v; 26, fo. 98v; TNA SP16/33/31, 42, 61.

But in or out of plague, people felt that the streets were getting more 'dangerous'. Londoners gauged growth by vagrants, street-sellers, thieves, or anyone else who lived rough on streets. People with no home almost always ended up somewhere suspicious: in some back-alley slum, squeezed into dim clammy rooms, huddled in 'secret corners', living without rules, magistrates immediately supposed. Independent lifestyles caused aldermen to lose sleep, like the spinster Marjery Carter who 'lived at her own hands out of service' selling apples in Westminster in 1615.[147] City leaders were caught by surprise when waves of women arrived after 1600. The city was so big that authority was out-of-joint where it mattered most in 'obscure' hideaways. Women were caught skulking outside service over and over again. Yorkshire-born Joanne Wetherall admitted that she had lived in London 'out of service' for three months in 1600, lately 'layeing' at Mrs Wynter's house near Ludgate for almost two months. Other 'light', 'loose', and 'lewd' women scraped by without submitting to laws for anywhere stretching from a few days to a year or more. Their independent lifestyles were linked to inevitable immorality. A constable said that the loose 'lodger' Anne Styring who lived 'out of service' was 'an idle and drunken woman'. Jane Langton, who lived cheaply in St Andrew Holborn 'without meanes and out of service', was 'suspected to be a woman of evil life'.[148] Magistrates could not fail to notice that many women without a service boarded with older spinsters and widows, much like a female guild, it seemed.

---

[147] WAC WCB/2, fo. 140.
[148] BRHA BHC 4, fo. 159; WAC WCB/2, fo. 137; LMA MJ/SR/806/56. See also BRHA BHC 4, fos. 243, 299, 348v, 349, 356, 362, 370; WAC WCB/1, fos. 56, 83, 123, 157, 158, 174, 247; WCB/2, fo. 29; LMA MJ/SR/517/65, 806/138; and my 'Masterless young people in Norwich, 1560–1645', in Paul Griffiths, Adam Fox, and Steve Hindle, eds., *The Experience of Authority in Early Modern England* (Basingstoke, 1996), pp. 146–86. Men were also brought to courts for being 'out of service'. See, for example, WAC WCB/1, fos. 115, 262, 272; WCB/2, fos. 97, 99, 134.

*Part II*

Crime

# 4  Crime: worlds

### Borders

Nabokov once wrote that '[t]he underworld was a world apart'.[1] Like him, men with power and pens four centuries ago thought of criminal communities around them as something apart, somewhere else, an otherness that we might well call an 'ideological cut' today.[2] This writing constructed alien criminal worlds on paper. Before 1660 surviving writing comes from only one side of the criminal divide: from magistrates, moralists, or hack-authors whose main aim was to say over and over again that 'criminals' were deviant, different, and distant. They believed that they wrote self-evident truths. There are no first-hand stories of criminal lives with a protagonist's care for feeling, though some scholars think that Moll Cutpurse has left us a *Life* in her own words.[3] No lower-class thief or vagrant put her/his life down on paper, although administrators and authors did it for them all the time. Clerks scribbled as suspects told stories. They often wrote quickly and might have missed what was being said, or perhaps they chose and chopped words later on when suspects were no longer in the room. Thousands of such depositions survive today, and we think of them as narratives framed by both their tellers and transcribers.[4] Other texts were published for the book trade. A continental rogue literature stretched east from Spain all the way across the German lands to Poland, and forked south to Italy. Countries added their own spin, but shared stock stories, characters, and themes, and some landmark texts were translated word-for-word across

---

[1] Vladimir Nabokov, *Lolita* (Harmondsworth, 1995), p. 170.
[2] Colin Sumner, *The Sociology of Deviance: an Obituary* (Buckingham, 1994), p. 299.
[3] *Oxford Dictionary of National Biography*, n.v. Moll Cutpurse.
[4] Laura Gowing, *Domestic Dangers: Women, Words, and Sex in Early Modern London* (Oxford, 1996), chap. 7; Ulinka Rublack, *The Crimes of Women in Early Modern Germany* (Oxford, 1999), esp. chap. 2; Malcolm Gaskill, 'Reporting murder: fiction in the archives in early modern England', *Social History*, 23 (1998), 1–30.

borders.[5] England, too, had its own rogue literature with numerous borrowings, but also with uniquely native cultural and environmental touches. This English *liber vagatorum* got off the ground with Robert Copeland's *High-way to the Spital-house* (1536). But the first real milestone came a little while later on with Thomas Harman's *Caveat for Common Cursetors, Vulgarly Called Vagabonds* (1566–7), a book that was copied for a long time afterwards. Harman and others described a finely graded underworld with ranks, roles, rules, and 'lewd lousy language'.[6] This underworld was a mirror-image of 'respectable' routine and work where authority counted. Like Harman, latter-day scholars tell tales of two cities: a settled one of clean-living citizens and a squalid 'parallel culture' of roughneck thieves and vagrants. 'A world apart' for sure; Robert Greene called rogues 'outcasts'. One scholar believes that they were 'no longer ordinary men of their times', but an alien troop marked out by their mobility, promiscuity, and vocabulary. Rogue writing was about an entire ethos, an 'anti-order' no less.[7] Other cheap print told life-stories from cradle to gallows with blow-by-blow

---

[5] Robert Jutte, *Poverty and Deviance in Early Modern Europe* (Cambridge, 1994), chap. 10; Peter Burke, 'Perceiving a counter-culture', in Burke, *The Historical Anthropology of Early Modern Italy: Essays on Perception and Communication* (Cambridge, 1987), pp. 63–75; Peter N. Dunn, *Spanish Picaresque Fiction: a New Literary History* (Ithaca, NY, 1993).

[6] Burke, 'Perceiving a counter-culture', p. 66. Quoting Thomas Harman, *A Caveat for Common Cursitors, Vulgarly Called Vagabonds*, 1566, reprinted in Arthur Kinney, ed., *Rogues, Vagabonds, and Sturdy Beggars: a New Gallery of Tudor and Early Stuart Rogue Literature* (Amherst, MA, 1990), p. 18.

[7] Mary Elizabeth Perry, *Crime and Society in Early Modern Seville* (New England, 1980), p. 32; G. M. Spraggs, 'Rogues and vagabonds in English literature, 1552–1642', unpublished PhD thesis, University of Cambridge (1980), pp. 9, 93; Robert Greene, *A Notable Discovery of Cozenage*, 1591, reprinted in Kinney, ed., *Rogues, Vagabonds, and Sturdy Beggars*, p. 177. Mary Perry writes that Seville was two cities: 'the one belonging to the oligarchy' and the 'city of the underworld' (*Crime and Society in Early Modern Seville*, p. 12). Important work on underworlds includes Julie Coleman, *A History of Cant and Slang Dictionaries, Volume 1, 1567–1785* (Oxford, 2004); Paul Griffiths, 'Overlapping circles: imagining criminal communities in early modern London', in Alexandra Shepard and Phil Withington, eds., *Communities in Early Modern England* (Manchester, 2000), pp. 115–33; Griffiths, 'The structure of prostitution in Elizabethan London' *Continuity and Change*, 8 (1993), 39–63; Ian W. Archer, *The Pursuit of Stability: Social Relations in Elizabethan London* (1991), pp. 204–15; A. L. Beier, *Masterless Men: the Vagrancy Problem in England, 1560–1640* (1985), chap. 8; Beier, 'Anti-language or jargon? Canting in the English underworld in the sixteenth and seventeenth centuries', in Peter Burke and Roy Porter, eds., *Languages and Jargons: Contributions to a Social History of Language* (Cambridge, 1995), pp. 64–101; John L. McMullan, *The Canting Crew: London's Criminal Underworld, 1550–1750* (New Brunswick, NJ, 1984); Lawrence Manley, *Literature and Culture in Early Modern London* (Cambridge, 1995), pp. 341–55; Bryan Reynolds, *Becoming Criminal: Transversal Performance and Cultural Dissidence in Early Modern England* (Baltimore, MD, 2002); Linda Woodbridge, *Vagrancy, Homelessness, and English Renaissance Literature* (Urbana and Chicago, IL, 2001); Gamini Salgado, *The Elizabethan Underworld* (Stroud, 1977); Norman Berlin, *The Base-String: the Underworld in Elizabethan Drama* (1968).

accounts of how small crimes led to Tyburn's tree. A last gallows speech was the source for pamphlets that blended grisly details with the quotidian humdrum of getting by, to make sure that readers saw themselves in gallows victims. If all went well, doomed felons urged crowds to stay on the right side of the law. It was now too late for the speaker who, however, hoped to be up in Heaven in the next hour or so. Not long after the last breath was sucked from swinging felons, their life-story and its ideological moorings were distributed far and wide in affordable pamphlets.[8]

Putting criminals between book-covers controlled their narratives. Moral coaching was a driving force, along with money and markets, so there is spice from the first page on to keep readers in high spirits. Rogue writing shocked and amused all at once, like something that is mouth-watering but forbidden. The accepted view today is that they cannot be trusted. They were not a feast of facts, but a mishmash of dogma, fiction, and slapstick. Modern critics were not always such doubting Thomases. One called Harman 'a sociologist' whose work was 'in most particulars correct'. John McMullan – a real-life sociologist – fell into the same trap with his anecdotal account of streamlined criminal societies with a 'distinctive language' and 'formal division of criminal roles'. He quotes large chunks from cheap print as if it was a trouble-free guide, and he is not alone.[9] The wheel has turned full circle now. Woodbridge warns us that 'rogue literature' is 'inadmissible as historical evidence' and no window on 'the real world'. Authors were 'axe-grinders', she says, who wanted to wipe out the 'rowsey, ragged rabblement of [rogue] rakehells'. There are no signs outside their pages that rogues had pecking orders, job specializations, a 'cant' language of their own, or any wish to turn the world upside down. In a nutshell, Harman and the rest made it all up as they went along.[10]

---

[8] Andrea McKenzie, 'Making crime pay: motives, marketing strategies, and the printed literature of crime in England, 1660–1770', in Greg T. Smith, Allyson May, and Simon Devereaux, eds., *Criminal Justice in the Old World and New: Essays in Honour of J. M. Beattie* (Toronto, 1998), pp. 235–69; Mckenzie, *TyBurn's Martyrs: Execution in England 1665–1765* (2007), chaps. 2 and 5; Thomas Laquer, 'Crowds, carnivals and the state in English executions, 1604–1868', in A. L. Beier *et al.*, eds., *The First Modern Society* (Cambridge, 1989), pp. 305–55; J. A. Sharpe, '"Last dying speeches": religion, ideology, and public executions in seventeenth-century England', *Past and Present*, 107 (1985), 144–67.

[9] A. V. Judges, ed., *The Elizabethan Underworld*, 2nd edition (1965), p. 495; McMullan, *Canting Crew*, pp. 131, 132–3.

[10] Woodbridge, *Vagrancy, Homelessness, and English Renaissance Literature*, pp. 11, 40, 6–11. Also quoting Harman, *A Caveat for Common Cursitors*, p. 109. See also Linda Woodbridge, 'Imposters, monsters, and spies: what rogue literature can tell us about early modern subjectivity', *Early Modern Literary Studies*, 9 (2002), 1–11; Jodi Mikalachki, 'Women's networks and the female vagrant: a hard case', in Susan Frye and Karen Robertson, eds., *Maids and Mistresses, Cousins and Queens: Women's Alliances in Early Modern England* (Oxford, 1999), pp. 52–69; J. A. Sharpe, *Crime in Early Modern*

None of us now, I think, believe that London was crawling with 'bawdy baskets', 'troll hazard of traces', or 'priggers of prancers'.[11] We meet them in rogue writing but nowhere else, although there are enough authentic sounding contexts to make this genre credible for its first readers. After all, there were 'runagate' boys all over London ('Kintchin Co' in cant), nimble thieves who pinched things through windows with hooks ('hooker'), and beggars who claimed to be shipwrecked sailors or acted deaf and dumb to con money ('a fresh-water mariner'/'dummerer'). Colliers did sell customers short with three-quarter full sacks. Con artists did swindle country bumpkins with card tricks and loaded dice. And sneaky tinkers did steal cutlery when people turned their backs. This is all to say that rogue writing is surely evidence for us, so long as we handle it carefully with back-up from other sources. Harman slipped in a passage about Nicholas Blount (alias Jennings), a 'counterfeit crank' beggar who was the talk of the town for a time in 1566. Senses of place also seem spot on at times. Thieves did mingle with 'worthy citizens' at 'Pauls' and The Exchange.[12] Cant words and other crime-titles in rogue-books, like nip, picker, rogue, or egyptian, crop up enough times in courtbooks to earn the title street talk. Nor do we have to look long for traces of theft and prostitution rackets, and there were also some largish groups of vagrants on the road.

But rogue works also created sharp 'ideological cuts' that split London's massive mess into tidy polarities like citizen/criminal or seedy/sound. Societies are imagined along boundaries like these that signify difference and unease. Foucault calls them 'confused, massive or transient polarities' that locate 'presences and absences' to define belonging and borders.[13] The underworld was one such 'cut', making 'criminals'

---

*England, 1550–1750*, 2nd edition (Harlow, 1999), pp. 144–5. See also the variety of opinions in the essays collected in Craig Dionne and Steve Mentz eds., *Rogues and Early Modern English Culture* (Ann Arbor, MI, 2004).

[11] All names/titles of rogues are taken from John Awdeley, *The Fraternity of Vagabonds*, 1561, reprinted in Kinney ed., *Rogues, Vagabonds, and Sturdy Beggars*, pp. 91, 93, 98; and Harman, *Caveat for Common Cursitors*, pp. 124, 137.

[12] Awdeley, *Fraternity of Vagabonds*, pp. 94, 95; Harman, *Caveat for Common Cursitors*, pp. 121, 128, 132, 133, 152–3; Greene, *Notable Discovery of Cozenage*, pp. 167, 182–4. There is more on Harman and Jennings/Blunt in A. L. Beier, 'New historicism, historical context, and the literature of roguery: the case of Thomas Harman reopened', in Dionne and Mentz, eds., *Rogues and Early Modern English Culture*, pp. 98–119; and Patricia Fumerton, *Unsettled: the Culture of Mobility and the Working Poor in Early Modern England* (Chicago, IL, 2006), pp. 40–3.

[13] Michel Foucault, *Discipline and Punish: the Birth of the Prison* (Harmondsworth, 1977), p. 143. See also Mary Douglas, *Purity and Danger: an Analysis of the Concepts of Pollution and Taboo* (1966), p. 114; Bronislaw Geremek, *The Margins of Society in Late Medieval Paris*, trans. Jean Birrell (Cambridge, 1987), p. 214; David Sibley, *Geographies of Exclusion: Society and Difference in the West* (1995), p. 183; Iris Marion Young, *Justice and the Politics of Difference* (Princeton, NJ, 1990), pp. 50–60, 170.

appear different.[14] There is comfort in putting them somewhere else, far away from citizens who toed the line all the time. But margins also create tensions and threats of troubling transgressions. Mary Douglas writes that there is stormy 'energy' around 'margins'. 'All margins are dangerous', she writes.[15] They are nearly always blurry, not the clean 'cuts' that their creators dearly hoped for. Nevertheless, magistrates did imagine separate lives for vagrants and thieves, not quite an 'underworld' perhaps, but something fairly specific nonetheless. Courtbooks refer to the 'vagrant', 'pilfering', or 'loose life'. There were people who lived by theft or scrounging hand-outs. People could live and look like criminals. Some offenders were said to appear 'like' loiterers, vagrants, thieves, or whores.[16]

Governors felt calmer if people caught in their net had real reasons to be in the city. Shifty people landed in court for 'not havinge any certyne or knowne trade of life', nor a 'good accompt of howe they lawfullie live', nor 'lawfull cause of theire repair or abode'. Nicholas Pulman landed in treble trouble in 1603: 'it appeareth that he is a nipper', the Bridewell court concluded, and a 'comon converser with cutpurses' who 'can geve no account of his life or of anie maintenance wherewith he should be kepte in any honest sorte'. Typical was Marie Downes who was locked up in 1608 'for leadinge a vagrant loose lyfe' without 'excuse'.[17] Neither outcast 'earn[ed] their bread with the sweat of their brows'. They slinked from one day to the next, 'skulking' without work. Richard Winter was 'accused to be a fellow that lives by shifting' in 1639, with nowhere to live. London is 'greatly pestered with idle and dissolute persons' who beg and steal to get by, the Crown moaned in 1631, and all 'so addicted to that lawless and intollerable kind of life that they will in no sort betake themselves to any course of honest labour'.[18] Work was a sure sign of falling in line. Courtbooks are packed with slackers like the 'comon rogue' William Bett, who would 'fale to no worke'; John Stephenson, who

---

[14] Sibley, *Geographies of Exclusion*, p. 183; Lydia Morris, *Dangerous Classes: the Underclass and Social Citizenship* (1994), p. 157; Ruth Mazo Karras, *Common Women: Prostitution and Sexuality in Medieval England* (New York and Oxford, 1996), chap. 5; Geremek, *Margins of Society*, chaps 1 and 9; Florike Egmond, *Underworlds: Organized Crime in the Netherlands, 1650–1800* (Oxford, 1993), chap. 1; Victor Bailey, 'The fabrication of deviance: "dangerous classes" and "criminal classes" in Victorian England', in Robert Malcolmson and John Rule, eds., *Protest and Survival: the Historical Experience: Essays for E. P. Thompson* (1993), pp. 221–56.
[15] Douglas, *Purity and Danger*, pp. 114, 121.
[16] BHC 1, fos. 81, 180, 182; 5, fos. 282v, 385.
[17] LMA Jour. 25, fo. 124v; Rep. 15, fo. 404; BRHA BHC 4, fos. 407v-9, 379; BHC 5, fo. 282v. See also LMA MJ/SR/804/71, 804/78; Rep. 23, fo. 552v.
[18] APC 1630–1, p. 260; BHC 8, fo. 262. See also BHC 3, fos. 98, 136v; 5, fo. 294v.

despite being 'a very stronge fellowe and whole in limbes' would 'fall to no labor'; and Nicholas Plocket, 'a man of no occupacon nor merchant nor merchants servant', who had been in London for five years in 1572 doing nothing.[19] People with nothing to do could only be up to no good. A sound life was a settled life in service or work with somewhere to call home. But people poured in and out of the city all day long, scrambling for work, moving from one house or job to the next. One parish gave an 'outlandish man' 1/6d in 1633 because he was 'sometime of good accompt' and sometimes not.[20] Some people could not be pinned down.

The most basic cut was the one that divided citizens from the ragbag unfree with no rights or roots in the city. Lawrence Johnson made up a Whitechapel address when he was stopped by Fleet Street watch in 1635, 'but [he is] in no service', the court found to his cost, nor 'anie house-keeper, [and] therefore is thought to be a vagrant'. Two men grabbed in a raid on a brothel in 1606 'were found to be masterles men and noe freemen' and were told to leave London at once.[21] The householder was the linchpin of society. He – it is always he – crops up in many by-laws. He was the cream of the community – 'able', 'honest', 'discreet', and 'substanciall' – paid rates on time, took office when his turn came round, moved through the ranks of guilds at the right speed, and stuck to sound religion.[22] Citizenship was a character reference, good enough to tip court cases. Hoping to get judges on his side, 'a householder of staid condicon and one of the liverie of his companie' poured scorn on his Star Chamber opponent, a 'sleight fellow of little or noe credit'. Another expected respect for being 'an ancient citizen' with a long track record of doing civic duties. I have never missed a subsidy payment in over thirty years, Maurice Petre said at the start of his Star Chamber bill of complaint in 1618, so that no one could doubt that he was a trusty Londoner. It doubly hurt Francis Derman – a St Bartholomew's governor – to be called 'a base attorney and threepenny fellowe' by someone much lower down the subsidy ladder. Subsidy men scored points in court through their status and economic muscle. Some suspects, like Roger Wade, claimed to be 'subsidie men', but were quickly trapped by their lies. One man who came to Bridewell 'to be bayle' for his friend was caught out when he could not say 'what he was ceased at the last subsedie'.[23]

---

[19] BHC 2, fos. 109, 206v; LMA Rep. 17, fo. 255v. See also BHC 2, fo. 173.
[20] GL MS 4457/2, fo. 316.   [21] BHC 8, fo. 44; 5, fo. 82.
[22] A. M. Dingle, 'The role of the householder in early Stuart London', unpublished MPhil thesis, University of London (1975); Archer, *Pursuit of Stability*, pp. 61–4, 206–8, 215–19.
[23] TNA STAC8 121/6; 187/1; 238/4; 126/10; 212/3; 233/15; LMA MJ/SBR/1, fos. 329, 352.

Crime: worlds 143

Unlike rootless criminals, citizens were 'ordinarie tradesmen' with a 'certaine place'. They were always victims. It was 'the good and best sorte of people' who were warned to watch out for thieves. Some priests sneaking up 'Prests Alley' after dark were 'more lyke theeves than true men'.[24] It was critical to keep this distinction rock solid for civic culture and confidence, even when citizens appeared in court for every crime under the sun. Magistrates hoped that these would be short-lived lapses with luck, although high numbers of citizen-criminals must have felt like an awful own goal at a time when civic 'fame' was tainted by vagrant floods. For this reason alone the criminal/citizen contrast was put across more forcefully, with some success. Citizenship was beefed up constantly as the fear of losing London became real.[25] It was for the good, magistrates felt, that people did not like to be lumped together with 'criminals'. Crime was a character smear, like any bad press. It was something to read or talk about, something that others did, not clean citizens. Some hit back with legal cases if they were called thief, rogue, or whore. They stood to lose credit in all senses of the word if this mud stuck. It was bad enough to rub shoulders with criminal riff-raff, as if touch alone contaminated. A clothworker told Star Chamber of his trauma when 'in most disgraceful manner' he was thrust 'into the dock with Newgate prisoners on trial for their lives'.[26]

At the opposite point of the compass to the 'best' was the 'beast'. One 'comon vagabond' was called 'an unruly idle beast' who brushed aside 'honest orders'. Katherine Watson sneered in a 'beastly and unseemely manner' when she was caught begging, telling one officer that she would make his 'guttes fall about his heeles'. Matthew Crossdall collected a hatful of labels in 1646: 'idle, lewd, uncivill', 'impudent', and last but not least, 'beastly'. Sara Guy was spotted 'fowlye and beastelye' pissing in a conduit in 1592. While women who left 'the frutes of their bodies' on steps and stalls were 'more unnatural and unkinde then brute beasts'.[27] The point, needless to say, was to distance such acts from decent people who rarely put a foot wrong. Roguish Richard Landes was called 'monstrous' in 1578, as was Austen Richard who 'vylely' beat her husband's apprentice. Heavy drinking Griffin Lloyd hit his wife 'inhumane[ly] and monstrous[ly]' one night in 1609. 'Monstrous' or 'barbarous' set 'brute'

---

[24] GL MS 1499; LMA Jours. 26, fos. 6–7; 25, fo. 305v; 27, fos. 240–0v.
[25] Cf. Craig Dionne's comments on the purposes of rogue writing in his 'Fashioning outlaws: the early modern rogue and urban culture', in Dionne and Mentz, eds., *Rogues and Early Modern English Culture*, pp. 33–61.
[26] TNA STAC8 233/15.
[27] BHC 1, fo. 11; 7, fo. 276v; 9, fo. 256; 8, fo. 151; GL MS 9064/16, fos. 59–9v; LMA Rep. 22, fos. 387–7v; Jours. 26, fo. 289; 29, fo. 177. See also LMA WJ/SR/NS/40/6.

bullies apart.[28] William Groom's gang were accused of 'inhumanlike accons', 'destructive to human society'. Masters and mistresses flogged their servants 'unchristianlyke' and 'unnaturallye', leaving some at death's door. Men could get away with being rough and tough, but mistresses lashed out 'contrarye to all womanly pytie' or 'honestye of womanhoode'.[29] Court- and street-talk is full of 'beastly' references. A Christ's Hospital beadle called Bridewell apprentices 'Bridewell doggs'. 'Beatle headed asses', someone else shouted at another time. A waterman called Elinor Gilnor 'frackle face toad' in 1633. While 'an ancient citizen', who was dumped in prison, alleged that officers called him 'Welsh dog', and taunted him all day long, bragging that 'they would make him glad to leap like an ape before they had done with him'.[30]

Unlike clean-living citizens, criminals did not stroll on streets or drop into shops to browse in 'honest' ways. They sneakily 'skulked', 'straggled', or 'shifted'. The vagrant pilferer, Thomas Tosser, was 'taken skulkinge att Anthomes Ordinary' in 1610. Three houses were pulled down in 1647 because 'dangerouse' people 'sculke[d]' in them and used them as hiding-places.[31] Nor could such people chat harmlessly or take time to walk innocently. They always 'lingered', 'loitered', and 'lurked', watching and waiting for opportunities to pounce. The Newgate ordinary – Henry Goodcole – wrote with concern about 'secret lurking malefactors'. Sickness and fevers also 'lurked'. Beggars 'lingered'. 'Pilferinge' people were caught 'loyteringe'. Religious rebels also 'loitered' in London, hoping to turn people away from 'true' religion. 'Romishe priestes and jesuites' 'lurked' in the city. 'Busy and ignorant schismatics' also 'lurked' there, meeting slyly in 'brewhouses and other mete [bad] places'.[32]

'Lurkinge' was sly, hinting at dangers unknown.[33] Ideas of crafty plotters trying to topple society were widespread. Neighbouring nations,

---

[28] BHC 3, fo. 350; LMA Reps. 23, fo. 31v; 29, fo. 5v; TNA SP12/164/80; LMA Jours. 20, fo. 341; 17, fo. 324v; 16, fo. 265v; TNA STAC8 200/13; 11/8; 21/7; 49/6; 71/17; 85/3; 152/22; 165/22; 187/1;190/13; 249/18.

[29] BHC 9, fo. 469; LMA Reps. 18, fo.325v; 20, fo. 315; 23, fo. 23.

[30] LMA MS 331–2–1; TNA STAC8 16/6; 187/1; LMA MJ/SBR/5, fo. 467. Cf. Mary E. Fissell, *Vernacular Bodies: the Politics of Reproduction in Early Modern England* (Oxford, 2004), pp. 80–2.

[31] BHC 5, fo. 419v; 9, fo. 320. See also BHC 7, fo. 95; 9, fo. 818.

[32] LMA Jour. 39, fo. 240; TNA SP16/193/69; BHC 5, fo. 241v; 6, fos. 27, 33v, 34, 34v, 36v, 37, 40, 431v; 7, fo. 335v; LMA Reps. 16, fo. 25; 20, fo. 412v; Letterbook S, fo. 65v; Jour. 26, fo. 297v; MJ/SBR/6, fo. 522; Nathaniel Hodges, *Loimolgia: Or, an Historical Account of the Plague in London in 1665*, 3rd edition (1721), p. 50.

[33] LMA Jour. 27, fo. 19. See also BHC 1, fo. 120; 5, fo. 335; 6, fo. 217v; 7, fo. 275v; 8, fo. 314v; 9, fo. 270; TNA SP16/455/102; GL MS 9064/19, fo. 35; LMA Jours. 18, fo. 139v; 27, fo. 29; 32, fo. 145v; 35, fos. 485–5v; 37, fo. 173; Reps. 20, fo. 320; 40, fos. 184v-5; LMA MJ/SBR/6, fo. 522.

traitors, and witches schemed round the clock. London, too, was fenced-in by traitorous suburbs, looking longingly at treasures over the walls.[34] The city was 'pestered and endangered' by 'stealth'. Thieves 'slipped' into shadows or 'creeped' into houses. They huddled 'in a crafty manner', plotting 'cunninglie'. Inmates also 'crept', and prisoners gave their guards the slip through 'conninge meanes'.[35] No trusty citizen would ever act like this. John Barker hung around shops 'slylie of purpose to steale', and paupers begged 'slyly' at church doors, guessing that people would be touched by suffering after good sermons. Almost all shady acts were described in similar terms. Libels were 'sly and subtle'. Brokers met 'slylie and underhand[edly]' to stop laws against their trade in 1622, drumming up support 'in subtill and secrett manner'.[36] Words like 'secret' turned people into ghostly 'creatures'. Small boys were put 'secretly' in houses to open doors for thieves after the last light was doused. 'Ydle vagabonds and valyant beggars' not living 'truely' lurked 'secreatly' in 'corners'. Bawds smuggled prostitutes 'secretly' into houses. Children were left 'secretly' on steps. Builders built 'secretly' after dark in 'obscure' nooks. Rumours travelled 'secretly'. Pockets were picked 'privily'. One author mentions 'private thieves'.[37]

Thieves were 'placed' in London but nowhere apparent. They 'dayly' trawled through London and disappeared after dark to 'lye' in 'secrett places' or 'obscure' crammed 'corners', where no one well brought up

---

[34] Carol Z. Wiener, 'The beleaguered isle: a study of Elizabethan and early Jacobean anti-catholicism', *Past and Present*, 51 (1971), 27–62; Ian W. Archer, 'Government in early modern London: the challenge of the suburbs', in Peter Clark and Raymond Gillespie, eds., *Two Capitals: London and Dublin, 1500–1840* (Oxford, 2001), pp. 133–47.

[35] LMA Jour. 24, fos. 225v, 263v; BHC 6, fo. 273; BRHA BHC 4, fo. 369v; LMA Remembrancia Book 8, fos. 59v-61; BHC 1, fo. 99v; LMA CQSF 118/interrog. Katherine Farr; Jour. 19, fo. 171; BHC 6, fo. 45; 8, fo. 28; BRHA BHC 4, fo. 407v. Star Chamber bills also said that people combined with 'craft': TNA STAC8 201/18; 200/13. See also TNA STAC8 311/9, people inventing debts through 'cunning devises'.

[36] BHC 5, fo. 411; LMA Rep. 40, fo. 71v; TNA STAC8 172/6; LMA Jour. 32, fos. 117–17v; GL MS 3018/1, fo. 99. See also LMA Rep. 18, fos. 404v-5; Paul Godwin, *Historie des Larrons, Or the History of Thieves. Written in French and Translated Out of the Original by Paul Godwin* (1638), pp. 42, 98, 113, 118, 195, 212; Anthony Fletcher, *Certaine Very Notable, Profitable, and Comfortable Similies* (1595), p. 84.

[37] BHC 7, fo. 291; LMA Jour. 17, fo. 42v; BHC 7, fo. 23; 9, fo. 345; LMA CQSF 129/16, 135/50; TNA SP16/485/110; 16/296/29; LMA WJ/SR/NS/32/47; MJ/SBR/5, fo. 79; Jours. 16, fo. 265v; 26, fo. 316v. See also BHC 7, fo. 71v; GL MS 6836, fo. 69v; LMA CQSF 104/19, 116/28, 129/16; Letterbook K, fo. 81v; Jours. 17, fo. 324v; 32, fo. 318; Rep. 20, fo. 503 ('private' groups of heretics); TNA SP16/485/111; GCL company minute book O3, fo. 697 (selling by candlelight in 'covert' ways); John Gee, *The Foot Out of the Snare; With a Detection of Sundry Late Practices and Impostures of the Priests and Jesuits in England* (1624), fo. T3a; *A Warning for House-Keepers, Or, A Discovery of All Sorts of Thieves and Robbers* (1676), p. 3; Phil Withington, *The Politics of Commonwealth: Citizens and Freemen in Early Modern England* (Cambridge, 2005), p. 201.

would spend one minute of time. Crooks also haggled for stolen goods in back street pubs.[38] Senses of place are loose; addresses rarely given. City rhetoric contained hazy images of dimly lit nooks with hundreds of hideaways. Vagrants 'lurked in corners'. 'Lewd' women met men in 'corners'; one 'lewd strumpet' 'played the whore with fellows in corners'. Foreign workers lived in 'obscure' crannies. Priests 'pried in bye-corners'. Unlawful printing presses pumped out pamphlets from 'obscure' or 'secret corners', and rumours started 'secretly' in far-flung 'corners'.[39] This secret seclusion was not for dishonest dealing alone. London's magistrates could also be 'crafty', fixing 'secrete and pryvye serches' to round up troublemakers 'in as secrete maner as may be'. Stealth was the key. Secrecy was a rule of thumb in civic administration.[40] Secrets were shields and a word along with 'privies' or 'privities' for genitalia and other things best left unseen. But vagrants and other bad apples were suspicious when 'secret', with reverse intentions to well-mannered citizens. There was otherness inside the walls and there were words for this at the time. Thieves 'nudged' citizens in markets, hoping to catch them off balance. They pried and peered into houses. Thomas Morgan was locked up for being 'a pryer into houses to pilfer'. Anne Williams also ended up behind bars for 'pryeinge where she may pilfer'.[41] Magistrates built boundaries repeatedly and insisted that the categories of citizen and criminal were poles apart in yet one more defence of civic identities as the value of London's 'freedom' slumped.

But did these 'ideological cuts' make a difference at the end of the day, or were they endlessly breached by citizens with not enough civic-mindedness to care? Why harp on about this desired distance unless there was little legroom to tell citizens apart from London's riff-raff? And from

---

[38] LMA Jour. 35, fo. 504; APC 1630–1, p. 260; BHC 9, fo. 850; TNA SP16/14/13. See also TNA STAC8 13/2; 311/9; LMA Jour. 35, fo. 411. Orders stated that pubs should not be allowed to open in 'corners' or anywhere else off the beaten track. See, for example, TNA SP16/282/12.

[39] LMA Jour. 35, fo. 261v; APC 1615–16, pp. 693–4; BHC 7, fo. 247v; Gee, *Foot Out of the Snare*, p. 73. See also LMA Jour. 17, fo. 42v; *The Execution of Justice in England and for Maintenance of Publique and Christian Peace* (1583), fo. Ciii; Robert Milles, *Abraham's Suite for Sodom: a Sermon Preached at Paules Crosse the 25th of August 1611* (1612), fo. E5r; John Lawrence, *A Golden Trumpet to Rowse up a Drowsie Magistrate: Or, a Patterne for a Governors Practise Drawne From Christs Comming to, Beholding of, and Weeping Over Hierusalem. As it was Sounded at Pauls Crosse the 11 of Aprill, 1624* (1624), p, 39; Gee, *Foot Out of the Snare*, p, 21; TNA SP16/5/119; HOL MP 21–10–1641; SCH company minute book C, fo. 266; TNA SP12/161/1; LMA Rep. 17, fo. 432v; TNA STAC8 187/1; 260/26; LMA Jour. 32, fo. 64v; APC 1615–16, pp. 483–4.

[40] Paul Griffiths, 'Secrecy and authority in late sixteenth- and seventeenth-century London', *Historical Journal*, 40 (1997), 925–51.

[41] BHC 6, fo. 28; 5, fo. 352. See also BHC 7, fo. 310.

the other side of the fence: can we dig deep in archives not rogue writing to find criminal cultures at this time? The next section wonders if people could make a living on the wrong side of the law. The one after looks at cases and words in archives to test the strength of thieving ties. We will also go back to crime maps and meet ringleaders and old hands at crime with skills. When all is said and done we are left with overlaps; the worlds of citizens and criminals crossed all the time.

### Living lewdly

It almost goes without saying that most theft was small scale. People stole 'small trifles' to get by on half-full stomachs.[42] Most migrants lived from one day to the next, not planning, just hoping. Geremek writes that 'one theft does not make a thief'. Lawrence Robinson said that he stole 'other mens goods' 'in meare necessity for want of victualls' (the court was not persuaded). Joseph Bentley took a bridle 'and sold it for sixpence for extreame want'. Two women were treated leniently for cutting 'calfe rumps' in markets 'because they did it for poverty'. One thief pleaded for pity after 'mere want' made him pilfer in the thick of the 'last great plague'.[43] This was a survival strategy, one way of not joining London's walking starving or vagrant dead. Others said that their crimes were momentary blips. Walter Turner would not have stolen a cloak, he appealed, if he had not been drinking all day long.[44] Temptation was a lamer excuse. One wag wrote that 'opportunity makes thieves', who pounced on the spur of the moment when shopkeepers turned their backs or something tempting sat at open windows or fell from carts. A pair of 'vagabonds' stole clothes draped over hedges to dry. Others sneaked into gardens. People were robbed after falling asleep on streets. While some plucky thieves dived into burning buildings. Fire called them like tolling bells. It did not take long for 'all the pilferers in the town' to get to the scene when the Banqueting House went up in flames in 1619, and royal servants saved some silver, or so they thought, by throwing it out of windows. Watches guarded smouldering houses in Broad Street after a 'greate and lamentable' fire broke out there in 1623, to 'keepe backe the multitude of idle people' who gathered like hawks, hoping to find something worth keeping in the rubble. Thomas Harrison threw his goods from a window as fire ripped through The White Horse alehouse in

---

[42] BHC 5, fo. 235v.
[43] Geremek, *Margins of Society*, p, 96; BHC 5, fo. 200; 8, fo. 177v; 7, fo. 26v; TNA SP16/107/36.
[44] LMA CQSF 102/interrog. Walter Turner.

148    Crime

Holborn, only to watch helplessly as thieves waiting below snatched them from off the street. Other thieves picked their moments more carefully, knowing that people would be at church or lining the streets for a 'royal passage', a good time for 'roberyes and other lewde and bad accons'.[45]

We do not know how many thefts were one-off acts. But in London, if nowhere else, we might expect to find people making livings from crime. Joan Fisher's father said that she lived 'by whoring and filching' in 1637. Two 'old [Bridewell] guests' – Henry Allen and Thomas Gardener – 'live[d] by villanie and pilfering'. A 'notorious theefe', living cheaply along Chick Lane, had spent four years stealing whenever he got the chance. Two 'comon vagraunts and comon pilferers in mens shoppes' – Margery Greene and Agnes White – admitted 'using pilfering' for seven years in 1599. Other Bridewell 'gessts' owned up to living by 'filchinge and shiftinge' or 'shiftinge and cosoninge' to make ends meet. Some lost count of their crimes. Jane Weston had 'picked and brybed' 'so often as the tymes cannott be numbered'. Francis Carter stole 'continually'. While Christopher Lusher was called a 'dayly pickpockett in markets' in 1635, and earmarked for a Virginia ship.[46] People made livings on streets, selling, stealing, and begging. William Morley said that 'hee must begge or steale'. Alice Miller had 'noe lodging but often in streets'. Dominic Chamberlain had 'continued a begger many yeares'. Winifred Rowse 'lived by begginge'. While 'dangerous' William Wiles had begged for five years. Others begged 'daylie' or 'continually'. Anne Scott was called 'a continuall begger' in 1600.[47]

Prostitution rackets also provided full-time jobs. 'Many lewd and loose persons' living on Turnmill Street ran 'notorious brothell howses' renting rooms to 'infamous queanes and whores' whose 'course of life' was 'prostituting their bodies unto the beastly lust of loose and dissolute persons'. It was said that husband and wife Gilbert and Margaret East 'cherishe' 'ill rule in their house' and 'live by it'; that John Shaw had 'no trade' to 'live by but bawdrye'; that Richard Wattwood 'hath none other

---

[45] *A Warning for House-Keepers*, p. 3; BHC 1, fo. 78v; LMA Reps. 17, fo. 321; 20, fo. 293; MJ/SR/505a/11–12; TNA SP14/105/40; LMA Jour. 32, fos. 232v; Rep. 10, fo. 266; BHC 7, fos. 290, 295; LMA Jour. 27, fo. 76. See also GL MS 4165/1, fo. 243v; LMA Jour. 36, fo. 59v; BHC 7, fo. 186v; 8, fo. 133; *The Diary of Henry Machyn Citizen and Merchant-Taylor of London From A.D. 1550 to A.D. 1563*, ed. John Gough Nichols, Camden Society (1848), p. 219.

[46] BHC 8, fo. 139v; 6, fos. 273, 328v; BRHA BHC 4, fo. 91v; BHC 1, fo. 94v; 8, fos. 92, 60. See also BHC 6, fos. 27, 28, 34, 148v; 7, fo. 205; BRHA BHC 4, fos. 10v, 275v, 322v, 419; LMA MJ/SBR/6, fo. 450.

[47] BHC 9, fo. 494; 8, fo. 160v; 9, fo. 637; 6, fo. 437; 9, fo. 420; 6, fo. 400v; 8, fo. 122v; BRHA BHC 4, fo. 159v. Thomas Lord told the Bridewell bench that 'hee beggeth ... victualls where hee can gett itt' in 1644 (BHC 9, fo. 122).

lyvinge' apart from the brothel he had run for eight years; and that Black Luce was 'a vilde bawde and lyveth by it'. The pimp Henry Boyer was called a 'bawde and comon' who 'useth yt daylie'. John Edward, who kept the Horse's Head at St Katherine's, gave up his day job to spend all his time running his 'bawdy'. A 'whore' who bumped into a Bridewell governor's servant in a Tower Hill alehouse in 1609, told him that 'she knewe not howe to lyve yf yt were not for suche young men as [he]'. 'Evill' Susan Carey – Sir George Carey's daughter-in-law – also 'live[d]' by 'young gentlemen'. Other 'whores' said that they had 'no other maintenance' apart from money from 'gentlemen'.[48] People spent long spells in these 'black economies'. Elizabeth Evans said that she had lived 'with th'use of' her 'bodye' for 'three or foure years' in 1598. Others spent three years, a little under two years, and eighteen months in the 'trade'. Many joined 'not of choice', one author wrote, 'but through fatal necessity' to get by.[49]

The stream of 'country wenches' coming with carriers caught the greedy eyes of 'agent[s] of corruption', like pimps who hung around drop-off spots with phony promises of jobs. Katherine Fuller, who ran 'a notorious bawdie house' in Clerkenwell, took 'countrie wenches from the carriers' and put 'them into gentlemens apparell' to 'plaie the whore'. It was hard to get away from a bawd's clutches when force and debt left new arrivals helpless.[50] It was a stark choice between thief or whore. Alice Sharpe, 'as badde as the best', who came to London to look for work, was

---

[48] LMA MJ/SBR/4, fos. 84–5; BHC 3, fos. 194, 95v, 127v, 10v, 280v, 102; 5, fo. 322; 8, fo. 159; BRHA BHC 4, fo. 39v. See also BHC 3, fos. 27v, 101v. Cf. the ordinances of the Southwark Stews, which refer to women who 'live by their body': quoted by Ruth Mazo Karras, 'The regulation of brothels in later medieval England', *Signs*, 14 (1989), 399–433, appendix.

[49] BRHA BHC 4 fos. 1 April 1598, 258v; BHC 3, fos. 100, 157; Robert Dingley, *Proposals for Establishing a Public Place of Reception for Penitent Prostitutes*, 1758, reprinted in Randolph Trumbach, ed., *Prostitution Reform: Four Documents*, Garland Series, Marriage, Sex, and the Family in England, 1660–1800, 22 (1985), p. 4. And see in the same volume, Saunders Welch, *A Proposal to Render Effectual a Plan to Remove the Nuisance of Common Prostitutes From the Streets of the Metropolis* (1758), p. 25. See also BRHA BHC 4, fos. 202, 258v; Jeremy Goldberg, 'Pigs and prostitutes: streetwalking in comparative perspective', in Katherine J. Lewis, Noel James Menuge, and Kim M. Phillips, eds., *Young Medieval Women* (Sutton, 1999), pp. 173–93, esp. pp. 176–8; Beier, *Masterless Men*, pp. 52–3; Tony Henderson, *Disorderly Women in Eighteenth-Century London: Prostitution and Control in the Metropolis, 1730–1830* (Harlow, 1999), pp. 16–18, 47–8, 182–9; Peter Earle, 'The female labour market in London in the late seventeenth and early eighteenth centuries', *Economic History Review*, 2nd series, 42 (1989), 328–53, esp. 331, 342–4; Donna T. Andrew, *Philanthropy and Police: London Charity in the Eighteenth Century* (Princeton, NJ, 1989), p. 121.

[50] LMA MJ/SR/510/33; [John Gwillim], *The London Bawd With Her Character and Life*, 4th edition, 1711, ed., Randolph Trumbach, Garland Series, Marriage, Sex, and the Family in England, 1660–1800, 17 (1986), pp. 141–2; Thomas Dekker, *The 'Honest*

procured by one Green's wife who told her that 'it is better to doe so then to steale'. 'Tis better for me and less hazardous to get my living by my tail than to turn thief', a fictional 'whore' muses.[51] For many there was no choice but to tread thin lines between work and vice, slipping and sliding from service to selling sex, at the mercy of masters and trade slumps. One of Dunton's 'rambling women' told him that she 'could not gain any creditable service' and fell into 'this horrid trade'. For her and others, prostitution was a short-term option until a better job or husband came along.[52] Not all women left brothels behind after they tied the knot, however. Jane Fuller had two illegitimate children by Sir Edward Baynton's brother 'before she was marryed', but this did not stop her from becoming one of late Tudor London's busiest 'whores'.[53]

Bawds and pimps could make money beyond the wildest dreams of day-labourers. Word was that one Maye's wife earned £100 'by bawdrey' in three years running a popular brothel near Aldgate. John Shaw's wife scooped £4 10s on just one busy night. Some keepers were in charge of little empires: Shaw had five brothels in the Whitefriars, Bishopgate Street, St Lawrence, Thames Street, and Finsbury; two less than Mistress Blunt, who ran three bawdy houses in Garden Alley, two more in Bishopgate Street, and one each in the 'Spittle' and St Katherine's, getting weekly rents of twenty shillings from each one.[54] Some brothels were rather on the small side. Ely and Thomas Fowles had three rooms only in their bawdy house in Mutton Lane Clerkenwell. Anne Wilkes had 'onelie' a chamber, kitchen, and garret in Northumberland Alley. While Agnes Parry lodged 'three young whores' at a time in Shoreditch. Other houses were bigger, some were even equipped with 'secret places' to hide 'whores' if ever officers came knocking at the door. One 'vyle, naughty, and bawdy' house in King Street had 'four chambers backwards'.[55] Some 'whores' had ties to more than one bawd and a shuttle service with pimps

---

*Whore, Part 2*, in Thomas Bowers, ed., *The Dramatic Works of Thomas Dekker*, 4 vols. (Cambridge, 1955–61), vol. II, 3:3, 6–7; 5:2, 381–2; Dekker. (with John Webster), *Northward Ho*, in Bowers, *Dramatic Works*, vol. II, 4:3, 95; Dekker (with John Webster), *Westward Ho*, in Bowers ed., *Dramatic Works*, vol. II, 1:1, 19–21; John Taylor, *A Bawd, a Vertuous Bawd, a Modest Bawd: As Shee Deserves, Reprove, or Else Applaud*, in *All the Works of John Taylor the Water Poet*, 1630, Scolar Press facsimile (1973), p. 95; John Dunton, *The Night-walker: Or, Evening Rambles in Search of Lewd Women*, 1696, ed., Randolph Trumbach, Garland Series, Marriage, Sex, and the Family in England, 1660–1800, 19 (1985), October 23, March 23–4. One of Dunton's 'nightwalkers' said that she had 'no [other] way left to get her bread': *Nightwalker*, September 3. Cf. my 'Structure of prostitution', 49–52.

[51] BRHA BHC 4, fo. 342v; [Gwillim], *London Bawd*, p. 11.
[52] Dunton, *Night-walker*, February 14–16; Henderson, *Disorderly Women*, pp. 15–16, 48–9.
[53] BHC 3, fos. 126v, 129v.  [54] Ibid., fos. 328v, 28v, 104, 188, 266.
[55] BRHA BHC 4, fos. 385, 429v-31, 440v, 39v, 9; BHC 3, fos. 188–8v, 20 June 1579. See also BHC 3, fo. 328v; BRHA BHC 4, fos. 27 Sept. 1578, 73; 5, fo. 257.

at the wheel let keepers pool prostitutes. Counts of clients ranged from six and fifteen to sixty or eighty 'in one daie'. Two whistle-blowers said that Blunt's 'bawdy' in St Katherine's was 'never emptie', and that Bowmer's in St John Street was 'never without whores' in 1578. Men 'have harlots as redely and comenly [as] vittels in vittelinge houses', they added. Dunton made notes on a keeper who 'borrow[ed]' prostitutes from 'neighbour bawds' if ever 'two or three sparks came in at a time'. John Shaw can be linked with twenty-three 'whores', and Jane Fuller with thirteen. Agnes Smith said that she had 'layen at Wattwoods, Marshalls, Jane Fullers, Martyns, Shaws, and other naughtie howses'.[56] Highest weekly rents topped twenty shillings. Alice Farewell spent thirty shillings for bed and board in Turnmill Street. Thomasine Breame gave Briary of the Old Bailey 'xxs a weeke for the bed of herselfe', her maid (Ann Jervis, another 'whore'), and servant Richard Rolles, who doubled as a pimp. Average rents were lower, somewhere in the 4s/6s belt. But few bawds went short. It was said that Black Luce 'had moche gayne', and that Gilbert East got 'much monye'. Small wonder that bawds were called 'welthye' or 'very riche', or that pimps got 'much' money for taking people to 'bawdys'. Thomas Nashe urged his readers to 'hoyse uppe baudes in the subsidie booke for the plentie they live in', although one keeper said that 'poverty drew him thereunto'.[57]

Keepers topped up rents with a share of takings. 'I see' 'whores', Nashe said, 'sharing half with the baudes'. Jane Fuller said that 'she had her half alwayes'; Shaw's wife 'had half every tyme'; while Dorothy Wise 'alwaies' got 'half'. Others settled for less. Farewell gave Fowkes 'xiid for being bawd' out of 'every vs she gained'. Richard Wattwood counted on getting 'iis or ii/vid at a tyme'. There were sliding scales. Mistress Wilkinson's share was twelvepence if Elizabeth Reynolds (a sadler's wife) got four or five shillings from 'gentlemen', and two shillings if fees climbed to ten shillings or more.[58] Some bawds got the lot. Katherine Roberts, who ran

---

[56] Dunton, *Night-walker*, October 27; BHC 3, fos. 121, 188–8v; BRHA BHC 4 fos. 228, 252; BHC 3, fos. 317v-19, 147, 20 June 1579; BRHA BHC 4, fo. 261v. See also BHC 3, fos. 102, 103, 107, 127, 158v, 224v, 277–81, 365v, 367v; 5, fo. 275; BRHA BHC 4, fos. 64, 101, 264v, 395–5v; GL MS 12806/2, fo. 134v; Archer, *Pursuit of Stability*, pp. 211–15; and my 'Structure of prostitution'.

[57] BHC 3, fo. 111; BRHA BHC 4, fo. 228; BHC 3, fos. 133v, 111, 188, 48, 104, 266, 134v, 122, 279v; Thomas Nashe, *Christ's Tears Over Jerusalem*, 1593, Scolar Press Facsimile (Menston, 1970), p. 78; BRHA BHC 4, fo. 257. Most brothel keepers who can be traced in subsidy rolls were assessed in the range of £3 to £5: Archer, *Pursuit of Stability*, pp. 215, 213. See also BHC 3, fos. 66, 67v, 114, 121, 161, 169, 170v, 188, 298.

[58] Nashe, *Christ's Tears Over Jerusalem*, p. 77v; BHC 3, fos. 128, 109, 220v-1, 127v; BRHA BHC 4, fos. 434, 430, 101. See also Robert Greene, *A Disputation Between a*

Captain Carewe's Smithfield 'bawdy', always 'toke all the money that was geven' to Margaret Warren, though she said she would 'geve her somewhat' now and then.[59] Pimps also made good livings. Wattwood bragged to another pimp that 'for his xs or xxs he can do as well' as Gilbert East; a snide quip that says something about the bad blood that existed between some vice-workers. Henry Boyer got five shillings for 'carrying' a maid to the Portuguese ambassador and a French crown 'for his labor' at another time. Pimps' fees ranged from four shillings all the way down to twelvepence: 'but xiid'. Roger, the pimp in Dekker's *Honest Whore*, 'never took under two shillings/four pence'.[60]

Fees stretched from a basement few pence up to ten pounds. Marie Donnolly got ten pounds from a single client over a few weeks. Thomasine Breame got this much for one afternoon's work with 'a good thick sett man with a full brest and a short statured man'. It took Elizabeth Foldes almost a year as a 'servant' in Long Lane to earn the same amount.[61] Breame's bumper pay-day was a one-off, but she picked up ten shillings at other times. Katherine Williams had 'sometimes xs, sometimes more and sometimes lesse'. Katherine Jones picked up anywhere from three to ten shillings.[62] Like Breame, she had ties to keepers and pimps who knew well-off clients. Prostitutes often dressed up at the high end of the market. Frances Baker said that Mistress Hibbens had wardrobes stuffed with silk gowns, velvet petticoats, and smart smocks, and dressed 'wenches' from 'top to toe' in classy clothes when 'gentlemen' called 'desyrous of gentlewomen'. Baker always 'putt off all her owne clothes' and slipped into genteel garments; one 'gentleman' gave her nothing after hearing that the clothes 'on her backe when he used her bodye' were not hers. Another bawd sent for a sadler's wife if 'gentlemen' or 'cyttyzens' came calling, and led her upstairs saying 'I have brought you a gentlewoman that wanteth occupying for that she hath an old man to her husband'.[63] Food and drink added to the bill. Keepers also pitched fees higher for virgins; Mistress Corbet sold Katherine Williams's 'maidenhead' to a merchant for forty shillings (some authors said that keepers switched young women to dupe clients). But two shillings or so was a more regular fee; apprentices paid less than skilled workers, for

---

*He-Cony-Catcher and a She-Cony-Catcher*, 1592, reprinted in Judges, ed., *Elizabethan Underworld*, p. 210; BHC 3 fos. 110v, 120, 161v-2, 221, 266, 274v-6; BRHA BHC 4, fos. 48v, 72v, 73, 84, 191v, 207, 221v, 248v, 270, 395v, 409, 429v-31.

[59] BHC 3, fos. 156v-7. See also BHC 5, fos. 26v, 372, 421.
[60] BHC 3, fos. 102v, 111v, 375v, 103v, 107, 213.   [61] Ibid., fos. 193v, 196, 213.
[62] Ibid., fos. 298-8v, 100-1, 129. See also BRHA BHC 4, fo. 434.
[63] BRHA BHC 4, fos. 64, 101. Some well-off clients gave fine clothes to prostitutes: ibid., fo. 68.

example.⁶⁴ But brothel ties bumped up costs. Women alone on streets in sleazy places like 'Whore Alley' in Moorfields lacked protection and pricing that shielded Breame and her like. Punk Alice, the 'mistress o' the game' in *Bartholomew Fair*, puts 'poor common whores' and 'privy rich ones' in different camps. Elizabeth Compe, 'a verie lewd queane' and 'old [Bridewell] gueste', said that she would be 'naughtie with anyone for iid'.⁶⁵

A common belief was that theft followed the 'business' 'verie closelie'.⁶⁶ Some vice-workers did top up earnings with theft. Mistress Berry, who ran a brothel in 'Codepece Rowe' (Whitechapel), 'carried' her lodgers to Cambridge to cut purses and pick pockets at fairs. Thomas Wise planned robberies sitting round the table in his bawdy house. Other bawds had sidelines receiving stolen goods. Mistress Corbet worked hand-in-hand with a pearl thief. Pheba Reynolds got in double trouble in 1609 for fencing and keeping a Whitechapel brothel.⁶⁷ Much of this second income was small beer, although the pimp Richard Rolles stole horses and ended his days dangling on the gallows. Gullible men were fleeced all the time. Mistress Cowell got thirty shillings from a gent's purse in 1603. The pimp Boyer admitted swindling a 'gent of my L[ord] of Oxford'. A 'whore' 'drew' men 'into lewd houses' and took money when their guard was down. Mary Lewis, an 'old' Bridewell 'customer', was arrested on Cheapside in 1631, 'enticing a man to drincke with her' as 'another picked 20s out of his pocket', an old trick of the trade. The 'horrible strompet' Jane Trosse 'pycked' £7 from a Spaniard in Stephen French's brothel on top of a twenty shillings fee in 1577, and she also stole 'iiii dobel pistoletts' from her host. Not long after she was in trouble for 'wild usadge' in Bridewell 'against the matron and the poore', and broke out of prison in 1579, stealing sheets and 'strikinge' the matron

---

[64] Ibid., fos. 395–5v; Griffiths, 'Structure of prostitution', 47. Cf. BHC 3, fos. 112, 375v; *The Wandering Whore in Six Parts*, 1660, ed. Randolph Trumbach, Garland Series, Marriage, Sex, and the Family in England, 1660–1800, 17 (1986), part 1, p. 11; [Gwillim], *London Bawd*, pp. 4, 121, 141, 145; Dunton, *Night-walker*, October 28, December 17.

[65] Jonson is quoted in Salgado, *Elizabethan Underworld*, p. 49; BHC 5, fo. 378. The distinction between street and 'bawdy' based 'whores' is neatly presented by Robert Greene in *The Second Part of Cony-Catching*, in Judges, ed., *Elizabethan Underworld*, p. 165.

[66] Nashe, *Christ's Tears Over Jerusalem*, p. 77v; *Amanda, Or the Reformed Whore*, 1635, ed. F. Ouvry (1869), p. 74; Dunton, *Night-walker*, October 27; February, epistle dedicatory; *Wandering Whore*, Part 3, pp. 7–8; Welch, *Proposal*, p. 13.

[67] BHC 3, fo. 33; BRHA BHC 4, fos. 101v, 389; LMA MJ/SBR/1, fo. 107. See also Nashe, *Christ's Tears Over Jerusalem*, p. 77; *Wandering Whore*, Part 3, p. 7; Dunton, *Night-walker*, September 4; December 25; January 22.

again.[68] Takings could also be high for cutpurses and pickpockets. Cutpurses scooped anywhere from sixpence to six pounds with one deft cut of a knife.[69] Some got even luckier. One gang took home £65 after a single day's work in 1630. Henry Waller, the ringleader of a gang of Dutch cutpurses, made off with £24 from a churchgoer's purse. Another cutpurse netted £6 after 'plucking a purse out of a mans pockett' in 1575 and pushing him into the river. While one Mowchachoe cut a purse containing two sovereigns, nineteen shillings, and a gold ring.[70] Pickpockets could also make off with princely sums. Frances Richardson was 'accused to be accessory to the stealing of 30li out of a mans pockett' in 1627. A pair of pickpockets got £140 from one pocket in 1631. Galfridus Emmes plucked £6 from one pocket and sixty shillings from another on the same golden day. Other loot ranged from a whopping thirty pounds all the way down to a lowly threepence. You 'cutte nothing but string', John Hancock told Owen Vaughan, after he cut a purse with just 'ixd in it'.[71]

The Bridewell court's weekly sittings allow us to follow people closely through its records to shed a little light on criminal lives. Most people appear only once and disappear for good, although this might not have been their only brush with the law. Many had only been in London for a short while, clueless and jobless. But many came back to Bridewell more than once, and some stay in sight for months or years. The longest stay in the books was for more than thirteen years. Joan Garroll was already known to the court when she made her first recorded appearance for nightwalking in June 1628, and we last see her in September 1641. She notched up thirteen other nightwalking charges, and also ended up in Bridewell for vagrancy seven times, eight times for pilfering or picking pockets, and one time each for 'breaking' prison, illegitimacy, sex, poking fun at 'a gent of good fashion', and skulking. Only her name is written down at other times, and perhaps a word about the outcome. The gap

---

[68] J. S. Cockburn, ed., *Calendar of Assize Records: Hertfordshire Indictments: Elizabeth I* (1975), pp. 133, 134, 138; BRHA BHC 4, fo. 395v; BHC 3, fo. 107; LMA CQSF 122/52; BHC 7, fo. 221; 3, fos. 103, 107, 224v, 365v, 367. See also GL MS 3018/1, fo. 65; BHC 3, fos. 63, 158v; 7, fos. 71v, 293v, 332; BRHA BHC 4, fos. 109v, 148, 409, 439. For more on Rolles see my 'Contesting London Bridewell 1576–1580', *Journal of British Studies*, 42 (2003), 283–315.

[69] For example, BHC 2, fos. 16, 94, 95, 181v, 182; 3, fos. 140v, 289; 5, fo. 383v; 7, fos. 96, 152, 195v; 8, fos. 10, 68, 263v.

[70] BHC 7, fos. 202, 242v; 2, fo. 95. Two thieves pocketed £18 in one day in 1636; another cut two purses on the bridge at one time, getting 4/6d: BHC 8, fo. 94; 2, fo. 95.

[71] BHC 7, fos. 43, 250; LMA MJ/SR/524/75; CQSF 94/12; BHC 2, fo. 95. See also BHC 6, fo. 295v; 7, fos. 38, 98v, 183, 256v, 339v; 8, fos. 88v, 179, 394; LMA CQSF 92/8, 93/4, 98/recog. Susannah Cobb, 102/interrog. Bazelius Litchpoole, 108/33, 115/26, 123/8, 129/16, 135/1; MJ/SBR/4, fo. 370; MJ/SBR/6, fo. 300; MJ/SR/524/38; WJ/SR/NS/30/2.

between her appearances was sometimes only a week or so. She was arrested in St Sepulchre thirteen times, four times on Fleet Street, twice in Cripplegate, and once in Farringdon Within, Cheap, and Holborn. Her home patch was a half-mile circle around Newgate. We know little about her except her offences, though her child was 'still borne' in 1629 and buried in Clerkenwell. She was 'with child' again one year later. Garroll was caught red-handed picking a minister's pocket six months later and shouted 'he that loveth a whore helpe helpe'; one helper punched a constable. She had a pass to go to Saffron Walden (Essex) in October 1632, but was still in London a month later, bribing watchmen. Another nightwalker said that Garroll bribed Marshal Fitch with 'a quart of wyne'. Garroll had a master in Holborn in early 1632, but when we next hear of her in July she had left Newgate on 'letters of transportacon', and was put to work until the next sessions 'or clse' sent to a ship. She never crossed the ocean, however, and was in Newgate in January 1638 as a 'condempned person'. But she avoided Tyburn's tree and was back in Bridewell little over a year later for pilfering and being out late. She 'will not bee reformed', the court groaned in May 1640. Garroll crops up once more in the next year, when she broke out of Bridewell with five other women.[72]

Anne Goodier/Lambe spent nearly eleven years in courtbooks from her first vagrancy charge in November 1630. She began with a blitz of five vagrancy charges in five weeks, and appeared twelve times for vagrancy in all, five times for nightwalking, twice for walking late, and once for cheating and mixing with men 'suspiciously'. The details of other offences were not noted. Like Garroll, she was a West End woman, with ten arrests in Farringdon Within, two more in Holborn, and one each in St Sepulchre and Fleet Street, and to the north and east in Aldersgate, Cripplegate, and Cheapside. She was in service in Moorfields at the time she was 'taken in the fields in an ill manner with a young man' in 1632, and was sent to St Thomas's in April 'to be cured of the fowle disease' but was still full of pox four months later. Goodier said she had 'lived in good sort' for eighteen months in a rented room in Chick Lane when she was found vagrant in 1635. The court let her go, hoping that she had turned over a new leaf. But in a carbon copy of Garroll's story she was locked up in 1636 after leaving Newgate on 'letters of transportacon'. She was set free in November and six months later was pregnant and married to Henry Lambe of Southwark, who signed a bond to leave London for

---

[72] BHC 7, fos. 78, 82, 98, 116v, 118v, 122, 136, 140, 141, 181, 188, 196v, 208, 226, 228v, 248v, 296v, 304v, 353v; 8, fos. 60, 61v, 77v, 92v, 159, 233v, 237v, 251v, 262v, 264, 292, 349; LMA CQSF 104/19.

five years after his bride was caught nightwalking: another broken promise. Goodier/Lambe was picked up after dark in April 1639, cracked jokes with officers, and said she was 'quicke with child' to get off lightly, although the matron found otherwise. The pox was a life-curse. She was twice sent to St Thomas's in 1639 for a cure. Her marriage may not have lasted long. She was called by her maiden name in January 1640 when jobless William Holden fathered her child. Goodier 'swore that she would not worke' when she was caught by the watch for the last but one time in the same month. 'Shee will not be reformed', magistrates complained.[73]

Susan Kendal/Locke chalked up nine years in Bridewell's books until her swansong in November 1638. She first attracted attention giving birth in prison after being 'thrust out of Blackfryers by the constable' with nowhere to go. She was arrested nine times for nightwalking, three times for vagrancy and theft, twice for picking pockets and walking late, and once for living 'loosely', leaving a child on a step, and illegitimacy (as well as other times when no offence is listed). Cheap ward was one of her patches, and she was also 'taken' in Bridge, Bishopgate, and Cripplegate, and left a child not far from the Royal Exchange in 1631. She did not hug the west walls like Garroll or Goodier, though half of her arrests were on their stomping grounds. Her Bridewell baby was stillborn – she shared that sadness with Garroll – and a stack of vagrancy and nightwalking charges followed. She was not sympathetically sisterly at Christmas 1631 when, pregnant again, she snatched 4/1d 'from the body of a pore women' who 'fell in labor' on a street. The court wanted to send her to Virginia in August 1632 after she was found walking late. But she stayed in London and was back in trouble five months later for the same offence, although she was freed as she was 'asked in church to marry'. Wedding banns did not stop her from walking late, however, as she was back in court a fortnight later. The clerk crossed out Kendal in July 1633 and put Locke in its place, but her husband was no shining example. She had come to get him out of Bridewell, but was put to work there instead. Henry Locke was an old-hand at the 'thieving trade', this time taking a sword from a shop. He helped himself to a cloak later on, and was one of a gang of eighteen men branded on the hand in Christmas week and locked up for six months. He tried to smash his way out with four other toughs, 'sawing' a 'great hole' in the porter's wall, and scaring the living daylights out of the porter's man. His wife, meanwhile, was back picking pockets.

---

[73] BHC 7, fos. 203v, 204v, 205, 207, 208v, 211, 221v, 271, 274v, 282v, 289v, 312, 328, 349v; 8, fos. 43v, 92v, 93v, 97v, 117v, 233v, 235v, 237v, 240, 248v, 274v, 340v, 345.

Crime: worlds 157

More theft and nightwalking charges followed until her last day in court in Winter 1638.[74]

### Trades and companies

We may never know why these women disappeared for good. The gallows might have been their last port of call, or perhaps they set sail for a colony or turned over new leaves and courts let bygones be bygones. Their brief lives stand out for the time they stay in sight, reminding us that crime was routine for some – nineteen-time vagrant William Campion was taken eight times by Marshal Fitch in three years – and that there were some longish alliances in crime worlds.[75] Rogue writing mentions 'bands', 'corporations', 'companies', 'fraternities', 'sects', or 'sorts' of thieves, mixing titles in the space of a few pages.[76] Group identities were not limited to the printed page, however. There are no pyramid shaped guilds of thieves in courtbooks, though there were some sort of pecking orders. One thief was called a 'principall cozener', and we come across titles like 'ringleader of a company'. But there are enough collective titles to rule in the likelihood of crime rings.[77] The preamble to a Parliamentary Act outlawing pickpocketing (1567) mentions a 'kind of evil-disposed persons commonly called cutpurses or pick-purses [who] confer together [and make] themselves [a] brotherhood or fraternity of an art or mystery' living by 'the secret spoil' of 'true' people.[78] Recorder Fleetwood called cutpursing an art and trade. A minor poet refers to a 'thieves trade' and 'cheating crew'. Alice Gregory was taught the thieves' 'trade' by her mother; a band of brothers joined the pickpocket 'profession' in 1628; and a Turnmill Street gang made thieving 'their profession'.[79] Fictional bawds also worked in 'trades'. A Bridewell witness spoke of the 'trade of bawdry'. Trade-talk described prostitution or brothel 'business'; clients

---

[74] BHC 7, fos. 139, 141v, 150v, 151, 193, 193v, 199v, 207v, 208, 210, 214v, 220, 226, 230v, 237, 242v, 254, 290v, 310v, 313, 315v, 336v; 8, fos. 57v, 103, 148, 210v.
[75] BHC 7, fos 139, 178, 182, 185, 193v, 195, 201, 209, 210v, 215v, 231, 234v, 235, 236, 238, 270, 275v, 278v, 290, 292.
[76] Harman, *Caveat for Common Cursitors*, pp. 110, 112, 115, 117; Awdeley, *Fraternity of Vagabonds*, p. 93.
[77] BHC 3, fo. 422; 7, fo. 32.; Godwin, *Historie des Larrons*, pp. 42, 211, 271.
[78] 8 Eliz. I c. 4.
[79] Quoted in John Strype, *A Survey of the Cities of London and Westminster: Containing the Original, Antiquity, Increase, Modern Estate and Government of Those Cities, Written at First in the Year MDXCVIII by John Stow ... Corrected, Improved, and Very Much Enlarged: and the Survey and History Brought Down from the Year 1633*, 5 books in 2 vols. (1720), V, p. 440; BHC 7, fos. 78v, 48; Humphrey Mill, *A Night's Search Discovering the Nature and Condition of All Sorts of Nightwalkers With Their Associates* (1640), pp. 251, 232; LMA MJ/SBR/5, fo. 80.

'had to do' or 'dealt' with 'whores'; pimps were 'brokers'.[80] There are other group words in records. 'Companies' of thieves worked together, and 'confederacies' of 'cutpurses, cuseners and pilferers' hung around playhouses.[81] Thieves landed in trouble for 'plotting', 'combining', or 'complotting', allegations that made 'faculty' or 'fraternity' rings seem credible.[82] Bridewell's bench said that Robert Browne 'cannot denye but that he [is] one of the facultie of cutpurses' (a nest of recusants in the Red Lion alehouse were called a 'facultie' in 1639). Cutpurses are often noted in collective descriptions. Four 'comon nips' were 'acquainted with all the cutpurses in towne' in 1620. 'Greate trouppes' of cutpurses squeezed into the Old Bailey yard in 1609, pressing deep into crowds, picking purses as people followed the twists and turns of trials. 'Greate multitudes' of cutpurses plied their 'trade' in built-up Middlesex a few years later.[83]

We should look for crime rings, never forgetting that people with pens and power often demonized these fears by making them more organized than they actually were. The rogue realm tells us this with its quixotic cast, but it still matters greatly when collective terms like 'faculty' appear in courtbooks. Magistrates surely read rogue writing, and we can imagine them sitting chatting about thieves' tricks. The Pickpocket Act with its talk of fraternities was passed a year after Harman wrote *A Caveat for Common Cursitors* (1566), and six years after Awdeley's *Fraternity of Vagabonds* (1561). The first pauper Act to note the term 'rogue' followed a little later in 1572. The time between these bills and books was short enough for ideas to run both ways.[84] Magistrates did come across thieving ties. Some thieves were called 'sharers' or 'fellows'. James Wilson and Thomas White were 'companions and sharers in cuttinge purses and picking picketts'. John Peacock 'shared' takings 'equally' with other pickpockets in 1629. Many ties were short lived, just one robbery long. But others lasted longer, like the three boys with a plan to rob books from shops: one 'cheapen[ed] books' while 'the other two stole away other

---

[80] BHC 3, fos. 128, 102v, 105v, 111v, 112. For examples of authors using 'trade-talk' see *Amanda*, pp. 41, 48, 49; Taylor, *A Bawd*, pp. 95, 99; Nashe, *Christ's Tears Over Jerusalem*, p. 77v; Dunton, *Night-walker*, February 14–16; John Twyning, *London Dispossessed: Literature and Social Space in the Early Modern City* (Basingstoke, 1998), p. 59.
[81] LMA MJ/SBR/3, fo. 102; MJ/SBR/4, fo. 555; Jour. 33, fos. 162v, 268; Remembrancia Book 1, fo. 325v.
[82] BHC 6, fo. 378v; 7, fo. 262v; 9, fo. 825; BRHA BHC 4, fo. 419; LMA WJ/SR/NS/29/56, 32/91.
[83] BHC 1, fo. 91v; GL MS 9064/21, fo. 62v; BHC 6, fos. 215, 22; 3, fo. 381; LMA Jour. 27, fo. 330; MJ/SBR/1, fo. 559. Gee called priests a 'troope and brood' (*Foot Out of the Snare*, p. 97).
[84] Woodbridge, *Vagrancy, Homelessness, and English Renaissance Literature*, p. 42 and chap. 1.

bookes'.[85] Thieves like the 'pilferinge fellowes' William Howard and William Monday knew each other for 'a longe time'. Thieves and 'whores' mixed all the time. Elizabeth Deacon mixed with Susan Kendal/Locke and other nightwalkers and thieves for three years, appearing six times with Julian Waterman, talking, drinking, stealing. Elizabeth Zeager stole 'a paire of silke garters' with Deacon, hung out with the 'comon pickepockett' Joan Palmer, and walked streets with Rebecca Ireland, who ended up in Bridewell twenty-four times in ten years.[86]

There are also words for aiding and abetting that imply support networks – 'supporter' for one. The fence Goodwife Brown was called 'a great supporter of cutpurses'. A husband and wife team were 'comon comforters of pickepurses and thefes'. Other 'help-words' included 'succourer', 'nourisher', 'receiver', 'agent', 'bulke', or 'helper'. One brothel keeper was dubbed a 'norrisher of a thousand whores'. Richard Wilson was called a cozenors' 'agent'.[87] There were words for teamwork, like 'confederate' or 'accessory'. People were 'party' or 'consentinge' to thefts. Anne Gannaway was 'charged by the Lady Tresom to have had a hand and consent with Peato and Sprye in robing her' in 1632.[88] 'Conversers', 'companions', and 'consorts' swapped ideas about cutting purses or picking pockets. Thieves also had 'accomplices', 'friends', 'followers', and 'frequenters'. Thomas Hunt was locked up in 1600 for 'haulinge after whores and cuttpurses'. Thomas Cooke was known to be

---

[85] BHC 6, fos. 126, 258v; 7, fo. 167v; For more examples of pilfering pairs and groups, see BHC 6, fos. 22, 108, 271, 352v, 392; 7, fos. 31v, 70v, 97v, 119, 182, 208v, 250v, 332v, 374; 8, fos. 17, 80v, 98, 149v, 204v, 254v, 335, 386; 9, fos. 30, 376 497, 626; BRHA BHC 4, fos. 19, 150v, 419; LMA CQSF 109/8, 116/19; MJ/SR/505a/14, 505a/16, 505a/32, 505a/64, 507/40, 523/57–68, 524/117–18; WJ/SR/NS/36/ 53–4; MJ/SBR/3, fo. 153; MJ/SBR/4, fo. 15.

[86] BHC 6, fo. 141. For Deacon and the rest, see BHC 7, fos. 80, 98, 163, 185v, 191v, 192, 192v, 196v, 199, 204, 205, 212v, 219, 221, 222v, 226, 237, 247v, 266v, 271 (Deacon); 133, 153v, 166v, 188v, 199, 202v, 204, 205, 212v, 213v, 219 (Bartlett); 152, 160, 194v, 207, 209v, 212v, 219, 222v, 226, 230, 235v, 249v, 250v, 258v, 266v, 289, 290, 328 (Waterman); 78v, 88v, 141, 150v, 151, 178, 190v, 192, 199, 204, 226, 231v, 243, 248v, 251, 254, 260v, 295v, 316, 342v, 348v (Zeager); 202, 251, 262, 312, 319, 342v, 349v, 364, 368v, 374v, 375; 8, fos. 11v, 13, 19v, 60, 62, 64, 98v, 120, 134v, 202, 239v, 255v, 298, 315 (Ireland).

[87] BRHA BHC 4, fo. 318v; BHC 1, fos. 108v, 47, 129v; 3, fo. 273; 6, fo. 332v; 7, fos. 40, 95v.

[88] For example, BHC 2 fo. 230; 3, fo. 289; 5, fo. 406; 6, fo. 22; 7, fos. 100, 262v; 8, fos. 96, 147, 224v, 323, 391, 157v; LMA CQSF 131/45 (confederate); BHC 7, fo. 43; 8, fo.4; LMA Jour. 16, fo. 341; CQSF 76/32, 96/8, 104/22, 108/38, 117/22, 121/22–3, 131/46; WJ/SR/NS/34/95, 37/98, 40/239, 44/219, 49/150; MJ/SR/505/90, 505a/69; MJ/SBR/2, fo. 349; MJ/SBR/3, fos. 18, 20, 430; MJ/SBR/5, fos. 30, 74, 197, 225, 415, 426; MJ/SBR/6, fos. 123, 397, 603 (accessory). See also LMA CQSF 126/4, 73/3, 93/26, 93/31, 93/35; WJ/SR/NS/35/79, 48/8, 49/11.

160    Crime

'a partaker with theeves'.[89] Some roles were carved out clearly, like the 'messinger betweene theeves' Margaret Hammond or the 'comon bayle' Robert Shaw.[90] Other members of the supporting cast included 'solicitors', 'setters', 'suers', and 'spies'. Anne Foster was a 'spy to bawds'; Edward Powell 'a setter to pickpockets'. A 'comon bawd' had a second string to her bow as 'a suer for rogues and cutpurses'. William Pallas was revealed to be 'a comon solicitor for pilferers [and] reputed receiver and abettor of them'.[91] Particular people were in good positions to give helping hands. The river offered escape routes, and enough watermen and lightermen helped out thieves to back up their rough reputations. Word reached Bridewell in 1579 that lighterman Samuel Chambers was always ready to row thieves across the river for a 'share' of their takings. Six Westminster watermen 'rescued' 'notable' cutpurse Owen Cannon from officers' clutches in 1632.[92]

London was not a thieves' paradise, but they could find safe harbours almost anywhere. Names and places often crop up more than once. Anne Hodgkins named five 'pickpurses' who rented rooms at Rawson's house on Seocle Lane in 1560. Nan Bradshaw named others who 'daily' dropped in at the Sun and Seven Stars near Smithfield Bars, and 'pickpurses' who also 'haunted' Rawson's house (he was jailed soon after). Richard Smithwick grassed on a cutpurse gang who met on weekends in a barn at the far end of Tuttle Street in Westminster in 1575, and he did not stop there, adding that 'a gret number of cutpurses' spent Saturday nights at a barn between Lambeth Marsh and the Bishop of Carlisle's house 'with dyverse whores thear with them', and that cutpurses also met at an alehouse 'beyond the Blewe Anker in Warwick Lane'. Two other thieves named Tuttle Street as a black-spot a little later.[93] Nowhere seemed safe. Recorder Fleetwood gave the Crown a list of 'harboring howses for maisterles-men and for such as lyve by thefte and other such like shifts' deep inside the city and rough suburbs. 'Into the hart of the city is

[89] BHC 6, fos. 24v, 128, 442v; BRHA BHC 4, fos. 177, 379; BHC 7, fo. 39v; 5, fo. 428; LMA CQSF 111/8, 112/42, 126/12; MJ/SBR/2, fo. 105; BHC 7, fo. 221v.
[90] BHC 1, fo. 143; 6, fo. 23v; 1, fos. 120v, 187v; 7, fos. 40, 106; BRHA BHC 4 fos. 146v, 223v, 376v; LMA MJ/SBR/1, fo. 329; MJ/SBR/2, fo. 59; MJ/SBR/4, fos. 38, 376; CQSF 92/11. For more 'bailers' see BHC 6, fo. 362v; BRHA BHC 4, fos. 27, 367v, 376v; LMA WJ/SR/NS/49/124.
[91] BHC 7, fos. 86, 85; BRHA BHC 4, fo. 52; BHC 7 fo. 87v. See also BHC 8, fo. 151; 3, fo. 392v.
[92] BHC 3, fo. 400v; LMA WJ/SR/NS/33/105–6. On watermen see Bernard Capp, *The World of John Taylor the Water-Poet, 1578–1653* (Oxford, 1994).
[93] BHC 1, fos. 79v, 90, 109; 3, fos 3, 34v. Nan Bradshaw also gave details about another house on Seocle Lane where 'comon bribers and theeves' spent a large part of the day. See also Lynda Ann Price, 'Parish constables: a study of administration and peacekeeping, Middlesex, 1603–1625', unpublished PhD thesis, University of London (1991), p. 19.

uncleanness crept', Nashe noted. 'Tis well knowne', Birdlime bragged in *Westward Ho*, that 'I have up-risers and down-lyers within the citty / night by night'.[94] London was hemmed in by thief-friendly alehouses to the west (St Andrew Holborn, for example, Fleet Street, St Clement Danes), north (Clerkenwell, for example, Cow Cross, Turnmill Street, or Shoreditch), and east (East Smithfield, for example, St Katherine's, Stepney). Nine cutpurses were taken in one swoop on 'the 3 Footestooles' in St Katherine's in 1578. A cutpurse ring 'lived' at the Green Dragon 'in the upper end of Southwark' in 1598. While Katherine Moore's mistress put up 'cutters and hackers' in White Cross Street in 1576; 'ther comes nether men nor wemen thither that are good', she said, 'the house is worse than the banckside'. Thieves also got a warm welcome in Richardson's alehouse in St Mary-at-Hill where they could always count on getting 'good chear' and beer in 1577. News reached Bridewell in 1579 that 'cutpurses, roges, and harlotts' met at the Blue Boar on Thames Street, and also at 'Clymer's house' in Smithfield. 'Greate numbers' of 'cutpurses' and 'cosyners' used the Savoy Hospital as a hang-out in 1579.[95]

Largish gangs had home-bases in various parts of the London area and ties to receivers who knew fencing pipelines like the backs of their hands. The king said that 'there would be no theeves if they had not their receipts' in 1616, aiming his royal arrow at 'base victuallers' with 'nothing else to live by' except their 'houses of haunt and receipt'.[96] A clutch of alehouse keepers were the cogs of a cutpurse gang who were based in Southwark, whose leading lights were all 'old gests' of Bridewell in 1575: including Jack of the Kitchen, John of Dulwich, one Mowchachoe, William Loggins, and Owen Vaughan. The gang got shelter from one Fellward who ran 'a sellar under a barbor' next door to St Thomas's Hospital; William Cook who put up cutpurses 'continuallie' in his house along Kentish Street; Goodman Franks who dined them, after thieving sprees, in his alehouse in Pepper Alley; and John Thorowgood, from St Nicholas Shambles, who laid on bacon, beef, and beer, and stood before

---

[94] T. Wright, ed., *Queen Elizabeth and her Times*, 2 vols. (1838), vol. II, pp. 249–51; Nashe, *Christ's Tears Over Jerusalem*, p. 77; Dekker, *Westward Ho*, 5:4, 246–53.

[95] BHC 3, fo. 273; BRHA BHC 4, fo. 18; BHC 3, fos. 45v-6, 167v, 380, 151, 152v; LMA Jour. 20, fo. 502. See also BHC 1, fo. 90v; 2, fo. 97v; 3, fo. 273v; 6, fo. 352v; 7, fos. 77, 249v; 8, fo. 398; BRHA BHC 4, fos. 151, 418; LMA CQSF 109/39, 121/55, 126/21; MJ/SR/508a/16, 514/34, 524/8; MJ/SBR/1, fos. 124, 459, 615; MJ/SBR/2, fos. 31, 294, 495; MJ/SBR/3, fo. 93; MJ/SBR/4, fos. 15, 615; MJ/SBR/5, fo. 197; MJ/SBR/6, fos. 51, 570; MJ/SBR/7, fo. 187; WJ/SR/NS/34/134, 39/174; WAC WCB1, fo. 284. Lady Mary Lynsey of St Martin-in-the-Fields was prosecuted for lodging 'lewd and incontinent' pilferers and pickpockets in 1635: LMA WJ/SR/NS/45/14.

[96] LMA Jour. 30, fo. 86.

his thieving 'boys' as they cut purses in London's markets. Landlords 'badd' or 'sett' cutpurses to steal, and 'changed' gold for money, putting up with grumbling from cutpurses about low exchange rates. There are many cases when we glimpse cutpurses meeting in alehouses to pass on tricks and tips and to hand knives around. This sounds cheery, but there were clear limits to this camaraderie. Threats clouded the atmosphere now and then. Thorowgood warned gang members that 'he would send for a constable if they would not give him rings'. Loyalties were often skin deep; some cutpurses saved their own necks by informing on 'companions'.[97]

A gang of Dutch thieves descended on London in 1626–7, and stayed for at least four years. We have the names of over twenty in this 'company'. One 'comon' Dutch 'pickepockett' came over 'with divers of the same kinde' in Winter 1628. Another had been 'a drummer in the warres' before crossing the channel to try his luck at cutting purses. Henry Derrick, from Rotterdam, was caught lurking 'under a gents window' in 1628, and said he was hanging on in London for a pass for the coast. There are native-sounding names among the Dutch – John Baron, David Reynolds, Walter Breame – aliases perhaps to cover their tracks. They mixed with English thieves and had a handful of ringleaders like Yarrin Manster, who was put behind bars for 'bringing up boyes to picke pockets' in 1630.[98] The leader of the pack was Henry Waller, who stays in sight for over five years until Winter 1631. He and three other 'notorious cutpurses and pickpocketts' were 'taken suspiciously together at the Spittle' in 1626 and set aside for soldiers. But Waller stayed on shore and was arrested in bustling Bartholomew Fair in 1627. He hired two men at 'ii vid a peece' to bail him out of prison. His name appears on a list of 'prisoners' to go to war in 1627, but he was spotted 'suspiciously' eyeing pockets in a church in the next year. Waller broke out of Bridewell but was quickly 'taken' and not allowed to talk to other prisoners after 'teach[ing] a little boy in the house to learne the art to pick pockets'. His gang bribed officers to keep out of harm's way. A marshalman was sacked after warning 'Waller and other pickepockets' when warrants were 'out for them'. Waller was picked up with two other Dutch pickpockets – Marseles Hudrix and Manster – in the new year, and was back in Bridewell three months later after picking a purse from a 'gent', and again at Christmas after another breakout with two cutpurses. He put pressure on John Prick for money to give 'slacke and fainte evidence against him' at Middlesex sessions in 1631. More thefts

[97] BHC 2, fos. 94, 94v, 95, 95v, 97v, 155v, 181v.
[98] BHC 7, fos. 97, 96, 101, 158v, 203–3v, 216v, 160v, 94v, 98, 99, 159v, 165, 414, 414v.

followed, including a near windfall when he almost got away with '24li', and another time when he picked a Bridewell governor's pockets. Waller 'made a mutiny' in Bridewell shortly after, 'sawing' through walls with two cutpurses and locking themselves in the lodge until a sheriff broke down the door. He was not a staunch friend and would turn stool pigeon to get out of sticky situations, 'promising to informe of others that are pickepocketts' to get out of prison in 1629, and naming five pickpockets who swooped on a church congregation with him in 1631. Waller also offered 'help' to trace lost purses; a hint that he ran rackets in stolen goods. He was not the only gang grass. John Moss 'promised to discover a number of dutch cutpurses that are now lately come over' in 1629, trying to talk his way out of trouble. While 'notorious pickpockett' Christopher Hewson was locked up in 1630 until he 'reveale[d] some Dutch cutpurses'.[99]

Waller's world was dangerous. There was honour amongst thieves, but it could fall apart in a flash if someone's freedom was at stake, and there were enough double crossers to keep thieves edgy. But even treachery reveals links now broken. The fact that some whistle-blowers could give long lists of names reveals criminal ties. Two pimps (Richard Wattwood and Robert Barlow) named twenty-three bawdy houses in 1578, and added 'that there are manye others' that 'they cannot remember'. John Shaw said that the 'pandar' John Byllyard 'knoweth all the bawdes houses and all the comon whores and many young men that useth them'. A 'bill' found in a cozener's pocket in 1578 named sixteen other cozeners. Thomas Gently revealed the names of seventeen 'pickepurses' (fourteen men and three women) at Bridewell in 1560, and owned up 'that he hath beene confetered' with them and 'hath seen them many tymes to doe that acte in dyvers many fayres and markets'.[100] People knew where to go to find brothels or thieves' dens. Two clients told John Shaw that if 'he had no good stuffe they could go to other howses and finde better'.[101]

Other key figures received stolen goods and were the last links in theft rings. Alehouses were handy places to haggle with people coming and going all the time. Landlords had neighbourhood names for trading stolen goods, often to their cost. Elizabeth Overberry dropped in at 'divers places' to sell silver spoons in 1601, before bumping into Mary Newborough on a street and selling them to her for thirty-nine shillings.[102] Others sold stolen goods directly to keepers. A silkweaver's

---

[99] BHC 6, fo. 422v; 7, fos. 39v, 40v, 41v, 96, 100, 158v, 160v, 184, 209, 242v, 244, 246, 249, 159v, 194; LMA MJ/SBR/5, fo. 241. See also BHC 7, fo. 134.
[100] BHC 3, fos. 317v-319, 119v, 320–0v; 1, fo. 91.
[101] BHC 3, fo. 121v.   [102] BRHA BHC 4, fo. 249.

servant sold stolen pots, dishes, candlesticks, and clothes to Robert Biggs who ran 'a victualling seller' in Fleet Street, and 'willed' him 'to bring what he would' for a fair price.[103] Traders and artisans turned to black markets for cheap goods or materials, and some built up long ties with thieves. Jane Weston admitted stealing from 'silke women' 'so often as the tymes cannot be numbered' in 1560, and said that she 'alwayes' sold stolen silk to haberdasher Thomas Lynte of Paul's Gate, who paid her 'farre under the trewe value' for it. A pewterer was put on trial in 1560 for being 'a comon filcher and receaver of such pewter as is stolen abroade'.[104] Almost equal numbers of men and women ended up in Bridewell for handling stolen goods, but the balance tipped towards women around 1600.[105] Women acted together in receiving rings, sometimes with men, and were leading lights in pawning rings and second-hand markets for household goods that often used alehouses as drop-offs. Like thieving, receiving could be a makeshift that often went on with lawful trade over alehouse tables or stalls. Larger London was a perfect place to resell goods in black- and second-hand-markets.[106]

Certain occupations picked up somewhat shady reputations for dealing with thieves, none more so than 'beggarly' brokers in charge of pawnshops, selling stolen plate in 'idle' and 'nedles trade', the not impartial Goldsmiths' groaned. Pawnshops and alehouses were twin evils that 'embolden[ed] all kinds of lewd and bad persons' to rob from 'true men', knowing that someone would pay them for their handiwork. Some brokers also had 'cunning' to melt down jewels and plate, wiping away evidence for good. Shifty 'cryers' for 'ends of gold and silver' were also called 'abettors' of thieves. Magistrates launched crackdowns on brisk traffic in stolen goods, and set up a 'registry of brokers' to keep up-to-date records of bargains and pawns to track down missing gold and silver. Many brokers slipped through the net, however, and set up shop outside the walls. London's leaders thought that receiving boomed in the

---

[103] Ibid., fo. 20v; TNA SP16/14/13.   [104] BHC 1, fos. 102v, 87.
[105] Figures are drawn from eight Bridewell books; there was one more male receiver: 44 to 43.
[106] Garthine Walker, *Crime, Gender, and Social Order in Early Modern England* (Cambridge, 2003), pp. 165–7; Beverly Lemire, 'Peddling fashion: salesmen, pawnbrokers, tailors, thieves, and the second-hand clothes trade in England, c.1700–1800', *Textile History*, 22 (1991), 67–82; Lemire, *Dress, Culture, and Commerce: The English Clothing Trade Before the Factory, 1660–1800* (1997), pp. 95–120; Michael Roberts, 'Women and work in sixteenth-century English towns', in Penelope J. Corfield and Derek Keene, eds., *Work in Towns, 850–1850* (Leicester, 1990), pp. 86–102, esp. pp. 93–5; McMullan, *Canting Crew*, pp. 23–4, 105–7.

suburbs, and drafted a bill for Parliament to extend the registry's 'compass' to three miles over the walls in 1610. But 'retayling brokers' remained a permanent pain, the 'ground and nurserie' of felonies and frauds, the Crown claimed two decades later. A string of City and Crown measures could not stop 'beggarly' brokers from handling stolen goods. Pawnshops were natural dumping grounds for thieves. On top of this, the 'broker' tag continued to be a synonym for trading loot. The wife of a Ratcliffe clothworker was accused to be 'a rec[eiver] and broker of stolen goods' in 1615. Mud stuck.[107]

The servant-turned-thief was a long-running problem, but increasingly attention shifted towards its 'real' roots: ravenous receivers. Without fences, Robert Greene wrote, thieves 'can do nothing', they would soon starve if they had nowhere to sell their spoils. Blame piled up on receivers. Women sneaked young maids into service to steal, a widespread problem by 1613 when 'women brokers' were slammed 'for placeinge maydeservants' in households for their own profit. Phyllis Lowe's 'practice' was to 'place maides in good houses to robbe their masters' and take them back afterwards to her house in Leg Alley until they found another service. She 'lyveth by that meanes', the Bridewell court heard.[108] Receivers (men and women) had special lines working with light-fingered servants. Magistrates noted that tatty rag-gatherers met with servants on the sly, 'animatinge and encouraginge them to robbe and spoile theire masters'.[109] Pushy adults leaned on young people; conventional job training, after all, was under the wing of substitute parents. Typical was the 'comon receiver', John Meme (clothworker), who took no notice of past warnings in 1559 when he was caught handling stolen goods from 'mennes servants and apprentices'. Alehouses again had leading roles. Two tapsters – Richard Durecke and Robert Bible – always took 'soche things as servants can bribe from their masters and children from their parents' in 1561. Some parents planted their children in service to steal whatever they could get their

---

[107] HOL MP 26–4–1610, 14–5–1610, 14–5–1621; LMA Jour. 32, fos 224v-5; WJ/SR/NS/ 41/52, 47/1; CQSF 121/40; MJ/SBR/2, fo. 150; GCL company minute books P2, fos. 217v, 229; Q2, fos. 159–60, 162v-3; R1, fos. 18–19; R2, fo. 149; APC 1616–17, pp. 355–6; SRPC (134), pp. 267–8; TNA STAC8 238/22; SP14/127/12, 16/318/15; BHC 7, fos. 23, 40, 53v, 60v, 72, 345v.

[108] LMA Jour. 29, fo. 20v; BHC 5, fo. 419; J. M. Beattie, *Policing and Punishment in London 1660–1750: Urban Crime and the Limits of Terror* (Oxford, 2001), pp. 38–9; Paul Griffiths, *Youth and Authority: Formative Experiences in England, 1560–1640* (Oxford, 1996), pp. 334–7; Tim Meldrum, *Domestic Service and Gender, 1660–1750: Life and Work in the London Household* (Harlow, 2000).

[109] LMA Jour. 25, fos. 101–2.

hands on. A number of husbands took charge of goods stolen by their wives.[110]

Thieves with no one lined up to take their spoils were in tight spots, needing to get rid of stolen goods quickly. Some got a pittance, others did not get even this small satisfaction. Ellen Browne showed a gold chain to a drunk Irishman in an alehouse who passed it round to tipsy drinkers. Drawing a blank, she next 'shewed' it to Elizabeth Jones who offered to sell it and meet her later in 'Powles' to give her a half share. But Browne never saw her again. One rogue turned to the first likely person he bumped into to sell a neckerchief, hoping to get three shillings.[111] Enough people and places recur for us to home in on situations where thieves bargained with receivers: pawnshop trade or alehouse barter, for example. Receivers coached thieves to steal; Dekker called receivers' shops 'academies of thieving'.[112] Experience counted. Veterans with standing knew London well. Talented thieves passed on skills. Wotton's 'school-house' for cutpurses near Billingsgate is the only one we have found this far back in time. A well-off trader who fell on hard times, Wotton changed course to 'rear' cutpurses and pickpockets in 'a new trade of life', with eyes for technique and ears for cant like the thick textures of rogue prose.[113] Thieves were drilled by seasoned artists. A joiner's son said that 'a servingman' living in an alehouse near Charing Cross 'taught him the maner of cuttyng a purse'. Fourteen-year-old Nicholas Adam's 'teacher' was the veteran pickpurse 'John of the Kechyn'. William Loggins 'firste entised' William Cooke and Richard Smithwick to cut purses. While John Pastell's 'firste teacher' was John White, though he needed extra coaching after his master boxed his ears as 'he colde not picke churche boxes so conyng as he wolde have hym'.[114]

Parents were supposed to hand down lessons to their children, but not how best to nick a purse or steal clothes. Alice Gregory's mother taught

---

[110] BHC 1, fos. 2v, 118. For other cases from a big pool see BHC 1, fos. 2v, 201; 2, fos. 12v, 147v; 3, fos. 290v, 414v; BHC 5, fo. 392; 8, fo. 1; BRHA BHC 4, fos. 20v, 143v, 278; LMA CQSF 91/177, 110/17; MJ/SR/36/130, 37/50; MJ/SRB/1, fo. 526; MJ/SRB/2, fo. 265; MJ/SRB/6, fo. 492.

[111] BHC 2, fo. 182v; 3, fo. 434. For other cases see BHC 1, fo. 112; 2, fos. 61v, 182v; 3, fo. 400v; 6, fo. 313v; LMA CQSF 117/14; MJ/SR/505/90, 509/91, 518/4, 524/8; MJ/SBR/1, fos. 33, 151, 293, 419, 516, 636; MJ/SBR/2, fos. 30, 132, 256, 336, 470, 494; MJ/SBR/3, fos. 124, 528; MJ/SBR/4, fos. 15, 438; MJ/SBR/5, fos. 213, 506; MJ/SBR/6, fos. 134, 482; WJ/SR/NS/30/75, 34/95, 35/72, 36/101, 38/33, 40/12, 40/41, 41/210, 41/225, 42/96, 44/12, 45/153, 47/27.

[112] Quoted in McMullan, *Canting Crew*, p. 106.

[113] Strype, *Survey*, V, p. 440. See also McMullan, *Canting Crew*, pp. 107–8.

[114] BHC 1, fos. 41, 31; 2, fos. 51, 22v. See also BHC 2, fo. 66v. Gregory also taught 'another boye called John Nayler' to cut purses. See also Reynolds, *Becoming Criminal*, pp. 87, 120.

her the pilfering 'trade'. Another mother helped her nightwalker daughter fleece men she picked up. Christian Roe stole a cloak from a man sitting supping with her in 1632, and her mother ran outside shouting 'murther' when he made 'a stirre for it'. Bridget Hambledon was locked up for 'mainteining her sonne' to pick pockets in 1633. George Raynton's mother 'caused him for feare of his liffe' to steal 'fyne lynnen clothes' from Mr Tenant's garden while his maids napped after a drinking binge.[115] No single family was a gangland, but there was some permanence when family members turned to crime. Magistrates heard of five brothers who belonged to the pickpocket 'profession' in 1628. William Fisher, called 'nip' by his mates, had a brother who was a cutpurse. Gang members and brothers Robert and Stephen Smith pinched the king's plate in 1638 (their father was also a 'suspected person'). Theft ran in families; prostitution too. Some sisters formed bawd/'whore' teams and some mothers were bawds to their own daughters.[116] Thieves also married each other, meeting in alehouses, boarding houses, barns, or fields, dancing, drinking, and flirting. There were one-night stands like those imagined in Harman's pages where his 'upright men' and 'doxies' have sex at the drop of a hat. But other relationships lasted for longer. There were husband/wife thieving teams, and some thieves who were guilty by association had harder jobs to clear themselves. Anne Bayly appeared at Bridewell in 1561 and pleaded not guilty to picking purses, but her 'late husband was a comon pickpursse' and she still mixed with his friends. Two vagrant women landed in deeper trouble after it emerged that one of them was married to a pickpocket and the other had lost her husband on the gallows. The husband of pickpocket Bridget Gibbs was charged with sexual assault in 1633. Grace Holland, who was caught walking late in 1640 after a week in the 'newe Bridewell', had a husband in Newgate waiting for trial. Love even bloomed in Bridewell; the minister was told that he could no longer marry prisoners without the court's blessing in 1606.[117]

Thieves also had tricks up their sleeves. Thomas Harbert broke up the boards on a stall one day as a 'nighte cart went by', so he would not 'be heard by any' standing nearby. Edward Dye was grabbed on the bridge 'cutting thinges from behinde horsemen'. Thomas Wright 'spread his hat

---

[115] BHC 7, fos. 48, 264; 8, fos. 130, 156v; BRHA BHC 4, fo. 389; BHC 6, fo. 257; 7, fo. 310; 2, fo. 290v; 1, fos. 117, 201, 216; 2, fo. 90.
[116] BHC 7, fos. 78v, 41v; 8, fo. 156v. See also BHC 7, fo. 202; 8, fo. 145; 1, fos. 187v, 188, 208; 3, fos. 117v, 130v, 136, 148, 153–3v, 162, 366; BRHA BHC 4, fos. 385–5v.
[117] BHC 1, fo. 140; 7, fos. 185v, 350; 8, fo. 312v. 5, fo. 89. See also LMA MJ/SR/508a/74; BHC 1, fos. 118–18v; 7, fos. 119v, 220, 350, 350v; 8, fos. 14, 193v; BRHA BHC 4, fo. 351v.

over 2 other hats' in a shop and grabbed the most expensive one. James Morrece was spotted at night 'with an yron instrument readie to breake open a doore'. More roughly, Edward Pink whacked someone with 'a gret crabtree truncheon' and took his cloak. Robert Wilkinson threw a snowball in a man's face to grab his cloak. Others had to think fast on their feet. A 'notorious' nip tried to shake off a chasing pack by shouting 'stoppe theef'. Thieves jostled people to get at purses or pockets in the tangle of bodies. James Bowner 'justled a woman' while his mate grabbed her ring in 1630. Others fell down on the ground to trip people and snatch something as they tottered off balance.[118] Thieves also drew crowds, knowing that there was cover in them. John Jeffrey sang ballads 'to drawe company togeather for his master to pick purses'. Others pulled pins from coach-wheels, and waited for people to spill out,[119] or stole 'under color' of job hunting or running errands. Some people never got back their kettles after thieves offered to fix them in their invented workshops. Henry Jones scouted for 'opportunities' when doing odd jobs in 1608. Mary Strange talked her way 'into mens howses under the collor of kindling of sticks' to take 'all she [could] come by'. John Davis stole shoes in 'shoemakers shoppes under color of enquirie for worke'.[120] 'Creepwindows', 'housecreeps', or 'shopcreeps' slipped into houses to let their accomplices in after families went upstairs to bed. Little eight-year-old George Schofield was 'put into casements by theeves'. John Stephen was caught 'lurking' in a house late one night waiting for an 'opportunity to lett in thieves'. A carman's wife was spotted 'comyng suspiciouslye to mens howses' after dark to draw latches in 1574, to let others sneak in once the streets emptied.[121]

Much of this took skill, daring, or cheek. Thieves had tricks, techniques, and tools. George Wilmott was 'suspected to bee a pickpockett' because he had 'the engines of a thiefe about him'. 'Daungerous' John Whetson had 'many cutpurse knives' when he was caught by a deputy. Others carried 'picklocks' or 'picklocke keyes'. 'Idle' John Bellmay had '4 picklocke keyes found about him' when he was stopped on a street in 1645.[122] Thieves also cut 'counterfeat keyes'. A Southwark locksmith was locked up 'for making keys' for thieves in 1618, one of them was a

---

[118] BHC 7, fos. 44v, 45, 84v, 158, 181v, 228; 5, fos. 77v, 421; 8, fo. 65v; 6, fo. 314v; 2, fos. 103, 177; BRHA BHC 4, fos. 54v, 315v; LMA MJ/SBR/4, fo. 400; MJ/SR/803/7.
[119] BHC 6, fos. 243, 259, 87; 5, fo. 353v.
[120] BHC 2, fo. 61; 5, fos. 242, 41v, 339v. See also BHC 6, fos. 141, 278v.
[121] BHC 7, fos. 373, 23v, 19, 291; 6, fos. 217v, 261v; 5, fo. 32v; 2, fo. 58v; BRHA BHC 4, fo. 369v.
[122] BHC 6, fos. 258v, 216v; 9, fo. 173. See also BHC 5, fo. 442; 6, fos. 5, 280, 407; 7, fo. 207v; 8, fo. 251v; BRHA BHC 4, fo. 54v; LMA CQSF 117/7; MJ/SBR/2, fo. 248; WJ/SR/NS/40/54, 40/179.

perfect fit for the Earl of Lincoln's lock. The 'pikyng knave', John Flower, was caught with 'a bonche of keyes of all sortes' in 1561. While two 'vagrant boyes' had a key for 'the kinges scullery dore' in 1634.[123] Others shaved sticks to steal from stalls or windows with hooks on tips for good grips. Daniel Jones raided shops after dark 'usinge a staff with a hooke att the end of it'. Thomas Tailor was caught red-handed putting a hook – 'made fitt to pilfer clothes' – 'in at a wyndowe' in 1576.[124] Lint or birdlime made money stick like gum. Walter Williams (the waterbailiff's son) had a stick 'noynted with lynt' to snatch money from goldsmiths' stalls in 1578. Richard Taylor was caught one night 'with birdlime on a sticke in a goldsmithes deske' in 1634. While Jeremy Wright dipped his fingers in 'lyme' to steal money out of boxes.[125]

'Liming' sticks first turns up at Bridewell in the 1570s and is still in use seven decades later, an old trick like 'false pocketts' or lock-wire. Barbara Orton had a 'false pockett in her petticoate' to stash cloth. A 'comon hat snatcher' had an 'instrument' to swipe hats. The 'comen roge' Cowetaile said that Crooked Legs had 'a great deale of wire'.[126] Old hands put novices through their paces, giving them tips on the job. It could take time to become a gifted cutpurse or cardsharp. Whether stealing or swindling with 'deceiptfull dyce' or cards, crooks could draw on rich street lore. Isabella Harding 'harbor[ed] Ned Duffill a notorious conicatcher'. Two 'comon decoyes and deceavers of people' lured 'a yong contry fellowe' into an alehouse 'with cards'. One case is a stock country-bumpkin tale. A cattle driver, Hugh Pare, who was said to be 'a simple countryman easy to be deceived', claimed that two 'common cheaters and cozenors' conned him out of £200 in a Gracious Street alehouse, asking him to drink with them, and plotting to make him 'senseless'. Ale flowed and they buttered him up with jolly 'carrouses and healths'. When he was 'half-drunk', the city slickers got out their 'false dice commonly called bars or flats' or 'high fullins'. One pledged to take his side to 'win monies', but true to the tale, Pare was left with nothing after the last throw of the dice.[127] Cony-catching was a money-spinning 'art'. Thomas

---

[123] BHC 8, fos. 1v, 42; 1, fo. 46; LMA MJ/SRB/2, fo. 504; BHC 1, fo. 117v; 7, fo. 358. See also BHC 6, fos. 27, 432v; 7, fo. 271v.
[124] BHC 6, fo. 351; 2, fo. 253; BRHA BHC 4, fo. 406v. See also LMA MJ/SBR/2, fo. 76; BHC 5, fo. 362v; 7, fos. 147v, 292; 8, fos. 51v, 259v; 9, fo. 354.
[125] BHC 3, fo. 350; 8, fo. 9; 7, fo. 246; 8, fo. 57; 9, fo. 366. A bawd in *Westward Ho* was called Birdlime.
[126] BHC 7, fo. 97v; 6, fo. 182; 2, fo. 434.
[127] LMA MJ/SR/508a/231; BHC 7, fo. 73; TNA STAC8 241/15. See also LMA Reps. 13ii, fo. 573v; 23, fo. 523; Jour. 19, fo. 353v; WJ/SR/NS/32/144; MJ/SR/506/5, 515/71, 525/80; MJ/SBR/1, fos. 457, 588, 639; MJ/SBR/2, fos. 70, 126, 331, 518; MJ/SBR/3, fo. 544; MJ/SBR/6, fos. 13, 84.

Buckmaster and Edward Bickerton made 'theire living by cheating with false cardes'. Abraham Folliott swindled '79li 17s 6d' from 'a duchman' with card tricks. Two tricksters conned £10 from a boy with 'false dyce and cards'. Francis Johnson 'lured' Richard Day to play 'one and thirty' in 1634, and tricked him out of £10. A gang of four swindled £8 from Hugh Davies in a game of 'tecketacke' two years later. While John Proof – 'a cheater of men by false arts and unlawful games' – fleeced twenty-one pieces of silver ('called rex dollars') from John Forbesse after wheedling him into a game of 'Most at two throws' in the same year. William Viner made money 'with false tallies by a tricke called the carrying of the colt'.[128] 'Cozening' or 'counterfeiting' covered many 'arts'. William Holland and Peter Constantine 'lived by' making and selling 'counterfett musk'. Fortune-tellers conned people with promises 'to bringe things loste home againe'. 'Cheators' switched fake or cheap jewells for pricey gems. John Gold 'cozened' with 'skeanes of copper instead of golde' in 1602; my master made me do it, he said. Thomas Beadley slipped a 'counterfett ringe' in a 'good rings place' in a goldsmith's shop in 1605; his pockets were stuffed with 'counterfet' stones.[129]

Few street discourses have survived from this time, although techniques and tricks imply shared knowledge. There are also splashes of thieves' cant in courtbooks from when suspects used words like 'lift' in the courtroom which were then written down by clerks. Courtbooks contain scores of 'nips'. Nip was also a nickname; one 'notorious cut-purse' was called 'nip' for short. 'Foist' also appears in records; two women were caught 'foisting' ten shillings from a pocket in 1620. Recorder Fleetwood noted that 'nipper' (pickpurse/cutpurse), 'foister' (pickpocket), and 'lift' (shoplifting) were 'terms of art' in Wotton's 'school-house'.[130] Other street slang suggests camaraderie and code, like nick-names. There are traces of rogue writing and thieves' speech in courtbooks. Not just names and titles, but tricks, techniques, and scenarios, like the slow befuddled bumpkin left holding nothing after the game of dice went awry. There is real life in rogue writing, enough at any rate to make some stereotypes stick. Without some ring of truth rogue writing would have been taken too lightly for a genre, we are told, that served as help-manuals to warn Londoners about thieves in their midst. More than enough people had the wool pulled over their eyes to

---

[128] LMA MJ/SBR/7, fo. 139; MJ/SBR/1, fo. 418; MJ/SBR/6, fo. 441; WJ/SR/NS/41/207, 46/189; MJ/SBR/1, fo. 487. See also LMA WJ/SR/NS/41/170, 42/88, 43/103, 46/137, 47/20, 47/68.
[129] BRHA BHC 4, fos. 309, 426, 310; BHC 5, fo. 76v. See also LMA MJ/SBR/1, fo. 417; WJ/SR/NS/36/161; CQSF 105/10, 106/24, 111/5.
[130] BRHA BHC 4, fos. 376v, 394; LMA CQSF 93/1; Strype, *Survey*, V, p. 440.

remind us that these cautions were essential elements of 'rough guides' to the city, and that rogue writing struck chords out on London's streets.

### Overlaps

No matter how often others saw thieves as something apart – black – or herded them to nether-regions – beasts – overlaps between citizens and criminals were plain to see. This was troubling for people who drew dividing borders. Little was comfortably clear cut, despite an annual flood of polarizing policy and prose. There were too many pimping craftsman, light-fingered traders, or other citizen-criminals for that, and too many officers who broke the law. Courtbooks contain countless warnings to relax categories of criminal as good-for-nothing drop-out and citizen as bright beacon of civic ethics. One vagrant was able to show that he was 'a freeman of London' and he was back at work the next day. Another vagrant got into magistrates' good books with a Bishopgate Street address and a City 'pencyon of fifty shillings yerlie'.[131] Some suspects got off the hook with jobs and enough of a salary to scrape by without hand-outs. I 'taketh paines by weedinge to gett a livinge', vagrant Dennis Wood said in 1619. A letter from Cambridge confirmed that William Bliss worked for 'the seconde coke' at Trinity College, and vagrancy charges were quickly dropped. Thomas Jones turned out to be 'an honest poore waterbearer att the conduite in Gracious Streate'. Alice Jefferson convinced the court that she was 'a laborious woman'. Servants, shoemakers, scholars, soldiers, sailors, tailors, glovers, drovers (up for the day), radish sellers, barber surgeons ('willinge to labor'), all walked free from court.[132] Jobs fixed them with an address and status. I have 'a house of [my] owne', vagrant William Sly said in 1604. John Duckett was freed four years later because he 'appear[ed]' to be 'a dweller'. Robert Wilcock had four things on his side in 1604: 'nothing could be found against him', he had 'a place of abode', 'labor[ed] for his living', and he 'live[d] in good sorte'. Agnes Stanley had a double defence: she had a house and husband across the river in Southwark.[133]

These offenders had footholds in London, some were rate-payers with voices and votes in vestries. Seemingly settled, they were allowed to go back home. Other offenders had well-heeled relatives and friends in high

---

[131] BHC 9, fo. 871; 5, fo. 191v.
[132] BHC 5, fo. 377v; 6, fo. 10; 5, fos. 439, 220v, 231, 376, 430, 431v, 432; 6, fos. 31, 94v, 160v, 400v; BRHA BHC 4, fos. 346v, 406v, 410; LMA Rep. 13i, fo. 115.
[133] BRHA BHC 4, fos. 442, 465; BHC 5, fos. 284, 181. See also BHC 5, fos. 242, 243, 281v, 297v, 300; LMA Rep. 14, fo. 263.

places. Humphrey Hitchcock, a vagrant 'brought from the bonfier in Cornehill', was a preacher's servant and 'kinsman to alderman Dixie's wife'. Frances Withers, who lived 'in lewdnes' for eighteen months, was Sir William Withers' daughter. A drunk caught roaring in 'idle company' turned out to be Lady Clifford's daughter. A leading bawd in mid-1570s London was married to 'the quenes wax chandler in The Old Baylye'. Mary Lord, 'an old running bawd', was 'kin to marshal Davis', who would take a leading role in the doomed expedition to the Isle of Rhe in 1627. One nightwalker tried to talk her way out of a sticky situation by claiming to be the niece of Bridewell's president. It must have been an awkward moment at Bridewell when it dawned on the bench that a vagrant standing before them was in fact the daughter of a 'late' Bridewell beadle. The sons of beadles, hangmen, and parish clerks ended up caught in Bridewell's net, along with the son of 'the king of Scotland's prynter', a ward deputy's niece, an unnamed 'greate mans daughter', and others who had parents 'of good meanes' or 'fortune'. Then, as now, good connections were handy things to have in a courtroom. Vagrant Charles Watson, who was 'taken' by the St Sepulchre watch late one night in 1632, was set free the next day when Mr Tito, 'one of the [Bridewell] governors', told his colleagues on the bench that he 'knew his father and some of his friends'.[134]

'Criminals' crossed spatial, residential, and work borders all the time. Londoners bought stolen goods at cut-rate prices, filled larders with food from sellers who were a curse for guilds, felt a warm glow after giving hand-outs, and rented cheap rooms to needy new arrivals. To cap it all, busy commercial concourses or any place where crowds gathered held magnetic properties for thieves, who walked the same city as citizens.[135] Citizens and criminals were locked in economic or social ties with give-and-take on both sides. Commercial sex was another apparent reciprocity. Even a shortened census of clients looks like a who's who of London society, with leading offices, titled big-wigs, and an army of apprentices. Names logged in Bridewell books include Mayor Spencer's son, Sir Owen Hoxton's second son, Alderman Pype's son, Alderman River's son, Alderman Starkey's apprentice, Alderman Bond's servant, a sheriff's servant, a 'hye constable', 'compter' clerks, the town clerk's clerk, 'a beare clark and meater of cloth in Yeldhall' ('comon doers with

---

[134] BHC 6, fos. 383, 424; 3, fo. 126v; 7, fos. 64, 21v; 6, fo. 352; 1, fo. 161v; 6, fos. 350, 369; 7, fos. 44, 73; BRHA BHC 4, fo. 127v; BHC 7, fos. 51, 75; 8, fo. 222v; 6, fo. 39; 7, fo. 297v. See also BHC 7, fo. 342v; 8, fos. 147, 159, 173v, 309, 315; BRHA BHC 4, fos. 11v–12.

[135] Cf. Judith Walkowitz, *City of Dreadful Delight: Narratives of Sexual Danger in Late Victorian London* (1992), chaps 1–2; Young, *Justice and the Politics of Difference*, pp. 239–40.

whores'), a Blackwell Hall 'sealer', a woodmonger in charge of Bridewell's wood wharf, 'gents' of the Inns, King's Bench attornies, a string of 'gentlemen and welthye men' and their servants, 'the lieftenants man of the tower', other royal servants, and a crop of foreign ambassadors' stewards, secretaries, and servants.[136]

Categories were blurred still further whenever officers took the side of offenders, helping them to get out of sticky situations or pocketing bribes, sleazy stories that will be left for Chapter 9. London's officers ended up on the wrong side of the law for much the same range of petty or raucous reasons that resulted in thousands of court appearances for men and women all over the city. A sheriff's sergeant, Christopher Ruddy, was locked up in Newgate in 1630 for stubbornly staying sitting in his seat after St Paul's vergers asked him three times to kneel down during the service. A pair of marshalmen were found among a crowd of rioters in 1608, egging them on, not rounding them up.[137] Badly behaved officers were subject to the same loose labels that were applied to vagrants and others in large numbers, like 'lewde', 'light', 'naughty', or 'bad'. They were caught 'misbehavinge' or 'misorderinge' themselves. Sheriffs' officers were warned that they would lose their posts if they ever 'unhonestly or lewdly use[d] and behave[d] themselves' in office. But not all of them took these warnings to heart, and they ended up out-of-office and out-of-pocket. Some officers were first suspended and later sacked after a string of offences. Bridewell beadles George Blower and Davy Fowler lost their jobs for 'abuses' in 1579 after taking little notice of warnings. Indeed, Blower was almost certainly the same George Blower who lost his 'place' as sheriff's yeoman in 1573 for not keeping his tongue in check: 'divers tymes' slandering the 'lord maiors courte' both 'publiquely' and 'secreatly', saying that it was 'no corte of recorde'.[138] He was not alone with his loose tongue. A constable was taken to task in 1616 for 'abusinge' men of 'good esteeme and reputacon'. One of London's leading traders, draper Maurice Abbot, was hopping mad after Marshal Walrond let drop 'scandalous speeches tending to [his] disreputacon and discredit' in 1623. Nothing could stem this flow of offences that ranged from felonies all the way down to trifling neighbourly nuisances. Walrond was ticked off

---

[136] BRHA BHC 4, fos. 48v, 67v, 70, 100v-1, 108v, 188v, 255v, 264v, 349, 361, 383, 390v, 430v; BHC 3, fos. 14v, 20v, 61v, 99v, 111v, 120v, 113v, 127, 134v, 199, 222, 262v, 280, 298, 320v, 355, 415. See also Mazo Karras, *Common Women*, pp. 95–101.

[137] LMA Rep. 44, fo. 176v; MJ/SBR/1, fo. 5.

[138] LMA Reps. 20, fo. 272; 23, fo. 517v; BHC 3, fo, 403v; LMA Rep. 17, fo. 432v. See also LMA Reps. 14, fo. 240v; 15, fos. 101v, 293; 16, fos. 70–0v; 17, fo. 244; 20, fo. 400v; 21, fo. 281; 23, fos. 91, 272, 441v-2; 34, fo. 367v; 59, fo. 317; MJ/SBR/2, fos. 312, 347; WAC F2001, fo. 114.

by aldermen in 1624 for building a house in the Old Bailey that leaned towards Newgate and blocked out the prison's light.[139]

Beer got the better of other officers and caused awkward moments. A parish acted quickly when it turned out that its constable was 'an ordinarye drunckarde'. Another looked back ruefully to the time when Constable Donne was 'often bestlie drunck' and unable to lift a finger to help anyone. Some watchmen drank all day long and were never in any fit state to watch. Drink also dragged down John Ashbury in 1560, 'sometyme hangman of Newgate', and 'a dronken quarelling knave'.[140] Drinking on duty was a great temptation for some; sex, as ever, was another. Officers were among many men who were prosecuted for fornication/illegitimacy. Beadle Broke fathered an illegitimate child and had 'either had vii basse children or ells had to dele with vii wemen lewdly'. He admitted to a prosecution for the same offence fourteen years earlier and living a 'lewde life' ever since. A Westminster beadle – Richard Shepard – who lodged two women in his house 'ever since his wifes decease', pleaded guilty to 'disordered living' and lost his job until he could convince the court that he was 'a new man'. A sheriff's sergeant was 'utterly dysmyssed forever' in 1572 for 'shameless disorder with keapinge company' with Shurlock's wife. Another sergeant took bail to let Cicely Bradshaw out of a compter in 1575 and 'had the use of her bodie' straight after. There was a steady procession of 'lewd living' officers through courts, including a watchman who raped a woman under 'cover' of searching her house.[141] One of Bridewell's 'ancient guests', 'lewd' Dorothy Woodward, came to the court there in 1621 to claim that Marshalman Peel had 'often' had 'the use of her bodye'. This was no overnight fling, Woodward said, as Peel 'many tymes would seke her out in Chick Lane' to take her to an alehouse for a drink and something to eat, and to a blind woman's house afterwards for sex, so often she said, that 'she cannot remember'. Whenever Woodward was locked up in Bridewell (a regular occurrence), Peel brought her 'stronge beere' each day at the hemphouse. She told Bridewell's matron that 'she was Peeles love'.[142]

---

[139] LMA Reps. 32, fo. 262; 14, fo. 299; 38, fos 6v, 206. For Abbot see Robert Brenner, *Merchants and Revolution: Commercial Change, Political Conflict, and London's Overseas Traders, 1550–1653* (Cambridge, 1993). See also LMA Rep. 17, fos. 433v-4; WAC WCB/2, fo. 45.

[140] LMA MJ/SBR/1, fo. 524; MJ/SBR/2, fo. 290; GL MS 9064/16, fos. 59–9v; BHC 1, fo. 74v; 9, fo. 583; WAC WCB/1, fo. 159.

[141] BHC 3, fos. 248–8v, 261v; WAC F2001, fos. 155, 156; BHC 3, fo. 338v; LMA Rep. 17, fo. 341v. See also BHC 2, fos. 47, 175; 5, fos. 112v-13, 118v; BRHA BHC 4, fos. 407, 417, 420v; GL MS 12806/2, fo. 108.

[142] BHC 6, fos. 249v, 250v.

There is evidence in this shady dealing that some of London's officers lived double lives, mixing in criminal circles, constantly conflating categories of officer/offender, and even, like Peel, becoming smitten with a woman he should have disciplined not kissed. Nor should we rule out existing friendships that were built up before someone took office. Other officers stumbled into vicious circles, unable to disentangle themselves without the risk of revelation. Whatever the motivation, many were on speaking terms with rough elements, slipping them tip-offs or sharing spoils after a robbery. Marshalman Dancy was dressed down by aldermen in 1596 after he 'lewdlye discovered his m[aste]rs secrett purposes' to surprise search 'suspityous and bawdy howses', so that his friends would not be caught unawares (he had once been caught by a marshal in a 'lewd house' late at night). Middlesex magistrates heard that Elias Faulkner 'misbehaved himselfe in his office of constableship' in 1618, 'by shareinge moneyes gott by lewde meanes and confederatinge' with 'persons of evill behavior'.[143] Officers gave other 'evill' people helping hands, a hiding place, or bed and board. Constable Cooke of Whitecross Street was 'reported to keep an alehouse and to be a harborer of theefs' in 1629. 'Evil' William Governor was found lodging in constable Gibson's house in 1614, and Gibson talked himself into deeper trouble by giving aldermen 'evill speaches' and was sent straight to Newgate. One of Newgate's stewards – Richard Davies – landed in deep trouble in 1637 when he did his best to bail two 'notorious' burglars.[144]

Largely lost now are off-the-record meetings when officers and 'suspect' people shared meals, knocked back beer, and talked long into the night. Two beadles were sacked when word circulated that they mixed 'with divers rogues for supporting them and for drinking'. A Bridewell matron, Dorothy Kennell, was spotted dropping into Pockey Faced Dall's house in seedy Turnmill Street in 1632, and she was already under a cloud for stealing from women in her charge and for holding parties in her house for prisoners and 'women of good fashion'. A decade earlier, Matron Millet's maid was known to be 'a comon broker' of the 'turnes and endes' of the worst sort of prisoners.[145] It is a mystery how Baxter of Golding Lane was picked to be constable and stayed in post for any amount of time in 1576. He was up to his neck in 'dirty work', and neighbours flooded Bridewell with stories of his 'lewd' loutishness as 'a company keper, banketter, and comfortor of lewde women and lewde

---

[143] LMA Rep. 23, fo. 560v; MJ/SBR/2, fo. 493. One of the king's messenger's was prosecuted for selling stolen goods: LMA WJ/SR/40/191.
[144] BHC 7, fo. 103v; LMA Rep. 32, fo. 4v; WJ/SR/NS/49/124.
[145] BHC 2, fo. 42v; 7, fo. 269v; 6, fo. 274v.

persons and a taker of bribes'. He 'and dyvers others often mett and banquetted' in bawdy houses in high spirits, bawds feeling shielded by the constable around their table. People said that he was 'a banquetter and a resorter to Raynbowes house and dyvers other lewde houses' in the area. Mrs Rainbow was known to be a veteran 'harlot' and she gave the constable a purse, handkerchief, and 'a pastie of venyson', amongst other things, to buy his support and silence. Baxter once got Rainbow and 'other like lewd persons' out of Bridewell with 'sinister' and 'subtill practizes', claiming that someone dropped dead of plague in her house two days ago, and others were now 'sick there of it'. A merchant gave ten shillings to Baxter to get him out of Finsbury gaol quickly with his 'harlot', so that no one would learn of his fall from grace. Baxter was clearly getting too big for his boots, feeling cocky as he managed to slip, not for the first time, through the magistrates' radar. But he pushed his luck too far in Lent 1576 when he tried to trick the curate of St Giles-without-Cripplegate to church Street's wife, 'a harlot'. Baxter was her 'frende' and 'comforter', neighbours said, and had somehow got hold of a 'certificate' for her child's christening. The curate smelled a rat, however, when the midwife gave the father a different name to the one from Baxter. He asked the constable 'what he knewe': don't fret, he said, I have sureties to keep the child off the parish. Street's wife turned up for the ceremony without a certificate, but Baxter walked in through the door right on cue with the proper paperwork (and yet another new name for the father). He tried to cool the curate's concerns: do not 'feare', I know 'her well enough'. But the curate was now in two minds: 'I will do it', he said, 'but I charge you' to take her to Bridewell when I am finished 'that it might be tried better'. But 'as soone as she was churched', Street's wife 'was gonne suddenlie out of the churche'. Bridewell's board thought that the case was too big for them to handle; it had 'many matters', they concluded, and turned it over to aldermen for their final word.[146]

Officers also bumped into London's 'low life' in alehouses and on the streets. 'What news at Bridewell and how is Jane Trosse?' the pimp Richard Rolles asked Michael Blower, a Bridewell beadle, when they met by chance 'at Paul's Gate' in Christmas 1577. The matron 'says she is very sick', Blower said. The pimp winced, 'she and I have been suer together for twelve months', he said, 'and I mean to marry her'. 'You will do well if you do', Blower said, not without friendly concern, 'for I hear that she is very sick'. Beadle and pimp then walked off together in the direction of the cathedral. Another day, another meeting: Rolles ran into

[146] BHC 3, fos. 64v, 68, 69v-70, 71v, 72v, 73.

Blower and Davy Fowler – another Bridewell beadle – and greeted them cheerfully, saying 'he would give them beer if he had money but he had none'. The beadles must have got out their purses that day, for we next see the three in high spirits, drinking and chatting in a Crump Alley alehouse.[147] These chance meetings may seem fishy, but the pimp passed good leads to officers that day. Blower and Fowler also called in to see the bawd-pimp Thomas Wise at his house on St Steven's day, 'being desired to come for breakfast'. Wise chatted good-naturedly, clearly he was at ease with his guests: 'he was much beholding' to Bridewell's 'honest, wise, and discrete' governors, he said, and 'would rather come before them to tell his tale than before any of his parish'. The pimp Henry Boyer also bumped into Blower 'severall tymes', and they seem to have got along fine.[148] Other officers had ties to bawdy-house rings. One was said 'to walke up and downe Holborne with divers harlots 3 or 4 at any time' by his neighbours and curate. Accusations heaped up, including one that he once arrested the pimp-keeper Richard Watwood to keep him out of Bridewell, and 'slandered the state of preachers and spiritual persons' and the mayor to boot. Mr Breech – Clerkenwell's high constable – was Gilbert East's landlord (a big fish in bawdy backstreets), and often dropped into his brothel, staying all night 'in naked bedd', spending 'xs or such a some in good chere'.[149]

Circles overlapped on what Geremek calls the 'fluctuating frontier' that separated 'conventional society' from its thin margins.[150] Like crossing streets, boundary hopping was routine and spontaneous. These 'border crossings', 'mediating bridges', or overlapping circles show the brittle vulnerabilities of categories like marginality, that fall apart once their tell-tale intrinsic ambivalence is revealed.[151] Janice Perlman wrote a book called *The Myth of Marginality* about Rio de Janeiro's slums.[152] Is marginality a myth of crime hot-beds and whiter-than-white citizens? It is certainly a *tendency* on both sides of the fence. Magistrates build borders and have the pick of the labels. People drift and fall into crime on the other side. We should stick with group-titles, with all the criminal ties and polish that we find in records. But these were never mere satellites of the

---

[147] TNA STAC8 B/11/18, Michael Blower, examination; BHC 3, fo. 303v.
[148] BHC 3, fo. 303v. [149] Ibid., fos. 328, 280–0v. See also BHC 6, fo. 374.
[150] Geremek, *Margins of Society*, p. 2.
[151] Griffiths, 'Overlapping circles'; Sibley, *Geographies of Exclusion*, chap. 3; Douglas, *Purity and Danger*, p. 168; Egmond, *Underworlds*, pp. 40–4; Heather Shore, 'Cross coves, buzzers, and general sorts of prigs: juvenile crime and the "criminal underworld" in the early nineteenth century', *British Journal of Criminology*, 39 (1999), 10–24, esp. 11, 15.
[152] Janice Perlman, *The Myth of Marginality: Urban Poverty and Politics in Rio de Janeiro* (Berkeley, CA, 1976).

citizens' patch. Anyone might one day step outside the law. 'All rob', one author said sardonically, 'and every trademan hath his way and particular craft for the deceitfull working of his owne ende'.[153] This border energy is the best test we possess that the underworld's margins were political not real. A landslide of labels never froze citizen/criminal categories that were experienced as fuzzy realities. This word-war was a perennial struggle in larger London. Magistrates sought peace in secure definitions, but this was a pipe-dream, better forgotten.

[153] Godwin, *Historie des Larrons*, p. 270.

# 5   Crime: words

### Name games

'But what art thou?' ailing Edmund asks disguised Edgar, his slayer, in *King Lear*.[1] This was a crunch question for the times. No other one was asked more often or caused more trouble if left up in the air. Anything uncertain unsettled City leaders. Lives needed noting. The criminologist Tannenbaum says that societies 'cannot deal with people [whom they] cannot define'. Imagine the panic in Common Council, then, when reports landed on tables in 1603 that 'lewd and ydle persons' had committed a string of 'divers outrages', who 'cannot well be described but by viewe and sight of them'; or when word spread in the next year about a scary gang of 'lewde and dangerous' stragglers, 'who cannot yet be described by any particular markers whereby they may be noted'. Three shifty-seeming nightwalkers were ordered to go back down to Bridewell's cells in 1644, 'untill Mr. Treasurer [can] be satisfied what they are'.[2] This need to know and name gave form to something shapeless. People were pinned down on paper with names, addresses, and jobs. Magistrates knew what to do if suspects stood in docks drenched in suspicion: name them, label them, end things in a verdict. Only then did they have identities to criticize (if necessary). Tannenbaum sums this up nicely in just one word: 'define'.

Examinations were all about evidence, but also getting biographies, important in cultures where good family backgrounds and hard slog in jobs could place people. With no name there was nothing to put on paper or in the margins of Bridewell's books where suspects' surnames were written down in columns. Clerks flicked quickly through them to sort previous prosecutions into biographies. Magistrates tried to string lives together. Ralfe Cowper 'set down in writinge his whole lyfe, falts, and

---

[1] William Shakespeare, *King Lear*, ed. R. A. Foakes, The Arden Shakespeare (1997), 5:3, 162.
[2] Quoted in Frances Heidensohn, *Crime and Society* (Basingstoke, 1989), p. 70; LMA Jour. 26, fos. 147, 240v; BHC 9, fo. 92.

evell behavior' after splurging his master's money on 'horemongering' in 1574. Richard Massie also put down his past on paper after coming to talk to a prisoner in 1575, though he said that they were old friends and he came 'to see howe he did', as any good friend would. Two 'incontinent livers' – Anne Flemming and Rebecca Gallyard – were put back in the cells for the time it took to get 'better informacon concerning theyre life'.[3] Questioning was adapted for certain crimes. In trouble for illegitimacy in 1575, Margaret Price was asked 'whether you ever had any childe or not? Who begott you with childe? Where did he the dede? What wordes or promyses was there betwene you and him? What gifts have you received?'[4] But issues stayed the same even if crimes did not. Dekker's 'inquisitor' in *Lanthorne and Candle-Light* (1608) asked women who were caught walking late: 'Where have you been so late?' 'Are you married?' 'What's your husband?' 'Where lie you?'[5] Like this inquisitor, courts trawled for pieces of lives to glue people in place. The same questions popped up over and over again: What is your name? Who is your master? Where do you work? Where do you live? Are you married?[6] A 'lewde' Herefordshire servingman was 'examynd of the ordre of his lyfe' since coming to London in 1565. Thomas Barnard was quizzed about the 'meanes he lived' by since arriving home on a ship: in Marlow 'ymediatetly after' for a fortnight, he said, in Maidenhead after that for a week or so, next in Flymwell Park for two days, and then with my mother in London ever since, except for a short spell in Newgate for taking money from my father-in-law. When hearing that Agnes Artors was soon to be married after falling in trouble for 'naughtie rule' in a Wood Street widow's house in 1561, Bridewell's bench wanted to check that it was a solid match. How 'woulde they live', she was asked. 'He is a barber and trusts to live well' she said. And where would they live? 'We have no house yet but shall have one in St Giles'. And was their 'weddinge apparell' 'theire owne'? 'Some of it is our own old clothes and some of it is borrowed'.[7]

There was more poking about in prisoners' lives after 1600 and more women than men were grilled, something that makes sense given the greater gendering of crime at this time. Women were asked questions about family, maintenance, and clean living, but with added edges of

---

[3] BHC 2, fos. 32, 191v; 7, fo. 48. See also BHC 1, fo. 192v; 2, fos. 45v, 99, 150, 152, 159, 175v, 179v, 191v, 202, 205; 6, fos. 209, 215; 7, fo. 48.
[4] BHC 2, fo. 79v.
[5] Thomas Dekker, *Lanthorne and Candle-Light*, 1608, The English Experience, 585 (Amsterdam and New York, 1973) fos. 42–2v.
[6] For example, BHC 1, fos. 4v-5, 187, 198; 5, fos. 301v, 306, 310, 310v.
[7] LMA Rep. 15, fo. 404; BRHA BHC 4, fo. 360; BHC 1, fo. 192v.

inevitable immorality, dependence, and extra expense. They should have been under the thumb of some man. Elizabeth Hall, who lived cheaply at The Boar's Head close by Bishopgate, told Bridewell's bench that her husband was away at sea in 1603, and was asked 'what maintenance she receaveth from him'. She said 'none', and her whipping was a foregone conclusion. Sailors' wives were often left in precarious positions as voyages dragged on. Margery Elliott – 'alias Prowdfoote alias Barrett' – was 'exa[m]ined how she liveth' in 1601, and said that 'her husband is gon beyond the seas as a master of a ship' and she made ends meet with 'needleworke'. Not so, 'divers of her neighbours' said; 'six or seven' men 'dayly resort' to her house, and one watched her standing at a window talking with a man who 'semed to give her money'. Another sailor's wife – Elinor Death – was asked 'wheare she dwelt' two years later, and said that 'she doth not knowe'. She was next asked 'what maintenance she hathe to live uppon', and could show no 'juste matter' of that either. The clerk jotted down that 'it appeareth plainlie to the cort [that] she liveth as an idle vagrant lewdelie and disorderlie'. Other women scraped by, they said, by cleaning houses or washing clothes, like Katherine Padgett who 'washed and starched for gentlemen'.[8]

Some life-stories from the cradle to court run on for two or three pages in the courtbooks. The bigger the biography the better. People with nothing should not have been in London at all. They could 'not excuse' themselves. Thomas Frank 'doth nothing about his life', magistrates complained, but runs and 'range[s] abrode' each day from dawn to dusk. Three vagrant 'lifters' were simply said to 'live all faulty'. None of them had a leg to stand on.[9] A common thread in courtroom examinations was the need to establish stable identities and the domestic security that could provide tickets out of prison. But names were the first piece of a puzzle. I will start – like the courts – with names and look at offences and labels later on. We have no work, so far, on naming in courtrooms. We count names, log them on polished data-bases, or follow them through time to trace continuous communities, criminal backgrounds, or religious leanings.[10] But I am drawn to the subversive qualities of naming and

---

[8] BRHA BHC 4, fos. 421v, 261v, 424, 407v (Death later said 'that she hathe bin married vi yeares' and her husband had gone to sea 'a year past' leaving her '35li for her maintenance', fo. 453). See also ibid., fos. 254v, 277, 282v, 299, 357, 362, 380, 388v, 415, 423v, 426, 434, 453.
[9] BHC 6, fo. 282v; 2, fo. 61; 6, fo. 367. See also BHC 6, fo. 294v; 7, fo. 205; 8, fo. 262; 9, fo. 415; BRHA BHC 4, fos. 344v, 406v.
[10] Nesta Evans, 'The descent of dissenters in the Chiltern Hundreds', in Margaret Spufford, ed., *The World of Rural Dissenters, 1520–1725* (Cambridge, 1995), pp. 288–308; Scott Bannister, *Names and Naming Patterns in England, 1538–1700* (Oxford, 1997).

182  Crime

attempts by magistrates to put things back in order with a name of their choosing, making one up to put on record the presence in court of a tight-lipped suspect. By name-games I mean steps taken by courts to tease out the names of people or to force-name them, and counter-moves by people in trouble to give nothing up, not even a name. If settled, identity puzzles could crack cases. If left up in the air, outcomes were rather less certain. Mary Douglas writes about the twisty knots of inexact 'half-identities', that get in the way of building biographies.[11] Only someone on the make or take did not care about names, like Humphrey Mill's quack: 'How e're it came, if I could get but one / I never car'd, or any man that came / which brought me money, I nere ask'd his name / Nor what he was, his life, nor where he dwelt / He had his will when I his money felt'.[12]

Like labels, names reveal, but they can also conceal and sometimes put magistrates on the wrong track. They were thought up by parents as life-long points of reference, but were also conferred by courts or parishes if one was needed for a payment or policy. Sometimes someone died suddenly with no name, not even a parish tag. 'A woman whose name was not knowne' was 'browght a bedd in the cage neare Whytechaple barres' in Christmas 1595. Whitechapel warders buried her still-born 'man chyld' but 'refused to bury' his mother until the ward intervened and ruled that 'it was meete and decent that she should be buried owt the way because she was a greene woman and could not be kept any longer above the ground'. 'Ye shaking woman' is mentioned only once in St Botolph-without-Bishopgate's accounts and we never hear of her again, anywhere. No names but identities made according to need or health: 'greene', 'shaking', pregnant, penniless. Bartholomew Need was given money to tide him over by one parish.[13]

Parishes needed names, if only for book-keeping, something that all of them took care to better after 1600.[14] No more so than when a child was left on a step or stall one night. Some mothers left notes with names: Andrew was 'laid' in St Bartholomew-by-the-Exchange 'with a note' of his name; Henry had 'a paper found in his bosome' by the church door in St Martin Orgar.[15] Any name would do if there was nothing else to go on. One parish paid fourteen shillings to nurse a 'child called the foundling'. Another took care of John and Elizabeth Foundling. St Michael Wood Street bought shoes and stockings for Michael Found. Goody Hallom

---

[11] Douglas, *Purity and Danger*, p. 96.   [12] Mill, *Night's Search*, p. 252.
[13] GL MSS 9234/5, fo. 154v; 4524/1, fo. 225v; 4383/1, fo. 352. Cf. David Postles, *Social Proprieties: Social Relations in Early-Modern England, 1500–1680* (Washington DC, 2006), pp. 46–54.
[14] Griffiths, 'Secrecy and authority'.   [15] GL MSS 4383/1, fo. 400; 959/1, fo. 225.

nursed Mary Foundher for four weeks in 1648. Another parish cared for Ann Chance who was found by chance.[16] Not much brain power was burned up naming foundlings: Andrew Ye Wall, Benet Finck, Olave Jurye, Jeremy Jurye, Michael Michael, Matthew Matthews, Matthew Milk Street, Blunt Milkstreet, Betty Pancras, Exchange Bartholomew, Bartholomew Exchange, Bartholomew Newcome In, Michael Cloister, Susan Conduit, Thomas Woodyard, Andrew Brewhouse, Joanne Foundbasket, Jane Steps, or Porch Wall, who was kitted out with clothes by All Hallows London Wall, were all named after the parishes in which they were found or nearby landmarks.[17] There were eight little Michaels and two small Quernes listed in St Michael le Querne accounts in 1652–3.[18] There was even some pride in names as saved infants revealed a parish with a heart in the right place, and some children managed to make it all the way to the crowning success of starting service with a master or mistress. Other names had ethnic splashes, like 'Mary Blackamore', who was given a shroud. Others followed physical or mental marks, like Blind Robin, Dumb Tom who was kept for seventeen years until the day a parish forked out for his funeral, Joan Madd, and 'Franck Foole' who got hose and shoes from St Botolph-without-Bishopgate, and who is probably 'Frank The Innocent' who got a hand-out not long after.[19]

Something could follow names, such as payments or prosecutions. Courts wanted clarity, anything diverse needed sorting out. 'Dissembling' muddled identities, leaving courts with tough jobs on their hands to test truths. John Lee was taken back to his home parish when he 'gave a wrong name' in 1632, to check that his name was 'registered by their minister'. Abigail Newman caused no end of mix-ups at Bridewell after being kicked out of a cook's shop and caught walking late. Justice Howard's letter on her 'behalf' came soon after, but 'being not found to be the woman she is' she was sent to him to be freed if he thought she was 'the woman she is', if not, she was to go back to prison. Vagrant Katherine Appleton gave her name as William in 1631.

---

[16] GL MSS 9237, fos. 49v, 51v, 56, 84v, 87, 90, 120; 2596/2, fo. 103; 524/1, fo. 79v; 593/4, 1640–1.
[17] GL MSS 5090/2, fo. 252v; 1303/1, 1682; 2895/2, 1628–9; 1016/1, fo. 207; 2596/2, fo. 50; 4409/1, fo. 137; 4409/2, 1661–2; 5018/1, fo. 70; 4383/1, fos. 369, 408, 415; 4071/2, fo. 167v; 818/1, fo. 319; 12806/2, fos. 392v, 398v, 415; 2089/1, 1638–9. See also Christopher Thomas Daly, 'The hospitals of London: administration, refoundation and benefaction, c.1500–1572', unpublished DPhil thesis, University of Oxford (1994), pp. 349–53.
[18] GL MS 2895/2, 1652–3.
[19] GL MSS 9237, fos. 57, 75v; 818/1, fos. 153v, 164v, 191v, 196v, 203; 2089/1, 1649–50; BHC 6, fo. 371; GL MSS 4524/1, fos. 170, 174; 12806/2, fos. 392v, 397, 398v, 399, 407v, 415.

184  Crime

While Mary Griffin sneaked pots from taverns 'in mens names for wyne'.[20] Disguise deceived, making crime more sinister. A vagrant 'with a vizard before her face' was whipped in 1599. 'Dangerous' Simon Webb, the leading suspect in a theft case, came to court with 'false haire'. The old-hand cutpurse Owen Cannon slipped out of Bridewell 'in a false perriwig and beard'. While Thomas Hayesley crept through his 'late' master's house wearing a 'false beard' in 1622, seeking something to steal to get his own back for the sack.[21] People dressed up to make good impressions in cultures that sized up character through clothes. Margaret Hussy landed in trouble after 'undertaking to be a fortune teller and borrowing clothes of a woman pretending [to be] married'. William Brett 'fayned to be a Dutchman' to talk his way into lodgings in 1575. A 'pryvye watche' hunted high and low for 'nyne or tenne persons disguised with honest apparell berring the behavior of gentlemen and honest men' in 1577. London's magistrates got sick and tired of beggars 'naming themselves to be soldiers' to bluff their way into citizens' pockets.[22] Names were 'abused' not just by snide slanders. John Rash was locked up in 1633 after 'abusing dyvers mens names' back home in Buckinghamshire by 'taking up' money 'in their names'. Nicholas Wood (alias William Stretch) was found begging and 'abusing the name of doctor Moulins a devine' in 1636, going round saying he was his son, bringing 'scandall upon' him, the clerk added, if anybody thought that a parson could have raised someone so low. John Stoole 'clean contrarie' called himself Richard Codde to con 'well disposed people' into giving him hand-outs.[23]

Disguise was all the rage on the stage for a lark and laugh. Students scuffled for plum seats to watch confusions untangle when *The Comedy of Errors* was put on at an Inn of Court.[24] Impersonation twisted identities and who knew which one was true. Two 'counterfeit' men landed in trouble in 1632 for imitating legitimate late night walking: one 'with a holbert' took the part of a 'watchman seeming to conduct the other to his dwelling colorably'.[25] Tom Kinder ended up at Bridewell in 1607 for 'counterfeitinge' Richard Appleyard's name. On the run from his master

---

[20] BHC 7, fo. 258; 8, fo. 69v; 7, fo. 248; 8, fo. 147v.
[21] BRHA BHC 4, fo. 123v; LMA MJ/SBR/5, fo. 254; BHC 7, fos. 135v, 136; 6, fo. 311. See also LMA MJ/SBR/2, fo. 275. Cf. *The Boke for a Justice of Peace* (1544), fo. 23v.
[22] BHC 7, fo. 188; LMA Jours. 20, fo. 366; 23, fo. 8v; BHC 3, fo. 94v; BRHA BHC 4, fo. 355. Cf. Godwin, *Historie des Larrons*, pp. 45, 53, 118, 272; WAC WCB/1, fo. 49.
[23] BHC 7, fo. 328v; 8, fo. 82. See also BHC 3, fo. 404v; 7, fo. 65v; 8, fos. 57, 62v, 105, 131, 331v; 9, fo. 380.
[24] Stephen Greenblatt, *Will in the World: How Shakespeare Became Shakespeare* (New York, 2004), p. 28.
[25] BHC 7, fo. 303.

in 1605, he got as far north as Yorkshire and tired and hungry knocked on Bartholomew Ramsden's door who was sure that he was the missing son of his near neighbour Appleyard. Here was a gilt-edged chance, Tom thought, too good to miss. Sent next door, he 'saluted' Appleyard's daughter 'by the name of sister Ann and she called him brother'. The phony brother also duped his new brother-in-law with his striking similarity to missing Richard, and Ann's mother 'acknowledged' that he was indeed her long lost son. 'By that occasion', the clerk noted, 'he took upon him that name', and like Arnold du Tilh in Martin Guerre's return, he settled into a cozy life with a new family. All this it seems to get away from a heavy-handed master. But back in London in 1607 for reasons now lost, Kinder/Appleyard was racked with guilt. Now on a vagrancy charge at Bridewell, he came clean about his masquerade: I am 'moved in conscyence to confesse the trewth lest [I] should deny [my] owne father and mother'. Anne Kinder had the final say one month later, calling Tom her 'natural son' and taking him home at long last.[26]

Tom Kinder was one of many who foxed courts with two names. Avery Johnson had a double defence in 1627 after she tried to bribe Bridewell's matron: 'she is found to have two names', the clerk noted, and changes her clothes inside out.[27] Like nicknames, aliases muddled identities, thought up in pressure-cooker situations to send police on wild-goose chases, as when three men gave 'false names' after rescuing a servant from a constable. This street strategy was exactly right for vagrants without histories in cities.[28] They had nothing to check unless they gave addresses within walking distance. Nor did they have any biographical scraps in passports. In some ways they had the upper hand and the odds were quite good that they would walk out of courts with their fake IDs intact. Many vagrants had hum-drum names, too many plain Jane or John Smiths to ring true.[29] But many thieves were caught trying to fool courts with aliases,[30] as well as a mixed bag of bawds, 'harlots', nightwalkers, cheats,

---

[26] BHC 5, fos. 185v, 194; Natalie Zemon Davis, *The Return of Martin Guerre* (Cambridge, MA, 1983).
[27] BHC 7, fo. 42.
[28] LMA MJ/SBR/5, fo. 32. Cf. the valuable work on aliases by David Postles, *Social Proprieties*, pp. 62–75. I am also grateful to David for allowing me to read his unpublished paper, 'The politics of naming and address in early modern England'.
[29] Cf. Martine Van Elk, 'The counterfeit vagrant: the dynamic of deviance in the Bridewell court records and the literature of roguery', in Craig Dionne and Steve Mentz, eds., *Rogues and Early Modern English Culture* (Ann Arbor, MI, 2004), pp. 120–39.
[30] For example, BHC 5, fos. 35, 105v, 136v, 206, 230, 344, 409, 420v; 6, fos. 359, 391, 400; 7, fos. 28v, 116, 284v, 373; 8, fos. 35, 100, 237v, 330v, 383; 9, fos. 14, 369, 793; BRHA BHC 4, fos. 29, 420; LMA MJ/SBR/7, fo. 126; CQSF 98/recog. Susannah Cobb, 113/35, 120/interrog. Freeze Brooman.

drunks, army deserters, runaway servants, bigamists, cross-dressers, and people on illegitimacy and fornication charges thinking about shrinking reputations and/or purses.[31] Some disguise-artists had several names at once. Bridewell's court had to sort out which of Mrs Sawmey's four names was the real one when word spread that she was a 'harlot' in 1579. It was tricky to get to the bottom of such cases. Elizabeth Walker, who knew 'most cutpurses' in London, also had four names. Anne Howe picked from six, including the one she gave the court – Arundel – that she took after 'a gentleman' locked up in King's Bench 'writt to her to do his busines and called her cosen Arundal'. Elizabeth Evans came clean in 1598, admitting she called herself 'sometime Dudley and sometime Carewe', with 'no reason [why] I tooke those names uppon me', she added.[32] It was a good day in court when aliases crumbled. Joan Yerly 'is also called Moulden' someone said in 1627. 'Old gessts', needless to say, found it harder to hide behind second names. William Tristram 'hath bene here before by the name of Roger Greene', a sharp-witted governor said in 1633. Edward Wadley 'was lately here by the name of Prett', another one said in 1638.[33]

Names could not be taken at face value. People reinvented themselves through disguise, trying to outwit magistrates. Like aliases, nicknames were also thieves' ID, with the added bonus for us that their use always hinged on acquaintance, recognition, and repeating. Nicknames tightened ties and also alllowed thieves to speak in jargon like cant that covered up their real names, identities, and actions.[34] Roguish Richard Reynolds was 'by nickname called Pondende Beefe'. Vagrant Edward Wills was 'otherwise called Small by a name the cutpurses call him'. 'Uncomely beastly' Anne Lewis was 'usually called Taumikin'. The 'comon nipp', John Gerrard, was 'commonly called Buttered Jack'. While a woman whom we know only as Anne was 'comonly called Kitchinstuff Nanne' by her companions.[35] 'Commonly' clearly suggests names with long shelf-lives, conferring other identities to the official ones in baptism

---

[31] For example, BHC 3, fos. 365, 374v, 436v; 5, fos. 49v, 100v, 265; 6, fos. 367, 375; 7, fo. 325v; 8, fos. 84, 112v, 237v, 331v, 351v, 367, 384v; 9, fos. 15, 38, 92; BRHA BHC 4, fos. 344v, 367, 381, 385v, 394v, 403, 418v, 420, 421v, 423v, 434, 438, 439, 449.

[32] BHC 3, fo. 409; BRHA BHC 4, fos. 179v, 131, 12v.

[33] BHC 7, fos. 41, 310v, 127. See also BHC 7, fos. 65v, 221, 366v; 8, fos. 57, 191, 350; 9, fo. 380; BRHA BHC 4, fo. 369; WAC WCB/1, fo. 49; LMA CQSF 96/4; Rep. 30, fo. 210; MJ/SBR/5, fo. 32.

[34] Norbert Schindler, 'The world of nicknames: on the logic of popular nomenclature', in his *Rebellion, Community, and Custom in Early Modern Germany*, trans. Pamela E. Selwyn (Cambridge, 2002), pp. 71, 72; Dave Postles, *Talking 'Ballocs': Nicknames and English Medieval Social Linguistics* (Leicester, 2003); Postles, *Social Proprieties*, pp. 62–75.

[35] BHC 6, fo. 230; 7, fos. 99, 62v; 6, fo. 279; LMA MJ/SBR/4, fo. 173.

registers. Nicknames crop up in nearly all criminal tableaux. We meet 'bawds' and 'whores' called Proudfoot, Bearfoot, Smallbear, and Nurse; thieves called Cowtail, Claribubbe, Captain Cowcomber, Hasty Jack, and Six-a-Clock; nips/cutpurses called Scanderbag, Mowchachoe, John of Dulwich, Flat Back, Jack of Bowbee, and Jack of the Kitchen; and vagrants/beggars called What You Will, Wicked Will Wells, Would Have More, Pinnace, Firebrand, and the more timorous sounding Herbert the Ruffian.[36] The same names crop up again and again. Mad Bess (a vagrant), Fair Bess (charged with sex in an alehouse), and Blinking Bess and Black Bess (both bawds), all appeared at the Bridewell court. Elizabeth White 'otherwise called Flounsing Besse a comen and abhomynable harlot of her bodie', appeared before aldermen in 1548.[37] More than one Long Meg turns up in the London area. The most notorious 'Megg' was a celebrity bawd at the start of Elizabeth's reign. Margaret Forster alias Marshal alias Taffety Meg was taken dancing 'at the Swanne taverne by the Spittle' with 'caveleers' one night in 1601. There were also many 'Malls' or 'Molls': Mall Neweberry, Irish Moll, and, of course, Moll Cutpurse.[38]

We rarely get more than names on paper, and not a word is said about the people who dreamed up nicknames in the first place, apart from suggestive group-titles like 'cutpurses', though we can imagine some wag shouting one out in an alehouse one night. A new bond was sealed that day. Nor did nicknames lack rhyme or reason, something random that might easily be forgotten. They did not need to be exotic to stick in memories. Most had roots in natural features, place, or ability, with something to say about backgrounds or bodies. Place was a common theme in this back-streets nomenclature. 'Cuntrie Nan' was a familiar face at Bridewell in 1600. Light-fingered Country Robin appeared there three decades later. Vagrant cutpurse Richard Waffoll was 'called Warwickshire' by his friends. Other names followed countries of origin. Irish Moll was put in Bridewell not long after Warwickshire. Irish Alice was caught picking pockets a little later, along with Irish James. Welsh Joan stole to keep hunger at bay, and the 'comon whore' Margrey

---

[36] BHC 2, fos. 94, 95, 97v; 3, fo. 434; 5, fos. 330v, 423; 6, fo. 389; 7, fos. 150v, 158v, 347v; 8, fos. 38v, 158, 257; BRHA BHC 4, fos. 31v, 37, 56, 101v, 158, 189v, 261v; LMA Rep. 12, fo. 511.

[37] BRHA BHC 4, fos. 424, 463v, 264v, 34; BHC 1, fo. 86v; LMA Rep. 11, fo. 451. Elizabeth Hicks alias Cooke alias Leyer alias 'Black Besse' told the court that she got married in Norwich some time ago and had had 'diverse children in wedlock', all now dead. See also Bernard Capp, 'Long Meg of Westminster: a mystery solved', *Notes and Queries*, 45 (1998), 302–4.

[38] BHC 1, fos. 42, 134v, 135v, 205, 208; BRHA BHC 4, fos. 229, 337v.

Gardener was 'comonly called Scotche Madge'. Nearer to home, the 'lewde pilferinge queane' London Stone was locked up in Bridewell after letting Black Jack have 'thuse and carnall knowledge of her body'. Other nicknames mocked neighbouring nations, dipping into a rich repertoire of jingoistic digs. A thief was called the Spaniard, because he was 'blacke'. While a prostitute was called 'French Megge', in the same way that the pox was thought at its source to be the seedy 'French disease'.[39] Bodies also gave ways to lump people together with similar features: tall, short, fat, thin, bad skin, crippled.[40] Size, shape, and age turn up in monikers like 'little' which slipped in all three: Little James (hat-snatcher), Little Robin (pickpurse), Little Meg (a 'runner' for bawds), Little Tom (cutpurse, pickpocket, hooker, and 'creeper in at windowes'), Little Alice and Little Nan (harlots), and Small Wills or Small Jack of Westminster. Cutting words about physical or mental traits reveal the rough no nonsense wit in this boozy culture. One thief was called Crooked Legs; another Bess of the Chest. Blinking Jane was caught on a step one night leaving a child. 'Pockey faced dall' was working hard in bawdy houses in 1630. While Whippet, I imagine, expresses respect for lightning speed.[41]

Nicknames had subversive tinges, not unlike topsy-turvy carnival jests. Some took swipes at the City or well-to-do, goading social betters. Vagrant Richard Hall was called Worshipful by his gang. Edward Powell was 'called The Witch of Powles' by his fellow thieves. Agnes Case was known as the Lady of Christ's Hospital by her friends, revelling in the sly dig against the showcase orphanage. Other haughty 'ladies' poked fun at the upper crust with false airs and graces. Vagrant beggar My Lady Will Have All was a 'comon [Bridewell] guest'. Anne Bartfield masqueraded as posh My Lady Bartfield, though she was better known at Bridewell for being 'a naughtie, lewd, and evell woman'.[42] No one contested their names, not according to the clerks' scribbles at any rate. There were no slanging matches. Some names express pride or

---

[39] BRHA BHC 4, fo. 296; BHC 7, fo. 417; BRHA BHC 4, fos. 52, 337; LMA MJ/SBR/5, fo. 197; BHC 7, fo. 246; LMA WJ/SR/NS/35/5; MJ/SR/525/62; BRHA BHC 4, fos. 410, 411, 430. See also Jon Arrizabalaga *et al.*, *The Great Pox: the French Disease in Renaissance Europe* (London and New Haven, CT, 1997).

[40] Cf. Schindler, 'World of nicknames', pp. 61 and 61–74.

[41] BHC 5, fo. 342v; 1, fo. 140; 2, fos. 262, 97v; 3, fo. 365; BRHA BHC 4, fo. 369v; BHC 3, fo. 434; 7, fo. 64; GL MS 12806/2, fo. 55; BHC 7, fo. 265v; BRHA BHC 4, fo. 337v.

[42] BRHA BHC 4, fo. 115v; BHC 7, fo. 349; 5, fo. 53v; 6, fo. 388v; 1, fos. 138, 209v. See also Schindler, 'World of nicknames', pp. 85–91; Schindler, 'Carnival, church, and the world turned upside down: on the function of the culture of laughter in the sixteenth century', in his *Rebellion, Community, and Custom*, pp. 93–145; Vic Gatrell, *City of Laughter: Sex and Satire in Eighteenth-Century London* (New York, 2006), chaps 5–6.

purpose in begging or pilfering. These were worlds where beggars became ladies. There are puns on tramping (Foot), snipes at well-off snobs (Would Have More), and some barbed fun. Colour and climate conveyed spoof senses of distance, a fringe-position quite fitting for 'whores' or thieves: Black Jack, Black Bess, Black Nan, Black Madge, Black Luce, or 'evel lyvinge' Cold Joan.[43] This is comic parody, but also code-names, known only by a select group, requiring recognition and repeating, reinforcing camaraderie one more time.

Silence was the last straw. Only Bridewell's governors stayed silent 'after the hammer strickes' to not 'molest' comrades leading examinations when trials were in full swing.[44] Some people in court for the first time had good reason to keep mum, as did debtors with creditors on their heels. Gervase Pogmore 'refused to tell his name' in 1609, 'because being in debte and daunger' he risked being locked up for a long time.[45] Other prisoners were suddenly struck down by memory loss or blamed the demon drink, looking on blankly as questions zipped past them. Nightwalker Margaret Owen was 'soe drunke she could not tell her name' at Bridewell in 1627.[46] Most silent suspects spoke after a while. 'Resolute' William Hudson 'refused to tell his name' after giving an officer a mouthful of 'abuse' in 1635 and ripping a beadle's band, but he caved in not long after. Joan Porter 'concealed her name' after lunging at Leonard Yonge with a knife in 1633. Vagrant William Frederick would not speak at all when he was brought to the Bridewell court, but he was whipped a little later, the clerk noted smugly, and 'then he spake', and screamed too.[47] Some plucky people stood their ground for longer. Patience was running thin with 'a tonguelesse man' in 1629 who 'cannot' or 'will not speake', the clerk scribbled crossly, but he spoke 'at last' he noted with some relief, and seems 'simple'. Five men were locked up by Parliament in 1653, including one 'who refuseth to discover his name' with a shrug of the shoulders. The stubborn mute was still not speaking six months later after at least eight attempts to squeeze something, anything, out of him.[48]

Some suspects let nothing slip and were let go after the court gave up trying to discover something about them, often with a 'noname' name. The 'notorious counterfeite' John Noname and vagrants Jane Nobody, 'Jone with no name', and 'John with no name' kept mum long enough for

---

[43] BHC 6, fos. 417–19; 8, fo. 82v; 1, fo. 45.  [44] BRHA BHC 4, fo. 93.
[45] BHC 5, fo. 349. See also TNA STAC8, 54/15.  [46] BHC 7, fo. 30.
[47] BHC 8, fo. 45; 7, fos. 344v, 140v. See also BHC 6, fos. 351, 402; 7, fos. 30, 127v, 173, 305v, 402.
[48] BHC 7, fo. 107v; BHC 9, fos. 620, 623, 625, 626, 628, 631, 633, 637, 640, 643.

the court to call it a day. 'No name', a 'lunatique', was earmarked for Bethlem in 1618.[49] No name, but there was something on paper to please the need to note. Other people got names for acting dumb. Jane Dumb went home without a whipping in 1625. John Dumbman got a shirt and pass to get back home to Yorkshire in 1622. John Dumb, who 'either cannot or will not speake', was caught begging at Lord Heath's door in 1632. While someone who is known to us only as 'Dumb Maid', who had not long left Watford, was arrested after snatching clothes and cash from her mistress in 1635.[50] There was pity for deaf and dumb strangers. A dumb vagrant was helped home 'where he maketh signes', pointing officers through London's maze.[51] Parishes gave hand-outs to get 'dumbe' drifters off their hands. A 'poore scholer' got a shilling after losing his hearing. A parish gave three shillings to 'twoe poore men' who 'had theire tongues cutt out by pyratts' in 1618. Hand-outs were also given to dumb men who had tongues cut out by Turks.[52] Some stories were touching, but parishes needed to be on their guard. Beggars and others got coaching in acting dumb. Two goodwives living along Long Lane 'taughte' Katherine Vaughan (who was caught sleeping under a stall in 1574) 'to fayne herselfe dom'. Another bogus mute was taught the trick by an old woman she bumped into 'by chance', who also gave lessons in faking blindness.[53] Most mute masks slipped sooner or later. Another John Dumb was turned in by prisoners working by his side, who told Bridewell's court that he could indeed speak after all in 1635.[54]

This Dumb was not the only unlucky beggar to open his mouth in the wrong place and wrong time. Roger Kerdesse, who took a boat from Ireland, 'dissembled he could not speak English', but 'forgetting' himself later 'he communed in English' in Bridewell's cells, and that was the end of his bluff. 'Dissembling' John Semprey from France got off lightly with a warning when he let a few words of English slip out in 1629.[55] But again there was sympathy if non-English speakers were not trying to con courts, even better if no one or 'nothing appeared' to point a finger at them. Diega Fernando, thought by the court to be a cutpurse, was 'not ponished *because* he could speake noe Englishe', and nobody charged him with

---

[49] BHC 6, fos. 289, 301, 217v, 336, 85. See also BHC 5, fo. 271v; 6, fos. 30, 171v.
[50] BHC 6, fos. 302, 402; 7, fo. 275; 8, fo. 41. See also BHC 8, fo. 178.
[51] BHC 7, fo. 350v. See also BHC 8, fo. 44.
[52] GL MSS 5090/2, fo. 283; 4409/1, fo. 150v; 818/1, fos. 100, 346. See also GL MSS 4524/1, fo. 144v; 4457/2, fo. 213v; 959/1, fos. 140, 157, 169; 818/1, fos. 85, 121v; 524/1, fo. 39v.
[53] BHC 2, fo. 29; BRHA BHC 4, fo. 467.
[54] BHC 8, fo. 44. See also BHC 1, fo. 183; 6, fos. 338v, 375; 7, fos. 222v, 275, 282; 8, fos. 53v, 79v, 178, 179v; 9, fo. 783; LMA Rep. 16, fo. 84.
[55] BHC 7, fos 328v, 121v. See also BHC 7, fo. 117.

anything. Joan Handrey, who could not speak a single word of English, got a pass for the Bristol Docks in 1638 to catch a boat back to Ireland. A parish gave sixpence to 'a poore man that could speake noe Englishe' in 1636. Once again attitudes that seem settled, this time that foreigners were scroungers, were far from fixed.[56] The conundrum in such cases was not the lack of English, it was the pretence to avoid an identity. Once more courts imposed identities through handy names, in this case along ethnic lines. John, Joan, Anne, and Mawdline Irish were all on the end of sharp lectures at Bridewell. Anne Irishwoman was caught vagrant in 1626. Jacob Dutchman was picked up begging in the same year. Some rovers did not even get a first name. 'A Grecian' was set free with a warning in 1625. A vagrant called 'a Portugall' was pushed into the army a week later.[57]

Courts needed names and prisoners needled courts by not giving them, choosing non-narrative strategies. Thieves handily forgot their sidekicks' names. Pregnant women forgot the names of their children's fathers all of a sudden until the peaks of panic and pain in labour when a midwife helped them to remember with a spine-tingling warning of Hell-fire.[58] Names gave leads and identities, the sort of reassurance that made one group of residents long for a name for their street,[59] and the sort of need that grew quickly in a culture that logged names more than ever before in tax lists, parish registers, bulky account rolls, bills of mortality, larger legal files, and countless censuses. Rows and rows of names for information, budgeting, policing, and policy-making in a sprouting surveillance culture.[60] The root of surveillance is a name, no matter how mundane. The complexities and consequences of legal name-games cannot be understood without this background of continually noting names and numbers. Magistrates were digging deeper for data. London was becoming a documented city. Londoners were listed by name, nation, age, address, job, wealth, health, religion, as the city grew bigger with each passing year. Names mattered more now if London was to be rendered legible. But new arrivals lacking metropolitan identities could evade counts and were harder to pin down. Magistrates missed much. There were more shadow people in London, not known to them. This was why magistrates felt

---

[56] BRHA BHC 4, fo. 467; BHC 8, fo. 178v; GL MS 4956/3, fo. 114v. See also BHC 8, fos. 20, 293v; BRHA BHC 4, fo. 467.
[57] BHC 6, fos. 336v, 350, 401v, 429, 437, 419v, 436v, 390v, 392.
[58] For example, BHC 1, fos. 86v, 188v; BRHA BHC 4, fos. 277v, 290v, 421v, 428v, 429, 445v. See also Laura Gowing, *Common Bodies: Women, Touch, and Power in Seventeenth-Century England* (New Haven, CT, and London, 2003), chap. 4.
[59] TNA SP14/69/36.  [60] See chap. 11 below.

queasy when someone without a name or history in London walked in through a courtroom door.

### Label landslides

'Thou worse than any name', Albany spits at Edmund who is now near death towards the end of the play.[61] This was something so shockingly vile that it could not be put in words. No label would do, only something new that needed to be thought up. This was another challenge of the times when magistrates drew up laws and guidelines; defining crime when change was a byword for the times and each day brought something new, leaving them struggling for words at times: 'who cannot yet be described by any particular markers whereby they may be noted'.[62] A landslide of labels fell on London's 'shady' people, even more quickly after 1600. Like maps or texts that tried to keep on top of changes by making them seem part of the urban fabric, this growing crime lexicon was an attempt to make better sense of London's metamorphoses. Brand-new crime-words described the latest troubles, finding all that was bad about London's sprint to becoming Europe's largest city. New descriptions were needed for the tidal wave of 'mean' hard-up paupers or the influx of women without men that seemed to get bigger year after year. Not for the first time City leaders went back to the drawing board for more relevant descriptions. The difference from earlier periods, however, was one of scope and scale, made clear in blanket criminalizations of the poor in the midst of a population boom and resource pinch around 1600 that made jobseekers take to the roads in droves from all parts of the land.[63]

It was easy to imagine this vagrant crush as a heaving homogeneous mass. Why sort through something so big and bad? 'At this presente a very greate number of idle, dissolute, and loose persons' living by 'unlawfull and indirect meanes' loiter 'idelie', magistrates took note in 1604, and some have 'latelie commyted verye fowle and notorious accons' but 'cannott well bee singled owt by themselves from the rest without the apprehencon of the generall number of that sorte of lewde people'.[64] Get them all in one go, they seem to say, tar each one with the same brush. But at other times magistrates were more exact, ordering round-ups or counts, or calling someone something specific. Perceptions of slides from the straight and narrow were put in snappy verbal brandings like lewd, loose, vagrant, or just plain bad. Once imposed, labels like these

---

[61] Shakespeare, *King Lear*, 5:3, 154.   [62] LMA Jour. 26, fo. 240v.
[63] Paul Slack, *Poverty and Policy in Tudor and Stuart England* (Harlow, 1988), chap. 5.
[64] LMA Jour. 26, fo. 156.

could stick with character glue. Often only a few letters long, their meanings stretched to cover all situations in which the poor broke the law. Very versatile, they were used by magistrates everywhere up and down the land because they summed up threatening existences in a quick word or two. And however quirky words like lewd might seem to us, they had the full force of ideology behind them and enough legal muscle for convictions. Labels could clarify the grounds on which to police, prosecute, and punish. Like names, they gave magistrates something to go on, by identifying someone or something that had once lacked any substance at all.[65]

We have some good work on labels like vagrant or whore and also on bridewells where many of the luckless labelled ended up,[66] but not much so far on the velocity or changing meanings of crime-tags.[67] But the number of labels with only one possible meaning could be counted on the fingers of one hand. This was a wordy culture after all; one where Erasmus had 150 different ways to say 'Thank you for your letter.'[68] Often lacking clear definitions, it is almost inevitable that crime-labels

---

[65] Cf. Lawrence Manley, *Literature and Culture*, p. 424: 'these anonymous creatures [vagrants, paupers, prostitutes] were the object of frequent searches and identifying schemes ... the London epigram was a response to social change; by sorting names and places it laid a lucid order over an obscure substrata of possibilities'. In *Fictions of Disease in Early Modern England: Bodies, Plagues and Politics* (Basingstoke, 2001), Margaret Healy says that 'it is not difficult to understand why plague was so frequently personified as a militaristic tyrant. In the absence of medical knowledge, metaphorical understanding such as this enables human beings at least to "get a handle on the problem": analogical reasoning [she continues], involved endowing a mysterious disease entity with human characteristics and motivations, provides a way of thinking about and articulating the "fight" against it, allowing individuals and societies to feel more in control' (quoting p. 62).

[66] Pioneering work on particular offences and penalties includes Robert B. Shoemaker, *Prosecution and Punishment: Petty Crime and the Law in London and Rural Middlesex, c.1660–1725* (Cambridge, 1991); Beier, *Masterless Men*; Joanna Innes, 'Prisons for the poor: English bridewells 1555–1800', in Francis Snyder and Douglas Hay, eds., *Labour, Law, and Crime: A Historical Perspective* (Oxford, 1987), pp. 42–122; Martin Ingram, 'Pain and Shame: themes and variations in Tudor punishments', and Paul Griffiths, 'Bodies and souls in Norwich: punishing petty crime, 1540–1700', both in Griffiths and Simon Devereaux, eds., *Penal Practice and Culture, 1500–1900: Punishing the English* (Basingstoke, 2004), pp. 36–62 and 85–120. Important work on meanings of 'whore' includes Gowing, *Domestic Dangers*, esp. chaps 3–4; Martin Ingram, 'Sexual manners: the other face of civility in early modern England', in Peter Burke, Brian Harrison, and Paul Slack, eds., *Civil Histories: Essays Presented to Sir Keith Thomas* (Oxford, 2000), pp. 87–109; and Bernard Capp, 'The double standard revisited: plebeian women and sexual reputation in early modern England', *Past and Present*, 162 (1999), 70–100.

[67] Cf. H. C. Erik Midelfort on meanings of melancholy in *A History of Madness in Sixteenth-Century Germany* (Stanford, CA, 1999), pp. 377–9; and Kathy Stuart on 'the label of dishonour' in *Defiled Trades and Social Outcasts: Honour and Ritual Pollution in Early Modern Germany* (Cambridge, 2000), p. 94.

[68] Greenblatt, *Will in the World*, p. 24.

would differ across time and place.[69] In what follows I will track the changing course and meaning of crime-labels in surviving Bridewell courtbooks up to 1658. These are broken records, however. They survive for the periods 1559–62, 1574–9, and 1598–1610, and for four decades after 1617, but we know next to nothing about court days for fully four decades of Bridewell's first century.[70] These silent years are a great loss, but they do not blur far-reaching and long-lasting trends after 1600. The following findings are taken from 50,277 cases when prisoners were labelled in Bridewell records: 5,137 cases come from the earliest decades (1559–62/1574–9), 12,466 from between 1598–1610, while 32,674 labels were pinned on people in the four decades before 1658. Bridewell has been called 'revolutionary' for its long-term impacts on penal cultures, but no less important was its leading role in disseminating crime-labels across London and beyond. Loosely defined anti-social acts were taken to the Bridewell court long before the 1610 Act that for the first time put fuzzy labels like disorderly or idle on the statute book. Edward Coke believed that this Act gave 'a general and large power' to magistrates to round up the rowdy poor.[71] Bridewell soon became the main lock-up for petty crimes in London, and before long it was also London's label factory. Bridewell governors had sweeping powers to arrest 'ydle ruffians', beggars, vagabonds, 'and all persons of yll name and fame'. The slightest and most general grounds would do. This amount of interpretation meant that the Bridewell court through its policing strategies and follow-up prosecutions took a leading role in London's word wars. Some words turned up in snatches of statute law, like rogue, vagrant, and idle. Others cropped up in London by-laws. Nightwalker had long had roots in the common law. There became little to stop the versatile use of labels, as guidelines in justices' handbooks urged that bridewells be used flexibly in generous interpretations of the 1610 Act.

In all I have followed 109 labels through Bridewell's first century. I make a note of the date and gender of the offender on the receiving end of each one, along with any information about the act or behaviour that

---

[69] Cf. my 'Meanings of nightwalking in early modern England', *The Seventeenth Century*, 13 (1998), 212–38; and 'Masterless young people in Norwich, 1560–1645', in Griffiths, Adam Fox, and Steve Hindle, eds., *The Experience of Authority in Early Modern England* (Basingstoke, 1996), pp. 146–86.

[70] There are, however, referrals from the Court of Aldermen to Bridewell in missing years, noted in Repertories, that give us ideas of proceedings in Bridewell's court.

[71] 7 Jac.1.c.4; Edward Coke, *The Second Part of the Institutes of The Laws of England* (1642), p. 730. The later significances of the Act are discussed in Shoemaker, *Prosecution and Punishment*, pp. 168–72; and Henderson, *Disorderly Women in Eighteenth-Century London*, p. 97.

made magistrates think that this was the right label for this offender and offence. With this I can build a time-series to show rates at which labels were used, and plot changing curves of this frequency tally to reveal shifts in meanings, in terms of gender or situations, for example. Sometimes someone was pelted with a hatful of labels. Thomas Tailor was called 'an idle wandering fellow vehementlie suspected to be a haker and a nightwalkinge fellowe' in 1603, and after his examination was 'found [to be] a vagrant' because 'he can geve no good accompt' of how he made ends meet. Elizabeth Fairclough was called a 'queane, an impudent slutt, a nightwalker', and 'notorious whore that daunceth and sheweth abhominable tricks before gents'. Like Tailor, she was smacked by six labels.[72] When this happens I count each label once, not trying to put one ahead of another. There are always snags in using written transcripts that come down through filtering processes. Any witness, clerk, or magistrate could tamper with words. Clerks were ventriloquists, pumping out words. They are permanent figures, always sitting writing with handbooks at their side, and no one else committed more terms to the court's collective memory. But the minutes made after each meeting were read aloud before the next court began business, giving governors a second chance to approve the labels that had been applied on the last court day.

The time-series shows contrasts in the way words were used that are miles apart. Not many stayed in records for the full century. Others are visible for short spans, and some appear once and are never seen again. Some suddenly turn up one day, seemingly from nowhere, and it is hard to know why because they had such short shelf-lives. But others were used over and over again. Vagrant appears 24,054 times in the courtbooks – almost half of the total tally: 47.8 per cent – and was a core word in the courtroom. Nighthunter, hedgehaunter, or lecher, on the other hand, all appear only once, almost like stray moral ad-libbings. Other words with one-day shelf-lives, like audacious, barbarous, inhumane, shameless, uncivil, or ungodly, look like the imaginative jabs of polished vocabularies, used to add more damning descriptions to legal labels. It caused more harm to call someone 'loose nightwalker' or 'incorrigible vagrant'. Some one-off labellings are simply baffling. Arlington Newington was brought to court in 1576 'for his unhappynes'. A lone woman was called a 'sluttish beast', and only one woman was called a witch on record.[73]

---

[72] BRHA BHC 4, fo. 406v; BHC 6, fo. 252.

[73] BHC 2, fo. 233v; 1, fos. 53v, 220v. The complete list of labels is as follows: abominable, arrogant, (living) at own hand, audacious, bad, barbarous, base, bawd, beastly, beggar, brave, briber, contentious, cozener-cheat, cutpurse, dangerous, desolate, desperate, detestable, disorderly, dissolute, distempered, drab, drunkard, evil, filcher, filthy, fine, forward,

196  Crime

Somewhere in between were a flock of words that turn up for a limited time in the courtbooks, ranging all the way from a handful of appearances to as many as several hundred or more. Just nine labels turn up in all nine surviving courtbooks up to 1658: beggar, cutpurse, idle, lewd, pilferer, receiver, rogue, suspicious, and unruly.[74] Five others crop up in eight books: cozener, evil, nightwalker, being out of service, and wanderer. Most of the remaining ninety-two labels slipped in and out of use, and we would have a better idea of why if the books did not tend to strip down entries to little more than name and offence after 1600, as more people poured into the court. It is hard to work with skimpy entries like 'Jane Dumbe, vagrant',[75] and explain why labels pop up now and then, with long intervals between appearances. Streetwalker, for instance, was first written down in the 1570s, but then went missing until more than five decades later when it made a late, last appearance. Vicious flickered briefly in the courtbooks in the late 1600s, but then sank without trace until a surprise solitary reappearance more than three decades later. We can imagine a description like vicious popping into the mind of one of the governors as he sat brooding over a case and character. In other cases a word took the place of another to bring certain situations to mind, in displacements that were not always precise. Vagrant was first used in the surviving Bridewell courtbooks in the mid-1570s at more or less the same time as use of the older vagabond plummeted from its mid-century summit when it was the routine term for banned movement. Vagabond vanished by 1600 as new ways emerged to describe travel without a pass.[76] Theft was also described differently. Briber and pickpurse were commonly used to pinpoint thieves around 1560, but each fell out of use

---

[74] gadder, haker, hedgeharlot, hedgehaunter, hooker, horrible, idle, ill, impudent, incorrigible, inhumane, intolerable, lascivious, lecher, lewd, lifter, light, lingerer, loathsome, lodger, loiterer, loose, lurker, lusty, malicious, masterless, micher, monstrous, nasty, naughty, nighthunter, nightwalker, ninner, nip, no account (of living), obstinate, (being) out of service, pack, picker, picklock, pickpocket, pickpurse, picksack, pilferer, ranger, receiver, rogue, rover, rude, ruffianly, shameless, shifter, shopcreep, shoplift, slut, stark, stout, straggler, streetwalker, stubborn, sturdy, suspicious, swaggerer, troublesome, turbulent, uncivil, ungodly, unhonest, unorderly, unruly, vagabond, vagrant, valiant, vicious, vile, wanderer, wicked, wild and witch. My term recidivist completes the list. I have squashed fourteen different labels implying recidivism into this catch-all term that were used on 5,928 occasions: 'comon' (3,533), 'old customer' (705), and 'old guest' (412) were the leading terms.
[74] I do not include recidivist in this list.   [75] BHC 6, fo. 402.
[76] Significantly, only early rogue texts used vagabond in their titles: John Awdeley, *The Fraternity of Vagabonds* (1561); Thomas Harman, *A Caveat for Common Cursitors Vulgarly Called Vagabonds* (1566), reprinted in Arthur Kinney, ed., *Rogues, Vagabonds, and Sturdy Beggars: A New Gallery of Tudor and Early Stuart Rogue Literature*, 2nd edition (Amherst, MA, 1990). Vagrant appears in earlier times. See Mazo Karras, *Common Women*, pp. 100, 16. Vagrant and vagabond were also used interchangeably. See, for example, LMA Jour. 19, fos. 171v-2.

by the mid-1570s, and two other titles used in early courtbooks followed not long afterwards: filcher and picker. A clutch of other terms emerged for the first time to plug these gaps, most notably lifter, ninner, nip, and pickpocket (in common currency by 1600). Pickpocket was not a timeless term, and it seems to have been a straightforward substitute for the now out-of-date pickpurse. The ebb and flow of these words could have come from new theft technologies or new spins in cant language. Theft-words like foist, lifter, or nip all had cant bloodlines.

Apart from clerks putting pen to paper, the origins of labels are almost always fuzzy. Some were brought to court by officers in descriptions of offenders who caught their eye, particularly if they had been knocked about by him or her, or if neighbours had tipped them off about offenders. They looked for the words to make a character smear or charge stick. A label might also have come to mind when witnesses described the tools and tricks of crime. Some skill-based labels like hooker, picklock, or shopcreep, squeezed data on technology into single words with roots in rogue writing. Other terms came from talk on streets or around tables. People used labels that turn up in court to poke fun, to wound people they did not like, or to comment on a piece of neighbourhood news. Some labels had a doorstep or street pedigree with links to legal-speak. Verbal drubbings and 'comon fames' that picked up speed on streets were peppered with labels that also led to whippings and warnings in Bridewell.[77] A 'gent' sneered at a stationer: 'thou are a pettifull roague and I will make thee sing ballads in Smythfeild upp to thy knees in dirt'. John Arden sniped at his daughter-in-law, calling her 'whore and queane', but he let slip that 'he hath a desire these tenne yeares to lye with her'. A spinster snapped at Patient Burrowes: 'thou art a base jade, kiss my arse thou base jade, thou pisspott jade, I will pay thy fatt arse thou jade'. Margaret Ashely rounded on her sister, calling her 'murtherer, jade, bawde, and witche' in 1635. Ann Manby, a tailor's wife, called widow Alice Stephenson 'pocki faced bitch and murther[er]' a couple of years earlier.[78]

These sizzling words poured out in temper tantrums, but they were also used far more soberly inside courtrooms. Street slang drew upon a smaller pool of words than that to be found in Bridewell's courtbooks, although we could add bad, bawd, bitch, harlot, idle, knave, lewd, light, loose, slut, thief, unruly, and vagabond from depositions taken at sessions

---

[77] The best thick descriptions of street talk include Gowing, *Domestic Dangers*, chaps 3–4; and Robert Shoemaker, *The London Mob: Violence and Disorder in Eighteenth-Century England* (2004), chap. 3.

[78] GL MS 9057/1, Archdeaconry of London General Examination and Deposition Book, 1632–8, fo. 115v; LMA CQSF 131/Thomas Knight, interrog., Frances Vernon interrog.; MJ/SBR/6, fo. 608; WJ/SR/NS/44/78, 41/110, 32/30, 41/112, 44/88.

on both sides of the walls and also from witness statements taken down at ecclesiastical courts.[79] This is both authentic street talk that we can imagine featuring in casual conversations and legal language in books and documents. But which came first? The trade between the two actually matters more. People picked up this talk from pamphlets, conversations, or when they came to courts. Street speech was absorbed into legal cultures, vocabularies, and laws. There were cultural crossroads between texts, speech, and legal jargon. Labels bridged social divisions, though they were often turned on the same people who used them all the time, just like Bridewell governors sitting in court, who picked them up from their own social circles, laws, handbooks, and other courtrooms where they heard cases as aldermen and justices. Clearly, labelling had many potential grapevines and mixed audiences. Bridewell's bench also had access to another label exchange: rising recidivism rates in their own courtroom. More 'old customers' and 'notorious gessts' made return visits to the Bridewell court from around 1620 than before, and a label was always at hand, lodged in the court's memory or books, when someone was pushed into the courtroom with an already remembered tattered reputation.

Labels can also be linked to passing new laws at either City or national levels (or both) covering anti-social acts that sprinkled labels through their preambles and main body. The use of disorderly, idle, and lewd in Bridewell's court, for example, soared after the 1610 Act with its blanket labels (see Appendix, Table 7a). Ninety-three suspects were called lewd between 1604–10, a lower annual rate (13.3) than the longer later period, 1618–34, when the behaviour of 1,052 offenders was so described (61.9). The annual rate of 'idle' suspects more than doubled over the same stretch of time: from 10.1 up to 22.7. The use of 'disorderly' also climbed: just seven suspects were called this before 1604 (0.4), and that number soared to 292 (6.0) over the next five decades. Again, the 1610 Act is a common denominator. Other laws also kick-started leaps in labelling. The big jump in the use of 'nightwalker' in 1638 came right after orders from the City government to crack down on women walking late.[80] A statute mentioned 'cutpurses' and 'pick-purses' in 1567, and this fits neatly with the time-line of these labels. Sudden 'vagrant' showers in the 1570s were precipitated by statutes passed in 1572 and 1576, as well as a string of by-laws over the same decade that used the new-fangled

---

[79] See also Robert B. Shoemaker, 'The decline of public insult in London, 1660–1800', *Past and Present*, 169 (2000), 97–131, esp. 114; Gowing, *Domestic Dangers*, esp. chap. 3; Martin Ingram, 'Law, litigants, and the construction of "honour": slander suits in early modern England', in Peter Coss, ed., *The Moral World of the Law* (Cambridge, 2000), pp. 134–60, esp. pp. 156–7.

[80] See my 'Meanings of nightwalking', 218–20.

Crime: words 199

term 'vagrant' rather than the old-hat 'vagabond'.[81] While the zenith of 'rogue' at Bridewell in the 1570s is linked to legislation and literature, coming after a statute that mentions this label for the first time (1572), and the publication of leading rogue tracts that gave the term publicity and colour.[82] Tabloid cant made labels accessible in glossaries with handy translations.[83] There are grounds to believe that cant crossed into everyday talk by 1700,[84] but well before then it cropped up in courtbooks, crime rings, and street talk. There were enough chronological overlaps between publishing, legislating, and labelling for us to see that labels had hybrid roots.

**Meanings of crime**

My work with words has also brought to light changes in meanings of crime after 1600 that appear from tracking label time-lines to see which ones were in the ascendant at particular points in time, and from swings in the application of labels to women and men. It might seem strange to try to pin down labels when one of their defining qualities was slipperiness. They were purposely pliant with 'large power', in Coke's words, to cover everything. A label's looseness is an advantage for magistrates, a point made at the time and today in work on vagrancy, madness, nightwalking, or prostitution.[85] But like their chronologies, meanings of labels were never steady, and two emerging senses of crime altered the nature of perceptions and policies after 1600.

The first was an environmental perception that put the roots of crime in London's quick growth. By environmental, I mean crimes that were understood to be both cause and consequence of the city's sprawl and squalour, and they emerged more vividly after 1600. Criminal and environmental horrors were twinned in explanatory theories. Crime upset London's air, health, and beauty, and significantly words implying

---

[81] 8 Eliz. I cap. 4; 14 Eliz. 1, cap. 5; 18 Eliz. 1, cap. 3.
[82] 14 Eliz. 1 cap. 5; Woodbridge, *Vagrancy, Homelessness, and English Renaissance Literature*, p. 42 and chap. 1; Spraggs, 'Rogues and vagabonds in English literature'; Ingram, 'Law, litigants, and the construction of "honour"', pp. 156–7.
[83] See the glossaries in Dekker, *Lanthorne and Candle-light*; and Harman, *A Caveat for Common Cursitors*. See too Gamini Salgado's 'Glossary of Underworld Terms' in his *Elizabethan Underworld*.
[84] Beier, 'Anti-language or jargon?', pp. 64–101, esp. pp. 92–3.
[85] See, for example, Thomas McStay Adams, *Bureaucrats and Beggars: French Social Policy in the Age of the Enlightenment* (Oxford and New York, 1990), p. 27; Griffiths, 'Meanings of nightwalking'; R. A. Houston, *Madness and Society in Eighteenth-Century Scotland* (Oxford, 2000), pp. 336, 350; Henderson, *Disorderly Women in Eighteenth-Century London*, pp. 76, 87, 88, 96; Shoemaker, *Prosecution and Punishment*, p. 168.

contagion covered criminals, as well as dirt, disease, plague, or the body.[86] Like rag-gatherers digging in rubbish for cast-off clothes or stinking inmates squeezing into clammy rooms, vagrants infected the city with crimes and stench. Law-abiding citizens could smell them on streets, and there was a real risk when it was believed that infection passed through the air, enveloping hapless Londoners. It was said that 'idell vacabounde' Peter Harris was 'a nasty filthy man', who 'stanke' so much that 'no man was able to abyde the ayre of him'. Beggars buzzing around St Paul's were 'a very greate annoyance and noysome in smell'. And it is no accident that streets were ordered to be cleaned of dirt and vagrants in the same sentence. Officers were told to 'clense' the streets of grubby vagrants and beggars.[87] Crime had always been dirty, of course. The Bridewell bench called 'bawdry' a 'stynckyng and filthy matter' in 1559. 'Lechery' was 'a foul, stinking, and detestable sin', Common Council said with disgust four decades earlier. 'Straungers' with no church who spent too much time 'haunting of playes out of the liberties' were 'comonlie unclene people'. Low-life lodgers lived 'filthily' in a cheap boarding house in St Botolph-without-Bishopgate in 1594.[88] Talk could also be 'filthie', this is what one sobbing woman said about wounding words that were spread about her in her neighbourhood in 1576. 'Stinkinge fellowe', a surgeon's wife snapped at Justice Shepard when he did not take her side in a case in 1633. Women often mixed dirt and seedy sex in their words when they wanted to hurt each other: 'durty slutt', one woman snapped at another who had offended her husband; 'filthie bawd', some shouted; 'filthie whore' others screamed.[89]

People smeared others with dirt, much like courts rammed home charges with adjectives implying filth/contagion. There were more of these dirt words after 1600 when bad living conditions became a leading explanation

---

[86] Sibley, *Geographies of Exclusion*, pp. 14, 18–19, 24–5; Thomas A. Markus, *Buildings and Power: Freedom and Control in the Origin of Modern Building Types* (1993), p. 146 and chap. 5; Alain Corbin, *The Foul and the Fragrant: Odour and the Social Imagination*, trans. Miriam L. Kochan with Roy Porter and Christopher Prendergast (Lemington Spa, 1994), p. 145; Georges Vigarello, *Concepts of Cleanliness: Changing Attitudes in France since the Middle Ages*, trans. Jean Birrell (Cambridge, 1988), chap. 10; Donald Reid, *Paris Sewers and Sewermen: Realities and Representations* (Cambridge, MA, 1991), pp. 20, 50–1; Joy Damousi, *Depraved and Disorderly: Female Convicts, Sexuality, and Gender in Colonial Australia* (Cambridge, 1997), pp. 28, 36, 43.

[87] Paul Slack, *The Impact of Plague in Tudor and Stuart England* (1985), pp. 26–8, 329–31; Mark S. R. Jenner, 'The politics of London air: John Evelyn's *Fumifugum* and the Restoration', *Historical Journal*, 38 (1995), 535–51; BHC 1, fo. 92; GL MSS 25,175, fo. 25; 12806/2, fo. 29v; SBHA Governors' Journal 5, fos. 49v, 77v; LMA Rep. 60, fo. 119.

[88] BHC 1, fo. 17; LMA Jour. 12, fos. 239–9v; Remembrancia Book 1, fo. 18v; GL MS 9064/14, fo. 5v. See also Frank Rexroth, *Deviance and Power in Late Medieval London* (Cambridge, 2007), pp. 288–9.

[89] BHC 3, fo. 63; LMA WJ/SR/NS/37/53, 39/6; D/L/C/218, fos. 99, 186, 210, 214.

of crime in London's by-laws and busiest court. By then distress about London's shoddy fabric was expressed in perceptions of street crimes, like vagrancy. Aldermen lamented that 'offences dayly more and more abound by reason that the city groweth dayly more populous' in 1610, and we could not ask for a tighter link between crime and growth than that.[90] Some scholars think that these links first appeared later in England's bulging industrializing cities. Gatrell for one believes that 'a critical displacement' took place around 1800 when for the first time 'change' was part 'of an *explanation* of crime, embedded in a broad thesis of social deterioration'.[91] These were clearly decades of shattering shocks, when even time changed.[92] But this was no new idea of crime. Change had long been linked to vice, vagrancy, and theft. Instant equations were drawn between 'extraordinary assemblies' of vagrants and rampant theft around 1600; vagrant and thief became one.[93] The city's crime-waves and most squalid living conditions anyone could remember were blamed on vagrants.

This is clear in Bridewell's books, our most complete catalogue of prosecuting street-crimes four centuries ago. The complexion of crime brought there changed after 1600. So much so, that even the books look different: no page looks the same as one from an Elizabethan book, the entries are by and large shorter, and as we thumb through the longer lists of names it dawns on us that more women were getting in trouble after 1600, even though the amount of sexual crime prosecuted tumbled (see Appendix Table 2a). Weeks or even months passed by without one prostitute appearing in the books, and their clients disappeared altogether after 1620. Only forty bawds ended up in court between 1618–32, and not one after 1632. While a measly eight pimps came there after 1605. This was a swift fall. Not quite overnight but quick enough to make us think that something important affected perceptions and policies. Sexual crimes were still coming to court in quite high numbers around 1600: a grand total of 104 'whoremongers' landed in the court in 1600–1 (ninety-seven prostitutes were prosecuted in 1559–60).[94] A more revealing index of the changing character of prosecutions/strategies is the big drop in the

---

[90] LMA Rep. 29, fo. 80v.
[91] V. A. C. Gatrell, 'Crime, authority, and the policeman-state', in F. M. L. Thompson, ed., *The Cambridge Social History of Britain 1750–1950: Volume III, Social Agencies and Institutions* (Cambridge, 1990), pp. 243–310, quoting pp. 251–2 (original emphasis). See also Peter King, 'The rise of juvenile delinquency in England, 1780–1840: changing patterns of perception and prosecution', *Past and Present*, 160 (1998), 116–66, esp. 157.
[92] E. P. Thompson, 'Time, work-discipline, and industrial capitalism', *Past and Present*, 38 (1967), 56–97; Hans-Joachim Voth, *Time and Work in England, 1750–1830* (Oxford, 2000).
[93] LMA Jour. 27, fo. 319.
[94] I have adapted figures for the Elizabethan court from Archer, *Pursuit of Stability*, p. 239, Table 6.1.

ratio of sex-crimes in Bridewell's overall caseload. In three sample years – 1559–60, 1576–7, and 1600–1 – Archer found that 45.68 per cent of all cases were sexual offences (the high point was 60.25 per cent in 1576–7). Over half of the court's time was spent on sexual offenders, as these probes tended to drag on longer than others, sometimes stretching to five or more pages in the courtbooks.

It was a different courtroom not long afterwards. Sexual crime slumped to under one-in-twenty of 29,744 listed cases in the four decades after 1618, dropping with each new decade: the lowest-point came between 1648–52 (3.34 per cent).[95] Prostitution prosecutions were rare occurrences by now. Sex was disappearing from the courtbooks. Illegitimacy cases barely ticked over with annual averages a little above one from 1640–60. While fornication, once a mainstay offence, was coming to court at only double this tiny rate. As with the sex-trade, the fall was sudden: 243 people were charged with fornication/adultery alone in 1600–1.[96] Sexual offending also plummets in the one surviving wardmote book for this time, and there is little sex in the ones we have from 1630 on.[97] In clear switches that parallel Bridewell business, wardmotes spent the largest chunk of their time dealing with the dangerous side-effects of growth: keeping watch on the streets, night lights, hygiene, tatty buildings, and the seemingly neverending downpour of inmates.[98] City quarter sessions records also show little sign that sex-cases were re-routed there from the Bridewell court; their staple load was still theft and street crimes. Nor is there much reason to think that the number of fornication, illegitimacy, or prostitution cases climbed significantly in London's church courts as some sort of counterbalance to the fall in cases at the Bridewell court, although much of the relevant work and counting in these records remains to be done.[99]

---

[95] Figures calculated from BHC 6–9.
[96] Archer does not give illegitimacy figures for Bridewell's court, though numbers were high before 1600, so the plunge in sexual crime is bigger than shown here.
[97] This is Cornhill Ward: GL MSS 4069/1–2. The next best book for these purposes is St Dunstan-in-the-West Inquest Book: GL MS 3018/1. There are a few other books and papers that give us glimpses of sixteenth-century wardmotes, when concern with immorality was greater than in wardmotes after 1650: see GL MSS 1499; 1509/2, 7–8; 2050/1; 4992/1; 9234/1–5.
[98] These developments can be traced in nearly all of the surviving wardmote books from this time. See, for example, GL MSS 68; 473; 1169/1; 2505/1; 4216/1; 9237. The most recent discussion of later wardmotes is in Beattie, *Policing and Punishment*, esp. chaps 2–3.
[99] Martin Ingram is currently working on the regulation of sex in early modern London, and he has guided me on seventeenth-century church courts in conversations and publications. See his 'Law, litigants, and the construction of "honour"', p. 154: 'The probability is that London and its suburbs had expanded so rapidly that the church courts were by then [early seventeenth century] slackening their grip on moral regulation far more than in most other areas'.

This turnaround followed a wholesale reordering of City policy and prosecution as London 'filled up'. But Bridewell's court never lost its pious loathing for slack morals and the burgeoning sex-trade, knowing full well that it was on the rise, even when numbers of pimps or prostitutes coming there dwindled to almost nothing. 'Bawdrey increaseth and raineth much in this city', the Bridewell court said in a letter to the aldermen in 1621, urging them to lobby hard for a 'stricter law' at the next Parliament. An 'Act for repressing of houses of bawdrey and comon uncleanness' was duly drafted in 1625 with strong City backing, but it could not drum up enough support to get onto the statute book, even though it anxiously pointed out that these 'houses' were dotted all through London.[100] The 1621 outcry was a boiling point after a build-up time of simmering frustrations when prostitution boomed but policies took other directions in order to meet London's growth head on. This was clearly a pragmatic policy shift that was rooted in first-hand 'experience', and it would have been a smart vote-grabbing move if free elections had existed. Nearly all Londoners could agree that rounding up leech-like vagrants, 'sweetening' smells, or patching up trashy tenements should have been top priorities. There was less agreement about taking legal action against sex-offenders, however, whether from the point of view of how best to spread thin resources around or from the partial perspectives of London's numberless 'whoremongers'. As long ago as 1582 John Howes – a friend of Bridewell – wondered if it was useful for the Bridewell court to spend well over half its time on the 'careful and diligent searchinge oute of mens wyves and other gallant gyrles' when everyone could see that vagrants swarmed all over the place.[101]

Howes's question struck a chord in the Guildhall. These were stingy times in London with not too much money to spare. But preachers still blasted 'whores' and 'whoremomgers' from their pulpits with righteous indignation, and magistrates kept on promising smarter policies to reverse falling morals. It is no fluke that vagrancy cases soared at Bridewell over the same time; almost like a see-saw, sex-crimes fall, street-crimes go up (see Appendix Tables 2a and 4a). Vagrants had been brought to Bridewell ever since its first day of operation. A little more than one-third of the offenders brought there in Archer's sample years were vagabonds/vagrants (36.2 per cent). This figure shot up to more than two-thirds of all cases between 1618–57 (67.6 per cent), and this near doubling is nowhere near real levels with the stronger

---

[100] BHC 6, fo. 224; HOL MP, 24–6–1625.
[101] R. H. Tawney and E. Power, eds., *Tudor Economic Documents*, 3 vols. (1924), vol. III, p. 441.

encouragements to courts to use summary justice to boot out vagrants.[102] The number of by-laws to get rid of vagrants also zoomed up after 1600. Bridewell's chief task was now to curb crimes that were the direct offshoots of London's rapid expansion. Charge sheets become long lists of vagrants, beggars, thieves, nightwalkers, work-shy layabouts, and shadowy people with no believable story of how they got by. Nearly nine-in-ten cases involved such people between 1640–60, and this figure never once fell below eight-in-ten over the 1630s. The common threads in these changing prosecution strategies were 'loose' movement, obscure lifestyles, sky-high crime, and cost-cutting in trains of thought that resulted in ecological nightmares of muck, infection, scruffiness, parasite tramps, and clammy inmates. Crime changed with the city. Howes's diagnostic hospital history was timely. He had been shrewd, and no one would have had much reason to ask his basic question five decades later. The nature of prosecutions at London's hardest-working court had shifted by a long way by then. Environmental explanations of crime proliferated in the London area and made a great deal of sense in these changing times.

The other emerging meaning of crime, not unrelated to the first, was a large-scale feminization of crime-labels after 1620, a time when more women were labelled in terms of numbers and in the greater likelihood that their characters or actions would be pinned down in labels that had once been more solidly masculine. Some labels changed character and now brought women more readily to mind. This was a time of telling shifts in ideas of gendering crime. Either more women were breaking the law or magistrates felt that this was so (or both). Women were now closely linked to crimes spawned by urban growth. For the first time in English records (so far consulted), female thieves outnumbered light-fingered men in Bridewell between 1642–58 (50.2 per cent: see Appendix Table 7c).[103] By then female pickpockets also topped men for the first time (57.5 per cent), numbers of women handling stolen goods more than doubled (averaging a little under 70 per cent in 1600–60), and equal numbers of men and women were called cozeners or cheats between 1634 and 1658. Female involvement rose steadily in each case, picking up momentum in each new decade. The quintessential street crime,

---

[102] See Faramerz Dabhoiwala, 'Summary justice in early modern London', *English Historical Review*, 121 (2006), 796–822; Paul Slack, 'Books of orders: the making of English social policy, 1577–1631', *Transactions of the Royal Historical Society*, 5th series, 30 (1980), 1–22; Henrik Langeluddecke, 'Law and order in seventeenth-century England: the organization of local administration during the personal rule of Charles I', *Law and History Review*, 15 (1997), 49–76.

[103] Cf. Beattie, *Policing and Punishment in London*, pp. 63–71, esp. p. 65, Table 1.4.

# Crime: words

vagrancy, also followed suit. A little over one-quarter of vagrants were women towards the end of the sixteenth century (28.6 per cent); a figure that climbed to nearly four-in-ten in the 1630s, and higher still over the next two decades (43.5 per cent). By now more women than men were pulled off streets through Bridewell's gate. Over half of arrested 'wanderers' were women after 1630, a time when the proportion of female nightwalkers was never less than 99 per cent (it had been lower a decade earlier). Women made up about three-tenths of all wanderers, beggars, nightwalkers, vagrants, rogues, and loiterers brought to the Bridewell court at the start of the seventeenth century; a figure that climbed steeply to 54.5 per cent in the quarter-century after 1634.

There were also sizeable rises in numbers of women called into question for leading shady lives. Words implying loose or shifty lifestyles took more feminine spins, including disorderly, idle, lewd, unruly, loose, and the phrase out of service (see Appendix Table 7c). A little over one-in-four of 'lewd' livers locked up in the 1570s were women. 'Lewd' was mainly masculine back then, but a U-turn followed, as over half of Bridewell's 'lewd' inmates were women by 1600 (57.4 per cent), and this soared to nearly 80 per cent in 1625–58, and peaked at 94.69 per cent in the decade after 1625. There was also a fourfold leap in ratios of women called disorderly: 51.1 per cent in 1625–55. Ratios of idle women almost doubled over the same period, rising to 45.6 per cent. While unruly women outnumbered unruly men, climbing from 22.2 per cent around 1600 to 55.8 per cent later on. Almost equal numbers of men and women could not give a sound 'accompt' of how they lived by 1640. More than eight-in-ten of all ill, loose, or out of service suspects after 1630 were women. But not all labels took on feminine tinges. Some stayed solidly male, including (in descending order of participation percentage points): lusty and ninner (100), masterless (95.8), dangerous (95.8), vagabond (94.4), stubborn (93.3), stout (90.9), sturdy (89), cutpurse (88.1), incorrigible (87.9), rogue (82), and nip (80.5), though not all solidly male labels stay in sight for a century. Nip or vagabond had disappeared by the time women took up more column inches in Bridewell books. Others slumped in the crunch time after 1620, including the once ubiquitous rogue. Some appear only a handful of times. All in all, larger numbers of women were labelled at Bridewell by 1650: 6,127 women were hit by labels in the quarter century after 1634 (56.8 per cent). Up until then men had been in the majority: two-thirds of labels dished out in 1574–9 landed on men, and slightly more in 1604–10 (69.38 per cent). In total, men were on the receiving end of 63.05 per cent of all labels noted up to 1634. What followed tipped almost eight decades of experience to new balances and formulations.

What had enough force to plunge women into this labelled limelight? Labelling processes are chain-reactions that grow insistent through repetition. To end up clearly defined, labels needed to be repeated over and over, like recurring chords that make songs stick in the mind. Repetition was key and if an impetus got off the ground its constant turning affected meanings. Once put in words and applied to certain groups on a regular basis, meanings pick up convictions of their own, becoming common currency in courts.[104] Another swing in the busy prosecuting at Bridewell was a sea-change in the nature of recidivism. Over eight-in-ten recidivists brought back there from 1635–58 were women; female recidivism had been on the rise since 1600 when it hovered at roughly half this level. But men made up over half of 'old gessts' only a short time before: 57.06 per cent in 1624–34. The stock recidivist was all of a sudden a woman. The Bridewell bench watched women walk into their court in droves, and the match between sky-high recidivism and the new nature of labels was no accident. A sequence of causes and effects linked higher female recidivism to thinking about the causes and characters of crime. These ideas sooner or later fell in line with recurring faces and facts in the courtroom, in large shifts of perception that were solidly rooted in the age, class, or gender of the bulk of Bridewell recidivists. Through repetition, recidivism altered understandings of crime-labels, building up knowledge about the nature of offences and offending at the same time. There were clear causal connections between mounting feminization and the near 1,500 female recidivists who stepped into the court from 1625–40. Yet recidivism is not a first cause. It is the outcome of repetition, not its roots. It had to follow something before it starts to exercise its pull. Once this happens and new momentums gain ground, it can soon become a driving force, and this was indeed the situation inside Bridewell after 1625 when streams of women were put on trial for offences that had once been thought of as male crimes for the most part. No wonder the matron asked for more living space for women prisoners in 1633.[105]

What altered the court's cultural antennae? Perhaps its complexion changed, and more moral-minded magistrates with tougher stances on sex and women took up seats there? Although there was a core group of regular attendees in the 1630s, there does not appear to be anything remarkably religious about them to make them stand out from their

---

[104] Cf. Donna Andrew and Randall McGowen, *The Perreaus and Mrs. Rudd: Forgery and Betrayal in Eighteenth-Century London* (Berkeley, CA, 2001), p. 63: 'Once such stories [about forgery cases] appeared in one paper, others tended to pick them up, and through repetition they gained conviction'.
[105] BHC 7, fo. 335v.

predecessors. The puritan minister, William Gouge, joined the bench in 1629, but he did not grab this golden opportunity to get down to work on 'domesticall duties'. Apart from coming to court for the cases of Mary Badham who cut purses in his church and two men and a woman who climbed into his back-yard late one night in 1640, godly Gouge hardly ever came to court, except on election days when the bench had a slap-up meal washed down with lashings of wine.[106] Religious leanings might be red herrings in any case, as immorality always concerned the court even as sex-cases slumped. It is also worth remembering that prosecution patterns after 1600 do not fit the 'classic' contours of a godly drive to change manners for the better, like the one Archer has noticed in the crackdown against prostitution in the winter of 1576–7.[107] Street troubles and living conditions took priority over everything else at the end of the day. The nature of female offending is also at odds with long-held views that couple it with sex. We might say that loose lifestyles summed up in labels like lewd had sexual meanings. Lewd smacks of sex. But like all other pliable labels, it could describe almost anything: thieves, thugs, ramblers, heavy drinkers, tiffs, as well as people charged with sexual offences, women more than men. Lewd was also used less around 1630 when its links with sex-offences was also weaker. Another label that is carelessly paired with sex, nightwalker, also had more general meanings covering suspicious actions.[108] Streets were identified with sexual disorder, danger, and pleasure, and patterns of female offending after 1600 reveal feminine aspects to urban culture and London's growing pains.[109]

I am not the first to spot changes in women's position in London's courts after 1600. Gowing spotted a revealing rise in female litigants at church courts over the same time when women were sent to Bridewell in higher numbers.[110] Something with enough muscle to change characters of crime altered material settings and perceptions. No single cause stands out in London's 'whirl', but more women were coming to the city to try and scratch a living. Proportions of female vagrants were on the rise long before the time after 1650 when we are told that London's sex-ratio

---

[106] Ibid., fo. 309v; 8, fo. 313v. Gouge sat on the bench for nearly two decades. A case of theft from the parish clerk of Gouge's parish was also 'referred' to him: BHC 8, fo. 331.
[107] Archer, *Pursuit of Stability*, pp. 253–4.
[108] Shoemaker, *Prosecution and Punishment*, p. 173; Griffiths, 'Meanings of nightwalking', 221–2.
[109] Laura Gowing, '"The freedom of the streets": women and social space, 1560–1640', in Paul Griffiths and M.S.R. Jenner, eds., *Londinopolis: Essays in the Cultural and Social History of Early Modern London*, (Manchester, 2000), pp. 130–51, pp. 131, 145–7.
[110] Gowing, *Domestic Dangers*, esp. pp. 32–8. Gowing writes that 'London's church courts saw a uniquely high level of female participation in litigation' (p. 34).

tipped towards women.[111] Feminine aspects of disorder led to a string of by-laws that put the blame for troubles stemming from messy growth on women's shoulders: including crackdowns on 'women brokers' who gave cheap room and board to maids knowing full well that they had no service (1606, 1613, 1635); action against 'lewd and wicked' women lining their pockets 'by the spoyle of others' (1614); steps against 'idle' women lodging in 'rooms and chambers' in 1635, whose main aim in life seemed to be tempting men to 'lewdnes' 'under pretence' of working for their living; and, starting towards 1600, but picking up more speed later on, repeated drives to license, limit, and label female street-sellers.[112] Pressure groups, among them Bridewell's bench, asked for tough action against ubiquitous vice and women who walked the streets in throngs. The bench pushed for a plan to sweep nightwalkers and other 'lewd women' off the streets in 1637, and action followed in the next year when Common Council warned constables 'to do their best endeavour' to round up 'lewd and loose wandering women in the streets' after dusk, and sure enough nightwalking cases peaked soon after.[113]

In some ways the streets belonged more to women. Unlike men who spent the day sitting still at workbenches or pottering around shops, making and fixing things, women quite literally walked to work up and down streets selling, walking to markets or to wash clothes or fetch water. Not just streets, but markets, alleys, lowly boarding houses, alehouses, and other meeting places teemed with women. No civic spot was immune. Not the Royal Exchange that hummed with women, or 'the seate in Paules Churchyard where the Lord Maior useth to sitt', on which the watch found vagrant Dorothy Wells one night in 1633, with the added offence (stain) that she was racked with 'the foul disease'.[114] Never a male preserve, streets were now imagined in feminine ways that were no less unsafe for that. Particular brands of metropolitan femininity were made by women themselves and by male magistrates lit by anxieties about 'loose' women. New understandings of streets were sharpened by surges in child abandonment and 'big bellied' vagrant women. They, too, were depicted in a language of labels, stigmatizations that were made razor-

[111] Roger Finlay, *Population and Metropolis: the Demography of London, 1580–1650* (Cambridge, 1981), pp. 140–2; D. V. Glass, 'Notes on the demography of London at the end of the seventeenth century', in Glass and R. Revelle, eds., *Population and Social Change* (1972), pp. 272–85.
[112] LMA Jours. 29, fo. 20v; 37, fos. 124v-5; Reps. 27, fo. 524; 32, fo. 7.
[113] BHC 8, fo. 108v; LMA Jour. 38, fos. 172–2v. See also for drives against nightwalking LMA Rep. 51, fos. 132–2v; Jour. 39, fo. 50v; BHC 8, fos. 275–5v; GL MS 3016/1, fos. 198–9.
[114] BHC 7, fo. 328. See also ibid., fos. 210, 321v.

sharp by the Infanticide Act (1624), with its bitter swipes at 'lewd' women.[115] There is nothing like the spate of orders about women walking, working, boarding, or breaking the law in sources stretching back to 1500. It must have been doubly heartbreaking for male magistrates, then, as rising female offending dovetailed with the degrading slump in the value of the masculine work 'freedom'. These ties between citizenship and remodelled cultures of urban women were among the burning issues of the times. Women with or without skills snatched work away from citizen breadwinners with mouths to feed. The old rules no longer applied it seemed. Urban and feminine identities were in stormy flux, caught nowhere better than in words of crime. The metropolitan authorities sprayed thousands of labels on people who did not live life by their book. And two tightly related anxieties dominated their perceptions of crime: London's evident growing pains and the women who seemed more troublesome at this point in time than ever before.

---

[115] 21 Jac.1.cap.27. The language of this legislation influenced labelling practices.

*Part III*

Control

# 6   Court days

### Contesting Bridewell

An artist whose name we do not know painted the moment when the king scribbled his signature on Bridewell's charter. The king sits in the centre of the portrait with his ministers on one side of the throne and a number of leading Londoners kneeling on the other side. These citizens seem steely faced, perhaps the grim state of the streets that brought them here in the first place is still on their minds. But they are also thankful. The king has an awkward half-smile, and a couple of his ministers look pleased. This was a hopeful moment, after all.

Bridewell was a comfort for the bulk of Londoners who felt glad that it was working for their good. They liked to be linked to its civic role and gave money to further its work. Bridewell soon became a by-word for control, but the opening of a brand new prison was not always welcomed by everyone, no matter how deep the need. Bridewell altered physical and mental landscapes for good. It now needed to be assimilated and opinions ranged from out-and-out support to deep loathing. We know much about the trials and tribulations of patients and prisoners, but people on the outside still seem mute.[1] Yet it is clear that their opinions were naggingly unpredictable. What else might be expected from people whose first port of call when they felt under the weather was more often than not an 'irregular' healer?[2]

Bridewell scared some people. Magistrates pinned their hopes on this if it was to become a heavy-duty deterrent that made people shrink from crime. Susan Moore was 'terrified' of going there in 1608 after telling Creed's wife that she was 'with child' by her husband. She was sitting drinking in a pub on Aldersgate Street when Mrs Creed stormed in and

---

[1] Cf. Mary Fissell, *Patients, Power, and the Poor in Eighteenth-Century Bristol* (Cambridge, 1991), chap. 8; Colin Jones, *Charity and Bienfaisance: The Treatment of the Poor in the Montpellier Region, 1740–1815* (Cambridge, 1982), chap. 6.
[2] See Margaret Pelling, *Medical Conflicts in Early Modern London: Patronage, Physicians, and Irregular Practitioners 1550–1640* (Oxford, 2003).

'threatened her that if she did not fynd another father for her child' she would dump her in Bridewell 'and have her whipt every court daye and work all the week' with just brown bread and water to live on. When a hospital beadle bumped into Sarah Lancaster at St James's fair in 1576 and asked her to walk with him to Charing Cross, she said that she was 'aferde' he would take her to Bridewell.[3] Bridewell became a black word to bully by. One pimp crowed that 'there was never a whore in England but if she kicked against him he woulde cause her to be brought to Bridewell'. Thomas Jones 'threatened' Jane Hilton 'to bring her to Bridewell' three years after she gave birth to a stillborn baby, getting meat and money from him all that time to keep quiet. The threat of Bridewell was dangled before 'whores' who fell out with clients and servants who got on the wrong side of masters/mistresses. Anne Allan's mistress warned her that she would 'serve' the next four years in dank Bridewell if she did not buckle down to her job. Some people conned others into thinking that they were Bridewell officers to intimidate them and/or pocket bribes.[4] And Bridewell was also a place of shame for 'honest' Londoners that left long-lasting stains. Only Bedlam could compare as a source for caricature on the page or stage. Authors saw Bridewell as a bleak prison stuffed with mucky vagrants and sleazy whores.[5] On paper and in gossip Bridewell's shame was sexual. John Lilburne's wife was bundled into a cell there with 'common sluts and whores whose society is a hell upon earth to one that fears the Lord', she said. The malicious glee of loose tongues sickened 'unfortunates' who rubbed shoulders with Bridewell's riff-raff. Another woman wept for her soul 'in this loathsome place accompanied with vile persons'. While the friends of a 'gentlewoman of good berth' plotted to free her from Bridewell, 'thincking bothe for theire owne reputacon and hers to avoyde the shame and infamy of so open and reproachfull a disgrace' as spending even one day locked up there.[6]

Tales of near-death thrashings, penny-pinching governors, maggot-laced food, and smelly bedding were bandied about not long after

---

[3] LMA D/L/C/218, fo. 159; BHC 3, fo. 67.
[4] BHC 3, fo. 187v; BRHA BHC 4, fos. 139, 293. See also BHC 3, fos. 67, 187v, 327v, 357, 389v, 400; 5, fo. 421; BRHA BHC 4, fo. 160.
[5] There are handy accounts of images of Bridewell and Bethlem in William C. Carroll, *Fat King, Lean Beggar: Representations of Poverty in the Age of Shakespeare* (Ithaca, NY, 1996), chap. 3, and Carol Thomas Neely, *Distracted Subjects: Madness and Gender in Shakespeare and Early Modern Culture* (Ithaca, NY, 2004).
[6] HOL MP, 21-2-1640; TNA SP16/451/106; LMA Remembrancia Book 1, fo. 153. See also TNA STAC8 288/14. Cf. Philip Massinger, *The City Madam*, in Philip Edwards and Colin Gibson, eds., *The Plays and Poems of Philip Massinger*, 4 vols. (Oxford, 1976), vol. IV, 2–94/10.

Bridewell first opened its doors. 'I almost starved there', the pimp Henry Boyer told Ann Ellis when the pair met on Warwick Lane in 1577. He said later that he was stuck in Bridewell for five long awful days with only 'thyn porredge and blacke breade as a dogge would skarse eat' and 'bare earth' to sleep on. A vagrant told his parents that Bridewell's 'breade and victualls' were only 'fit for doggs'.[7] Bridewell was turned into a figure of fun or scorn in the wrong hands. Other hospitals were also lampooned and lambasted, and not one of them escaped getting its name dragged through the mud. Heads turned on New Fish Street in 1552 when a woman walking from the bridge 'develyshlye' shouted at the top of her voice: 'Alas that ever she was born for her two children were taken from her' by coldhearted Christ's governors, and one of them was now 'murdered and the other [is] almoste ded'. Gossip-lines hummed around Newgate Market in 1571 when Mistress Blundell spread word that sick children were not getting any comfort or care in Christ's. Rumours reached aldermen two decades later that the hospital governors had cooked the books for some time. The class gap between 'haves' and 'have-nots' also sparked bitter words. 'Rich mens children' are 'preferred here and poor mens children [are] rejected', Goodman Jagger snapped at Christ's in 1577. Christ's forked out 8/9d in 1596 to cover costs when it took a woodmonger to court after he gave its board the sharp end of his tongue.[8] There are fewer outbursts against other hospitals, in existing records at any rate. But they had their edgy moments too. 'Privie back-bitying' by 'busybodies' heaped scorn on St Bartholomew's in 1552: what good has it done since it opened, these grouches asked, the 'poor and afflicted' still swarm in streets, blocking traffic, soiling air, and draining money like a drip-feed. 'The slaundre is so widespread that a narrow remedy cannot amend it', the hospital's board mused, spin-doctoring was now needed, and they 'thought [it] good' to ask the mayor to 'publishe' the rules and regulations of the hospital to the four corners of the city to put people in no doubt that it was doing a good job in extremely trying circumstances. St Thomas's 'board' was also on the receiving end of some 'ill speeches' and 'false and slanderous reporte[s]'.[9]

A noteworthy thing about these anti-hospital words is that most come from the second half of the sixteenth century, on paper at any rate. We

---

[7] BHC 3, fo. 214; TNA STAC5 B/108/33, Henry Boyer, examination; BHC 5, fo. 420.
[8] LMA Letterbook R, fo. 227v; GL MSS 12806/2, fo. 61v; 12806/3, fo. 7; 12806/2, fo. 173; 12819/2, 1595–6, n.p. See also GL MS 12806/2, fo. 208; LMA Rep. 13ii, fo. 177v.
[9] SBHA 'The Ordre of the Hospitall of St Bartholomewes in West Smythfield in London', fos. Av-Avir; LMA Rep. 13ii, fo. 203; H1/ST/A1/3, fo. 116v. See also Christopher Thomas, Daly, 'The hospitals of London: administration, refoundation, and benefaction, c.1500–1572', unpublished DPhil thesis, University of Oxford (1994), p. 175.

can only read surviving sources, but if they have any value then Bridewell was the most controversial of the '4 hospitals' by some distance, even though Christ's was the heaviest drain on civic charity and finances towards 1600 when money was short and troubles spiralled.[10] As with the other hospitals, however, the number of words aimed at Bridewell dropped after 1600, evidence that Bridewell became more accepted across the length and breadth of the city as time passed. The decades after 1550 were without doubt the stormiest times when many minds were not yet made up. Not only were there more anti-Bridewell slurs, but they were consistently more toxic. Bridewell split opinion like no other hospital. Its bench were called 'men of much worship and wisdom' in one set of 'house'-rules (1557); far from it, a barber's wife shrieked in 1560, they are heartless 'murtherers'. Bridewell's founder – Edward VI – was called a 'godly' prince and a true pilgrim; not so, said a thief who snatched a cloak and hat from a man on the street, and 'cursed' Bridewell and its 'founder'.[11] Bad publicity was the last thing that Bridewell needed in its early rocky decades, as it was at the bottom of the hospitals' pecking order, and there was always competition for dwindling resources. Bridewell's legal footing also caused concern, as we shall soon see. 'Wild' words were bad enough on their own, but they were also picked up by crowds now and then, and travelled from one person to another, getting more spicy and harmful with each retelling. A woman was 'well whipped' in 1559 after Bridewell's bench claimed that she was caught 'rayling most unhonestlye and slaunderouslye upon this house and its governors openly in the hearyng of five hundred persons'. Worse still, a preacher blasted Bridewell from London's most public pulpit – Paul's Cross – in 1558. His 'rashe and slanderous' speech gave an over-the-top blow-by-blow account of the savage 'beatynge of an apprentice' inside Bridewell that left him clinging to life. The story was already spreading quickly as a City lobby hurried to the Lord Chancellor to see if there was anything that he could do to stop this 'false reporte' and clear Bridewell's name from any blame.[12]

There were many such public-relations exercises all the way through Bridewell's first century, as for some Londoners Bridewell was a heavy-handed intrusion in their lives, keeping watch over intimate matters and dishing out sharp penalties, not always fairly, it seemed. Manners and morals were hotly contested, a clash of opinions neatly summed up in 1577 when William Aldersley greeted drinkers in a Cheapside pub saying 'I woulde Bridewell weare downe and the stewes up agayne', or when a

[10] Daly, 'Hospitals of London', pp. 339, 359. [11] BHC 1, fo. 87v; 8, fo. 212v.
[12] BHC 1, fo. 17v; LMA Rep. 14, fos. 14, 24v, 29v.

bunch of 'whores' plotted to hang themselves there dreaming that Bridewell would be 'put down' by the resulting bad press two years earlier.[13] Bridewell had troubled relations with London's citizens from its first day. It was opened in their name, as a royal gift to the 'maior, coialtie, and citizens', who also named its governors.[14] But it was run by a ring of governors who claimed to occupy the moral high ground. People were always falling on the wrong side of the law. A list of 'whoremongers' from Bridewell's courtbooks looks like a cross-section of the metropolitan population.[15] Bridewell was on a collision course with citizen-pests right from the start. The bench felt that they were peering into a bottomless pit of immorality and sex took up more time in court than anything else in its first half-century.[16] Many brothel haunting citizens felt bitter about this moral meddling. Bridewell's bench were busy moral bees, swooping on houses and alehouses, trampling over citizens' rights. We will never know how many felt this way, but it was surely high and crossed class lines. The Earls of Leicester and Worcester had close links with the vice-trade in the 1570s. Leicester took the side of 'whores' in court cases; while Worcester received rents from a busy brothel – Worcester House – that was run by Mistress Higgins under his wing, and he once waged law to stop it being shut down. 'Gentlemen' also rescued 'harlots' from Bridewell and the clutches of its officers. Henry Machyn made a note in his diary about some 'gentyllmen and ruffelars and servingmen' who stormed into Bridewell waving swords in 1559 to free 'serten women' and traded punches with constables, doing 'myche besenes', Machyn added.[17]

There was no sitting on the fence. Sex split opinions. One point of view was that rounding-up prostitutes and their clients was a nuisance and a waste of time and resources that distracted attention away from the real problems spawned by fast growth. People followed this line for different reasons: a serial 'whoremonger' and a highly thought of hospital governor both asked out-loud whether crackdowns on vice should be a top priority. Goldsmith Anthony Bate, 'the vilest and rankest whoremonger' in all London, one pimp said, took the Bridewell bench to the Star Chamber to clear his name after allegations of 'whoremongering' and to quiz Bridewell's process from start to finish, in a case that dragged on for

---

[13] BHC 3, fo. 192; 2, fo. 110.   [14] TNA STAC5/B/21/3, Anthony Bate, bill of complaint.
[15] See above, pp. 172–3.
[16] Ian W. Archer, *The Pursuit of Stability: Social Relations in Elizabethan London* (Cambridge, 1991), p. 239, Table 6.1.
[17] LMA Rep. 19, fo. 198; Archer, *Pursuit of Stability*, p. 232; *The Diary of Henry Machyn Citizen and Merchant-Taylor of London From A.D. 1550 to A.D. 1563*, ed. John Gough Nichols, Camden Society (1848), p. 194. See also BHC 3, fos. 242, 246, 296; LMA Rep. 20, fos. 285v, 298v.

three long years (1577–80).[18] Bate's bill complained about Bridewell's slender legal roots, fishy policing and courtroom processes, crooked officers who took bribes at the drop of a hat, and its vendetta against citizens. He said that he, like others, was hounded day and night by Bridewell. Some well-heeled citizens took his side through thick and thin, plotting in alehouses, putting pressure on witnesses. A handful were fellow goldsmiths. In Bate's case a gang of citizens started a small war with Bridewell. Bate, who called himself a 'citizen and goldsmyth of London', took the part of a champion of citizens' rights, a tireless crusader against sleaze, and a shining civic knight in armour who was licking his wounds after a series of scandalous allegations. Bridewell's treasurer, Robert Winch, denied at Star Chamber that 'cytyzens' had been unfairly 'called in question of there reporte, fame, and credit' since he took his post on 'mere suspition' of 'incontinencye' or 'willful accusacion' by 'dissolute persons'. He also fended off charges that he 'compelled manye of good creditt to compounde', and 'wynked at open, knowen and confessed adulteryes, malefactors, and felonies' at exactly the same time as he wrongly 'afflicted godlie and vertuous cytyzens', like Bate.[19] Bridewell, Bate claimed, had turned its back on London's citizens.

Bate's case ended with his drubbing in Star Chamber and abject apology before the aldermen: 'I have many ways greeved and offendyde famous and honorable' Bridewell, he whimpered, tears streaming down his cheeks, 'for which I am veary sorye' and 'pytyfullye crave pardon'.[20] Bate got trounced, but the case caused splits in London, letting loose cross-currents of opinion about citizenship, morality, and the law. The City was washing its dirty laundry in public again. Bate's case was the talk of the town in some circles. William Aldersley bumped into William Gold in 1577 and 'asked him what newes he had hearde of Anthony Bate?'[21] The Bate case clearly touched raw nerves at a time in the mid-1570s when Bridewell launched crackdowns on vice.[22] Not everyone backed this hard-hitting line. Aldermen asked the Crown to bring the case to a speedy close in 1579 as it caused 'great troubles, threateninges, and daunger of assaultes' to Bridewell's bench.[23] Marie Donnolly (a 'whore') said that the brothel-keeper Thomas Wise and two pimps – Williams Mekens and Jasper Wrey – met at Gilbert East's bawdy house to 'talke of Anthony Bate', and one day she heard Wise 'threaten' to 'beate' Bridewell's

---

[18] The Bate case is the cornerstone of my 'Contesting London Bridewell, 1576–1580', *Journal of British Studies*, 42 (2003), 283–315.
[19] TNA STAC5/B/53/40, Robert Winch, interrogatories.
[20] LMA Rep. 20, fos 11v, 115v-16.  [21] BHC 3, fo. 192.
[22] Archer, *Pursuit of Stability*, pp. 253–4.  [23] BL Additional MS 48019, fo. 151.

Court days 219

treasurer and clerk if he bumped into them.[24] No single Bridewell governor got as much abuse as Winch. John Richardson was taken to court in 1577 for 'vyolently' punching him as he sat 'quyettly' on his Cheapside doorstep. A woman called governor Clark 'a turkey cocks nose' and Winch a 'turke' and 'a ten pence' in 1578. George Greene filed sureties in the same year after he was caught taunting the treasurer. While a weaver was locked up for poking fun at Winch, though he said the 'slaunderous words' 'came from a whore's mouth' and not his own.[25]

One year after Bate grovelled in front of the aldermen, squirming as he said sorry, John Howes, who sat on Christ's board, wondered why Bridewell spent so much time clearing up sexual offences when grubby vagrants flooded London. This was *the* pressing problem of the day, he said. Howes was a friend of Bridewell, and wrote a glowing history of the hospitals in 1582, though it did not lack criticisms. He gave a cooler and shrewder analysis of Bridewell up to that date than Bate.[26] But each of them cast doubt on the strategy of chasing sex-offenders for different reasons. Howes could take his arguments to the aldermen's table where he felt at home. But this was not Bate's home-turf. He was once picked for his guild's livery, but he climbed up and tumbled down the ladder on the same day, losing his 'room' due to unpaid debts.[27] He was not a City bigwig but his opinions counted for people who thought that sex was none of the magistrates' business. Bridewell was a burden for such people, and twisted by double standards. Asked to curb vice, some governors grabbed chances to meet 'lewd' women, they said. Pimps and prostitutes claimed that treasurer Winch set the 'rankest' example. Although he took his place on the bench alongside puritans, Winch was not a lily-white character, some said. A pimp scattered stories that he made regular return trips to 'lewd women'. 'Harlot' Agnes Williams said that Winch paid for room and board for prostitute Thomasine Breame in Paternoster Row, and 'showed lewd women great favor in Bridewell', letting them come and go 'at liberty'. Another 'whore' added that Breame ruled the roost at Bridewell with a green light to leave 'when she listed'. Breame lived snugly on Paternoster Row, a bawd said sourly, 'pleasantly going at her pleasure'. Breame herself said that she had 'been abused by Mr Winche, and that he had kept her at a house nere Paules'.[28]

Much mud was slung at Bridewell while Bate's case was hanging in the balance. Winch may have been the target of a smear campaign, but not

---

[24] BHC 3, fo. 196.  [25] LMA Rep. 19, fo. 211v; BHC 3, fos. 321–1v, 347v.
[26] See above, p. 203.  [27] GCL company minute book L, fos. 147, 150.
[28] BHC 3, fos. 242v-3, 246; TNA STAC5/B/108/33, Agnes Williams, Jane Robinson, Joanne Higgins, examinations.

one of these slurs was new. All had been levelled at Bridewell before. Bate's case with its little hill of documentation lets us dig deep into bribery, bullying, and double-dealing. A clerk claimed that Winch netted bribes from brothel-loving merchants and coaxed 'many sums of money and clothes' from well-off 'gents' to keep them safe from arrest. Pimp William Mekens boasted that 'he could go to Mr Winche and fetche 3 or 4 crownes of [him] when he had nede'. Another pimp – Henry Boyer – told a parson that Winch 'unhonestlye ryfled twoe cutpurses which were brought to Bridewell'; one lost thirty shillings, the other was missing seven pounds. The eldest son of the queen's cousin – Lord Hundson – also lashed out at Winch: 'the world will judge him to be one of the worst members that can live in a commonwealth', he snapped, with all his 'cloked faultes'.[29] He was not the only Bridewell big wheel said to line his pockets with bribes. One woman 'shamefully' called the bench crooked 'bawds', who pooled pickings from 'whores'. A bricklayer was in deep water in 1577 for saying if he gave the bench 'iis for a brybe he shoulde not have bene any more trobled'. James Reade said that 'poore' apprentices were slung out of Bridewell in next to no time unless their parents or parish were able to pay an extra 'three or fower poundes'. Double-standards were stock themes in pot-shots at Bridewell. 'Beggarly harlots are ponysshed' there all the time, a fishmonger growled in 1560, 'and the riche eskape'. Wealth could always buy softer or suspended sentences, if need be. 'Sisters' are 'imprisoned and whipped', one ballad quipped, 'but not the London prentises and other men of good fashion'.[30]

There is a grain of truth in these gloomy depictions of Bridewell by sulky prostitutes, pimps, and hard-done-by citizens. Not all charges were brushed aside as tall tales or settling of scores. Reade's protests led to inquiries. Stories of wrongdoing were believable, even in the mouths of slippery characters, because similar charges circulated at other times. Bridewell was rocked by sloppiness and scandals of its own making down through the years: irregular discharges of prisoners, bribes, fee-fiddling 'house' officers, matrons skimping on diets, stewards cooking the books, 'inhumane crueltie' to 'poore and sicke prisoners', 'house' officers stealing prisoners' possessions, having sex with others, and mixing with thieves and 'old whores' in and out of the building. Matron Millet's

---

[29] BHC 3, fos. 280v, 187v, 242v-3; TNA STAC5/B/103/33, Giles Cannon, examination; LMA Remembrancia Book 1, fos. 37–7v.
[30] BHC 1, fo. 38; 3, fo. 257; 9, fos. 189–90; 1, fos. 51–1v; 'Whipping Cheer', in Hyder E. Rollins, ed., *A Pepysian Garland: Black-Letter Broadside Ballads of the Years 1595–1639, Chiefly From the Collection of Samuel Pepys* (Cambridge, 1922), pp. 39–43. See also LMA Rep. 19, fo. 338; BHC 1, fo. 38; 3, fos. 173, 176, 214; 5, fos. 108v, 116; 7, fo. 35v; 8, fo. 23; BRHA BHC 4, fos. 331v, 391; HOL MP 21-12-1640.

charge sheet stretched over a couple of pages in Bridewell's courtbook: she received stolen goods from prisoners, took money 'for favors', helped herself to their clothes, 'winked' at 'their lewdness', mixed with 'people of ill fame' at alehouses and other 'suspected places', dished out 'inhumane crueltie' to 'poore and sicke prisoners under her charge', and let people have round-the-clock 'accesse to close prisoners' for a fee.[31] And Bridewell even became London's biggest brothel for six months in 1602 (right in the middle of two campaigns to confirm Bridewell's charter in Parliament) when it was put under the wing of 'undertakers' (private contractors) led by Thomas Stanley, under whose 'misgovernment' 'lighte and lewde' women wearing 'gorgeous apparell' 'sat and supped' with wealthy gentlemen in the 'fairest roomes', tucking in to lavish meals of 'crabbs, lobsters, artichoque pyes and gallons of wyne', and peeling off after in pairs to 'private' rooms.[32]

Bridewell spawned speculation, hardly a surprise when so much went on behind its high walls, including proceedings in a court that took people to task for scattering its 'secrets', among them a nosey beadle who sneaked in one day when the bench was deep in 'private conference'. Only the treasurer and clerk were trusted with keys to the court in 1599, and the porter kept a look out at the door to make sure that no 'strangers' slipped in before they were 'called'. The 'eldest beadle' guarded the door in 1643 after 'disturbances' caused by slipshod 'dorekeepers'. The matron had a lot of explaining to do in 1634 after bribing the 'clarkes man' to let her know what the bench said when others came forward with incriminating stories about her crooked conduct.[33] Secrets mattered at

---

[31] BHC 6, fos. 133–3v, 274v. See also BHC 1, fos. 137–7v; 7, fos. 88v, 363v, 365v; 8, fos. 29v, 81, 309v, 311v; BRHA BHC 4, fo. 162.

[32] BRHA BHC 4, fos. 345v, 284, 296v, 313v, 314v, 313, 314, 316–16v, 302v, 310v, 317v, 319, 324v-5, 326v, 331v, 332v, 365, 389, 398v; BHC 5, fo. 362v; LMA Reps. 25, fo. 281; 26, fos. 35v, 37, 296v, 313v, 314v, 331. The 'Undertakers scandal' is fully described in Gustav Ungerer, 'Prostitution in late Elizabethan London: the case of Mary Newborough', *Medieval and Renaissance Drama in England*, 15 (2003), 138–223, esp. 182–191.

[33] BHC 8, fo. 20; 9, fo. 32; BRHA BHC 4, fos. 55v, 93v; GL MS 33013, C, fo. 23. Bridewell was not the only 'closed' court in the city. Other hospitals also ran internal affairs in courts inside their walls, as did guilds and the College of Physicians. See Daly, 'Hospitals of London'; Pelling, *Medical Conflicts in Early Modern London*; Ian Anders Gadd and Patrick Wallis, eds., *Guilds, Society and Economy in London, 1450–1850* (2002); Caroline M. Barron, *London in the Later Middle Ages: Government and People, 1200–1500* (Oxford, 2004), chap. 9. Beadles also guarded the door of St Thomas's court where only the clerk was 'privy' to 'talk' about 'the affairs of the house'. Christ's had a garden where governors took breaks from the court to 'confer privately': LMA H1/ST/A1/1, fo. 44; H1/ST/A1/3, fo. 167v; H1/ST/A1/4, fo. 51; H1/ST/A1/5, fo. 130v; GL MS 12806/2, fo. 67; Daly, 'Hospitals of London', pp. 284, 286. Cf. My 'Secrecy and authority in late sixteenth- and early seventeenth-century London', *Historical Journal*, 40 (1997), 925–51.

Bridewell. The courtbooks were locked in a 'stronge place' with one key that the clerk kept safe and sound. No one could take 'bookes or bonds' out of 'the house' without the treasurer's blessing. Other secrets, seals, and revenues were put in a locked box or 'greate chest' for safe keeping.[34] Blabbing could cost a whipping, a steep fine, or the sack. Secrets also spawned speculation. Bridewell seemed big and bleak. Curiosity set minds racing. In this chilly climate that missed even the moderating hand of a jury, what did those high walls hide? The lack of close outside scrutiny led to Inquisition-like images in some minds of pitiful, quivering prisoners who caved in after blood-curdling threats and horrid handling. Stories of sleaze and rough handling spread and with each new one it became harder to pick out fact from fantasy. A beggar tried to squeeze some sympathy with 'great lamentacon and crynge, seyinge he hath been whipped at Bridewell for askeinge for the heavenlie fathers sake'. Twelve of Margaret Greenwood's 'honest' neighbours all went along to Bridewell in 1560 to say that she had 'vilely slaundered' the governors and 'order' of the 'house', spreading stories that she had been 'whypped' there 'untyll she might borne her fynger in her flesh'.[35]

A second complaint about Bridewell reached the Star Chamber a decade after Bate put Bridewell on its stage, this time of a harsh and hasty whipping before any proof was brought to court. Jane Neville alleged that a sheriff who was nursing a grudge against her took her to Bridewell on a trumped-up charge that she was 'a naughtie strumpet and harlot' who kept 'verye ungodly rule in her howse' at all hours. She was never given a chance to put her side, she said later in Star Chamber proceedings, even though she asked for some time to bring 'witnesses for defense of [her] cause'. The sheriff and governors who watched her whipping were asked if she begged to be 'spared' until she could 'produce proofs', and whether anyone seemed 'glad' as the whip cut her back. One governor, Henry Tayleford (clothworker), said no one gloated except for the sheriff, who 'was no sorrowful man to see her whipped'. There is more to this case than first meets the eye. One Bridewell governor said that Neville did not plead for time to show she was 'honest'; another said that

---

[34] BRHA BHC 4, fos. 76v, 94; BHC 9, fo. 2; LMA Rep. 15, fo. 23v. Other hospitals kept records in chests and gave keys to a chosen few. Common Council told 'governors of every hospitall' in 1567 'to 'provyde a stronge and sure chest' to be put 'in the most substancialie fastened and surest place of your house', with three locks and keys to be kept by the president, treasurer, and most 'aunciente governor'. See LMA Jour. 19, fos. 67–7v; GL MS 12806/2, fo. 94; SBHA Governors Journal 1, fo. 168; 'The Ordre of the Hospitall of St Bartholomewes in West Smythfielde in London', fos. C4v-5; LMA H1/ST/A1/4, fo. 92.

[35] BHC 2, fo. 72; 1, fo. 95.

she did. We hear of 'generall informacon' that she ran a 'brothel howse', and that her neighbours talked about her all the time. Two people who gave evidence against her were now locked up in the Fleet prison, the last stop for many debtors and cheats: one was a recently ejected Bridewell treasurer who cooked the books (Roger Warfield), and the other was the same sheriff who looked on smugly as the whip whacked Neville's back. This case also got into gentry gossip, the last thing that the City needed. Jane Neville was in fact highly placed in society, as wife of the claimant to the Latimer barony, and beneath the surface and beyond the Star Chamber documents there lies a sordid story involving a sheriff who was imprisoned and fined for his actions and who, for a while at least, compromised magisterial authority and Bridewell's standing.[36]

Bate's case planted seeds of doubt about Bridewell process. He lost the final judicial decision, but there were enough stories of wild whippings, heavy-handed pressure to wring confessions, and corruption, to make the City fear the impact of the case on 'public opinion', not least because it was backed up by others before and after. Henry Boyer told Ann Ellis that he confessed lies at Bridewell out of 'feare of famyshenge'. 'I think it will come to the quene to ende it', the pimp mused. Later on when quizzed at Star Chamber about Bate, Boyer added that the governors warned that he would be 'whipped at a cart's arse' with forty lashes every Saturday until he gave them the answers that they wanted to hear. A second pimp – Richard Rolles – was asked why 'he slaundered Bate at Bridewell' with tall tales: I was 'kept [there] v dayes' and 'threatened to be whipped', and 'therefore I did', he said. Phyllis Russell stuck solidly to her story that she spoke 'wordes and confession againste Katherine Hughes' in 1576 'for feare of punnishment'. The brothel keeper/pimp Thomas Wise was also grilled about Bate at Bridewell. The bench wanted to know if Bate had had sex and supper at his house with Thomasine Breame in Christmas week 1576. Wise stood his ground: Bate did not set foot in his house with her, he said. But as time dragged on and Winch and the rest of the bench put pressure on him, Wise caved in, 'partlie by threats and partlie by promyse of rewards', and 'promysed' the treasurer 'that he would saie whatsoever he would have hym saie'. Later on, gripped by guilt, Wise dragged his bruised body from friend to friend, making 'lamentacon unto

---

[36] TNA STAC5 N15/10, Henry Tayelford, Henry Webb, Thomas Skinner, Roger Warfield, John Cacher, examinations; 'the maysters of Brydewell', interrogatories. I must thank Ian Archer for information on Jane Neville and the wider ramifications of this case. See also Richard Crompton, *Star-Chamber Cases, Shewing What Cases Properly Belong to the Recognizance of that Court. Collected for the Most Part Out of Mr Crompton, His Booke, Entituled The Jurisdiction of Divers Courts*, 1630, The English Experience, 723 (Amsterdam and Norwood, NJ, 1975), p. 19.

them with weepinge eyes that that he was compelled to accuse' his good friend Bate 'of matters [that] he never knewe' anything about.[37] Bridewell is a danger here rather than the reassurance that it ought to have been for citizens. It bulldozes suspects in these stories and tosses the rule of law aside as an awkward irrelevance. One line of attack in Bate's case was to chip away at the legal integrity of 'holy' Bridewell, blending scaremongering with a number of sharp criticisms of process that were also made by skilled scholars with expert legal training. Bate and his cronies homed in on ironies and irregularities in Bridewell's process. 'Why did you examine Rolles privatlie' in 'yor owne house', Winch was asked at Star Chamber (after hearing Bate and others), 'and what was the meaninge of yor private conference?' Why did you not summon some of 'the graver sort of governors' to your house for the examination? There were also accusations of witness-tampering. Star Chamber wanted to know what pieces of the case were wheedled out of witnesses by the governors before 'publick examination' at Bridewell.[38] 'Publick' is safe and above board here; 'private' is dangerous and implies not playing by the book. The Star Chamber would not give Winch an inch: did you 'perswade' Breame 'to confesse matters of adultery and indecency before her open examinacon before [the rest of] the governors?' they asked, trying to sort out what was proper and improper practice.[39]

These concerns come from one bulky case with more than a fair share of double-crossers and double-dealers, although this was not the only time that such charges were made. Bridewell's fuzzy legal status had long been a bone of contention in legalese and less-polished street talk. Lawyers and labourers could both talk about Bridewell as either a comfort or curse, depending on which side of the fence speakers stood. It was a prison with a court that, unlike anywhere else, could police, prosecute, and punish in a single sweep, without any screening authority, like a justices' warrant. Bridewell was new, highly visible, and apparently arbitrary. The bench was formally constituted to hear cases, with broad 'power and aucthoretie' to 'searche, enquyre, and seke owt' 'all ydell ruffians and taverne haunters, vagabonds, beggars, and all persons of yll name and fame' in the London area, and drag them to Bridewell to face the bench, who could punish people 'as shall seem good' to their 'dis-

---

[37] BHC 3, fo. 214; TNA STAC8 B/103/33, Henry Boyer, examination; BHC 3, fos. 207, 244v; TNA STAC8 B/21/3, Anthony Bate, bill of complaint.
[38] TNA STAC5 B/53/40, Henry Winch, articles, answers.
[39] Ibid. See also TNA STAC5 B/108/33, Thomasine Breame, articles; B/11/18, William Stackford, interrogatories.

cretion'.[40] This might seem solid on paper, but the charter was not a ticket to police, prosecute, and punish at will, commentators said. The nub of the matter was that it was never backed by Parliamentary Act and for this reason lacked legitimacy, even though it was stamped with a royal seal.

Bridewell's shaky legal standing was also chewed over in both print and manuscript. A key critical commentary appeared in the 1580s, although there are question marks about both its authorship and date. A copy in the Guildhall Library (London) has the title *A Brief Treatise or Discourse of ye Validity, Strength, and Extent of the Charter of Bridewell ... Worthily Composed by Mr Searjant Fleetwood, Sometymes Seirjant at Lawe*: this is William Fleetwood, London's recorder. A copy in the British Library, however, is credited to Francis Bacon with the title *Discourse upon the Commission of Bridewell*, an ascription shared with the editors of a standard edition of Bacon's *Works*, published in the third quarter of the nineteenth century.[41] As recorder, Fleetwood would have been familiar with the nuts and bolts of Bridewell process. He had a seat on the bench and attended court sittings. He was a very active recorder, getting involved in

---

[40] Quotations from the charter and other documents are from *The Thirty-Second Report of the Charity Commissioners of England and Wales*, Per Acts 38 Geo.3.c.91 & Geo.3.c.81, part IV, 1840 (219), xix (hereafter *Charity Commissioners Report*), pp. 390, 389; *John Howes' MS, 1582, Being A Briefe Note of the order and Manner of the Proceedings in the First Erection of the Three Royal Hospitals of Christ, Bridewell, and St Thomas the Apostle*, ed., William Lampiere (1904), pp. 56–60; Francis Bacon, *A Brief Discourse Upon the Commission of Bridewell*, in *The Works of Francis Bacon*, eds., J. Spedding *et al.*, 14 vols. (1857–74), vol. VII, p. 512; GL MS 6, *Memoires Historicall Relating to the 5 Principall Hospitals in London*, fo. 6v; William Waddington, *Considerations on the Original and Proper Objects of the Royal Hospital of Bridewell Addressed to the Governors* (1798), pp. 9–10; GL MSS 33001; 33003.

[41] GL MS 9384, *A Brief Treatise or Discourse of Ye Validity, Strength, and Extent of the Charter of Bridewell and How Far Repugnant Both in Matter, Sense, and Meaninge to the Great Charter of England. Worthily Composed by Mr Searjant Fleetwood, Sometymes Seirjant at Lawe*; BL Harley MS 1323, fos. 127–38v; Spedding, *Works of Francis Bacon*. There are three other extant copies of this treatise without identified authors, the earliest surviving copy – in the Huntington Library, San Marino – is dated before 1593. This is the copy that Alan Stewart uses in his new edition for the *Oxford Francis Bacon*. Spedding dates Bacon's *Discourse* to 1587, a dating also followed by Daniel R. Coquillette, *Francis Bacon* (Stanford, CA, 1992), pp. 25–8. The manuscript in the Guildhall Library, attributed to Fleetwood, is a later copy. There are many minor but no major differences between this and the British Library copy, written, we think, a little later. There is the intriguing possibility that the treatise has been mistakenly attributed to Fleetwood because it appears with a small work by him on the office of a justice of a peace in the same formulary, now at the Huntington. Authorship of the *Treatise* or *Discourse* is still controversial. Alan Stewart tells me that there is 'no compelling evidence' for either candidate (personal communication: 20 April 2006). Coquillette writes that the *Discourse* was 'almost certainly by the young Bacon' (indeed, it is his first surviving legal work): *Francis Bacon*, 25. I am grateful to Alan Stewart for his guidance on this matter, and to Harriet Knight for her hard work in uncovering manuscripts relating to it. I hastily concluded that

the nitty gritty of policing, going out on searches and travelling deep into London's shady areas. Aldermen asked him to go through Bridewell's charter with help from legal counsel in 1577 to draw up an exact account of what the bench 'maye doe by force of the letters patent graunted by King Edwarde the sixth' (a short entry in a Common Council journal in 1579 notes, with no expansion, 'things in their [i.e. Bridewell's bench] power to do', and if a list was drawn up it was not written down). But there is no direct link to the *Discourse/Treatise*, although the aldermen's instruction sounds like a call for clarity out of some concern for Bridewell's legal standing.[42]

Whoever he was, the author of the *Discourse/Treatise* dug deep into the past for yearbook cases, statutes, and other grants with bearing on the matter-in-hand to argue that Bridewell's charter lacked legal standing as it only had backing from royal letters patent. He did not mince words: 'the king's charter may not change the law' and the king cannot 'change any one point of the Great Charter' (Magna Carta). 'In matter, sense and meaning', therefore, Bridewell's charter was 'repugnant' to the law of the land.[43] Bridewell was legal Bedlam without parliamentary consent. The possibility of suspects being dragged there on 'slight cause' without the legal comfort of a justices' warrant was the nub of the matter. The author of the *Discourse/Treatise* made the acerbic point that cases 'on accusation of whores taken by governors' were not 'sufficient to call any man to answer', in words that echo Bate not long after his case came to an end. Searching for statutes, he turned up almost forty that made the 'wisdom and discretion' of handpicked justices a legal imperative. One – 43 Ed. 3 – was referred to more than once to clinch the case: 'No man', it said bluntly, can 'be put to answer without presentment before justices of the king'. Everything else was mere 'error'. The proof of the pudding was that royal commissions had been revoked because they had led to arrests without warrants, and Bridewell lacked a watchdog like a jury. No court 'ought' to meet 'in any close or secret place', the author of the *Discourse/Treatise* warned, drawing to a close, all 'inquiry ought to be by juries'. 'I thus conclude', he said, that not even someone with 'great knowledge of

---

Bacon was not the author of the *Brief Discourse* in my 'Contesting London Bridewell', 293, got my dates mixed up, and even accused Bacon of plagiarism when evidence is not at all clear.

[42] LMA Rep. 19, fos. 170–0v, 193; Jour. 20(2), fo. 510v. The most accessible guide to Fleetwood 'as policeman' is the series of letters he sent to Burghley about searches, amongst other things, that are collected in T. Wright, ed., *Queen Elizabeth and her Times*, 2 vols. (1838). With a seat on Bridewell's bench and the most important legal position in a City government that needed Bridewell for crime crackdowns, it would seem like a colossal own goal for this *Treatise* or *Discourse* to have been authored by London's recorder, although he was qualified to do so.

[43] Coquillette, *Francis Bacon*, p. 26; GL MS 9384, fos. 3v, 5v, 4v, 5.

law' had a leg to stand on if he tried to 'defend' Bridewell's commission. Six decades later when all royal 'arbitrary' institutions/processes were sitting ducks, the author of *Brief Collections Out of Magna Charta* (1643), helped himself to large chunks of the *Discourse/Treatise*: a royal charter is 'void', he wrote, if it 'is repugnant to the maximes, customes or statutes of the realm'.[44]

But Bridewell was not just a target for seasoned legal eagles. 'The charter of the house was not worthe iid, no it was nothing worthe', William Guy sneered in 1577. 'This house has no aucthoritie to sende' for me or my wife, James Fareclowe bragged in 1579, after his wife had been summoned to the court for 'lewde behavior' and for renting rooms to 'ruffians' on a daily basis.[45] London's leaders were shaken by this vulnerability, and took steps to spell out Bridewell's precise powers to build shields against criticisms, starting, not surprisingly, in the thick of Bate's case, when the recorder sat down with others to make a list of the 'things' in Bridewell's 'power to do' (1579). This was a stepping stone for a move to get solid statutory support for Bridewell's charter within a wider claim for statutory status for the charters of the other three of the '4 hospitalls'. A panel of governors was 'ordered' to draft 'a bill' that was 'exhibited to the Parliament for the ratification of the charters of the hospitals' in 1579, though it sank quickly, not even reaching a first reading.[46] There is an excellent chance that a case like Bate's that revealed so many cracks before different audiences on streets and one of the highest courts in the land triggered such defensive actions. At the same time as the bill was winging its way into Parliament's wastebasket, a fifty-three clause Common Council Act spelled out Bridewell's powers and responsibilities in textbook detail over ten long pages in a Journal (1579). This Act expressed in simple and straightforward prose the rule that Bridewell's bench should never act above the law: 'Suche things as be not in the power of thaldran or his deputye but in the power of the house of Bridewell by vertue of their charter', it said, 'shalbe delivered to the governors of Bridewell to be by them executed and reformed so farre as they maye according to the lawe'; anything outside their 'power' was to go without delay to the Court of Aldermen

---

[44] *Charity Commissioners Report*, p. 400; GL MS 9384, fos. 6, 5v-6, 9–9v, 7, 6v, 9v; BL TT E38(12) *Brief Collections Out of Magna Charta: Or, the Knowne Good Old Lawes of England* (1643), p. 4.
[45] BHC 3, fos. 183v, 405v.
[46] LMA Rep. 19, fos. 170–0v; 193v; Jour. 20(2) fo. 501v; BHC 3, fo. 428; Geoffrey Elton, *The Parliament of England, 1559–1581* (Cambridge, 1986), pp. 78–9. See also LMA H1/ST/A1/3, fo. 207v; GL MS 12806/2, fo. 249.

or a justice.[47] The 'valydytye of ye [Bridewell] charter' was put to the test across the river in Southwark two years later. Revealingly, given that justices' warrants had been a crux of the controversy concerning Bridewell, aldermen ordered, later in the same year, that whenever Bridewell governors or 'offycers' brought warrants to City justices 'to be sygned for thapprehendenge of eny malefactor', the justice must sign it at all times, regardless of whether or not he was one of the governors of the 'howse of Brydewell'.[48] This attempt to tighten procedure emerged in the same climate in which John Howes made up his mind to write the first ever history of the '4 hospitalls', which 'putt in wrighting certaine abuses in ye governmente of the poore in this present tyme'.[49] If Fleetwood penned the *Treatise* then he would have done so at about this time when Bridewell's charter was under fire. If Bacon did write his *Discourse* in 1587, as experts on his work have suggested, then he sat down to write it at a time when the fuss about Bridewell's shaky foundations had settled down a little, at least if entries in Common Council Journals and Court of Aldermen Repertories are anything to go by.

Yet little had been settled by the failed parliamentary lobby in 1579 and doubts about Bridewell's legal standing never faded, despite the best efforts of the City to seek greater clarity in the storm of Bate's case and its aftermath.[50] Each Bridewell governor was expected to know the fine points of the charter. The clerk read out 'the chief poynts of the charter once every quarter' from 1599 on, and they were put in a 'table' hung up on a wall in the courtroom not long after.[51] Bridewell's bench put a series of questions to Lord Chief Justice Popham in the next year to try to sort out their lingering jurisdictional confusion, having first sounded him out at a dinner party given by the mayor: could they sign warrants to authorize raids on suspicious places, was their 'discretion' entirely above board, could they in 'discreccon' punish people through bodily discipline and fines, and, lastly, could they 'take bonds of evill offenders for their appearance and also for their good behaviour?' Popham's answers did little to soothe anxieties, and a second bill 'for confirmacon of the charter' was drafted in 1601 after yet another meeting with him. This one

---

[47] LMA Jour. 20, fo. 501v. The Act was passed in August 1579. Three months earlier 'the residue of the Booke devised for the settinge of the poore on worke in Bridewell was redd to the Comon Counsell. The same booke is nowe agreed uppon [the entry continues] and well liked of and that it shalbe (as it is) preferred to the consyderacon of' the Privy Council: Ibid., fo. 483.

[48] LMA Rep. 20, fos. 259, 325. See also GL MS 12806/2, fo. 297v.

[49] *John Howes' MS*, p. v.  [50] LMA Rep. 20(2), fo. 259.

[51] BRHA BHC 4, fos. 94, 111. See also BHC 5, fo. 166; 6, fo. 275v.

stumbled through a first reading but fell at the next hurdle.[52] The clerk tipped off the bench about a number of 'doubts' he had spotted in the charter 'fitt to be reformed' three years later, although he did not jot them down. But a third Parliamentary lobby soon gathered steam after a speedily convened meeting of aldermen in 1604. Bridewell's treasurer and clerk called on 'councell learned' with the charter to draw up 'an act of parliament for confirmacon of the charter'. A draft bill was tabled before Parliament, but once again the end result was nothing but frustration.[53] The next crunch moment came nearly four decades later in 1641 when the clerk copied passages from the charter relating to Bridewell's 'government', and drew up a list of 'queries and cases as are doubtful and necessary' for the bench to look into. They were still noting questions 'concerninge' the charter nine months later, seeking guidance from legal experts, and setting up a sub-committee to pour over their 'advice' and report back to the full bench.[54] The last bid to put Bridewell on a firm statutory footing in this period came in 1647, four years after the publication of *Brief Collections Out of Magna Charta*, but even in a world turned upside down by revolution the outcome was another big let down for the City and Bridewell.[55]

Four bills led only to disappointment in City circles and Bridewell's court remained in legal limbo all the way through its first century. Justices' warrants had almost sacred status for Bridewell's critics. They were safeguards against all sorts of legal abuses. Nobody needed to tell that to the aldermen, recorders, and justices who sat on Bridewell's bench as well as on the Old Bailey and Guildhall sessions benches, working with warrants all year round. This know-how was helpful when doubt was cast on Bridewell's legality. Aldermen's advice and their place in the Bridewell court was not noted by legal pundits at the time, although it might have been a small reassurance. In matter of fact, City by-laws ordered Bridewell to have at least one justice present in court to hear certain cases: cases when house-officers were 'beaten or misused' on duty (1576), or shifty alehouse-keepers gave room and board to 'wicked persons' who were said to be responsible for the 'increase in [theft and] harlotts and consequently bastards and diseases', which ought to have

---

[52] BRHA BHC 4, fos. 196v, 274; LMA Rep. 25, fos. 312, 324; *The Journals of All the Parliaments During the Reign of Queen Elizabeth Collected by Sir Simonds D'Ewes*, 1682, rev. O. Bowes (Shannon, 1973), p. 648; T. E. Hartley, ed., *Proceedings in the Parliaments of Elizabeth I, Volume III, 1593–1601* (1995), pp. 354, 421; David Dean, *Law-Making and Society in Late Elizabethan England: the Parliament of England, 1584–1601* (Cambridge, 1997), p. 250.
[53] BRHA BHC 4, fos. 440v, 441v, 460.   [54] BHC 8, fos. 324, 352, 353, 355v.
[55] LMA Jour. 40, fos. 206, 211. See also SBHA Governors Journal 4, fos. 313v-14.

been settled by 'soche nomber of justices' as was 'required by the statuts'.[56] There is some patchy evidence that Bridewell was receptive enough to make more use of justices' warrants at times when its charter was queried. Just under 16 per cent of 39,516 recorded Bridewell committals were made by justices. One-in-twenty of these cases came along these lines around 1560, a figure that then edged up to almost one-in-ten by the mid-1570s when Bate began his Star Chamber case. The peak in these committals came three decades later, shortly after two botched bids for statutory support, when 31.63 per cent of suspects were brought in by justices' warrant (see Appendix Tables 8a and 8b). This figure soon fell, but never below earlier levels, and climbed again to one-quarter in 1634–42, before slipping over the next decade. The last charter bill (1647) did not reverse the fall in warrants, but the large leap around 1600 came when Bridewell's process was put to the test once again. Steps had been taken two decades earlier to tighten committal by justices, a year when the black publicity from Bate's case still lingered.

The amount of discretion given to Bridewell's bench in the charter was another sticking point. Almost all work on dispute-settlement in the sixteenth and seventeenth centuries contains a step-by-step sketch of how discretion had bearings on all stages of process, making it flexible enough to meet the circumstances and characters of each case. This is seen as a good thing that softened the full force of the law and gave people the benefit of the doubt.[57] But discretion also had a darker side in the wrong hands, and was used to settle scores in malicious allegations.[58] Another dimension to this much darker side of discretion emerged whenever it was placed in the shakier hands of courts with slender or contested status, like the one inside Bridewell. Discretion is a keyword in Bridewell's charter, and the author of the *Discourse/Treatise* zoomed in on it with pin-point precision.[59] But City magistrates still urged Bridewell's bench to prosecute and punish as it saw fit at their 'pleasure',

---

[56] GL MS 12806/2, fo. 154; LMA Jour. 20, fo. 502.
[57] Cynthia Herrup, *The Common Peace: Participation and the Criminal Law in Seventeenth-Century England* (Cambridge, 1987); J. A. Sharpe, '"Such disagreement betwyx neighbours": litigation and human relations in early modern England', in John Bossy, ed., *Disputes and Settlements: Law and Human Relations in the West* (Cambridge, 1983), pp. 167–87.
[58] See, for a later date, Douglas Hay, 'Prosecution and power: malicious prosecution in the English courts, 1750–1850', in Hay and Francis Snyder, eds., *Policing and Prosecution in Britain, 1750–1850* (Oxford, 1989), pp. 343–95. Steve Hindle writes about malicious recognizances in 'The keeping of the public peace', in Paul Griffiths, Adam Fox, and Hindle, eds., *The Experience of Authority in Early Modern England* (Basingstoke, 1996), pp. 213–48.
[59] GL MS 9384, fo. 4v.

or 'as shall seeme beste' to their 'discretions'. The bench was told to 'sort' the sick, sane, and vagrant poor 'att their discrecon' in 1587 (the same wording was used in 1644, one year after the disapproving *Brief Collections* was published), and to follow 'best discrecons' to take care of vagrants in 1624. Elizabeth Bradley was whipped 'by their discression' in 1573 after 'wishinge' out loud that the mayor burn in Hell, 'sayinge that he never did any good nor never will'. The bench was also asked to look into 'the ordre' of 'lewde' John Thomas's 'lyfe' in 1565 and deal with him 'accordyng to his deserts'.[60]

The word 'discretion' turns up in all sorts of situations in the Bridewell court: giving hand-outs to vagrants, settling surgeons' wages, or sacking ministers.[61] It also shows up in the day-to-day running of other hospitals and guilds when decisions needed to be taken about top-up fees for beadles, for example, the terms of leases, paving, hand-outs, repairs, clerks' fees, changing house-rules, letting patients out for a short spell on 'needful business', diagnosis, or even the best way to clean 'privies'.[62] These 'boards' also used 'discretion' to tackle trouble, as when St Thomas's handed over a woman who had spent time alone with a man to the matron, 'to use her discretion in correcting her', or when Christ's took a hard line on a watchman who was caught having sex with his maid.[63] The difference of course is that thousands appeared at Bridewell, and many left there smarting and seething. Bridewell was in the legal limelight week-in-and-week-out and it is no wonder that it got a bad press, only the High Commission and Star Chamber got more. Like Bridewell, they were touchy symbols of royal prerogative justice and were early victims of the Revolution's revenge. But there was no talk of getting rid of Bridewell in these topsy-turvy times. It had become far too important for the fight against rising crime in the capital city.[64]

---

[60] LMA Reps. 21, fos. 475v-6; 57, fos. 98–9 (1st pag.); 39, fos. 2–2v; 18, fo. 90v; 15, fo. 404. See also LMA Reps. 14, fos. 236v, 267, 304v, 534; 15, fo. 500; 16, fos. 175–5v; 18, fos. 170–0v, 391; 20, fo. 394; 21, fos. 19, 577v; 23, fo. 560v; 39, fos. 2–2v; Letter Book V, fo. 92; Jour. 20, fo. 500; BHC 3, fo. 331; 5, fo. 385; 8, fo. 175; TNA STAC5 N15/10, John Cacher, examination.

[61] BHC 6, fo. 18v; 8, fo. 42v; 9, fo. 26.

[62] GL MSS 12808/2, fos. 182–2v; 12806/3, fo. 360; SBHA Governors' Journal 1, fos. 19, 19v, 183v, 184; Governors' Journal 3, fos. 209v, 279v; Governors' Journal 4, fos. 42v, 219; LMA H1/ST/A1/2, fo. 9v; H1/ST/A1/3, fo. 74v.

[63] LMA H1/ST/A1/3, fo. 49; GL MS 12806/2, fo. 112; LMA Rep. 12, fo. 481v; D/L/C/ 214, fos. 160–1; H1/ST/A1/4, fo. 33v; GL MS 12806/2, fo. 180v; SBHA Governors' Journal 1, fo. 168v.

[64] See H. E. Phillips, 'The last years of the Court of Star Chamber, 1630–1641', *Transactions of the Royal Historical Society*, 4th series, 21 (1939), 103–31. Pelling compares the College of Physicians' court to Star Chamber: *Medical Conflicts in Early Modern London*, pp. 291–2.

232  Control

But stains covered Bridewell like oil on an ocean, even the sand that it dredged from the Thames was called 'nought' by a peeved bricklayer in 1578, who added that Bridewell will 'answer it before the best in Englande' if he was locked up.[65] A stream of 'scoffinge' and 'sawcy' words mocked Bridewell from all walks of life, but on paper it flowed more freely before 1600.[66] I wonder if this resulted from a greater acceptance of Bridewell by Londoners as time passed. Needless to say, many citizens supported a new prison that for them embodied civic ethics, though we do not often hear this being said. That anti-Bridewell words were spoken is no surprise, but we should remember that some were reported by concerned citizens, numbering twelve in one case, who felt that it was their duty to turn these loudmouths in.[67] Strangely enough some prisoners enjoyed their time in Bridewell, one so much that she would not leave her cell when she was set free; another told his friends that 'he had as good be in Bridewell as any wheare ells because there he could have his roast meate and a gowne to putt on'.[68] Attitudes were never inevitable or stable. But what caused 'bad' words to fall above all else was Bridewell's shifting priorities revealed in its caseload (see Appendix Table 6a). The amount of sexual crime tumbled after 1600. Bridewell's leading priority now was to curb crimes directly related to speedy growth, like vagrancy, and nearly everyone could rally to this cause. Each new day brought more vagrants and theft boomed. All citizens lost out when the freedom of their city was of 'little worth'.[69] Bridewell's value was readily realized by a grateful population when it took the lead in policing 'environmental' crimes that were both symptoms and symbols of hazardous growth. Far fewer people felt it necessary to contest the uses to which Bridewell was being put after 1600. Opinions had settled down for the most part, although there were still some qualms and spats. Unease about legal status lingered. There was still work to do, including another bid for a statute for the charter in 1647. But only a small fraction of Londoners ever witnessed court days, to see for themselves what the court routinely got up to, putting people on trial, but not without care for the letter of the law.

---

[65] BHC 3, fos. 293v, 294.
[66] Other cases include BHC 1, fo. 11; 2, fos. 145v, 189, 191v-2; 3, fos. 173, 176, 184v, 189, 218, 328, 331, 331v, 345v, 396; 5, fos. 162v, 324, 380v; 6, fos. 120v, 126v, 149, 236, 287v, 419; 7, fos. 42, 121v; 8, fos. 45, 169v, 212; BRHA BHC 4, fo. 127.
[67] BHC 1, fo. 95.   [68] BHC 5, fo. 68; BRHA BHC 4, fo. 280v.
[69] TNA PC2/42, fos. 305–6.

## Court days

The rules of law were never absent at Bridewell, whatever some commentators and complainants said. There was law all around the courtroom. The clerk was asked to buy 'the last edicon' of 'the statutes at large' in 1634, and had it close at hand at all times. A junior town clerk got ten shillings each year from 1599 on to copy Court of Aldermen orders related to 'this house'.[70] But the records that we hold today are not neutral. They speak first and foremost for the Bridewell court. The clerk chose words carefully when he was taking notes, and sat down afterwards picking out what to put in the courtbook and what to leave out, framing entries to create sound images of procedure. Most court sittings began with clerks reading aloud the minutes of the last meeting for anyone present to have a final chance to amend anything. Bridewell's bench clearly felt that it was worthwhile to keep a clean account of their handling of suspects, that emphasized legalism in proceedings.

The court almost always met behind closed doors inside Bridewell,[71] though there were times when it was forced to gather elsewhere. Plague drove the bench to Stationers' Hall for election day in 1645 and a few court days after as it blazed through the precinct, and the court also met in governors' houses for election dinners or audit meetings in other plague seasons.[72] Governors sat on one side of the room, the clerk took notes, put papers in order, and found people in the books if asked. The bench was picked from a pool of leading lights in the City, guilds, parishes, or wards: hospitals limited membership to wardens of the dozen great guilds or masters of lesser ones in 1628.[73] Numbers on the bench stayed steady

---

[70] BHC 7, fo. 371; BRHA BHC 4, fo. 69.

[71] BHC 9, fos. 32, 475; 3, fo. 425v; BRHA BHC 4, fo. 55v. Thomas Ellwood has left us a description of the courtroom from the later seventeenth century. 'The first flight [of stairs] brought me to a fair chapel on my left hand ... I went up a storey higher which brought me into a room which I soon perceived to be a court-room ... observing a door on the farther side ... [I] opened it ... but I quickly drew back, being almost affrighted at the dismalness of the place; for besides that the walls quite round were laid all over from top to bottom in black, there stood in the middle of it a great whipping-post, which was all the furniture it had. In one of these two rooms, judgment was given, and in the other it was executed on those ill people who for their lewdness were sent to this prison, and there sentenced to be whipped' (*The History of the Life of Thomas Ellwood*, ed., C. G. Crump (1900), p. 94). For other hospital courts see Daly, 'Hospitals of London'; Carol Kazmierczak Manzione, *Christ's Hospital of London, 1552–1598: 'A Passing Deed of Pity'* (Selinsgrove, 1995), chap. 2.

[72] BRHA BHC 4, fo. 191v. See also BHC 2, fo. 80v; 3, fos. 252, 293; 8, fos. 95, 324, 332, 35v; 9, fos. 212, 216, 221, 223; TNA STAC5 B/11/18, William Stackford, interrogatories; E. G. O'Donoghue, *Bridewell Hospital, Palace, Prison, and School*, 2 vols. (1923, 1929), vol. II, chap. 1.

[73] GL MS 12806/3, fo. 443. Citizens who had fined for sheriff or served a stint as ward deputy also appear on lists of potential governors: ibid., fo. 343; GL MS 12806/4, fo. 46.

for a while, edging up slowly from twelve to nineteen over the first two decades, before leaping to twenty-seven in 1577, charging to fifty-four in 1579, staying around fifty a decade later, and hitting new peaks soon after: seventy-eight in 1610 and ninety-four in 1612. The bench boasted many City dignitaries at one time or another: mayors, aldermen, deputies, justices, recorders, sheriffs, marshals, and high-ranking military men when the country was split by war. Divines also had seats on it: four in 1605, five a few years later.[74] This array of influence provided pipelines to the Court of Aldermen, quarter sessions, and ruling bodies in guilds, wardmotes, and vestry rooms. The exact ratio of aldermen seesawed: three aldermen to eighteen governors in 1575, nine to fifty-one in 1589, seven to seventy-eight in 1610, and a lowly four to ninety-four two years later.[75] The alderman-justice-governor built up knowledge of social issues and policies over a couple of decades or so of service, and it was handy to have the ear of London's leading legal official (the recorder). Bridewell often took advantage of its links to lobby the City government, asking aldermen to nudge the next Court of Aldermen about the 'Bethlem business', for example, the 'speedie' discharge of prisoners by justices that only created more troubles, shortfalls in poor rates, or the 'evils' caused by keeping 'cavaleers and prest men' in 1645.[76] Nor is it any surprise, given Bridewell's omnibus role in social issues, to see the City calling on its bench again and again to sit on scores of committees, sometimes making up one-third or more of members. There was always a Bridewell group on City think-tanks that checked to see that Poor Laws were followed to the letter,[77] to round up vagrants and spruce up alleys,[78] clean up 'controversyes' in Newgate and other prisons,[79] and to come up

---

[74] For example, BHC 9, fos. 39, 210, 710; LMA Reps. 17, fo. 58v; 19, fo. 179; 20, fo. 119v; 22, fo. 290v; 27, fos. 132v, 274–4v; 29, fo. 124; 31(1), fos. 165–7; 32, fos. 184v-6; 45, fo. 494. Bridewell boasted five mayors in seven years from 1587–93. For divines see LMA Reps. 21, fos. 469v-70; 23, fos. 295–6; 27, fos. 84–6v; 29, fos. 290v-2; 30, fos. 385–7. Cf. Daly, 'Hospitals of London', p. 288.

[75] See, for these and supporting statistics, BHC 3, fos. 252v, 343; GL MSS 12806/1, fos. 24, 35, 49; 12806/2, fos. 15, 19v, 24v, 29, 32, 36v, 43, 53v, 78v, 93v, 110v, 134; LMA Reps. 14, fos. 216–17; 18, fos. 429v-31; 19, fos. 241–2v, 494v-6; 20, fos. 114–14v, 235–6v; 21, fos. 469v-70; 22, fos. 100–0v; 23, fos. 295–6; 27, fos. 84–6v; 29, fos. 290v-2; 30, fos. 385–7.

[76] BHC 6, fo. 126; BRHA BHC 4, fo. 176; BHC 5, fo. 178v; 8, fo. 362; 5, fo. 324v; 7, fo. 256; 9, fo. 213. See also BHC 6, fo. 406v; 7, fo. 264; 8, fo. 336; 9, fo. 368; BRHA BHC 4, fos. 125, 163v.

[77] LMA Reps. 18, fo. 97v; 20, fo. 483; 45, fos. 45, 164v, 234v; 47, fo. 52v; 56, fos. 119v-20.

[78] LMA Reps. 18, fos. 127–7v, 267v, 332, 389; 19, fos. 4, 234, 395; 21, fos. 470v, 475v; 22, fos. 252v-3, 173v, 330v; 23, fos. 185, 235, 483v; 33, fo. 55; 38, fo. 114v; 40, fos. 60v, 71–2; 43, fos. 154v-5; 51, fo. 78v.

[79] LMA Reps. 17, fo. 81v; 19, fo. 322v; 20, fos. 25v, 74v; 21, fos. 75v, 78, 117v, 253v, 336v, 368, 400, 514v; 22, fos. 5, 88v, 94v, 126v, 158v; 28, fo. 153; 47, fo. 96v.

Court days 235

with guidelines for policing, street-sellers, and plague months,[80] as well as a stack of other troubles that all had law, order, health, quick growth, and London's physical fabric in common: tatty buildings, rowdy alehouses, cheap 'foreign' labour, inmates, sabbath-day sins, catholics, coal, corn, clothing, water supply, walls, walks, 'wicked women', and a plot of land to bury Tyburn's dead.[81] Nor is it a surprise to see Bridewell proposing policies to the Guildhall in its spheres of influence: to take action against 'bawds and the practice of bawderey', for example, 'nightwalkers and lewd weomen' walking after dark, or vagrants rambling loose on streets.[82]

Under a 1599 house-rule only the clerk could be present in court with the governors for examinations. Other officers and officials had to stay outside the door, unless called. The porter was told to 'cleere the court' in 1650 as prisoners trooped in, and to stand guard at the door unless a bell rang to tell him that he was needed. A porter or beadle hovered around the door, keeping an eye out for trouble. Only one governor was to speak at one time and courtesy was counted on.[83] But the court still had its fair share of troubles. Some prisoners were dragged in kicking and screaming, and not all calmed down. Robber Elizabeth Greene stormed into court 'in a commaunding way' in 1636 and 'challenged' the bench. Linen-thief Toby Butler also taunted the bench, saying that 'he would not work although they hanged him'. Thomas Walker dived on a beadle in court. Thomas Venables pulled out a knife after he heard his sentence 'and swore that he would kill himselfe or whomsoever should lay hould on him'. While Alice Benjamin, who pulled off 'a piece of the matrons husbands beard', 'resisted' officers and vowed to 'scratch and strike them': no more than 'stomackfulnes', the clerk scribbled scornfully. Other people were 'extraordinary ungracious and stubborne' in 'the face of the court', barking 'disobedient words', 'cursing' the court, blaspheming God 'here at the table', and yelling 'wicked oathes in the hearing of the court'.[84] The court wanted to avoid bad press at all costs. The core

---

[80] LMA Reps. 16, fo. 422v; 17, fo. 425; 21, fos. 53, 542v; 23, fos. 72, 125v, 185, 233, 505v, 524, 546v, 573; 28, fos. 42, 124v, 214v, 261; 29, fo. 215; 30, fo. 133; 32, fos. 172–2v, 186v; 34, fos. 57, 59 (2nd pag.), 102–2v, 125v-7; 40, fos. 170v-1; 46, fo. 105v; 47, fo. 265; 56, fos. 22v-3.
[81] LMA Reps. 25, fo. 5v; 27, fo. 366; 28, fos. 29v, 201, 314v; 29, fos. 125, 277v-8; 30, fos. 24v-5, 291; 31(1), fos. 44v, 142; 32, fos. 7, 65v; 33, fo. 32v; 34, fos. 69v, 89v-90; 36, fos. 4, 172; 38, fo. 38v; 44, fo. 89v; 45, fo. 424v; 46, fo. 387v; 47, fos 2–2v, 9, 56v, 91v; 48, fos. 333, 340v, 648.
[82] BHC 6, fos. 224, 272v; 8, fos. 108v, 347v, 376v, 378v, 380v; LMA Reps. 16, fo. 340; 19, fos. 426–7, 490; 25, fo. 99v; 33, fo. 55; 38, fo. 114v.
[83] BRHA BHC 4, fos. 68, 93–3v; BHC 9, fo. 475.
[84] BHC 8, fo. 92v; 7, fo. 121v; 8, fos. 169v, 136v; 7, fo. 349v. See also BHC 3, fos. 218, 406; 5, fos. 324v, 337v, 338v; 6, fos. 278v, 286, 419; 7, fos. 42, 67, 126v; 8, fos. 45, 169v, 212, 213.

concern of anti-Bridewell legal lines was committals without warrants. But people were called into question for following dubious methods. John Budde was locked up for not bringing William Convey 'imedyately before a justice' after arresting him in 1554. Warrants were the nub of Star Chamber cases when rogue officers made arrests without one.[85] Proper process was a sticking point. Bridewell's court asked aldermen to intervene in autumn 1617 when prisoners were no longer coming from Newgate by justices' warrant 'or noate'. A constable was sent straight back to Sir William Wade for his warrant when three Shoreditch women arrived merely on his command in 1609. One warrant was 'not thought sufficient' because it was 'not directed to this house'. Another was 'not good' and a marshal hurried to the mayor to get a 'sufficient' one. Anthony Tiffin's brother-in-law – a constable – brought him to court in 1617 for hanging around Charing Cross begging, but the bench 'thought it not fitt' to lock him up without a warrant and let him go home, impressed, they said, by his 'good habit' and university background. The fence Michael Buffet was not questioned in the same year until a warrant arrived from a justice.[86]

Process seems sound in the courtbooks. We know how someone ended up in Bridewell in 39,516 cases with details like the names of officers, masters, or parents, or a note on warrants (see Appendix Table 8a). More than six-in-ten were snatched on streets, caught red-handed by public officers, or turned in by neighbours. More often than not constables, beadles, deputies, marshals, or watches acted on their own authority, by-laws, or on policing clauses in Bridewell orders. None of this was noticed by anti-Bridewell hawks. We already know that justices sent in 16.79 per cent of offenders to Bridewell, but they also had a hand in bringing people there by other routes: a little under 5 per cent of committals were signed by Bridewell's bench, president, treasurer, or individual governors. Magistrates wanted justices' hands on Bridewell warrants. Aldermen were 'moved' by a hospital lobby in 1581 to order that justices 'of what hospital soever he be' may sign Bridewell warrants if no justice from that 'house' was in the room.[87] High-ranking City officials put 9 per cent of inmates behind Bridewell bars. Even when a warrant was missing, there were justices sitting in Bridewell giving their blessing when one was signed and sealed. There were official imprints stamped all the way

---

[85] LMA Rep. 13i, fo. 113v; TNA STAC8 187/1; 54/15; 71/17; 102/17; 104/17; 128/18–19; 150/22; 159/23; 162/10; 190/13; 228/8; 230/3; 233/15; 238/22; 297/20. See also BHC 5, fo. 337v.
[86] BHC 6, fo. 9; 5, fos. 376v, 101; 6, fos. 210, 7v, 19. See also BHC 8, fos. 93v, 328v.
[87] GL 12806/2, fo. 297v; LMA Rep. 20, fo. 235.

through process. The Crown handed over trouble-makers (1.14 per cent). Parliament also used Bridewell to lock up the king's followers and religious radicals after 1642, along with deserters, and other trouble-causers (0.33 per cent). Bridewell's court is not a rogue tribunal in its own pages. There was legal-mindedness in prose and process, and even an idea of a 'good arrest'. A 'gentleman' was 'arrested at the Compting House' in 1576, 'and yt was a good arrest', the clerk added at the end of the entry.[88]

So there were good and bad arrests. A beadle was taken to task after 'forcibly' grabbing Elizabeth Vaughan's 'wearyng apparell' as she headed for Kentish Street one night in 1560 'of his owne auctorytie', and put her in the cage until the next morning (he paid her gaol fees out of his own pocket).[89] Some cases never reached court if they were 'light' or 'slight' or evidence seemed too thin. They ought not to have 'bene brought hither for this offence', the bench said tetchily in 1634, when three women were charged with 'plotting' to scare Mr Chamber and his wife 'by making a noise to cause them to thinke theire were spiritts' haunting their house. 'No matter here declared worthye of ponnishment of this house', the bench ruled when it got another flimsy case. 'The matter was but lighte', they said on another day.[90] But it was never easy to get to the bottom of cases with stacks of slurs, lies, and attempts to settle scores. There were malicious committals to Bridewell and Bethlem, prisoners left cleared after being 'falsely and wrongly accused'. Thomas Frank was put in Bridewell by his own father in 1575 for no 'cause' it later came to light. He was locked up for three weeks after his father said that he would bring proof of his son's 'lewde' life within a fortnight. The pieces of this puzzle soon fell into place. The son had watched an attorney's wife slip into his father's room, heard him tell her that she was 'the onelie joye' that he had in the world, and learned that his father had drafted a new will that left everything to his new lover and nothing to his mother/wife. So the son who knew too much was put out of the way in Bridewell. A cobbler got in trouble in 1574 after conning the bench to put his wife in Bethlem, 'sayinge she was made beinge not madde', so that he could live alone with his 'harlott'.[91]

Something else for the bench to ponder was Bridewell's place in the city's tangled jurisdictions. The court had to watch its step and make sure that it did not tread on rival authorities and patches, and always see that crimes not within its scope were sent somewhere else more fitting. Church courts frowned on Bridewell's trespass on their age-old right to

---

[88] BHC 3, fo. 52v.   [89] BHC 1, fo. 91v.   [90] BHC 7, fo. 359; 1, fos. 158, 197; 2, fo. 233v.
[91] BHC 1, fo. 88; 2, fos. 217–19, 47.

wipe out immorality. Howes wrote in 1582 that Bridewell 'did somewhat abridge the ecclesiasticall courtes of theire jurysdiction', so that 'the governors were never in quyet' but had to fend off 'proces' 'for [one] cause or other' in 'every terme'. London's bishop apparently called Bridewell 'a rude and irreverent place' run by 'undiscrete' men 'of filthy bawdry' in 1579, a crunch year as Bate's case dragged on, and 'not mete' to hear incest charges against parson Eaton, who 'very filthilye abused his bodie' with his daughter while he 'taught her the latine tonge in bed'. Yet the bench knew enough about legal niceties to move illegitimacy and bigamy cases to 'high commissioners' in 1578. Other cases fell by the wayside as they were 'causes current' in 'spirituall courts'. A 'cause of incontinency' ground to a halt in 1604 after word arrived that it 'ys dependinge in the ecclesiasticall court'. The bench 'dismissed' Katherine Cuffe's case against an Inner Temple cook 'out of this house' in 1599 upon learning 'that the matter was first begun in the spiritual court', and also turned to church commissioners for rulings in borderline cases. It heard that Margaret Porter (alias Smith) 'often went abroad in mans apparell' in 1633, and was 'the overthrow of divers persons by her lewd course of life', but news arrived of a church court warrant for her arrest. A meeting with 'Bishops Court' bureaucrats followed, and the case stayed with Bridewell, not the only time that tiffs were settled good-naturedly. News leaked that there was 'a process out of the arches' for Bridewell inmate Peter Goodson to go through public penance after fathering a second illegitimate child on Judith Thompson in 1635, and so two governors met with Dr Duck – a church court commissioner – to double-check that this was for his 'first fact', leaving Bridewell free to punish him for his 'last fact'.[92]

Bridewell's powers to punish people in public also caused trouble and were later limited, but the bench had never had a free hand in the first place. A City order (1556) said that only the Court of Aldermen should 'appoynt and ajudge' the 'open punishmente' of 'notable and haynous' crimes brought to Bridewell, unless two justices and the mayor had already given 'assente'. New 'house'-rules in 1557 said that the signatures of six governors were needed when 'open' reprimands were handed out. City checks were tightened later when aldermen-governors were told to bring all 'examynacons' of people sentenced to public shame to the Court of Aldermen for its backing, 'according to law'.[93] Two 'comen

---

[92] *John Howes' MS*, p. 72; BHC 3, fos. 412, 323, 330v, 411v; 7, fo. 353; 8, fos. 37, 67v; BRHA BHC 4, fos. 3v, 460, 60, 71. The Inner Temple cook was later put on trial at Guildhall Quarter Sessions.
[93] LMA Rep. 13ii, fo. 463v; GL MS 'Legal Cases and Opinions Concerning the Mayor's Powers to City Magistrates to Commit Offenders to Bridewell' (1842), fo. 15; LMA Rep. 14, fo. 372v.

vagabonds' were 'whipped naked' through 'open streets' at a cart's tail in 1562 after their case was moved to the Guildhall. Aldermen 'wholly' backed Mabel Gower's punishment in 1567 after she was caught red handed leaving a 'younge childe infant' in Lothbury, so long as Bridewell asked for their go-ahead if it chose to punish her in public.[94] There is not a word from aldermen in other 'open' penalties: the 'comen harlotte', 'drunkarde', and 'evill and beastlye person', Anne Carter, was whipped 'at a stake' outside her house in 1578 with no word from aldermen. But another alleged 'harlot', Dorothy Johnson, was 'appoynted to be tried with a jurye and carted' in the same year.[95] Public penalties were given from 1579–98 (though the books are lost), as aldermen asked Bridewell's porter to get a cart 'at hys owne charge' in 1582 to whip 'roagues and lewd persons from Brydewell', and the court handed Alderman Ryder a 'note' about two women who left children on doorsteps, 'to move' the mayor 'that they might be openly punished'.[96] But public penalties at Bridewell disappear over the next few decades, unless we think of tough work on the riverside or streets as stage-managed exposure. Prisoners were now whipped behind Bridewell's high walls.

Nor did Bridewell want to make trouble for itself by taking cases outside its jurisdictional reach. 'Masterlesse' Robert Browne was 'discharged' in 1562 after his 'accusers' added other 'matters' that were 'without the commission' of the 'house'. The bench 'wolde not meddle with yt', the clerk noted. A case was shelved four decades later because it 'did not concerne this court'.[97] Bridewell's best interest was to cultivate good working relations with other courts, guilds, and the Guildhall. This was a two-way process with both sides trying to play by the book. When William Chapman gave the Fishmongers' wardens 'hard words' in 1594 after they did not give his tearaway apprentice 'open punishment', he was told that 'the howse cold not well punishe him for yt' since he had already 'beene punnished for the same falte by imprisonement in Bridewell'. Some things were also best left to livery companies or masters. When Nicholas Goff tried 'to cutt his owne throate' in 1627, the court thought 'it not fitt to meddle with him' as he was an apprentice and better left to the care of his 'frends' and master.[98] There were brokers between Bridewell and other courts who could help to iron out problems: guild

---

[94] LMA Reps. 15, fo. 500; 16, fo. 308. See also LMA Rep. 17, fo. 165v.
[95] BHC 3, fos. 332v, 319. In other cases the court sentenced people to public punishment but spared them that ordeal after they agreed to pay a fine or some of their friends came along to petition the court on their behalf. See, for example, BHC 1, fo. 64; 3, fos. 411v, 412v.
[96] LMA Rep. 20, fo. 337v; BRHA BHC 4, fo. 125.
[97] BHC 1, fo. 207; BRHA BHC 4, fo. 116.    [98] GL MS 5770/1, fo. 33; BHC 7, fo. 34v.

240  Control

leaders on Bridewell's bench, along with important people from wards and parishes, aldermen, and justices, all bringing first-hand experience of policies and politics from elsewhere.

There was also a sifting process to make sure that serious offences were sent to higher courts. Accused/suspected felons were put back in the cells until they could be sent to justices. A runaway 'pilferinge wenche' was sent to City sessions in 1575, 'for the matter in parte towchethe fellonye'. Two men were taken to the recorder for close questioning 'touching fellony'. Another thief took a 'bed of a greate value' in 1635; 'it is felony', the court said.[99] Some felonies slipped through the net, but most were spotted and sent to the proper place at quarter sessions, although some were handed back to victims. Alice Potter was suspected of felony in 1635, 'which is not conceaved proper to be heare examined', and so the case was left 'to the discrecon of them that prosecute'. Arresting officers continued other cases. A marshal was asked to 'presente the law [for] fellonie' against Thomas Phillips after he was brought to court yet again 'for counterfeiting himself dumb' and running up and down begging in 1622.[100] The bench often made up its mind quickly. The same constable who brought in George Parnott for pinching a bedspread in 1622, was told to take him to a justice because 'the busines [did] not concern' Bridewell. Robert Lee was sent straight back to a justice after he was picked up 'upon the hue and cry' for felony. While John Dade's master was told to take him back to a justice in 1632, since he had been charged 'with things that concerne not this house'. The court also turned to the recorder for advice if it felt that 'the punishment of this house is not sufficient for [the] fault'.[101]

Not all felons were sent to a justice or to Newgate on the same day that they appeared in court. Some were left in Bridewell until the next sessions or until a 'house'-officer managed to get in touch with a justice. Bridewell's bench also saved some people from the gallows. Peter Newsam was locked up there in 1642 'to keepe him from the gallowes'. Exactly two decades earlier, and in line with the tumbling domino theory of criminality that less serious crimes would one day lead to the gallows, William Flood and Godfrey Chapman were 'ponished for a warning' in 1622 'to save them from the gallowes being notorious nipps'. John Mekins was not so lucky in 1562 after he was caught 'unlawfully companyeng' with Ellen Clarke, and 'yt fell out' that he had 'most vilely, abhominablye and most ungodlie misused, misbehaved [and]

---

[99] BHC 2, fo. 112; 6, fo. 137; 8, fo. 36v. See also BHC 3, fos. 112v, 158v.
[100] BHC 8, fo. 35v; 6, fo. 266.
[101] BHC 7, fo. 273v; 6, fos. 215, 221; 7, fo. 258; 5, fos. 285v, 161v; 7, fo. 154v.

Court days 241

misordered' himself with her two children 'in such sorte that they were swollen moste piteouslie', and he was quickly switched to Newgate prison, 'arrayned, condemned', and swinging from Tyburn's tree shortly afterwards. Elizabeth Brian, who killed 'the child within hir' with a 'warme' drink, was likewise handed over to a justice in 1605, and she also ended her days dangling on the gallows. A number of suspected robbers, muggers, and murderers were also locked up in Bridewell for a while until the truth 'be further known'. A woman who was caught 'with a young man with her hand in his codpisse' one night in 1637, was not allowed to leave Bridewell after word arrived that 'shee standeth indicted of felony'.[102]

There is sometimes no word of any further action when suspected felons were put behind bars in Bridewell, although it is hard to believe that the fates of Abraham Delabew, who pinched £60 in 1641, or 'outragious' Mary Jennings, who tried 'to kill her owne child', were left up to Bridewell alone. A thief who helped himself to £19 was also locked up there along with a clumsy horse-thief, and no more is said about either of them.[103] More often, however, clerks noted that serious offenders were to be handed over to Newgate or a justice, and many felons made this trip along Fleet Street: thieves more times than anyone else, along with cozeners, counterfeiters, receivers, recidivist rogues, rapists, bigamists, muggers and brawlers, jailbreakers, a handful of suspected murderers, and others who were not listed with a specific crime next to their name.[104] A large number of 'lesser' offenders also ended up in the hands of justices: including adulterers, bawds, bastard-bearers, careless carmen, drunk nightwalkers, cheeky servants, idle layabouts, lewd livers, spirits, vagrants, and some rogues who were sent to get 'burned' on the

---

[102] BHC 8, fo. 391; 6, fo. 294v; 1, fo. 218v; 5, fo. 30; 7, fo. 22; 8, fo. 117v. See also BHC 3, fo. 339; 8, fos. 14v, 132, 348.
[103] BHC 8, fo. 348; 9, fo. 459; 5, fo. 317; 9, fos. 366, 746.
[104] For examples of thieves, BHC 2, fos. 12v, 149v; 3, fo. 173v; 5, fos. 4v, 202, 305, 439; 6, fos. 5, 175, 304, 423v; 7, fos. 105v, 304v, 372; 8, fos. 10v, 112v, 201v, 398; 9, fos. 158, 255, 364, 470, 594, 742, 878; pickpockets, BHC 5, fo. 123v; 6, fo. 125; 7, fos. 58v, 310; 8, fos. 10, 206; 9, fo. 717; burglars, BHC 6, fo. 216v; 7, fo. 60; 8, fo. 327v; nips, BHC 6, fo. 325v; cutpurses, BHC 2, fos. 16, 109, 183; 3, fo. 392v; 6, fo. 118; 7, fo. 242v; cozeners/counterfeiters, BHC 2, fo. 68; 3, fo. 363; 5, fo. 264; 6, fo. 152v; 7, fo. 241v; 8, fo. 335v; 9, fos. 645, 742; receivers, BHC 7, fos. 28v, 365; recidivist rogues, BHC 2, fo. 98v; 3, fo. 151v; 6, fo. 338; 7, fo. 364; rapists, BHC 1, fo. 218v; 3, fo. 295v; bigamists, BHC 5, fo. 131; 9, fo. 420; muggers and brawlers, BHC 5, fos. 108, 437v; 7, fo. 49; 8, fos 63, 257, 370v; 9, fos. 211, 506, 755, 883; jailbreakers, BHC 7, fo. 373; 8, fo. 57; 9, fo. 518; no noted crime, BHC 3 fo. 302v; 5, fos. 146, 443; 6, fos. 31v, 160, 225, 278, 321, 397; 7, fos. 24v, 216v; 8, fos. 322, 368v; 9, fos. 347, 623, 727; suspected murderers, BHC 3, fo. 346; 9, fos. 28, 449.

shoulder.[105] There is frustratingly little in Bridewell's courtbooks to tell us why some small-scale offenders were sent to higher courts, when many more stayed locked up inside Bridewell. Recidivism clearly made a difference now and then, but even repeat offenders also came back to Bridewell again and again, some more than twenty or thirty times, and were dealt with on the spot rather than facing the sort of sterner treatment that awaited them in a justices' parlour. Some pigheaded prisoners who did not shrink before the court were more likely candidates to be handed over to higher authorities, but not even this was a rule of thumb.

There were other sorting processes inside Bridewell. An 'accessary to the drowning of a man' was sent back to the cells until he was needed 'to give evidence to the coroner' in 1640. On other occasions hot-tempered apprentices were turned over to guilds.[106] Other wayward apprentices were handed over to the Chamberlain's Court. A crossbow-maker's apprentice, who ran away from his master, was sent there after the bench ruled that 'the busines' was 'not fitt for this house but more properly belonged to the chamberlaine'. Like light-fingered George Medcalfe, Ralph Martyn was sent to the chamberlain in 1607 'to be dealt with', 'being an apprentice'. Other young runaways, loudmouths, and thieves made the same trip, as well as others picked up after curfew or begging on streets.[107] But once again more domestic disorders were handled quickly within Bridewell, and there seems nothing remarkable on paper about the cases that were moved to the chamberlain, even the apprentice who ran away seventeen times.[108] The reasons for sending cases to the chamberlain are rarely stated, although a spate of referrals in winter 1634–5 suggests that this was the preferred option for a short time then. The Court of Aldermen was the only other City court that took over a fair number of Bridewell cases, among them bribery, 'beating' constables, illegitimacy, sexual abuse, theft, anti-authority taunts, cozening, begging with false passports, and sheltering plague victims.[109] Yet again there is nothing out of the ordinary about these offences. All of them could have stayed at Bridewell up until a final sentence.

---

[105] For example, BHC 3, fo. 335; 5, fos. 158, 440; 6, fos. 61, 208, 384v; 7, fos. 50, 229v, 319v; 8, fo. 293v; 9, fos. 367, 622, 717, 882. See also Robert B. Shoemaker, *Prosecution and Punishment: Petty Crime and the Law in London and Rural Middlesex, c.1660–1725* (Cambridge, 1991).

[106] BHC 8, fo. 285; 5, fo. 159; 6, fo. 352.

[107] BHC 6, fo. 346; 7, fo. 36v; 5, fo. 168. See also BHC 3, fo. 364; 7, fos. 117v, 291, 366v; 8, fos. 7, 105, 194, 255, 324v, 395; 9, fos. 7, 167, 216, 367, 476, 570, 633, 749, 804, 813, 827, 850.

[108] BHC 9, fo. 804.

[109] BHC 1, fo. 178; 3, fos. 72v-3, 90, 257, 344, 397v; 5, fo. 405v; 6, fos. 161, 169.

Bridewell procedure was not watertight. There was too much traffic in and out for that. There were hitches, slip-ups, and sleaze. Not all admissions/discharges were noted down by porters on duty; some pocketed bribes to let prisoners slip through the gate. The bench also tried to keep track of the exit and entry of prisoners. If justices sent for suspects by 'warrant or command', officers were told to tell the treasurer before offenders left Bridewell. The mayor was 'humbly desired' to write warrants when asking for inmates in 1643, after Bland, a 'notorious' pickpocket, left 'before court' without 'official' say-so: the porter owned up that it was a 'usual course' to simply accept the word of the mayor's officer, and through this looseness 'many great malefactors may escape', the court noted. The porter was told to never again 'deliver' suspects without warrants fifteen years later, unless they were brought in overnight for 'examination' first thing in the morning by a justice, and even then one of the beadles was not to leave the suspect's side until a justice made a ruling. The porter was also asked to keep an up-to-date 'booke' of the names of offenders and officers, to make sure that rules were followed at all times.[110]

### Rules of law

The mixed results of orders like these is no indication that the bench did not try hard to follow proper procedures. A legal appearance was important, needless to say. Once inside Bridewell, suspects were searched, bodies were examined for signs of sickness or evidence, and suspects quizzed further if necessary. (Bridewell was one of three London prisons where traitors, heretics, robbers, or murderers were tortured.[111]) Some examinations stretched over a few days or weeks, but not all took place inside Bridewell. Some suspects were quizzed by constables or deputies before they were dropped off there, the rich evidence that some officers brought to court shows that they had already spent time building cases. Suspects or witnesses were also questioned at governors' houses or the Royal Exchange, where four governors quizzed Mary Cooper in 1600 after talking and trading had finished for the day, 'to knowe the father' of her new-born twins. A woman was instructed to go to Governor Gardener's house one afternoon in 1575 to give evidence against John

---

[110] BHC 5, fo. 33v; 9, fos. 56, 863.
[111] John H. Langbein, *Torture and the Law of Proof: Europe and England in the Ancien Regime* (Chicago, IL, 1976), pp. 83–6, 94–123. The other two were The Tower and Newgate (used only twice in 1557 to get confessions from counterfeiters). Racks and manacles were the most frequent form of torture at Bridewell. See LMA Rep. 23, fo. 57v, for a case involving 'seditious libells'.

Hitchin.[112] These were not quickfire question-and-answer sessions but full-blown examinations, although most took place in Bridewell after suspects had been locked up for a night or more. Starting in 1579, four governors spent 'two howres at the leaste in the daye' questioning prisoners picked up in 'the [overnight] first serche'.[113] There were a number of grapevines to tap. The clerk leafed through the books when a suspected recidivist showed up, jotting down the dates and details of earlier appearances. Governors also jogged their memories, including those who sat on sessions benches. 'House' officers also gave evidence against 'old gessts'. Prisoners mixed together in cells and workrooms, and some turned informant. But there was a downside to this mingling, because it could also lead to intimidation. Prisoners knew who were the tough nuts to crack, and bullies and ringleaders of crime rackets stood out in the crowd in the cells. With so many recidivists making return trips to the cells after 1625, it is easy to imagine thieves or others who worked together on the outside forming tight groups. Prisoners with incriminating tales about others were warned to keep their mouths shut or to lead the bench along false trails. With this in mind precautions were taken to keep prisoners who had not yet gone through examination somewhere out of reach of known thieves and racketeers. The matron was told to 'suffer none to talke or have conference with any prisoners' under her wing before they were questioned by governors and to make sure that they got no letters from outside.[114]

We have one clear advantage over the people who took pot-shots at Bridewell all that time ago. Unlike them we can actually hold the courtbooks in our hands to read them and take note that Bridewell's bench took care as a rule to try and keep their processes above board. The courtbooks also tell us that questions of proof and truth could make or break cases at Bridewell, as elsewhere. The clerk made a point of noting whenever proof seemed clear or lacking beyond any shadow of a doubt. An open-and-shut case took less time to decide and the bench could feel sure that its verdict was the right one. The court was on even more certain ground when offenders were caught red handed. There was little that suspects could say in their defence once the bench made up its mind that proof 'apered evydently' against them or was 'manifest' or 'good and evident'. 'Naughtie lewde and evell' Anne Bartfield 'stoutlie' denied 'whoredom' charges in 1562 after she was caught in a 'baudes' house, but her chances of winning the case disappeared completely when

---

[112] BRHA BHC 4, fo. 191v; BHC 2, fo. 131v. See also BHC 2, fos. 10, 36, 80v, 204–4v; 3, fos. 53, 337; 5, fos. 277, 421, 428v.
[113] LMA Jour. 20, fo. 501v.   [114] BRHA BHC 4, fo. 94; GL MS 33013, fo. 25.

witnesses made 'manifest things she hathe done'. Elizabeth Palmer also 'stowtly denye[d]' that she was a 'comon harlot' in 1560, 'but in the end it was so duely proved to her face', the clerk noted, a little self-righteously, 'that she could not but confesse yt'. Four decades later it was 'very apparent' that Ralph Lowe ran a bawdy house where a 'queane' was locked up in a room with a man, and 'evidentlie proved' that 'ill and lewd' Elizabeth Griffin 'used to goe in mans apparrell' through London's streets.[115]

The words proof and truth crop up a lot in Bridewell's courtbooks and were not taken lightly. A case needed to be driven home, and if this could not be achieved then there was a good chance that suspects would leave Bridewell with no more than a warning. Rose Owen was put back on the road to Wales in 1560, in spite of concern that she looked to be 'a suspect person', since 'ther apered no matter [against her] but only great presumpcions'. Gabriel King also walked free after he was charged with 'lye[ing] with Clare Hudson' in 1629, as 'the evidence was not thought competent but circumstance'. Elizabeth Hope had lived in a seedy house along Suffolk Lane for a good while and there were strong grounds to think that she was 'evell', but she admitted nothing and her case was dropped, 'althoughe many suspicious matters were alleaged against her', since 'nothing was or colde be at this tyme proved'. Anne Carter was 'sente in as a comon harlotte' in 1575, but the evidence against her was also thin: I only 'offended in thoughte but not otherwise', she said, and she was set free after a few days of hard work after no one came 'to give evidence against hir'.[116] The court convicted quickly in many cases, but others were incomplete, and the bench took more time, hoping to get the last piece of proof. Time was not on Elizabeth Adams's side when midwives 'seinge her' strongly 'suppose[d]' that she was 'with childe' in 1562, and the court told her to come back one month later 'for that the matter wold not appeare in short tyme'.[117] John Skinner's first wife was given an extra week to 'bring forth' proof when she filed bigamy charges against him in 1578. The prime suspect when a purse 'was lost on the bridge' in 1605 was 'kept till further proofe come againste him'. The likelihood was high that John Stanhope had 'stollen certeine taffety' in 1624, but he was put back in a cell since 'the evidence' was not 'yet full'. Four suspects were told to come back to Bridewell three days later

---

[115] BHC 1, fos. 209v, 44v, 84v, 85, 86; BRHA BHC 4, fos. 270v, 317, 351v, 409v.
[116] BHC 1, fo. 106v; 7, fo. 152v; 1, fo. 212v; 3, fo. 187. In another case, however, 'great presumptions' were enough for a guilty verdict: BHC 3, fo. 54v.
[117] BHC 1, fo. 201v.

because although 'the busines' seemed 'lewd' to the bench, it was 'not yet rype'.[118]

Charges were often dropped at Bridewell for 'wante of good proof'. The bench ruled that Evan Richards was 'not to be detained here without proofes' in 1636. Mary Smith was also set free in 1637 because her accuser could not 'certainly say' if she was the thief who pinched a pan from his stall.[119] Cases crumbled when there was 'no fact', 'no fault', 'no accusation', 'no matter', 'no cause', 'no testimony', or 'no evidence' to make charges stick. Other suspects were cleared because there was 'no proof' or no 'evident', 'due', 'manifest', 'certen' or 'just proof' of their guilt. The court even freed a couple who had spent the night together in an upstairs room 'suspiciouslye', after coming to the conclusion 'that there is noe facte proved'. Joan Smith got off the hook in 1561 when John North was 'found in her house with his codpece downe', but nothing at all 'naughtie' happened she said, and it 'fell out that he thorowgh her licence was there onlye to ease himself and noe otherwise'. Elizabeth Castle was released one year later when a theft charge 'did not fullie falle out true against her'. Like other shelved cases, there was 'nothing appearing' or 'brought' to court, nothing 'alleged', 'objected', 'proved', or 'worthy' of the court's time. 'It appeareth not plainly', the bench summed up in other thin cases. Many stories did not stand up to close scrutiny and were 'not thoughte to be true'. It was alleged that a tapster at the Hanging Sword in Fleet Street had 'sondry wyfes' scattered in nearby counties, but the court took his side saying that 'all things did not apere to be true that is reported of him'.[120]

There seemed too little or pretty nearly nothing to answer in too many cases for comfort. 'The matter was but lighte', the bench ruled in one case, impatiently. 'Taken in the house of Carre the bawde along Longe Lane' in 1562, Mary Turner was told 'that this tyme ther was no matter greatlie to charge her with'. Other cases were dropped because there seemed to be 'no speciall matter' to answer for.[121] Mere suspicions were not usually enough to get convictions in Bridewell's court. The bench still freed homeless 'lewd' Robert March after three spoons went missing from a room people said he had just that minute left because 'there is noe proofe [against him] but suspicon'. Two nightwalkers were

---

[118] BHC 3, fo. 348v; 5, fo. 60; 7, fo. 121v; 6, fo. 90. See also BHC 1, fo. 24v; 5, fo. 316.
[119] BHC 3, fo. 313; 8, fos. 92, 100v. See also BHC 8, fo. 128.
[120] BHC 1, fos. 1, 30v, 38v, 77v, 88, 97v, 111, 120v, 133, 134v, 154, 210; 2, fos. 187, 237v, 259; 3, fo. 303; 7, fos. 238v, 293; 8, fos. 93v, 251; BRHA BHC 4, fos. 92, 281, 397v, 407, 466v.
[121] BHC 1, fos. 197, 216v, 136. See also BHC 5, fos. 111, 385; 6, fos. 3, 194v, 431v; BRHA BHC 4, fos. 9v, 407v.

also released after the bench felt that there was no good reason to keep them there any longer 'but only words'.[122] Even old hands and 'comon customers' could get the benefit of the doubt in flimsy cases. The bench agreed that 'Christian alias Margaret Manbigh alias Margaret Bradley' was 'undoubtedly' a 'lewde and naughtie woman' in 1559, but she was still allowed to go back home with just a warning because there 'apereth no proofes for this tyme'. Even 'old gessts' could strike it lucky if no one came along to press charges or give evidence against them. Two 'nightwalking huswyfes', who were caught hanging around Cheapside after dusk hoping to 'intice yonge people', were released from the cells in 1618 since there was 'no accusacon cominge againste them'.[123] Other cases collapsed because not a single accuser bothered to turn up at court or there was little substance in what they said. People said that Jane Gold helped herself to some of her master's goods in 1657, but the bench made up its mind that he 'cold charge her with nothing' firm enough to make any charges stick. Charges were also dropped against Elizabeth Mott in 1576 after she 'utterlie denied' that she had stolen 'a litle dogge' because 'none cometh against hir'. While William Johnson was also escorted out of Bridewell with a warning in 1602 after no one came 'to prosecute any matter against him' and there was no 'sufficient matter extant' to keep him any longer.[124] Governors sometimes took accusers to one side or officers called round to their houses to see if there was really any point in proceeding any further with a case. The mixed results of these conversations are clear in the long list of cases that never got as far as a verdict.[125]

There was also an expectation that people in the dock would stand up for themselves if they felt hard done by: they would protest their innocence, query evidence, provide alibis, appear hurt. William Mills, who was alleged to have stolen some silk from a 'shoppe in Chepe', was 'well whipped' after he 'would not fully and cleerelie excuse himselfe' in 1562.[126] Stuttering or silence could both be taken as evidence that suspects were unsure of themselves and their stories, or that they were trying to hide something significant. Whenever possible, however, the bench tried hard to pin solid evidence on prisoners to leave no messy discrepancies behind after a case drew to a close. The odds were stacked

---

[122] BHC 8, fos. 382v, 178. See also BHC 1, fo. 191v; BRHA BHC 4, fo. 134.
[123] BHC 1, fo. 25; 6, fo. 25v. See also BHC 1 fos. 108v, 134v.
[124] BHC 9, fo. 789; 2, fo. 220v. See also BHC 1, fos. 120v, 160, 198; 2, fo. 259; 5, fos. 52, 111, 153v, 233, 272v, 345; 6, fos. 203v, 253, 321v, 344v; BRHA BHC 4, fos. 14, 112v, 299, 376v, 467.
[125] For example, BHC 6, fos. 23, 240v, 293v, 381v, 430v; 8, fos. 48, 92, 139v, 152v, 187, 223v, 247v, 284v, 327v, 358, 384, 411; 9, fos. 353, 420, 442, 511, 542, 603, 637.
[126] BHC 1, fo. 202.

heavily against John Cockley when he was charged with 'cutt[ing] lead pypes' in 1618 as he was carrying lead pipes when he was arrested: there 'was great apperaunce' of his guilt, the bench noted, with confidence. Walter Haynes was whipped when someone stole silk garters from a haberdasher's shop, and officers searched him from top to toe and found a tell-tale tool-of-the-trade hidden in his clothes: 'a cutpurse knyfe'.[127]

Pausing for proof was quite common. Examinations and confessions were read back to prisoners to let them check that words had not been put in their mouths, and to give them a chance to go through their stories once more. Helen Cordell, who was caught in Grizelle Addingsell's brothel in 1610, said that 'she was druncke when Mr deputie Hodgson took her examination and did not knowe what she had spoken and affirmed' that day. The industrious pimp Henry Boyer had his 'confessions' 'rede unto him' at Bridewell in 1577. Mary Deane (alias Ranyton) from Scotland listened as her 'examinacons' were read aloud in court in 1600, and was 'sensured' and 'ponished' after she admitted that they were true. Others caved in and confessed after hearing their accusers' words.[128] Some suspects trapped themselves with tall tales, blunders, or inconsistencies. The court was always digging for giveaway discrepancies: stories, dates, times, or places that did not match up. Some stories were a shambles. Vagrant Myles Minnie, who had a suspicious sum of money in his pockets, 'coulde make no good answere' and was 'taken doublinge in his tale'. Elizabeth Gryse was 'proved contrarie in her sayenges' in 1575. Suspected pickpocket, Elizabeth Overbury, said that she was caught walking late because she had had no luck going to an Aldgate alehouse to bargain with carriers for a ride. But fortune was not on her side in court either, as a governor called her story an 'excuse' because it was common knowledge 'that those carriers never come on Wednesdaies'. Some couples contradicted each other when taken aside and asked the same questions. Vagrants John and Elizabeth Thompson said that they were man and wife in 1619, but were 'found different in theire tales': she said they had been married for six years, he thought that it was six months since their wedding day. Thomas and Margery Llewellyn also had foggy wedding memories: she said they married six or seven years ago in Wales and Richard Fisher gave her away, and they dined in his house afterwards; he said that his 'kinsman' in the Forest of Dean gave her away and arranged the wedding feast. Another couple's claims were said to be mere 'small tales'.[129]

---

[127] BHC 6, fos. 28v, 98.
[128] BHC 5, fo. 421; 3, fos. 240–1v, 242, 242v-3, 41; BRHA BHC 4, fo. 194v.
[129] BHC 5, fo. 413; 2, fo. 105; 6, fos. 109v, 209; 7, fos. 119v, 280; BRHA BHC 4, fos. 87v, 367–7v.

But the court did not always have to work hard to outsmart suspects. Some confessed at once, out of remorse. John Boyes 'openlie and voluntarilie' confessed that 'beinge a maryed man' he forgot 'his dewtie towards God and the world' in 1574 and 'lewdly used' Elizabeth Palsted 'many tymes' 'carnalie'. The clerk made a note that Thomas Browning 'comethe of himselfe and acuseth himselfe that he hathe had the use of the bodie of Johan Totley'. Oliver Mason 'confessed of his own mynde' that he 'abused' his sister-in-law more than once in 1560. Others came of their 'voluntarie will' or 'voluntarilie' owned up. Some penitent prostitutes broke down in tears.[130] Prisoners spoke of troubled consciences. Others confessed to save their own skins. In other cases, it took time and often some pressure to get prisoners to confess. A few strong-willed suspects held out for a while. Elizabeth Helinge and Richard Harrison both confessed that they were 'naughty' together in 1579, but not before they 'first with horrible execracons denied it'.[131] Torture was out of the question, of course, but there were milder ways to wring confessions from someone. John Fisher was put back in the cells in 1575 until he told 'the trothe' and put down in 'wryghtinge' 'howe, of whome, and whoe, and which waie he hathe consumed and spente' his master's goods. Elizabeth Rodes was also locked up in the same year until she told 'the trothe what resorte hathe used to hir howse'. The 'pickyng and michyng harlot' Thomas Hall 'stubbernly' dug in his heels and would on no account 'confess' nor 'submyt himself' in 1559 and was put back to work to make him think again.[132] On a slightly different tack, witness William Libie was kept in Bridewell in 1576 because 'he wolde not declare the truthe before' about Elizabeth Walker, but 'did bolster' her, saying that she was his 'kyneswoman', 'he knowinge well that she was a harlott' all the time.[133]

A timely whipping could also help to squeeze out a confession, although here there was a thin line between acceptable and heavy-handed coercion. The clerk noted that the 'comon pickpurse' Anne Hodgkins 'would confesse nothing untyll she was well ponished' in 1560, and then she blew the whistle on others. 'Masterlesse' Thomas Loggyn, who was picked up 'in suspicion of pickyng a pursse', also 'stoutly denyed yt untyll he was duely whipped'.[134] The bench had other things up its sleeve if the whip was not enough. There were also threats of divine displeasure, and

---

[130] BHC 2, fos. 39, 36v-7; 1, fo. 64; BRHA BHC 4, fos. 335-5v. See also BHC 3, fo. 302; BRHA BHC 4 fos. 274, 299v, 50, 74.
[131] BHC 3, fo. 366.
[132] Ibid., fo. 99v; 2, fos. 194v, 200v; 1, fo. 1. See also BHC 3, fo. 45v; 5, fo. 7.
[133] BHC 2, fo. 222v. [134] BHC 1, fos. 79v, 107. See also BHC 1, fo. 78v.

some people suddenly started to speak as soon as mention of Judgment Day was slipped in. Elizabeth Matthew was warned that she must 'no wyse slaunder or declare an untruwthe' against a man who was charged with having sex with her when his wife was out of town, 'as she wolde answere before God at the dreadful daye of judgemente'. She was also told that she was bound by 'corporall othe' to tell the truth. When the prostitute Marie Donnolly was put 'face to face' with her bawd Margaret East in 1577 and asked about money changing hands between them, the bench 'charged [her] to saye the truthe and not to charge anybodye falselye', as one day she would 'answere before almightie God'. Joan Tailor reeled off slanders about her master later on in the same year, and each one of her allegations was double-checked by the court. But when she was 'examined' for a second time 'and threatened with the judgements of God', she stuck solidly to her story, and said that all that she had said about her master was indeed true.[135]

As in other courts, suspects were not always helpless. They had certain rights and strategies, and tilted the stories in the courtroom to win over the bench.[136] They could come out on top if they put their case staunchly enough or doggedly refused to confess. The clerk noted jadedly that Insham Dukcett 'would tell noe other tale' except that she did no wrong after she was caught 'suspiciously' under a bed with 'counterfeat keys' in 1559. 'Naughtie' light-fingered George Hampton also stood his ground and was freed even though 'the matter was suspicious'. The same thing happened to Elizabeth Hope one week earlier, who admitted 'nothinge althoughe manye suspicious matters' remained unanswered.[137] The bench did not give up easily, however, and sometimes staged face-to-face encounters between accuser and accused, often turning authority upside down: servants pointed fingers at masters/mistresses,[138] children put the blame on parents,[139] women stood up to men,[140] wives and husbands crossed swords,[141] rape-victims faced up to rapists,[142] and

---

[135] BHC 2, fos. 118v-19; 3, fos. 197-7v, 239.
[136] Recent work on narrative strategies includes Laura Gowing, *Domestic Dangers: Women, Words, and Sex in Early Modern London* (Oxford, 1996), chap. 7; Ulinka Rublack, *The Crimes of Women in Early Modern Germany* (Oxford, 1999), esp. chap. 2; and Malcolm Gaskill, 'Reporting murder: fiction in the archives in early modern England', *Social History*, 23 (1998), 1–30.
[137] BHC 1, fos. 46, 213, 212v. See also BHC 1, fos. 4v, 12v, 180.
[138] BHC 1, fo. 84v; 2, fos. 125v, 188v-9; 3, fos. 164v, 177, 180v, 212, 219, 270, 319, 342, 351v, 364v, 371, 384v, 390v, 396.
[139] BHC 1, fo. 117.
[140] Ibid., fos. 138, 156; 2, fo. 81; 3, fos. 5v, 9v, 54v, 60v, 75, 134, 244, 307v, 316; 6, fos. 49v, 95, 233, 252; 9, fo. 298; BRHA BHC 4, fos. 413v, 446, 464.
[141] BHC 3, fo. 301.   [142] Ibid., fos. 361-1v, 415.

prostitutes sparred with pimps, bawds, and well-to-do clients.[143] Some testified at great risk to themselves: Judith Varrante's mistress made her 'go with a priest' for money and 'threatened' to punish her 'as all shall take ensample by' if she 'disclosed this matter'.[144] John Lane and Margaret Noble stood 'face to face' in the courtroom 'before the maysters' and she 'stifflie' said to his 'face' that her child was his, 'and that he gott yt of her in her fathers house', shutting windows before he took her to bed. When John Dawson was charged with 'most filthilie' raping nine-year-old Anne Smith in 1576, she told him 'to his face' that 'he abused hir bodie on his bedd three tymes', and a surgeon's wife who 'searched' her said she had 'bene hurte by a man' and was 'not whole', but 'swelleth inwarde in the seacret parte' with a risk 'that it will ron uppe' into her belly 'if it be not loked to' at once. In her second such confrontation, Marie Donnolly stood 'face to face before William Breech' and the Bridewell bench, 'called him by his name', and 'advouched to his face' that he gave her gifts for sex. The bench was troubled because she was known to be 'lewd', and so a second man was 'brought' to court 'in a cloke lyke [Breech, and she was] asked whether she knewe Breech or not': she said that 'she did not', but that she would 'as soone' as she saw him.[145] The impact of these face-to-face encounters was such that a silkweaver 'offered' that if Priscilla Elliott charged 'him to his face then he would acknowledge' having 'thuse of her body', even though he 'denieth utterlie that ever he had it'.[146] Thieves and 'lodgers' of 'comon harlots and vagabonds' were also lined up next to their accusers in the courtroom to help solve cases.[147]

Bridewell process changed now and then. New methods were tested and old ones fell by the wayside. The word 'proof' crops up more often after 1600, when there is also more in the courtbooks about 'voluntary' confessions, more use made of justices' warrants, more cases dropped owing to thin evidence, and more weight placed on keeping records secret and in good order. Each of these developments had something to do with doubts about Bridewell process that were always present, but were also liable to become more pronounced at certain times, like the time around 1600 when two attempts were made to get statutory backing for the charter. On the whole, Bridewell courtbooks give the impression that concern about strong-arm tactics and legal process grew after 1600.

---

[143] BHC 1, fos. 14, 15, 84, 84v, 87, 111, 136–7, 188v; 2, fo. 127; 3, fos. 72v, 197–7v, 225, 239, 277v-8, 283v.
[144] BHC 2, fos. 155v-6v. See also, for example, BHC 2, fos. 3v-4, 73v, 127v, 134v-5, 143, 220, 239v; 3, fos. 28, 49v-50, 58v-9, 66–6v, 83, 88v-9, 389v; 5, fo. 207.
[145] BHC 1, fo. 156; 2, fo. 233; 3, fo. 205v.    [146] BRHA BHC 4, fo. 446.
[147] BHC 1, fos. 8v-9; 3, fos. 242v, 344v; 6, fo. 365; BRHA BHC 4, fos. 10v, 87v.

The consistent legalese from one courtbook to another is significant, but there was also something to be gained by looking legal, and this is reason enough to be cautious when summing up court days at Bridewell. On the other hand, there were fewer storms about Bridewell's legal standing after the third botched bid for Parliamentary recognition in 1604. This is the impression drawn from City and Bridewell records at any rate. There were fewer jurisdictional spats and steps to tighten up process. Vagrants still snarled at Bridewell, but the number of Londoners who ended up in a court for pouring scorn on Bridewell and its charter dwindled to almost nothing, a silence that on paper at least is evidence that opinions warmed towards Bridewell once it concentrated the major part of its resources on holding back vagrant floods.

# 7 Bodies

**Bodies**

There were scores of bodies in Bridewell at any one time, working, suffering, and resting. Bodily discipline was the order of the day there from sunrise to sunset. Inmates were put to work in the hope that they might change for the better and meanwhile spin or make pins, buttons, brushes, or tennis balls. Work was tedious, dirty, sweaty, and sticky in stuffy hemphouses or outside shifting sand or cleaning ditches. Vagrants were not coupled with good hygiene. Dirt stuck to them like a second skin, magistrates thought, and their clothes were caked with filth and sweat. A deputy was told to bring a 'rogue' back to Bridewell 'in cleane clothes'. Prisoners had soap to scrub themselves and their clothes were washed every four days or so to get rid of lice. An oven was made 'to destroy' the 'vermine of the prisoners' in 1632.[1] More softly, bodies were nourished, healed, and cleaned with running water.

Bodies were also bashed and battered. Work was bruising and there was a crop of accidents. A surgeon got 6/8d 'for curing a womans head hurt at the mill' in 1628, and a scale of fees 'for sudden cures happening within the house' was drawn up in 1629.[2] A lot of blood was spilled after whips lashed backs. The sound of the lash and groans of flogged prisoners that continued long into the night were acoustic cues to toe the line. Bodies were also maimed by torture, mainly in the decade after 1589 (according to Langbein's work on warrants).[3] Bridewell's harsher side was always on view. People walking in the yard saw stocks standing in a corner to show them what lay in store if they broke house-rules. Rowdy patients were whipped at a 'cross for correction' at Christ's, a 'cross' at

---

[1] BHC 6, fo. 389v; 5, fo. 60; 8, fo. 377; 6, fo. 338v; 9, fos. 34–5; BRHA BHC 4, fo. 313. See also BHC 6, fo. 389v; BRHA BHC4, fo. 7v.
[2] BHC 6, fos. 66, 134v; BHC 5, fo. 35v. See also BHC 5, fos. 14v, 303.
[3] Langbein, *Torture and the Law of Proof*, pp. 83–4, 111–19; TNA SP12/268/10; LMA Rep. 23, fo. 57v. See also Jonathan Andrews *et al.*, *The History of Bethlem* (1997), p. 117.

St Bartholomew's, and 'cross or place of correccon' at St Thomas's.[4] 'Bad' prisoners were 'shackled', 'manacled', 'fettered', or kept 'close' in Bridewell, as when John Bingham was ordered 'to be kepte a close prisoner' by the lord chief justice in 1606, 'and noe body to speake with him', he added. A 'room' was 'made over the gatehouse' to keep 'close prisoners' 'in security' in 1626. 'Rude' Frances Wootten was 'putt in a turret' in 1641 until she became 'quiet'. William Hurst's leg was strapped to the 'myll' by a 'long chayne' to make sure that he mixed with no one and worked 'contynually' after the watch stumbled on 'comon harlots and vagabonds' in his alehouse. John Gwynne, 'a prisoner convict and mutinous in Newgate', was 'kept at worke in chaynes and fettered' in 1618. Thomas Venables ended up 'mannacled and fettered with irons' in 1637 after lunging at house-officers with a bottle.[5]

But bodies were not just physical things, leaking smells and sickness, hurting, or taking on board sustenance. Outward appearance was a 'window on the soul'. Governors combed bodies from head to toe for guilt marks on skin, in giveaway expressions, and clothes or hair-styles not in 'outward conformity' to status- and gender-codes.[6] Margaret Williams, who was caught walking around midnight in 'very suspicious manner' with a man, was 'thought by her habitt' to be 'a comon enticer of men'. Alice Wickham was 'suspected' to be up to no good 'by reason of hir fondnes in attire' in 1575.[7] Innocence or guilt were seen in faces, gestures, or clothes. Anthony Tiffin was no beggar, Bridewell's bench said in 1617, because he dressed in 'good habit' like a 'scholler'. Rose Cornish was cleared of theft by her 'outward comertures'. A charge that Jane Yeomans was a bad servant was dropped because 'shee appeared to bee of civil cariage'. Other suspects tried to con courts. 'Comon bawd' Margaret Greet was locked up in 1561, even though 'in countenance she

---

[4] SBHA Governors' Journals 3, fo. 45v; 2, fo. 39v; GL MS 12806/2, fo. 247v; LMA H1/ST/A1/2, fo. 86; H1/ST/A1/3, fo. 35; H1/ST/A1/4, fo. 147. See Kevin P. Siena, *Venereal Disease, Hospitals, and the Urban Poor: London's 'Foul Wards', 1600–1800* (Rochester, NY, 2004), pp. 89–92, who argues that St Thomas's took a harsher line against 'poxed' patients, whipping them after their cure from 1599 on.

[5] BHC 5, fo. 97; 6, fo. 414; 8, fo. 35v; 1, fos. 8v-9; 6, fo. 58v; 8, fos. 136v, 132. See also BHC 5, fos. 206v, 229v; 8, fo. 151; BRHA BHC 4, fos. 236, 354.

[6] Quoting Edmund Bolton, *The Cities Advocate*, 1629, The English Experience, 715 (Amsterdam and Norwood, NJ, 1975). p. 40. See also Paul Griffiths, *Youth and Authority: Formative Experiences in England, 1560–1640* (Oxford, 1996), pp. 221–33; Ann Rosalind Jones and Peter Stallybrass, *Renaissance Clothing and the Materials of Memory* (Cambridge, 2000). Tatty clothes were also linked to insanity. See R. A. Houston, *Madness and Society in Eighteenth-Century Scotland* (Oxford, 2000), p. 150; Andrews et al., *History of Bethlem*, p. 334.

[7] BHC 2, fo. 91v; 8, fo. 130.

would seem to defend herself'.[8] Courts also put two and two together to make 'whore' or 'whoremonger' when skin was covered in tell-tale signs of the pox. A servant was soundly whipped in 1576 when it 'openlie appered' that he was 'a comon horemaster' 'for that he is filthilie deseazed with the pocks'.[9] Other signs of criminal pasts were hard to camouflage like brands on hands that singed skin like a loathed tattoo. John Mayfield was spotted dropping a child in Bishopgate Street and he was 'known by his burnt arme' to be a 'comon beggar'. Some bodies were coated in marks like pebbledash. The vagrant 'notorious theefe', John Garrett, had been 'burned in the hand sundry tymes in Newgate'.[10] Like paper, bodies had spaces to put data that might come back to haunt a recidivist standing in the dock one day.

Bodies had bits and pieces that were hard to hide and once revealed could clinch cases. Magistrates just needed to roll up sleeves, check teeth, or hear someone speak. A squint eye could give the game away. Pen portraits of suspects were sent to wards in the hope that an eagle-eyed officer might spot someone. Some were no more than a line long with scraps about clothes or build. Others were longer and zoomed in on skin, hair, height, or voice. John Anderton, who was on the run after taking plate in 1603, spoke 'like a stranger but an Englishman borne'. A thief who swiped 'great somes' from his master was 'a northern man' who 'speaketh very brode and northenly'.[11] Distinguishing marks were also pointed out. Another light-fingered servant – Robert Carlyle – had a glass eye, cut lip, and spoke 'through his nose'. Clement Sly, who broke out of Newgate in 1612, had one eye. The Gunpowder plotter, Thomas Percy, 'stooped somewhat in the sholders' and had 'longe footed small legges', and 'the culler of his beard and head mingled with white heares but the head more white than the beard'. Eliza Leicester, who pinched 'a greate chaine of gold', a horse, and 'writings' from a royal officer in 1604, had been 'latelie hurte' in the head 'in twoe or three places'. Another thief at large, Gervase Stanley, had 'pocke holes in his face', 'a small scarr upon his forehead, and a great ould cutt healed upp in the forefinger' of one hand. Sir Griffin Markham had a 'maymed' hand and a big nose. The horse-thief Edward Launcelott and priest William Watson both had squints: if the priest reads 'anie thing he putteth ye paper neare to his eyes', his pen-portrait said.[12] A 'privy search' was set up in 1571 to look in alehouses for Ellen Shawe, who was 'somewhat grosse and of a middle

---

[8] BHC 6, fo. 7v; 1, fo. 143v; 6, fo. 240v; 1, fo. 8.   [9] BHC 2, fo. 231.
[10] BHC 7, fo. 105; 6, fo. 350v. See also BHC 5, fo. 433v; 6, fo. 389; 7, fos. 116, 157, 231, 277v, 344v, 361; 8, fos. 44, 335v, 374v; LMA CQSF 91/10; MJ/SBR/4, fo. 406; MJ/SBR/6, fo. 450.
[11] LMA Jours. 26, fo. 143; 20, fos. 393v, 113; 30, fo. 281.
[12] LMA Jours. 29, fo. 186v; 28, fo. 305; 26, fo. 264v; 30, fo. 281; 27, fo. 6; 26, fo. 118v.

stature, full facyd, blacke browed with two brode teathe' poking out of her mouth 'somewhat blacke'. She was dressed in 'a red petycoate wth a white upper bodye' and an old 'colored cassocke', rounded off with 'an overcast' smock with 'two l[ett]res for her name' sown on it. Henry Field, who broke out of prison after a 'high offence' against the king in 1623, was 'of a middle stature', 'above fortie yeares of age', with a 'leane' face, a few 'pockholes about his nose', 'verie hollowe' eyes, a sallow 'complexione', 'brownish' hair, 'a light collor' beard 'somewhat forked and thinne of haire', and dressed 'in a leather suite of does skynne'. One mayor was hot on the heels of his 'skowringe woman' after she ran away with 'fower [of his] trencher plates' and four gilt-edged silver spoons. He quickly got descriptions out to the wards: she is from Gloucestershire, 'aboute the age of xxii yeares', with 'a full face', 'high coloure complexicon', and hair 'of a sadd colour'.[13]

Beards were fashionable and attracted comments like 'lyttle', 'thyn', 'small', 'cutt shorte', 'neer cutt', 'close cutt', black, yellow, flaxen.[14] Note was made of height, hair, and build: tall, small, 'low', 'reasonable', or 'midle stature'. One priest on the run was 'of midle stature inclyninge to the lower sorte', 'not leane nor corpulent but betwixt bothe'. One offender was 'slender'. Others were 'well sett', 'thick sett', or 'gret guttey'. Legs stretched from little to 'bigge', 'very stronge and gret'. Hair was 'flaxone', red, yellow, 'darke browne', black, or 'betwixte alborne and flaxen'. John Anderton's hair was 'upright before and is cutt somewhat short'. Another offender had 'nere polled' yellow hair. Faces were lean, round, and full. Complexions were 'sanguine', 'bleak', pale, or bright. Fugitives had on blue, russet, red, green, 'sad gray', 'sad greene', 'skye cullored' 'shepes colored' caps, hats, hose, doublets, jerkins, cloaks, coats, and slippers. Light-fingered Gawen Udall, wore 'a new mingled colour cloth somewhat darkishe' with green stockings. Clothes were 'comely' or 'not comely', or in a 'marriner's' style. 'Whoremonger' Anthony Bate decorated himself from head to toe like a Christmas tree: his hat blazed with a 'gret [gold] broche', one hand glittered with two rings topped off with 'blewish stones', and the other one sparkled with 'three jenners of golde together'.[15] These descriptions could change from

---

[13] LMA Jours. 19, fo. 379v; 32, fo. 145v; 33, fo. 198v.

[14] For beards see Will Fisher, 'The Renaissance beard: masculinity in early modern England', *Renaissance Quarterly*, 54 (2001), 155–87; Fisher, 'Staging the beard: masculinity in early modern English culture', in Jonathan Gil Harris and Natasha Korda, eds., *Staged Properties in Early Modern English Drama* (Cambridge, 2002), pp. 230–57.

[15] LMA Jours. 19, fos. 124, 194v; 20, fos. 189, 113, 366, 393v; 26, fos. 118v, 143; 28, fo. 305; 30, fo. 281; 35, fo. 260v; 37, fo. 130v; 39, fo. 306; Letterbook V, fo. 189v; BHC 3, fo. 215v. See also LMA Jours. 19, fos. 134, 136; 20, fos. 455, 471; 26, fo. 134; 32, fo. 273v; 36, fo. 20; 39, fo. 295v; Letterbook V, fo. 199v; WJ/SR/NS/39/10.

Bodies 257

one day to the next if new information came to light. The fugitive priest William Watson liked his beard long but 'informaccon' was 'given [days after his getaway] that nowe his beard is cutt'. Henry Field was wearing 'a leather suite of does skynne' when he first broke out of prison, but changed clothes later and was now dressed in a dark green suit, magistrates warned.[16]

Bodily features provided evidence and help with policing, but wounds or weakness could also move the Bridewell bench to 'pitty and remorse'. Poorly prisoners or others in low spirits could get pity, and penalties were softened, suspended, or scrapped if suspects were 'weake' or 'feble'. Helen Wheeler was drugged by Doctor Buck's 'good draft' of ale and pills in 1606, and 'veary merry' had sex with him, but her punishment was delayed until 'she growes stronger'.[17] Sick, crippled, or blind suspects also got off the hook. 'An idle knave' walked free as he was 'corrupte with sycknes'. The court followed a beadle's lenient line in 1575, who 'for pitties sake' did not arrest a 'soare diseased' woman who roomed in a brothel. 'Very greene' Ann Marshal was set free after a 'mischaunce' when her master 'abused' her. Mary Lyster also walked free with a warning as she was 'blinde and could not see to labor'. Anne Carr was spared the shame of riding in a cart because she was 'diseased with bleadinge continuallye', though she was 'well whipped'.[18] Carers were also allowed to go home to look after sick relatives. Phillidelfa Parris left with only a caution after a neighbour said that her husband was 'sick of the plague'.[19] Nightwalkers, thieves, bawds, harlots, vagrants, and others who left children on steps and stalls were freed if they were 'great with chyld'.[20] Age also made magistrates think carefully. Both old and young could get off lightly. Young people were spared if their little lapse seemed out of character, and they had time on their side to get back on the right track. 'Best to bend while tis a twig' was a piece of proverbial wisdom. 'Now they will bend, now they be pliable', another author added, maxims backed up by a tumbling cards account of criminality in which one crime followed another like clockwork.[21] Elderly people, on the other

---

[16] LMA Jours. 26, fo. 118v; 32, fo. 167v.
[17] BHC 5, fo. 90v. See also BHC 3, fos 413v, 437; 7, fo. 338v.
[18] BHC 1, fo. 98; 6, fo. 402v; 2, fo. 186v; 1, fos. 182, 215; BRHA BHC 4, fo. 96. See also BHC 1, fos. 65, 80v, 193v; 5, fos. 1, 2, 12, 20v, 27, 34, 252v, 305, 355, 410v, 434; 6, fos. 3, 12, 16, 22v, 24, 440; BRHA 4 fos. 354v, 371, 373v, 375, 387v, 391, 395, 464v, 465, 465v, 564v.
[19] BHC 5, fo. 212v.
[20] For example, BHC 1, fos. 24v, 29v, 42, 87v, 99, 212v, 217; 5, fos. 29, 34, 442v; 6, fos. 14v, 443; 7, fos. 346, 346v, 349v; 8, fo. 2v; BRHA BHC 4, fos. 368, 371, 383, 464v, 465v.
[21] BHC 1, fos. 95, 113v; 3, fos. 203v-5, 347v, 348v; 5, fos. 7, 48, 50v; 7, fo. 308; BRHA BHC 4, fos. 371, 383v; F.R., *A Collection of English Proverbs* (Cambridge, 1670), p. 61; Richard Shelford, *Lectures or Readings Upon the 6 Verse of the 22 Chapter of Proverbs*

258    Control

hand, were sometimes set free because they were frail or needy. Grizelle Bradley (alias Starkey) – a 'rag woman' – was allowed to go home 'without po[nishment in 1602] by reason of her age and impotency'. Alice Peel owned up 'that she had a yonge man in bed with hir' one night in 1574, who 'had thuse of hir bodie thrise', but she was let off with a warning since she was 'an old woman and had no better grace'. A vagrant dodged a whipping 'by reason of his age', as did a 'verie old' bawd.[22]

The signs of age were enough for a sympathetic hearing. There was also leeway for people in deep dark moods. Bridewell's court thought it best to lock up Frances Reynolds 'in safetie' in 1623, after she twice tried to drown herself in the Thames, 'over the iron pikes att the drawe bridge'. Elizabeth Jones also jumped in the river with her 'prettie young child': 'the devil urged her', she said.[23] Rules were relaxed for 'crazed', 'crackbrayned', 'silly', 'symple', light-headed or 'idle headed' suspects. Nicholas Weed was softly 'admonished' after lodging 'comon harlots' because 'he seemed a very natural foole'. One vagrant caught walking late got sixpence rather than a whipping because 'he seemeth a simple harmlesse fellowe'. Little time was spent on John Munch who stalked people, spouting gibberish about 'fabulous dreames': he is 'a playne dunsticall cuntry fellowe', the court said.[24] Parishes gave helping hands to 'fooles', and covered the costs of putting 'mad', 'distracted', or 'lunaticke' people in Bethlem or home-care.[25] The same bench doubled up for Bridewell and Bethlem, overseeing admissions, weeding out the insane. John Crosshaw was put in Bethlem in 1609 after he 'cursed his father and rayled egregiouslie upon my lord maior' and seemed 'lunatique'. Elizabeth Rathborne was kept on there after 'about 18 monethes' in 1624, as she was 'not yett fitt to goe abroad'.[26] Timid and tame simpletons were sent to prison or let go. 'A silley ideot boy' walked free in 1652;

*Concerning the Vertuous Education of Youth* (1606), p. 126. See also my *Youth and Authority*, esp. pp. 40–54. Cf. mitigation in felony trials: J. M Beattie, *Crime and the Courts in England, 1660 – 1800* (Oxford and Princeton, NJ, 1986), chap. 8; Peter King, *Crime, Justice, and Discretion: Law and Social Relations in England, 1740–1820* (Oxford, 2000), chaps 7–8.

[22] BRHA BHC 4, fos. 383, 380, 338v; BHC 2, fo. 39. See also BHC 1, fo. 113v; 3, fos. 203v-5, 347v, 348v; 5, fos. 7, 50v; BRHA BHC 4, fos. 371, 382v, 465.

[23] BHC 6, fos. 329v, 382v.

[24] BHC 1, fo. 3; 5, fos. 416v, 87; 1, fo. 25; 5, fos. 360, 401v; 6, fos. 12, 21v, 440v, 442v.

[25] GL MS 4524/1, fo. 170. See also GL MSS 4524/1, fos. 115v, 161, 243v; 590/1, fo. 170; 593/2, fo. 83; 878/1, fo. 97v; 1124/1, fo. 213; 1568 fo. 325; 3146/1, fos. 6v, 205; 4071/2, fo. 130v; 4956/3, fo. 188; 6552/1, fos. 97, 248v; 7674, fo. 50; 9237, fo. 143v; Andrews *et al.*, *History of Bethlem*, chaps 9 and 18; Peter Rushton, 'Idiocy, the family and the community in early modern north-east England', in David Wright and Anne Digby, eds., *From Idiocy to Mental Deficiency: Historical Perspectives on People With Learning Disabilities* (1996), pp. 44–64.

[26] BHC 5, fo. 338v; 6, fo. 368v. See also Andrews *et al.*, *History of Bethlem*, pp. 331–41.

as did 'a cilly weak wench' in 1657.[27] The bench tried to pin down the line between insanity and idiocy, picking from a mix of words to describe unsteady states. The late-night rambler Samuel Chambers was 'not well in his wits' but not lunatic either, and was sent to a healer for a 'cure'. Most prisoners 'found to be frenzie' were set free, but not William Wetton, who was 'kept at ease' after heckling preachers in 1606. 'Crackbrayned' people were also freed, as was 'somewhat distempered' Robert King. 'Crazed' prisoners were not as alarming as 'lunatiques', and rarely ended up in Bethlem or on the end of sharp punishments, including awkward cases like Peter Delight who, 'crazed in his braines', marched through London playing tunes on a fife 'with a boy before him striking a drumme', all the time warning bystanders to 'take heed' of 'doctrine'; or a waterbearer who 'threaten[ed] the death of divers watermen'.[28] Mitigating medical and mental states were handled kindly on the whole. But Bridewell's bench was always on guard for bogus bodies and minds that were hard to spot in the hands of skilful actors like 'notorious counterfeit crank' beggar Edward Fetherton.[29] People tried to con courts by faking madness, lameness, lost limbs, or war wounds, putting cloths on heads and groaning about splitting pain. 'Counterfeit criples' tried to dupe citizens, as did women who stuffed bundles of rags under their clothes to make 'packed up' bellies to pretend that they were pregnant.

**Medical grids**

The court took a different tack if lumps under clothes were not rags. As with female felons sentenced to death, pregnant women guilty of lesser crimes were treated more softly and many got away with a warning, and some mothers-to-be got hand-outs.[30] People showed up in all conditions at Bridewell. The surgeon took 'care to cure the hands' of branded Newgate prisoners in 1648.[31] Some suspects were on the verge of collapse. Others limped through the gates, but not vagrant William Clay who had 'noe leggs'. One vagrant boy had toes 'almost rotted off'. Robert Wilbrome was 'a broken man'. Other vagrants had scurvy or 'dead

---

[27] BHC 9, fos 534, 824.
[28] Jonathan Andrews, 'Identifying and providing for the mentally disabled in early modern London', in Wright and Digby, eds., *From Idiocy to Mental Deficiency*, pp. 65–92; BHC 5, fos. 94, 108, 53v, 75, 85 118, 153v; 8, fos. 14v, 175, 279v; 5, fo. 88v; 6, fo. 40; 9, fo. 664.
[29] BRHA BHC 4, fo. 296v.
[30] For example, BHC 1, fos. 24v, 29v, 42, 87v, 99, 212v, 217; 5, fos. 29, 34, 442v; 6, fos. 14v, 443; 7, fos. 346, 346v, 349v; 8, fo. 2v; BRHA BHC 4, fos. 368, 371, 383.
[31] BHC 9, fo. 854.

palsey'. Martin Hart came from Devon 'to gett himself cured of the kings evill'. Some vagrants walked chilly streets 'naked' or partly clothed, risking infections. 'Three forren naked vagrants' were 'clothed' at the 'howses' charge in 1602. Nine women were given shoes, waistcoats, smocks, bands, 'coyses', and hose at one time in 1618. Many more vagrants got new breeches, shirts, smocks, and stockings to replace their tatty clothes.[32]

Not everyone left Bridewell alive. There was a graveyard for people who dropped dead inside its walls, but surgeons were shared with other hospitals and Bridewell got its own in 1580. There was a 'sick dyett' and 'sick ward' with just six beds in 1618.[33] Sick prisoners were sent to other hospitals, and a medical grid stretched over London, as pauper patients and prisoners were ferried from prison to hospital.[34] This became the established means for caring for the sick 'poor' who ended up in Bridewell; whose bench said that they sent their 'lame, sore, sicke, and weake people' to other hospitals 'for their cure according to [their] foundacon and institucon'.[35] Bridewell sent more sick 'poor' over the river to St Thomas's than on the shorter trip up Fleet Street to St Bartholomew's. Only a few prisoners were sent outside to healers (on record at least). Lockley's wife picked up four shillings each time she healed 'one of the pores heddes' in 1579. Mistress Stone took care of an apprentice laid low with 'the kings evill' in 1642. Matrons also 'looked to' sick inmates, though more fees are logged to surgeons for 'cures' and 'dressings'.[36] Parishes also sent people to and from hospitals, paying for board, clothes, and care. The costs of running hospitals were eased now and then by parish collections, one-off gifts, or charity baskets. The most common route to a hospital bed was a parish referral. Half of all orphans who ended up in Christ's from 1556–92 were sent from parishes (250/502) or streets 'without comfort' (125/502).[37] Beadles, 'messangers',

---

[32] BRHA BHC 4, fos. 332v, 348.
[33] BHC 5, fo.409; 6, fos. 23, 25v, 26, 45v, 48, 82v, 97v.
[34] The fullest study of the hospitals' early history is Daly, 'The hospitals of London'. See also Siena, *Venereal Disease*, chaps 1–2; and Paul Slack, 'Hospitals, workhouses, and the relief of the poor in early modern London', in Ole Peter Grell and Andrew Cunningham, eds., *Health Care and Poor Relief in Protestant Europe, 1500–1700* (1997), pp. 234–51.
[35] BHC 9, fo. 504.
[36] Daly, 'Hospitals of London', p. 261; BHC 3, fo. 436; 8, fo. 394; 7, fo. 235v. On female healers see Pelling, *Medical Conflicts in Early Modern London*, chaps 5–6; Siena, *Venereal Disease*, pp. 55–60. The most recent study of London's 'medical marketplace' is Patrick Wallis, 'Competition and cooperation in the early modern medical economy', in Mark S. R. Jenner and Wallis, eds., *Medicine and the Market in England and its Colonies, c. 1450 – c. 1850* (Basingstoke, 2007), pp. 47–68.
[37] Admissions figures are taken from GL MSS 12806/1–2; quoting GL MS 12806/1, fo. 18v.

lobbies, or warrants went from parishes to hospitals to get beds for their sick. Costs could be high: five shillings 'for continuing Cakebread in the hospitall', 7/8d for a boy with a broken leg. Parishes also helped out sick stragglers crying on streets, locked in cages overnight, or cringing in church porches or 'howse[s] of office', and for burials if one of their flock died in hospitals.[38] They also settled apothecaries' accounts, surgeons' fees, and healers' or 'phisick' bills. One gave four shillings to 'a poore man' with nothing left to his name after spending 'all his meanes upon surgeons', without luck.[39]

This looks like a decent-sized framework of care, though we could count the number of key institutions on one hand. St Bartholomew's started off with 100 patients, but was swamped with 180 by 1588, and lifted the ceiling for patient numbers to 120 with thirty more in the 'owte houses'. The number had only dropped to 160 by 1590, and complaints about overspills continued in the next century.[40] An upper limit of 100 was set at St Thomas's in 1561 when patient numbers rose to 140. Numbers hovered around 120 for a while, but zoomed upwards to 151 by 1565. Seasonal limits came in soon after: 100 in summer and 'six score' in winter. But numbers soon bounced back to higher levels: 150 in 1572. Grumbling about surplus sick continued, and the cap was put at 200 in 1624: 'nine score' in summer and 'eleven score' in winter. A decade later the board insisted that numbers 'be reduced to a certainty' once more: 'twelve score' in summer this time and 'fourteen score' in winter. There were clear-outs of 'incurables' and others 'lurking in the house upon no cure', and steps to weed out hangers-on from lazarhouses who were now 'whole'.[41] A 1564 count showed that 1,916 children had been 'admitted' to Christ's since it opened in 1552: '733 of them deade' and 866 'put to service'. The number of orphans and urchins in Christ's

---

[38] GL MSS 590/1, fo. 160; 3146/1, fo. 60; 4524/1, fo. 13v; 818/1, fo. 7v; 2088/1, 1612–13; 593/2, fo. 80; 6552/1, fos. 163v, 177; 577/1, fo. 79; 5714/1, fo. 208v; 593/2, fo. 154.

[39] GL MSS 4071/2, fo.86v; 3146/1, fos. 17, 96v, 107, 104, 113, 117v, 125v; 4524/1, fo. 161v; 1176/1, 1656.

[40] SBHA Governors' Journal 1, fos. 5, 93; 3, fos. 27, 46v; 4, fos. 31v, 219v. Siena provides figures for patient numbers, and writes that 'on an average day in 1622 one would expect to find 182 patients in the main hospital and 55 patients in the two outhouses combined'. The number of 'pox' patients in the outhouses climbed after that, almost doubling within a decade (Siena, *Venereal Disease*, pp. 70 and 98–9).

[41] LMA H1/ST/A1/3, fos. 18v, 48vff., 91v, 114, 219v; H1/ST/A1/4, fos. 77v, 137v, 150v; H1/ST/A1/5, fos. 20, 40, 43v, 50, 59v, 136; H1/ST/A1/2, fo. 114; SBHA Governors' Journal 3, fo. 6. Siena estimates that there were roughly 278 hospital beds in St Thomas's by 1660, 52 for venereal patients (*Venereal Disease*, p. 73). See also Daly, 'Hospitals of London', pp. 296–7.

rose from then on: 344 children were 'remaining here', annual reports said in 1570–1, 627 in 1585–6, and 665 in 1597.[42]

London was growing at a cracking pace, and a hospital bed-count perhead would turn up dismal disparities. But the value of the hospitals exceeded the sum total of beds. They were symbols of civic pride with roles in responses to rapid growth, referred to almost automatically as the '4 hospitals'. The 'howses' are all 'one intercorporacon', aldermen said in 1590, 'and if one should fayle in performance' of 'dewties and services required by theyre chartre the same might hazard the state of all the hospitals'. They did indeed give each other helping hands with loans or leases. St Bartholomew's and St Thomas's swapped land and shared surgeons and medical expertise. They set up a joint meeting on 'cutting' for 'the stone' in 1622 that led to a 'treaty of communication', and also held joint talks 'about ordering' 'physic and surgery' of the 'poor' in each hospital.[43] As well as pooling knowledge and resources now and then, the '4 hospitals' sent inmates to other 'houses' for care, punishment, or work. Bridewell and Christ's began to swap pests not long after they first opened, when illegitimacy and child abandonment cases were still heard at Christ's. A Southwark woman, who was whipped at Bridewell for 'forsaking' a child on a street, was sent on to Christ's 'for further reformacon'. Vagrants, beggars, and young runaways all went in the opposite direction.[44] Christ's also sent sick people to the other hospitals for care and cure, and drew up a template warrant for passing its 'lame or diseased' orphans and urchins across the grid.[45] Other hospitals sent sick waifs and strays to the orphanage. 'Lunatiques' were switched to Bethlem if medicine and surgery were no longer enough. Plague victims were taken to pesthouses from the '4 hospitals', and some seriously sick people were put in lazarhouses.[46] Aldermen also sent lame, 'ympetent' and poxed people to one of the hospitals, like Christian Appelly, 'a poore woman'

---

[42] GL MS 12819/2, 1563–4, 1570–1, 1585–6, 1597–8. Numbers were also on the rise after 1620. See GL MSS 12806/3, fos. 209–10v; 12806/4, fos. 34–7, 312–15, 568–72.
[43] LMA Rep. 22, fo. 184v; GL MSS 12806/1, fos. 28v, 59; 12806/4, fo. 349; 12819/2, fos. 23v, 25; SBHA Governors' Journal 4, fos. 344v, 349; LMA H1/ST/A/1/3, fos. 66, 86v; H1/ST/A/1/4, fos. 94, 160v; H1/ST/A1/5, fos. 14, 50.
[44] GL MSS 12806/1, fos. 4v, 41v, 55; 12806/2, fos. 2, 34v, 36, 56v, 71v, 77, 83v, 91, 112, 118v, 230. See also GL MS 12806/2, fos. 43v, 70, 100v, 106, 125v, 299v, 335v.
[45] GL MS 12806/2, unpag. (end of book). See also Daly, 'Hospitals of London', p. 356.
[46] LMA H1/ST/A1/1, fos. 4ff., 9v; H1/ST/A1/3, fos. 128v, 143; H1/ST/A1/4, fos. 54, 169; BRHA BHC 4, fos. 53, 390v, 396v; GL MSS 9237, fo. 57; 4383/1, fo. 448; 878/1, fo. 271v; 4423/1, fo. 151; 4385/1, fo. 219; 4180/2, fo. 76; 524/1, fo. 48; 5090/2, fo. 233; 5018/1, fo. 76; 1568, fo. 646; 593/2, fo. 168v; 2596/2, fo. 91; 959/1, fo. 163v; SBHA Governors' Journal 2, fo. 78.

of Portsoken, who was admitted to St Thomas's in 1577 'to be cured and healyd of the dysease callyd the poxe wherewith she is grened'.[47]

The number of transfers between hospitals is enough for us to see a grid stretching across London with links to parishes, prisons, and the Guildhall. It was handily flexible with patients and prisoners shuttling back and forth.[48] Bridewell turned to other hospitals for medical assistance, money, or medicine. St Bartholomew's and St Thomas's were asked to share the costs for hiring a surgeon for Bridewell in 1580 to 'cure' 'impotent and dysesed' people; this will be 'a great ease', they were told, as prisoners would not now need to take up one of their beds. Complaints from the first year included eight sore mouths, four sore hands and two sore throats, eight ulcers in legs, cheeks, and arms, two leg tumors, two swollen legs, broken heads and arms, and other knocks on feet, fingers, chins, and groins.[49] Three men filled the surgeons' post over the next two years: Edward Bailey picked up £6 13s 4d as well as a salary from St Bartholomew's. Other surgeons followed in quick succession. Thomas Cole's annual salary was pitched at £3 6s 8d in 1597, although salaries fell afterwards: William Wright and John Quince got sixty shillings in the 1620s. Not many men stayed in post longer than two years, although Wright stayed for a handful and died in post in 1632.[50] Surgeons also got fees for individual cures. Wright was paid 6/8d 'for curing' a woman who hurt her head in the mill. Another surgeon got twenty shillings for 'dressing' another mill casualty.[51] This all changed in 1635 when the bench ruled that surgeons would only get paid for cures listed in 'bills' from now on. John Meredith got 'no fee' except 'reasonable allowance for his cures and businesses' when he became surgeon in 1643. 'Surgeons bills' were jotted down in annual accounts: £11 in 1643, £14 in 1645 for tending to prisoners of war, £8 12s 6d 'for cures done to the poor' in 1647. And surgeons still got one-off bonuses: Doctor Nurse got a whopping £20 in 1655 for his 'extraordinary paines' in caring for an above average number of 'lunatickes'.[52]

---

[47] LMA Rep. 19, fo. 266. See also LMA Reps. 18, fos. 274v, 326v; 19, fo. 464; 20, fos. 132, 422; 21, fos. 215, 220v; 22, fos. 40, 224–4v.
[48] Margaret Pelling, *The Common Lot: Sickness, Medical Occupations, and the Urban Poor in Early Modern England* (Harlow, 1998), pp. 197–8.
[49] SBHA Governors' Journal 2, fos. 190–0v. Cf. Daly, 'Hospitals of London', pp. 145, 260–1.
[50] SBHA Governors' Journal 2, fos. 173v, 178v, 185, 195v, 196, 176; BHC 6, fo. 395; 7, fos. 159, 287.
[51] BHC 7 fos. 66, 35v, 134v, 303; 8, fos. 46v, 57, 321; BRHA BHC 4, fos. 366v, 376.
[52] BHC 8, fo. 42v; 9, fo. 12; GL MS 33063/1, Christmas 1643, Ann 1645, Michaelmas 1647; BHC 9, fo. 724. See also BHC 8, fos. 46v, 57, 321.

It is not always clear why someone with a sore head or lame leg went elsewhere, when others stayed in Bridewell for care. Entries are often no more than a sentence long. Perhaps a prisoner's health took a turn for the worse, or the surgeon had heavy loads and no time to spare. One norm was that disease should be 'curable', if not people were sent back. A Spanish prisoner of war was sent to St Thomas's 'to be cured of his disease if he be curable' in 1601, and after cure 'to be safely brought [back] agayne'. Thirteen more Spaniards were sent there over the next few months. The sick vagrant Richard Ward also went there but was soon back in Bridewell when found to be 'uncureable', as was Elizabeth Hoare who could not be cured in 1600.[53] Most prisoners stayed for short spells in other hospitals, but it was a long-term switch for some. It took St Thomas's doctors three long years to decide that Elizabeth Nicholls was 'uncureable'. While 'notorious roague' Robert Atkinson was there for a 'long' time in 1619 after timber fell on him.[54] As with the Spanish captives, prisoners were supposed to go back to Bridewell 'after cure'. Two pickpockets sent to St Thomas's in 1640 were 'resent hither when they were well'. John Wither was 'trusted' to come back 'to worke' after 'his cure of his scauld head' in 1657. Charles Davey returned after being 'cured of the pocks' in 1598, but he slipped away before he was punished. While John Stapleton, on trial for pinching his master's goods in 1575, was also sent to another hospital on the understanding that he would 'be sente back againe' 'when he is whole'.[55] St Bartholomew's took in pickpockets, pilferers, vagrants, beggars, nightwalkers, and 'harlots' from Bridewell, along with apprentices with 'sore leggs' or 'scald' heads, one had care for 'a fistula in his eye'. An inmate who had 'long since' broken an arm and 'thighebone' was sent 'to be cured', though it was felt that he would never 'be his owne man' again.[56] Numbers sent to St Thomas's outstripped the slim column going to Smithfield by over one-in-ten by 1600. The treasurer was given 'discrecon' to send prisoners to a hospital in 1635, but only St Thomas's was listed as a potential destination.[57] Bridewell sent all sorts of prisoners to St Thomas's 'for cure': vagrants, beggars, thieves, nips, cheats, runaways, army deserters, strumpets,

---

[53] BRHA BHC 4, fos. 251, 284, 299, 177v, 301. Parishes also paid to move their sick from Bridewell to a hospital: for example, GL MSS 6754, fo. 52; 2968/2, fo. 7v; 577/1, fo. 94v.
[54] BHC 6, fos. 253v, 125. See also BHC 5, fo. 429; 8, fo. 394.
[55] BHC 8, fo. 308; 9, fo. 798; 3, fo. 92v. BRHA BHC 4, fo. 40v. See also BRHA BHC 4, fo. 156v.
[56] BHC 9, fo. 746; 5, fo. 347; 1, fo. 155v. See also BHC 5, fos. 225v, 285v, 294, 339, 414v; 6, fos. 66v, 391v, 409v, 427; 7, fos. 5v, 82, 172v, 223, 314; 8, fos. 10v, 398; 9, fos. 113, 140, 200, 289, 292, 393, 511, 562, 640, 651, 769, 813, 850; BRHA BHC 4, fo. 364v.
[57] BHC 8, fo. 42v.

queens, lewd livers, and dangerous or disorderly people, as well as sick Turks, apprentices, and 'poor' boys and wenches.[58] 'Scalled heads' and lameness are noted more than any other condition, except for the pox. Four people with 'scalled heads' went to St Thomas's over a few days in 1632.[59] Others ended up there with bad limbs, rotting toes, scratched eyes, scurvy, falling sickness, and king's evil. A nightwalker had 'a dangerous sore legg'. A 'poore maide' was 'diseased in the throate'. A vagrant had 'his arme out of joynt', and another had 'a canker'. Beggar Mary Smith had 'the itch'. A 'leprous girle' turned up in court one day, while John Matthews was sent over the river 'to be healed of the white scowle'. But most of the sick Bridewell prisoners who followed him to St Thomas's lacked an exact diagnosis or they were simply called 'diseased'.[60]

To be 'healed' or 'cured' appears at the end of nearly all such orders. There was a real expectation that the grid would do good and that punishment would follow later if need be. But traffic did not all flow in one direction, as Bridewell also gave its fellow hospitals helping hands, taking in their unruly patients, though this made up as little as 0.17 per cent of recorded committals (sixty-nine). St Bartholomew's sent one troublemaker more than its cousin institution: runaways, thieves, and bullies in the main, though one couple were found having sex there. Some were quickly sent back after a dressing down. Zachary Panton, 'one of the poore of St Bartholomews', was brought to Bridewell by the 'hospitler' for 'ill rule and pilfering', whipped on the spot, and 'sent thether agayne'. Thomas Edwards, an old-hand beggar and 'incorrigible boy', who ran away from St Thomas's and 'will not be cured of his scald head', was whipped and sent back there. Others were put in Bridewell for a few days or more, like Samuel Tench who was caught 'robbing' from 'the poore' in St Bartholomew's, and boasting that 'hee had 30 times the use of the body' of his master's maid in 1623.[61] There was a concern that diseases would spread like wildfire through the prison population. Thomas Richardson, who bungled a robbery in 1630, was speedily sent away with a pass when it seemed that he was 'likely to infect the house'.[62] People with pox were often sent back to other hospitals as quickly as

---

[58] BRHA BHC 4, fos. 283v, 290v, 295v.  [59] BHC 7, fos. 286v, 287v, 289v, 292.
[60] BHC 8, fo. 299; 7, fos. 105v, 77v; 9, fo. 52; 7, fo. 86; 9, fo. 680; 5, fo. 127v. See also BHC 5, fos. 34, 161, 285v; 6, fos. 289, 436; 7, fos. 25, 86, 243, 298v, 335; 8, fos. 19, 60, 147, 211, 297v, 334; 9, fos. 30, 88, 150, 345, 468, 544, 622, 648, 700, 804; BRHA BHC 4, fos. 14v, 213, 371, 465v.
[61] BHC 6, fo. 242v; 3, fo. 180; 8, fo. 334; 6, fo. 325v. See also BHC 1, fos. 207v, 218v; 2, fo. 236v; 5, fos. 379v, 409v; 6, fos. 90v, 91, 269v, 288; 7, fos. 222v, 304v; 8, fos. 8, 57v, 58v, 326; 9, fos. 31, 354; BRHA BHC 4, fos. 141v, 157, 173v, 427; Daly, 'Hospitals of London', pp. 260–1.
[62] BHC 7, fo. 189.

possible. 'Lewde harlott' Emme Wynott, who was 'full of the french pox', was whipped and returned to St Bartholomew's on the same day in 1602. A 'Barts' beadle brought three 'lewde' men and one 'lewde woman' to Bridewell in 1604, and took them back shortly after as each had 'the evill disease'. Some people with pox stayed longer, like Anne Percy, 'a notorious roague infected with the frenche disease'. But this was rare.[63]

A long line of sufferers with the 'filthie' or 'fowle disease' passed from Bridewell to another hospital (a few were sent to surgeons somewhere else). There was no room left in the 'foul ward' in St Bartholomew's in Spring 1634 or in 1642 when 'sweatwards' filled up quickly. Almost one-in-five patients treated at St Bartholomew's in the seven decades after 1622 had the 'fowle disease'. One 'sister' (Goodwife Sworden) treated 'pox' on the side, picking up two shillings 'and halfe a sheete' in 1601 to 'tend and cure' a woman with pox in a boarding house.[64] Not many days went by without someone turning up at Bridewell 'dirty' and infected, like the 'filthy adulterous woman' with the 'filthy and diseased body', who was sent to St Thomas's in 1603.[65] Some came back again and again. The 'notorious queane', 'notorious nightwalker', and 'notorious whore', Joan Moulden, often turned up at Bridewell with the 'fowle disease' in 1620–6.[66] A crop of 'poxy' 'queens', 'comon harlotts', 'nawghtie vile whores', and 'comon horemassters', thieves, cheats, fishwives, beggars, and vagrants also appear in records with the pox. Sex was the crux of the matter in most cases. Susan Goldsmith was riddled with pox in 1638, 'having had three bastards', the clerk noted. A bigamist joined her in the hospital with the pox.[67] Alice Haynes, who roomed in 'bawdys', was unlucky enough to pick up the pox from a surgeon living in Lambeth.[68] People became infected in similar situations for the most part. Questions about how they 'came by' the pox were often the leading lines in examinations. Cicely Bennet said that she thought she caught the 'fowle disease' at Black Bess's house near East Smithfield (a red-light area). Elizabeth Cobham picked up the pox from Mr Scorie, who paid for her

---

[63] BRHA BHC 4, fos. 337, 354v, 95, 120, 162v, 232; BHC 6, fo. 269v.
[64] SBHA Governors' Journal 5, fos. 44, 73v; BRHA BHC 4, fos. 270–0v; BHC 3, fo. 341. On the treatment of pox in St Bartholomew's and St Thomas's see Siena, *Venereal Disease*, chap. 2. William Clowes, a St Bartholomew's surgeon in the 1570s, said that over 1,000 people were healed of pox there in five years, and that at least half of all patients were admitted with pox: 'I speak nothing of St. Thomas's Hospitals and other houses in the city', he added, 'wherein an infinite number are daily in cure'. See Daly, 'Hospitals of London', pp. 183–4, quoting p. 184.
[65] BRHA BHC 4, fo. 373.   [66] BHC 6, fos. 205v, 248, 380v, 423.
[67] BHC 8, fo. 152v; 1, fos. 120v, 175v, 182v; 2, fo. 231; 3, fo. 405v; 5, fo. 57v; 6, fos. 154v, 250v; 8, fos. 28, 330v; BRHA BHC 4, fos. 52, 328, 354v.
[68] BRHA BHC 4, fo. 430.

food and board in Elizabeth Burrow's sleazy lodging house (seven groats each week). A tailor was 'greved' after he 'was burned' by a 'harlotte' in 1578. The prostitute Jane Trosse got the pox from the pimp Richard Rolles in a widow's house in Charing Cross, not long after he got out of Newgate. Others caught the 'disease' on one-night stands, or from someone who lived in the same house, their master or mistress, or a relative or friend who dropped in all the time.[69]

Like other things, the pox was often treated by joint efforts between the hospitals. But it was rarely completely smooth sailing. Hospitals were not just supportive of each other, they also fell out now and then, hardly surprising as they competed for the same resources and there were never enough pieces of the cake to go round. Each one of 'the 4 hospitals' had its own rules, purse, and needs, and was quite prepared to put its own interests above all else. There were limits on teamwork, therefore, and what mattered most to each 'board' was its own budget, or how many hard-up inmates were draining resources. So there were some splits in the hospitals' union, however hard it was reiterated that they were the '4 hospitals'. Some were long running, though others were shorter and limited to a couple of the hospitals: a quarrel about costs 'for clearing a bastard child from the city' was limited to Christ's and Bridewell in 1578. But all four hospitals were wrangling over alderman Hawton's handsome £200 legacy two decades later. The sparks for other spats included bickering beadles, beadles' fees, lazy beadles who did not do their duties or 'walks', wills, turnovers from lands, leases, legacies, or rents, corn stocks, orphans' 'porcons', surgeons' bills, and caring for 'younge girles' or 'poore and diseased persons taken upp in the streete'.[70]

A few more serious squabbles touched thornier issues concerning terms of 'foundacon and institucon', for example. The Bridewell board was up in arms in 1641 after hearing that St Thomas's was turning away 'diseased poore' sent there from the prison as soon as they showed up at the gate. The clerk met with the mayor to 'put' him 'in minde to move' aldermen to put a stop to these 'abuses'. But this was only a quick-fix step, it seems, as Bridewell was again complaining a decade later that other hospitals would not take in their 'lame, sore, sicke, and weake' prisoners at all, or dumped them back out on the streets without cure, 'contrary to the[ir] foundacon' and the 'charitable intencon' of the 'founder'. This

---

[69] Ibid., fos. 424, 270–0v; BHC 3, fos. 341, 204; 5, fo. 110.
[70] GL MSS 12806/2, fo. 215; 12806/3, fo. 34. See also LMA Reps. 19, fo. 354v; 23, fo. 537; 45, fos. 547–7v, 548–51v; SBHA Governors' Journals 2, fos. 213, 254; 3, fos. 13, 159v, 285; GL MSS 12806/2, fo. 226; 12806/3, fos. 23v-4, 66, 197v; 12806/4, fo. 133; LMA H1/ST/A/1/4, fos. 67v, 139; BHC 9, fos. 12, 29, 109, 113; Daly, 'Hospitals of London', p. 8.

time it was Bridewell's president who 'moved' aldermen to issue rulings that no one ever left a hospital without proper care.[71] A lack of beds and dwindling funds in other hospitals had led to these bans on Bridewell's walking wounded. But money had long been a sticking point in relations between the hospitals. John Island – Bridewell's fourth surgeon in three years – was out-of-pocket for 'curinge' broken arms and legs in 1583, and St Bartholomew's blamed colleagues at St Thomas's, who had not yet paid their share of his salary and bills, even though their 'house' was of 'better ability'. A settlement was struck not long afterwards, but the hospitals were again at loggerheads over the surgeon's salary less than a year later, the Smithfield 'house' again claiming that it was 'lesse able' to cover costs.[72] But settlements only ever papered over the cracks for a while. Financial snags and tiffs dragged on. The 'Barts' board took a stand ten years later when William Pickering 'made sewte' for 'the surgions roome of Brydewell': we have 'bine longe charged' with the 'whole stipende', they said, sounding weary and exasperated, once more pointing fingers at their sister institutions.[73]

To make matters worse, there was a barely concealed snobbishness on the part of Christ's governors (especially) when it came to scoring points in the struggle for resources. There was a pecking order, at least in the minds of some boards, when they went cap in hand to the City for assistance. Christ's claimed that it was the most deserving of the hospitals when it was short of money in 1599. We only comfort 'the best poor kind of people', its board bragged with little fraternal feeling, unlike 'the other hospitals' who 'spend the profits of their lands on foul persons, country people, and such like, but very little on citizens of London which this house altogether does relieve'.[74] Christ's had what looked like a leading status from the start: citizens could think well of the hospital that dished out pensions and was more bound up with the public expression of civic identities than any other one, its children turning up in neat blue clothes for the funerals of citizens, and lining up in a smart blue line at Spital sermons. In addition, early general meetings of all hospital boards were held at Christ's, and 'evidences' and 'notes' from the other hospitals were stored in Christ's chests, until each took charge of its own affairs and

---

[71] BHC 8, fo. 336; 9, fo. 504.  [72] SBHA Governors' Journal 2, fos. 238, 240, 254.
[73] Ibid., fo. 104.
[74] GL MS 12806/3, fo. 40. The same board ruled later that children born 'without the liberties' could not be admitted, 'according to ancient orders of this house', 'except it be upon very great consideration' (fo. 105v) (see also fo. 321). Beadle Thomas Stone landed in trouble in 1579 for 'his speech touching the taking in of children not born in this city', saying that they should 'starve in the streets' rather than 'be taken in' (GL MS 12806/2, fo. 232v).

archives later on.[75] But Christ's governors clung to the upper hand when necessary, even in the likelihood that their hospital was pounded by critics as time passed because it was the biggest drain on civic resources.[76] But they also had some justification on their side, as there was a rank order in rituals with Christ's at the head. Christ's treasurer walked 'in the first place' at an alderman's funeral in 1633, 'as anciently has been accustomed', records reported, with St Bartholomew's treasurer behind him 'in second place'. Later, at the dinner in Draper's Hall, Christ's governors sat snootily 'at the upper table', their compatriots from St Bartholomew's and St Thomas's lined each side of the hall, while Bridewell's board did not even get a table in the hall, but had to settle for seats in the next-door parlour, straining to hear the speeches from the other side of the door.[77] Over time each hospital came to carve out its own identity, and antagonisms always remained (along with sharper spirits of self-preservation), lingering like sporting rivalries at times: 'Bridewell doggs', a Christ's beadle snapped, as a bunch of his 'boys' 'challenged' the Bridewell 'boyes' in church one day.[78] But as with the team spirit among the hospitals, however, we should not exaggerate the scale of the clashes that sometimes strained their relations. Scrapes are always likely when more than one self-interest is involved in any matter. That said, however, a system emerged over time, and magistrates knew where to send London's sick, mad, and bad. The '4 hospitals' quickly became rhetoric themselves, I argued earlier, but something that was both discursive and physical, with a real part to play in responding to growth.

### Touch and search

Bodies were not only put in the hands of surgeons with medical missions. They also contained evidence from top to toe, of medical conditions naturally: a vagrant said 'she had a plague sore upon her', but close checks found that it was 'another fowle disease', one evidently more shameful than the 'infeccon', and she was not alone in tricking courts or hospitals to avoid the slur of pox.[79] But bodies also contained legal data. Magistrates and parishes often called on 'poor women', midwives, or goodwives to 'searche' maids in the main to check whether or not they were 'with

---

[75] Daly, 'Hospitals of London', pp. 314–23; LMA H1/ST/A/1/3, fo. 216v; SBHA Governors' Journal 1, fos. 97, 108v; LMA Reps. 13ii, fo. 363; 16, fo. 167.
[76] Daly, 'Hospitals of London', pp. 339, 359.   [77] GL MS 12806/3, fo. 575.
[78] LMA MS/331–2–1.
[79] BHC 5, fo. 293v; 8, fo. 23. See also Siena, *Venereal Disease*, pp. 36–54. Claude Quetel argues that attitudes towards the pox sharpened after 1600: *The History of Syphilis*, trans. Judith Braddock and Brian Pike (Baltimore, MD, 1990), pp. 73–5.

childe' or had recently had sex. Courts turned to midwives for help in illegitimacy cases, to establish pregnancies and get the names of fathers from mothers in childbed, and sometimes asked for second opinions if matrons found nothing. These mostly middling women took leading roles in policing women's bodies when asked, propping up patriarchy, or those aspects that were of most concern to them: children, male violence, and how reputations of all women were at stake if one fell short of male standards.[80]

Back in Bridewell there were 'searches' when matrons or midwives checked claims about pregnancy, sex, or rape. Up until the mid-1570s the court sent some women up Fleet Street to be 'searched' by Christ's matron.[81] But searches mostly took place inside Bridewell after that with matrons in charge. When Elizabeth Fellows slipped away from her master's house to spend nights with a carman in 1602, the court asked the matron 'to serche her because she seemed to be an awdacious incontinent woman'. The bench's hunch was right: she was 'found to be with childe'.[82] The matron also came to court if women in the dock claimed to be 'with child' to get softer treatment. Elizabeth Conway (alias Steward), who was 'taken' walking late, was not yet 'with child', the matron said, but was 'within a weeke of quickening'. Another matron advised that 'the matter wold not appeare in short tyme' in a case from 1562. Only a handful of women told the truth.[83] A number of women were found 'clear': nightwalker Jane Cannon, who would 'not be reformed', was 'found not with child' in 1646; Elizabeth Ouncestead, who was suspiciously locked up in a room with a man and a warm bed in 1641, 'never knew man'; while Rachel Hoggard, whose master said that she spread stories that 'hee had the use of her body 3 times', was 'founde cleare' in 1637. But many more were caught out by the matron's touch and 'found to the contrary', including vagrant Mary Fox with 'noe settled habitacon or course of life', women who 'played the harlott' or skulked

---

[80] GL MSS 577/1, fo. 44; 593/2, fo. 71; 1016/1, fo. 91; 4180/2, fo. 81v; 2596/2, fo. 131; LMA MJ/SBR/1, fo. 232; MJ/SBR/2, fo. 226; MJ/SBR/5, fo. 156; WJ/SR/NS/48/37; BHC 8, fos. 175, 255. Cf. Laura Gowing, *Common Bodies: Women, Touch, and Power in Seventeenth-Century England* (New Haven, CT, and London, 2003), chap. 5; Gowing, 'Ordering the body: illegitimacy and female authority in seventeenth-century England', in Michael J. Braddick and John Walter, eds., *Negotiating Power in Early Modern Society: Order, Hierarchy, and Subordination in Britain and Ireland* (Cambridge, 2001), pp. 43–62, esp. pp. 46–51; Doreen Evenden, *The Midwives of Seventeenth-Century London* (Cambridge, 2000), pp. 170–1. Parishes also paid for 'searches' in Bridewell: for example, GL MS 5018/1, fo. 47. On the social background of midwives see Evenden, *Midwives of Seventeenth-Century London*, pp. 16, 71–2, 170, and chaps 4–5.
[81] For example, GL MS 12806/2, fos. 105, 237v.   [82] BRHA BHC 4, fo. 322.
[83] BHC 8, fo. 239v; 1, fo. 201v; 8, fos. 199, 344v.

out of service, nightwalkers, beggars, sabbath-breakers, heavy drinkers, thieves, and other vagrants.[84] Matrons (and midwives) also 'searched' bodies when infanticide or rape charges came to court, or when women were accused of leaving children to see if they had given birth lately. A Silver Street midwife testified that 'a boye childe' born 'dead' in Henry Dissell's house in 1576 had been dead in the womb for 'aboute xiiii daies', and 'was not murthered but dead borne'. Two midwives found solid body-proof that Martha Brookbank had wrongly accused an apprentice of fathering a child on her, as she 'never had noe child'. Sometimes seeing was enough, without touch. Helen Rowse, a sailor's wife from St Katherine's, cut 'the hear from her secreats' in 1600 for 'her guestes to drincke for tobacco', and danced long into the night with just her smock on. The matron confirmed all that was in the charge, although Rowse claimed that her hair was not used as a tobacco substitute.[85]

These 'searches' followed specific charges for the most part. But at other times the court acted on suspicions alone, women were in the wrong place at the wrong time, and made inevitable connections in this manmade culture between women living alone or drinking late and immoral sexualities. The number of sexual offences slumped at Bridewell after 1600, but these links were no weaker for that. Even as numbers tumbled, the court conducted some virginity/chastity 'searches'/'tryalls', pulling women in off streets in situations that stirred suspicions, instructing matrons to check if they were 'maides' or 'noe maides'. The first such 'search' on record was in Winter 1602 and the last in 1645, though they had fizzled out about a decade earlier.[86] There are ninety-five on record, but their impact was more than mere numbers. There is also a seven-year gap after 1610, and the first decade was the peak time for these invasive touches. In verbal and follow-up physical trials, women stood before the court, suffering stares and suspicions from men digging for 'dirty' data with a whipping-room next door. Some gave no ground and hit back with conviction, countering charges in last-ditch efforts to save a last ounce of reputation. The clerk noted that Bridget Laman 'absolutlie denied all and

---

[84] BHC 9, fo. 336; 8, fos. 354, 144, 189v. See also BHC 7, fos. 190v, 253, 295v, 338v; 8, fos. 58v, 102, 137v, 175v, 189v, 199, 233v, 255, 298, 338, 344, 388; 9, fos. 282, 336; BRHA BHC 4, fos. 116v, 303v. In 1560 St Thomas's board ordered that 'no woman is to be received into the house' unless the matron or surgeons had 'searched' her 'to see whether she be with child or no': LMA H1/ST/A1/1, fo. 25v. See also LMA H1/ST/A1/5, fo. 74.

[85] BHC 3, fo. 2; 7, fo. 148v; BRHA BHC 4, fo. 173. See also BHC 2, fo. 233; 5, fo. 139; 7, fo. 187; 8, fos. 97, 136, 176v; Martin Ingram, 'Child sexual abuse in early modern England', in Braddick and Walter eds, *Negotiating Power in Early Modern Society*, pp. 63–84, esp. pp. 70 and 82–3.

[86] BRHA BHC 4, fo. 336; BHC 9, fo. 191.

standeth verie directlie upon it'; that Bridget Evans said she was 'a maide' in 1609 and 'stoode verie confidentlie upon it'; and that Mary Barbor, who left a child at the 'end' of Carter Lane in 1603, 'standes upon her maidenhead'.[87] Not all were telling the truth at this nerve-wracking time. Both Barbor and Evans were found 'too light' or 'no mayde' (Laman's is the one search with no written outcome). Nightwalker Susan Phillips 'tould a faire tale', the court thought in 1610, 'and affirmeth confidentlie that she is a mayde, but was found otherwise'.[88]

In all, sixty women were found to be 'noe maide', 'light', 'unhonest', 'untrue', 'otherwise', 'contrary', 'faulty', or 'harlots' (70.21 per cent), and only four admitted that they were not 'maids' from the start of their examinations in Bridewell. Only one woman was found to be 'greate with childe'.[89] What did women do to earn this invasive treatment at Bridewell? Just over one-in-five of them were said to lead 'suspicious', 'loose', or 'lewde' lives, or they were not able to give a believable account of how they lived from one day to the next. Another five had no service and were up to no good, the court concluded. More than a quarter of the 'searched' women were caught walking after dark, and there were eleven vagrants in their ranks, six 'whores', another six who were snatched in bawdy houses, five thieves, two women who were caught bringing food to prisoners in Bridewell, another pair who were arrested sitting drinking in an alehouse, and a 'verlet'. In all three-in-ten of the 'searched' women were suspected of sex-crimes. 'Loose' Gertrude Bostock was 'founde to lighte and very comon'. Margaret Moxen was 'found to be scant sounde' and admitted to the court that she had twice had sex with a player's son. Elizabeth Hutchinson, 'a suspected comon harlot', was caught in a brothel and 'not found to be as shee should'. Margaret French sounded 'sure' at her 'first coming' to court in 1608, and 'said she was a maide and would stand upon it', but back in court a little later she admitted giving birth to 'two bastards' in the not too distant past.[90] Biographical scraps show that most 'searched' women were single and lacked visible support and a good reason to be in London. Nightwalking Ann Cooley was a rare case of someone with a convincing story who got softer treatment: she had roots in Salisbury, was 'sure' to a Dutchman, and worked spinning 'silver' on Bishopgate Street, a job that her 'kinneswoman' (married to a royal musician) helped her to get.[91] But many more women lived in the restless worlds of cheap lodging, multiple moves, and slipping in and out of service. Marie Barbor rented a room in Seacoal Lane and 'paid a penny

---

[87] BHC 5, fos. 428v, 356v; BRHA BHC 4, fo. 397.   [88] BHC 5, fo. 428v.
[89] Ibid., fo. 119v.   [90] BHC 6, fo. 334; 8, fo. 159v; BRHA BHC 4, fo. 345v.
[91] BHC 7, fo. 286.

a night'. Agnes Healey, who was taken drunk 'ranging the streets' in 1603, had been 'out of service' for five weeks. Peternella Jackson was spotted sleeping under a stall in 1634, and said she was 'noe maide', but offered little else about her life. Another 'no maid', Elizabeth Dorley, could 'not shewe howe she liveth' in 1603 and was told to leave London at once. Some women had only been in the city for a week or so. Others were about to leave for good. Alice Evans, who had 'no certaine place of dwelling', had already handed a bundle of her clothes to a Bristol carrier for the trip back home when she was found to be 'no maide' in 1603.[92]

The court used different words at times, 'noe maide' was more common in the first two decades of 'tryalls', while 'light' was used more often after 1620. Why 'maid' when in fact many of these women were maids of a different sort in households, although sometimes rootless, living on patriarchy's edges out of service? 'Maid' muddled meanings. Thief Dorothy Cox turned out to be 'a mayd out of service' in 1606, and the matron found that she was 'no maide' (she admitted sex with 'one who was executed at Tyburne the last sessions').[93] 'Maid' implies honesty in chastity, and chaste maids were idealized daughters of virtue in conduct books and on the stage. 'Maide', then, was what young working women ought to be, settled in service and under the thumb of a man. A 'maide' played by the conduct book. When Anne Brooke (alias Hutton) ended up in Bridewell in 1604 on a trumped-up charge of living incontinently, she said that 'she is a maide and hath lived honest ever hitherto', and sure enough the matron reported that she was 'a maide'.[94] No woman wanted to be called 'noe maide' and have it on paper to follow her through life. Joyce Reynolds tried to bribe the matron in 1638, promising her two shillings if she would tell the court 'that she was a mayd' to let her start again with a clean slate. Hush money did not work in this case, however.[95] In others women argued different senses of honesty to stop slurs sticking. Mary Taylor was caught red-handed in bed with Richard Moss 'committinge fornicacon' but still 'affirmed herself to be a mayde and stoode confidentlie upon her purgacon'. The matron found otherwise and told the bench that she had not long since had a child. Taylor did not give up, however: 'she notwithstanding mainteyneth her honest behaviour', the clerk noted, saying that 'she hath honestlie demeaned herselfe in dyvers services in good mens howses'. Work with respectable masters meant

---

[92] BRHA BHC 4, fos. 397, 418v; BHC 5, fo. 321; 8, fo. 1; BRHA BHC 4, fos. 356, 434. See also BRHA BHC 4, fos. 366, 366v, 385, 388v, 421; 5, fo. 122v.
[93] BHC 5, fo. 128v.   [94] BRHA BHC 4, fo. 454.   [95] BHC 8, fo. 189v.

more than sexual slip-ups for decency in Taylor's view, or it at least evened out the damage.[96]

The proportion of women found 'cleare' or 'maides' fell after 1617.[97] 'Maides' did not walk free from the court, however, though many did even if they had committed an offence. The court let Elizabeth Parson go back home to Hornsey after she was 'fownde truelie a mayde' in 1610. Another vagrant 'maide' – Frances Jefferson – was given fourpence and a smock and told to leave London. Pilfering Ellen Davies had a lucky let-off in 1607 when she was found to be a 'maide', as the court believed she had robbed 'upon malice'.[98] Other 'maides' were set free even if suspicions still lingered. Mayhem Adams, who was spotted sitting 'veary suspicously' on 'a paire of staires' one night in 1606, was sent back home after the matron gave her a clean bill of morality, even though she lived nervously out of service. While Anne Whitacre, who was caught snooping on Aldersgate Street after midnight and was out on bail after admitting having sex with an 'ambassador', was freed when the court heard that she was a 'mayde' and no one came along 'to accuse her'.[99] Other 'maids' were less lucky and ended up with a whipping and/or a spell in a cell. Anne Eliffe was charged with 'playeinge the queane' with 'a verie boy' in 1609 and 'spoyl[ing] him', but stuck to her story and 'confidentlie den[ied] that she ever had to doe with him or he with her'. The matron 'founde' that she was not 'in any suche case to spoyle him', but she was still whipped for 'appearinge to be a va[grant] ydle queane'. Mary Ichenor was also 'found to [have] never bene nought[y] of her body' a decade later after mixing with 'lewde' men, but she was put back in prison after refusing to go home to Bermondsey.[100] It could also help 'noe maides' to tell the truth from the start, as when Mary Brougton was caught walking late by a marshal in 1632 and admitted that she was 'noe maid' without putting the court to the trouble of a 'search'. She was let off with a warning word because no 'particuler thing' was 'objected against her'.[101]

The women 'searched' did not commit dramatic crimes, and situations leading to their arrests were not dramatic enough to lead to new directions in investigations. They came to court for the same reasons as the much larger number of women who were never 'searched'. The 'searches' were linked to broader gender troubles, but there is nothing remarkable about the date of the first one: 1602. There is no order to start the ball rolling, and no sudden surge of suspicious women coming to court. There are only a couple of lines and not a single word of explanation. Nor will we find a

---

[96] BHC 5, fo. 355v.   [97] BHC 8, fo. 144.
[98] BHC 5, fos. 435, 103, 165v. See also ibid., fos. 41v, 42, 93.
[99] Ibid., fos. 118; 8, fo. 298. See also BHC 5, fo. 345; 6, fo. 215.
[100] BHC 5, fo. 374; BHC 6, fo. 120. See also BHC 6, fo. 215.   [101] BHC 7, fo. 272v.

word about the 'searches' in Court of Aldermen records. Their roots lie deep in Bridewell's process, though there was no new matron in 1602, who might have tipped off the bench of a better way to get evidence from bodies. And to muddle matters still further, 'searches' tail off at the same time around 1635 when the number of female offenders soared and a spate of by-laws dealt directly with women's crimes. This should have been a boom time for 'searches' according to perceptions and policies. There is no order to bring 'searches' to an end, and no nasty mix-up or botched 'search' scary enough to stop them at once. Perhaps something now lost would fill in some gaps for us. But what might have made a difference as 'searches' slowed down was the large leap in female recidivism in the decade after 1625, when eight-in-ten of Bridewell's 'old gessts' were women. A likely impact of this returning train might have been less need to establish the facts of lives and bodies. Some evidence suggests that 'old customers' were less likely to be 'searched' than new faces in the courtroom.

Weeks or even months could slip by without a 'search' in Bridewell, but they did go on there for over four decades, and nothing else can tell us so much about female bodies there. They produced physical evidence to back up the cultural assumptions held by men on the bench. Not one woman challenged the outcome of her 'search', although some insisted that they were 'maids'. They tried to outfox the court and questioned its core assumptions about them if they failed. Perhaps most women doubted that matrons would find anything incriminating. Others, who knew themselves to be 'maids', saw a chance to leave the court vindicated, even though they felt offended. Women had more bodies of evidence than men for Bridewell's court.

## Punishment

We think of whips when we think of punishment inside Bridewell, and perhaps long bouts of hard work also. But bodies were not just physical things. People thought and felt inside these shells, and work was believed to be a moral correction that trained thoughts for the better. Likewise, emotions did not suddenly freeze when whips stung backs. Pain was not only a shock to the skin and systems, it was thought to be cultural and a matter of minds, turning thoughts with sharp spasms. Pain's shock was meant to make people feel better not bitter. Cheapside's whipping post was revealingly called the 'post of reformation'.[102] There was much more

---

[102] Esther Cohen, 'The animated pain of the body', *American Historical Review*, 105 (2000), 36–68, esp. 42; LMA Reps. 20, fo, 293; 23, fo. 60. Cf. Peter Lake and Michael Questier, 'Agency, appropriation, and rhetoric under the gallows: puritans, romanists, and the

to whippings than violence and no neat split between bodies and minds, as Foucault and others after him have taught us. Such a split would have seemed strange to religious reformers who made minds their top priority or advocates of spiritual medicine to soothe suffering, or in legal systems where mind-acts like amendment were considered to be good outcomes and character could make all the difference. Bodies and emotions were coupled, as in Erasmus's visual-verbal remark that the 'outward honesty of the body cometh of the soul well composed and ordered'.[103] People from all walks of life were asked to delve deep into their souls by the reformed religion, and magistrates and ministers agreed about the need to reform black sheep. Affecting souls was a leading aim in judicial process, all the way to 'last dying words' on gallows, coaxed by ministers to offer doomed felons solace in salvation. Correcting small character faults followed on from ideas that first flaws were the roots of awful felonies, unless reform stopped the rot. This slide started with sloppy morals and soon picked up speed. It was critical to nip crime in the bud. Touchstone lectures Quicksilver his apprentice in *Eastward Ho*, who is shortly to hang on Tyburn's tree: 'You see the issue of your sloth. Of sloth comes pleasure, of pleasure cometh riot, of riot comes whoring, of whoring

state in early modern England', *Past and Present*, 153 (1996), 64–107, esp. 71; Elizabeth Hanson, *Discovering the Subject in Renaissance England* (Cambridge, 1998), pp. 24–55; Thomas Adams, *The White Devil, Or the Hypocrite Uncased* (1613), pp. 22–3: clean disordered sinews 'by correction, relieve them with punishment, and so recover them to the life of obedience'.

[103] Andrew McRae, *God Speed the Plough: the Representation of Rural England, 1500–1660* (Cambridge, 1996), p. 67; Margaret Healy, *Fictions of Disease in Early Modern England: Bodies, Plagues and Politics* (Basingstoke, 2001), esp. pp. 28–34; Rublack, *Crimes of Women*, pp. 44–5; Christina Vanja, 'Madhouses, children's wards and clinics: the development of insane asylums in Germany', in Norbert Finzsch and Robert Jutte, eds., *Institutions of Confinement: Hospitals, Asylums, and Prisons in Western Europe and North America, 1500–1950* (Cambridge, 1996), pp. 117–32, esp. p. 126; Carole Rawcliffe, *Medicine for the Soul: the Life, Death and Resurrection of an English Medieval Hospital* (Stroud, 1999), esp. pp. 161, 170. For some contemporary indications see the Edwardian *Exhortation to Good Order*, quoted by McRae, *God Speed the Plough*, p. 120; *The Diary of Ralph Josselin, 1616–1683*, ed. Alan Macfarlane, British Academy Records of Economic and Social History, New Series, III (1976), pp. 39, 58, 114, 438, 600; Edward Heron, *Physicke for Body and Soule* (1621); John Strype, *A Survey of the Cities of London and Westminster: Containing the Original, Antiquity, Increase, Modern Estate and Government of Those Cities, Written at First in the Year MDXCVIII by John Stow ... Corrected, Improved, and Very Much Enlarged: and the Survey and History Brought Down from the Year 1633*, 5 books in 2 vols. (1720), V, p. 257; *The Arraignment and Burning of Margaret Fern-seede, for the Murther of Her Late Husband Anthony Fern-Seede* (1609), fo. B2. Erasmus is quoted in Martin Ingram, 'Sexual manners: the other face of civility in early modern England', in Peter Burke, Brian Harrison, and Paul Slack, eds. *Civil Histories: Essays Presented to Sir Keith Thomas* (Oxford, 2000), pp. 87–109, at p. 93. See also Jones and Stallybrass, *Renaissance Clothing*, esp. chap. 1; Patricia Allerston, 'Clothing and early modern Venetian society', *Continuity and Change*, 15 (2000), 367–90, esp. 367.

comes spending, of spending comes want, of want comes theft, of theft comes hanging.'[104] It was only a matter of time unless work and whipping swayed small-time thieves or work-shy layabouts to toe the line. Antisocial acts or character faults were corrected in Bridewell for good with any luck. 'In a word', one author observed, even the most badly behaved 'profligates' can be 'saved' from 'infamous deaths' on the gallows with help from bridewells.[105]

Work and whipping were not just bodily disciplines. Work was character building and whipping made people think about what they had done and might one day become. The leading legal handbook of the day urged justices to put offenders in bridewells, so that 'by labour and punishment of their bodies their forward natures may be bridled, their evil minds bettered, and others by their example terrified'.[106] Care for character change had been evident ever since Bridewell first opened. House-rules made it clear that people were locked up there 'for theire reformacon'. Reformation was *the* burning issue of the day all through Bridewell's first century, and reforming manners was a long-running aim.[107] It would seem strange if this did not affect the modus operandi in houses of correction or 'reformation', as the one in Acle (Norfolk) was aptly called. The sharpest legal mind of the early seventeenth century said that few are shut up in 'the house of correction or working house but they come out better'.[108]

Pious words were spoken in Bridewell's court, chapel, and catechism classes in godly 'admonicions' or 'exhortacons'. A matron was sacked for a string of abuses in 1622 that included 'not endeavouring to reforme' women under her wing, 'but winking at their lewdnes'. The court asked 'a

---

[104] G. Chapman *et al.*, *Eastward Ho*, 1605, Tudor Facsimile Texts (New York, 1970), fo. G3v. Cf. W. Chappell, ed., *The Roxburghe Ballads*, Ballad Society, 14 vols. (1869–95), vol. III, part 1, pp. 1–5, 25–8, 36–41; J. A. Sharpe, *Crime in Early Modern England, 1550–1750*, 2nd edition (Harlow, 1999), pp. 230–3; Lincoln B. Faller, *Turned to Account: the Forms and Functions of Criminal Biography in Late Seventeenth- and Early Eighteenth-Century England* (Cambridge, 1987), chaps 2–3 and 5; Philip Rawlings, *Drunks, Whores, and Idle Apprentices: Criminal Biographies of the Eighteenth Century* (1992), esp. pp. 19–22.

[105] Robert Moss, *A Sermon Preach'd Before the Right Honourable the Lord Mayor of London, the Court of Aldermen, and the Governors of the Several Hospitals of the City, at the Parish Church of St Sepulchre ... in Easter Week* (1709), p. 15.

[106] Michael Dalton, *The Country Justice* (1661 edition), p. 122. Cf. Kathy Stuart, *Defiled Trades and Social Outcasts: Honour and Ritual Pollution in Early Modern Germany* (Cambridge, 1999), pp. 143–4; Robert Jutte, *Poverty and Deviance in Early Modern Europe* (Cambridge, 1994), p. 169.

[107] LMA Jour. 20, fo. 502v; Martin Ingram, 'Reforming manners in early modern England', in Paul Griffiths, Adam Fox, and Steve Hindle, eds., *The Experience of Authority in Early Modern England* (Basingstoke, 1996), pp. 47–88.

[108] Edward Coke, *The Second Part of the Institutes of the Lawes of England* (1644), p. 729.

reverend preacher of Gods word' (Mr Egerton) to 'convert' two 'famous harlots', Ellen Bedford and Mary Newborough, in 1603. They gave 'good eare' to his 'good instrucons', but Mary 'in outward shewe seemed to have the more repentinge and meltinge hart'. Character change was expected from all people, regardless of background or breeding. Heavy-drinking governors were banned from court in 1639 until their colleagues were 'truly' sure of their 'reformacons'.[109] Pliant and penitent people got softer handling. Agnes Manori said that Alviza Pavenla had 'the carnall use of her bodie', but was punished 'with some moderation' after 'see-minge penitent'. Others escaped punishment altogether for seeming 'sorrowful' or 'penitent', and pledging not to 'offend in the like faulte againe'. Frances Richardson was caught walking late but was spared whipping after 'her faithfull promise of amendment of her idle life'. Drunk Francis Taylor vowed to 'become a new man' in 1639 after daily troubling his master and mother. Other drunks, loudmouths, night-walkers, or surly servants escaped lightly after giving word to lead better lives.[110] There were also grounds for hope if people were put back under the thumbs of household heads. A 'nightwalker' was set free in 1641 after her husband 'promised to keep her at home and reforme her'. 'Bad' Anthony Ferris was handed back to his master after scratching his face, 'in hope that hee wil become a better servaunt'. Marriage also raised expectations of a brighter life. Mary Austin wriggled free from a fornication charge in 1600 by 'beinge verie penitent for her evell life' and also saying that she was 'ready to marrye, whereby [the court said] she may become an honest woman'.[111] These were mind-acts calling for character change, although still tied to bodies through punishment if things did not work out. Minds mattered at Bridewell. Some inmates talked about their stormy consciences or how remorse either made them give themselves in or file cases. Elizabeth Pennyfeather said that it was concern for 'her owne creditt' that 'moved' her to reveal 'a most filthie and notorious synne of adulterye committed by Agnes Fisher' in 1602, because she could not 'in conscience' 'conceale so vile a facte'. Joseph Yarner also turned over his thoughts, saying that he 'repent[ed]' of his 'fault' straight after having sex with Joanne Angel, and found comfort in another bed, alone.[112]

---

[109] BHC 6, fo. 274; 8, fo. 226v; BRHA 4, fo. 346.
[110] BRHA BHC 4, fos. 337, 12v, 193v, 447, 467v; BHC 5, fo. 361v. See also BRHA BHC 4, fos. 5v, 47, 95v, 419v, 451. Some petitioners wrote of their 'true sorrow and repentance' when begging royal ministers for help to get out of Bridewell. See, for example, TNA SP16/451/106.
[111] BHC 8, fo. 356; BRHA BHC 4, fos. 334v, 175v.
[112] BRHA BHC 4, fos. 335–5v, 436.

Movement into bridewells is often imagined like revolving doors, with inmates only staying for the time it took to get warned and whipped. They did not leave lasting impressions on inmates, then, no matter what their rules said. A surge of vagrants after 1600 put an end to this high hope in the long run.[113] But not all offenders were shunted in and out of London Bridewell. Revealingly, it was called a 'prison' holding 'prisoners'. One woman was locked up from sunrise to sunset in 1603 after having sex with a man who was not her husband. But Lodowick Bowyer was locked up for the rest of his life to stop him 'infect[ing] others of like lewd life'. Edward Sanderford was also given a life sentence in 1642, almost certainly because he was a political prisoner in highly charged times.[114] Clerks noted how long someone had been locked up now and then, but apart from chance comments the only way to know the length of these stretches is to find a record of release. I have a small sample of 200 sentences to give us an idea of the length of time prisoners spent in Bridewell. There are a lot of short-stays: vagrants, young runaways, thieves, nightwalkers, scolds, sex-offenders, and badly behaved children and servants, who were locked up for a handful of days to shake them up a little. All spent less than a week in the cells; three days is the most mentioned short stay. A little under one-quarter walked free after a few days. Another thirty-two spent a week in Bridewell. In all, fewer than half of these sentences were for a week or less (80/200). Six-in-ten prisoners stayed for longer than a week, and some spent even longer there. 'Lewd' Joan Leech (alias Canon), who was sent in by Parliament's purger, Pride, in 1649, was ordered 'to worke for a yeare'. A gang of five men were sentenced – 'per Act of Parliament' – 'to remaine att labor for one whole yeare' in 1650. The court warned the 'comon nightwalker' Martha Jackson that she would be locked up for a full year 'if ever shee came in againe'.[115]

A year in prison is not a soft option, even today. Other prisoners spent over six months in Bridewell's cells. Joan Dunning was locked up for falling out with neighbours in 1641, and was still behind bars seven months later. Frances Knott spent eight months in prison for 'gadding' in 1559. Another 'gadder', Bridget Abell, worked in Bridewell for six months in the next year. Light-fingered Henry Morgan was locked up for a little more than six months in 1642: 'a great while', the clerk noted in the

---

[113] This is the line followed in Joanna Innes, 'Prisons for the poor: English bridewells 1555–1800', in Francis Snyder and Douglas Hay, eds., *Labour, Law, and Crime: a Historical Perspective* (Oxford, 1987), pp. 42–122; and A. L. Beier, *Masterless Men: the Vagrancy Problem in England, 1560–1640* (1985).

[114] BRHA BHC 4, fo. 422; BHC 8, fo. 351; 9, fo. 1v. Bowyer was locked up in Bridewell 'by order of Star Chamber', and was fined a whopping £3,000.

[115] BHC 9, fos. 376, 436; 8, fo. 404.

book. Radicals Lodowick Muggleton and John Reeve were handed six-month sentences a decade later with a threat to lock them up for longer if they still spouted their dangerous doctrines.[116] A higher number of trouble-makers stayed behind bars for one, two, or three months. A 'straggling' woman was locked up in Bridewell for two months in 1559, as was a woman who sold flesh in Lent: 'a longe ponyshment', the clerk added this time. Vagrant Anne Darke spent two months in Bridewell. A vagrant nightwalker worked for three months there in 1606, three weeks longer than Ellen Holland, who was caught red-handed stealing from her master in 1638.[117] A mixed group of beggars, nightwalkers, vagrants, drunks, pickpockets, and pilferers were all locked up in Bridewell for around a month. A woman walked free in 1606 after a month in the cells, 'in regard' of her 'longe imprisonmente and repentance' for her 'lewdnes'.[118]

These sentences might seem on the short side, though we should not do these sums by today's standards when longer sentences are the rule and pass by unremarked, unless unfair. A month or more of tough work behind high walls might have been a scary prospect in a society that was still not used to soft or stiff custodial sentences. 'Mere fear' of Bridewell was a threat that was often used to get people to follow the rules.[119] Bridewell was not a cheery place. Prison, Geoffrey Mynshul wrote in 1638, was 'a grave to bury men alive', 'a little world of woe', 'a map of misery', and 'stinks more than the lord mayor's dogge-house or Paris Garden in August'.[120] Clerks noted that a month was a 'long' time or that six months was a 'great while', and sometimes they simply scribbled that prisoners had spent 'a longe tyme in the house', they had 'ben longe in this house', or had spent 'a greate while' there. All hinting that prison was painful, that losing freedom for a month was frightening, and that an idea of 'long' imprisonment existed, different to today, but no less tough for that.[121] And the number of short three or four day stays dropped after

---

[116] BHC 8, fos. 354, 389; 1, fos. 28v, 29v, 63v; 8, fos. 362, 383; 9, fo. 628. See also BHC 1, fo. 82; 5, fos. 33, 102, 109; 6, fo. 39v; 8, fos. 175v, 329; 9, fo. 257; BRHA BHC 4, fos. 192v, 232v, 237v.

[117] BHC 1, fos. 42, 63; BRHA BHC 4, fo. 260; BHC 8, fo. 175v.

[118] BHC 5, fo. 30v. See also BHC 1, fos. 35v, 73v; 5, fos. 101v, 229, 249v; 6, fos. 34, 39v; 8, fos. 215, 249, 329, 377v, 383, 405, 414; 9, fos. 341, 342, 343; BRHA BHC 4, fos. 79v, 189v.

[119] Innes, 'Prisons for the poor', p. 105. See also my 'Bodies and souls in Norwich: punishing petty crime, 1540–1700', in Simon Devereaux and Paul Griffiths, eds., *Penal Practice and Culture, 1500–1900: Punishing the English* (Basingstoke, 2004), pp. 85–120, esp. p. 104.

[120] Geoffrey Mynshul, *Characters of Prisons and Prisoners* (1638), p. 3.

[121] BHC 5, fos. 30v, 98v, 102, 106; 8, fos. 363, 377v, 379, 383; 5, fos. 64, 109, 293, 300; BRHA BHC 4, fos. 207v, 241v, 242, 257, 345v, 352, 392, 396.

1620. The court still singled-out particular people for stiff sentences, even if the bulk of offenders did not spend more than a morning there. The doors kept turning for many, but not for all, and the court sorted out offenders for short or long stays, acting prudently and selectively, on a case-by-case basis.

Not much separates short- and long-stay prisoners in terms of offences. They all committed small slip-ups or character flaws. The nature of the offence mattered less than an offender's character and track record. Recidivists got shorter shrift and longer stretches, like 'lewd' Leech sent in by Colonel Pride: she 'will not bee reformed', the court moaned. 'Comon pickepockett' Richard Gladwell was locked up for three months in 1646: 'often here', the clerk noted.[122] With limited space in cells the court chose who to lock up for longer stretches, and the likelihood of character change ranked high in priorities. Some recidivists would never change for the better and wasted resources. Three men with nothing to live on were taken in 'a house of ill fame' in 1634 and were treated differently in court: one was 'not knowne here' and was warned and freed, but the other two were 'comon pilferers' with giveaway brands on hands, and they were both locked up for a month.[123] Some long-stay offenders came from other courts in London. City and Middlesex quarter sessions sent offenders who were often locked up for a month or more. A group of five men got six-month sentences, while a woman was jailed for one year in 1651. The number of thieves sent from sessions after branding or lesser charges of petty felony edged up after 1600, as elsewhere. They were sentenced to a month or longer of 'hard labor', though longer stretches were not rare.[124]

Prisoners also ended up in armies. The Crown asked the City to round up 'strong bodied' or 'able young' vagrants when it needed troops, not doddering old tramps.[125] Large numbers were requested: 1,000 for the Palatinate in 1625, 6,000 for 'the king of Sweden' in 1631, and 3,000 for the Scottish Wars.[126] This was one way of cleaning London. 'Great good' follows pressing 'idle and loose people', the Crown said in 1601. 'Tapsters, ostlers', 'lewd' watermen and other tarred jobs were also targeted for the press. Lists of 'straungers' were drawn up in 1580 for

---

[122] BHC 9, fos. 376, 254; 6, fo. 235v.   [123] BHC 7, fo. 360.
[124] BHC 9, fos. 807, 420, 511, 801. John Beattie analyses the growing number of petty larcenists sent to Bridewell after 1660 in *Policing and Punishment in London 1660–1750: Urban Crime and the Limits of Terror* (Oxford, 2001), pp. 24–33, 95–7.
[125] LMA Jours. 22, fo. 321; 35, fo. 316; TNA SP16/195/33; APC 1601–4, p. 145; LMA Jours. 22, fo. 321; 33, fo. 23; Rep. 23, fo. 25v; Remembrancia Book 8, fos. 28v-9.
[126] LMA Remembrancia Book 8, fos. 29–31, 123v-4; Jour. 35, fo. 316; TNA SP16/195/33.

an army to cross the Irish Sea.[127] Officers swooped on cheap boarding houses, alehouses, and 'tobaccoe houses' to get ward quotas. Pressed men stayed in Bridewell before leaving for the coast: 100 vagrants rounded up in pubs were left there after surprise 'searches' in 1640; another seventy-eight were left in 1599 for the Low Countries. Bridewell officers got bonuses for guarding soldiers 'in the yard' in 1600; the damage bill after one press reached £22 15s 8d. Other pressed men stayed in Leadenhall. Anne Crosby got in trouble 'for the fowle sinne of whoredome most shamelessly amongest the soldiers att Leadenhall' in 1624 (some Newgate felons also had the choice to go to war to save their necks).[128] Bridewell prisoners signed up for armies in dribs and drabs, though sixteen were pressed on one day in 1604 and fourteen at a single sitting for the Low Countries in 1605. Thirty-six more were shipped to 'Swethland' in one go in 1609.[129] Captains took all sorts from London's basements (see Appendix Table 9c): vagrants, rogues, cheats, cutpurses, pickpockets, bowling-alley addicts, heavy-drinkers, hat-snatchers, jail-breakers, work-shy layabouts, suspected felons, acquitted felons, and tinkers. Four-in-ten of all pressed men from Bridewell were vagrants. Some 'old customers' ended up in armies. The expert cutpurse Stacey Powell took press money in 1632. 'Lewd' and 'idle' Abraham Aliborne, who had been 'burned in the hand', was pressed into 'the service of the state' in 1643. Eight pickpockets were pressed in one batch in 1631.[130]

In all, 820 men joined armies from Bridewell between 1604–58. Numbers fell over time: only thirty-seven were pressed between 1634–42, just twelve over the next seven years, and not a single one in 1649–58. Some would-be soldiers were turned down if unfit to 'bear arms'. Wards set up second presses in 1640 after pulling in a second-rate crop of 'unfit' men. Lame Anthony Harley was below par in 1608. Humphrey West was 'not fitt to goe for a souldier' in 1627 because he was 'often druncke'. Recruit Henry Wyatt was given a pass to go home in

---

[127] APC 1601–4, pp. 145, 27–8, 74–5; LMA Jours. 33, fo. 23; 39, fo. 68v; TNA SP16/195/15; LMA Rep. 20, fos. 90, 117.
[128] TNA SP16/450/26; BRHA BHC 4, fos. 80, 158v; BHC 9, fos. 200, 213; 6, fo. 383. For felons see TNA SP12/28/63, 12/229/84, 14/107/27, 14/111/146, 14/140/28, 14/170/28, 14/184/54, 14/188/44, 16/59/58, 16/183/16, 16/188/86. Cf. K. J. Kesselring, *Mercy and Authority in the Tudor State* (Cambridge, 2003), pp. 32–5 and 83–7. Some compter inmates were also sent to the wars: for example, TNA SP/12/185/84.
[129] BHC 6, fo. 392; BRHA BHC 4, fo. 429; BHC 5, fos. 64, 352v; 6, fos. 183, 183v; 7, fo. 43. See also BHC 5, fos. 86v, 105v, 192, 211, 347v, 395v; 6, fos. 391, 424, 436; 7, fos. 41v, 45, 141v, 232v; BRHA BHC 4, fos. 36v, 87, 171; *Letters of Philip Gaudy of West Harling, Norfolk, and of London, to Various Members of his Family, 1579–1616*, ed., Issac Herbert Jeayes (1906), pp. 120–1.
[130] BHC 7, fos. 232, 282; 9, fo. 61.

1621.[131] Apprentices could not join up without their masters' blessing. Two who 'offered themselves to be prest' were locked up when their story fell apart.[132] People could not be shoved into armies against their will. This was in name at least a choice, but the alternative of scraping a living on streets was not a bright one. Records reveal people 'willing', 'desirous', or 'content' to put their name down for the press (though two men were pressed for 'souldiers for Denmark againste theire wills' in 1627). The Crown sought 200 'voluntary soldiers for Ostend' in 1601. Vagrant Robert Addis 'was willing to be a soldier voluntary' in 1628. Four vagrants were 'desirous to go for souldiers to the low countries' in 1632. A cutpurse was 'sent for a souldier' by 'his owne consent' in 1637. While two East India Company 'garblers' who pilfered 'the best nutmeggs and other spices' 'agreed' to be 'prest for soldiers' in 1624.[133] There was a choice on the table, but the press was not popular. One observer heard 'murmurs' in 1639 as captains looked for soldiers. A constable was bullied when 'pressing' soldiers for Scotland a year later. William Mosten 'abused the seriant of States' when he walked up and down banging a drum 'for voluntaryes' in 1629. Ludowick Holland, vintner at the Welsh Harp in Grays Inn Lane, mocked a captain who came for vagrants in 1606 and left empty-handed after Holland talked them out of it. Some did U-turns, like the thief Richard Ayre, who 'at first desired to goe', but had second thoughts later.[134] Others deserted after taking press money. Francis Ancotts was caught sliding down a rope dangling from a Bridewell window in 1627. 'Grub the marshals man' ran a racket substituting 'prest souldiers'. 'Idle queane' Gillian Wallinger got 'soldiers released for money' in 1625, saying they were her husband.[135] Raw recruits bolted clutching press money. John Hunt gave Sir George Fleetwood's officers a wrong name and the slip after taking press money. Some apprentices took press money from a captain in 1604 for beer money. One observer blasted the 'usual custom of divers of the ruder sort' after getting a shilling 'to jeer and bragg that they will drink for his majesty's sake'. Some 'rude' rabble took money from more than one

---

[131] TNA SP16/195/33; BHC 7, fo. 438; LMA Jour. 39, fo. 70; BHC 5, fo. 266v; 7, fo. 225; 9, fo. 115. See also BHC 7, fo. 22v; LMA Jour. 22, fo. 321; Remembrancia Book 8, fo. 28v.
[132] BHC 7, fo. 46.
[133] Ibid., fo. 41v; APC 1601–4, p. 145; BHC 7, fos. 67, 251, 367; 8, fos. 133, 334; 5, fo. 139v.
[134] CSPV 1636–9, p. 524; LMA MJ/SBR/7, fo. 93; BHC 5, fo. 139v; 7, fos. 136v, 298v, 128v. See also BHC 6, fos. 382, 397; 7, fos. 41v, 114v, 128v, 349v; 8, fo. 136v.
[135] BHC 5, fos. 46v, 39; 6, fo. 401v. See also BHC 5, fos. 28, 77, 233, 303; 7, fos. 97, 229, 288v; 8, fos. 131, 133, 414; 9, fo. 59; BRHA BHC 4, fos. 62, 234v, 373v; LMA Rep. 21, fo. 580v; Remembrancia Book 8, fo. 28v; TNA SP14/181/53, 16/455/102; LMA MJ/SBR/4, fos. 550, 604.

captain. Richard Hedger duped six captains in 1643. Other deserters sold their new army clothes at the first opportunity.[136] Troops also caused trouble once on the road, stealing, brawling, or looking for chances to run away. 350 men set out for Chester in 1600 but only 140 made it to ships, while another troop of 200 was cut to sixty by the time it reached the docks. Some soldiers slipped over the side of ships. There were also mutinies on ships moored in the Thames. John Trenitt sparked one on board Captain Lostley's ship in 1627. Mutinies also hit Bridewell. A pair of 'sturdy roagues' who had just been 'tryed at Newgate uppon theire lives' and pardoned for the press started one there in 1626.[137] Reprisals were swift. Four deserters stood on the gallows in 1627 casting dice 'for their lives'. Magistrates wanted 'extraordinary' and 'exemplary correction' to 'terrify' others when a mutiny broke out in 1627; the ringleaders were put on the Tower Hill pillory and all had an ear chopped off.[138]

Nor should we forget that transportation was more commonly used at first to get rid of small-fry offenders. Bridewell looms large in its first few decades. This all began with an agreement between the City and the Virginia Company in 1618 to sweep up homeless boys and girls to give them a fresh start overseas with promises of fifty acres of land and corn and cattle at the end of their training: at age twenty-four for boys and twenty-one or marriage for girls (the age for boys dropped to twenty-one in 1619). Exactly 100 children set sail for Virginia from Bridewell in 1619, with other shiploads following soon after. Children from hard-up homes were also sent overseas to 'ease' burdens on poor families. More boys sailed on these first ships: seventy-six 'boys' and twenty-four 'wenches' left on the first one.[139] Pauper parents were told that handouts would be stopped if they kept their children at home. A royal ruling gave authority to punish stubborn parents in 1620. Another 100 boys were shipped in two batches in 1622.[140] Parish collections covered

---

[136] BHC 8, fo. 131; BRHA BHC 4, fo. 456; TNA SP16/354/113; BHC 9, fo. 67. See also BRHA BHC 4, fos. 79v, 145; LMA Jours 22, fo. 107; 35, fo. 356v; 39, fo. 70v.
[137] SRPJ (12), pp. 32–4; (281), pp. 667–9; LMA MJ/SBR/5, fo. 39; APC 1599–1600, pp. 620–1; TNA SP16/450/58; APC 1628–9, p. 33; BHC 5, fo. 43; 6, fo. 421.
[138] APC 1627, p. 257; TNA SP12/202/8. See also TNA SP16/61/2.
[139] LMA Jour. 30, fos. 374, 382, 396, 397v; BHC 6, fo. 101v. See also Robert C. Johnson, 'The transportation of vagrant children from London to Virginia, 1618–1622', in Howard S. Reinmuth, ed., *Early Stuart Studies: Essays in Honour of David Harris* (Minneapolis, MN, 1970), pp. 137–51; Joanna Innes, 'The role of transportation in seventeenth- and eighteenth-century English penal practice', in Carl Bridge, ed., *New Perspectives in Australian History* (1990), pp. 1–24. See also Abbot Emerson Smith, *Colonists in Bondage: White Servitude and Convict Labour in America, 1607–1776* (Chapel Hill, NC, 1947), chaps 5 and 7.
[140] LMA Jour. 31, fos. 125–5v, 128v, 129; APC 1619–21, p. 118; LMA Rep. 36, fos. 170, 196v.

clothing and shipping costs: £7 3s 4d from St Helen Bishopgate for the 'Virginia busines' in 1619; a little less from St James Garlickhithe for shipping 'children to Virgeny'; and a lot less from All Hallows Staining 'for Virginia boys'.[141] Parishes also added money for clothes, apprenticeship fees, travel to the dockside, or for preachers who took the word to the New World. One forked out 8/6d 'for a suite of apparel, a capp, hose and shoes for William Smith', who was shipped to Virginia in 1622, and six shillings to cart another boy to a ship docked at Gravesend.[142] Parishes spent similar sums all through the 1620s and after, and later on paupers were also given help to get across the sea to Barbados. By now whole families were setting sail for a second chance in a new place; one parish spent three pounds to put William Caxton and his family on board a ship to Virginia in 1650.[143]

Bridewell started to ship trouble-makers on its own initiative as early as February 1618, when a boy who would not be 'ruled' was kept until a ship was ready to set sail.[144] Other courts were also quick off the mark; two Newgate felons were spared from the gallows in 1619, so long as they took a ship for Virginia. London's first surviving sessions files are wrapped in casings with lists of felons earmarked for ships rather than death scribbled in now faded ink.[145] Patchy records mean that we will never know the true numbers, but more petty offenders crossed the Atlantic before 1650. Bridewell books list 1,106 trouble-makers kept for boats between 1618–58. Not all boarded ships, however, as these are orders not outcomes. But most of them are never heard of again. Numbers dropped from a high point in the 1620s but still stayed steady. Only one-in-ten people transported were women before the mid-1630s, but this then doubled between 1634–42, and climbed a little more by 1658 (24.28 per cent).[146] Nearly all settled in Virginia in the first decade or so, but numbers sailing for the Caribbean edged up from the mid-1620s on with a fall after 1635 (see Appendix Table 9b). One thief, Philip Trumball, was

---

[141] LMA Jour. 30 fo. 396; Reps. 35, fo. 58; 36, fos. 196v, 275; GL MSS 6836, fo. 95v; 4180/1, fo. 196; 4956/2, fo. 283v. See also GL MSS 1124/1, fo. 27; 4383/1, fo. 218; 878/1, fo. 132; 4423/1, fo. 91; 4385/1, fo. 128v; 590/1, fo. 104v; 4071/2, fo. 46v; 645/1, fo. 34; 4409/1, fo. 129; 4956/2, fo. 314v; 1432/3, fo. 127v; 959/1, fo. 137v; 4051/1, fo. 21; 2601/1, fo. 14v.

[142] GL MS 4524/1, fos. 201v, 206. See also GL MSS 4423/1, fo. 199; 951/1, fo. 63; 1303/1, 1636; 4071/2, fo. 97v; 6574, fo. 114; 6552/1, fo. 163v; 4180/2, fos. 9v, 18; 4524/1, fos. 182, 190v, 256; 4409/1, fo. 163; 959/1, fo. 146v.

[143] GL MS 3146/1, fo. 17. See also GL MSS 6552/1, fo. 212; 3146/1, fo. 29v; 1568, fo. 662.

[144] BHC 6, fo. 28v.

[145] LMA CQSF 88/membrane. See also LMA CQSF 126/membrane; 127/membrane; 128/membrane; TNA SP16/391/116; Smith, *Colonists in Bondage*, chap. 5.

[146] In all, 918 men and 190 women (17.15 per cent) agreed to go overseas to the colonies.

shipped to the East Indies in 1640. Only one vagrant boy and four 'poore vagrant girles' were sent to New England, all in 1643, but destinations were rarely jotted down by this time.[147] There were many court days when no one was sent to a colony. Like soldiers, prisoners were shipped in dribs and drabs, though largish groups were sometimes sent at a single sitting: sixteen on one day before Christmas 1619, thirteen on another busy day two months later, and sixteen more over two consecutive court days in 1631.[148] A hodgepodge of offenders were put on ships, but most numerous by far were vagrants (see Appendix Table 9a): in cases where offences are recorded, over six-in-ten prisoners 'kept' for ships were vagrants (63.10 per cent).[149] Others who set sail for the New World included nearly 100 thieves, forty-one people caught walking after curfew, twenty-six nightwalkers, twenty-one badly behaved servants, forty-five beggars, five cheats, one drunk, and a single ballad-singer.

Also like pressed men, prisoners were not transported against their will. To stay on the safe side, clerks nearly always noted that prisoners gave their 'owne consent' and were 'willing' to set sail, noting that Thomas Wallins, who begged to get by, 'will goe to a plantacon and he may goe'.[150] The appearance of choice mattered in an institution whose legal standing was questioned now and then. Capham Strange 'came hither and offered himselfe to goe to Virginia with Captaine Tucker', the clerk wrote in 1629. A vagrant pilferer was kept 'at his owne request' until a ship was ready to sail in 1632, 'if any will take him', the clerk added. The old-hand pickpocket Richard Braithwaite was 'willing to goe beyond the seas' in 1632.[151] People had straight choices. John Wilton was told to get a service soon or get on board a ship bound for Virginia. A pilfering 'houseboy', Richard Webb, was put to work until he made his mind up to either 'go to a plantacon' or get his sister to find someone willing to take him as an apprentice.[152] Some women already had husbands across the ocean, but not all of them were anxious to join them. The bench had a sneaking suspicion that 'lewd' Elizabeth Whelpston was up to no good when she was caught walking late in 1630, and it took bail

---

[147] BHC 8, fo. 318v; 9, fos. 22, 25. The clerk simply starts to note that people were shipped 'overseas'. This is the case with 15/155 cases from 1627–34, 114/215 in 1634–42, and 343/350 from 1642–58. When we do have a good number of destinations the balance between North America and the Caribbean is as follows: 1618–26, Virginia 381/Carribean 7; 1626–34, Virginia 85/Carribean 53; 1634–42, Virginia 73/Carribean 27.
[148] BHC 6, fos. 163, 172v; 7, fos. 238, 238v.
[149] We have the offences of 721 people who agreed to go 'overseas'. In another 432 cases we only have information about the officer who brought the offender to court or no specific offence is listed in courtbooks: 122 offenders were simply said to be 'old prisoners'.
[150] BHC 8, fo. 413.   [151] BHC 7, fos. 148v, 275, 276.
[152] BHC 6, fo. 171; 8, fo. 313. See also BHC 8, fos. 238v, 241, 349; 9, fos. 361, 654.

to get her to sail to the 'Somer Islands' (Bermuda) to join her husband. There was less shilly-shallying with Elizabeth Clarke, who 'promised' to sail on the next ship to Barbados where her husband now lived, after she was caught taking '16 ells' of 'packing lynen' from a draper's shop.[153]

One rule of thumb was that young people could not board ships without a parent's or master's blessing. Thomas Busley, a 'vagrant pilfering boy', could not board ship until the court learned if 'itt bee certainly knowne' if he is an 'apprentice of London'. A house officer talked with Robert Park's master in 1628 'to see if it be true' that he gave him his go-ahead to sail to Virginia. John Seaman's master was glad to get him off his hands on a boat to Barbados after he robbed his 'goods' in 1632. James Johnson's mother and master were 'well contented' to let him sail to Barbados in 1648. One master talked his apprentice out of 'goeing to a plantacon' in 1639, even though he was eager to go.[154] A parent's word was enough in other cases. William Leicester and James Walker were 'willing' to work in the colonies, but their 'mothers said that they would only agree if they offended again', and took their boys home with them. Martin Bowyer was caught walking late in 1639 and said that he was 'willing to goe to a plantacon if his father will' let him. A couple of pilferers and a pickpocket sailed with their 'friends' consent for their 'exportacon'.[155] There was little that the court could do without 'willingness' to go, apart from bending the rules and putting pressure on people to get on board a boat. 'Lewd' Richard Newman was told to work for as long as it took to get him to agree to 'go to sea' in 1657.[156] He felt hard done by, but pressure was rare. Other offenders dug in their heels. Three vagrants 'will not goe to Virginia', the clerk scribbled in 1628, 'all to work'. 'If she be not transported of her owne desire', the court ruled in the case of the 'comon nightwalker' Mary Monday a decade later, 'she must be punished'. The 'nip' William Bragg would not 'go to Virginia' in 1620 and was whipped and put to work.[157] Might was not right and not even 'old gest' Bragg who had been 'diving into pockets' for a long time could be forced on board a ship. A captain appeared at quarter sessions in 1654 for keeping George Giles ('a youth about 13 or 14 yeares') 'on shipboard against his will and without his parents consent'. There was also a last-minute attempt to stop Joseph Cock crossing the ocean in 1657: Bridewell's court told the porter

---

[153] BHC 7, fo. 184v; 8, fo. 251v. See also BHC 8, fo. 159.
[154] BHC 9, fo. 341; 7, fo. 84v; 8, fos. 243v, 246v; 7, fo. 262; 9, fo. 334; 8, fo. 234. See also BHC 7, fos. 85v, 275, 345v; 8, fo. 320; 9, fos. 503, 714, 783, 805.
[155] BHC 8, fos. 194, 239, 384, 40, 57v. See also BHC 6, fo. 235v; 8, fos. 40, 401; 9, fo. 798.
[156] BHC 9, fo. 794. Newman agreed to go to sea with Edward Gethin a couple of weeks later with his mother's 'consent': ibid., fo. 798.
[157] BHC 7, fo. 81v; 8, fo. 239; 6, fo. 185v. See also BHC 7, fo. 86v; 8, fo. 237; 9, fo. 1.

to rush to the dockside after hearing that he had been 'betrayed' and was on 'shipboard' against his will.[158]

The City also bargained with merchants to ship pests overseas. A deal was reached with Mr Hurst, who lodged in an alehouse in Newgate Market, 'to transporte twelve vagrant boyes to Virginia' in 1642, 'whoe are willinge to bee transported thither'. Both sides shared the costs as a rule; merchants covered room and board at Bridewell from time to time. Some scrawny prisoners were turned down because merchants wanted healthy people for the long voyage. A thief was told that 'none comes for such litle boys' as he in 1638.[159] Merchants signed contracts, but there was a breed of crooked trader who took people overseas against their will. Richard Paler told Bridewell's court that he had royal 'authority' 'to procure men to be transported' in 1635, but someone remembered that not long ago he took 'some men' to ship overseas and no one knew what happened to them. Edward Coteene, who lived on the waterfront, got in trouble in 1640 for 'secretly enticing and conveyinge away 2 apprentices beyond sea', and bribing two boys to cover up their disappearance by taking 'the oath of allegiance in their names'. He might have been called a 'spirit' soon after, someone who 'took up' children for the colonies. 'Spirits' first turn up at Bridewell in 1641, when 'spirits' Robert Clarke and William Pratin were put to 'hard labour' for 'taking up young boyes and fellowes'.[160] Almost thirty crop up in my records, and nearly two-thirds were said to be 'idle', 'lewde', 'suspicious', or 'dangerous'. Two 'dangerous' vagrant 'spiritts' were charged with 'stealing children to send them beyond seas' in 1646. 'Spirits' stole 'children', 'litle children' (one only four-years-old), 'young boyes' and, in one case, 'youthes to sell them to worke'.[161] Merchants are mentioned more than once, and some 'spirits' set up supply lines for traders looking for cheap cargo. 'Idle' 'spirritt' William Hellick took 'boyes' to merchants in St Katherine's dock. Another, Anne Wilton, was charged with 'selling' children.[162] We know next to nothing about 'spirit' networks, but there was money to be made at all stages up to the dockside and last port-of-call overseas. 'Spirits' were 'seamen' and 'marriners' from the eastern fringes in the main, although

---

[158] LMA CQSF 125/25; BHC 9, fo. 810.
[159] BHC 8, fos. 405, 185v. See also BHC 7, fos. 86, 334v, 8, fos. 46v, 60, 150v, 331v; 9, fos 209, 623. Bridewell usually paid for clothes and gave a payment to the merchant.
[160] BHC 8, fo. 61v; LMA MJ/SBR/7, fo. 168; BHC 8, fo. 324v. On 'spirits' and stealing children see John Wareing, 'Preventive and punitive regulation in seventeenth-century social policy: conflicts of interest and the failure to make "stealing and transporting children and other persons" a felony, 1645–1673', *Social History*, 27 (2002), 288–308.
[161] BHC 8, fos. 324–4v; 9, fos. 8, 256, 261, 667, 196, 266, 294, 343, 649, 717, 745, 766; LMA CQSF 114/4. See also BHC 9, fos. 196, 319, 333, 428, 648; LMA CQSF 123/17.
[162] BHC 9, fos. 373, 697.

one lived south of the river.[163] They rubbed shoulders with merchants all the time, building bonds, getting to know who might buy stolen children for a nice price.

People also 'stole away' after agreeing to cross the sea. Bridewell 'old guest' William Loggin was caught red-handed 'cutting gould fringe' from a purse after he 'stole away' on the dockside after agreeing to leave Newgate for a Virginia ship. 'Lewde' Lucretia Lea, a 'comon' pickpocket who 'enticed' men 'to lewdnes', fooled magistrates three times in six months with phony promises 'to goe beyond seas'.[164] Others jumped ship. William Garford, a vagrant with a brand on his hand, leaped over the side of a ship soon after leaving Gravesend in 1634, but was back in Bridewell shortly after and again kept for Virginia. Two vagrants slipped away from a ship when it docked at The Isle of Wight in 1637, but were caught in London a little later. Prisoners leaving Newgate with letters of transportation lingered at the risk of a quick hanging. Frances Richardson, a veteran vagrant thief and 'condemned person' who 'should have gone beyond seas', was kept in Bridewell until further order in 1634. Robert Aspinall was sent to Newgate in 1641 when word reached Bridewell that he was 'outlawed for felony' after running away with 'l[ett]ers of transportacon'.[165] Some plucky people got back from a colony before their sentence ended. A thief who should have been in Virginia was caught sneaking into Sir Edward Sackville's house in 1622. While Richard Simpson was not long back from St Christopher's Island when he was arrested for bullying passers-by in 1630. They were not the only ones to slip back over the sea only to land in Bridewell's court once more.[166]

Bridewell's bench had more options to deal with offenders by 1600, certainly more than judges who made life-and-death decisions in higher courts. Bridewell's description as a 'house' nicely sums up how punishing petty crime became more of a 'private'/indoors matter since the day it took its first batch of prisoners.[167] Whipping was used all the way through its first century, but it is hard to plot its course. Clerks sometimes note that prisoners were punished or 'put to work' or 'labour' with nothing else

---

[163] LMA CQSF 114/14, 122/60, 125/25. See also LMA MJ/SBR/7, fo. 168.
[164] BHC 6, fo. 187; 7, fos. 342, 345, 359, 364v. See also BHC 6 fos. 127v, 71v, 241v; 7, fo. 153; 9, fos. 846, 872.
[165] BHC 8, fos. 17, 136v, 5; LMA MJ/SBR/7, fo. 193.
[166] BHC 6, fo. 281v; 7, fo. 205v. See also BHC 6 fo. 274; 7, fos. 156v, 271v; 8, fos. 144v, 375.
[167] Innes, 'Prisons for the poor'; Paul Griffiths, 'Introduction: punishing the English', in Devereaux and Griffiths, eds., *Penal Practice and Culture*, pp. 1–35, esp. pp. 22–6. Pieter Spierenburg writes that 'the emergence of houses of correction, bridewells and similar institutions constitutes the foremost example of the retreat of the elements of publicity

added. The courtbooks do not tell the full story, however. The clerk missed people and not all cases made it to court anyway, as the bench had more leeway to punish people without the rigmarole of going to court after landmark summary justice rulings. Many whippings have slipped our notice for good, though there is less whipping on record by the middle of the seventeenth century. Whipping was moving away from the public gaze.[168] Bridewell was a linchpin of this creative cycle, although it was not without hitches. More petty thieves were whipped out in the open towards 1700, and whipping rates bounced back later on in the eighteenth century after earlier downswings.[169] With the opening of Bridewell, courts in London, and later elsewhere, now had a bigger range of penalties for 'lesser' offences that blended 'public'/'private' and bodily discipline/reformation in creative ways.

and infliction of physical suffering': 'Introduction', in Spierenburg, ed., *The Emergence of Carceral Institutions: Prisons, Galleys, and Lunatic Asylums, 1550–1900* (Rotterdam, 1984), pp. 2–8, quoting p. 5.

[168] Cf. Ian Archer's work on the treatment of fornication/adultery and vagrancy cases at Bridewell in 1576–7 and 1600–1: *Pursuit of Stability*, pp. 240–1, Tables 6.2 and 6.3.

[169] Whipping over the 'long' eighteenth century in London is covered in Beattie, *Crime and the Courts*, pp. 461–4, 485–7; Beattie, *Policing and Punishment in London*, pp. 444–7; Robert B. Shoemaker, 'Streets of shame?: The crowd and public punishments in London, 1700–1820', in Devereaux and Griffiths, eds., *Penal Practice and Culture*, pp. 232–57; Greg T. Smith, 'Civilized people don't want to see that kind of thing: the decline of public physical punishment in London, 1760–1840', in Carolyn Strange, ed., *Qualities of Mercy: Justice, Punishment, and Discretion* (1996), pp. 21–51.

# 8 Policing: people and policy

### Getting rid of Dogberry and Elbow

Thanks largely to Joan Kent's work on policing we ought by now to have got rid of the stereotypes of the dithering clown constables Dogberry and Elbow who traipse through *Much Ado About Nothing* and *Measure for Measure*. This was dry caricature, but believable. Comic constables were stock literary characters at the time, and there were enough bumbling officers across the land for them to be instantly recognizable. But we might remember that Dogberry did a good job. He brought a pair of 'villains' before Leonato and got money for his 'care'. Elbow also took a 'parcel bawd', 'hot-house' patron, and thief into custody.[1] The pair are nowhere near representative of constables, whose performances ranged anywhere from careful to careless, and they should remain as paper caricatures if we always pick out their funny sides, forgetting perhaps that Elbow served in his post for seven-and-a-half years, although steps were being taken to replace him as the play draws to a close.[2]

Yet much previous work sees early modern constables as second-rate amateurs for the most part, neighbours who served by turn for one year only and were not even paid for their troubles. It is often said that a system staffed by part-time amateurs must have had flaws, and left unsaid that to improve it needed to become 'professional'. This is largely due to interpretations that see policing through time as an inevitable progress from lackadaisical Tudor constables to career policemen three centuries later, whose appearance owed little to advances before 1800.[3] More recent

---

[1] Joan Kent, *The English Village Constable 1580–1642: a Social and Administrative Study* (Oxford, 1986); William Shakespeare, *Much Ado About Nothing*, 5.1, 297; *Measure for Measure*, 2.1 58–61; 3.1, 273–4, in *The Norton Shakespeare Based on the Oxford Edition*, eds. Stephen Greenblatt *et al.* (New York and London, 1997). Cf. Clive Emsley, *The English Police: A Political and Social History* (Harlow, 1991), pp. 9–10, 13; H. C. Evans, 'Comic constables – fictional and historical', *Shakespeare Quarterly*, 20 (1969), 427–33.
[2] *Measure for Measure*, 2.1, 228–42.
[3] Ideas about policing's historical development are described in Douglas Hay and Francis Snyder, 'Using the criminal law, 1750–1850: policing, private prosecution and the state',

work, however, has revised images of ham-fisted early modern policing. Innovations remodelled organization and techniques around 1700 and after, so much so that some scholars now say that 'traditional' parish procedures met expectations, and that loud voices spoke up in support of the status-quo when police-reform was put on the table.[4] But questions still linger, and London still lacks a full study of its police over the century before 1660. Even after Archer's close work on Elizabethan law and order and Price's PhD on constables in built-up Middlesex, the suggestion remains that little was done to improve policing in London before 1660.[5] But there are also rosier views from the same time. John Earle for one thought that the constable was 'very carefull' 'in his office'. 'There is not the least misdemeanour or inconvenience', James Howell bragged in 1657, 'but there be officers in every corner of the city to pry unto them and find them out'.[6]

Nor was having a foot in the community as a neighbour a bad thing. It brought a past of local relations to office, for better or for worse. Policing must also be considered in terms of what its effectiveness meant for people at the time, as most officers were elected by wards, parishes, and precincts in which they lived. This local colour was an advantage because people soon got to know officers and offenders in their part of London. Disputes were often settled without warrants and prosecutions, leading to endless complaints from the Guildhall about lax policing when in fact it was flexible and melded to neighbours' needs much of the time. Most beats were on the short side, taking in some medium-sized streets with a

---

in Hay and Snyder, eds., *Policing and Prosecution in Britain, 1750–1850* (Oxford, 1989), pp. 3–52; Beattie, *Policing and Punishment* chap. 2; Clive Emsley, *The English Police: a Political and Social History* (2nd edition, 1996), pp. 1–7; Leon Radzinowicz and Roger Hood, *A History of English Criminal Law and its Administration from 1750*, 5 vols. (1948–86), vols. II–V.

[4] See Beattie, *Policing and Punishment*; Ruth Paley, '"An imperfect, inadequate, and wretched system"? Policing London before Peel', *Criminal Justice History*, 10 (1989), 95–130; Elaine A. Reynolds, *Before the Bobbies: the Night Watch and Police Reform in Metropolitan London, 1720–1830* (Basingstoke, 1998), chaps 5–8; Andrew T. Harris, *Policing the City: Crime and Legal Authority in London, 1780–1840* (Columbus, OH, 2005); Tony Henderson, *Disorderly Women in Eighteenth-Century London: Prostitution and Control in the Metropolis, 1730–1830* (Harlow, 1999), chaps 5–6; Clive Emsley, *Crime and Society in England, 1750–1900*, 2nd edition (1996).

[5] Randall McGowen, 'The Bank of England and the policing of forgery 1797–1821', *Past and Present*, 186 (2005), 81–116, esp. 81–5; Archer, *Pursuit of Stability*, chap. 6; Lynda Ann Price, 'Parish constables: a study of administration and peacekeeping, Middlesex, 1603–1625', unpublished PhD thesis, University of London (1991). There is a very balanced summary in Emsley, *English Police*, pp. 8–15.

[6] John Earle, *Micro-cosmographie, Or, A Peece of the World Discovered in Essays and Characters*, 5th edition (1629), fo. F11v; James Howell, *Londinopolis: an Historical Discourse or Perlustration of the City of London, the Imperial Chamber and the Chief Emporium of Great Britain* (1657), p. 391.

few alleys running off them, and the smallest parishes within the walls were roughly an acre in size. People often stayed put in one place for a while, as the turnover rate of population was low in the London area.[7] Modest sizes and a core of long-term stayers meant that people knew who to go to if something went wrong. Officers, likewise, had a resident's knowledge of rumour mills, rowdy houses, back alleys, and black sheep in their neck of the woods, and a friendly word in the ear was often more effective than a warrant. This neighbourly side-stepping of City/criminal law was London's 'two concepts of order', a shared preference for settling spats within communities, not with warrants but words or something stiffer, if need be.[8] One-in-ten householders held office at any one point in time, taking post 'by turn from house to house', and some served for long stretches more than once.[9] As constables, churchwardens, overseers, or jurymen, they had close experience of crime and poverty. A Star Chamber witness spoke of a life time of office in St Sepulchre, his home for thirty-two years, serving as scavenger, constable, collector, and churchwarden, when his turn came round. In St Dunstan-in-the-West, as elsewhere, it was expected that people would have served a spell as constable before taking up post as churchwarden.[10] This office ladder was a stepping stone to a seat in the vestry, which became smaller and more secretive as time passed, creating tight ties between office-holding, power, and 'middling' men. Showing willing to take office was an obligation for middling men by now.[11] They picked up news in and out of

---

[7] Vanessa Harding, *The Dead and the Living in Paris and London, 1500–1670* (Cambridge, 2002), p. 35; Jeremy Boulton, *Neighbourhood and Society: a London Suburb in the Seventeenth Century* (Cambridge, 1987), pp. 110, 116–17, 120–38; Roger Finlay, *Population and Metropolis: the Demography of London, 1580–1650* (Cambridge, 1981), pp. 45–8.

[8] Keith Wrightson, 'Two concepts of order: justices, constables and jurymen in seventeenth-century England', in John Brewer and John Styles, eds., *An Ungovernable People: the English and their Law in the Seventeenth and Eighteenth Centuries* (1980), pp. 21–46.

[9] GL MS 1431/2, fo. 21; Valerie Pearl, 'Change and stability in seventeenth-century London', *London Journal*, 5 (1979), 3–34. Cf. J. F. Merritt, *The Social World of Early Modern Westminster: Abbey, Court, and Community, 1525–1640* (Manchester, 2005), p. 105.

[10] TNA STAC8 160/16; GL MS 3016/1, fos. 380–1. Cf. Price, 'Parish Constables', p. 94; Merritt, *Social World of Early Modern Westminster*, p, 104.

[11] GL MS 3016/1, fo. 422; Paul Griffiths, 'Secrecy and authority in late sixteenth- and seventeenth-century London', *Historical Journal* 40 (1997), 925–51; Steve Hindle, *On the Parish? The Micro-Politics of Poor Relief in Rural England, c.1550–1750* (Oxford, 2004); Merritt, *Social World of Early Modern Westminster*, chap. 4; Joan Kent, 'The rural "middling sort" in early modern England, circa 1640–1740: some economic, political, and socio-cultural characteristics', *Rural History*, 10 (1999), 19–54; H. R. French, 'Social status, localism, and the "middle sort of people" in England, 1620–1750', *Past and Present*, 166 (2000), 66–99; Keith Wrightson, 'The politics of the parish', in Paul Griffiths, Adam Fox, and Steve Hindle, eds., *The Experience of Authority in Early Modern England* (Basingstoke, 1996), pp. 10–46; Beattie, *Policing and Punishment*, pp. 146, 118.

office, mixing with other office-holders, sitting in vestries, or talking around dining tables. Talk soon turned to running parishes when ratepayers/office-holders bumped into each other. These men were the parish purse-strings and leading property owners with most to lose if they did not do a good job. As in other walks of life, respectability counted for much in cultures that conflated economic and social credit. Office ladders were another potential knock to pride, as the distribution of office shadowed wealth.[12] Most constables counted on having credibility with the leading lights of the parish, and their standing was prominent enough to figure in visual validations of social ranking, like church seating plans that mention a 'constables pew'.[13]

Governors wanted sound middling men to serve as constable. St Bride's Fleet Street chose its constables from the 'auncientest parishioners', while Westminster constables needed letters to back up their 'sufficiency and fitnesse' in 1612.[14] But there were also claims that constables could not read, that they spoke out of turn, ran rowdy alehouses, 'haunted harlots', and even egged on rioters. Magistrates complained again and again that some constables lacked the required social standing.[15] There was also concern that many first choices allowed second-rate hired men to step into their shoes; a lack of care that put parishes in tricky positions, as it was felt that such needy substitutes could not have been up to the task. Parishes also milked election fines to excuse men elected for extra revenue by picking people who were in no position to take office, a boon for cash-poor parishes when fines reached £5.[16] Some of the men chosen were 'auncient', 'weakely bodyed', 'distracted', or racked with gout. Thomas Rich hobbled about on crutches; another was seventy-five-years-old; another, nine years younger, was tortured by 'the stone'. Some had done a stint elsewhere, or were shortly leaving to live somewhere else. Others said that they would fall on hard times as there was no one else who could take their place in their shop.[17] Outright refusals to serve were few and far between, however, and rebels usually caved in after a while.

---

[12] Craig Muldrew, *The Economy of Obligation: the Culture of Credit and Social Relations in Early Modern England* (Basingstoke, 1998), chaps. 6–7; Boulton, *Neighbourhood and Society*, pp. 139–41, 268; Steve Rappaport, *Worlds Within Worlds: Structures of Life in Sixteenth-Century London* (Cambridge, 1989), pp. 256, 258–9, 348–9, 367; Archer, *Pursuit of Stability*, p. 64.

[13] GL MSS 9235/2, fo. 477v; 878/1, fo. 237; 6386, fo. 116; 2968/2, fo. 354v.

[14] GL MS 6544/1, fos. 15, 40v; WAC WCB1, fo. 167; GL MS 877/1, fos. 45, 73–4.

[15] TNA STAC 8 21/7; 160/6; 85/3.

[16] GL MSS 877/1, fo. 53; 4069/1, fo. 214v; 1431/2, fo. 409.

[17] GL MSS 4524/1, fos. 142v-3; 2968/2, fo. 136; 4216/1, fo. 103; 6554/1, fos. 40v-4, 183v-5v; 4415/1, fo. 211; 3570/1, fo. 76; 4526/1, fo. 11; LMA Rep. 55, fo. 340v; MJ/SBR/5, fo. 482.

Most duly paid fines, a one-off fee effectively to dodge office forever. 'Xii phisicons' of 'the colledge' each paid 20/3d 'for a man' when they were 'chosen constables' in 1538. One pick paid a £6 fine 'for neighborhood sake'.[18]

Parishes appeared content to pocket fines before 1600, so long as 'hable' people filled the gap.[19] But they felt more unease about stand-ins later on, making links with deeper troubles. Magistrates coupled authority and competence with wealth and standing. A vestry on busy Fleet Street moaned in 1599 that many 'disorders have of late arisen by taking of fines and dispensing with people of the better sort', and ruled that no one should be allowed to fine except 'by warrant' or if 'weakness' left them crippled. A riverside parish doubled fines after suffering 'daily smites of most men to be spared' in 1613.[20] Wardmotes told constables to serve 'in person' in 1614, but if they had reason to step down they would be 'lyable' if ever their hired hand was 'faultie'. A report from aldermen deputies that was read out at Common Council in 1621 spoke anxiously of the 'great hinderance' when 'many of the more able and better sort of the citizens' passed the baton to 'meane men'. They drafted an act for the next meeting, noting that London was now 'more full of able and suffi-cient men to bear the office of constable' than ever before. Only 'strangers and others exempt by law' should fine, and deputies had the last word on substitutes if the choice fell on sick or frail men, or 'urgent cause' like going overseas 'on affaires' led to absences.[21] This act set a course for the rest of the century. A later effort to put a blanket ban on substitutes sank without trace, it was now better to think of ways to work with them. John Beattie has found groups of (mostly) artisans, who made livings standing in year after year when well-off men fined around 1700. There was almost certainly a similar pool of volunteers living in London a century earlier, although we know much less about them, who created fewer setbacks than stinging outbursts against them would lead us to believe.[22]

Some would-be constables claimed prior privilege as exemption, and although their numbers were relatively modest, some of these disputes were serious enough to land on the Privy Council's table. Others were settled with healing words. When Thomas Marten got 'a writt of privilege out of Star Chamber' for discharge from serving in office in 1621, a substitute was picked to take his place 'after conference' with the parish.

---

[18] LMA Reps. 10, fos. 81, 181; 23, fo. 32v; GL MSS 4383/1, fo. 75; 877/1, fo. 53.
[19] LMA Rep. 19, fo. 421.   [20] GL MS 3016/1, fo. 33.
[21] LMA Rep. 32, fo. 26v; Jour. 31, fos. 318–18v, 352–2v. It seems that the mayor approved deputy constables before this Act was passed: Archer, *Pursuit of Stability*, p. 222.
[22] GL MS 4060/1, fo. 184; Beattie, *Policing and Punishment*, pp. 134–50; Archer, *Pursuit of Stability*, p. 222.

Robert Williamson ruled himself out of serving when he was chosen constable in Castle Baynard ward in 1619, because he was a Chancery clerk and proctor of the Court of Arches. But aldermen were able to 'perswade' him 'for neighborhood sake' to follow 'ordinary rules and orders' like previous proctors, and he 'freely relinquished' his writ.[23] Such suits were another source of funds through fines with good-natured neighbourly words. A Common Pleas attorney fined 'in a neighbourly way'. Two Prerogative Court proctors whose work called for 'continual attendance' each paid £3 'to continue neighbourhood and love'.[24] A spate of cases from around 1570 put foreigners in the spotlight. John Box (Dutchman) 'persisted' with refusals to serve in 1567, but changed his mind after a meeting between the Spanish ambassador and aldermen. Wards were warned at the same time to 'understand' what 'strangers being an householder have done' when their turn came to serve. A follow-up order told 'straungers' to serve in person or (probably preferably) to get an 'honest Englishman as his deputie'.[25] Some privilege cases drained money and time, as when a Temple 'person' at long last 'yielded' to take up a post in 1658 after hearings before St Benet Paul's Wharf vestry, the Court Moot, the mayor and ward alderman, quarter sessions, Temple Crown Office and, finally, the lord chief justice at the end of the line, at his home in Lincoln's Inn. Such cases also troubled London's top brass. Common Council asked for lists of 'persons' of any 'condition' with claims to be 'exempted' from office in 1641.[26] Touchy matters like honour or jurisdiction flared up when royal officers got involved. For a long time, it was said in 1637, Tower 'servants' had not filled parish posts 'through continual [royal] service', but now London's leaders said, humming with indignation, ten were 'troubled to bear office' and locked up after failing to appear in court as ordered to put the case for their defence. The City would not concede any ground to them as they kept 'open shop and trade' for their 'advantage', like other freemen, but without doing parish duties. Tempers cooled after privy councillors ruled that no one, no matter what their day jobs, should be spared from City office, 'both for their own good as that of the city'.[27]

Constables were not from the lowest rungs of social ladders in the main. Most ranked in the top one-third income bracket in subsidy rolls,

---

[23] SBHA Governors' Journal 4, fo. 49; LMA Rep. 34, fos. 65–5v.
[24] GL MSS 4415/1, fo. 148v; 877/1, fo. 127. See also GL MSS 4415/1, fo. 35v ('a cornmeter of the city'); 3016/1, fo. 53 (Earl of Dorset's servant); 3570/2, fo. 50 ('King's wayters at the Custom House'); LMA Rep. 59, fos. 81–1v (King's Bench attorney).
[25] LMA Reps. 16, fos. 255v, 262v, 270v, 257v; 18, fo. 326.
[26] GL MS 877/1, fos. 165–6; LMA Jour. 39, fo. 181.
[27] LMA Remembrancia Book 7, fos. 211–13; TNA SP16/368/76.

although they were a mixed bunch that included skilled craftsmen and merchants. Little St Bartholomew's constables in 1600–30 included a goldsmith, plumber, joiner, brewer, tailor, merchant, and gentleman. Parishes purged people of low status or sloppy morals. Servants or alehouse keepers were let go on such scores, as happened to Thomas Mugg, a 'domesticke servant', in 1627.[28] Beadles were barred from keeping alehouses and were ordered to have 'a certificate' of 'good life and conversation' to be a candidate for office, signed by some of their 'better' neighbours.[29] It is possible that some constables did not serve long enough to pick up the nuts and bolts of the job. A vestry voted whether they should serve for one or two years in 1630, and more hands went up for one.[30] But some stayed in post for longer. Warm tributes oozed for one officer for his 'verie good and substanciall service for manie yeares'. A beadle got a golden handshake 'for his civility to the parish'.[31] Marshals, among them Pordage and Walrond, chased vagrants for more than a decade. William Davis was still serving as marshal two decades after he first took up the post in 1619, although he had gaps in his service, including one in 1627 when, because of his 'experience and sufficiencie', the king thought fit 'to ymploye him' as 'provost marshall of his armie in the Isle of Rea'.[32] Ward deputies, beadles, and warders, also served for long stretches; Worthington of St Mary Woolnoth stayed in the beadle's position for two decades.[33]

Some officers turn up year after year in records and reveal the potential for periods of stability in office.[34] The name of arresting officers is often noted in Bridewell's books. Not many appear for decent stretches of time, but there is a good run of names for the decade after 1617. Tracing surnames is tricky, so I limit myself to officers given the same parish/ward

---

[28] Ian W. Archer, 'Governors and governed in late sixteenth-century London, c. 1560–1603: studies in the achievement of stability', unpublished DPhil thesis, University of Oxford (1988), pp. 283–5; LMA Reps. 28, fo. 64; 47, fos. 82v-3; 59, fo. 42; MJ/SBR/4, fo. 528; SBHA Governors' Journals 3, fos. 172v, 268v; 4, fos. 5, 67, 102, 148, 167, 183v. Cf. Price, 'Parish Constables', p. 97: 'None of the qualified officers appear to have been wealthy, but on the other hand, none of them were destitute or beggarly.'

[29] GL MS 9680, fo. 45; WAC F2003, fo. 150; WCB2, fo. 78.

[30] GL MS 1264/1, fo. 41v.    [31] LMA MJ/SBR/4, fo. 211; GL MS 5090/2, fo. 287.

[32] For William Davis see BHC 6, fo. 111; LMA Reps. 39, fo. 286; 41, fos. 351v-2v; APC 1627, p. 165; TNA SP16/455/102.

[33] Archer, *Pursuit of Stability*, p. 67; GL MSS 1002/1; 2999/1. Warder Sparrow of St Botolph-without-Bishopgate also served for over a decade (4524/1, fos. 135v, 219v). Roger Phillips served at least eight years in St Mary Aldermanbury (1584–91), but there is a gap in records afterwards (3556/1, fo. 172ff.).

[34] Cf. work on countryside constables: Kent, *English Village Constable*; Keith Wrightson and David Levine, *Poverty and Piety in an English Village: Terling 1525–1700* (Oxford, 1995), pp. 104–6.

298    Control

affiliation all through a recorded career. My figures are on the low side because names were not always jotted down, and Bridewell's records are missing from 1610/17 and run dry after 1628 when names were rarely noted. Some constables appear for long spells: Browne (Cheap) stays in sight from Autumn 1618 to Spring 1625, Parkinson (Farringdon Without) went back and forth to Bridewell for six years, while Waller (Farringdon Within), Studley (Fleet Street), Lee (Farringdon Without), and Mould (Walbrook), stay on paper for five years.[35] Others remain in records for up to four years. These old hands were often drawn from west wards. Allen, Bradford, and Cook all walked beats in trouble-prone Farringdon Without. Foster policed Cheap's buzzing streets. While Dicher kept the peace in cash-poor Cripplegate.[36] Dowling kept an eye on Queenhithe's riverside for at least two years. Needler policed vagrant-ridden Bridge for the same stretch, while Walker turns up in Cordwainer, near to the heart of the city, for four years.[37] Beadles, warders, and deputies all appear for similar lengths of time. The shortest stay for a deputy was four years and the longest nearly eight. Beadle Balthasar was on duty in Newgate Market for at least four years. Beadle Holland in Bread Street for three. While Warder Slater did daily laps of Bridge ward for at least as long as eight years and probably more.[38] These terms were long enough to settle into the job. Some officers also switched posts. Slater was Bridge's warder in the mid-1610s and constable there a decade later, when a pair of Slaters

---

[35] BHC 6, fos. 71v, 128, 154v, 336, 344v, 351, 352, 387v, 391v, 393 (Browne); 6, fos. 265, 279v, 289, 299, 314, 318v, 323, 327v, 337, 337v, 425v, 441; 7, fo. 38v (Lee); 6, fos. 185, 240v, 250, 255, 323, 336, 340v, 342, 348v, 349, 356, 386 (Mould); 6, fos. 169v, 175, 178, 184, 192, 199v, 200, 201v, 207v, 210, 216v, 217v, 218v, 220v, 222v, 226v, 227, 230v, 232v, 233v, 235v, 239v, 255, 255v, 256, 258v, 259v, 261, 262v, 269, 438v (Parkinson); 6, fos. 298v, 299v, 301v, 314v, 317, 322, 326v, 335v, 340v, 346v, 350, 354v, 356v; 7, fos. 38v, 47v (Studley); 6, fos. 122v, 126v, 129v, 131v, 143, 145, 148, 151v, 155, 155v, 191, 319v, 338, 338v, 347, 353v, 355, 356 (Waller). Parkinson may have been in office for as long as nine years: constable Parkinson of Fleet Street is recorded making an arrest in December 1617 (BHC 6, fo. 23).

[36] BHC 6, fos. 166, 181, 181v, 186, 191, 192, 196, 198, 198v, 199, 201, 214, 217v, 218, 222v, 232, 240, 242, 245v, 247v, 248v, 249v, 257v, 263 (Allen); 6, fos. 41v, 46v, 57v, 61, 62, 62v, 68v, 70v, 78v, 83, 87, 95, 96, 119, 133v, 135, 136v, 144, 146, 147, 149, 164 (Bradford); 6, fos. 120, 122, 126, 133, 157, 238v, 267v, 278v, 287, 292, 292v, 293, 294, 303, 305, 309v, 310v (Cook); 6, fos. 263, 273, 282v, 287, 292, 292v, 293, 293v, 294, 304v, 305v, 308v, 329, 333v, 338v, 352, 352v, 356 (Foster); 6, fos. 55, 59v, 60, 62v, 67, 72v, 74v, 86v, 88, 89v, 94v, 99v, 126v, 129, 133, 143, 146v, 199v, 217 (Dicher).

[37] BHC 6, fos. 245v, 254v, 256, 264, 268, 273, 291, 295, 300v, 324v, 339, 340, 342, 345 (Dowling); 6, fos. 339v, 355v, 364, 387, 390, 397v (Needler); 6, fos. 290v, 298, 310, 320, 329, 330, 334, 340, 342, 349, 353v, 362v, 367v, 430 (Walker).

[38] BHC 6, fos. 137, 151, 204v, 237v, 272v, 292, 334v (Balthasar); 6, fos. 112, 122v, 235v, 245, 245v, 273v, 276v, 309v (Holland); 6, fos. 17v, 30, 32, 36v, 38, 40, 42v, 51, 52v, 55, 56v, 57v, 58v, 61, 64, 65, 72v, 73v, 84, 90v, 102v, 105v, 119, 121v, 133, 275v, 275v, 326, 387 (Slater).

served side by side. Constable Needler – also of Bridge – may be the deputy of the same name who crops up two years after the constable disappears.[39] Some constables served second or third spells.[40] There is also a likelihood that some served in more than one ward. Is it a fluke that officers called Hubbard served in Queenhithe and next-door Castle Baynard after 1620, or that someone called Mould was constable in Dowgate in 1618–20 and over the ward border in Walbrook from 1620–5? Constables crossed borders in other ways, making arrests in more than one ward. Browne grabbed suspects in both Cheap and Bread Street in the 1620s, Waller in Farringdon Within and Cheap, and Cook in both Farringdon wards. Yet aldermen ruled as far back as 1538 that officers should stick to their own wards and not 'meddle' in others, after a prickly incident when Vintry ward complained that next-door Dowgate's constables constantly crossed the dividing line between the two wards.[41]

There was no standard yardstick or magic number of arrests to measure efficiency. But we can count the times when named constables were credited with arrests at Bridewell. These totals poorly reflect effort as often only office and location were jotted down. More active constables, needless to say, came from trouble-prone areas: Parkinson (41 arrests), Bradford (35), and Allen (34) all policed the Fleet Street area. Not far behind were Carter and Statfield (29), Cook (25), and Clayton (24), all from Farringdon Without. Waller notched up twenty-seven arrests, mainly in and around Paul's Churchyard. Dicher and Foster (25 arrests) kept the peace in the next-door wards of Cripplegate and Cheap. Some periods were noteworthy for bursts of activity. Constable Clayton dragged twenty-four people to Bridewell from Farringdon Without over sixteen months. Statfield sent twenty-eight prisoners there in one year from the same ward, while constable Nash rounded up seventeen suspects in Bridge in a little less than one year. Others were steadier and unspectacular, lagging behind but solid servants still the same, like Creecher in the Blackfriars, who made trips to Bridewell with ten suspects between 1621–2, Mould who walked half-way across the city with fourteen suspects in tow in five years from Walbrook ward, and Constable Walker, who took twenty suspects across the shorter distance from

---

[39] BHC 6, fos. 339v, 355v, 364, 387, 390, 397; 7, fos 122, 262 (Needler). Slater is called a warder at BHC 6, fos. 275v, 387; and a constable at BHC 6, fos. 275v, 326.
[40] Officers who seem to follow this pattern of office-holding include Browne from Cheap ward, Slater in Bridge, and others who served in Farringdon Without: Carter, Cook, and Parkinson, for instance.
[41] LMA Rep. 10, fo. 87.

Cordwainer in a little under four years.[42] Many officers did a good day's work. Hemmings of Tower led seven suspects across the city on one day in 1621. Davies brought six suspects from Queenhithe to Bridewell on 17 March 1621, while Lodwin pulled off a minor miracle in getting nine women and seven men there from Newgate Market on a cold wintry day in 1622.[43] Beadles and warders also chalked up a few dozen arrests. Warder Slater of Bridge matched anyone else, taking thirty-five suspects to Bridewell in twenty months. Ward deputies were steadier on paper at any rate. Whitwell took twenty-three people to Bridewell in four years, Hickman eighteen in a little more time, while Stanguish took fifteen suspects there in six years. Certain officers or parishes and precincts built ties to Bridewell, and it is no surprise that Farringdon constables from London's rowdiest parts top the table of Bridewell arrests.

Like today, most officers were paid for their work. A deputy constable in All Hallows London Wall got thirty-five shillings for six months' 'salary'.[44] Wages were not the same across the board. Wards, parishes, or hospitals could set their own rates. Hospital beadles were better paid than ward ones on the whole, getting five marks in 1569. A Bridewell beadle got £6 in 1577, although St Thomas's paid one pound less, and 'Barts beadles' only got £4 three decades later.[45] But salaried officers policed round the clock, funded by rates, though some householders refused to give anything when collectors came knocking.[46] 'Bedles of beggers' got a groat for each day's work in 1549. A parish raised the beadle's wage to twenty shillings quarterly in 1600, but another slashed theirs to £2 a decade later. Ward beadles and warders got similar amounts. Warder Sparrow picked up £3 in 1624 (plus £1 quarterly 'to looke to inmates'). Another got sevenpence for a day's work in 1630. Forty shillings was the most regular recorded annual salary for warders from 1600–50, although one got £5 4s 3d in 1638, a plague year with a lot of overtime.[47] Marshals had the highest wage. William Davis got a whopping £96 13s 4d in 1619. Henry Fitch had £30 less a decade later and a new marshal's salary was pegged at £80 in

---

[42] BHC 6, fos. 318v, 324, 339v, 354, 355, 355v, 356 (Nash); ibid., fos. 216, 255, 255v, 256v, 257, 260, 261v, 262v, 263 (Creecher).
[43] Ibid., fos. 229, 225, 307v.    [44] GL MS 5090/2, fo. 167.
[45] LMA Rep. 12, fo. 129; GL MSS 2968/1, fo. 349v; 2968/2, fo. 156v; 559/1, fo. 12; 951/1, fo. 69; 12806/2, fo. 38v; 12, 806/4, fo. 136; BHC 3, fo. 240; LMA H1/ST/A3, fo. 30; H1/ST/A/4, fo. 12v; SBHA Governors' Journal 4, fo. 96.
[46] GL MSS 4216/1, fo. 86; 4069/1, fo. 198v; 4069/2, fo. 265.
[47] GL MSS 4524/1, fos. 135v, 219v; 942/1, fo. 21; 1303/1, 1630–1; 951/1, fo. 41v; 1279/2, fo. 184v; 5090/2, fos. 171, 210, 252v; 3556/1, fos. 172, 205, 235. A parish paid £5 5s to its 'blue cote warder' in 1624: 951/1, fo.66. Another paid its warder 3/3d weekly: 9680, fo. 59. Cornhill watchmen got thirty shillings quarterly in 1660: 4069/2, fos. 282, 283, 326, 377.

1643.[48] The City and hospitals linked pay to performance. Bridewell beadles got a rise in 1642 for 'better encouragement' to work 'diligentlye and duely'. Marshals' salaries shot up by £20 in 1650, in token of 'extraordinary paines'. Cornhill watchmen each got a slice of a £4 13s quarterly 'encouragement' at one time.[49]

Officers also got top-ups for tasks over and above the call of duty. Some beadles got £1 extra for 'extraordinary paines', and bonuses for tasks ranging from checking coal supplies to whipping vagrants for up to sixpence at a time. They also pocketed a few pence for turning out at citizens' funerals, and fourpence at one time from fines paid by each nightwalker they arrested.[50] As well as whipping vagrants, constables got fees (sometimes several shillings) for carting or whipping offenders, ducking scolds, and dragging 'hoores', thieves, vagrants, 'Duchmen', and 'Spanyards' to prison or trial, or out of the city. On one trip, St Katherine's constables traipsed across the city with twenty-four vagrants in tow.[51] Like warders, constables also picked up bonuses for guarding plague struck houses or putting plague victims in pesthouses. Marshalmen also helped shut up 'infected houses' and took the sick to pesthouses and prisoners to lock-ups.[52] Their bosses also got bonuses for dropping off 'visited persons' at pesthouses, 'sendinge awaye' 'Turkes' and 'Scottishmen', policing vagrants, and taking charge of collections for maimed soldiers.[53] Watchmen got top-ups for 'watchinge' after a fire (5s), taking suspects to prison, and guarding gates, soldiers, felons (2s), 'a madman' slumped in an alley (2/6d), coals (6d), lead falling from a church roof (8d), holes (6/8d), and ladders left in streets.[54]

---

[48] BHC 6, fo. 21; LMA Jour. 40, fo. 73; City Cashbook 1/2, fo. 48.
[49] LMA Jour. 40, fos. 42, 77–8v; Rep. 56, fo. 140v; SBHA Governors' Journal 4, fo. 47v; GL MS 4069/2, fo. 285; LMA Reps. 60, fo. 136; 54, fos. 271v-2; 56, fos. 22v-3; Jour. 28, fo. 264.
[50] SBHA Governors' Journals 4, fo. 299; 5, fo. 77v; GL MS 2089/1, 1646–7 (coals); LMA Rep. 12, fo. 402; GL MSS 9680, fo. 24v; 2968/1, fo. 455; 1279/2, fo. 165; 4524/1, fo. 96; 4383/1, fo. 49 (whipping); SBHA Governors' Journal 3, fo. 106v; GL MS 12806/2, fo. 509 (funerals); LMA Rep. 57, fo. 80v; GL MSS 878/1, fo. 288v; 4423/1, fo. 199v; 5018/1, fo. 32; 662/1, fo. 154 (nightwalkers).
[51] GL MSS 9680, passim; 2991/1, 1663–4; 4457/2, fo. 85; 3146/1, fo. 116; 4524/1, fo. 112; 6552/1, fo. 218v; 6836, fos. 73, 212; 4457/2, fo. 22v; 4956/3, fo. 171; 959/1, fo. 176.
[52] GL MSS 2991/1, 1636–7; 951/1, fo. 66v; 818/1, fo. 134v; 7674, fo. 26; 590/1, fo. 250; 3907/1, 1636–7; 4071/1, fo. 152; 5714/1, fo. 65v; 1124/1, fo. 155v; 4241/1, fo. 458; 4385/1, fo. 227v.
[53] LMA Reps. 27, fo. 273v; 28, fos. 133, 268, 272; 29, fos. 32, 143, 257, 301v; 31(1), fo. 5; 44, fo. 233v; BHC 5, fo. 97v; GL MSS 6574, fo. 132v; 1002/1, fo. 519; 645/1, fo. 39; 645/2, fo. 67v; 2596/2, fo. 39; 959/1, fo. 140; 4956/3, fo. 27v; 4385/1, fo. 151v; 590/1, fo.145.
[54] GL MSS 4524/1, fo. 91v; 3556/2, fo. 144; 1303/1, 1641; 9680, fos. 6, 10v, 12v, 24, 30v; 9080/7, 1658; 4383/1, fo. 181; 3907/1, 1638–9; 1002/1, fo. 325; 5018/1, fo. 38v; 3556/2, fo. 144; 9680, fo. 12v; 4457/2, fo. 152v; 2895/2, 1657–8; 4409/1, fo. 254; 4409/2, 1655–6.

Nor were top-ups the only perks for London's officers. Bridewell beadles lobbied hard for a French crown taken from a cutpurse hanged at Tyburn in 1604. Arresting officers could claim a cut of confiscated spoils.[55] Officers also got loans in hard times. A 'diligent' beadle was loaned £4 to cover the cost of house repairs. Beadle Willard got ten shillings after losing his purse with 'a quarters wages in it'.[56] 'Gifts' also helped make ends meet when prices soared. Hospital beadles often got something extra in 'dear' times; such top-ups became routine additions to Bridewell pay. Some long-serving retirees also received hard-luck money. 'Long servant' John Pierce got a weekly pension from Christ's in 1632. Even marshals fell on hard times. Nicholas Bestney got a £2 loan from Bridewell as he starved in King's Bench prison in 1641, a decade after his sacking. Marshal Parker soon slid into hardship after losing his post in 1632 (having 'given over his trade' to take it), but his luck changed when he got a £20 City pension and takings from two freedom admissions. Widows also got helping hands. Marshal Pordage's widow was given a pension after his 'untymely accident' in 1627 and was still getting it three decades later.[57] And there was sick-pay for on-the-job injuries. A beadle got money to tide him over when a bull trampled on him at a conduit. One warder received hand-outs for two years after breaking his leg in a 'parishes service'. A marshalman got fifty shillings after 'a hurt received on the lord maiors day'. While Marshal Davis had a 'gift' of forty marks in 1623 after a 'hurt' from 'a fearefull fire', and was given time off to go to Bath 'for the better recovery of his health' in 1629. Officers also received hardship pay in plague times, as reward perhaps for staying put in post as others fled to the safer countryside.[58]

Officers had coats or other insignia to help them stand out in a crowd. 'Special marks' also included staffs hanging outside their homes, like the blue lamps that once guided people to police stations. Constables hung up staffs or another 'apparent signe to demonstrate their office' for people to 'take knowledge' to know where to go for help. How 'frequently peace is broken' if staffs are not hung out, aldermen noted in 1617, warning that they must hang 'continually' from sunrise to sunset 'in open view', so that

---

[55] BHC 5, fo. 3v; LMA H1/ST/A4, fo. 75.
[56] GL MS 12806/3, fo. 442; LMA H1/ST/A4, fos. 69, 101; BHC 9, fo. 400; GL MS 33063/1, Michaelmas 1643, Christmas 1643, Michaelmas 1645, Christmas 1645, Christmas 1648; 878/1, fo. 77; BHC 8, fo. 122; LMA Rep. 29, fo. 17v.
[57] GL MS 12806/3, fo. 333. See also SBHA Governors' Journals 4, fo. 135v; 5, fo. 40; BHC 5, fo. 93; 8, fo. 351; LMA Rep. 51, fo. 303v; BHC 8, fos. 275v-6; LMA Reps. 51, fos. 303v-4; 41, fo. 161v; Jour. 41, fo. 163.
[58] LMA Rep. 17, fo. 222v; BHC 8, fo. 81v; GL MS 2991/1, 1639–40, 1640–1; LMA Reps. 38, fo. 333v; 43, fo. 282; GL MS 33063/1, Michaelmas 1645. See also BHC 3, fo. 15; 5, fos. 176, 341v; 6, fo. 18; BRHA BHC 4, fo. 293; SBHA Governors' Journal 3, fo. 81.

'every man having occasion to use a constable may readily finde their houses' (constables could have faced a ten-shilling fine if they did not hang out their staff).[59] Staffs added to iconographies that displayed authority all day long. Linen-draper William Hawkins was angry when Anne Granger came for her deposit for handkerchiefs she no longer wished to buy in 1634. 'Base queane', he snapped; 'durty slut', his wife chipped in as she disappeared out of the door. She did not get far before he pounced to grab the handkerchiefs from her hands, and when 'she cried out theeves and murther, murther', Hawkins told the gathering crowd that he was a constable chasing a thief. Granger, however, said she would obey him only if he 'shew[ed] his authority', asking 'where his staff was'. His game up, Hawkins headed home with a court date to follow soon after.[60] Bridewell's beadles wore 'blewe coats' when going 'abroade'. Warders also walked beats in blue, although one parish plumped for bright yellow coats.[61] Marshalmen dressed in coats or 'madillyons', and also had spruce new uniforms for the mayor's swearing-in (and the Duke of York's baptism in 1634).[62] Beadles and warders had staffs/staves for weapons and crests. Hospital beadles carried 'tipstaves' on 'rounds' to 'be known for officers'. Marshalmen and watchmen carried less cumbersome halberds or 'partisans', but a thump from one of these could send suspects spinning to the ground.[63]

## Linking lines

Wards were split into 242 precincts, each with a constable, although Stow counted 238 constables in his *Survey* (1598).[64] Vagrancy seemed so crushing in 1613 that eighty-five householders were picked to walk

---

[59] LMA Rep. 30, fo. 245; Jours. 30, fo. 129v; 31, fo. 68; 34, fo. 9v; GL MS 4457/2, fos. 81v, 98.
[60] LMA WJ/SR/NS/29/95.
[61] BHC 6, fo. 297v; GL MS 4457/2, fo. 213; BHC 9, fos. 360, 872; SBHA Governors' Journals 1, fo. 86; 2, fo. 58v; GL MSS 12806/2, fo. 38v; 3146/1, fo. 44; 2968/2, fo. 195; 4180/1, fo. 175; WAC E2416, fo. 210; F2003, fos. 192–3 LMA Jour. 28, fo. 278 (beadles). GL MSS 1176/1, 1662; 3146/1, fos. 6v, 86; 4524/1, fo. 131; 942/1, fo. 55; 878/1, fo. 58; 4457/2, fo. 116v (warders).
[62] LMA Reps. 23, fo. 503; 28, fo. 279v; 29, fos. 104v, 298; 48, fo. 247; Jour. 40, fo. 73; BHC 6, fo. 111.
[63] LMA Letterbook S, fo. 138; Jour. 28, fo. 278; GL MSS 4180/1, fo. 175; 4524/1, fo. 183; 2968/1, fo. 169 (beadles); 1046/1, fo. 29; 4457/2, fo. 129; 1002/1, fo. 338; 4956/2 fo. 137; 3556/1, fo. 195v (warders); LMA Reps. 22, fos. 22v, 486 (constables); 23, fo. 503; 40, fo. 346v; Jour. 28, fo. 278; BHC 6, fo. 111; GL MS 4180/1, fo. 175 (marshalmen/watch).
[64] John Stow, *The Survey of London* (1598), ed. H. B. Wheatley, revised edition (1986); LMA Jour. 29, fo. 120v (229 is the number given in this order from 1613).

through wards from dawn to dusk with 229 constables. Each ward got three except for the crime hot-spots Bridge and both Farringdon wards, which got double the standard share, and better-off Lime Street and Bassishaw, which each got two extra hands.[65] Each ward also had a warder, beadle, and deputy (often long-term residents with key roles in local affairs[66]). On top of this, 543 watchmen were spread unevenly through wards in 1643, according to perceptions of risk: one-quarter watched in trouble-prone Farringdon Without alone.[67] Provost marshals took up post towards 1600 when job losses, biting inflation, and rumoured and real riots shook London. Two City marshals followed soon after with six 'men' at first (and three or four later on), who did daily laps of the east and west halves of the city.[68] We can also add bellmen, who looked out for fire and trouble as they walked after dark, ringing time; trained bands who lined streets and fields in tense times; and informers who snooped around 'foreign' workers, for example, or Protestant dissenters after the return of the king in 1660.

Numbers went up and down, but somewhere near 800 men policed the square mile in 1643, more than the 767 officers who policed the city's streets in 2000–1.[69] Then, as now, however, people in authority wanted more not less policing. Eight extra 'bedells of beggars' took up post in 1569. A parish got two extra constables in 1642 when its 'old tyme' allocation was no longer enough.[70] London's policing systems had linking lines of organization and accountability long before the reforms after 1700. They helped London respond to troubles, putting key institutions in tight relations with each other, beginning with the Guildhall and stretching out with purpose to courts, hospitals, wards, middling men sitting in vestries who worried all week long about dwindling finances, all the way down to lowly precinct constables. Policies, petitions, and tip-offs all moved up and down these lines. Each officer had a place, though links loosened if someone forgot to do his job or orders or good advice did not sink in. But the roles and rules of office always changed to cope with developing troubles. London's leaders were resourceful, sometimes taking steps hard on the heels of a new vagrancy statute or prodding from

---

[65] LMA Jour. 29, fos. 120v-21v.  [66] LMA Jour. 28, fo. 278; Rep. 30, fo. 294v.
[67] LMA Jours. 40, fos. 75–6; 29, fo. 120v.
[68] BHC 6, fos. 111–14v; LMA Jour. fo. 73; Reps. 23, fos. 503, 524, 526v, 529v; 60, fos. 119, 136; Jours 22, fo. 347v; 33, fo. 268; APC 1616–17, pp. 193–4; 1627, p. 165.
[69] LMA Reps. 11, fo. 325; 16, fo. 450; 22, fo. 337; Letterbook R, fo. 14; Jour. 40, fo. 45v; The City of London Police Annual Report, 2000–1, 28. William Maitland put the tally of constables (241), beadles (32), and watchmen (672) at 945 in the early eighteenth century: *The History of London From Its Foundations by the Romans to the Present Time* (1739), p. 515.
[70] LMA Jour. 40, fos. 45v-6.

privy councillors. A City committee was set up soon after the 1572 statute to put it in force and devise 'new orders if nede require' ('articles' were passed not long after). Time after time, the City said that its anti-vagrancy steps followed strategies stated in statutes. Parishes and wards were also 'put in mynde' at other times to act on vagrancy clauses in Books of Orders.[71] Printers busily printed passes to send vagrants back home, pumping out 1,200 at one time around 1600 and 1,960 at another not long after.[72] Few years passed without at least one committee looking long and hard at policing. Some were one-off brainstorming sessions, but more often committees met for the time it took to produce something, as in 1578 when ten aldermen (among them four Bridewell governors) met several times over 'wyne' with twelve leading citizens (including five more Bridewell governors) to devise 'good meanes' to get rid of 'all sorts of roagues, vagabonds, and beggars'. These Guildhall think-tanks were part of attempts to improve policing, and they always included a number of wise-heads from the hospitals who had hands-on experience of vagrants and their habits. A City task force met 'constantlie' with Bridewell's 'masters' in 1626 until they 'perfected' the 'businesse' of coming up with a 'course' for 'freeing and cleering' London's streets of begging vagrants. The wide-ranging report that followed was one of a series that led to important policy changes in crunch times.[73]

Large-scale City acts made it clear that policing vagrancy was never imagined separately from other troubles that stemmed from growth. 'Clearing' and 'cleaning' London was neatly double-edged wording, involving stability and sanitation at one and the same time. There were single-purpose vagrancy orders, but just as often policing measures were part of sweeping policy packages that covered 'clearing' and 'cleaning' streets, alleys, dirt, decay, and inmates, as well as dangerous and dirty vagrants. Policing was planned along this broad front, in conjunction with health and hygiene improvements. Lengthy orders linked policing, punishment, prison, hospitals, census findings, night watches and lighting, environmental controls, and clean-up campaigns. 'Bokes' for 'orderyng of the pore people' (including policing disorderly poor) were issued in the sixteenth century. Individuals, with safety in mind, also thought up

---

[71] For example, LMA Reps. 10, fo. 287; 14, fo. 402v; 16, fo. 519v; 18, fo. 389; 21, fo. 126v; 39, fos. 1v-2; Letterbooks R, fo. 64v; T, fo. 151v; Remembrancia Book 8, fos. 113v-14; Jours. 11, fo. 337; 12, fo. 239; 17, fo. 42v; 21, fo. 406; 22, fo. 245; 23, fo. 74; 25, fo. 227v; 30, fo. 395.
[72] LMA Reps. 26(1), fo. 96; 26(2), fo. 428v; 25, fo. 110v.
[73] LMA Reps. 18, fo. 97v; 21, fo. 470v; 19, fo. 395; 21, fo. 470v; 22, fos. 252v-3; 23, fos. 185, 483v; 33, fo. 55; 38, fo. 140; 40, fo. 72; 43, fo. 154v; 45, fo. 234v; 46, fo. 150v; 51, fo. 78v.

plans (with help) to cut vagrancy. Sir Martin Bowes (an alderman with ties to the hospitals) 'devysed' a 'proclamayccon' in 1557, giving authority and a salary to a 'pensioner' from each parish to 'dryve out' beggars.[74] From an early stage initiatives like this one involved the hospitals. Christ's took a leading role early on, as London's poor relief scheme was centralized in the hands of its bench for a while.[75] The mayor asked the 'hospityalls' to 'devyse good meanes' to drive out 'the greate number of vacabonds' in 1568, and his successor four years later turned first to St Bartholomew's board for guidance to 'abolyshe' the hordes of 'comon beggers and dezeassed' street stragglers.[76]

But more complex courses were needed as troubles multiplied with growth. A 'special courte of aldermen' ran through 'the boke of articles for the relief of the poore and abolishinge of roges and mastlerles men lately devised by the Bishop of London' in 1572: 1,000 copies of 'articles' to put an end to begging were sent round to parishes in the next year. Not for the first time a bulky order – this one stretching to thirteen clauses – was passed shortly after to stop vagrants crawling through the city with harm in mind. Some of this was familiar stuff, but other parts were newer; a 'surveyor' or 'deputie' (working in tandem with constables) walked the rounds in parishes – 'where he thinketh best' – and handed vagrants to constables; 'espieinge' vagrants, constables were told to take them to the next parish from where they were passed to the next-in-line on the shortest route out of the city; parishes were told to comb pauper houses in alleys for 'newe inmates' each fortnight at least; wards were warned to check that cages were sturdy enough to hold vagrants overnight; and watermen were warned not to bring tramps and beggars across the river.[77]

Policing orders were passed at regular intervals from then on, each with some adjustment in the light of experience. Some were built into giant orders, like the fifty-three clause Common Council Bridewell orders (1579), which required 'speedy' searches for vagrants. Bridewell's role was spelled out in detail: healthy vagrants were quickly moved on (whippings waited for anyone foolish enough to sneak back), citizens were told to help catch vagrants or risk a steep fine, and wards were told to keep cages, stocks, and whipping-posts in good repair.[78] Nor was it odd that such an all-encompassing social policy was subsumed under the heading 'Brydewell', because the hospitals had become indispensable to policing.

---

[74] LMA Rep. 11, fos. 224–5; Letterbook S, fo. 137v.
[75] This centralized poor relief scheme is described in full in Archer, *Pursuit of Stability*, pp. 159–61.
[76] LMA Rep. 16, fo. 340; SBHA Governors' Journal 2, fo. 79.
[77] LMA Reps. 17, fo. 259; 18, fos. 110v, 127–7v. See also LMA Jour. 20, fos. 323–3v.
[78] LMA Jour. 20, fos. 499v-501, 502v.

The 1579 act, like others afterwards, set out roles for each one, with few differences from the first 'Orders for the Hospitalls'. Bridewell was given more policing tasks over time, most notably in campaigns to limit street selling. More 'Orders for Roagues' followed in 1587 in which Bridewell is a clearing house: vagrants and others brought there after 'daye searches' were 'seene by the governours' who 'sorte[d]' them into categories – 'stowt and stronge', 'small strengthe', 'sycke, sore, and lame', 'cureable', 'masterless', 'vacabond'. The court's final word sent some stragglers to sick-beds, others to work, and the rest on the road back home. Emerging strategies sought better co-ordination with neighbouring justices/counties, so that each one followed the same script. Aldermen were given 'a [newe] prynted booke of lawes and ordynances' for 'clearynge' London, to make sure that no ward had excuses for not following Guildhall guidelines. This 1587 act was the basis for a later 'report towching the hospitalls' (and policing) in 1644, that once again clarified the flow of people to each hospital. Before then, this four-fold flow was ratified again in a lengthy by-law of 1625 (and again in the next year), the same year that yet another vagrancy order again emphasized the vital role of hospitals as the receptacles of London's rootless sick and vagrants.[79]

Policing orders changed through time, new names or labels appeared as meanings of crime shifted, and special attention was sometimes paid to ballad sellers/singers, fishwives, or broom-sellers. New roles were also carved out for offices that had been around for a while, along with more recent innovations, most notably marshals who, with constables, emerged as *the* busiest law and order officers after 1600, bringing between them over 95 per cent of suspects brought to Bridewell after 1625. New touches were added, as when alderman-governors of hospitals were asked to be 'att theire hospitalls' to 'dispose' of vagrants.[80] Far from being rusty, then, policing was bolstered by a string of improvements. True enough end results did not always meet desired goals, but these steps were not the marks of a lackluster system. Far from it, the century before 1660 was a purple time for thinking about the nature of policing. It was better co-ordinated by 1660, although the frustration of seeing offenders skip over county lines remained, and more accountable, critical here was the role of 'overseers' in keeping tabs on officers. More 'searches' were set up to ferret out a growing range of suspect people. Information was tapped in a variety of ways, and there was more counting to discover the extent of

---

[79] LMA Reps. 21, fos. 475v-6; 57, fos. 98–9 (1st pag.); 39, fos. 1v-2v, 2v-3v, 38v-9; 40, fo. 71–2.
[80] See below, chap. 11; LMA Rep. 39, fos. 1v–2.

troubles. And last but not least, more attention was paid to night lighting and watches.

Constables were lynchpins of law and order, always 'attendant in the parish'.[81] No one expended full-time energy clinching cases with detective science, but we see constables rushing to crime scenes, rummaging for clues, going from house to house to ask questions, getting evidence for a later day in court. Some got to scenes so quickly that they could later tell courts that they found warm imprints of human figures on tousled beds. 'Beggers feare him more than the justice', John Earle remarked in 1628.[82] Bridewell books let us walk the streets with officers. A regular run of City orders told constables to 'walk the rounde' or 'ronne' through wards; 'not once or twice but all daie long', Common Council said in 1635. Constables had 'warding' days, taking turns to walk 'rounds'. They routinely set watches and counted numbers to see if anyone was missing, and checked that lanterns were burning outside front doors. With beadles, they spent the most time compiling 'returns' or counts of suspect people and suspicious places. Constables also took leading roles directing 'searches' that, needless to say, covered the full range of London's troubles: surprise swoops to round up recusants, 'romishe priests', inmates in 'Jelly Alley' and other dank places, 'mayds' or 'singlewomen' 'not in any service', suspect 'strangers', and vagrants and 'masterless men'.[83]

Constables had leading peace-keeping roles, but not enough notice has been paid to others who also made arrests, like watchmen, warders, beadles, marshals, aldermen, deputies, or 'speciall officers' who were given specific tasks by the City or guilds. 'Speciall persons' were hired to catch vagrants from time to time, to police particular patches on Sundays when beggars headed for churches, or to 'take' anyone seeking lodgings in the Savoy in 1579; a 'nursery' of crime, Common Council called this once grand hospital.[84] Special officers also hunted down 'goodes forane bought and solde', and strangers slipping into London to work in nooks and crannies and street-sellers. Four were hired to seize banned brushes in 1606, and two confiscated linen sold in 'open' streets

---

[81] LMA Jour. 20, fo. 323.   [82] Earle, *Micro-cosmographie*, fo. F11r-v.
[83] LMA Jours. 36, fo. 1; 37, fo. 49v; GL MSS 6552/1, fo. 121; 4524/1, fo. 131v; 2956/1, fo. 192; 3556/2, 1658; LMA Jours. 28, fo. 95; 39, fo. 243v (catholics); GL MSS 6552/1, fo. 241; 9237, fo. 72; 4524/1, fo. 266v; 4383/1, fo. 314; 5090/2, fo. 262; 4956/2, fo. 291; LMA Jours 35, fo. 252 (inmates); 37, fo. 125; GL MS 645/2, fo. 52v (maids); LMA Jour. 33, fo. 6; Letterbook R, fo. 310; TNA SP12/47/57 (strangers); LMA Jours. 25, fo. 255; 26, fos. 68, 293; 27, fos. 70, 137, 300v, 380; 28, fo. 304; 29, fos. 259–60; 30, fo. 394 (vagrants); GL MS 4524/1, fo. 115; LMA Jour. 26, fo. 12v (shady houses).
[84] LMA Rep. 22, fos. 258v-9; Jour. 20, fo. 501v.

by hawkers in 1611–12.[85] Inmates, 'devided' houses, and carts zipping along streets were among other troubles put in the hands of 'speciall' officers.[86] In a similar category were warders who stopped 'wronges' to the 'walke', walls, rails, trees, grass, and ditches in newly renovated Moorfields in 1609: including checking that vagrants were sent packing and grass did not 'growe amock'.[87]

Like 'special officers', informers were hired by various authorities to deal with the troubles caused by London's growth and it is no accident that their numbers rose after 1600.[88] Informers snooped around inmates, for instance, 'forryn' workers, and almost anyone else who fell foul of penal statutes or a parish or guild. They gathered evidence and went to courts with, they hoped, case-winning testimony. Perhaps best known to us are Hugh Alley 'and his partnyers', who were handed near carte blanche powers by the City to curb hawking and forestalling markets in 1600, and had bumper pay-days, £28 at one time in 1601. Alley had a textbook informers' career for over a decade, chasing 'alien' workers or brewers who sold beer at excessive prices.[89] More mundanely, 'one halfe' of 'engrossed' fish and fruit put on sale at Billingsgate in 1561 was given to 'the fynder', and anyone uncovering 'forrein buying and selling' got a 'halfe of forfeitures' in 1646.[90] Parishes also hired informers to regulate Sunday tipplers and traders, victuallers trading on the sly, or children left

---

[85] LMA Jour. 20, fo. 503v; GCL Company Minute Books O3, fo. 438; P2, fos. 224v, 227v; LMA Reps. 27, fos. 314v-15; 30, fo. 68; See also LMA Rep. 16, fos. 127v-8; GCL Company Minute Books O2, fo. 255; R2, fo. 128v.

[86] GL MSS 4487/1, fo. 468; 819/1, fo. 154v; 943/1, fos. 38v, 191v-2v; 3908/1, fos. 56v, 58v; 1453/1, fo. 52v; 5444/1, fos. 233, 236; 12806/3, fo. 47v.

[87] LMA Rep. 29, fos. 13v-14, 225; GL MSS 942/1, fo. 15v; 6836, fo. 74v; 4457/2, fos. 96, 98, 101v; 5090/2, fos. 171v, 174; 4241/1, fo. 199; 1568, fo. 419; 7673/1, fo. 367v; 645/2, fo. 10v; 4409/1, fo. 72; 4457/2, fo. 189.

[88] For informers see M. G. Davies, *The Enforcement of English Apprenticeship, 1563–1642: a Study in Applied Mercantilism* (Cambridge, MA, 1956), chaps 2–3; M. W. Beresford, 'The common informer, the penal statutes, and economic regulation', *Economic History Review*, 2nd series, 10 (1957), 221–38; Archer, *Pursuit of Stability*, pp. 137–9; Malcolm Gaskill, *Crime and Mentalities in Early Modern England* (Cambridge, 2000), pp. 165–73; Dean, *Law-Making and Society in Late Elizabethan England*, pp. 204–7; Shoemaker, *Prosecution and Punishment*, chaps 9–10.

[89] For example, LMA Rep. 34, fo. 576v; MJ/SBR/1, fos. 89, 100, 109, 112; WJ/SR/35, 167–8; GL MS 4813/1, fo. 93. For Alley and 'partners' see LMA Reps. 24, fos. 137, 351v, 435, 459; 25, fos. 246v, 150v-2; and Ian Archer's account of Alley and the markets in *Hugh Alley's Caveat: the Markets of London in 1598*, eds., Archer, Caroline Barron, and Vanessa Harding, London Topographical Society, 137 (1988), pp. 15–29. The Fishmongers' Company gave 'Alley and his partners' twenty shillings in 1601 for moving on fishwives with 'comon sittings in Cheapside and other marketts': GL MS 5770/1, fo. 289. For Alley as informer, see Archer, Barron, and Harding, eds., *Hugh Alley's Caveat*, pp. 18–27.

[90] LMA Letterbook T, fo. 32; Jour. 40, fos. 189v-90.

by mothers for others to keep. Some went back to the same mole. John Philimore appears in St Sepulchre (Middlesex Division) accounts for several years in succession, 'informinge againste' unlicensed victuallers.[91] Informers or 'agents' (a title from 1636) also caught catholics, including some who set up a church in secret in 1594. Hearing about the 'bold and frequent repair' to mass in 1630, the Crown hired Humphrey Crosse to 'observe and apprehend' daring 'papists', someone with experience who had rounded up two priests and seven jesuits in a single swoop on a house in Clerkenwell two years earlier.[92]

Informers were essential elements in policing before 1600, though they drew bad feelings. Artisan 'strangers' said that they were 'daily molested' by meddling informers, and got backing from foreign ambassadors now and then. The City was supportive of native workers, but the Crown had milder attitudes to 'aliens', mindful that for a long time it had given safe haven to protestants at risk overseas.[93] But all could join in the chorus against prying informers who greedily pocketed statutory forfeitures. Muck spread and informer became a dirty word. Hugh Williams was insulted when he was called an 'informer, a raylor, a drunkard and what not' in 1629. The aptly named Christopher Hitter said he would 'beat' anyone who prosecuted Sabbath-day laws. A yeoman from Turnmill Street was caught 'abusing' an informer 'for defective measures' in 1614.[94] Informers took bribes without scruples, many said, even though laws banned compounding without permission, and royal and civic orders targeted 'abusive' informers. But none of this stopped 'abuses'. Thomas Wright was trapped taking bribes when 'informing against vitlers' in 1615. An embroiderer was caught 'cheating divers' under 'collor of an informer' in 1633. A Wapping man ended up in court for 'informing and compoundinge without leave', while a porter was ordered to 'bring forth his confederates [who] joined with him to deceave' people 'under colour of being informers of penall laws'.[95] Such fraud added to

---

[91] GL MSS 593/2, fo. 144; 4524/1, fos. 248v, 255; 951/1, fo. 30v; 1303/1, 1630–1; 2895/2, 1654–5; 9080/1b, 1647–8; 9080/2, 1649, 1650, 1651; 9080/3, 1652; 9080/4; 7706, fo. 8v.
[92] TNA SP12/268/75; LMA Remembrancia Book 8, fo. 98; APC 1629–30, p. 307; 1627–8, pp. 379–80. See also HOL MP 6–9–1641; P. R. Harris, 'The reports of William Udall, informer, 1605–1612', *Recusant History*, 8 (1965), 252–84.
[93] TNA SP14/87/78; 16/39/59. See also Andrew Pettigree, *Foreign Protestant Communities in Sixteenth-Century London* (Oxford, 1986).
[94] HOL MP 10–3–1621; GL MS 5770/2, fo. 750; LMA Rep. 33, fo. 328; MJ/SBR/2, fo. 57. See also LMA Rep. 33, fo. 321; MJ/SBR/2, fo. 39; G. R. Elton, 'Informing for profit: a sidelight on Tudor methods of law enforcement', *Historical Journal*, 11 (1954), 149–67.
[95] LMA Jour. 20, fo. 189; SRPC (204), pp. 472–80; LMA MJ/SBR/2, fo. 218; MJ/SR/523/169; WJ/SR/NS/38/71; MJ/SBR/2, fo. 333. See also D. R. Lidington, 'Parliament and the enforcement of the penal statutes: the history of the Act "In Restraint of Common Promoters" (18 Eliz. I, c.5)', *Parliamentary History*, 8 (1989), 309–28.

already ambiguous attitudes towards informers: pariahs for some, yet used by the City to enforce laws for gain so long as controls were put in place, and able to get redress if someone took exception to their 'meddling'.[96] Rewards were also used to spur investigators and informing by officers. One officer got £10 after tracking down 'principal engrossers of coals' in 1623.[97] City and Crown dangled rewards in front of people long before the statutory rewards created in the 1690s, hoping that more prosecutions would soon follow.[98] A City Act to stop 'burglaries [and] robberies' by 'retayling brokers, broggers and hucksters' in 1623 offered £5 to anyone who 'first gave informacon'. With vagrants swarming in 1634, justices gave rewards 'out of parte of the monies' to 'incourage' people to 'informe and prosecute'. One quarter of each ten shilling fine paid by constables who left vagrants to wander was put aside for prosecutors in built-up Middlesex in the same year. Rewards also helped to get to the bottom of particular cases. Four marks was offered for information about the 'lewd fact to disclose the doers' after 'lewd and disordered persons' 'defaced' seats in the Royal Exchange in 1577. A sailor picked up twenty shillings from the City after he 'disclosed' a 'horrible conspiracye of murder' of 'honest' sailors by 'wycked marryners' in 1567.[99]

Rewards also gave a lift to thief-takers and rackets in receiving stolen goods, and if these seem less than in eighteenth-century London, this may be the result of skimpier evidence.[100] Robert Tittler has traced the careers of John Pulman and his sidekick William Elder, who were both called 'thieftakers' at City Sessions in 1609, and (with Alexandra Johnson) has sketched the potential for thief-taking.[101] Newgate keepers got justices' warrants when people lost purses of 'great value' towards 1600, giving them authority 'to take up all the nips and foists' and 'let them lie [in Newgate] while the money be re-aunswered to the party'. Recorder Fleetwood infiltrated cutpurse rings at this time and kept lists to 'know

---

[96] Archer, Barron, and Harding, eds., *Hugh Alley's Caveat*, pp. 26–7.
[97] LMA Rep. 42, fo. 312v.
[98] Cf. Beattie, *Policing and Punishment*, chap. 8; Tim Wales, 'Thief-takers and their clients in later Stuart London', in Paul Griffiths and Mark S. R. Jenner, eds., *Londinopolis: Essays in the Cultural and Social History of Early Modern London* (Manchester, 2000), pp. 67–84.
[99] LMA Jours. 32, fos 224v-5; 36, fo. 203v; MJ/SBR/6, fo. 16; Jour. 20, fo. 341; Letterbook V, fo. 82v.
[100] Cf. Beattie, *Policing and Punishment*, chap. 5; Wales, 'Thief-takers and their clients'; Ruth Paley, 'Thief-takers in London in the age of the McDaniel gang, c. 1745–1754', in Hay and Snyder, eds., *Policing and Prosecution*, pp. 301–41.
[101] Robert Tittler, 'Swaddon the swindler and Pulman the "thief-taker": crime and variations in the great metropolis', in Tittler, *Townspeople and Nation: English Urban Experiences, 1540–1640* (Stanford, CA, 2001), pp. 156–76; Alexandra F. Johnston and Robert Tittler, '"To catch a thief" in Jacobean London', in E. B. DeWindt, ed., *The Salt of Common Life* (Kalamazoo, MI, 1995), pp. 233–69.

what new be sprung up this last year and where to find them if need be'.[102] The morning after his pocket was picked in 1614, a 'gentleman' called on Mary Markham (better known to us as Moll Cutpurse) and asked her for her help to find the thief, 'knowing her before', he said later, 'and having heard by these meanes [that] many who had their purses cut had been helped and divers malefactors taken'. This is a telling glimpse of a scam run along similar lines to Jonathan Wild's 'clearing house' that traded in stolen loot a century later, and is further evidence of the existence of rackets in returning stolen goods for profit. Dorothy Stevens was said to be 'confederate with Will Hart', who conned 'divers' people in 1633 'under pretext of helping to know of divers losses'. A 'gent' took Rody Chester to court in 1635 for taking his purse stuffed with thirty shillings. He was drinking with her and another woman at 'The Signe of the Clawe' next to Westminster's bowling alley, he said, and after they left he found that his purse was missing. He bumped into Chester three days later and told her that he had lost his purse 'in her company', and she replied that she 'would help him to his money againe', 'if he wold be contented and say no more'. Margaret Evans came clean at Westminster Sessions in 1637, saying that if he had been prepared to give her 'three pieces', she would have helped John Gwyllimas to get back forty-three pounds taken from him by the 'notorious' pickpocket Frances Chickley. Evans was part of the 'conspiracy', justices decided, and she was soon on her way to the 'New prison'.[103] Small beer perhaps, but thought-provoking insights, nevertheless, into events replayed elsewhere that show us how thieves could work hand-in-hand to wheedle money from victims and also help magistrates crack cases.

Examining the role of constables alone cannot give us a full sense of the potential of policing. That can only emerge when informers and thief-takers are included, along with inputs from other officers, who sometimes served for longer than constables, prominent among them beadles, whether appointed by hospitals, parishes, or wards. Before Bridewell (and after) 'beadles of the beggars' stood in wait at a gate or handy 'corner' to pounce on rogues. Hospitals with their own beadles and powers over 'beadles of beggers' had a key role in tackling vagrants. Beadles divided 'walkes', policed wards, taking time to cover each street, magistrates hoped, and had days and times to guard the bridge in 1563. The number of 'beadles of beggars' was doubled to sixteen in 1569.

---

[102] Archer, *Pursuit of Stability*, pp. 236–7, quoting Robert Greene, who Archer believes is a reliable source; Wright, ed., *Queen Elizabeth and Her Times*, vol. II, 74.

[103] TNA STAC8 124/4; BHC 7, fo. 355; LMA WJ/SR/31/3, 48/8. For Moll Cutpurse see Gustav Ungerer, 'Mary Frith, alias Moll Cutpurse, in life and literature', *Shakespeare Studies*, 18 (2000), 42–84; *Oxford Dictionary of National Biography*, n.v. Moll Cutpurse.

Bridewell's role grew as time passed, and it was handed authority in 1591 to 'sende' for beadles from other hospitals to drive out 'roagues and beggars'.[104] Beadles continued to 'clear' streets long after this, an extra twenty-six were chosen in 1612, and told to 'spend their time wholly in walking' their 'limitts everyday from one hower before' sunrise until one hour after sunset. Not everything went as planned, however; rate collections fell far short of the amount needed for salaries, and householders claimed that beadles did 'litle or no service'. Magistrates took little notice and later in the same year instructed each ward to appoint a beadle and 'so many more' 'according to the greatnes' of the ward.[105] Beadles had heavy workloads. Ward beadles often ran through names of watchmen at the 'meeting' and 'breakinge' of watches to check that no one was missing. They were also asked at various times to pay particular attention to policing inmates, street-sellers, women leaving children on streets or steps, and alehouses open late or while church services were taking place.[106] Like constables, they also went from house to house to count and check 'forreigne poore'. The minutiae of week-long work in parishes is noted in accounts that log payments to beadles for writing down names in subsidy books and muster lists, fetching warrants or indictments, knocking on landlords' doors to get them to sign bonds, finding aldermen to sign 'ye poore roule', cleaning cages, making sure that the poor did not lack 'fuel' in cold winter months, tending fire 'engines', taking trips to check that nursing children were in good health, 'carrying away' church 'soil', keeping churchyards 'quiett and free from noise' in service time, and checking hawkers and carts carrying 'household stuff'.[107]

Beadles were expected to be Jacks-of-all-trades, but always with a clear role in policing streets. This was also true with warders who, amongst

---

[104] LMA Letterbook R, fo. 14; Rep. 11, fo. 325v; SBHA 'The Ordre of the Hospitall of St Bartholomewes in West Smythfield in London', E7–8; Governors' Journal 2, fos. 194v-5; GL MS 12806/2, fos. 15v-16, 38v; LMA Reps. 16, fo. 450; 22, fo. 337. See also Edmund Howes, *Annales, Or, A Generall Chronicle of England Begun by John Stow: Continued and Augmented With Matters Forraigne and Domestique, Ancient and Moderne, Unto the End of the Present Year, 1631* (1631), p. 41. For beadles in late medieval London, see Rexroth, *Deviance and Power*, pp. 61–7 and 191–8.

[105] LMA Jours. 28, fo. 278; 29, fo. 5v. See also LMA Jour. 20, fo. 500v; Rep. 31(1), fo. 26; H1/ST/A1/4, fo. 46v; GL MS 3570/1, fos. 4v, 12v; SBHA Governors' Journal 4, fos. 47v, 115.

[106] LMA Jour. 40, fos. 77–8v; H1/ST/A 1/4, fo. 46v; H1/ST/A 1/5, fo. 120; Rep. 12, fos. 239v, 509v; GL MSS 3016/1, fo. 537; 4487/1, fo. 441; 6544/1, fos. 38, 65v, 72; 943/1, fo. 38; 12806/2, fos. 38v, 388; 1046/1, fo. 38; 4570/2, fo. 306.

[107] WAC F2003, fos. 192–3; GL MSS 2968/1, fos. 20v, 247; 2968/2, fo. 315v (subsidy books/muster lists); 4385/1, fos. 119v 147, 264v, 300v; 590/1, fo. 254v; 4457/2, fo. 324; 5090/2, fo. 270; 5713/1, fo. 129v; 1124/1, fo. 50v; 7673/2, fo. 62v; 4241/1, fo. 435; 1002/1, fo. 490v (warrants and indictments); 4385/1, fo. 205v; 951/1, fo. 162 (signatures); 4457/2, fo. 314v; 4241/1, fo. 365; 1303/1, 1636; 2895/2, 1637–8; 3907/1, 1632–3; 4409/2, 1648–9; 959/1, fo. 221; 3356/2, 1654 (cages, coals, and fire engines);

314   Control

other things, helped set up daytime warding ('daye watches') before watches came on duty. Warders were chosen by wards but the City hired auxiliary warders from time to time. Parishes chose 'dayly warders' in 1611 as vagrants poured into London. Warders headed to Mercers' Chapel first thing in the morning in 1625 for 'dirreccon' from Sir Thomas Middleton to help marshals 'cleere' up vagrants.[108] Wards were posted on the riverside and at corners and gates at break of day from 'daie to daie' when 'extraordinarie' throngs of rogues clogged streets in 1610. Warders guarded each gate in 1623 to 'better clear' vagrants. 'Day wards' were also set in tense times like Kett's planned march on London, if plague hit hard, or when soldiers and sailors milled about swearing revenge for long overdue wages.[109] Numbers of warders were rarely noted, though we have figures for central and west wards (where the need was felt to be greatest) from 1640: twenty warders for Bassishaw, fifty for Coleman Street, sixty in Farringdon Within, Cripplegate, and Cheap, and eighty in Farringdon Without and Castle Baynard.[110] Like beadles, warders had other duties on top of stopping vagrants, including 'looking after' lighting. One picked up four shillings to 'looke to precinct lanthornes' for 'the whole yeare' in 1651, and sixpence for 'bread and beere when hee hanged upp the lanthornes' in the next year. Warders also went round houses to note the names of inmates, watched women who someone thought might leave a child, got rid of vagrant 'great bellied women', stopped rowdy 'footeball' play, and took turns on 'warding Sundaies' to see that nothing disturbed divine service.[111]

Aldermen deputies took a lead in co-ordinating local strategies, not least because their superiors were often away all day on City matters.[112] They worked with local officers, enforcing by-laws and giving policy advice. They also got involved in the nitty-gritty of running wards: 'viewinge' paupers, 'makinge' subsidy and residents books, 'warding', checking

3146/1, fo. 112v; 5018/1, fo. 8v; WAC F2003, fos. 50, 192–3 (remaining tasks). St Martin-in-the-Fields beadles walked 'frequently up and downe in the streetes' and kept a 'booke' of 'all vagrants passed away': WAC F2003, fos. 192–3.
[108] LMA Jours. 28, fo. 264; 33, fos. 20v, 163v, 250v; 34, fos. 9v, 75v, 87, 157, 248v; 35, fo. 270v. See also LMA Jour. 37, fo. 254; Rep. 21, fos. 126v, 240; TNA SP14/75/54; GL MSS 1509/2/7; 113/1, fo. 65v; 4165/1, fo. 10.
[109] LMA Jours. 30, fo. 283v; 32, fo. 192v; 28, fo. 63v; Reps. 12, fo. 113v; 13i, fos. 68–8v, 129v. See also LMA Jours. 17, fo. 164; 26, fos. 98, 273v; 27, fos. 275, 422; 28, fo. 116v; 33, fo. 304; 34, fos. 16v, 76, 224v, 297v; Reps. 12, fo. 395v; 13ii, fo. 463; 17, fo. 242; 40, fo. 72.
[110] LMA Jour. 39, fo. 143.
[111] SBHA Governors' Journal 3, fo. 106v; GL MSS 1303/1, 1650–1, 1651–2; 3016/1, fos. 250, 537; 952/1, fo. 88; 6544/1, fos. 38, 59, 65v; 4524/1, fo. 219v; 4570/2, fos. 306, 314, 322; LMA Jour. 28, fo. 160v; GL MS 4051/1, fo. 95.
[112] The role of aldermen/ward deputies is emphasized by Archer, *Pursuit of Stability*, pp. 67–8, and in his discussion of social policy and crime in chaps 5–6.

that trained bands were 'weaponed', and giving advice about loans, rents, hand-outs, or costs to send children across the sea to Virginia.[113] People often came running to deputies if something went wrong. With aldermen, they could 'redress' wrongs 'within' their 'power by lawe' brought to them by residents. It was a deputy who cleared up the mess when a collector for the poor refused to do his job in St Botolph-without-Aldgate in 1632; another 'caus[ed] new rayles to be sett upp in Moorfields' in 1616 and 'a strong' gate at 'Bedlem'; and Deputy Grafton saw that Morgan Sampson's wife was thrown out of the ward for 'incontynence and vycious levynge' in 1555.[114]

Marshals, as stated, made a big difference to policing, criss-crossing the city with their teams (another patrolled Southwark's streets). They were men of some standing: 'gents', cordwainers, merchant taylors, and the like.[115] From the first their role was seen in terms of the heavy vagrant 'problem'; Marshal Walrond was given two extra 'able' men in 1617 (doubling their number at a stroke), as 'multitudes' of vagrants streamed through the gates.[116] Bridewell's triplicate role as policeman, prosecutor, and punisher was embodied in the decision taken in 1619 to give it responsibility for a marshal, 'a proper work' by its 'foundacon', the City said, although it also looks like cost cutting. William Davis was Bridewell's first marshal and the next job was to draw up 'directions' for him and 'four servants'. They were told to 'dailie' 'devyde themselves' to catch vagrants and take them to the nearest constable or Bridewell. Davis was told to keep a 'true note' in a 'booke' of each vagrant handed to a constable. Marshals also policed the 'howses of persons notoriouslie suspected' for 'lewde and incontinent life', or any other house where vagrants or felons might get a room, and 'walked' through watches, when asked. Davis also kept lists of the 'names and homes' of constables, 'to find them readilie upon all occasions'. These 'direccons' were 'open-lye redd' at the next Court of Aldermen and each alderman was handed a copy to see that they were followed in his ward.[117] Marshals made

---

[113] For example, GL MSS 1176/1, 1599; 2968/2, fos. 16, 119; 878/1, fo. 58; 2596/1, fo. 190v; 4071/1, fos. 125, 136, 149v; 4071/2, fos. 73v, 86v, 97v, 125v, 155; 6574, fos. 31, 96v, 97, 101, 101v; 2895/1, fo. 241; 1002/1, fo. 515; 4409/1, fos. 137v, 138, 150, 150v, 156v, 157, 163, 170.
[114] LMA Jour. 20, fo. 501v; Reps. 46, fo. 320v; 32, fo. 368; 13ii, fo. 289v.
[115] LMA Reps. 39, fo. 286; 41, fos. 161v, 351v; 51, fos. 303v-4; 56, fo. 129.
[116] LMA Rep. 33, fo. 88. See also Strype, *Survey*, V, pp. 432–3.
[117] BHC 6, fos. 110v, 111, 112v-13v, 114v; LMA Rep. 34, fos. 102–2v, 125v. See also LMA Reps. 38, fo. 204; 39, fo. 2v; 40, fo. 71v; 60, fo. 119; TNA SP16/187/54. Marshal Davis and his first four 'servants' – a fishmonger, goldsmith, joiner, and skinner – were ordered 'not at any tyme' to 'prejudice' Roger Walrond, 'the mediate [City] provost marshal': LMA Rep. 34, fo. 102v.

impacts, but not without cost: City leaders winced at the hefty 'yerely charge' of £289 13s 4d for marshals in 1627. The City had taken back responsibility for both marshals by then, but there was no question of getting rid of this costly load.[118] Their 'daily' laps of the city had become integral to structures that gave backbone to policing. They were 'overseers' as well as investigators, keeping an eye on other officers, and taking reports directly to aldermen and Bridewell. Marshals became in effect London's eyes and ears, adaptable for any trouble, and more besides. A single order in 1626 told them to crack down on vagrants, street-sellers, catholics, rough alehouses, 'houses of incontinencie', and lax constables, warders, rakers, and scavengers, as well as checking that residents were told to hang out 'lanthorne and candlelight', and that the markets and streets were 'cleered in the evening'.[119] Admittedly, marshals trod on the toes of other officers prickly enough to grumble – with vagrants – about this new power on the streets. But, in spite of the mixed abilities of incumbents, a system evolved after 1600 in which marshals played leading roles. One sign of their effectiveness is how quickly they became hate-figures for vagrants, and the reason for this is plain to see in courtbooks that show their heavy involvement in day-to-day policing.[120]

Military muscle sometimes seemed the best way to keep order at certain times. 'A lawe martiall' was set to round up 'rebells and other upstyrrers' as news arrived of Kett's rebellion in 1549. Lieutenancy commissions with power to 'leavy' troops under 'expert captains' boosted defences when 'rebells' and 'traytors' plotted to bring down the government. Trained bands also turned out in tense times like the stormy Shrovetide season or when out-of-pocket soldiers or sailors converged on London for back pay.[121] The Crown sometimes selected provost marshals if 'unlawful assemblies of rogues and vagabonds' threatened the peace, a likely situation when men poured back after wars with little to do. The first thought was to appoint a provost marshal when 'many robberies and fellonies' and other 'horrible crimes' shook London 'day and night' in 1618. Plague was another crunch time when provost marshals were often asked to take over law and order, as in 1603 when problems grew more quickly than the plague that killed more than one-

---

[118] LMA Rep. 41, fos. 212v-13. Aldermen thought for a while about transferring costs for one marshal back to Bridewell in 1627, but it was clear by now that the cost was too steep for 'any hospitall' to bear, and from then on it was 'raysed by comon councell' (ibid., fo. 217).
[119] LMA Rep. 40, fos. 183v-5.
[120] See, pp. 324–25, for antagonisms between marshals and vagrants.
[121] LMA Letterbook R, fos. 26v-7; Jour. 23, fos. 3–3v; Rep. 14, fos. 32v, 34v; Jours. 33, fo. 268; 34, fo. 35v; 39, fo. 127v; Griffiths, *Youth and Authority*, pp. 147–61.

in-five Londoners.[122] As troubles brewed on London's edges after 1600 – described as 'greater [than usual] swarms of vagrants' – magistrates co-ordinated strategies by appointing provost marshals in nearby counties. Your troubles will be less, the Crown told the City in 1616, if surrounding counties are 'first well cleared of dangerous people'. Captain Bardsley had the bright idea of inventing the post of provost marshal of the 'new incorporation' for himself in a letter to the Crown in 1637. It was certainly worth a try, as by then the porous counties and 'monstrous' suburbs had long been seen as the reason why many 'misliving people' flocked to the city.[123] Magistrates imagined defensive shields circling London, with justices and provost marshals at the helm. And although they were never robust enough to keep London vagrant free, they do offer support for the view that there was some thoughtful analysis of crime control at this time.

### Ambivalences and abuses

Like larger London, policing had scores of parts and traits, and there can be no single interpretation of how well police did their job, only ambivalences. But this fuzziness has not stopped scholars calling policing one thing or another, mostly inadequate and amateur, even though many officers had steady spells in office. With so many on duty at any one time the performance record across the city was bound to be patchy. Officers also committed abuses and suffered at the hands of others. This single word, abuse, sheds light on many aspects of policing, and with it we see constables at their hard-working best or crooked worst. Like today, the two sides of abuse stretched from smug arrogance to nervous vulnerability. Abuse is open to several interpretations: what should we say about constables who came through scrapes with hostile hecklers or ended up black and blue after a tough arrest? On-the-job injuries and insults were antagonisms, but they also show that officers took their tasks seriously enough to risk pain and danger. They did not look the other way when trouble brewed or someone called for help. This amount of abuse can be a measurement of care in the line of duty, but also points to another ambivalence at work: a mix of attitudes towards officers. People laughed back then and still laugh today when Dogberry ambles on stage. Name-calling

---

[122] LMA Jours. 22, fo. 347v; 24, fos. 225v, 263v, 328v-9; 33, fo. 268; TNA SP12/240/59; 12/261/70; 14/3/63; SRPJ (161), pp. 360–2.

[123] APC 1615–16, pp. 693–4; 1626, p. 371; TNA SP16/372/10. See also APC 1616–17, pp. 193–4; 1626, p. 288; 1626–7, pp. 306–7; TNA SP14/91/32; 16/36/36; 16/455/102; PC2/46/158.

318    Control

and cat-calling were two likely responses. But people were also afraid of what might happen next if they were caught doing wrong. A waterbearer's wife tipped off a court that a widower who lived a few doors away from her would not let women leave his house by the front door at night, 'for feare of being apprehended by a constable'.[124]

Some officers were singled out for threats and taunts, but many ended up licking their wounds after a spell in office. The 'creple but verie desperate rogue', John Stadborne, whacked a warder 'exceedinglie' with his crutch when he tried to arrest him in 1631, and would 'have beaten out his braines' and bit 'off a peec of his legge' if he had not been strapped to a cart and wheeled to Bridewell. He was not the only 'creple' to hit a warder with a crutch, and more than a few tried to bite a chunk from a warder's hand, like Richard Turner who was found hanging around in 1609 with a ticket to get into a hospital that was two months out-of-date.[125] Many arrests turned nasty. A Walbrook warder was 'struck downe' in the 'kennel' by a wooden-legged drunk in 1606, who 'resisted all officers that came neer him'. Hugh Beades was so drunk when he pinched 'a piece of bacon' that 'sixe or seven men could hardlie restraine him'. The only way to calm John Webb after a drinking binge was to tie his legs together. Another drunk vagrant missed when lunging at a constable with his knife and toppled into a 'kennel'; and someone caught red-handed robbing books also missed a constable and stabbed himself in the side.[126] Others were strapped in a cart for their own good. Vagrant Diana Matthews, who tried to 'cheat' a 'country wench', was strapped in one after flinging dirt and punches at officers. John Street, who suddenly started spitting at startled shoppers and pulling things from stalls in a market, was also tied to a cart. Ballad singer Richard Kempsall would not budge an inch 'until the marshall got a carte' to drag him to Bridewell. While fake 'creple' John Griffin was bundled into a cart after he 'bad the proudest marshal' to arrest him in the Cloth Fair.[127] Officers grabbed anything handy to get trouble-makers to a lock-up. Hugh Jones was wheeled to Bridewell on a wheelbarrow after taunting warders in 1618; 'unruly' Thomas Burges was taken there 'upon mens backs' in 1627.[128]

---

[124] GL MS 9057/1, fos. 108–8v.    [125] BHC 5, fo. 351v; 7, fo. 237; 5, fo. 339.
[126] BHC 5, fos. 100v, 122v; 7, fos. 63v, 95v, 265. See also BHC 5, fos. 46v, 100v, 109, 130v; 8, fo. 235; LMA CQSF 133/31; Rep. 40, fo. 410v; MJ/SBR/1, fos. 121, 125v; MJ/SBR/2, fos. 41, 522; MJ/SBR/6, fos. 66v, 109; MJ/SBR/7, fo. 335; MJ/SR/522/122, 198; WAC WCB/1, fo. 43. Cf. Jennine Hurl-Eamon, *Gender and Petty Violence in London, 1680–1720* (Columbus, OH, 2005), pp. 97–105.
[127] BHC 8, fo. 9v; 6, fo. 46v; 7, fos. 35v, 53.
[128] BHC 6, fo. 49; 7, fo. 45. See also BHC 6, fos. 100v, 230, 440; 7, fos. 38v, 166, 220v, 274.

People also ran away when they saw officers coming along the street or to escape from custody after arrest, squeezing through holes in walls, climbing onto roofs, scrambling over 'the tiles' to get away from the hand of the law. Some suspects slipped away after being left in a constable's house until a justice could be found to sign a committal order.[129] Not all of them escaped for good, however. Abraham Proff gave watchmen the slip after they caught him being 'naughty' in a street with Agnes Hill one night in 1608, but he only tasted freedom for 'about an hower' until the same watch came across him sitting on a stall.[130] Friends or bystanders also jumped in to help people who had been arrested. Elizabeth Wilson of Wapping 'called upon people to rescue her' as she struggled with officers. 'He that loveth a whore helpe helpe', Joan Garroll shouted when she was caught red-handed picking pockets. Brothers rescued brothers, masters rescued apprentices. The cry of 'prentices and clubs' was an alarm-call for apprentices, we are told, who came running to pluck their mates from officers. John Sherborne was called a 'comon' 'rescuer of others from officers'. John Evans nearly killed a marshalman with a hammer when he dived in to help a vagrant who was trying to wriggle out of his grip.[131] Officers were also caught off-guard when crowds turned up out of the blue. Alice Rogers raised a 'tumlte in Smithfield' in an attempt to drag 'an arrant thief' from officers and waded into the scrum herself, 'tearing their bands'. A 'gent' was killed when twelve vagrants ganged up to free a man who had been arrested on Fleet Street in 1631.[132] A number of 'knights in shining armour' rescued 'strumpets'. John Barber of Dorchester swooped on two officers as they marched 'a lewde strumpet' to Bridewell in 1582. A group of Temple 'gents' ganged up on a marshal with 'a lewd woman' in tow. While Richard Edmunds told a marshalman that the 'lewd woman' in his custody was his wife, and 'stroke up' his heels, leaving him helpless on the floor as he disappeared into the crowd with his new friend.[133]

---

[129] BHC 2, fos. 109v-10, 111; 3, fos. 109v, 328, 400v; 5, fo. 286v; 6, fos. 15v, 49v, 152v, 205v, 280, 353v, 430v; 8, fo. 349; 9, fo. 548; LMA MJ/SBR/4, fos. 125, 380; MJ/SR/514/82; CQSF 110/46.
[130] BHC 5, fo. 260.
[131] LMA MJ/SR/505/67; BRHA BHC 4, fo. 212v; LMA MJ/SBR/2, fo. 279; BHC 6, fo. 58v; 8, fo. 224v; 6, fo. 337; Griffiths, *Youth and Authority*, p. 162. See also TNA STAC8, 178/2; BHC 5, fo. 426; 8, fo. 224v; BRHA BHC 4, fos. 393–5; LMA Remembrancia Book 1, fo. 102v; Reps. 14, fo. 167v; 16, fo. 307; 20, fo. 333v; 23, fo. 96v; 42, fo. 306; CQSF 77/22, 110/15–16, 131/96; MJ/SBR/1, fos. 253, 618; MJ/SBR/2, fos. 87, 520; MJ/SBR/4, fo. 258; ; MJ/SBR/5, fo. 179; MJ/SBR/7, fo. 56; MJ/SR/505/144, 515/52, 522/123, 806/135; WJ/SR/NS/41/76 45/77, WAC WCB/1, fo. 262.
[132] BHC 6, fo. 343v; LMA MJ/SBR/1, fo. 256; BHC 7, fo. 252v.
[133] LMA Rep. 20, fo. 285v; MJ/SBR/2, fo. 218; Rep. 23, fo. 432v; BHC 7, fo. 267v.

Constables should have been able to count on neighbours to give helping hands, but not everyone came running if they called. One bystander refused to help a constable catch a 'disorderly' carman and threw the warrant 'in the durt'. When a constable asked a carman for help to catch 'a comen rogue' in 1608, he pushed him in a ditch and 'strook the marshal and his man'. Other officers also got unneighbourly cold shoulders.[134] This was a 'dailie' hitch by 1632 when 'diverse constables' complained that they were 'dailie misused and not assisted in doinge their offices' by neighbours. Six months later, Common Council told ministers to 'move' people from the pulpit to step in to help constables if they got into any trouble.[135] People also ended up in court for not helping out when hue and cry was raised, or for holding back the chase to help someone get away. William Hussey got the better of a 'fresh pursuite' in 1629 when an alehouse keeper forced his pursuers to run 'halfe a mile' out of their way when he would not let them chase him through his fields, for fear that they 'should 'tread downe his fences'. Even felons found friends in tight spots. A landlord lost his licence in 1630 after letting a murderer sneak away 'without pursuite' after he killed someone in his alehouse along the Strand.[136] Another concern was that someone nursing a grudge after arrest might bring a counter-suit to clear his name and claim costs. The mayor gave William Belfeld a glowing reference for his defence in such a case in 1580. He was 'a verie discrete honeste man' and 'carefull', adding that this was not the first such story that he had heard in his seven months in office: 'I do dayly receve many complaints', he said, 'vexing of officers by sute and charge is of late become a very comon practise', so that 'honest men' nervous of 'quarelling suites' were 'werey of doing their duties'.[137] Vexatious suits continued without much pause, however, and the situation became so serious that when a man roughed up Constable Wade as he arrested his wife in 1637 and got 'a writt out of the common pleas' to sue him for false arrest, aldermen ruled that from now on the City solicitor would defend such cases at the City's cost for 'better encouragement' to officers to 'doe their duties'. Beadles and marshals also managed to get financial backing if writs landed on their doorsteps. Parishes also met defence costs some of the time. St Sepulchre (Holborn

---

[134] LMA CQSF 83/40; Rep. 28, fo. 283v. See also BRHA BHC 4, fo. 137; LMA CQSF 83/101; Rep. 27, fo. 125; MJ/SR/505/190, 519/79; MJ/SBR/1, fos. 135, 587; MJ/SBR/2, fo. 441; MJ/SBR/3 fo. 94; MJ/SBR/5, fo. 527; MJ/SBR/6, fos. 160, 472; WJ/SR/NS/33/61, 46/149; WCA WCB/2, fo. 87.
[135] LMA Jour. 26, fos. 27, 82–2v.
[136] LMA MJ/SBR/5, fos. 45, 166; MJ/SBR/1, fo. 55; MJ/SBR/3, fo. 79; MJ/SBR/6, fos. 483, 543.
[137] LMA Remembrancia Book 1, fo. 45v.

Policing: people and policy 321

division) spent a whopping £10 to defend one of its officers from a malicious counter-suit.[138]

The Guildhall worried about escapes and counter-suits, but there were other reasons for concern when not a single week passed by without someone standing in a dock for harming officers. 'Dissolute, idle, and lewd' Margaret Lewis flung 'a bowl of blood' in a constable's face in Billingsgate in 1628 and taunted a 'gentlewoman in the street'. Other muggers turned violent after heavy drinking sprees. All that John Bird could say when asked 'what moved him' to rescue 'a lewde suspicious woman' in 1605, was that 'he was druncke and knewe not what he did'. She was 'druncke and did not know' what she was doing, nightwalker Margaret Fisher said, after 'scratching' a beadle's cheek and lunging at him 'with a great pynne'. 'Bad' Robert White beat up a constable who tried to break up a 'great' band 'of idle people' he gathered in the 'open streets' by banging a drum.[139] Officers were tripped up, thrown downstairs, punched, kicked, stabbed, and left dazed with 'broken heddes'. Some were left at death's door, 'in great danger' of their lives. A few tackled raving vagrants waving swords in the air, threatening to skin them alive. Others were told that their houses would be burned down or guts spilled. After doing her best to 'entice' a beadle, Elizabeth Laurence said that she would 'burne his house' down. Edward Bentley butted in when a beadle arrested a 'nightwalker' in 1617, saying 'he should answer it with the best blood in his belly'. 'Idle and lewd' Mary Barker 'dare[d] and outface[d]' all constables. Some people longed to get even. Vagrant Francis Roberts 'shook' the 'rule in his hand' at a beadle, shouting 'I will be even with you'. Thomas Gunter, who robbed 'poore people' with 'a cudgel', growled that a deputy 'was as good as he'.[140] Niggling neighbourly rows could also spill over into office. Thomas Parkinson called a constable a 'rogue and rascall' in 1614, and yelled that 'he would meet with him' after he stood down from office. 'Shit on [Whitechapel]

---

[138] LMA Rep. 51, fo. 40v; GL MS 3146/1, fo. 113v. See also GL MSS 3146/1, fo. 18v; 2968/2, fos. 299v-300; LMA Reps. 10, fo. 63; 19, fo. 298v; 29, fo. 185; 33, fo. 341v; 37, fos. 151–1v; 38, fo. 120v; 44, fos. 228v-9; 45, fo. 284; 49, fo. 210v; Remembrancia Book 1, fos. 319–19v; MJ/SBR/1, fo. 5; MJ/SBR/6, fo. 452; BHC 7, fo. 30; HOL MP 19–2–1629, 1–12–1640, 1–3–1641, 10–8–1641.

[139] BHC 5, fos. 9v, 354; LMA Rep. 31(1), fos. 51v-2; GL MS 9064/14, fo. 90.

[140] BHC 8, fo. 411; LMA Rep. 33, fos. 182v-3; BHC 6, fo. 232; BHC 7, fo. 35v; 5, fo. 428v. See also BHC 1, fo. 160; 2, fo. 171v; 3, fo. 436; 6, fos. 61v, 428; 7, fos. 68, 366v; 8, fos. 98, 290, 382v; 9, fo. 524; BRHA BHC 4, fo. 420; LMA CQSF 78/46, 109/39, 120/31, 130/26, 132/58; Reps. 19, fo. 388; 21, fo. 539; 23, fo. 457v; 29, fo. 383v; 51, fo. 40v; 53, fo. 13v; MJ/SBR/1, fo. 616; MJ/SBR/2, fo. 505; MJ/SBR/3, fo. 315; MJ/SBR/5, fo. 529; MJ/SBR/6, fo. 591; MJ/SR/509/115, 512/70; WJ/SR/NS/31/49, 44/188, 49/115; TNA STAC8, 34/7; 260/16; SP14/130/5–7.

churchwardens', Alice Saunders screamed, because they 'wilbe jacke owte of office' one day soon. People also alleged that officers used their position to settle old scores. A scrivener said that a constable 'overcharged him in the subsidye booke above his betters' in 1603 to get his own back for losing an earlier argument.[141]

'Ill language' crackled in a bawdy chorus that abused officers or 'braved' them in words implying sharp antagonism. Michael Moore was called a 'comon maunder' and 'greate abuser' of 'officers in the streetes' in 1640. 'Kiss my arse', a Westminster loudmouth barked at a constable, and other officers had the same invitation. 'Rogue' was another choice jibe for goading officers, along with 'knave' or 'fool'.[142] 'Ill words' zipped through the night air in alehouses and bawdy houses when officers tried to close them down for the night.[143] 'Hot' words also poured out on doorsteps when officers came to search for suspect people or stolen goods. A merchant's servant got 'a dossyn good lashes with a rodde' for not owning up to being a Frenchman and telling Aldgate's deputy to 'serche also his tayle and to kysse it' when he made house-to-house searches in 1563. Things turned ugly quickly on doorsteps when officers were 'resysted and evyll intreated'. William Harwood yelled that 'he wolde not so doo neither for kynge or quene and caste hott mettell' on a constable's head when asked to open his door. Another peeved householder shouted that he would kill anyone who set foot over his door. Others used stalling tactics, keeping officers talking to buy time while friends slipped out of a back door or window.[144] Words also flew when officers tried to distrain goods to cover debts or fines and defaulters went on the warpath.[145]

---

[141] GL MS 9064/14, fo. 130v; WCA WCB/2, fo. 69; SBHA Governors' Journal 3, fo. 233.
[142] BRHA BHC 4, fo. 394; BHC 8, fo. 24; LMA MJ/SBR/6, fo. 299; MJ/SBR/4, fos. 375, 421; MJ/SR/506/61, 515/36; WCA WCB/1, fo. 214; BHC 8, fo. 228v.
[143] LMA MJ/SBR/2, fo. 215; MJ/SBR/1, fos. 34, 81, 173, 230; MJ/SBR/2, fos. 60, 420, 460. See also BHC 3, fos. 6v, 236, 433; 5, fos. 28v, 294, 407; 6, fos. 99v, 423; 7, fos. 71v, 349; 8, fos. 45, 411; 9, fos. 500, 695; BRHA BHC 4, fos. 300, 390, 457; LMA Reps. 11, fo. 429; 14, fo. 523; 16, fo. 534v; 21, fo. 578v; 40, fo. 70; 51, fo. 201v; CQSF 78/32, 104/55, 112/4, 124/72; MJ/SBR/1, fos. 34, 429, 565, 639; MJ/SBR/2, fos. 72, 255, 520; MJ/SBR/3, fos. 17, 296; WJ/SR/NS/30/22, 33/149; MJ/SR/505/72, 515/36, 523/209; WCA WCB/1, fos. 32, 121; WCB/2, fo. 38.
[144] LMA Reps. 15, fo. 275v; 10, fo. 123; TNA STAC8, 230/3. See also BHC 2, fo. 188; 3, fo. 282; LMA Reps. 12, fo. 428v; 20, fo. 220v; 25, fo. 110v; CQSF 76/4, 106/4; MJ/SBR/1, fos. 309, 592; MJ/SBR/2, fo. 257; MJ/SBR/4, fo. 545; MJ/SBR/5, fo. 377; MJ/SBR/7, fo. 22. MJ/SR/505a/32, 509/109, 523/97; WJ/SR/NS/44/65; TNA STAC8, 274/7. Churchwardens also ran into trouble. See, for example, GL MSS 9064/14, fo. 181; 9064/17, fo. 12v; 9064/20, fos. 10v, 175v; 9064/21, fos. 12v, 136v; BRHA BHC 4, fo. 279v.
[145] LMA CQSF 106/42; Reps. 40, fos. 380–0v, 382v, 391, 400v, 413v-14; 41, fos. 57, 90v, 132v, 358v; MJ/SBR/1, fo. 399; MJ/SBR/2, fo. 307; MJ/SBR/5, fo. 260; TNA STAC8, 228/8.

Hotheads also ripped up warrants. Gartwright Gray 'snatched' a warrant 'out of a constables hand' and 'tore it all to pieces' when he came to question her about the man in her house 'that is not her husband'. 'I charge yow in the king's name to kisse my tayle', a Whitechapel silkweaver told an officer who served him a warrant. 'Idle warrant', someone else sneered as an officer drew near to try and arrest him. While a broker snapped 'that he did not care for his warrant' when a constable came to his house to search for stolen goods.[146] Uniforms were also fair game in hostile words that were tailored towards the symbolic status of clothes or weapons. 'Gownestave' was one such mocking word, along with 'knaves with long staves'. Agnes Wilson focused on clothes when berating beadles in 1608: 'Yf ever she is po[nished, she shouted] she would cutt their cloaks from off theire backes'. 'Outragious' Anne Phillips ripped 'the watchmens bands and clothes' when she was taken staggering along a street after a day-long drinking binge, and it took four men to 'bringe her downe' and into custody (much is made of torn bands or clothes in such cases).[147]

All officers were in the firing line. Beadles received their fair share of abuse.[148] Sheriffs and their sergeants suffered less in the records, but also got into scrapes. One sheriff was called a 'thief'; another 'a pollinge gentleman'. 'Dailie drunckard' Roger Paston could no longer 'beare stronge drinke', he said, and lost his temper 'upon smale occasion' after being 'sore wounded with a grievous blow' to the head when he 'was a serjant at mace'.[149] Deputies also suffered bruises and cheek,[150] and warders picked up poundings: they were pelted with brickbats and belted with 'great crabtree cudgells', stabbed, scratched, pulled by beards, and shoved 'headlong' down steps. 'Notorious pilferer' Alice Butler told a warder that she would cut his throat. Warders were always among the walking wounded when the curtain came down on another Shrovetide rout.[151] Constables received more abuse than anyone, but nothing

---

[146] BHC 7, fo. 77; BRHA BHC 4, fo. 167v; LMA MJ/SBR/2, fos. 52, 147, 45; WJ/SR/NS/ 46/90. Others demanded to see warrants: for example, TNA STA8 21/7, 104/17, 124/4.

[147] BHC 5, fos. 346v, 304v; 1, fo. 154; LMA MJ/SR/515/36; Rep. 25, fo. 227; CQSF 115/1; BHC 2, fo. 68v; 5, fo. 405v; 6, fos. 116v, 204v.

[148] For other examples see BHC 1, fos. 85v, 209; 5, fo. 316v; 7, fos. 11, 62, 110, 273v, 366v; LMA MJ/SBR/6, fo. 44; Rep. 11, fo. 98; WCA WCB/1, fo. 34.

[149] BHC 1, fo. 14v; LMA Rep. 17, fo. 464v; GL MS 9064/17, fo. 79. See also LMA MJ/ SBR/5, fo. 358; Reps. 9, fo. 20; 22, fos. 290, 422v; 27, fos. 4v, 275; 42, fo. 306; CQSF 95/17; 95/118.

[150] BHC 1, fo. 144v; 3, fo. 400; 5, fos. 238v, 355v; 6, fos. 115v, 230, 261; LMA CQSF 129/ 59; Reps. 15, fo. 53; 16, fo. 534v; 20, fos. 55, 238; 22, fos. 20, 389v.

[151] BHC 6, fo. 440v; LMA Rep. 27, fos. 17v, 175v. See also BHC 5, fos. 59v, 184v, 395v, 433v; 6, fos. 30v, 78, 167, 349, 402; 7, fos. 108, 165v, 246, 334v; 8, fos. 123v, 131v, 221v; 9, fo. 115.

matched the spite levelled at marshals. 'Notorious vagrant' Constantine Rich 'abuseth all officers [Bridewell heard] and especiallie Mr Marshall'.[152] It did not take marshals long to become arch-enemies of people wary of their new powers. A few months after their first patrol in 1596, aldermen noted that marshals had 'been deverslye abused' by 'unruly and disordered persons as well with threatenings as with reprochfull speeches as by resistance and open violence'.[153] William Shigwell, 'one of her mats gromes', knocked on Marshal Simpson's door on a May morning in 1596, 'calling him rogue and threatening to cutt his flesh'. He was not the only one to toss 'rashe and unseemely speeches' in this inaugural year. 'Beard the marshals', James Gilman shouted, when one placed 'xiid for prest money' in his hand. Roger Clarkealter fired 'vile' words against Marshal Read before 'many people' in 1596, after hearing him order a constable 'to carry three sturdy' vagrants to Bridewell. A 'constable was not to be made a beadell' at a marshal's beck and call, he snapped, 'the marshal and his knaves were hired' for dogsbody duties, he added for good measure, telling Read that his 'beste knave' was lower than 'the worst boy' in my house. 'My masters', Clarkealter said to the milling crowd, if we are not careful marshals 'will raigne and rule over us', and he struck a chord, as 'some loose people', 'animated' by his goading, picked a fight with marshalmen. There is perhaps more to Clarkealter's prickliness than meets the eye, as he may be the officer of the same name with a chip on his shoulder about the marshals' new powers (aldermen had been tipped off that constables did not help marshals).[154]

No other officer had more contact with 'street people', and a number of marshals stayed in post for a decade or longer, becoming well known to almost anyone with a reason to dodge the law. 'Look out, here comes a marshal', must have been a regular refrain. It is not hard to imagine how marshals turned into hate figures in certain circles. Vagrant John Steele 'vowed to pistoll' a marshal in 1619. Another marshal got a 'cuck[ing]' in the next year. Marshals and their men were attacked with hammers and knives; one rabble-rouser 'cryed kicke him downe' as a crowd threw snowballs at a marshal in 1635.[155] Ill will grew as marshals made many more arrests in the 1620s. They were busybodies some said: a 'maid in the

---

[152] BHC 6, fo. 78v.
[153] 'A proclamation for the aide and assistance of the two marshalls of this citie' (LMA Jour. 24, fo. 150v).
[154] LMA Rep. 23, fos. 538v, 508v, 521v, 548–8v.
[155] BHC 6, fo. 146; 7, fo. 206v; 6, fo. 337; 7, fo. 46; 8, fos. 24v, 28v. See also BHC 5, fo. 59v; 6, fos. 121, 349, 430; 7, fos. 45, 198, 305; 8, fo. 35; LMA Reps. 23, fo. 508v; 28, fo. 283v; MJ/SBR/2, fos. 217, 417; MJ/SBR/6, fos. 121, 224, 430; MJ/SRB/7, fos. 45, 147v, 283v.

street' called them 'rogues and meddlers with that they had nothing to do with' in 1629. 'Roguetaker' was another pet slur that brought marshals down a few pegs to the level of mucky rogues and street-sweepers. A vagrant cripple called one marshal 'roguetaker' in 1629. Judith Alexander also called him 'roguetaker' a week later.[156] Marshal Pordage picked up a string of knocks, and some could not hide their glee when he was murdered in 1627. Mary Pitts said it 'was a pity' that someone should be 'hanged for killing a marshal'. Cutpurse Margaret Barter was either gloating or making threats in sneering 'that the marshal was a dead man' in 1628. Richard Deane had a pistol hidden in his clothes when he was taken in 1629, and admitted that he wanted to kill Marshal Bestney (and Provost Marshal Heath). Things seemed particularly ugly around the time of Pordage's killing. A juggler was the 'ringleader' of a gang of 'idle people' who poured 'scalding water' over marshalmen in the same year that Pordage was murdered. Branded vagrant Thomas Hill said that he and 'his company' were 'like to have killed' Marshal Davis a week later. Bestney had to bear up to other death threats; a vagrant told him that he hoped 'to be his death' in Spring 1629. A month earlier, not caring that he was standing in the Bridewell court, Hugh Turrell snapped that 'if he had him out of this place he should make him know what it was to challenge him'. Bestney was also once 'chocked' by two women who tried to pick his pocket, and not long after became the butt of taunts that he took bribes.[157]

It was not this ugly all of the time. Marshals could count on support from most civic-minded citizens who wanted quiet streets. But abuse did not always flow one way. Officers also fell on the wrong side of the law. Constables were taken to task for 'carelesse negligence' and 'general neglect'. They were considered so 'remisse and carelesse' in 1602 that they needed to be 'putt in mynde' of their duties. London's leaders were running out of patience again in 1632, when for the third time in two months they criticized wards and parishes for their nonchalant attitude to 'careles' constables.[158] Magistrates hired 'overseers' from time to time to keep an eye on officers. William Browne was paid £10 to 'oversee' constables in 1581 (but he, too, was sacked for laziness). Wards picked 'sufficient and discrete' people to write weekly reports noting times when

---

[156] BHC 7, fos. 104, 120, 123.
[157] Ibid., fos. 26, 29, 32, 35v, 52v, 79, 105v, 120, 123, 151; TNA SP14/124/102; LMA Rep. 41, fo. 43.
[158] LMA Jours. 26, fos. 37v, 49–9v, 186v; 38, fo. 125; 33, fos. 20v, 216v; 34, fo. 238v; 35, fo. 520v; COL/AC/08/1, fo. 46; GL MS 1509/7. See also LMA Jours. 26, fo. 337v; 32, fo. 241v; 35, fos. 252v, 515v; 36, fos. 162, 239; 37, fos. 126v, 414; 38, fos. 24–4v, 308; 49, fo. 386v; MJ/SBR/1, fo. 547; MJ/SBR/6, fo. 225; GL MS 3016/1, fo. 161; TNA PC2/43, fo. 432; PC/2/44, fos. 480–1.

constables failed to catch vagrants in 1602. Future marshal Roger Walrond was told to 'take care' that 'everie constable' did his 'dutie' in 1603, and he was given the same task as provost marshal twelve years later. Informers shadowed constables in Middlesex in 1618, not without opposition, and this might explain why a beadle from St Martin-in-the-Fields ended up in Newgate 'at the instance' of two informers for speaking up in defence 'of the constables of the parish'.[159] More commonly, other officers filled the role of 'overseers'. Beadles took 'dailie' 'diligent care' over constables in 1602, and wrote weekly 'perfecte' reports of their efforts to expel vagrants (aldermen, in turn, wrote monthly 'notes' on beadles). Warders were given this task three decades later, and it is likely that friction followed when colleagues snooped on each other. These cross-purposes explain why marshals, without roots in parishes, took over the main role in arresting officers who let vagrants slip through their hands – 'not done their best endeavors' was the usual phrase.[160]

Little was more perplexing in this 'overpeopled' city than stories about constables who did not lift a finger when vagrants walked past them. 'Careles constables' were prosecuted in batches nine strong at times (paying a standard ten shilling fine).[161] But their number is steady not spectacular. City leaders usually heard about such sloppiness from marshals, who were asked to bring all 'negligent' constables before aldermen in 1615. Some cases seem harsh, as when William Mess got in trouble for not rounding up a group of four vagrants in 1633.[162] Magistrates were keen to come down hard on 'carelesnes'. Other cases were more clear cut. One constable ended up in court in 1628 for not helping 'an infant of the age of halfe a yeare' who he found one morning alone in Hyde Park. Another got into trouble for not whipping a group of 'vagrant boyes' at the post in 1633. Other bumbling constables let murderers, horse-thieves, adulterers, and rioters slip out of their custody. Constable Collins of St Clement Danes let Richard Lee go, even though he had a justice's warrant to arrest him after he led 'an outragous ryott upon the Lady Lewkenor' in 1614. Other officers ended up behind bars after bungling arrests, or not 'executing' a warrant, or hue and cry.[163] A marshal

---

[159] LMA Reps. 20, fos. 169v, 220v; 32, fo. 36v; Jour. 26, fos. 49–9v, 111; MJ/SBR/2, fo. 497; WCA F2001, fo. 130v.
[160] LMA Jours. 26, fo. 37v; 35, fo. 252v; WJ/SR/NS/47/192; Rep. 23, fo. 527.
[161] For example, LMA Reps. 23, fo. 529; 28, fo. 111; 30, fo. 124; 33, fo. 241; 39, fos. 184–4v; 44, fos. 197, 217v–18; 45, fo. 178; 46, fo. 205v; 49, fos. 177v–8; BHC 6, fo. 376; 7, fos. 182, 376.
[162] LMA Reps. 33, fo. 43; 32, fo. 36v; WJ/SR/NS/39/166.
[163] LMA MJ/SBR/4, fo. 615; BHC 7, fo. 334; LMA MJ/SBR/2, fo. 75. See also GL MS 3018/1, fos. 65v, 85; LMA Reps. 14, fo. 294; 22, fos. 369–9v; MJ/SBR/1, fos. 101, 595,

watched from a distance as a constable 'seemed to excuse' a vagrant 'poyntmaker' whom he had stopped on Kent Street in 1627. Novice officers were also outfoxed by streetwise suspects. One constable stupidly let someone suspicious go in 1622 after a neighbour 'promised' that he would make sure that he appeared in court at a date not yet fixed. Another constable was quite content to take a suspect's word that he would turn up in court without sureties, and he was never seen again. Aptly named Peter Free 'foolishly suffered' David Griffin to skip court after 'taking two mens words for his personal appearance'.[164] Acting more like neighbours, some officers covered up crimes or turned a blind eye: one ended up in court in 1617 for not stopping begging or 'unlawful games' by his neighbours at Whitsun Ales, letting women walk 'in great companies' to beg money, as they had done in all past years, he said, in a defence that got him nowhere.[165]

Nor did beadles always toe the line. They were often warned to take more care to round up vagrants, and some were arrested for letting prisoners go or not turning up for duty.[166] Warders also went missing from their posts, and made half-hearted efforts to catch vagrants. One refused point blank to take a vagrant to Bridewell when a marshal handed him over. Another stood his ground 'obstinately' when he was reprimanded by a vestry for carelessness. The blame for the 'swarms' of vagrants was also put on lax warders and beadles. A parish said that 'great want of a warder or beadle' led to a surge in the number of children abandoned on streets.[167] Marshals and their teams were also taken to task now and then. They were hauled over the coals for not taking vagrants to deputies or constables in 1596; a complaint that resurfaced in later years. The situation was so serious in Spring 1642 that 'divers' Bridewell governors told aldermen that marshals and constables did not round up vagrants 'as they ought to doe', only a handful of 'impotent people' were brought in 'now and then', they said, and 'notorious and lewd' troublemakers with enough money for a bribe were either 'lett alone' or put in a compter cell for a short while without work or 'correction'. The two marshals – William Davis and Henry Fitch – were ordered to 'walke

---

635; MJ/SBR/2, fos. 29, 204, 509; MJ/SBR/4, fo. 556; MJ/SBR/5, fos. 202, 499, 527; MJ/SBR/6, fos. 167, 565; MJ/SBR/7, fo. 187; MJ/SR/505/145, 515/35, 528/38; WJ/SR/NS/36/162, 45/43, 46/83; TNA SP16/415/17.

[164] BHC 7, fo. 44; LMA MJ/SBR/5, fo. 427; MJ/SBR/6, fo. 558; WCA WCB/1, fo. 154.
[165] LMA MJ/SBR/2, fo. 460.
[166] LMA Jour. 28, fo. 284; Rep. 15, fo. 461; BHC 1, fo. 101v; 8, fo. 347v; 9, fos. 322, 766–7; LMA Rep. 50, fo. 298; GL MS 5570/2, fo. 195; WCA F2003, fos. 171, 185, 203, 306; WCB/1, fo. 240.
[167] BHC 6, fo. 236; LMA MJ/SBR/6, fo. 357; GL MS 3016/1, fo. 207; LMA Jours. 33, fo. 20v; 35, fos. 112, 138, 278; GL MS 4216/1, fo. 149.

through all the streetes' each day and bring vagrants to Bridewell; one of them was to go to each meeting of the Bridewell court for guidelines for 'cleeringe the streets'. But the pair took no notice and lost their jobs 'forever' one year later. Trust in marshals slumped to rock bottom in that year when it also came to light that Richard Parker was still drawing a salary, even though he had been out of office for 'many yeares'.[168] Like constables, some marshalmen let suspects (or pressed men) slip away for a fee or, like Bestney's 'man', Copestake, they were caught napping as a prisoner sneaked out of Bridewell. Magistrates thought that Dr Lambe's life might have been saved in 1628 if two marshalmen had sent word straight away to an alderman or sheriff to break up the 'tumultuous assemblye' howling for Lambe's blood.[169]

Not many could match Davis and Fitch for nerve, but there was enough negligence and sleaze to lend credibility to complaints and caricatures of London's fumbling front-line defences. With so many places to fill, somewhere in the region of 800 officers in 1643, it is inevitable that some undesirables slipped through the net. Some were weeded out: one constable was dismissed after it became known that he 'standeth indict for iiii assaultes'.[170] But heavy-handed officers were taken to court by people with hair-raising stories of 'violent hands' and 'violent pull[ing]' in the course of arrests. A ninety-two-year-old woman was ill-treated in a case so shocking that it reached the lofty heights of the House of Lords in 1640.[171] Other officers dished out 'ill language' with as much acid wit and irreverence as any verbal sharpshooter on a street or doorstep. They talked back to people above them. One constable told a justice that it is 'a hard case when his adversary shall be his judge'. Another one with a bee in his bonnet stood in the mayor's house jeering at him with 'very lewd speeches' in 1605. Two sheriff's officers stopped the coach carrying 'the ladie mayoresse' and her daughter in 1656, unbridled the horses, and shouted that the coachman had knocked down and killed a child, when

---

[168] LMA Jour. 24, fo. 113v; Rep. 55, fos. 410v-11; Jour. 40. fo. 48v; BHC 9, fo. 23. See also TNA SP16/415/17; BHC 6, fo. 253; 7, fos. 66, 310. It was said that marshalmen watched as Lambe was murdered by a crowd in 1628, and that they did not send word to higher officers to come and disperse the 'tumultuous assemblye' and save Lambe's life (LMA Rep. 42, fo. 213v).
[169] BHC 7, fos. 66, 310; LMA Reps. 42, fo. 213v; 33, fo. 169v.
[170] LMA MJ/SBR/1, fo. 377.
[171] HOL MP 1-12-1640. See also, for example, LMA MJ/SBR/1, fo. 377; MJ/SBR/5, fo. 156; CQSF 112/40; Reps. 20, fo. 272; 23, fo. 140; WCA WCB/2, fo. 99. There are other cases in the sources, including grisly stories of violence by officers in Star Chamber cases, although we should remember that these accounts are only one side of a case that could contain several versions of the same story: see, for example, TNA STAC8 21/7; 65/1; 68/20; 124/4; 187/1; 190/3; 190/3; 238/4; 274/7; 288/14.

nothing of the sort had happened 'her ladyshipp' informed the aldermen sitting in their court. Aldermen and their deputies were also taunted by junior officers. Guidelines for sheriffs' officers were devised to nip trouble in the bud in 1634: they were not to treat one another or anyone else 'uncively' in either 'word or deede'. They had a chequered past. One sergeant – John Bradley – was locked up in Newgate 'with a payre of boltes upon his legges' in Armada year after 'veary lewdelye abusing James Dalton esquyer the auncientest of the fower comon pleaders with vearye unseemeleye speaches in the Guildhall'.[172] Officers did not always get along. Constables came to blows with sheriffs' men at times; one did not lift a finger to help a sergeant when he was mugged by a gang, even though paving stones were covered in his blood.[173] There was edginess about jurisdictional niceties and pecking orders, not least when City and Crown officers traded insults: one constable stood a step away from the lord keeper and mocked him in 'presumptuous and insolent words'.[174] 'Hot' words sometimes rained down on junior officers from above. Marshals fell out with their 'men' now and then. Three marshalmen were quizzed at Bridewell 'for their neglect' in 1630 and in their defence each said that they 'dare not execute their places as they ought to doe for feare of the marshals'. There are good grounds to think that this was not made up, as Nicholas Bestney, one of the 'bullying' marshals in their time of 'feare', was kicked out of office by the City in 1632 after a string of 'ignominious and reprochfull speeches' lashing out at Bridewell's bench, calling them 'rogues' more than once. He was dumped in Newgate and was still there five months later with debts piling up.[175]

A bill was tabled in Parliament in 1626 to put an end to sleaze among officers. Corruption stopped justice in its tracks, some said, but the bill never got as far as the statute book.[176] Some officers still acted as if they were above the law, lining their pockets with bribes, arresting blameless people for 'no cause', dragging others into custody without warrants, and

---

[172] LMA MJ/SBR/7, fo. 43; Reps. 64, fos. 63–3v; 27, fo. 160v; 48, fos. 311v-12v; 21, fo. 536v. See also LMA MJ/SBR/5, fo. 428; Reps. 10, fo. 9; 13(ii), fo. 449v; 15, fo. 49; 16, fo. 145v; 20, fo. 363v; 21, fo. 307v; 23, fo. 582v; 29, fo. 53; 30, fo. 116; 33, fo. 238; 40, fo. 60; 47, fos. 154v-5, 358v. Twelve constables in Langbourn were locked in a 'controversie and variance' with the deputy of the ward in 1566 after they committed a 'misorder': LMA Rep. 16, fos. 70–0v.
[173] LMA Rep. 15, fo. 380; MJ/SBR/1, fo. 431; Reps. 48, fos. 311v-12, 316; 15, fo. 380; 42, fos. 42, 306; 40, fo. 60; 54, fo. 294v; 21, fo. 536v.
[174] LMA Reps. 48, fo. 119; 33, fo. 112v; TNA STAC8 1/38. See also LMA Rep. 32, fo. 193v.
[175] BHC 7, fo. 193v; LMA Rep. 46, fo. 297; BHC 7, fos. 265v, 273v.
[176] HOL MP 20-2-1626.

teaming up with thieves or bawdy-house rackets to make money on the side. High and mighty officers trampled over law and etiquette. John Holmes from Cow Cross was put on trial for 'unlawfully arresting' the Newgate ordinary and collector of 'last dying words' of felons Henry Goodcole on a Sabbath day in 1626, and 'extorting xis in money from him by colour of fines'. Other officers made money by giving prisoners room and board in their own homes or a nearby alehouse for a while without bail; time that was sometimes spent coaxing bribes. Aldermen heard that sheriffs' officers 'comonly make theire owne houses and diverse alehouses to bee receptacles for prisoners' in 1648: a note in the margin reads, 'serjeants and yeomen not to keepe prisoners in theire owne houses'. 'Tables' of 'orders' were hung up 'in each compter' to get them to toe the line, but four months later four 'seargants' admitted keeping people 'att their houses severall daies' after arrest on writ without bail, not bringing them to a compter to 'deposite theire monies' as due process required. This was a long-standing hindrance: sheriffs' officers appeared as defendants in Star Chamber cases, charged with holding people against their will and demanding money with menaces. One Londoner said that a sheriff's sergeant took the post 'to profit by it'; another claimed that a sheriff 'for money would do anything for him'.[177] These were Star Chamber stories from one side of a case and cannot always be taken to be true. But there were many times in the week when officers had opportunities to top up their wages with a bribe. A Southwark beadle stood in shame in the pillory in 1572 'for discoveringe of the queens secrets in the watch and for extorcon done in his office'. 'Comon whore' Joanne Young said 'that when she was attached to go the counter [in 1575] the bedell of the warde had of hir at one tyme xviiid' and took two groats from two men 'at another tyme'. One of Marshal Fitch's 'men' let 'idle' Bridget Merrick go in exchange for her coat. A maidservant bumped into Beadle Hobson in St James Fair in the next year, and 'afferde' that he would take her to Bridewell, gave him the three pennies in her purse after he asked her 'what money she had for a good fellowe'. Three pennies seems a poor return for

---

[177] LMA MJ/SBR/4, fo. 376; WJ/SR/NS/41/27; Reps. 59, fos. 160, 248, 251v; 33, fo. 169v; 41, fo. 375; TNA STAC8 54/15; 71/17; 98/13; 102/17; 110/12; 128/81; 159/23; 200/22; 230/3; 233/15; 238/22; 297/20 (some Star Chamber cases also involved constables and beadles). Something of Goodcole's authorial career and standing can be gleaned from J. A. Sharpe, '"Last dying speeches": religion, ideology and public executions in seventeenth-century England', *Past and Present*, 107 (1985), 144–67. Aldermen heard that sheriffs' officers were 'takyng upon theyme to arreste men in churches in the dyvyne service tyme' (LMA Letterbook R, fo. 282). See also LMA MJ/SBR/1, fo. 369; MJ/SBR/2, fo. 172; MJ/SBR/6, fo. 454; Reps. 17, fo. 356; 21, fo. 59v; 27, fo. 366v; 30, fo. 323v; 46, fo. 202v; 51, fo. 352v; 52, fo. 178; WCA WCB/2, fo. 99.

taking such a risk, although one constable took just three half-pennies from Arthur Malmes in 1620.[178]

It is difficult to come down strongly on one side or the other in questions about the quality of policing in London four centuries ago, because that might miss essential ambivalences. We cannot rely on counting alone to see if ineffectiveness trumps effectiveness or vice versa. Bribes by nature are underhand, and we can never know how much good police-work has escaped our notice. But it is worth saying that London was better policed in the century before 1660 than existing work would lead us to believe. Even the abuse aimed at officers appears ambivalent, as it is a sign that some risked ridicule or even life and limb to keep order. But there is also the chorus of complaint to consider, so constant that it was reiterated almost word for word from one year to the next. That said, however, we would never use only the repetitive patter of complaint to judge policing today, since magistrates never stop complaining.[179] A common complaint was that there was never enough money to go round: Londoners did not always fully back new developments, as when word reached Common Council in 1626 that people thought that extra beadles had been 'elected without their liking'. The City lumbered under heavy 'continuall charges'.[180] Usually when something went wrong with a new directive it had as much to do with dwindling finances, rather than any lack of effort by magistrates. The City was more short of money than resolve or ingenuity. Abuses and troubles there were and plenty of them, but London muddled through these troubled times, albeit in a permanent condition of friction. And if we use neglect, sleaze, or slip-ups as litmus tests, then all police-forces at anytime or anywhere will be found wanting.

---

[178] LMA Rep. 17, fo. 249v; BHC 2, fo. 63; 7, fos. 193, 236, 317; LMA CQSF 90/8. See also BHC 3, fos. 46v, 67; 5, fos. 46v, 164v; 7, fo. 317; 8, fo. 338; TNA STAC8 65/1; 233/15; LMA MJ/SBR/5, fo. 280; WJ/SR/NS/31/22, 36/163.
[179] Cf. Harris, *Policing the City*, p. 10: 'The period between 1780 and 1830 saw these criticisms [of London's night-watches] constantly recycled'.
[180] LMA Jours. 29, fo. 5v; 28, fo. 278.

# 9 Policing: night battles[1]

### 'Terrors of the night'

'The terrors of the night', Thomas Nashe said chillingly, 'are as many as our sinnes', and the 'sinnes of the night surmount the sinnes of the day'. Nashe was thinking of ghosts, hair-raising dreams, creaking doors and floors, and fire and crime in the pitch black dark. 'My house is mighty dangerous, having so many ways to come in', Pepys mused, after a friend had told him that he and his wife trembled in bed 'night after night', hearing 'noises over their heads upon the leads', thinking panic-stricken thoughts about thieves creeping over roofs, looking for windows left carelessly open. Pepys tossed and turned in bed all night long, 'thinking every running of a mouse really a thief'. Simply seeing someone leaving a dark house through a back door made pulses beat faster.[2]

More care was needed in night's 'dead time' as danger always lurked somewhere in the shadows. Night-time was more dangerous, people were more on edge and more sensitive to the slightest tap or rattle in night's quiet. Law-abiding Londoners liked to be locked in their houses in an envelope of security as they slept in bed, leaving nothing to chance. Anne Owen made the careless mistake of leaving 'her masters door wyde open' at midnight, and she found herself in court within a week.[3] London should also have been sealed tightly, gates locked, walls even more imposing in the dark, and alert watchmen wide awake looking out for anything or anyone that moved in the dark. The Aldgate watch was

---

[1] My thanks to Carlo Ginzburg, *The Night Battles: Witchcraft and Agrarian Cults in the Sixteenth and Seventeenth Centuries*, trans. John and Anne Tedeschi (Baltimore, MD, 1992).
[2] Thomas Nashe, *The Terrors of the Night, or a Discourse of Apparitions*, 1594, in *The Works of Thomas Nashe Edited from the Original Texts*, ed., R. B. McKerrow, 5 vols. (1910), vol. I, pp. 346, 386, 356; *The Diary of Samuel Pepys*, eds. R. Latham and W. Matthews, 11 vols. (1970–83), vol. VI, p. 25; GL MS 25175, fo. 19v. See also Pepys, *Diary*, vol. VII, pp. 197–8. The best work on the night at this time is A. Roger Ekirch, *At Day's Close: Night in Times Past* (New York, 2005).
[3] GL MS 25175, fo. 21; BRHA BHC 4, fo. 57v.

332

hauled over the coals one night in 1551 for leaving 'the wyket of the gate stondynge open all night' with the key in it.[4] Terrors were more magnified at night, as if people let down their guard in sleep. Fire seemed more terrible against night's black canvas than daylight white when there were also more people around to rush to the scene to douse the flames. Watch out for small sparks that can start fires at any time of the night, magistrates warned, and do not light 'hot presses' or take 'lighted' torches into haylofts, and never 'hammer' metal in forges after nine at night.[5] In addition, there were specific conceptions of night crime, more dangerous because of night's thick cover. 'There is no thief that is halfe so hardie in the day as in the night', Nashe said. Night was 'the favourer of theeves', one author noted gloomily. 'Watchman what seest thou by night?', John Lawrence asked in 1624: 'Do you not see revelling, dauncing, and banquetting till midnight? ... carding, dicing, drinking and swearing all night? ... the theefe stealing, the murderer stabbing, the cozenors cheating, the prodigall wasting, the profane spending'?[6] People worried when their loved ones stayed out late in the chancy night. Pepys wrote 'vexed' at nine one night when his wife was not yet back home, keeping his fingers crossed that she was not in any danger. He also fretted when he walked through rough areas of the city after dark, and sometimes side-stepped shady characters or turned another way to go home. 'It was dangerous to go [out] at night because of robbers', Alessandro Magno noted warily in 1562.[7]

Another good reason not to be out late was that people walking in the dark risked arrest after the curfew hour. Anyone outside at night without reason or permission was potentially criminal and suspicious. Mawdelyn Brunt was caught 'walkinge late like a rogue' one night in 1576; while Magdalene Differy and Sara Faircloth 'were [both] taken suspiciously' in 'the nature of nightwalkers' in 1632.[8] Nightwalking had long been an

---

[4] LMA Rep. 12, fo. 397.
[5] LMA Jour. 22, fo. 388v; BHC 7, fo. 97v; GL MS 4069/1, fo. 27. See also GL MSS 473, fo. 8; 25175, fos. 16, 21.
[6] Nashe, *Terrors of the Night*, p. 347; Paul Godwin, *Historie des Larrons, Or the History of Thieves. Written in French and Translated Out of the Original by Paul Godwin* (1638), p. 186; John Lawrence, *A Golden Trumpet to Rowse up a Drowsie Magistrate: Or, a Patterne for a Governors Practise Drawne From Christs Comming to, Beholding of, and Weeping Over Hierusalem. As it was Sounded at Pauls Crosse the 11 of April, 1624* (1624), p. 42. See also Moss, *Sermon*, p. 14.
[7] Pepys, *Diary*, vol. VI, p. 49; vol. III, p. 201; vol. IX, p. 172; 'The London Journal of Alessandro Magno 1562', eds., Caroline Barron, Christopher Coleman, and Claire Gobb, *London Journal*, 9 (1983), 136–52, esp. 148. See also TNA STAC8 30/17.
[8] BHC 3, fo. 3v; BHC 7, fo. 298. For other cases see BHC 1, fo. 167; 2, fos. 204, 217v; 3, fos. 87, 336, 411v, 420v, 424; 5, fos. 90v, 108, 225v, 267; BRHA BHC 4, fo. 202; LMA WJ/SR/39/47–8.

offence, but many more nightwalkers were taken to court after 1600, and nearly all of them were women after 1620, a scenario that fits neatly with the greater gendering of crime around this time.[9] This is not to say that men could drift through dark London with the sort of freedom that daylight might bring. They also got into trouble for walking in the streets after the curfew hour, although their offence was not normally termed nightwalking in seventeenth-century London. Courts relied instead on simple statements about men being 'taken in the watch' or 'wandering late', along with anything else that seemed incriminating, as when William Gardener was caught by the Westminster watch in 1617 and could not adequately explain why he had six chickens in his hands.[10]

Just as there was illegitimate movement by day – vagrants and the like – there was also limited legitimate movement in 'dead nyght'. Nightworkers should not have started their work until after the first ring of the curfew bell. 'Gongefarmers' were told not to carry any loads of 'odour' until after nine at night. 'Nightmen' did not start work before eleven in summer and ten in winter in 1624 (these times had been one hour earlier in 1588). 'Soil' could not be taken out of the city before ten. Butchers could not carry tubs of 'guts, blood, offal, entrails, or other filths' on Southwark's streets before ten in Winter 1635. While 'nightworkers' worked late 'scouring' the town ditch from Aldersgate to Newgate in 1583.[11] We also catch sight of 'nightworkers' in the records after they did something wrong. 'Nightmen' emptied 'ordure in the streets' in 1624, and 'donge, odure and other fylth into the comon sewer' in 1591. 'Lewde' 'gongfarmers' made 'diverse laystalls' near 'conduit heads' in 1610, 'corrupting' the water. While John Sadler was caught 'carrying' 'beasts offells' on streets at 'unseasonable houres' two years later.[12] Some people who were stopped by the watch said that they were on their way home after a long and late working day. While a clothworker who was stopped on Elbow Lane by officers around nine said that he had just finished a day-long stint of 'hard labour'. Other night-owls said that they had been working late washing,

---

[9] Paul Griffiths, 'Meanings of nightwalking in early modern England', *The Seventeenth Century*, 13 (1998), 212–38.
[10] WAC WCB/2, fo. 45. See also BHC 3, fos. 53, 311v, 333v, 339, 384, 385, 418, 423v, 433; 6, fos. 250v, 272v; WAC WCB/2, fo. 138; LMA Lord Mayor's Waiting Book 1626–36, fo. 18.
[11] Strype, *Survey*, V, p. 306; LMA Reps. 38, fo. 220; 21, fo. 544; 25, fo. 83; CLRO/05/389/001, 1635; GL MS 12806/2, fo. 326v. Pudding carts were not allowed on streets after nine at night; merchants were told to leave the Exchange by six in winter and seven in summer in 1632; and 'no waterman or whiryman' was allowed to row 'in the Thames in the night time' in 1584 without 'good cause' or the 'fare' of some 'honest person': Strype, *Survey*, V, p. 307; LMA Reps. 46, fos. 70-0v; 21, fo. 36v.
[12] BHC 6, fo. 377v; LMA Reps. 22, fo. 262v; 29, fo. 153v; WAC WCB/1, fos. 177–8. See also BRHA BHC 4, fo. 398; LMA WJ/SR/39/175.

'scowering', or checking that a cow had calved. One man said that he was hurrying to Sandwich with an urgent letter; the Swallow brothers said that they were rushing back to Essex to get 'provision for the quenes house'. Women also left the house late to go to a friend's 'labor'. A silkweaver, who was caught knocking on a door after midnight, said that 'his wife was [inside] keeping one in childebed'.[13] Work, prayer, and healing were all good reasons to be out late at night. The minister of St Bartholomew's was given a key to a 'little wykett gate going into the churchyard' in 1570, so that he could come and go 'at all tymes' to 'visitt the sick and deseased'.[14] There also seemed to be little harm done when Elizabeth Jacob was sitting at her door with Dorothy Mytton near midnight one night in 1591, 'talkinge neighborlye together', not causing anyone else trouble, just up talking a little late perhaps.[15]

Allowances were usually made for people who had some social status on their side. Lord Fielding clearly expected to pass through London's streets untroubled at 1 am one night in 1641, and he quickly became piqued when his coach was stopped by the watch, shouting huffily that it was a 'disgrace' to stop someone of such high standing as he, and telling the constable in charge of the watch that he would box him on the ears if he did not let his coach carry on back to his house. 'It is impossible' to 'distinguish a lord from another man by the outside of a coach', the constable said later in his defence, 'especially at unreasonable times'.[16] A relaxation of rules explains how Pepys sauntered around the city almost at will at night. He often left alehouses to go home around midnight (once as late as 2 am: 'very late', he added in his diary), sometimes singing: Mrs Rebecca 'would needs have me sing' and I 'did pretty well', he noted smugly.[17] Pepys walked home 'late' from coffee-houses, playhouses, and after dancing deep into the night, and one game of cards dragged on well past midnight.[18] He often got back from visiting family or friends before midnight, though sometimes he was still out as late as 2 am (dinner with the lord mayor ended at eleven one night).[19] He also stayed behind late at

---

[13] TNA STAC8 251/23; BHC 8, fos. 100v, 231; 5, fo. 20; 2, fo. 242v; 6, fos. 293v, 422; 5, fo. 107v; 6, fo. 311; 7, fos. 36, 368; LMA Rep. 16, fo. 107; TNA STAC8 296/9.
[14] SBHA Governors' Journal 2, fo. 68.   [15] LMA D/L/C 214/95.
[16] HOL MP 29-6-1641.
[17] For example, Pepys, *Diary*, vol. I, pp. 19, 26, 37, 38, 209, 216, 234, 244, 248, 261, 281; vol. II, pp. 8, 61, 65, 71, 138, 156, 220, 222, 373; vol. IV, p. 261; vol. V, pp. 142, 191; vol. VI, pp. 199, 311; vol. VII, p. 18.
[18] For example, ibid., vol. I, pp. 40, 43, 253, 309, 323; vol. II, pp. 3, 39; vol. V, p. 37; vol. VII, pp. 347, 424.
[19] For example, ibid., vol. I, pp. 46, 173, 254; vol. II, pp. 60, 123; vol. III, pp. 82, 166, 273; vol. IV, pp. 53, 78, 100, 103, 104, 188; vol. V, pp. 19, 120, 230; vol. VI, pp. 106, 156, 297; vol. VII, pp. 56, 166, 372; vol. VIII, pp. 100, 167.

work, leaving his office at or after midnight at least forty-two times, getting home 'very late' or 'pretty late' when most people would have been sound asleep in their beds. Pepys took a coach or walked home on nice nights, walking pleasantly, sometimes with a skip in his step, not caring it seems whether or not he bumped into the night-watch.[20]

Pepys had official standing to fall back on, but others less lucky needed a good excuse if caught walking late. A lock up was the only option for a goldsmith who was picked up 'very late in the night' and had no 'good account where he had bene so late'.[21] Others said that they were late getting home from a play or dinner with friends. The watch came across Agnes Grey 'sitting' at Whitefriars gate after dark, who said that she had 'parted late' from supper with her brother and 'could not gett in' to the city. Others out late were too scared to go home, they said, having lost their master's pie in one case and brooms in another. Some were lost or new to the city with no place to go to, and were found sleeping under stalls or curled up in a 'corner'. There was some sympathy for Francis Stone, 'a pretie boy' whose master had 'lately died of the sicknes'; Frances Hassels who was lost in a reverie, 'discontented for her sweetheart'; another late walker who had been 'robbed and hurte in the streate'; and perhaps even for an apprentice who said that he was 'loath' to go home and face the music because it was getting so late.[22] Some people had to think on their feet, some more lamely than others. Ellen Finch rustled up the excuse that she was 'somewhat late to seeke her husband'. One man said that he was 'goeinge towards his lodgeing'. A goldsmith rather recklessly revealed that 'the sickness' was in his house 'and so inclosed in the daytime he went abroad in the nighte'. An apprentice said that he had been 'drinckinge with a countreymen', but had 'never before [been] so late out'.[23] The watch saw through some stories. Elizabeth Harvey was taken one night at midnight in 1635, 'pretending to goe fetch a midwife'. Elizabeth Gryse was going home after 'supping in Southwarke' with a 'countryman who promised her lodgings', she said, but she 'loste him' 'by chaunce' in the middle of a melee: far-fetched, watchmen thought, and sure enough she was 'proved contrarie in her sayenges'. A couple, who 'three tymes

---

[20] For example, ibid., vol. I, pp. 190, 300; vol. II, pp. 50, 101: vol. III, pp. 129, 239, 280; vol. IV, pp. 21, 182, 252, 381–2, 437; vol. V, pp. 7, 72, 200, 305, 359; vol. VI, pp. 1, 96, 108, 143, 321; vol. VII, pp. 24, 188, 216, 418.
[21] LMA CQSF 121/33.
[22] BHC 5, fos. 24, 379v; 8, fo. 148v; 6, fo. 291v; LMA WJ/SR/NS/44/18. See also BHC 5, fos. 20, 248v, 378, 440; 6, fos. 1v, 394; 7, fo. 316; BRHA BHC 4, fo. 96v; LMA WJ/SR/NS/41/16.
[23] BHC 8, fo. 41v; 5, fos. 51v, 288v, 440. See also BHC 8, fo. 169v.

passed' through a watch in 1622, claimed to be 'goeinge for a midwife', but it quickly emerged that there was 'noe such thinge'.[24]

The message should have been loud and clear to all Londoners: there were real reasons to walk to work at night and accidents or emergencies that needed immediate attention, but ideas of 'unlawful' tyme after dark changed the nature of law and order. People walked along dark streets or lingered in 'lewd' houses in 'ill hours', 'undue tyme', or 'unlawful' and 'unseasonable houres'. Ann Norton still shivered as she told Star Chamber how she tried to get to sleep one night in 1620, as men of 'mean quality' kept popping in and out of the house next door at 'unorderly' times, scaring neighbours as late as 2 am: 'extraordinary hours', she said, and 'the fittest time to discover such suspicious persons'. St Dunstan-in-the-West precinct ordered Henry Naylor to not 'keepe his fence scole at unlawfull howers' in 1565.[25] Like Ann Norton, people spoke of a time after nine, when decent people should have been resting inside, slowing down, getting ready for good deep sleep. This was considered to be 'due tyme', a twenty-four-hour-long cycle of work, rest, and sleep with curfew at day's end to mark the moment of rest. A Star Chamber witness, who was seeking to draw attention to the more odious nature of crimes committed after dusk, spoke of 'the dead time of the night when all good subjects should be at quiet taking their natural rest in their beds'. A Lincolnshire 'gent', boarding in the Green Dragon alehouse in Bishopgate, said that he went up to his 'restful bed' about 10 pm one night for 'necessary repose for recreation of his tired and wearied body', but he was rudely awakened a little later by a gang who rushed into his room and pulled him from his bed. Bed was the proper place for law-abiding Londoners in the hour or so before midnight, and anyone outside without good 'cause' was inevitably suspicious.[26]

Sleep should have followed regular rhythms night after night. Too much was almost as bad as not enough sleep. 'When Sampson was asleepe he was betraied', John Lawrence warned, 'and if you slumber long our cities will be wasted', so 'take heede you give not your eies to much sleepe'. Too little sleep, on the other hand, was bad for health, and

---

[24] BHC 8, fo. 61v; 2, fo. 105; 6, fo. 282v. See also BHC 5, fo. 108.
[25] TNA STAC8 200/13; GL MS 3018/1, fo. 14v. See also GL MSS 12806/4, fo. 145; 3146/1, fo. 69v; 4069/1, fo. 118v; 3018/1, fo. 82v; 5770/2, fo. 847; 25175, fo. 7; LMA Reps. 15, fo. 395v; 20, fo. 1v; 49, fo. 52v; MJ/SBR/2, fo. 495; MJ/SBR/4, fo. 456; MJ/SBR/5, fo. 291; MJ/SBR/6, fo. 559; MJ/SBR/7, fo. 315; WJ/SR/38/116, 47/37; WAC WCB/1, fos. 177–8; BHC 1, fo. 167; 2, fo. 217v; 6, fo. 418; 7, fo. 130; 8, fo. 262; 9, fo. 409; BRHA BHC 4, fo. 453v.
[26] TNA STAC8 303/7; 152/22. For 'due tyme', see LMA Reps. 12, fo. 324v; 59, fo. 146; Jour. 39, fo. 356; GL MS 25175, fos. 18, 21.

might let down the body's guard against plague: 'plague hath taken men', one author cautioned, 'by sitting up too late and so drying and inflaming the blood and weakening nature'.[27] London could ill afford to have half-asleep workers stumbling through the day in bad moods, dozing on the job, and making mistakes. Behaviour by night and day ought to have been as different as black and white. Night's black was meant to be foreboding, and night was the time to be safely locked inside. Day was a busier and jauntier time when people had good reason to be outside, shopping, picking up things for work, or nipping out for one or two beers with friends, but no more. Nashe referred to 'darke night and cheerfull daylight'. Elizabeth Bull and Raffe Lewes attracted adverse attention because they lived their lives in reverse patterns to rules set down by magistrates: 'keepe[ing] house all daye and walke[ing] the streets most part of the night'.[28] It meant something else entirely to offend at close of the day in 'unlawfull time'. Magistrates and moralists thought in terms of strict polarities of day and night. The 'disorderly' 'damned crew' of 'roaring boys' broke barriers by 'turn[ing] the day into night and the night into day' in 1617, with their twenty-four-hour-long jamboree of 'swaggering' drinking and violence. On more modest scales, but to similar effect, aptly named Joseph Light from Fetter Lane ranted and raved 'bothe nyghte and daye' in 1597, no matter what time it was, and a chandler was punished not long after 'for receiving apprentices to drinck and take tobacco by day and by night'.[29]

Night should not have been turned into day, nor day night. Nonetheless, opposite points of view disputed whether or not home was the only place to be after curfew. People even took issue with time, questioning accuracy, refusing to follow the commands of the clock. What was the significance of the 'tumult in ye church about ye 8 a clocke bell' in St Antholin Budge Row parish in 1634, its cost, noise perhaps, or maybe the fact that people were told to go home so early in their opinion, when the night was still young?[30] Night offered cover, a chance that was too good to miss for the 'asymbulle of men and women' who met 'at night' for 'Englys serves and prayers and lectorne' in 'Bowe chyrche-yerde' in 1555, or someone who was building a house in breach of building rules, if only he could keep the noise of hammering down. Fishmongers and fishwives 'forestalled freshe fishe' at the dockside or bartered in alehouses in Billingsgate

---

[27] Lawrence, *Golden Trumpet*, pp. 40–1; *The Shutting Up Infected Houses as it is Practised in England, Soberly Debated* (1665).
[28] Nashe, *Terrors of the Night*, p. 347; BRHA BHC 4, fo. 28.
[29] TNA STAC8 62/13; GL MSS 3018/1, fos. 63v, 64v; 4069/1, fos. 137v, 140. See also LMA CLA/046/01/001, fo. 6.
[30] GL MS 1046/1, fo. 185v.

around midnight and later for fish to sell at a profit in the morning. Some sneaks hid in the dark at doors and windows to eavesdrop on neighbours chatting inside to pick up any juicy or incriminating talk and gossip. Others were caught 'casting' 'lewd libels' in the night, hoping that there was more chance that no one would see them dropping their acidic lines in the dark.[31] And all of a sudden 'a grete noyse' might pierce the night air, spoiling sleep, sending officers scuttling to the source. People living along Cheapside woke with a start one night in 1564 when a 'tumult' of trumpets shattered the peace and quiet of their rest. Two boys who rang a steeple bell 'in the deade of the night' in 1556 got a stiff lecture from aldermen. A wax chandler stupidly 'range one of the grett bells in Seynt Sepulchres churche' in 'maner of an alarm in grett terror of the people', in a year (1559) when the political nation was once again holding its breath.[32]

Sometimes animals made the noise at night: 'Up betimes about 4 a-clock', Pepys bellyached in 1667, 'waked by a damned noise between a sow gelder and a cow and a dog'.[33] But more likely it was someone working late into the night, a drunk stumbling home, or some domestic spat that descended into caterwauling. A couple living on Holborn Bridge ended up in Bridewell in 1562 after 'grett[ly] disquietinge' neighbours many nights in a row, with their 'moste ungodlye scolding' at 'unlawfull howers and beating' on walls and doors. John Alden stayed 'up all nighte', his neighbours grumbled, 'makinge great noise and uproare' to their 'terror and disturbance'. Another sort of noise cut short sleep in St Paul's 'Peti Canons' in 1598, when a group of women 'masquers' broke open the college gate one night after midnight, 'with their minstrel', and 'dawnsed around the court' waking up all inside. Six women landed in trouble afterwards, including Isabel Parker, the wife of St Paul's bellringer.[34] No one was allowed to blow horns or whistles after nine. Smiths, pewterers, founders, or anyone else whose work was noisy were told to down tools until four in the morning or else risk a three shillings fine. Some Cornhill upholsterers paid a price for their 'great noyce' in 'beatinge' feather beds 'late in the eveninge and earlie in the morninge' in 1609. John Malen and Robert Railton, from the same ward, were taken to

---

[31] TNA SP16/296/29; Machyn *Diary*, p. 79; GL MS 5770/2, fos. 263–4, 563, 611, 647, 847; TNA STAC8 284/23; SP12/273/57.
[32] LMA Reps. 15, fo. 395v; 13(ii), fo. 432v; 14, fo. 189. See also LMA Rep. 28, fo. 197.
[33] GL MS 1499; Pepys, *Diary*, vol. VIII, p. 313.
[34] BHC 1, fo. 218; LMA MJ/SBR/7, fo. 20; GL MS 25175, fos. 7, 21, 25. See also LMA MJ/SBR/1, fo. 535. Another group of neighbours complained that Mr Golding in St Paul's 'peti canons' kept his gate open 'very late' to let in lodgers in 1598, whose loud 'knockinge' woke up people 'at theire rest' who 'kept due howers': GL MS 25175, fo. 18.

task for 'hammeringe of theire metall in theire shoppes not onely in the daye but also in the night'.[35] Nor was singing or any other sort of 'revelling' allowed after curfew, although this did not stop Pepys one night in 1666, who sat singing in his garden with his wife and friend until midnight in 'fine mooneshine', neighbours not minding, it seems, opening their windows. Others, not so lucky, ended up in court for 'singeinge bawdie songs' late at night. James Angel, a Westminster musician, played 'loud instruments' late into the night with others in 1643, fooling his neighbours into thinking that they were Westminster's waits.[36]

Not everyone followed the rules after dark, then, and some diehards held altogether different ideas of what the night was for. Why hurry inside like submissive schoolchildren the second the bell rang when there was still some drinking to be done, deals not yet struck with prostitutes, card games to play, songs to sing, or scores to be settled? Each night watchmen dealt with London's noisy, boozy, bawdy cultures. Some people spilled onto streets, shouting, fists flailing. Drunks staggered home late, singing and shouting at the top of their voices, like John Simpson who walked home 'whoopinge and hallowing' with a bellyful of drink one night in 1609. 'Drunk' Cuthbert Foster had people living along Tuttle Street in Westminster scrambling from their beds when he raised a hullabaloo coming home from an alehouse in 1613, 'crying murther', while 'evell' Cuthbert Carlyle's neighbours could not get to sleep at midnight one night because of the din next door as he bawled 'dronke in halfe ransie'.[37] People of all ages stayed up late at night to drink, dice, and dance, no matter what by-laws said. People like the group of Westminster men caught playing 'slydthrift' late one night in an alehouse; a pest from St Dunstan-in-the-West, who had a gang playing 'unlawful games in hys house at all hours in the nyght'; Margaret Payne, who lived along lively St John Street, and sold 'bottle ale' 'at all houres'; the surgeon James Heyden from St Clement Danes, who sat playing tables for nineteen hours in a victualler's house; and Edward Allen in Tower ward, whose rowdy 'comon victuallinge house' was packed with 'idle and evill disposed persons att unlawfull tymes', who 'daily' mocked curfew by

---

[35] Strype, *Survey*, V, p. 307; GL MS 4069/1, fos. 116, 118v, 161, 27. See also Emily Jane Cockayne, 'A cultural history of sound in England, 1560–1760', unpublished PhD thesis, University of Cambridge (2000), pp. 234–6, 241–7.

[36] Pepys, *Diary*, vol. VII, p. 117; BHC 5, fo. 378; 7, fo. 74; LMA WJ/SR/NS/41/19. Westminster's waits also complained about Angel: LMA WJ/SR/NS/41/94. Pepys also attended 'a puppet-play' in Lincolns Inn Fields after nine one night in 1663: *Diary*, vol. IV, p. 265. See also Machyn, *Diary*, p. 145.

[37] BHC 5, fo. 376; WAC WCB/1, fo. 238; BHC 1, fo. 211v.

'tumultuously' drinking, 'scowldinge, brawlinge, and misbehavinge' after midnight, causing 'fierce and terrible disturbances', 'clamors', 'strifes and discords'. One of William Bright's neighbours in Hart Lane, Covent Garden, saw footmen standing at his door most nights with cloaks in their hands, waiting patiently for their masters who were inside carousing with 'light women'.[38]

Many night-owls were high-spirited, rough, and resilient with entrenched lifestyles, and kept coming back for more camaraderie and pleasure. An officer told Bernard Fisher to go home from a Cow Lane alehouse at nine one night, only to find him in another one up the lane an hour later. A beadle who took Jane Kibble in the Nag's Head on the same lane at 'unseasonable hours', said that she was 'often' seen 'late in the streetes'. While Edward Moody admitted that 'contrary' to his master's 'trust', he gallivanted around the dark city in 1576, 'takinge my pleasures making mery with others', he said, naming nine. He also let slip how he 'often tymes' crept out of his master's shop window, 'leavinge [it] unmadfast', and headed for The Bell in Distaff Lane where there was 'comenly a noyse of muscyons and dawnsinge all nighte' and a dice-game in a corner.[39] We will never know what proportion of people painted London red at night. Nor do courtbooks give us close tallies of arrests for late bingeing and boozing because constables could take on-the-spot fines from 'drunckard[s] in the night'.[40] But we can be sure that this number was high and that there were words that were used more than others to describe bawdy antics at night. There is a particular resonance in one – swagger – that concisely expresses the happy-go-lucky high-jinks of drunk men that can turn violent without warning. Fishmongers' apprentices hung around Limehouse 'alehowses and other bad places' on 'the Thameside' in 1614, 'swaggeryng [and] drynkyng' with 'lewd women'. An alehouse-keeper was taken to court for serving 'swaggers' in 1605. A group, including an Eastcheap butcher, 'much delighted', it was said, in spending nights in taverns or dicing houses, often heading home 'overcome and distempered with wine', 'swagger[ing] in streets', heckling passers-by, singing loudly. Famously, there was the group of well-to-do

---

[38] LMA WJ/SR/NS/43/45; GL MS 3018/1, fo. 9; LMA MJ/SBR/2, fo. 214; WJ/SR/NS/45/39, 45/41; CQSF 110, Edward Allen information; WJ/SR/NS/48/20. See also LMA MJ/SBR/1, fo. 80; MJ/SBR/2, fo. 147; MJ/SBR/3, fo. 351; MJ/SBR/5, fo. 291; MJ/SBR/6, fo. 559; WJ/SR/39/104, 47/126; CQSF 106/54; Reps. 27, fo. 117; 31(1), fo. 38v; BHC 5, fos. 164v, 346v; 7, fo. 315; 8, fo. 158v; 9, fo. 143; BRHA BHC 4, fo. 453v; TNA STAC8 296/9; SP16/423/85; GL MSS 3018/1, fos. 67v, 97v, 106; 4069/1, fos. 21v, 216, 234v.
[39] BHC 8, fo. 147; 7, fo. 258v; 3, fos. 138v-9.   [40] GL MS 6552/1, fo. 170v.

'swaggerers' called the 'damned crew' or 'roaring boys', who raised the roof all through the night.[41]

With drink flowing there was always a danger that things could easily turn ugly in a flash. The 'roaring boys' or 'damned crew' caused one ruckus after another in early seventeenth-century London. We see them in one Star Chamber case banging on the doors of the house of two heiresses, hoping to get their hands on their inheritance, shouting at the maid who rushed alarmed to the door, 'God's wound you whore open the door', throwing stones at windows, breaking some, 'roaring out ... come out your bawdy house, common base twopenny whores', 'all the world knows' that you are 'burnt tail whores [who] might be had for a pot of beer'.[42] Other rough roisters appear in the sources, rapiers drawn, spoiling for a fight. Violence and vandalism were par for the course after a heavy drinking bout. After a brawl one night in The Devil of St Dunstan spilled over into Fleet Street, a gang went up and down the street, one witness said, 'determined to assault whoever came that way'. 'Kill hym my love, kyll him my love, stabbe him', 'lewde' Katherine Ratcliffe yelled when her lover got into a fight with 'a man of my Lord Riches' on Field Lane in 1609. Watchmen were always coming across roughnecks like Fagg Huffum and Edward Courthop, who were found 'fighting and quarelling' in the streets late one night. Night's 'rude and riotous rabble' broke bones, 'hedds', windows, walls, doors, and sleep, all part of early modern London's noisy rough nocturnal scenes, that were played out night after night without pause.[43]

## Lighting

This was one battle that magistrates could never win. London was never quiet at night; there was always someone somewhere causing noise and trouble. And so magistrates did their best to warn people about night's 'terrors' and dangers and passed measures each year to improve night lighting and policing, with some success. The rest of this chapter concerns this effort to keep order after dark, notwithstanding some violence,

---

[41] GL MS 5770/2, fo. 99; BHC 5, fo. 48; TNA STAC8 296/9; SP14/7/29. One 'roaring boy' – John Goodier – was a member of Middle Temple. Another, Edward Rippington, received a Bachelor of Arts from Oxford, and said that he would have got his MA, but he was encouraged to go to London to become a nobleman's servant: TNA STAC8 62/13.
[42] TNA STAC8 62/13.
[43] TNA STAC8 190/8; BHC 5, fo. 350v; LMA CQSF 124/95–5. See also GL MS 4069/2, fo. 389v; BHC 5, fo. 335; 6, fo. 250v; 7, fo. 304v; 9, fo. 59; LMA CQSF 110/8; Reps. 10, fo. 66; 11, fo. 385; 27, fo. 180v; WJ/SR/34/45, 41/65, 45/46, 48/21; MJ/SBR/1, fo. 115; MJ/SBR/2, fo. 22; MJ/SBR/5, fo. 20; MJ/SBR/7, fo. 162.

rowdiness, and determined drinking. It was important to impose the idea that day and night were different in terms of work, bodily health, and 'fitting' conduct, and something that all offenders shared in this view of crime was a deep aversion to light. 'A general principle it is [Thomas Nashe wrote, that], hee that doth ill hateth the light'. Humphrey Mill called nightwalkers a 'brood of darknesse that do hate the light'.[44] Thieves hid in thick crowds to fleece people by day, taking care to work unseen, away from the glare of open light. Turning out light was a natural thing for anyone to do who was up to no good. Katherine Pangman 'vouched' in 1577 that Elizabeth Bagles and Robert Edwards were 'suspitiously together from ix a clock at night til one a clocke'; they had a candle with them, she said, 'but it was put out' after a while and they 'taried an ower in the darke alone'. Agnes Higgins, who was 'abused' in a shoemaker's house by a cooper's servant in 1576, claimed that he 'never came to her but by dark night when they never had any light'.[45] Throwing light into shadows was a response to 'deeds of darknesse'. Light was linked to safety in lanterns lighting London's main streets or carried by watches as identification marks. The absence of light was a tonic for thieves or anyone else who needed the dark for cover. 'Many mischiefes and assaults' occur between 'fyve and nyne of the clocke at night', magistrates noted in 1624, 'by reason' that 'little or noe light' shines on streets. 'Oftentimes and especially in the winter tyme the evenige beinge darke', common councillors said in 1627, 'idle, lewd, and vagrant persons' emerge from their hide-outs if 'lanthorne and candlelight is not hunge out', and the number of 'burglaries' and 'robberyes' shoots up. They also said that murder, felony, and other 'mischievous acts' were 'deeds of darknesse' in 1639, when asking once more for improved lighting.[46] Light that seemed pure was linked to the 'expelling and abolishinge of vice' and cleaning up of vagrants and filth from London's streets.[47]

The history of London's night lighting is usually and not unfairly told with heavy emphasis on the four decades from the Common Council Act (1695) that put 'publick lights' in the hands of the private Convex Light Company and lighting legislation that was passed by Parliament in 1736,

[44] Nashe, *Terrors of the Night*, p. 386; Humphrey Mill, *A Night's Search Discovering the Nature and Condition of All Sorts of Nightwalkers With Their Associates* (1640), p. 276. See also Nicholas Breton, *The Good and the Badde: Or Descriptions of the Worthies and Unworthies of this Age* (1616), fo. E4r. For later comments that show continuity, see Daniel Defoe, *Augusta Triumphaus: Or, the Way to Make London the Most Flourishing City in the Universe* (1729), p. 27.
[45] BHC 3, fos. 231v-2; GL MS 12806/3, fo. 144.
[46] LMA Jours. 33, fo. 140v; 34, fo. 168; 39, fo. 363.
[47] LMA Letterbooks V, fo. 69v; S, fo. 50; Jours. 23, fo. 156; 13, fos. 428v-9; 14, fos. 121v, 159, 198; 19, fo. 10v; 20, fo. 521; Rep. 13(i), fo. 2.

that allowed individual wards to bargain with any company to get the best deal for street-lighting. As with London, other leading cities on the European mainland became brighter with better night lighting, beginning with Paris in 1667.[48] Before then, many scholars say, streets were dimmer and more dangerous at night. The implicit assumption in much work so far is that left to citizens to light lamps, London before bright commercial oil lamps was a dimly lit city, a pale light at best that did little to reveal sneak thieves lying in wait in shadows. This is true up to a point, so long as we note willingness in the Guildhall to recognize flaws before 1660 and plan improvements. Like policing, lighting was not neglected. It posed problems, but there are some revealing continuities deep into the next century when crime remained linked to a lack of light. Street lighting was not year-long or even round-the-clock in winter's longer nights before 1660. Beadles commonly did their rounds around six on 'dark nights', knocking on doors to tell householders to hang out 'lanthorne and candle-light'. For how long exactly is uncertain, because by-laws did not always follow the same schedule: some allowed lights to flicker out at the curfew hour (nine, normally), while others called for longer light, and some told householders that each candle should keep 'burninge soe long as [it] will endure'.[49]

The effect of all this light is difficult to measure, although there was plenty of griping about neglect from the Guildhall and elsewhere. 'The greatest parte of the ward' do not hang out lights, Cornhill wardmote complained in 1615. The same ward was angered by 'no light' at the Royal Exchange in Winter 1574, when 'divers [people were] taken comyttinge fornicacon' in the dark. 'Often presented and not amended', ward leaders noted crossly, but a decade later Lady Gresham herself made her first appearance for the lack of 'lanthornes in thExchange', that was said to be 'dangerous for passers-by'.[50] Foot-draggers clearly resented the cost and trouble of putting out light each winter night, although the City took

---

[48] 9 Geo. II, c.20. See also Beattie, *Policing and Punishment:*, pp. 207–25; Malcolm Falkus, 'Lighting in the dark ages of English economic history: town streets before the Industrial Revolution', in D. C. Coleman and A. H. John, eds., *Trade, Government and Economy in Pre-Industrial England: Essays Presented to F. J. Fisher* (1976), pp. 248–73; and E. S. de Beer, 'The early history of London street lighting', *History*, 25 (1940–1), 311–24. For lighting elsewhere see Ekirch, *At Day's Close*, pp. 67–74, 332–7; L. S. Multhalf, 'The light of lamp-lanterns: street lighting in seventeenth-century Amsterdam', *Technology and Culture*, 26 (1985), 236–52; Craig Koslofsky, 'Court culture and street lighting in seventeenth-century Europe', *Journal of Urban History*, 28 (2002), 743–68.

[49] LMA Jours. 26, fo. 179; 33, fos. 6, 140v; 34, fo. 29; 36, fo. 181; 27, fos. 291v, 417; 29, fos. 15v, 60v; 36, fo. 181; 39, fos. 8, 363; Reps. 13i, fo. 2; 51, fo. 332v.

[50] GL MS 4069/1, fos. 140, 191v, 14, 31, 47, 51v. See also LMA Jours. 34, fo. 29; 35, fo. 360v; 36, fo. 181; 38, fo. 1v; Rep. 25, fo. 24v; GL MSS 4069/1, fos. 49, 56, 60, 104, 181; 3018/1, fo. 69v; Howell, *Londinopolis*, p. 393.

steps to see that candles were fairly priced (if the Butchers' wardens 'were wyse', Richard Benyon snapped in 1577, 'they wolde not agree to the lorde mayors pryce for tallowe').[51] A carpenter 'grevously wounde[d]' a constable who 'requyred' him to 'hange owte a lanthorne' in 1578. William Copley slammed his door shut in a constable's face when he was asked to do the same thing almost six decades later.[52] Not everyone appeared to be civic minded enough to light lanterns, and even as they burned in the expectation that thieves would shrink away, plucky 'cutters' made off with lanterns even though they were exposed in the glare of the light. 'Lanterne cutter' Robert Hyame was 'taken with three lanthornes' late one night in 1619. John Skull, who was caught 'about nine [at night] cutt[ing] downe two lanthornes' in Winter 1637, was said to have been 'bestly druncke'. Lanterns were also a tempting target for vandals. Two 'maryners' landed in trouble in 1550 for 'bet[ing] down lanthornes' at 'mens dores'. St Michael Cornhill vestrymen woke up one morning in 1578 to the bad news that their 'great glass lantern' had been smashed up in the night.[53]

There are only a few lantern cutters in the sources, but apathy created larger problems that upset residents but were not avoided by magistrates. People living on London Bridge petitioned aldermen in 1637 about the 'small light' along the bridge at night, 'which by reason of the closenesse of the place [the petitioner's said]', with 'houses hanging over the streetes, could hardly be seene'. For remedy they asked for 'seven greate lights' that would give 'sufficient light' for 'neighbours and passengers'.[54] With theft on the rise in 1634, common councillors instructed wards and precincts to provide a 'great lanthorne' in winter, 'over and above' their 'ordinary lights'. One year later, the same body sent round an order for precinct lanterns to provide light all through the city long after midnight (until 4 am), to give 'comfortable passage' through the streets.[55] Precincts and wards had long had charge of larger lanterns, but after 1600 magistrates tried harder to improve provision. Wards had for some time taken responsibility to provide public lighting, placing lanterns for safety in selected strategic spots. Cornhill sought assistance to hang lights 'in the winter nights' at 'St Peter's churche dore and St Peters alleys dore [in 1590] for that those places are dangerous for the passers bye'. The same

---

[51] LMA Rep. 19, fos. 201, 203. A butcher's servant was prosecuted for striking a tallow chandler who 'desired' to 'buy tallow at the price menconed' by the mayor: LMA Rep. 34, fo. 565v.
[52] LMA Reps. 19, fo. 388; 50, fo. 60v.
[53] BHC 6, fo. 92; 8, fo. 151; LMA Rep. 12, fo. 278v; GL MS 4072/1, fos. 18, 19. See also BHC 2, fo. 41; 6, fo. 216v; 9, fo. 3; LMA Rep. 16, fos. 434–4v.
[54] LMA Rep. 51, fo. 332v.  [55] LMA Jours. 36, fo. 10; 37, fo. 128.

ward put a light 'about [St Michael's] cloyster' four decades later, as it was the place 'most fitt' to give light to all that 'passe or goe' from the churchyard. An alderman gave Bread Street ward a costly large lantern in 1604, that was fixed to the wall at the east end of the church, and a matching lantern was hung up on the west wall near Soper Lane end a few years later.[56]

Precinct lanterns burned for longer through the year (sometimes all year round) and far later at night (often until after midnight) than the lanterns that were hung up by householders. St John Zachary parish covered the costs for a 'great lanthorne' to 'hange out till morninge' in 1634. Precinct lanterns with 'great candlelight' burned all through the night across the city until the start of the working day in 1642. One parish paid Mr Potter 2/6d 'for hanging out the lanthorne for one yeare'.[57] Ward lanterns, precinct lanterns, parish lanterns, 'comon lanthornes', 'night lanthornes', 'glasse lanthornes', 'great lanthornes', and 'large lanthornes', lit up walkways across London. They sometimes stood on streets or steps, but more often they were handily located in churchyards, perched on top of church steeples, or burning on church porches, doors, 'ends', or 'corners', hanging up on hooks, 'hornes', poles, chains, or branches. St Botolph Billingsgate attached 'a fair glass lantern' on 'the corner of the church against Botolph Lane' to 'give light' from 14 August all the way through to 1 April. While St Christopher-le-Stocks hung a 'newe great lanthorne' on the church door in 1626.[58] Lanterns were also placed prominently on street 'ends' and corners, or in back alleys and yards: in 'Pudding Lane end', for example, 'Crooked Lane end', 'Soper Lane corner' and 'end', 'Spy Corner', Blackhorse Alley, and Bell Yard.[59] Light also shone from prominent buildings, like the Guildhall (where 'a fayre lanterne' blazed through the entire 'wynter season' on the porch to 'gyve lyght' to all passers-by), the Royal Exchange (though not all the time, as we have seen), Blackwell Hall, and in market-places and on landmarks like conduits. Lanterns also burned late in porter's lodges in the hospitals, right next to the gates.[60]

---

[56] GL MSS 4069/1, fos. 52, 196; 4992/1, fos. 351, 353.
[57] GL MSS 590/1, fo. 150v; 6552/1, fo. 250; LMA Jour. 39, fo. 363; GL MS 1568, fo. 365.
[58] GL MSS 3556/2, 1642; 943/1, fo. 31; 4423/1, fo. 107. See also GL MSS 559/1, fo. 65; 6552/1, fo. 229v; 4383/1, fo. 281; 4423/1, fo. 168v; 1046/1, fo. 139v; 2968/1, fo. 413v; 4071/1, fo. 135; 4072/1, fo. 22; 942/1, fo. 83; 1568, fo. 614; 590/1, fo. 159v; 1240/1, fo. 74; 4214/1, fo. 43; 642/1, fo. 56; 1002/1, fo. 345; 645/1, fo. 106v.
[59] GL MSS 942/1, fos. 136v, 148v, 174; 3146/1, fo. 126; 1176/1, 1639; 1046/1, fos. 46v, 123v, 127, 151, 176; 6552/1, fo. 249v; 2895/2, 1642; 878/1, fos. 283, 289v; 1568, fo. 357; 4457/2, fo. 352v; 662/1, fo. 159v; 3016/1, fo. 201; 2593/1, 1636, fo. 5; 6836, fo. 143v; 5018/1, fo. 30.
[60] LMA Reps. 18, fo. 433; 22, fo. 318; 23, fos. 4v, 462, 505; GL MSS 4069/1, fos. 14, 31, 42, 54; 2895/2, 1624–5, 1625–6; 33063/1, Xmas 1646, Mich. 1647, Mich. 1648; 12806/4, fo. 174.

Wintry London did not just rely on householders to light main streets to stop 'thieves and desperadoes' in their tracks or to help people get back home without stumbling in the dark or falling victim to 'terrors'.[61] Watchmen walked with lights, and along with watermen and boys are seen guiding people home in the dark with 'links' and 'lights'. John Thomas made money by 'carry[ing] lincks to gentlemen about the cort' in 1633. Pepys was often 'lit home' by a boy when walking home late, though 'linck boys' also fell on the wrong side of the law. Word got round that William Powell 'carryeth lincks to light gents to bawdy houses' in 1618. A young 'runaway' was 'taken lighting one with a lincke from Blackfryers playhouse' a decade later. While Thomas Duncan was 'taken' late one night in 1637, 'with a linke lighted on the topp of his head'.[62] These mobile lights flickered along dark streets, warning watchmen (and others) that someone was coming. Nothing this far back in time matched the brighter lights of later decades, but the impact of night-lighting was not negligible in London four centuries ago. 'Honest' people welcomed it with open arms, and the link between better light and safety was a given. It is quite easy to be lukewarm about London's pale night-lighting, but that does not get us far. Attempts to make the city brighter and safer before 1660 ought to be acknowledged. In fact, London was a better lit city by the middle of the seventeenth century. Starting around 1600, Common Council routinely issued lengthy orders for dusky winter nights in early November, that always began with warnings about sneak vagrants and burglars 'lurking' in dark 'corners' and shadows, followed by detailed instructions to wards, parishes, and householders for lighting lanterns (at doors or windows and 'daylie continued' until March 1), setting the curfew, the time to begin and break watches, and orders to search 'suspect' houses and clean streets.[63]

The time of lighting was deeply embedded in senses of time. 'There [Whitehall] till after candle-lighting', Pepys scribbled in his diary in 1668, telling time by candle-light.[64] People knew the hour when lanterns came on. Time was also rung by bellmen crying lanterns and curfew bells that

---

[61] GL MS 4992/1, fo. 12; Lawrence, *A Golden Trumpet*, p. 41.
[62] LMA WJ/SR/38/3; BHC 6, fos. 22, 30; 7, fo. 52; 8, fo. 109v; Pepys, *Diary*, vol. II, p. 60; vol. III, p. 180; vol. VI, pp. 27, 340; vol. VII, p. 100; vol. VIII, p. 3; vol. IX, p. 172. See also 'London Journal of Alessandro Magno'; Howes, *Annales*, p. 1040; BHC 6, fos. 161v, 381v, 423v; 7, fos. 218v, 355; 8, fos. 51, 146v, 273, 331v, 368v; GL MSS 4409/1, fos. 112, 277v; 1002/1, fos. 212, 219.
[63] For example, LMA Jours. 26, fos. 274–4v; 27, fos. 1–1v, 95–5v, 191v-2, 308v-9; 28, fos. 120–0v, 263–4; 29, fos. 259–60, 283–4v; 31, fos. 261v-2; 35, fos. 10, 360v-1; 39, fo. 142v.
[64] Pepys, *Diary*, vol. IX, p. 299.

informed people that it was now high time to get home.[65] Nine was the usual time when curfew cut movement to a bare minimum of vital workers and peace-keepers. With rest came noise controls to bring the day's socializing and work to an end. Alehouses were instructed to stop serving at eight or nine and raids by officers checked that the last customer had gone home. Magistrates also warned householders to get their apprentices and servants safely inside by a certain hour; foreigners were also subject to household curfews.[66] The first bellman was appointed in 1555/6 to stop at 'lane ends' to 'give warning' about fire and candlelight, and to urge Londoners to help the poor and pray for the dead (they were also 'locker up[s] at night', Geoffrey Mynshul said in 1638).[67] Two 'honest, sadd and discrete' bellmen divided the city into east and west halves in 1568, 'watching nightly' from nine until four in winter and three in summer, 'contynually ringinge' their bells 'and pronouncynge certayne words' (bellmen picked up £4 in salary in 1635). They rang time in regular rhythms, that were soothing perhaps for anyone awake late: 'I sat up till the bell-man came by with his bell, just under my window as I was writing of this very line and cried "past one of the clock, and a cold frosty, windy morning"', Pepys wrote, sitting up late in 1660.[68] Parishes paid sextons, staffbearers, and others to ring 'the curfewe bell', and records refer to '8 and 5' or '9 and 5' bells: no 'peal' to last longer than an hour, St Michael Cornhill vestry said in 1608 (fifteen minutes, another parish instructed six decades later).[69] This time-calling chorus was completed with the clang of gates shutting at nine or ten, depending on the season (and only opened on 'urgent occasion' or for people who were 'known to be honest'), and unlocked for the new day no earlier than 4 am. Pepys walked home late one night in 1667 and found the gates shut and a rumpus in nearby Newgate prison, 'some thief having broke open prison', he noted later in his diary. A surgeon 'wound[ed]' Newgate's porter when he stood his ground and 'would not suffer hym to passe through' the gate

---

[65] Cockayne, 'Cultural history of sound in England', pp. 141–2, 236–7; *The Manner of Crying Things in London* (1599?).

[66] LMA Reps. 11, fo. 331v; 12, fos. 91v, 99; 17, fo. 372; 21, fos. 59v, 330v; Letterbook R, fo. 11; Jours 21, fo. 356; 23, fos. 114v, 123; 39, fos. 84v, 253v; 41, fo. 212; GL MS 12806/2, fo. 258v. 'Due tyme' for closing down alehouses for the night was 10 p.m. in a Common Council order from 1642: LMA Jour. 39, fo. 356.

[67] Strype, *Survey*, V, p. 393; GL MS 4992/1, fo. 12; Maitland, *History of London*, p. 153; Mynshul, *Characters of Prisons and Prisoners*, p. 42.

[68] LMA Rep. 16, fos. 422v, 433v; Pepys, *Diary*, vol. I, p. 19. See also LMA Letterbook V, fos. 205, 213v; Rep. 34, fo. 182v; City Cashbook 1–2, fo. 40.

[69] GL MSS 4457/2, fo. 88v; 4072/1, fo. 100; 819/1, fo. 143v. See also GL MSS 4072/1, fo. 157; 9068, fos. 152, 208; 3016/1, fo. 289; 1240/1, fo. 74.

at 'xi' in 1583.[70] Christ's Hospital gates were slammed shut at six in the evening in 1574 ('and none to come in after except a very urgent cause', governors said), and at eight at night in winter and seven in summer in 1637. A Star Chamber witness said that ten seemed like an 'unusual' time for anyone to try to get into the Tower, as he supposed that most people knew that the gates were always shut earlier at eight.[71]

### Watching

Citizens should have been able to sleep soundly this late at night, but things did not always work out that way. Watches were supposed to be on guard all through the night, however, with black staffs 'to be known by', in one parish.[72] But watchmen were frequently lampooned and lambasted. 'Drowsie' was John Lawrence's word of choice; 'slender' and 'weak' were also bandied about in caricatures of toothless and spineless bunglers, needy enough to pocket a few pennies to stand watch, but not hardy enough to see out the entire night.[73] Policing after dark was a nightmare of sorts. London was huge by the standards of other cities and a powder keg in the talk of the times. Bad enough by day, many said, London was more dangerous at night, so watches gathered at their meeting places and 'greate' precinct lanterns burned until daylight. Watches were set all year long for various periods of time in winter and summer in line with the time of sunrise: 8 pm to 3 am, eight to four or five, nine to four, five, or seven, and ten to four or five.[74] 'Contynuall watch' was set 'nyghtly' for the 'saufeguard' of the city. Some were 'standinge watches' situated in strategic locations. But it is not always clear whether watchmen walked about the streets or stood still on guard, although the clear inference over time is that they were expected to walk through their precincts/wards.[75] Far from being haphazard, 'the distribucon and placinge' of watches was a matter for careful attention. Local officials were told to put watchmen in 'places

---

[70] LMA Reps. 11, fo. 331v; 12, fos. 95, 324v, 328v, 395v; 20, fo. 445v; 21, fo. 577v; 59, fo. 146; Letterbooks K, fos. 19, 404v; R, fos. 8v-9, 259; Jours. 15, fo. 243; 16, fos. 247, 333v; 21, fo. 356; 23, fo. 6v; 40, fo. 41; Pepys, *Diary*, vol. VIII, p. 371.
[71] GL MSS 12806/2, fo. 101v; 12806/4, fo. 174; TNA STAC8 190/131.
[72] GL MS 819, fo. 6v.
[73] Lawrence, *Golden Trumpet*, p. 100. See also Price, 'Parish constables', pp. 102–3. For abuses by and against the watch see below, pp. 353–7.
[74] For example, LMA Jours. 13, fos. 428v-9; 16, fo. 365v; 20, fo. 150; 28, fo. 252v; 35, fo. 167; Reps 11, fo. 192v; 12, fo. 95; 20, fo. 412v; 21, fo. 577v; Letterbooks R, fos. 8v-9; S, fos 63, 118.
[75] For example, LMA Reps. 10, fo. 144; 11, fo. 440; 12, fos. 179, 298, 395, 518v; 13(i), fo. 112; 14, fo. 519v; 16, fos. 86v, 518v-19; 17, fo. 427; 18, fos. 138v, 296v; 20, fo. 412v; 21, fo. 330v; 22, fo. 335v; Letterbooks K, fos. 194–4v; R, fo. 259; V, fo. 264; Jours. 20, fo. 150; 28, fo. 252.

as have moste neede' for London's 'safe and sure keepinge', and to have 'dyligente regard to the Thamys syde', landing places, gates, and all major crossroads.[76] The numbers on watch were tailored to need, and watchmen were not evenly divided across the city, but were thinner on the ground in areas that had less significant histories of disorder: eleven in Lime Street in 1643, for example, ninety in overcrowded Cripplegate Without, a dozen in Bassishaw, eighty in busy Bishopgate, sixteen in the city centre in Cornhill, and 130 in trouble-prone Farringdon Without. Watches were boosted at each gate in the panic and confusion that followed the Gunpowder Plot, ranging from twenty watchmen at Moorgate to thirty-five in Newgate.[77]

'Ordinary watches' were topped up with extra 'dylygent' watches when there was felt to be more danger: extra watchmen were appointed for two weeks at one such time in 1547, for the coming weekend at another in 1582 when a flood of 'roages' was forecasted, and 'until further order' at other times when trouble was in the air. Householders were also put on alert to guard the streets if needed: some were told 'to be readdie' within 'one howers warninge' in 1593.[78] 'Doble watches' were also posted all over the city when sudden bursts of vagrants or theft raised concerns. Watches were doubled in Christmas 1623 'to secure passengers from theeves'. Sometimes no reason was given, on record at any rate. 'A good and substantiall double watch' was set 'for sundrie and important reasons' in Winter 1626; a 'nightly' watch was set in 1641 for 'some special causes' that were not divulged.[79] But reasons are clear at many other times. Watches were 'dowbled' when Kett seemed certain to turn his attention to London in 'the tyme of comocon' in 1549, and other times when politics was on a knife edge and the talk was of rebels and revolts: Somerset's 'arraynment' in 1551, for example, the 'tyme of the rebellyon of Wyatt and his complices', the Gunpowder plot, the epidemic of enclosure riots in 1607, and the 'tymes of great distruccon and eminent daunger' during the Revolution. A 'treble watch' was set as crowds swarmed around Parliament in January 1642, and a 'double watch' stood up to feverish crowds when Strafford was put on trial.[80]

---

[76] LMA Jour. 26, fo. 70; Rep. 54, fo. 181v; Letterbooks R, fo. 34v; S, fo. 79v; X, fos. 93v-4; GL MS 12806/1, fo. 4; HOL MP, 3-5-1641.
[77] LMA Jours. 40, fos. 75–6; 27, fo. 14v. See also LMA Jour. 26, fo. 70.
[78] LMA Reps. 11, fo. 267v; 20, fo. 320; 23, fo. 51v; Jours. 16, fos. 91v, 333, 365v; 20, fos. 185, 388.
[79] LMA Jours. 33, fo. 199; 39, fo. 193v. For other examples see LMA Reps. 11, fo. 274; 13(i), fo. 122v; 17, fo. 249v; 19, fo. 413v; 55, fo. 402; Jours. 16, fo. 163; 20, fo. 113; 28, fo. 84; 31, fo. 343; 33, fo. 245v; 34, fo. 297v; 35, fo. 96v; 39, fo. 273v; 40, fo. 308v.
[80] LMA Rep. 12, fos. 98v, 114v-15, 149–9v; Letterbook R, fos. 32v, 34v-5; Reps. 12, fo. 420; 13(ii), fo. 174; 13(i), fos. 120v, 156; Jours. 16, fo. 257; 27, fo. 14v; 39, fos. 185v,

Policing: night battles 351

The City, needless to say, did not need government to hang in the balance to boost night patrols. Watches were strengthened in boisterous Bartholomew Fair, 'solempne fasts', 'duryng the syttyng of the Parlyament', at fierce fires that drew thieves like magnets, when stormy 'mutinies' rocked Newgate Prison in 1640, when the queen went to 'supp' with the mayor in 1634, and at the 'demyse and death' of monarchs.[81] Additional watches were also set and London's gates were 'fast shutte' at high points in the festive and ceremonial calendar, such as 'Maye Eve', the Vigils of Saints John, Paul, and Peter, and the once grand Midsummer Watch, which was stripped down to a duller 'ordinary doble watch' ('no goinge watche', alderman said) in 1569, 'withowt lights, drones, musicall instruments', or the elegant trimmings of years gone by.[82]

Magistrates also set up surprise 'privy' searches, often planned a couple of hours ahead. 'This night and twyse every weke untyll Xpmas', aldermen said when setting up a search in 1550; next Friday, they said in 1594, planning a few days ahead of time to swoop suddenly on 'suspected' people. Catch them off guard, governors told officers, storm suspect houses at 'unknowne times uppon the sudden', 'every weeke once at the least'. Some searches were one-off efforts to catch someone in particular or to clamp down on vagrants, but plans were also made for weekly or fortnightly follow-up searches.[83] Searches were often set as soon as word spread of disorders, as when six men who broke out of Newgate prison in 1615 were known to be 'lurking' in 'obscure' nooks. More often, however, plans were made after a sudden surge of trouble: thieves, vagrants, masterless men, nightwalkers, 'loyterers', strangers, and murderers were

---

238v, 264, 266, 273v, 331v; 40, fos. 271v-2; CSPV 1607–10, p. 14; 1610–13, p. 764; William Gough, *Londinium Triumphaus* (1682), p. 343; *The Diary of John Evelyn*, ed., E. S. De Beer, 6 vols. (Oxford, 1955), vol. III, p. 331.

[81] LMA Jour. 30, fo. 228; Rep. 18, fo. 413v; TNA SP14/4/76; LMA Jour. 39, fos. 147v, 262, 281; Rep. 9, fo. 46v; Jours. 32, fo. 232v; 39, fo. 59; 36, fo. 217; 35, fo. 302v; Letterbook R, fos. 262–2v; CSPV 1623–5, p. 879.

[82] For example, LMA Reps. 12, fo. 328v; 13(i) fo. 156v; 15, fo. 433v; 18, fo. 197; Jours. 15, fo. 334; 16, fo. 383; 17, fo. 122v; 20, fo. 405; 31, fo. 313; 35, fo. 446v; 38, fo. 241v (May Eve); Reps. 17, fo. 335v; 21, fo. 299; Letterbooks R, fos 9, 260v; V, fo. 175; Jours.16, fo. 388; 26, fo. 352; 30, fo. 192v; 33, fo. 129; 37, fo. 207v (Vigils of Saints John, Paul, and Peter); Reps. 11, fo. 445v; 15, fo. 446; 18, fo. 389v; Jours. 16, fo. 247; 19, fo. 346v; 20, fo. 412; 27, fo. 250v; 29, fo. 216; 35, fo. 485v; 39, fo. 325 (Midsummer). The 1569 Midsummer Watch order is noted in Rep. 16, fo. 475v. Four years before the ending of the old Midsummer Watch in 1569, aldermen were told to see that constables 'doe not prepare ... eny matter of cressett, lyght, drape' or other 'mynstrelsye' on May Eve, but simply set a 'good, sadd and substancyall doble watch' (LMA Rep. 15, fo. 434). See also Strype, *Survey*, V, p. 256, 393; Howes, *Annales*, p. 595. For policing measures in Shrovetide see my *Youth and Authority*, pp. 154–8.

[83] LMA Reps. 12, fo. 418; 23, fo. 152; 11, fos. 379, 390; 12, fo. 111; 13(i), fo. 107v; Jours. 17, fo. 88v; 19, fo. 291; 26, fo. 240v; 32, fo. 318v.

352    Control

all targeted at various times, to be 'exactly examined of their lyving and behavior'. Other searches were in effect press gangs hunting for 'stronge, apte, and able' vagrants (and others) to 'serve' overseas. People taken on suspicion in searches were usually held until next morning, when they were taken before a justice. 'Devide' into groups, deputies in charge were told in 1610, make sure it is 'carefullie done aboute 3 of the clocke', look 'especiallie' in 'hyred' chambers, and bring anyone found to the mayor by 7 am. Alehouses, 'pennye hostelries', bowling alleys, and 'dyssing howses' were all singled out as likely places to find suspects.[84] The idea was to pounce quickly before anyone caught wind of what was happening. Out on 'narrow search' to round up 'gunners' and 'seafaring men' in 1639, officers were told to move 'in the privatest manner that maybe lest any taking notice' steal away. Ward leaders were directed to 'devide' their 'company' by precinct and start searches at the same time 'with all speed and secresie', or 'with as much secrecy as you may'. Word sometimes slipped out, however. Michael Holt landed in trouble in 1629 'for giveinge notice to M[ist]riss Holland that the constable was comeinge unto her house to search for lewd people'.[85] Magistrates also extended their net with 'generall privie searches' in nearby counties, as in 1615 when the Crown called for weekly or twice-weekly 'sudden' searches after a spate of robberies. Synchronization was the key, so that word did not zip round that searchers were on the way. Royal ministers told the City and neighbouring justices to search 'suspected places' 'sudden[ly]' and at the 'same instant' in 1616.[86]

We are often left in the dark about the end results of searches, except that there were times when suspects were dropped off at Bridewell from one. Recorder Fleetwood had a smooth night's work in Winter 1582, when he led a search party that found 'not one rooge stirring'.[87] But there are signs that not everything went according to plan. There were jurisdictional tangles that needed sorting out when adjacent wards or precincts squabbled about setting watches: two constables, from Cornhill and nearby Aldgate, fell out on watch in 1564. In other cases arrangements caused concern for City and Middlesex magistrates, including a situation in 1634 when two next-door parishes on the

---

[84] LMA Jours. 29, fo. 394; 17, fos. 67, 88v; 28, fo. 38v. See also LMA Reps. 12, fo. 487; 13(ii), fo. 349v; 14, fo. 378; 16, fo. 511; 19, fo. 394v; Letterbook X, fo. 11; Jours. 17, fo. 342v; 18, fo. 309v; 19, fo. 364v; 20, fo. 456v; 21, fo. 395; 26, fo. 393; 27, fo. 380; 29, fo. 394; 31, fo. 315; 34, fo. 283v; 35, fo. 504; 37, fo. 423; 39, fo. 221; TNA SP12/188/54, 12/191/5, 12/252/42.
[85] LMA Jours. 38, fo. 309; 39, fo. 237v; 32, fo. 318v; MJ/SBR/5, fo. 45. And see LMA Jours. 19, fo. 291; 20, fos 223, 252; 35, fo. 21v; Rep. 16, fo. 448; TNA SP12/188/74; APC 1601–4, pp. 74–5.
[86] APC 1615–16, pp. 211–12, 693–4; LMA Rep. 48, fos. 54v-5; TNA SP12/188/74.
[87] Wright, ed., *Queen Elizabeth and Her Times*, vol. II, p. 166.

Middlesex border pooled watchmen, taking turns to watch over both parishes. Magistrates heard in 1615 that, sticking to 'ancient custome', constables in 'particuler precinctes' would not cross precinct lines, even if they were hot on the heels of suspects; they were told to watch in future, 'withoute makinge question of lymitte or precincte'.[88] Watchmen were on the receiving end of much criticism. Most years saw a number of complaints from the Guildhall about low standards and follow-up precepts to try to put things straight.[89] Particular wards were sometimes singled-out for a tongue-lashing. Aldermen blasted below-par watches in Bishopgate in 1645.[90] But more often fingers were pointed at wards and parishes in city-wide complaints. To make matters worse, not all watch-rates were paid in full or on time. 'We greatly marvel that any man will be so slack' for 'a general good', the Crown said in 1630, linking the latest surge of vagrants to dwindling watch-budgets as rates yielded disappointingly low returns.[91] The working day often began at the crack of dawn and turning up for watch-duty did not appeal to everyone who also had dayjobs, like the people living on the edges of Paul's Churchyard who refused to watch when their turn came round in 1579. An innkeeper on St John Street called the Cow Cross constable 'slave' and the beadle 'villaine', and added that he 'wished they were both hanged', when they asked him to take his turn to watch in 1615. One man said that he could not watch in 1654 'because of colds and aches in his bones' picked up 'in the commonwealth's service' from lying on the cold ground in open fields.[92] Other unwilling watchmen were rather more foolhardy. A draper told a constable that his horse would watch instead of him as he had better things to do. When Daniel Mabbes was asked 'where his weapon was to watch with', he snapped back that 'itt was in his codpiece'. 'If he must watch', a woodmonger's apprentice said one night in 1640 when his master asked him to take his turn for him, 'he would turne rebel with his fellowe apprentices'. There was tension in the night air in the middle of the 'commotion time' in 1549, when word spread that two constables had been harshly punished for neglect that did not seem serious to their 'fellows', who did 'moche murmor and grudge', muttering 'that they wyll no more watche'.[93] Would-be watchmen also claimed exemption

---

[88] LMA Rep. 15, fo. 380; MJ/SBR/6, fo. 91; MJ/SBR/2, fo. 156.
[89] For example, LMA Reps. 21, fo. 397; 22, fo. 86v; 56, fos. 84v-5; Jours. 14, fo. 123v; 19, fo. 247; 26, fo. 71; 31, fo. 68; 32, fo. 127v; 35, fo. 438v; 36, fo. 10; 37, fos. 212, 231v, 258v; 38, fo. 233v; 39, fo. 140v.
[90] LMA Rep. 57, fo. 77v (2nd pag.).    [91] APC 1630–1, p. 137.
[92] LMA Rep. 20. fo. 45v; MJ/SBR/2, fo. 215; GL MS 3016/1, fo. 417. See also LMA WJ/SR/NS/44/260, 46/15, 47/207–9, 49/101.
[93] LMA MJ/SBR/2, fo. 400; MJ/SBR/6, fo. 353; MJ/SBR/7, fo. 114; Rep. 12, fo. 103.

through privilege to get off the hook, 'under [mere] pretence of custom' aldermen said, when people living in alleys, courts, and yards in Bishopgate tried to shirk their watch duties in 1616. Royal servants and others living in exempt places also refused to watch. But not many got their own way, and most ended up paying fines or taking their turn as asked, and their numbers – never large anyway – dwindled over time.[94]

But many night-watches missed one or two men from time to time, and the City complained about 'slender watches' and the weedy ramshackle bands who showed up to watch who were clearly not up to the task. Magistrates reeled off the qualities of model watchmen – 'discrete', 'sad', 'substancyall householders' 'well and defensybyle harnassed' – and left no one in any doubt that numbers should never be made up by 'boys or other light persons'. But trusty able-bodied watchmen seemed to be thin on the ground at times, if we accept all of the allegations and characterizations in City complaints. Running their eyes over watch lines, aldermen saw row upon row of 'aged' and 'weake' men without weapons, muscles, or wit. Common councillors were nervy in 1609 when reports reached them that watches were made up 'for the most parte' of 'poore and meane persons bothe in estate and capacity'. Middling men, who preferred a good night's sleep, hired 'aged and weake' stand-ins to take their places. Some beadles landed in trouble in 1643 for taking a few pennies from householders 'to exempt them from watching', and filling their shoes with riff-raff.[95] Caricature and complaint apart, there are clumsy and sleepy watchmen in the records, like the watchmen who left 'the wyket' of a city gate 'open all night'. A shoemaker stole a 'halbert' from a watchman snoozing on a street in 1639. Watchmen on roads leading to London had a reputation for clumsiness in the late-1580s.[96] It was a temptation on cold winter nights to slip away early from watching stations to catch some sleep. Constables in charge sometimes let watches go home early. 'The late placinge and early dischargeing' of night-watches concerned Common Council in 1609 and again three decades later when someone sent out to spy on watches reported that they 'breake up longe before they ought'. 'The greatest parte of the constables' broke up watches 'earlie in the morninge' at exactly the time 'when most danger' was 'feared'

---

[94] LMA Rep. 32, fo. 248. See also LMA Reps. 10, fo. 2v; 12, fo. 245v; 20, fo. 45v; 23, fo. 249; 33, fo. 165; Jour. 20, fo. 501; CQSF 92/17, 114/45, 122/47, 131/63–4; MJ/SBR/1, fo. 570; MJ/SBR/2, fo. 441; MJ/SBR/3, fo. 15; MJ/SBR/4, fo. 626; MJ/SBR/6, fo. 68; WJ/SR/29/129, 31/49, 33/155, 35/179, 37/172, 39/175; GL MS 3016/1, fos. 198–9; WAC WCB/2, fo. 45.
[95] LMA Reps. 12, fo. 102v; 20, fo. 462v; Jours. 13, fo. 349; 16, fos. 17v, 91v, 264; 17, fo. 32; 18, fo. 216; 22, fo. 48; 24, fo. 18; 37, fo. 212; 28, fo. 18v; 38, fo. 217; Rep. 56, fo. 94v.
[96] BHC 8, fo. 269v; LMA Rep. 12, fo. 397; TNA SP12/192/22.

in the long night, leaving the dark streets to thieves. The 'ill ordering' of watches led to more 'misdemeanours', 'mischiefes', 'outrages', and 'burglaries and robberies' in 1613. Far from stopping crime, sluggish watches 'incorage[d]' 'loose and idle persons' to think that they could easily escape detection.[97]

We can imagine watchmen on chilly nights counting off the hours until sunrise. Alehouses offered some warmth, even after curfew bells told people to drink up. A group of watchmen sneaked into a 'vitlers' house one night in 1617 and stayed 'drinking and taking tobacco all night longe'. Ezechias Colebrooke hammered on an alehouse door in the Old Bailey around midnight one night in 1628, shouting for beer, and pulling down the sign with his 'watch bill' when no one stirred inside.[98] Like other officers, watchmen could become the focus for trouble themselves, adding to the hullabaloo at night instead of ordering others to keep the noise down and go to bed. And as by day, there were more than a few crooked officers policing the streets at night, quite happy to turn a blind eye to trouble for a bribe. Watchman Edward Gardener was taken before the recorder with 'a comon nightwalker' – Mary Taylor – in 1641 after he 'tooke 2s to lett' her 'escape' when he was escorting her to Bridewell late at night. Another watchman from over the river in Southwark took advantage of the tricky situation people suddenly found themselves in if they stumbled into the watch, 'demanding money [from them] for passing the watch'. Tempers were sometimes short on watching nights as tiredness got the better of some, which might explain why one hot-headed Queenhithe constable fired off a volley of verbal abuse when the mayor and sheriffs came riding through the ward one night in 1613 to check that all was well with the watches.[99]

Watchmen were also on the receiving end of abuse, something that is no surprise from what we know of the high spirits of London's bubbling night-life. High jinks in alehouses often led to trouble with watchmen, when drunks, nightwalkers, prostitutes, and others kicked up a fuss. One nightwalker bit off a chunk of a watchman's thumb in 1607. Joanne Dickinson also sank her teeth deep into a watchman's hand when she was found creeping in a cellar, and knocked down another one 'with a boxe of the eare'.[100] Watchmen had their legs pulled, their bodies bruised,

---

[97] LMA Jours. 27, fo. 168v; 38, fo. 217; 28, fo. 18v; 29, fo. 14; 28, fo. 18v. See also LMA Jours. 14, fo. 123v; 19, fo. 247; 24, fo. 170; 26, fo. 71; 32, fo. 127v; 35, fo. 438v; 36, fo. 10; 37, fo. 258v; 38, fo. 233v; 39, fo. 140v; Reps. 21, fo. 397; 31(1), fos. 33–3v; 56, fos. 84v-5; MJ/SBR/2, fo. 441; GL MS 6544/1, fo. 129v; APC 1628–9, p. 397.
[98] LMA MJ/SBR/2, fo. 441; Rep. 42, fo. 219v.
[99] BHC 8, fo. 338; LMA CQSF 131/99; Rep. 31(1), fo. 94v.
[100] BHC 5, fo. 207; 7, fo. 34.

and their lives threatened by 'extreame outrage[s]'. A Farringdon constable stopped John Strone – 'one of William Druris men' – on a street 'between x or xi of the clock in the watche' one night in 1550 with 'a naked sworde all bloodie' in his hand after 'a fray at Holborn Brydge', who was in no mood for pleasantries and admitted that along with his master he had also been arrested a few days previously and 'trusted', he said, 'to see the daye when he sholde be even' with London's mayors and sheriffs. Dennis Cornelius from Moorgate was sitting chatting with his sister around eleven one night in 1637 at her house in Hart Street, Covent Garden, when all of a sudden a gang of 'gentlemen' stormed in through the door and ransacked her cellar for beer and mutton. One grabbed his sister by the throat, others broke glasses and pots, and on their way out one of them (he later turned out to be Richard Tailor who had grabbed hold of Cornelius's sister by her throat) called his well-dressed friend by the name of Mr Dowbleday. 'Lets have no names', Dowbleday said quickly to shut him up, although it was now too late for him, his mask had slipped. Back on the dark street, Dowbleday's gang (thought to be twenty strong) with swords drawn walked straight into the watch on Long Acre – seventeen strong – and after some gruff words a fight broke out with Dowbleday again in the thick of things. He wrestled a halberd from a watchman and beat him on the head with his sword. Soldiers also picked fights with watchmen. Privy councillors heard that troops 'enterprised to beat the watches' in 1600. While things turned so sour in 1649 after some skirmishes between soldiers and watches, that City leaders asked General Fairfax to step in and keep his rank-and-file troops in line.[101] Nightwalkers and watchmen also had relations that bordered on flirtatious coaxing at times. Some nightwalkers had comic encounters with officers, that show cheek and sometimes no small amount of confidence in the outcome. Dorothy Clifton offered to 'prostrate herself' to a constable who caught her walking late. Katherine Harris, another 'comon nightwalker', 'offered a pinte of wine' to a constable who questioned her at night, and asked him to 'goe into a house where she sayd that they might doe anything'. Martha Mammoth told another constable that he was 'a man of fashion', and offered to ditch the man she was with and go home with him instead. Mary Paris (alias Williams) 'unseemely' 'seize[d]' a beadle who was 'making water ag[ains]t the wall'. Anne Birch slipped

[101] LMA Rep. 12, fo. 224; WJ/SR/NS/50/24–5; APC 1599–1600, pp. 203–4; LMA Rep. 59, fos. 339v, 343. See also BHC 5, fo. 118v; 6, fos. 106v, 266v, 360, 436v; 7, fos. 135, 325; 9, fo. 132; GL MS 4069/2, fo. 501v; LMA CQSF 113/9, 116/98, 124/28; Reps. 12, fo. 224; 20, fo. 73; 28, fo. 163; 31(1), fo. 7; 47, fo. 123v; MJ/SBR/1, fos. 99, 534; MJ/SBR/2, fos. 205, 418; MJ/SBR/4, fo. 631; MJ/SBR/5, fo. 508; MJ/SBR/6, fo. 398; MJ/SR/505a/94, 525/41; WJ/SR/39/31, 40/123, 46/94, 47/60, 49/89; TNA SP/16/451/21.

her hand into the same beadle's 'breeches' on another day when he was again 'makeing water' on a wall. Other women draped themselves over officers' shoulders, nestled up to them jokingly, and took them by the hand to lead them off for a drink.[102]

Again abuse is double edged, bringing to light strengths and weaknesses. Stories of violence, heckling, and teasing show officers taking tasks seriously, stopping suspects, asking questions, risking injuries and insults. Tables of arrests from Bridewell courtbooks show that watchmen had a hand in a large number, and it is likely that some attributed to a single constable were in fact the work of the whole watch. A St Giles constable said that he was always on his sharpest look-out around 1/2am, as this was 'the fittest time' to snatch 'suspicious persons'. Watches rounded up people out late and walked straight into rowdy scenes, like the watchmen who stumbled upon Margaret Harding and a servingman 'strivinge' after she nipped his purse. Other watches came across couples having sex in streets; one picked up a couple 'suspiciouslie' in 'a house of office'. Another scooped up twenty-three 'roggs, maysterless men' and vagrants in one busy night in 1578. Knowing the lay of the land, watchmen often made arrests in spots where late-night revellers gathered.[103] Drinkers were caught in surprise swoops on alehouses, and drinkers staggering along dark streets were sitting ducks. One of Lord Cromwell's footmen was 'taken somewhat overseene in drincke' by the watch in 1606.[104] Suspicious couples, thieves, masterless men and others were dragged from cellars and houses, some of them from their beds. Elizabeth Rose was disturbed by the watch 'lyenege on [a] bed with George Langley' in 1574, while her husband, a watchman, was out on watch himself.[105] Bellmen also made arrests when they walked through the city ringing time at night. Ellis Dixon, 'a scholem[aste]r' who taught children 'to write and cifer about Paules Chaine', was 'twice taken' at night by the St Sepulchre bellman 'with queanes'.[106]

Running counter to cutting satire about bungling lightweight watchmen (with 'one foot in the grave', Defoe said mockingly in 1729) is some evidence that people did not relish bumping into the watch. Alice Furres said that she had been 'verie fearefull' when the watch knocked at the

---

[102] BHC 6, fos. 249v, 250; 7, fo. 304v; 8, fos. 104, 173, 201v, 239, 365. See also BHC 6, fo 102; 7, fos. 154v, 218, 281v; 8, fos. 98, 103, 104v, 233v, 239v, 243, 245v, 411; 9, fos. 25, 31, 282, 459.
[103] GL MS 12806/1, fo. 5; BHC 2, fo. 178; 7, fo. 91; 8, fos. 50, 58, 376; 9, fo. 623; TNA STAC8 200/13; LMA CQSF 130/8; Rep. 19, fo. 536. See also BHC 2, fos. 92, 249; 5, fos. 20, 24, 27, 107v, 109v, 248v, 288v, 291v, 351v, 370v, 378, 378v, 414v, 422, 439, 440.
[104] LMA Rep. 20, fo. 375; BHC 5, fos. 85, 440, 282; 6, fo. 10.
[105] BHC 2, fo. 51v. See also BHC 5, fo. 66v; 7, fo. 295v; 8, fo. 379v; GL MS 9064/20, fo. 140v.
[106] BHC 5, fo. 67.

door of a house where she was up late in company with others, and so she 'hid herselfe in the kitchin in the place where the wasshebowle was sett'. She was not the only one who scrambled to look for somewhere to hide when the watch knocked on the door. A carpenter locked himself in a chest when the watch arrived on his doorstep, having had a tip-off that he was sitting up late 'suspicouslie' with a woman. There was clearly some respect for watches from people on the wrong side of the law. Others slipped into hiding places in dusky alleys, or sought shelter in houses 'for feare of the watch'. Sybil Old admitted that she paid someone a penny to hide in a house when she saw watchmen walking in her direction. One man warned another in 1576 that it was 'very dangerous' to lodge a woman in his house overnight 'for feare lest she should be found by the watche'.[107] There are also many accounts of watches asking stiff questions of people they caught out walking after curfew to get an 'accompt where [they] had bin or the cause' of why they were walking along the streets so late. Nor did watchmen shirk from calling London's upper-crust to account, as Lord Fielding found out to his cost (and 'disgrace') in 1641. Pepys, somewhat hypocritically, took a dim view of the 'frolic and debauchery of Sir Ch. Sidly and Buckhurst' in 1668, 'running up and down all night with their arses bare', he chided, fighting 'and being beat by the watch and clapped up all night', and the lord chief justice 'hath laid the constables by the heels to answer for it next session', Pepys said sounding peeved; 'a horrid shame', he added.[108]

James Howell bragged about 'the excellent nocturnal government of our city of London', in a letter to a friend in 1620.[109] Typical Howell hyperbole, perhaps, but a caution nonetheless against dismissing the watchmen as nothing but reluctant mediocrities. Aldermen saw the need to improve watching and lighting the streets that was frequently expressed in terms of swift growth in the moving 'multitudes of roagues and vagabondes', rising 'robberyes [and] burglaryes', or panic in times of plague.[110] They took steps each year to 'better enlarge and strengthen' watches: improved co-ordination throughout the city, for example, or tighter supervision.[111] Little seems remiss or moribund here, judging by

---

[107] Defoe, *Augusta Triumphaus*, p. 47; BHC 5, fo. 280; 2, fos. 57, 153, 233. See also BHC 2, fo. 178v; 3, fo. 149; 5, fos. 29, 280, 297; 6, fo. 36.
[108] LMA Rep. 42, fo. 36; HOL MP 29-6-1641; Pepys, *Diary*, vol. IX, pp. 336–7. See also TNA STAC8 14/350/5–7.
[109] James Howell, *Familiar Letters or Epistolae Ho-Elianae*, 3 vols. (1903), vol. I, p. 36.
[110] For example, LMA Jours. 27, fos. 291v, 367v, 379v; 30, fo. 89v; 35, fo. 10; 26, fo. 124v.
[111] For example, LMA Reps. 12, fo. 531; 13(ii), fo. 196; 17, fo. 376v; 31(1), fos. 3-3v, 164v; 54, fos. 271v-2; 56, fo. 22v; Jours. 29, fos. 121-1v; 40, fo. 55v; Letterbook R, fos. 11, 70v, 265.

what was possible in the light of available resources. Magistrates showed some resolve to get from dusk to dawn as smoothly as possible. They did not always succeed, but calls for reform never dried up, and some led to tangible improvements: bellmen were added to London's night-forces, for instance, and more care was paid to bigger and better lanterns. Another step in the right direction was building 'watch howses' as the country lurched towards revolution after 1640. A City committee was asked to look into the question 'what watchhouses are necessary' and where 'for the safety of this cittye' in 1642. Workmen began building watch houses in strategic spots soon after: one sat prominently on Tower Hill in 1644.[112] They provided assembly-points for watchmen to gather to hear orders for the night ahead, somewhere to shelter from 'extremitye of wind and weather', and holding-places for suspects until morning when justices examined the night's catch. Progress was slow, but snippets in sources show that there were watch houses next to Temple Bar (1648), 'neere the Granaryes' by Bridewell (1648), 'neere Moregate' (1648), and next to St Paul's south door (1649). They were not big; the one on St Paul's south side was a 'litle house' and the one near Moorgate was 'a small house or shed'. This was a time of experimentation, and people (including those in authority) were learning how to make best use of these new structures in their midst. A pauper from Bridewell Precinct with nowhere else to live was allowed to 'lodge in the watch house' in 1646. The City's tenant living 'over the gate' at Temple Bar 'lockt upp' the watch house in 1648, certain that he was within his rights to do so, but he was looking for somewhere else to live not long after.[113]

He turned out to be wrong and the watch got their house back, but the City tenant's case is a neat microcosm of the 'problem' of improvement and reform: it took time to get something off the ground and not everything worked out as magistrates planned. Progress was often irritatingly slow, but it was hardly ever negligible. London had a system of night policing in place before 1660, although it was improved over the next century through better lighting, administration, finances, and better and more regular salaries.[114] But the essential elements of the night-watch were performing competently by the middle of the seventeenth century. There would always be aggravated senses of danger in the dark, no matter what magistrates said or did. That is as true in London today as it was four

---

[112] LMA Jours. 39, fo. 361v; 40, fos. 40–2; GL MS 9237, fos. 90, 95, 102v. See also Beattie, *Policing and Punishment*, pp. 186–7.
[113] BHC 9, fo. 268; LMA Reps. 59, fos. 184v, 225, 324v; 60, fo. 23.
[114] See esp. Beattie, *Policing and Punishment*, chap. 4; Reynolds, *Before the Bobbies*; Paley, '"An imperfect, inadequate, and wretched system"?', 95–130.; Harris, *Policing the City*.

centuries ago when heavy late drinking, sex with strangers, and 'roaring boys' were all part of night's rich recurring theatre that pulsed no matter what watches did. Carola's fatalistic opinion about getting rid of night-time vice in Milan springs to mind: 'you dive into a well unsearchable', he told the Duke in Dekker's *The Honest Whore, Part 2*.[115] In London, likewise, it was an impossible dream to 'clean up' the night. Like London's growth, the question of its vibrant night-time cultures became one of containment over time, not reversal, and certainly not elimination. No amount of purging would ever have been adequate enough for that. The pragmatic position for City magistrates to take was simply to try and make sure that nothing ever got so out of hand after sunset that the night descended into pandemonium.

---

[115] Thomas Dekker, *The Honest Whore, Part 1*, in Thomas Bowers, ed., *The Dramatic Works of Thomas Dekker*, 4 vols. (Cambridge, 1955–61), vol. II, 4:2. 106.

## 10 Policing: process and prosecution

### Crimes with and without victims

There is currently a lack of balance in work on policing and prosecution in the early modern period. In a nutshell, it tips too heavily towards the efforts of private people. Time after time we are told that the private prosecutor was the 'central agent', 'backbone', or 'mainstay' of criminal justice. 'Private prosecution' was 'the paradigm case' before the Metropolitan Police Act (1829).[1] John Beattie argues that the judicial system's 'capacity to discover, arrest, and prosecute offenders' was 'entirely undeveloped' as late as 1700, and detective work was 'left to the public' and 'efforts of victims'.[2] Other scholars couple the leading role of private prosecutors with part-time police-work to argue that policing was shoddy

---

[1] Beattie, *Crime and the Courts in England*, pp. 38, 216; Douglas Hay, 'The criminal prosecution in England and its historians', *The Modern Law Review*, 47 (1984), 1–29, esp. 4; Hay and Snyder, 'Using the criminal law, 1750–1850', pp. 3–52, esp. p. 24; Reynolds, *Before the Bobbies*, p. 71; Tim Hitchcock, 'The publicity of poverty in early eighteenth-century London', in J. F. Merritt, ed., *Imagining Early Modern London: Perceptions and Portrayals of the City from Stow to Strype, 1598–1720* (Cambridge, 2001), pp. 166–84, esp. p. 171; David Taylor, *Crime, Policing, and Punishment in England, 1750–1914* (Basingstoke, 1998), p. 109; Gwenda Morgan and Peter Rushton, *Rogues, Thieves, and the Rule of Law: the Problem of Law Enforcement in North-East England, 1718–1800* (1998), p. 30; Shoemaker, *Prosecution and Punishment*, p. 216. See also Emsley, *Crime and Society in England*, pp. 178–93; Julius R. Ruff, *Violence in Early Modern Europe, 1500–1800* (Cambridge, 2001), p. 90; Hindle, *The State and Social Change in Early Modern England*, p. 121; Bernard Capp, *When Gossips Meet: Women, Family, and the Neighbourhood in Early Modern England* (Oxford, 2003), p. 282; Sharon Howard, 'Investigating responses to theft in early modern Wales: communities, thieves, and the courts', *Continuity and Change*, 19 (2004), 409–30, esp. 411.

[2] Beattie, *Policing and Punishment in London*, p. 85. Beattie comments that 'No public body had the responsibility to investigate crimes, to detect offenders, or to gather the evidence that would sustain a prosecution. All of that was left to the victim' (226). See also Hay and Snyder, 'Using the criminal law', p. 16; Harris, *Policing the City*, pp. 14–16, 34; Mark Goldie, 'The unacknowledged republic: officeholding in early modern England', in Tim Harris, ed., *The Politics of the Excluded, c.1500–1850* (Basingstoke, 2001), pp. 153–94: 'There was no police force' in the sixteenth and seventeenth centuries 'beyond the ability and willingness of a community to exercise its own force, and no prosecution without neighbourly cooperation' (quoting pp. 155–6).

four centuries ago. Gaskill, for one, writes that the 'criminal law depended on informal and amateur policing, privately initiated suits, and trials by jury, [and] as a consequence its enforcement was often random, inefficient, and unfair'.[3] Constables often appear as less important than neighbours or victims who, it is said, took the leading roles in clearing up crime in the sixteenth and seventeenth centuries. Indeed, some scholars link a decline in the involvement of 'private' citizens in policing to an increase in the role played by 'public' officers. A 'gradual professionalization' of policing over the course of the eighteenth century and after was partly made possible by a significant drop in 'active community involvement'. Constables appear less active or effective when neighbours are thought to have taken the lead.[4] But London's public officers did not take back seats before 1700. They were active in making arrests and clearing up crime, and must now be put back in the thick of the action.

My argument is relatively simple: public bodies like parishes had large involvement in starting and funding cases in the sixteenth and seventeenth centuries. There were no trained detectives this far back in time, but London's officers were instructed to always check prisoners' stories, for example, to search high and low for suspects, and to question them after arrest. They did the legwork whenever parishes (or other public bodies) tried to track down offenders. While being nowhere near 'top-drawer', skills to collect information or catch suspects were not 'entirely undeveloped'. Nor was private prosecution the 'paradigm case' all of the time. Prosecution also appears to have been in a state of some flux six centuries ago. Judicial systems under Henry V (1413–22) have been called 'reactive'; they did not start the ball rolling but followed up on actions by private people.[5] Yet the balance had supposedly tilted to public

---

[3] Malcolm Gaskill, 'The displacement of providence: policing and prosecution in seventeenth- and eighteenth-century England', *Continuity and Change*, 11 (1996), 341–74, esp. 342, who notes that 'the twin principles of amateur policing from above and voluntary prosecution from below were not substantially replaced until the second half of the nineteenth century' (361). Cf. Hitchcock, 'Publicity of poverty', p. 172.

[4] Faramerz Dabhoiwala, 'Sex, social relations, and the law in seventeenth- and eighteenth-century London', in Michael J. Braddick and John Walter, eds., *Negotiating Power in Early Modern Society: Order, Hierarchy, and Subordination in Britain and Ireland* (Cambridge, 2001), pp. 85–101, esp. p. 100; Dabhoiwala, 'Sex and societies for moral reform, 1688–1800', *Journal of British Studies*, 46 (2007), 290–319, esp. 291. Others warn us not to diminish the significance of neighbourhood surveillance after 1700, although there was considerable social strain. See, for example, Donna Andrew, 'The press and public apologies in eighteenth-century London', in Norma Landau, ed., *Law, Crime, and English Society, 1660–1830* (Cambridge, 2002), pp. 208–29.

[5] Edward Powell, *Kingship, Law and Society: Criminal Justice in the Reign of Henry V* (1989), pp. 65–6. Barbara Hanawalt writes that 'villagers and townspeople had the primary responsibility for insuring [sic] the good behaviour of their neighbours, and for identifying,

prosecution between 1300 and 1350 after a series of royal 'law enforcement drives' in highly charged times. How long this push lasted is another matter. Klerman calls the six centuries after 1300 'the return of private prosecution', though not many would go this far back in time for its roots.[6] It has long been argued that the Metropolitan Police Act (1829) was not the result of a smooth progress from one stepping stone to the next; it was instead a more haphazard process.[7] This is also the case with the development of prosecution through time. There is in fact good reason to think that public prosecution was rising five centuries ago. Langbein has drawn attention to the role of 'prosecuting' justices who after the Marian bail and committal Acts took leading roles in gathering evidence, binding suspects, accusers and witnesses to appear in court, and prosecuting offenders. Attorney generals also guided some cases through Star Chamber and were in effect prosecutors in State trials. Justices took the chair to hear summary cases when there were few victims in the room.[8] A little over one-in-ten Staffordshire felony cases in 1750–1800 were brought by public authorities; the bulk involved rioters, forgers, coiners, and clippers shadowed by special agents.[9] Treasury solicitors and under secretaries of state also took part in building and funding cases against rioters, smugglers, and blacklisted printers and publishers after 1700, when steps were also taken to lighten

---

pursuing, catching, imprisoning and trying felons': *'Of Good and Ill Repute': Gender and Social Control in Medieval England* (Oxford and New York, 1998), p. 2. Cf. her *Crime and Conflict in English Communities, 1300–1348* (Cambridge, MA, 1979), pp. 32–9.

[6] A. J. Musson, 'Turning King's evidence: the prosecution of crime in late medieval England', *Oxford Journal of Legal Studies*, 19 (1999), 467–79, esp. 474–6; Musson, *Public Order and Law Enforcement: the Local Administration of Criminal Justice, 1294–1350* (Woodbridge, 1996), chap. 8; Daniel Klerman, 'Settlement and the decline of private prosecution in thirteenth-century England', *Law and History Review*, 19 (2001), 1–65, esp. 7, 8: 'Private prosecution regained its dominant role in early modern times and in turn gave way to public prosecution in the last two centuries'.

[7] See, most recently, Beattie, *Policing and Punishment*, esp. Part II.

[8] 1&2 Phil. & Mar.c.13 (1554–5) and 2&3 Phil. & Mar.c.10 (1555); John H. Langbein, *The Origins of Adversary Criminal Trial* (Oxford, 2003), pp. 40–7; Langbein, *Prosecuting Crime in the Renaissance: England, Germany, France* (Cambridge, MA, 1974), chaps 1–5. On summary justice see Peter King, 'The summary courts and social relations in eighteenth-century England', *Past and Present*, 183 (2004), 125–72; King, *Crime and Law in England 1750–1840: Remaking Justice from the Margins* (Cambridge, 2006), pp. 15–39; Faramerz Dabhoiwala, 'Summary justice in early modern London', *English Historical Review*, 121 (2006), 796–822; Shoemaker, *Prosecution and Punishment*.

[9] Hay and Snyder, 'Using the criminal law', pp. 21–3: who note that 'although parish constables were prosecuting a small proportion of cases, they were mostly offences against themselves or serious non-property offences, like murder, and only very rarely concerned theft against individuals' (quoting p. 21).

the load on private prosecutors by meeting their costs from public purses.[10]

Magistrates often complained about the trouble that was caused when prosecutions were left in the hands of victims with no money or time to go to law, who also had other ways to get their own back. Robert Selby ended up in court after his pocket was picked because he let the thief go once he got his money back. Robert Wynch also let a thief off the hook; he was a fellow silkman, he said, with a family to care for. Middlesex justices were angry with Henry Carpenter when he dropped charges against two pickpockets after they gave him back his thirty shillings.[11] Others turned to witches or wizards to track thieves, although the law said they 'cheated people of their money'. Two men conned people by offering to find stolen goods with the help of 'a figure' in 1613. An apothecary landed in court in 1611 for 'taking upon him to tell where stolen goods should be found'. Mabel Gray from Westminster said that neighbours 'advised' her 'to goe to a cuninge woman' in Southwark after she lost some spoons in 1637. She spent a shilling just for advice to go to a 'cunning man in Lukeners Lane', who got two shillings and another shilling in drink for a tip to visit a third sage, Mr Tunn in Ram Alley, another 'cunning man'. Tunn took five shillings and three shillings worth of wine from her for his magical appraisal of where matters now stood: 'the thiefe was in the howse that had the spoones', he said, 'and the spoones should come agayne they should not knowe howe and be laid in the same place from whence they were taken'.[12] Victims also did their own spadework. Joan Mosse, who stayed out late mixing with bad company, was questioned by the Earl of Pembroke who had her on his list of suspects after he lost linen from his cupboard in 1633. Courts told accusers and victims to act quickly and fairly to see justice done, and bound them over with witnesses to press charges. Yet suspects still walked free when accusers did not show up. John Coumgton left court in 1641 after 'no prosecutors appeare[d] against him' for stealing a hand-iron. John Clasey had a stroke of luck when no one turned up to prosecute him after he helped himself to canary wine in 1638. Like masters who did not press charges against servants,

---

[10] See Beattie, *Policing and Punishment*, chaps 5 and 8; Wales, 'Thief-takers and their clients', pp. 67–84; Malcolm Gaskill, *Crime and Mentalities in Early Modern England* (Cambridge, 2000), chap. 5.
[11] LMA WJ/SR/NS/33/116; BHC 7, fo. 172; LMA MJ/SR/524/22. See also LMA MJ/SR/508a/23; BHC 8, fo. 382v; J. A. Sharpe, 'Enforcing the law in the seventeenth-century English village', in V. A. C. Gatrell *et al.*, eds. *Crime and the Law: the Social History of Crime in Western Europe Since 1500* (1980), pp. 97–119; Beattie, *Policing and Punishment*; Hindle, *State and Social Change*, p. 130.
[12] LMA MJ/SBR/1, fos. 418, 640; MJ/SBR/2, fo. 96; MJ/SBR/7, fo. 82; WJ/SR/NS/50/22.

victims took pity on people in their charge or care. Other cases were dropped after bullying, although a shopkeeper who lost a pewter pot still pressed charges against John Barlow after he spat in his face.[13]

There is another imbalance in work to date: almost all interpretations about the development of policing and prosecution since 1550 are drawn from felony cases.[14] Like contemporary pamphlets, historians mostly cover serious or shocking crimes like witchcraft, murder, or grand larceny. But this perhaps leaves out somewhere over 95 per cent of prosecuted crime (or possibly more) from narratives of the development of policing. We have some fine work on petty crime,[15] but it has had too little influence on debates about the nature of policing and prosecution. This remains a felony tale in the main. Shoemaker guesses that one-in-ten cases at Middlesex courts were felony cases in 1660–1725, but the overall figure from across the land will be higher because of the stack of corporation and manor courts hearing minor cases week in and week out.[16] So, the exact balance cannot be known, not least because many petty crimes were handled in a flash by cheaper and speedier summary justice. The number of hard-up beggars or small-time thieves was much greater than 'out-of-the-ordinary' cases involving witches, highway robbers, or murderers. Martin Ingram calls 'lesser' crimes like vagrancy or idleness 'commonplace'.[17] They were run-of-the-mill slip-ups and character

---

[13] LMA WJ/SR/NS/38/4; BRHA BHC 4, fo. 203v; BHC 8, fos. 327v, 161v; 2, fo. 68; 7, fo. 75v. See also BHC 8, fos. 92, 229, 302v, 368v, 384; 9, fos. 361, 445, 518, 603, 789; BRHA BHC 4, fos. 308, 467. Cf. Beattie, *Policing and Punishment*, chaps 2, 5, and 8.

[14] Cf. my 'Introduction: punishing the English', and 'Bodies and souls in Norwich'.

[15] A pioneering study is Shoemaker, *Prosecution and Punishment*. See also Archer, *Pursuit of Stability*, chap. 6; Beier, *Masterless Men*; Innes, 'Prisons for the poor'; Martin Ingram, 'Shame and pain: themes and variations in Tudor punishments', in Devereaux and Griffiths, eds., *Penal Practice and Culture*, pp. 36–62; Ingram, '"Scolding women cucked or washed": a crisis in gender relations in early modern England?', in Jenny Kermode and Garthine Walker, eds., *Women, Crime, and the Courts in Early Modern England* (1994), pp. 48–80; Ingram, 'Juridical folklore in England illustrated by rough music', in Christopher Brooks and Michael Lobban, eds., *Communities and Courts in Britain, 1150–1900* (1997), pp. 61–82; Paul Slack, 'Vagrants and vagrancy in England, 1598–1664', *Economic History Review*, 2nd series, 27 (1974), 360–79; Marjorie Keniston McIntosh, *Controlling Misbehaviour in England, 1370–1600* (Cambridge, 1998); and my 'Bodies and souls in early modern Norwich'; 'Masterless young people in Norwich, 1560–1645', in Griffiths, Adam Fox, and Steve Hindle, eds., *The Experience of Authority in Early Modern England* (Basingstoke, 1996), pp. 146–86; and 'Meanings of nightwalking in early modern England'.

[16] Shoemaker, *Prosecution and Punishment*, p. 6: 'The impact of misdemeanour prosecutions was felt in all corners of society. Perhaps nine times as many defendants were involved in misdemeanour prosecutions as in felony cases, and they came from a wider range of social classes than other types of litigation' and 'included a far more diverse collections of offences than felonies'.

[17] Ingram, '"Scolding women cucked or washed"', quoting p. 60.

faults; the everyday excesses and eruptions of bodies, streets, markets, and households, more spontaneous, more 'ordinary', and massively more numerous than felonies.

The misleading impact of felony cases on current understandings of the historical development of policing is equally apparent in the fact that theft was the most commonly prosecuted felony by a long way. Proportions see-sawed, but theft was never less than eight in ten of all felony cases.[18] Its numerical weight has unduly shaped our senses of policing in the past for the simple reason that theft always has a victim, someone feeling a loss strongly enough to go to court. These are histories with victims, and their implications for how we interpret policing need great consideration. The bulk of crimes had no victims, there was no one at hand to rush to an officer or court with something to report and prosecute later. Most petty crimes did not hurt someone's pocket or body, and their policing was often quite different from the process followed in felony cases. Theft was a little more than 15 per cent of all offences that were brought to Bridewell in the five decades after 1605.[19] When private prosecutors did come along to Bridewell it was usually to chase thieves, like Mrs Anthony and Goodwife Saunders who went there one day in 1574 to follow through their claim that Martin Pynnots had 'beguiled' them 'of there yarne and also spoyled them both of their clothe'. Others were advised by the bench to go to a justice for a warrant to search for lost goods or take their suspect to another court.[20] Mothers of illegitimate children came along to challenge men face to face who said that they did not father their child. Parents, masters, and mistresses also asked the bench to lock up their wayward family members, although Bridewell was not used to confine domestic firebrands on anything like the scale that household heads in mainland Europe used *lettres de cachet* to put pests behind bars: less than 0.2 per cent of all committals were made by masters, parents, or relatives.[21] In all, victimless crimes formed a clear majority of the 'lesser' lapses brought to Bridewell, something that we also find at the Norwich Mayor's Court, for example, or any other court with vagrant-heavy caseloads.[22]

---

[18] Beattie, *Crime and the Courts*, chap. 5; King, *Crime, Justice, and Discretion*, chap. 5; Sharpe, *Crime in Early Modern England*, chaps 3 and 8.
[19] See also Shoemaker, *Prosecution and Punishment*, pp. 52–77.
[20] BHC 2, fo. 46v; 7, fo. 368; 6, fo. 380v. See also BHC 8, fo. 9.
[21] Catharina Lis and Hugo Soly, *Disordered Lives: Eighteenth-Century Families and their Unruly Relatives*, trans. Alexander Brown (Oxford, 1996), chap. 1; Pieter Spierenburg, *The Prison Experience: Disciplinary Institutions and their Inmates in Early Modern Europe* (New Brunswick, NJ, and London, 1991), pp. 234–7.
[22] See my 'Masterless young people' and 'Bodies and souls in Norwich'.

Unlike felony, then, this is mostly history without victims. Petty crimes were often down to someone's shortcomings or rootless situation. It was almost always public authorities who brought spendthrifts, beggars, and sex-offences to trial. Most misdemeanours upset something broadly construed in terms of societal norms of the 'public good' or 'public peace' (and purse). It is society at large that suffers for the most part, and turns to public officers to try and put things right. Shakespeare's Dogberry nabbed two 'villains' in 'the prince's name', and watchmen with him at the time ended up being their named 'accusers'. Walking through streets after dark when they should have been in bed, these 'villains' threatened the public peace. Similarly, Elbow grabbed sleazy-seeming people from an 'ill house', and came across a 'strange picklock' in the pockets of a suspicious looking pedestrian and put him in the care of a deputy who continued the public investigation.[23] Nobody lost anything here or was attacked. Nor did anyone bring accusations apart from officers on the spot. No one lost anything who might have followed matters through to a close in court. These cases were in the hands of public authorities.[24] Colchester town leaders brought cases 'more frequently and speedily' around 1600 in their war against vice. Metropolitan magistrates were cracking down on prostitutes and 'disorderly' houses two centuries later, issuing warrants under vagrancy/house of correction laws (1610, 1744) to search 'suspected' houses. Parishes picked up prosecution costs, but public bodies had been turning to the law all the way through the sixteenth and seventeenth centuries as well.[25]

Private individuals and public authorities could choose different ways to get satisfaction in or out of the courtroom. Summary justice was one short-cut that was taken by magistrates. Similarly, the profile of Bridewell committals slants heavily towards City authorities, justices, and officers: a mere 0.05 per cent of all committals can be laid at the door of 'private' people. Bridewell was a key resource for public officials and officers, something that is confirmed in other work on street-crime and houses of correction in the early modern period, which also shows the heavy

---

[23] *Much Ado About Nothing*, 3.3, 22–3; 4.2, 30; *Measure for Measure*, 2.1, 61; 3.1, 273–4.
[24] See also Shoemaker, *Prosecution and Punishment*, pp. 6, 218; and, for a later century, Jennifer Davis, 'Prosecutions and their context: the use of the criminal law in later nineteenth-century London', in Hay and Snyder, eds., *Policing and Prosecution*, pp. 398–426, esp. p. 420.
[25] Laquita M. Higgs, *Godliness and Governance in Tudor Colchester* (Ann Arbor, MI, 1998), pp. 259–60; 7 Jac. 1, c.4; 17 Geo.II.c.5; Henderson, *Disorderly Women in Eighteenth-Century London*, pp. 92–3, 95, 149–50, 160. See also Shoemaker, *Prosecution and Punishment*, chap. 7; Rublack, *Crimes of Women*, pp. 36–42; Stuart, *Defiled Trades and Social Outcasts*, pp. 97–8.

involvement of public authorities in policing and prosecution.[26] Not enough work has been done so far on the role of parishes in preparing and prosecuting cases. We will see parishes covering the costs of investigations and examinations, and taking cases to court later on. But first I want to spend some time on the situations and actions that gave rise to court cases, homing in on the points of arrest to observe London's officers and courts handling victimless crimes. Officers got tip-offs, swooped on offenders, and raided suspect houses. Magistrates marshalled evidence to build cases, not unlike the way they gathered information in more serious cases to prepare the tightest case possible.[27] But far from cutting back on the role of victims or neighbours in bringing offenders to court, however, I would like to strike a better balance between their contributions and the efforts of London's officers. Neighbours frequently worked hand in hand with officers to crack crimes, and their joint efforts only serve to jumble the categories of public and private with respect to policing. All in all, we will end up with a more complex sense of prosecution and policing in the early modern period, but it will also be more accurate for that.

### Neighbours

Many constables got on with the job of keeping the peace with little trouble, choosing to arbitrate, caution, or prosecute. The best way to restore order was not always to wage law, but to soothe strains with wise warning words or third-party arbitration. Constables often chose whether to enforce law and felt that it was better to settle disputes with words not warrants, acting like mediators as well as law enforcers.[28] They were neighbours but also linchpins of law in the places they lived, and caught between two stools: neighbourly protocols on the one hand and their oath of office on the other. Constables embodied counter-claims of inward-looking communities

---

[26] Cf. Shoemaker, *Prosecution and Punishment*, pp. 216–18 and chap. 7: constables, the night watch, overseers of the poor, and churchwardens were probably responsible for 'the majority of commitments to houses of correction' (quoting p. 216). See also Paul Slack, *Poverty and Policy in Tudor and Stuart England* (Harlow, 1988), chaps 5 and 7; Slack, *From Reformation to Improvement: Public Welfare in Early Modern England* (Oxford, 1999), chap. 2; Nicholas Rogers, 'Policing the poor in eighteenth-century London: the vagrancy laws and their administration', *Social History*, 24 (1991), 127–47; Innes, 'Prisons for the poor'; Beier, *Masterless Men*, esp. chap. 9; Griffiths, 'Bodies and souls in early modern Norwich'.

[27] Hindle, *State and Social Change*, p. 121. Hindle has the 1554–5 committal statutes in mind when noting that 'recognizances required by magistrates in committal hearings compelled the production of prosecution evidence in every felony trial'. Prosecution, he continues, 'came to be supervised by officers of the state'.

[28] Sharpe, "Such disagreement betwyx neighbours"', pp. 167–87; Sharpe, 'Enforcing the law in the seventeenth-century English village'.

and the criminal justice system.[29] The conflation of neighbour and constable in a single person muddles distinctions between private and public law enforcement. The law seems almost personal when officers slip between these roles.[30] Nonetheless we should be careful not to imagine all constables as caught in some sort of paralysis, unsure what to do when balancing neighbourly ties against the clout of the state. Westminster constables presented 120 of their neighbours at a single sessions in 1637.[31] They seemed quite prepared to get on with the job in hand, presumably not unafraid to rock the boat for the sake of public order. And it is also possible to exaggerate the extent of this tug-of-war, as state and community had common aims, in the Poor Law, for example. Dwindling parish funds and pressures from above to discipline the poor strengthened these mutual interests over time.[32]

Trusty neighbours were a blessing. 'And indeed a very greate comoditie it is to have an honest neighbor dwell by a man', John Bridges told the Paul's Cross crowd in 1571, 'no lesse annoyance to be matched with an ill neighbor'.[33] Neighbourhoods were physical areas, but also sets of cultural and social values by which people living cheek-by-jowl assessed each other. Good neighbourhood involved support, not falling out, and sticking together through thick and thin. A parish clerk was moved enough to write a little ditty, which he copied into the vestry book: 'Even as stickes may easily be broken / So when neighbours agre not then ther is a confucion / But a great many stickes bound in one boundell will hardly be broken / So neighbours being ioyned in love together can never be severed'. Some older Cornhill residents felt hard done by when 'yong men' leap-frogged over them into wardmote seats, pointing out that the 'union and brotherly love (among the neighbourhood which is as a wall and defence to this ward) is broken'.[34] First-class neighbours lived side by side 'in unity and charity', and sought 'to gain love and good opinion', and kept an eye on each other. In an ideal world all would agree to nip

---

[29] The most important statement of this dilemma is still Wrightson, 'Two concepts of order', pp. 21–46. See also Kent, *The English Village Constable*, chaps 7–8.

[30] Herrup, *Common Peace*.

[31] LMA WJ/SR/NS/47/207–9. Presentments were for not coming to church, scolding, keeping 'ill rule', running unlicensed victualling houses, giving room and board to inmates, and refusing to watch and ward.

[32] Hindle, *State and Social Change*. See also Michael J. Braddick, *State Formation in Early Modern England, c.1550–1700* (Cambridge, 2000); Wrightson, 'Two concepts of order'; and Wrightson and Levine, *Poverty and Piety*, chaps 5–7.

[33] John Bridges, *A Sermon Preached at Paules Crosse on the Monday in Whitsun Weeke Anno Domini 1571*, (1571), p. 97.

[34] GL MSS 943/1; 4069/2, fos. 271v-2.

disputes in the bud.[35] If no notice was taken people clubbed together to cast aspersions or, if all else failed, to go to law. We should not romanticize these neighbours. Many lived on top of each other and fell out over something shared. They bickered about dirt, smells, noise, gutters, wells, windows, walkways, animals on the loose, or fire-hazards like hanging thatch. A row between a hospital governor and a Star Chamber clerk about hanging clothes to dry in an alley ran on for years with each side moaning that wet laundry brushed against their skin, spreading infection that was worse in the wind. Neither was neighbourly enough: the clerk had a 'contentious spirit' of 'hated and unsociable neighbourhood', but he gave as good as he got, calling the governor 'more quarrelsome than neighbourly', without the smallest speck of 'neighbourly love and friendship'.[36]

Even with such spats, neighbourliness was appealed to again and again in goliath London when black sheep fell out with their neighbours. 'Disorderly' Thomas Godden's neighbours paid twelvepence to leave him in Bridewell each week. John Ashberry tossed 'pisspotts and bowles of pisse on [neighbours] heads and into their windows' in 1561. While 'comon curser' Elizabeth Beeston upset neighbours with 'stinking blood and other filth' in 1641.[37] And sometimes we hear underneath condemnations the voices of neighbours on high horses, calling themselves the 'better', 'honest' or 'worshipful sort' of people, passing moral judgment on the common herd below them. Men of 'good reputacons' put Ambrose Molineux on trial in 1622 'for abusinge himselfe divers ways towards honest neighbors'. 'Honest' neighbors dazed by 'gret greefe in conscyence' took 'whoremonger' Joseph Locke to court in 1595.[38] Whatever the

---

[35] Paul Griffiths, *et al.*, 'Population and disease, estrangement and belonging 1540–1700', in Peter Clark, ed., *The Cambridge Urban History of Britain: Volume II, 1540–1840* (Cambridge, 2000), pp. 195–233, esp. p. 225; Boulton, *Neighbourhood and Society*; W. K. D. Davies and D. T. Herbert, *Communities within Cities: an Urban Social Geography* (1993), p. 34; David Garrioch, *Neighbourhood and Community in Paris, 1740–1790* (Cambridge, 1986), pp. 30–1; Keith Wrightson, *English Society, 1580–1680* (1982), p. 62; David Warren Sabean, *Power in the Blood: Popular Culture and Village Discourse in Early Modern Germany* (Cambridge, 1984), p. 28.

[36] SBHA Governors' Journal 3, fo. 233; TNA STAC8 21/7; 11/8; 93/8; 126/10. See also Archer, *Pursuit of Stability*, pp. 78–9; Gowing, *Domestic Dangers*, pp. 22, 117; Garrioch, *Neighbourhood and Community*, pp. 34, 54; D. V. Kent and F. W. Kent, *Neighbours and Neighbourhood in Renaissance Florence: the District of the Red Lion in the Fifteenth Century* (New York, 1982), p. 3; J. R. Farr, *Hands of Honour: Artisans and their World in Dijon, 1500–1650* (1988), pp. 151, 164–5, 169.

[37] BHC 9, fo. 128; 1, fo. 155; LMA MJ/SBR/7, fo. 186. See also LMA Reps. 13i, fo. 323v; 17, fo. 228v; MJ/SBR/1, fo. 644; MJ/SBR/2, fo. 518; MJ/SRB/4, fo. 694; D/L/C/218, fo. 100; CQSF 120/19; GL MSS 9057/1, fo. 115v; 3018/1, fo. 99; BHC 3, fo. 405v; 6, fo. 282v; 8, fo. 334v.

[38] BHC 6, fo. 282v; GL MS 3018/1, fo. 60v.

source, neighbourly outpourings could make or break cases, even felony trials where they could help win softer sentences or pardons. The 'comon voice and fame' or 'publique and common speache' was evidence enough for convictions. Neighbours' words counted, as when it was 'affirmed by his mistris and divers honest neighbors' that a French apprentice sauntering through the streets in women's clothes 'did yt upon a merriment to fetch oysters'.[39] People on the wrong side of the law walked free after 'good reporte', 'earnest sute', or 'entreaty' by 'divers' or 'a grett number' of 'good and honest' neighbours.[40] Edward Dorte brought 'above xxtie men and women' to Bridewell 'to testifie' for his brother's 'honest and good behavior'. A barber's wife's good name was saved by over twenty 'neighbors and wemen whome she kept in childbedd', who said 'that she is cleane and honest' after her husband tried to lock her up for 'burning him'. 'Manie substantiall' neighbours in Wood Street pledged that Alice Good had lived 'well and honestlie' for thirty-five years when it was said that she had sex 'divers and sundry times' with her husband's apprentice.[41]

These neighbourly views nearly always emerged after a steady build up of comments. When asked to define a 'comon fame' in 1608, Rebecca Handley called it 'a publique and comon speech of a thing'; asked the same question, Randal Brooks said a 'publique and comon speache or report of many people'. A 'noted' bad name could stick for a long while, once 'comonly accompted and taken'.[42] Even London's neighbourhoods were mostly small with long memories. Oliver Hasseldon said that Anne Cunningham to his 'certeyne knowledge and hearing' had been 'an incontinent person of her body' for six years, and he had 'heard it often reported' that she mixed with Dutchmen 'incontinently'. William Wolfe knew that it was Henry Goomer who called Grissel Fish 'a whore having byn a neighbor of his these ii yeares and being well acquainted with his voice'.[43] Chit-chat quickly spread to eager ears; ready-made grapevines

---

[39] BHC 5, fo. 198v; LMA D/L/C/214, fos. 78, 431, 437–9; D/L/C 218, fo. 84; WJ/SR/NS/ 39/175; GL MSS 9057/1, fos. 115v, 121v; 9064/14, fos. 30, 157; 9064/16, fos. 8, 171; 9064/17, fos. 20, 245; 9064/19, fos. 34, 162; 9064/20, fos. 3, 230v; 9064/21, fo. 139; 3018/1, fo. 10v; Beattie, *Crime and the Courts in England*, chap. 8; Capp, *When Gossips Meet*, chaps 5–6; Herrup, *Common Peace*, chap. 6; Shannon McSheffrey, *Marriage, Sex, and Civic Culture in Late Medieval London* (Philadelphia, PA, 2006), pp. 150–63.

[40] BHC 1, fos. 17, 12, 70v; 3, fo. 357; 5, fos. 169, 302v; 8, fos. 8v, 334v; LMA H1/ST/A/3, fo. 200; Rep. 11, fo. 396; TNA STAC8. 57/7. See also LMA D/L/C/217, fo. 201; WAC WCB1, fo. 170.

[41] BHC 2, fo. 229; 3, fo. 327; BRHA BHC 4, fo. 15v.

[42] LMA D/L/C/218, fos. 133, 178; D/L/C/214, fo. 429; D/L/C/218, fo. 100. See also Phil Withington, *The Politics of Commonwealth: Citizens and Freemen in Early Modern England* (Cambridge, 2005), pp. 202–9.

[43] LMA D/L/C/218, fos. 5, 90.

existed around shopping stalls, alehouses, doorsteps, and tables. People rushed next door with juicy gossip. A Shoe Lane shoemaker 'heard words' that men at Mistress Lane's 'evill' house along the same street 'doe nothing under halfe a peece'. Tongues wagged even after a 'fame' became formalized in sworn statements. Thomas Creed's wife stormed into an Aldersgate alehouse accusing Susan Moore with 'fearce' gestures that she was 'with child' by her husband, saying she would dump her in Bridewell on brown bread and water and week-long hard work. True to her word, she filed a complaint and gossip gathered speed. A 'publique examinacon of the matter' by a justice was 'talked of' by 'many people', and later 'talked of publiquely' before the mayor. Ever since, a court heard, 'ther is a comon and publique fame bothe in the parishe' and 'divers other parishes in London', that Creed and Moore spent time 'incontinently' together.[44]

Not all crimes were good material for neighbourly tittle-tattle. We hear little about vagrancy or theft, for example, in charges of lack of proper neighbourly behaviour or thoughtfulness. There were limits to what some neighbours acted on for something to bloom into a 'publique fame', however spicy or unsavoury. Vagrants did not set gossip-lines buzzing. Domestic spats, on the other hand, were talked about all the time. Like servants who 'defyled' their master's house by having sex under his roof, scandals marred community reputations.[45] Prudence Prue's mistress told her 'that there was a scandal raised on her' as word spread that her 'late lodgers' dead baby lay 'unburied' in her house for two days. 'A comon fame of incontinency' against Susan May said that she locked herself away with her husband's apprentice, and after she snubbed their cautions, neighbours 'told their landlord that they would not stay in their house if he did not speedily take some course of reformacon'. Elizabeth Gwyn 'was suspiciouslie taken' with a cartmaker in 1575, and said that 'he had his hande under hir clothes and meante theare to comyt the facte yf they had not ben letted by the next neighbours'.[46] Neighbours cared above all else about the shame of sex, when whole streets could get bad names for having a cluster of bawdy houses. Next in line came public disorder, like heated quarrelling, brawling, or drinking sprees. Neighbours put on shows of strength at Bridewell. Twenty of Nicholas Dixler's neighbours said he was impossible to live with. Sixteen neighbours filed complaints about 'evill', 'beastly', drunk 'comon harlot' Anne Carter in 1578, and 'suspitious' Katherine Poley who ran a house of 'evil resort' in Holborn, whose husband wept 'xxtie tymes' at her 'lewdnes'

---

[44] BHC 8, fo. 253v; LMA D/L/C/218, fo. 163.   [45] BHC 2, fos. 21–1v, 38v.
[46] GL MS 9064/19, fo. 53v; BHC 2, fo. 136; LMA WJ/SR/NS/39/8, 33/77, 35/74, 36/98.

and tried to hang himself with 'black threde'. Other neighbourly lobbies were smaller – seven, six, five, four – but no weaker for that. Three neighbours told how 'dyvers persons' called at Anne Lewis's house around midnight when her husband was away, even after she was warned to 'leve' it off. Neighbourly sound and fury was not taken lightly. Hearing 'a noyse of neighbors about the dore' when he was lying in 'sinful' bed with Agnes Brooke in 1576, John Banks tried to squeeze under the bed, 'for feare he should be arrested', but much to his dismay his breeches 'were so gret he cold not gett under the bed'.[47]

Shameful slurs cut deep but also pressing was concern to help legitimate families get by. Boozing men squandering family budgets grabbed attention, as did out-of-work sponging husbands or bossy wives. A parish locked up work-shy Edward Robinson in Bridewell after he 'riotouslye' wasted 'all his goods' and pawned his wife's belongings.[48] Domestic disorders were not fitting in well-run parishes. Child-, servant-, and wife-beaters were told to turn over new leaves. A currier was locked up for beating his wife 'in very inhumane and monstrous manner' after coming home drunk 'to the great disquieting' of neighbours. People on Chancery Lane 'exclamed' on a stonecutter's wife 'for inhumanely beating' a child 'and almost starving it' in 1633.[49] Women often brought sex-crimes to courts. 'Divers' women accused John Young of incest and his wife of living 'a very evel lyff'. William Harwood witnessed how two women banged on his door, 'shaking and telling what beastlines there was' in Walter Swaine's house up the street. He 'peeped in at the cranny of the doore', and saw Swaine get up after sex with his daughter, fill a dish with beer and give it to her, who 'drunke it to her father and he to her againe'. Neighbours burst in on crimes when something caught their eye or 'great noysse' sent them scurrying next door. Agnes Fryddy 'cryed' loudly when she was raped by three men in 1560, and 'by that meanes neybors had understandinge thereof'. Noises alerted Bridget Uppley that something was wrong next door, and she gathered some 'neybors' together who looked through a window as a bookbinder's wife and her lover climbed out of bed to get dressed. Anthony Hewetson was dozing in bed in 1603 when he heard his landlady and someone 'jumblinge and

---

[47] BHC 3, fos. 53, 332v, 265, 46v, 2v. See also LMA Reps. 13i, fo. 130v; 16, fo. 91v; BHC 3, fos. 340, 399; GL MS 3018/1, fos. 50v, 58, 216.
[48] BRHA BHC 4, fo. 27. See also BHC 2, fo. 249v; 3, fo. 360v; 8, fo. 129v; 9, fos. 128, 299.
[49] LMA WJ/SR/NS/39/113; Rep. 29, fo. 5v. For master/servant disputes see my *Youth and Authority*, chap. 6. For cases of gossip about abusive husbands leading to arrests: BHC 1, fo. 74; GL MSS 9064/15, fo. 203v; 3018/1, fo. 91v; LMA D/L/C/214, fo. 137; Reps. 15, fo. 407; 16, fo. 91v; 31(1), fo. 24; BHC 3, fos. 107v-8, 392; 7, fo. 325; WAC WCB 1, fo. 250. See also Capp, *When Gossips Meet*, chap. 6.

bustlinge togeather' in the entry below his window.[50] Other tip-offs of 'lewd couplings' included 'creaking' and 'cracking' beds. Margaret Stansby looked out of a window into Harrow Alley one night 'and sawe by chance' a spurrier on top of Richard Medley's wife, 'neare the beds feete', making the bed shake. Two women chatting on a doorstep looked across the street into a neighbour's house and saw his wife having sex with another man. Neighbours peeped into Luce Barnaby's 'house of bawdry' in 1623 and saw 'such a sight as thou never saw standing against a post with clothes up to her mouth'.[51] People came to courts to tell of shocking sights seen through holes in walls and doors, keyholes, across alehouse tables, in gardens, or right in front of their eyes, as when three Whitechapel neighbours watched Lawrence Ashely 'filtheley abuse himselfe in shewinge his privie members' a little way across the street. Thomas Wood's neighbours arrived too late after they spotted him through a window dangling from a cord strapped to the staircase, even though he was still 'very warme' when he was cut down.[52]

People also overheard slanders, scaremongering, or poor-taste jokes from someone close by. Aldermen, nudged by the Crown, asked all alehouse keepers to 'give a good eare' to their 'gestes' to note down the names of 'spredors of rumors, false words, and sedicyous tales' and report them at once in highly charged times in 1554. Thomas Brown was locked up in Newgate in the same year after his neighbours 'credably' reported that he 'sedyciously rayled againste the hole cytie sayeinge that the hole cytie were trayters and rebels'.[53] Some taunts were meant to be heard by as many people as possible. Margaret Hyde was sitting on her step working one day in 1591 when Margaret Head startled her: 'before thow comest to London', she shouted, you 'played the whore in Wales'.

---

[50] BHC 2, fo. 143v; 7, fo. 319v; LMA WJ/SR/NS/40/6; BHC 1, fos. 53, 32; BHC 3, fo. 390v; BRHA BHC 4, fos. 134v, 289v, 353–3v.

[51] TNA STAC8 57/7; BHC 2, fo. 71v; BRHA BHC 4, fo. 22. See also SBHA Governors' Journal 3, fo. 265v. Curtains regularly appear in probate inventories around 1700: see Lorna Weatherill, *Consumer Behaviour and Material Culture in Britain, 1660–1760* (1988), p. 40; Carl B. Estabrook, *Urbane and Rustic England: Cultural Ties and Social Spheres in the Provinces, 1660–1780* (Manchester, 1998), p. 149.

[52] BHC 2, fos. 49, 74, 78, 254v; 3, fos. 16, 46–6v, 161, 402; 5, fos. 21, 313v; 7, fo. 340; 9, fos. 204, 301; BRHA BHC 4, fos. 43v, 134v, 246–6v, 257, 261v; LMA WJ/SR/NS/30/9. Cf. David Turner, *Fashioning Adultery: Gender, Sex, and Civility in England, 1660–1740* (Cambridge, 2002), p. 155.

[53] LMA Reps. 13i, fo. 130v; 13ii, fo. 202. See also Adam Fox, *Oral and Literate Culture in England, 1500–1700* (Oxford, 2000), chaps 6–7; Martin Ingram, 'Ridings, rough music, and mocking rhymes in early modern England', in Barry Reay, ed., *Popular Culture in Seventeenth-Century England* (1985), pp. 166–97; Alastair Bellany, *The Politics of Court Scandal in Early Modern England: News Culture and the Overbury Affair, 1603–1660* (Cambridge, 2002), chap. 2; Gowing, *Domestic Dangers*, chaps 3–4.

Answer me, Head hounded her, and shout your answer so 'neighboures maye heare whatt you saye'. Hyde said that Head spoke 'openly in the alley that all the neighboures thereabowts might heare her'. Slanders were often spoken in the heat of the moment or at the wrong place and time. Margery Nowell scoffed about a workmate when walking with Edward Muffin in Islington Fields in 1575: 'she is a witche', she sneered, and never 'had a heare on her privie members', and she found herself in court soon after with seven more of her neighbours in attendance who readily gave other examples of 'hir lewde words'. Neighbours also overheard 'frothie words' on greens, outside windows, or from the other sides of thin walls.[54] Such neighbourly 'meddling' could backfire if hotheads sought revenge. A St Sepulchre butcher thumped some of his neighbours after they had taken him to task for his rowdy house and all-night parties. Some with scores to settle scattered 'ill rummers and slaunderouse talke'. Gossip spread like wildfire from 'talebearers' like Agnes Taylor who went from neighbour to neighbour 'makinge great dissention' in 1604. Loose talk was dangerous in the wrong hands, and a 'fame' could take on meanings that were never intended. William Ewen of St Botolph-without-Bishopgate spent most of the day in alehouses rather than earning his living with his cart, 'tell[ing] againe any such thing that he shall here amongst the neighbors and made matters worse' by sowing 'sedition and stuff amongst' them, causing them to fall out repeatedly.[55]

But despite these risks no one should doubt the onus that was placed on people to stamp out trouble and bring cases to court, and that some people in London took these obligations seriously. Citizens were expected to go to courts when wronged: the City was satisfied when a husband dragged his wife to Bridewell, saying that she was 'a comon harlot', or when masters took action against light-fingered servants.[56] Citizens had a duty to tackle trouble inside or outside households: to take vagrants to the nearest constable or risk steep fines, for example.[57] Peacekeeping gave citizens more active roles than later on. This is all to say that saddled with duties to look out for the peace and purse, it is no wonder that neighbours got involved in legal process from start to finish. But this is more apparent when crimes had smarting victims. It is not easy to squeeze most crimes into neighbourhood/policing paradigms. The

---

[54] LMA D/L/C/214, fos. 5–7, 23, 25, 75; D/L/C/217, fo. 37; D/L/C/218, fos. 80, 182; BHC 2, fo. 186; 3, fos. 12v, 63, 316–16v, 350; LMA Rep. 14, fo. 195.
[55] LMA CQSF 91/18; GL MS 9064/16, fos. 12v-13; LMA D/L/C/218/22.
[56] BHC 1, fos. 6, 14, 71, 198v; 2, fos. 11, 255; LMA Reps. 13i, fo. 131; 13ii, fo. 202; 14, fo. 245; 19, fo. 171. Cf. Gowing, *Domestic Dangers*; Griffiths, *Youth and Authority*, chaps 2 and 5–6.
[57] LMA Jour. 20, fo. 500v.

next section does not leave neighbours behind, but it does start to piece together pictures of policing and prosecution that give large roles to public authorities. How did a word in a neighbour's ear become a prosecution? At what stage did public authorities step in to 'formalize' this fuss with authority and warrants?

### Investigations

Neighbours hardly ever acted alone. They teamed up with officers to take suspects to court if all else failed, and we should not imagine neighbourly interventions as lacking the backing of officers. Warning words or peace-making had more clout with support from an alderman or other officer. 'As Abraham toke Agar' so can I 'take another woman' by 'reason of the want' which is in my wife 'by reason of her age', a brewer told All Hallows the Great vestry, when his neighbours and parish officers joined up to charge him with keeping a 'harlot' on the side. The brewer knew his Bible well, and 'almost in effecte certyfyed the vilde dede by scripture for that his wife is not able to serve his torne', horror-struck vestrymen said later at Bridewell, in a case in which it is impossible to tell officers and neighbours apart. John Webb, a Southwark broom-man, was sitting supping in an alehouse in St Clement Danes one day in 1635, with his brooms stacked up against the door when, in the middle of his meal, he looked out of the window with a start as he saw John Greene pick up his brooms and start running up the street. Greene had a headstart but the brooms were heavy and inside a minute Webb 'overtook' him, tripped him up, and flagged down a constable to take the broom-thief into custody. He was not the only Londoner who charged up a street shouting 'stop thief', hoping that a constable would hear him and come running to the spot at once.[58]

Policing more often than not was a joint enterprise between neighbours and officers. Six parishioners and four constables searched Maudly Wall's house in 1575, hoping to catch a curate who was a constant caller there late at night, but he disappeared in the nick of time, as they found 'his book' on the table, cloak on the bed, his 'shoes standinge in the chimney corner', and 'the printe of twayne' in a still 'warme' bed.[59] Tip-offs from members of the public helped to crack cases. David Pynfold 'laye in bedd with one Elizabeth night by night' until St Olave Street's deputy 'had intelligence of it' through a spicy 'comon fame'. A Clerkenwell constable said that 'his neighbours came and told him' that Jane Dey had just given

---

[58] BHC 3, fos. 254, 264v; LMA WJ/SR/NS/44/5–6, 44/9. See also LMA CQSF 133/50; Rep. 23, fo. 72; SBHA Governors' Journal 4, fo. 135; BHC 3, fo. 324.
[59] BHC 2, fo. 74v.

birth to an illegitimate child in 1600, 'and wished him to go to a justice for a warrant'. Bridewell was the first port of call for beadle Agar after 'divers' people 'tolde him' that a hosier 'had a woman between vi or vii of the clocke everie mornynge in his garden'. Elizabeth Evans's neighbours told the deputy about her 'lewde life' after she 'slenderlye regarded' their 'friendly admonition' in 1598 and continued to stay out with men past midnight.[60] This tip-off/arrest sequence was a regular route to court. A pewterer smelled a rat when John Price dropped into his shop to sell him a dish, and he realized that it belonged to Sheriff Wright, and Price was soon Bridewell bound. John Daniel had a word with a deputy after watching women come and go from John Barker's house several nights in a row in 1575, to ask that 'serche mighte be made'. He took the law into his own hands soon after seeing Barker with a woman at his door, however, and his skin was saved by a beadle when he 'cried out' loudly as Barker lunged at him with a sword. Deputies were often in the thick of inquiries, speaking with neighbours, interviewing suspects, collecting stories. They knew neighbourhoods intimately, and worked with neighbours each day to run wards, as when the deputy and 'substantiall inhabitants' of St Sepulchre parish rounded up a gang of brawling servants in 1602. Wardmotes worked closely with City courts, and aldermen were at hand to take cases to one if required.[61] The grass-roots experience of middling men in office meant that there was someone nearby who knew what to do if warnings or warrants were required. They also put their knowledge of the neighbourhood and its people to good use, often acting on their own hunches, but not always correctly. A constable had doubts straight away in 1593 when James Dagger and Roger Pepper brought him 'news of bad report' that Marmaduke Butler and Margaret Durrant were 'naughty' together, because he had known for some time that she took 'great paines' to 'labor hard for her living'. Something was not right, and he did not want to 'drawe' her 'into discreditt withowt desert'. He asked the pair to bring the woman who 'brought up this report' and listened as she heaped shame on Durrant. Her 'quality' worried him next to diligent Durrant, and she talked herself into trouble, 'in effect' owning up to being bawd to the pair, as bad as the sex itself, the constable lectured, and he 'doubted' that her 'creditt was such that creditt might be given to hir words'. But he

---

[60] GL MS 9064/19, fo. 182; BRHA BHC 4, fos. 12, 185; BHC 2. fo. 188v.
[61] BHC 7, fo. 257; 2, fos. 77–7v; BRHA BHC 4, fo. 307; See also BHC 2, fos. 10, 69, 154, 230; 3, fos. 60, 326; 5, fo. 327; 7, fo. 136; LMA CQSF 131/22; GL MS 3018/1, fo. 57. Elbow handed a suspect to a deputy: *Measure for Measure*, 3.1, 273–4. For examples of aldermen making arrests or working with neighbours, see BHC 2, fo. 188; 3, fo. 355v; BRHA BHC 4, fo. 307; LMA D/L/C/214, fo. 429; WJ/SR/NS/33/77, 40/6; Reps. 13ii, fo. 323v; 15, fo. 407; 23, fo. 72.

gave her a last chance: he would 'give creditt unto hir if she coulde bringe forth any person of creditt' to back 'hir good behavior'. Dagger and Pepper, meanwhile, were told to keep mum, so that Durrant's 'doings and meetinges' might be better 'espied owt' for 'good proofe'. But the constable got it wrong on this occasion, and Butler and Durrant both appeared before the wardmote a little while afterwards.[62]

Teamwork between neighbours and officers did not end suddenly once a case reached court. Magistrates looked for 'pregnant testimony' from people and police to clinch cases. Sixteen neighbours turned up at Bridewell with their deputy at one time to make sure that a 'comon harlot' was put behind bars.[63] Courts also sent letters to parishes for information, and officers sometimes called at the house of someone who knew a suspect. After Hannah Streetly was caught walking late one night, a beadle chatted with one of her friends 'to knowe of what report shee is'. Peternella Jackson was found crouching under a stall after dark in 1634, and locked up until a letter was sent to Mr Jackson of The Temple 'to know what she is'. A deputy was asked to have a word with a vagrant's uncle to check his story. Another officer was sent to make sure that Solomon Arnold really did work with a bricklayer in St Katherine's Lane in 1652. And a beadle called on Mr Dicewell in Bishopgate Street in 1639 'to enquire whether it be or no', after Ann Parfield bumped into the watch and explained that she had been 'scowering' at his house and left late.[64] A lot of groundwork was done by beadles. One went across the river with a prisoner 'to seeke out the owner of the table cloth w[hi]ch hee stole'. Others also visited crime-scenes to get particulars of offences or to test 'the truth of yt'. A beadle took John Philips back to the market where he swiped beef and bacon to get him to point out the stall from where he grabbed the meat.[65]

Magistrates could take the lead in cracking theft cases. Moll Cutpurse was once led up and down Cheapside by officers who stopped in goldsmiths' shops to ask if anyone recognized her and if she had ever tried to sell them stolen plate. London's 'comen crier' walked through the city in 1579, 'crying' a stolen basin so that the 'right owner' could take the case over. A parish forked out a shilling 'cryinge a ringe that was founde in the churche'.[66] Magistrates more commonly took the initiative in offences that were not 'interpersonal' acts. Parishes and wards were often very

[62] BHC 6, fo. 90; 7, fos. 48, 96; LMA D/L/C/214, fos. 437–9.
[63] BHC 6, fo. 425; 3, fo. 332v.
[64] BHC 5, fo. 165v; 9, fo. 580; 8, fo. 231; BRHA BHC 4, fo. 54.
[65] BHC 5, fo. 67; 2, fo. 83v; 5, fo. 156. See also BHC 1, fo. 24v; 2, fo. 139v; 3, fo. 361v; 5, fos. 378, 411v; 7, fo. 22; 8, fos. 62v, 176v.
[66] TNA STAC8 124/4; BHC 3, fo. 389; GL MS 2088/1, 1612–13.

involved in 'searches' set up by City magistrates to track down offenders, sometimes targeting particular people on the run, or rounding up vagrants, for example, 'evyll persones', 'lewd' women out of service, rioters, or rumour-mongers. Individual wards and parishes also set up searches of their own, or approached the Guildhall for help to set one up. Hospitals also needed help to track offenders down from time to time. Beadles 'divers times' carried children who had been left at Christ's Hospital door through the streets in 1587, hoping to pick up some information about the parents. A 'yonge infant' with a broken neck was found in a pew in St Peter's Cornhill one day in 1612, and magistrates told a midwife 'and other sadd and discrete women' of the parish to walk through the streets to try to trace the 'lewd' woman who put him there. The head of 'a new borne child' was dumped in a 'grasseplatt' somewhere in St Botolph Aldersgate in 1639, and a search was set up at once for the 'mother murderer' who had seemingly vanished into thin air.[67] Experience taught magistrates and officers that such 'malignant mothers' often sought out hiding places in alehouses and 'howses of lodging or resort of suspect persons', and that the 'greatest number' of them 'goe under the name of maidservants'. Information on women who had not long given birth was always helpful to catch offenders, even more so if they could not say where their child was at that particular point in time. Wards called on the expert help of midwives to catch 'fowle' mothers. When a 'new borne' baby was found dead in a Blackfriars street in 1628, officers were told to move 'suddenlye in the secretest manner they cann to procure mydwyfes or other skillfull women' to 'viewe and search the bodyes of all maidservants and other womenkind as there shall be any cause to suspect'.[68]

It was usually left up to individual parishes to make a start to track down 'fowle' mothers. Parishes paid for investigations, examinations, warrants, and court fees. This was public detective work that led at the end of the day to prosecutions that were brought in the name of public bodies. There was no one else to start proceedings. Parishes would arrange for search parties when a child was found somewhere within its bounds.[69] A record of fees and payments to cover the costs of these searches is logged in the accounts of many parishes, and they also give us some nice details about the composition and conduct of searches.

---

[67] GL MS 12806/2, fo. 388; LMA Jour. 18, fo. 64v; Rep. 15, fo. 120v; Jour. 38, fo. 299.
[68] LMA Jours. 26, fo. 289; 29, fo. 177; 32, fo. 318; 35, fo. 21v. See also LMA Jours. 28, fo. 158v; 36, fo. 181; 38, fos. 40, 101, 172, 258v; 39, fos. 52, 81, 134, 192, 304.
[69] GL MSS 6574, fo. 205v; 4180/1, fo. 70; 4409/1, fos. 29v, 153v; 2596/2, fo. 15v; 3146/1, fo. 52v; 1303/1, 1601.

There are times when only one officer is listed as taking charge of a search, beadles more than any other, although 'bishops officers', clerks, sextons, warders, and watchmen are also named as the lone leaders from time to time.[70] Hospital beadles also gave wards and parishes helping hands. Bridewell beadles picked up 9/8d from a parish in 1589 to cross the city to 'seek owt the mother of a child' left in a churchyard.[71] The names of other men (and one time a boy) are also listed when parishes set out to hunt for 'malevolent' mothers.[72] But women were nearly always included in parish search parties, just as they had leading roles in getting 'big bellied' vagrants out of parishes. These widows or 'goodwives' for the most part could look for tell-tale signs on bodies and perhaps had a sixth sense of the best places to look for missing mothers. Women are listed in accounts receiving payments for 'bringing word' of runaway mothers, 'for discovering the matter', and also for giving evidence in court after a successful search. Nurse Martin was paid ten shillings in 1641 'for her paynes in bringing to light the mother' of a child left to the care of St Stephen Walbrook. The same parish also spent 7/6d for a four-day search in 1585: two shillings for a beadle, 3/6d for a woman for 'carryeing' the child, and another two shillings 'for fyer for the chylde'. While Goodwife Pith pocketed eight shillings for travelling to Thistleworth and other places in 1635 to look for the mother of an abandoned child.[73]

Time after time the sources let us watch women carrying abandoned children through London's streets with officers at their side, asking questions of people who might know something, searching faces for clues. There was stirring symbolism in this parade of mothers carrying 'lost' children in images that appealed to tender motherly love and rock solid family ties. Perhaps someone would recognize the babe in arms. The search party kept walking, trying to jog memories to see if anyone could remember a single woman who gave birth in a hushed room one day whose child was now no longer with her. Goodwife Clement got twelve-pence for leading a child through a number of funerals on the trail of a mother, presumably burials of young women whose mourners might

---

[70] For beadles see GL MSS 4383/1, fo. 350; 4385/1, fo. 38v; 1046/1, fo. 117; 2088/1, fo. 50; 2895/1, fo. 253v; 1016/1, fo. 73v; 1279/2, fo. 132; 3556/1, fo. 237; 577/1, fo. 22. For some other officers see GL MSS 4409/1, fo. 153v; 593/2, fo. 72; 6574, fo. 109v; 2596/2, fo. 15v; 4383/1, fo. 367; 1176/1, 1641; 3556/2, 1644; 4051/1, fo. 33; 590/1, fo. 224.
[71] GL MSS 4992/1, fo. 331; 1046/1, fo. 38; 4524/1, fo. 52; 1176/1, 1592; 5090/2, fo. 100v; 2895/1, fos. 231v, 240; 3556/1, fo. 184; 2596/1, fos. 178v, 182v; 6574, fo. 20.
[72] GL MSS 2999/1, 1675–6; 1176/1, 1641; 662/1, fo. 148v; 2601/1, fo. 14v; 4071/2, fos. 85, 156, 199v; 3146/1, fo. 52v; 4524/1, fo. 62.
[73] GL MSS 593/4, 1640–1; 4409/1, fo. 237; 593/2, fo. 73v. See also GL MSS 6574, fo. 205v; 3146/1, fo. 88v; 878/1, fo. 246; 6552/1, fo. 250; 4383/1, fo. 420; 4423/1, fo. 144; 4071/2, fo. 136v; 4409/1, fo. 232v; 4570/2, fo. 317; 524/1, fo. 99; 9080/7, 1658; 4524/1, fo. 52.

Policing: process and prosecution 381

recognize the child, and her search party was completed by a beadle and sexton who picked up 2/6d to share. The same two officers crossed the river with another woman not long after, this time to draw attention to a child who had been found crying on a stall in the late afternoon, and again they focused on funerals, 'to make it known', perhaps after a tip-off, that the mother was from Southwark. One parish gave Christ's beadles six shillings for a long six-day search in 1586, and a warder's wife received two shillings for 'carrying' the child for four days, 'to learne the mother of it'. Widow Hedge picked up five shillings in 1649 'for carryeinge' a child all through the city and its edges, 'to see if shee coulde fynde out the mother of it'. Some searches continued late after dusk. St Benet Fink purchased '3 004E' in 1629 so that officers could continue to search for the parents of an abandoned child after nightfall.[74] Parishes also checked the details of births in the records of other parishes, trying to find the one piece of information that might link a child to a mother. One parish gave a nurse and two other women two shillings when they travelled to Peckham in 1583 to hunt through records to 'prove' that a child had been 'borne thear', and fourteen shillings at another time to two men who travelled all the way to Hertford for the same reason.[75]

Parishes also paid 'cryers' to 'crye the child' through streets for fees that climbed to six shillings, the amount paid to a nurse when she walked all day long 'crying the Lambeth child' for St Botolph Billingsgate.[76] Another parish printed 'ticketts' at a cost of 6/8d to help track down a missing mother. Others hired informers or rewarded their own officers for good detective work. St Stephen Walbrook handed over £1 'to the informers that directed us to the mother' of a child in 1628, and a beadle picked up three shillings for 'finding her out'. James White was £1 richer after 'discovering one that had laid Judith Cornhill' in St Michael Cornhill in 1647.[77] The number of searches noted down in parish records soars after 1600.[78] Chances might seem slim, but a surprising number of

---

[74] GL MSS 6574, fos. 62, 66; 3556/1, fo. 184; 4409/2, 1649–50; 1303/1, 1628–9. See also GL MSS 4071/1, fo. 133v; 4071/2, fo. 120; 1046/1, fo. 10; 593/2, fo. 126v; 2596/1, fo. 208; 6574, fo. 76; 1303/1, 1661; 4383/1, fo. 304; 4423/1, fo. 61; 6836, fo. 129.
[75] GL MS 4524/1, fos. 52, 62. See also GL MSS 5090/2, fo. 256; 593/4, 1630–1.
[76] GL MS 942/1, fo. 212. See also GL MSS 5714/1, fo. 178; 2999/1, 1673–4; 5018/1, fo. 8v.
[77] GL MSS 2895/2, 1660–1; 593/2, fo. 144; 4071/2, fo. 156. See also GL MS 959/1, fo. 175v.
[78] For some examples, GL MSS 577/1, fo. 144v; 590/1, fo. 245v; 4383/1, fo. 360; 4071/2, fos. 167–7v; 4051/1, fo. 169; 4423/1, fo. 185; 1303/1, 1639; 5714/1, fo. 180v; 2088/1, 1596–7; 1568, fos. 337, 699; 1002/1, fo. 310v; 4180/1, fo. 199v; 4956/2, fo. 119; 2956/2, fo. 50; 1432/3, fo. 80; 959/1, fo. 190; 662/1, fo. 68v; LMA MJ/SBR/1, fo. 532; MJ/SBR/3, fo. 567.

mothers were tracked down. More than a few parishes counted their blessings after reporting successful outcomes when mothers and children were brought back together. 'Joan the oyster woman' got sixpence from a parish in 1636 'for carying a child to Algate'. St Mary Aldermary handed back '4 found children' to their mothers, after spending £2 3s 3d to track them down over a single year (1659). Nor did matters always end if search parties arrived back empty handed, as some parishes continued the chase and turned to courts to get warrants for further help to discover mothers or for rulings about child-care. Only one parish on record gave up the chase after a mother 'could not be found', although others did call off searches without giving any reason.[79] Parishes needed to be resilient because money was at stake, and whatever the costs of searching the long-term benefits were imagined in years to come when children were no longer burdens on parish coffers. A parish spent six months hunting down Margery North's parents, first getting a warrant to question Goodwife North and Nurse Spooner in Christmas 1646 after hearing that North had spent some time with the nurse as her delivery date drew nearer. Mary Hall picked up five shillings four months later after confirming that North spent time at the nurse's house, although Spooner said that she never 'sawe the parents of the childe'. But soon after the parish happily reported that the true parents were indeed North and her husband, and that it was 'freed of the further charge of that childe by this discovery'. 'A fowndling' was left on a doorstep in St Helen Bishopgate on Maundy Thursday night with no trace of the mother. The parish put the child to nurse, but the broken-hearted mother came back for her child a little later and mother and child were 'happely mett', to the great relief of parish leaders who helped the pair to get back home to Shoreditch.[80]

Public bodies also guided investigations when officers brought in a note or word of tatty buildings that looked like they might come crashing down, lodgers squeezed into dank rooms, or noisy alehouses. Parishes often followed up on City-led inquiries, as when St Benet Paul's Wharf reported 'Mr Jackson's life and conversacon' to aldermen.[81] But they did not need to be jolted into action, often acting as problems cropped up in their own back-yards. St John Zachary paid 4/6d to track down a husband who ran away from home in 1609, leaving his family behind to fend for themselves. Another parish covered the costs to trace a runaway wife. St Peter Westcheap gave a beadle sixpence 'to search the woman that

---

[79] GL MSS 1002/1, fo. 515; 6574/1, fo. 203v; 5090/2, fo. 70. See also GL MSS 3146/1, fo. 88v; 4423/1, fo. 156v; 6836, fo. 76; 590/1, fo. 100v; 1303/1, 1646–7; 5090/2, fo. 284; 4071/2, fo. 156; 6574, fo. 89; 1002/1, fo. 351v; 4570/2, fo. 272; 818/1, fo. 193v.
[80] GL MSS 2991/1, 1646–7; 6836, fo. 89v.   [81] GL MS 878/1, fo. 356.

knewe the man that died in the streete'. A deputy got sixpence from a parish in 1624 'for discovering a fellow with a counterfeitt passe' in their midst.[82] Illegitimacy was another matter when child-care was at issue. Parishes chased fugitive fathers, one spending 19/3d 'for horse hire and dyet' to send two men to Watford to corner absentee father Henry Hayward. Another forked out twelve shillings to bring back Thomas Austin, who 'gott his maide with childe' and for a warrant for his pending trial. The Court of Aldermen or a parish usually spearheaded chases with good success rates. As well as clearing up crime, they also solved riddles about dead bodies on streets or washed up on the riverside. One parish gave 'the cryer' a shilling 'to cry a man who was found drowned on Botolphe Wharfe' in 1617.[83]

### Arrests

We often just get short matter-of-fact notes of the name, office, and patch of arresting officers in the cold legal calculus of Bridewell courtbooks when arrests were put into words by clerks, but we do not always get all three at the same time, and sometimes we have only a slim scrap or nothing at all. That said, however, the laconic entries gathered together in their thousands by Bridewell's clerks give us a sample of 39,516 cases drawn from eight surviving courtbooks, when the source of a committal was noted down (see Appendix Tables 8a–8d): an officer (often), a justice (less often), the City (roughly half as often as a justice), or another court or prison (sometimes).[84]

No other set of records from anywhere in the city gives us a bigger or better profile of court committals. Bridewell's cells were kept full by officers in the main: almost two-thirds of committals were the result of an arrest by one of London's officers (63.64 per cent/25,147 cases). The second largest source was a justices' warrant, but it lagged far behind (16.79 per cent/6,635 cases). Next in line was the City and its officials (9.03 per cent/3,570 cases), and after that we are dealing with one or two

---

[82] GL MSS 590/1, fo. 55v; 3146/1, fo. 11; 4524/1, fo. 220; 645/2, fo. 56.
[83] GL MSS 4051/1, fo. 77; 6836, fo. 159v; 942/1, fo. 70. Cf. GL MSS 3146/1, fo. 123; 1046/1, fos. 117, 127; 1016/1, fo. 190; 4180/2, fo.70; 4956/3, fo. 228; 1432/3, fo. 164; Griffiths, *Youth and Authority*, pp. 267–89; Capp, *When Gossips Meet*, chap. 4; Tim Meldrum, 'London domestic servants from depositional evidence, 1660–1750: servant-employer sexuality in the patriarchal household', in Tim Hitchcock, Peter King, and Pamela Sharpe, eds., *Chronicling Poverty: the Voices and Strategies of the English Poor, 1640–1840* (Basingstoke, 1997), pp. 47–69.
[84] The sample is drawn from BHC 1–2 (1559–62/1574–6) and 5–9 (1617–58).

384    Control

percentage points or less.[85] Only thirty-nine people were put in Bridewell by parishes or wards, all before 1620. Guilds also used Bridewell sparingly to deal with problem apprentices (eight in all). Three victims marched their assailants to the prison. Two prisoners came along to Bridewell 'voluntarily'.

We should bear in mind that officers could still have roles in some of the 14,369 committals not laid directly at their door, either by making arrests – after warrants signed at Bridewell, for example (counted under Bridewell in my tables) – or by helping to move prisoners to Bridewell from somewhere else – a beadle dispatched from Bridewell to bring prisoners from Newgate perhaps, or City officers bringing someone from aldermen. Consequently, there is more to officers' roles here than first meets the eye. These figures are also aggregates that take no account of likely changing patterns. Indeed, breakdowns show that the role of officers grew around 1620 at the same time as vagrants swarmed in larger numbers, parishes took more notice of grubby inmates and abandoned children, and more women were trapped in Bridewell's net. Three-quarters of suspects standing in the dock between 1617–25 were taken prisoner by officers (10,090/14,601). This figure fell to a little over two-thirds in 1626–34 (67.86 per cent), and kept falling over the next two decades, dropping to under half of all committals in the long years of revolution and republican rule. In spite of what we might think, the number of committals also fell sharply in these troubled times for reasons that are not clear. There was no pause in the tempo of troubles, but the court was meeting less often, weekly sittings were the rule of thumb by now.[86] Rising resort to summary justice made a difference after 1630, with many suspects not appearing in courtrooms or courtbooks. There was no new lock-up for petty offenders inside the walls, no large-scale growth in prison space, and no sign in quarter session records of a sudden surge in cases that might have made up for Bridewell's slide.

Something did change outside the walls, however, when the decision was taken in 1614 to open a house of correction on Bridewell's jurisdictional patch in built-up Middlesex, and plans were afoot for a new and larger house of correction to the west in Tothill Fields by 1622. From the moment each was ready for its first inmate they provided places for people who might otherwise have gone to Bridewell.[87] The fall in the number of

[85] City and Middlesex quarter sessions sent in 798 suspects between them (2.06 per cent); the Crown or royal court sent in 446 (1.15 per cent); 317 prisoners were sent from another prison, mainly Newgate, or house of correction, mainly Middlesex (0.82 per cent).
[86] BHC 7, fo. 345; 8, fos. 327, 349v.
[87] The Middlesex house of correction was located in Clerkenwell and completed by 1615 with help from the City. 'Orders for the government of the howse' were passed in 1615

officers bringing suspects to Bridewell in the 1630s was offset by the larger number of warrants signed by justices and Bridewell officials that in all likelihood were served by the same officers who no longer appear in paperwork. There was also a jump in the share of committals from City officials in this decade, but nothing like the fivefold rise in times of revolution and republican rule, when three-in-ten suspects noted in records were put in Bridewell by the City. This City activity almost single-handedly counterbalanced the nose-dive in proportions of committals from officers, with a little help from quarter session referrals that doubled to 6 per cent. It seems that London's leaders took more initiative in times of deep political trouble, but the new Corporation of the Poor (1649) did not take any arrests or prosecutions away from Bridewell: coaching children to be trusty and honest adults was the prime goal of its flagship workhouse, not getting vagrants out of London, and only a handful of trouble-makers were sent to Bridewell from the Corporation.[88] When all is said and done, however, perhaps the most startling statistic to emerge from Bridewell committals is the big drop in numbers after 1630, that almost certainly had something to do with internal Bridewell procedures (and the steady spread of summary justice) and, later on, the ripple effects of the stormy 1640s and 1650s on City processes (including Bridewell's partial conversion into a prison for radicals and heretics).[89]

Also liable to change was the prominence of particular officers in bringing suspects to Bridewell (see Appendix Table 8c). Deputies brought in almost seven-tenths of all suspects arrested by named officers in the first two books, more than any other officer, but their participation rate tumbled over the seventeenth century to a little over 2 per cent in the 1630s, and as low as 0.75 per cent after 1645. Beadles were close behind deputies in the first few years, but soon took a back seat over the next nine decades, apart from a spurt of arrests in the 1600s. Constables brought in

and 1616: LMA MJ/SBR/2, fos. 117, 120, 242–3, 244–5, 273–4, 410–11; Rep. 32, fo. 120; Jour. 29, fos. 123–13v. For Tothill Fields house of correction see WAC F2001, fo. 114; F2002, fos. 53, 55, 57; E13, 1622–3; E14, 1624–5; and Merritt, *Social World*, p. 284.

[88] See Valerie Pearl, 'Puritans and poor relief: the London workhouse 1649–1660', in Donald Pennington and Keith Thomas, eds, *Puritans and Revolutionaries: Essays in Seventeenth-Century History Presented to Christopher Hill* (Oxford, 1978), pp. 206–32, esp. pp. 223–30.

[89] On London and the Civil War see Ben Coates, *The Impact of the English Civil War on the Economy of London, 1642–1650* (Aldershot, 2004). Coates gives more coverage to social policy in his PhD thesis, 'The impact of the English Civil War on the economy of London, 1642–1650', unpublished PhD thesis, University of Leicester (1997); and in his 'Poor relief in London during the English Revolution revisited', *London Journal*, 25 (2000), 40–58. See also Stephen Porter, 'The economic and social impact of the Civil War upon London', in Porter, ed., *London and the Civil War* (Basingstoke, 1996), pp. 175–204.

only one-in-ten of Bridewell suspects in 1559–62, and a touch more in 1574–6. Watches do not appear to have been very busy early on, shepherding just twenty-seven suspects there in the first six years of records, but their efforts are likely to be under-reported, as on a number of occasions, impossible to decipher from terse entries, names of constables in charge are jotted down rather than the watch itself.[90] Marshals are nowhere to be seen in early books, needless to say, although their time would soon come. Nor do warders make an appearance until four decades after the first batch of prisoners arrived at Bridewell. What alters beyond any shadow of a doubt in these policing snapshots is the virtual takeover of arrests by constables and marshals in the seventeenth century. More than 95 per cent of suspects who were brought directly to Bridewell from London's streets and shady houses after the mid-1620s were caught by either constables or marshals and their teams (96.63 per cent – 9,997/ 10,346).[91]

This is all from Bridewell's books and we can only see what clerks wrote down. We can almost take it for granted, however, that this is not a complete picture (particularly with the fall in recorded committals after 1630). It is Bridewell's story but also London's: there was nowhere else to take out of luck vagrants, except one of the smaller compters, and we know little else about them. Bridewell was London's lock-up, and only Bridewell has the courtbooks that let us appreciate, however imperfectly, what it was like to be under arrest, placed behind bars, and put on trial, often for little more than the skinniest suggestion of being 'suspicious' or 'lewd'. Bridewell also gives us unique archival angles on policing London's streets, and what it shows is a clear reorientation of policing towards constables and marshals as troubles grew. Marshals 'carried' more than 4,000 suspects to Bridewell in the quarter century after 1617 (and this number is a low estimate as they had express orders to hand over vagrants to the nearest constable). Constables brought in 12,051 suspects over the same period and their role had grown since the late sixteenth century; they were listed as being responsible for almost half of all committals from 1604–10. These figures alone suggest that City leaders gave long and hard thought to the issues of policing, and that with Bridewell as their named lock-up in most cases/orders, they made greater use of constables and marshals in planned strategies to cope with quick growth. Warders also crop up more often around 1600, but became rare visitors to

---

[90] This must explain, for example, why there is not one recorded committal by watchmen from 1634–42, the preference being to mention constables alone.

[91] If we go back to 1617 we would see that constables and marshals were named as arresting officers in 18,672 out of 21,336 cases (87.51 per cent).

Bridewell after 1625.[92] It was not just the nature of crime that was reassessed as London lurched from one troubled decade to another. Policing was also reconceived and reorganized along different lines, and the new alignment of constables and marshals in City policies and strategies is clearly seen in Bridewell's books.

Arrest tables give us neat patterns, but we must go back to the books to learn more about moments of arrest. Our knowledge of this unwelcome touch on the shoulder is seldom deep, but officers often acted alone (or are named alone at any rate), but also in pairs and groups of watchmen. Many suspects were already known to them, most likely after contacts reaching back over years in neighbourhoods. All sorts of fishy behaviour raised suspicions, leading officers to shadow someone on streets or burst into rooms with warrants. Acts behind closed doors were 'private' and always spawned suspicions. One officer knocked three times on a door and took the silence that followed as a sign that someone was up to no good. Another hammered on the door when the 'comon harborer of great bellied whores' Margaret Ketteridge shut herself up 'in a closed room with ii knaves and another whore'. Other people cowered under blankets or under stairs, trying to stay out of sight.[93] And as we have already seen, lack of light was thought to indicate something amiss if people were found fumbling in the dark, and anyone walking late could face stiff questions. Certain situations also stirred suspicions, such as people slumped asleep in alleys or on doorsteps, places linked with abandoning children. A beadle and a Bridewell governor spotted Blinking Jane sitting on a step one night in 1570 'with a young child on her lap' and an 'open' breast at a house where Alderman Ramsey had once lived near Stocks market. They both had the same thought; that she might slip away and leave the child on the step, and she ended up behind bars after questioning, no matter that she denied ever thinking such a thought (a constable also looked on in another case when a woman left a child on a doorstep).[94]

Anyone coming along to Bridewell to talk to a prisoner was immediately suspicious by association. Elizabeth Giles came to speak to 'mistress Anne' in 1561 and was recognized 'by chance' by a 'lewd' woman 'of this

---

[92] Warders brought 213 suspects to Bridewell in 1604–10 (7.88 per cent of committals), and 339 in 1617–26 (3.08 per cent), but not one (on record at any rate) in 1634–42. The activity of watches also increased and fell away in a similar pattern: watchmen were listed as arresting officers in 605 cases in 1604–10 (22.40 per cent), and 944 in 1617–26 (8.59 per cent), with a fall after that.

[93] BHC 9, fo. 159; LMA D/L/C/214, fo. 54; MJ/SR/505/182; BHC 3, fo. 331; LMA MJ/SR/510/34. See also BHC 8, fo. 91v; 9, fos. 596, 740; LMA MJ/SR/505, fo. 284; MJ/SR/522, fo. 2.

[94] BHC 1, fo. 162; GL MS 12806/2, fos. 54v-5; BHC 5, fo. 364v.

house', Ellyn Remnaunt, who tipped off officers that she was a well-known 'comon harlot' to her certain knowledge. Another visitor, Alice Bell, also never ended up going home on the day she went to visit her sister in Bridewell. Her history doomed her, as she was known there to be 'a bawd at her own house' and 'at Longe Megges at Redriffe'. Some cutpurses also ended up behind bars after knocking on the door of the porter's lodge to see if there was any chance of a chat with one of their mates in the cells.[95] People also found themselves in tricky spots if they were found with large sums of money in their pockets or purses and had no credible explanation for their sudden windfall. Bridewell's bench 'thought [William Ball] to be a cutpurse' for the simple reason that 'he hath always good somes of money' in his pockets, 'some tymes xs and sometimes xxs'. Nor did it help at all if prisoners were dressed in scruffy clothes when their pockets were stuffed with money. The shapes of prisoners' bodies could also let the cat out of the bag, as when begging women stuffed rags under clothes to con people into thinking that they were pregnant to get a few pennies. But smart clothes could also land people in trouble, because 'fondnes in attire' was not something that magistrates coupled with people low down on social ladders, and stylish clothes worn by 'common women' were taken as tokens that they were socially mobile courtesans. Both rags and riches could set suspicions racing. A constable tailed a suspicious seeming straggler for some time along a street, after 'observing his mean estate and thinking [that] he must have been a vagrant'.[96]

Other offenders were caught red-handed. A constable stumbled on a man panting on top of a woman on 'stones at London Bridge'. Elizabeth Doyson was found with her hand deep in a codpiece. Two officers caught Mary Tuss and Edward Holderness 'in the very acte'. There was little that a minister could do when he was found 'suspitiouslye' with 'his hose downe' and a woman 'abedd'. Nor was anyone in any doubt what was going on when a partly clothed couple were caught cringing in a room with two beds, one warm, the other cold, or when Angellet Norman was 'taken in the act of incontinency in the streete' at midnight by a beadle: 'fye beasts are you not ashamed', he said.[97] Pickpockets were caught with

[95] BHC 1, fos. 134v, 208; BRHA BHC 4, fos. 367v, 376. For more on Remaunte see Bernard Capp, 'Long Meg of Westminster: a mystery solved', *Notes and Queries*, 45 (1998), 302–4.
[96] BHC 1, fo. 170; 2, fo. 91v; TNA STAC8 251/23; BHC 6, fo. 7v ; BRHA BHC 4, fo. 125v.
[97] BHC 9, fo. 159; 6, fo. 301; 2, fo. 229; 7, fos. 278v, 334, 334v; 3, fo. 322v. See also GL MSS 9064/17, fo. 18; 9064/19, fo. 53v; BHC 2, fo. 230; 3, fos. 180, 392v; 5, fos. 2v, 118v; 6, fo. 186; 7, fos. 280v, 347v; 8, fos. 91v, 228, 304v, 391, 402.

hands deep in others' pockets; cutpurses were also grabbed 'on the job', a clumsy cut alerted the owner of a purse, or someone happened to keep their eye on a suspicious character hanging around well-dressed 'gents' in markets. Thieves were taken shaking under beds or on quays cutting open mealsacks. One thief was stopped walking down the stairs of a house 'with a bulke under his armes'.[98] Other would-be thieves never even got the chance to commit their crime. Thomas Powell was 'taken early' one morning in 1631 with a ladder in 'a carpenter's yard', and a sharp-eyed constable noticed the brand on his hand. John Powesse was spotted climbing up a ten-foot-high wall to rob a house after sunset. Nicholas Matfield was lost for words when he was caught 'suspiciouslie' upstairs 'in Alderman Hellins house'. Adulterers were also taken crawling into houses; a haberdasher's wife was found 'creeping through a gutter wyndowe' in 1560, dressed only in her 'pettycote and barelegged', although she claimed that she had only 'a purpose of evyll doing'. But there was no escaping the very awkward fact that she was remembered to be a 'notorious harlott' who had been found 'faultye' three times before.[99]

Like neighbours who rushed next door after hearing cries, officers ran to the scene after hearing someone shouting 'stop thief', loud banging on doors, and 'pitiful outcries and lamentable groans'. Joseph Leake settled himself into bed one night tucked in 'between' Frances Richardson and his wife, Richardson not liking the situation one bit and 'in feare of her lyfe', suddenly started screaming 'murther' loud enough for a passing constable to hear, who smashed down the front door of the house and rushed upstairs.[100] On watch one night in Aldgate in 1579, a constable knocked at the door of Margaret Grey's 'comon bawdie howse' after hearing something suspicious inside. 'Coming to the dore', Grey 'harde his voyce' and recognizing it straight away 'would not open' the door but ran upstairs 'hasteleye' urgently whispering: 'fye for shame make amende have ye not done the constable comes'.[101] One advantage in a city of neighbourhoods and constant chattering like London is *knowing* about people and places in local areas. Constable Collie plucked two vagrants from a house, which was, he said, 'the greatest howse of ill resorte in all that quarter'. Officers also knew, by dint of walking streets day after day, the likeliest places to find vagrants gathering or resting, finding young runaways and beggars slumped in doorways or behind stalls: one was easy

---

[98] LMA CQSF 106/15; BHC 7, fos. 309v, 340; 8, fos. 169, 180, 251v, 270, 284v, 299, 344.
[99] BHC 7, fos. 236, 328v; 6, fo. 437; 1, fo. 197.
[100] LMA WJ/SR/NS/44/9; BHC 5, fo. 297; TNA STAC8 190/13; 21/7; 251/23; BHC 7, fo. 264.
[101] BHC 3, fo. 346.

to pin down, as he was found slouched on the floor of a constable's shop after a drinking binge.[102] Constables trailed people along the streets when something suspicious caught their eye. One took Dorothy Agar and a merchant into custody after following them at a distance 'for a long time from Cheapside to Leadenhall': they would unquestionably have been 'nought[y] together', the constable added, but 'passengers' brushing by them kept cutting short their caresses.[103]

Some people were unlucky enough to do something wrong in an officer's shop, not knowing the true identity of the proprietor, or made a disastrous snap decision to rob off-duty officers. Constable Collier bumped into Joan Baker on Cheapside one day in 1579, who in friendly fashion offered him some nuts to munch and fell into talk 'as he stodde by here in the street amongst others', all the time waiting for an opportune moment to pick his purse from his pocket. Constables also pounced on loudmouths who spat tart insults and threats, little knowing that an officer was in hearing range. Two constables and three people 'of good credit' listened as reckless John Crowshawe called a woman 'whore', thinking that there was no one around to hear him. Simon Dunway was also overheard speaking 'daungerous words' on a misty night in the edgy atmosphere of January 1642 as rumours raced round the city and everyone worried about what would happen next in England's political blizzard: 'kill him', he muttered darkly, 'and 'ile kill another for this is a bloody night'.[104] Beadles also show up in Bridewell books arresting vagrants and others caught meandering aimlessly along streets, 'harlots' walking on 'darke' lanes, 'ruffyans', nightwalkers, and couples having sex out in the open without a care in the world, it seemed. They also kept ears open for warning yells and words spoken out of turn. Mary Little, 'a comon nightwalker', boasted that she had had sex with a 'gent' who gave her a ring, unaware that Beadle Ashwell standing nearby heard every word.[105] Beadles, as we saw in the last but one chapter, worked side-by-side with deputies, taking complaints and dropping off suspects for examination. Anne Buck shouted so loudly late one night in 1622 that her neighbours, sick of her constant howling, 'called' the deputy from his bed

---

[102] BHC 2, fo. 193v; 3, fo. 187v.
[103] LMA Rep. 18, fo. 33v; BHC 7, fo. 332; LMA Rep. 11, fo. 353v; BHC 2, fo. 16; 3, fos. 49v–50; 7, fo. 373; 8, fo. 344v; BRHA BHC 4, fo. 21v; GL MS 9680, fo. 26v; TNA STAC8 249/18. For watches see chap. 9. And for examples of churchwardens making arrests see GL MSS 9064/15, fo. 80; 9064/16, fo. 50; 9064/19, fo. 35; LMA Rep. 13ii, fo. 322.
[104] BHC 6, fos. 99–100v; 3, fo. 427v; 5, fo. 385; 8, fo. 364.
[105] LMA CQSF 126/49; Rep. 12, fos. 79, 495v; BHC 2, fos. 18, 146v; 7, fo. 278v; 8, fo. 344v.

to calm her down.[106] A deputy's scene-of-the crime inquiry was often a key stage on the road to court. Inmates, vagrants, pickpockets, rapists, and papists, are all among the offenders on record who were taken before deputies for questioning. Some owned up without the tiring rigmarole of a full-blown examination. Deputies sorted through the two sides of a story, if they were doing their job properly, to decide if a case was strong enough to answer in a courtroom, and they often gave evidence later in court. Deputy Gonnell stood in court and said that Elizabeth Brush 'asked a man what he lacked and whether he lacked a fair woman or not' in 1575. Deputies also raided shady houses, one time snatching four women of 'lewd conversacon' in a single swoop, one was found quivering inside a chest.[107]

Crimes also happened right in front of their eyes (or doors or windows). One deputy rounded up a group of rabble-rousers when a 'tumult' boiled over outside his front door. Another arrested Dorothy Cleyton – already 'knowne [to him] to be a harlott' – and John Hicks when he saw them 'kissinge together lewdly' on the street outside his house one night in 1576. John James was 'taken' lurking in Deputy Westwood's garden in 1629 (Westwood was also a member of Bridewell's bench at the time).[108] Nor was he the only Bridewell governor to catch rogues red-handed in his garden. No less a figure than 'hot' puritan William Gouge caught three 'vagrants and suspicious nightwalkers' 'climbing over a yard' into his house in 1640, one with a knife in his pocket, not knowing that the author of *Domesticall Duties* (1622) was watching them through a window. Gouge also marched a cutpurse to Bridewell in 1633, who was 'taken in the act' of cutting a purse in a pew in his Blackfriars church as he boomed from the pulpit. Bridewell's treasurer was strolling along Cheapside in 1635 when two vagrants suddenly burst into song, 'singing lewd songs' at the top of their voices, and the vocal vagrants were soon behind bars with the help of a nearby officer. In fact, all members of Bridewell's bench had been told to 'call the next constable' if they bumped into 'rogues or beggars' (1582). There was always a quota of deputies on the bench, and they often dipped into ward gossip when it seemed worth it. Richard Grafton brought word about 'certayne evell persones' living 'lewd' lives in Bishopgate to the Court of Aldermen in 1554. Members of Bridewell's staff also had a hand in bringing in some suspects, as when the matron

---

[106] BHC 6, fo. 292v.
[107] BHC 2, fo. 142. See also LMA D/L/C/214, fo. 429; Reps. 16, fo. 373v; 19, fo. 231; BHC 2, fos. 204–4v; 3, fo. 53; 5, fo. 421. For deputies see TNA STAC8 233/15; BHC 5, fo. 428v; 6, fo. 312v; LMA Reps. 13i, fos. 95–5v, 114; 19, fo. 231; GL MS 12806/2, fos. 94v, 238v.
[108] BHC 8, fo. 48; 3, fo. 393; 7, fo. 151v.

'found' the 'naughty harlot' Margaret Bloke in a bawdy house in 1560, who was questioned at Bridewell not long after but allowed to go home later because 'she had the pocks and a sor legg' (records do not tell us what the matron was doing in a brothel in the first place).[109]

There does not appear to have been a multitude of dim-wits on the beat in sixteenth- and seventeenth-century London. Quite the opposite, many officers used skill and cunning to trap suspects. Jane Whitehorn gave constable Weekes 'a potte of beere' in 1640 and led him to a cook's house from where the pair walked up Wood Street to the Barbican, the constable still sticking to his cover, but he grabbed his opportunity as they drew near to the compter and took her straight in through the door. Another constable 'fayen[ed] himselfe to be in drinke' when he bumped into Dorothy Morton late one December night in 1627, and suspecting she was up to no good he went with her to 'The Blew Boare in Gutter Lane' and followed her up to a 'chamber' where she would 'have lyen with him', but he arrested her as they walked upstairs. It is not clear whether Humphrey Newman was a constable, but he duped Alice Dartnell and took her into custody in Bridewell after she dropped into his shop in 1579 and asked him if 'he had any children'. I was jesting, she said later, but 'for tryall of her', Newman asked 'if I wolde coulde you helpe me with one then'. By 'chaunce' I can, she said, and mentioned Mother Jeye's house in St Andrew Undershaft – 'a lone woman' who 'lyved by the almes of the parishe' – 'wher he mighte [go with her and] be as bolde as with his own wiffe' for forty-five minutes with beer to quench his thirst. I would take you to my house, she added, but 'the skypjacke' my husband 'woulde come lepinge in'. Mildred Allen made the big mistake of 'enterteyn[ing]' Marshal Bestney in the street one winter night in 1628, 'not knowing' who he was. Bestney acted the part of a 'whoremonger' to lead her along, but marched her off to Bridewell as soon as he learned that they were heading for a glazier's house on Shoe Lane, 'w[hi]ch is reported to be a lewd house', he said later in court. Marshal Fitch was sitting in an alehouse five years later within earshot of Joan Holt and Elsie Child, who were chatting over drinks about their plans to swindle men to 'accuse them of incontinencie' and then take money from them as a 'composicion'. Holt and Child were standing in the Bridewell dock a day later, as the marshal told his story to the court.[110] We do not know if Fitch was working undercover that day, snooping around alehouses, hoping to pick up leads on the sly, though marshals were well known by others (and was

---

[109] BHC 8, fo. 313v; 7, fo. 309v; 8, fo. 60; GL MS 12806/2, fo. 279v; LMA Rep. 13ii, fo. 229; BHC 1, fo. 88.
[110] BHC 8, fo. 281; 7, fos. 54, 100, 317; 3, fo. 419v.

the matron who brought in Bloke also working undercover?). But there are some undercover operations in the sources, like one to round up nightwalkers in Spring 1639 not long after a by-law was passed against women walking late. Fifteen nightwalkers were put in Bridewell by four Cheap constables on one busy night, and in most cases the constables told the same entrapment story, rounding it off with a line on how they would have been led to a 'private' bed, room, house, or place if they had not revealed their true identities.[111] Netting fifteen nightwalkers in a single manoeuver was hardly typical, but similar tactics were followed over and over again. And once in court officers continued cases by giving evidence and using their knowledge of London and its low-life to clinch prosecutions. Some of them also brought prosecutions in their own name and on behalf of the public interest against vagrants, nightwalkers, or other offenders, and like Dogberry's watchmen, they were the named accusers in the record.

## Prosecutions

A tiny fraction of Bridewell committals were made by household heads and other individuals, including a handful of victims. All the rest came from some sort of public officer or official in the main. Again, in most of these cases there were no clear victims except for the public peace of the city. Vagrants, to take one example, went through the Bridewell process from arrest to punishment without ever coming into contact with anyone apart from the officers who arrested them, asked them questions about what they were up to, and brought them to court where, if it came to a case, the only people in the courtroom might have been the bench, a beadle, a clerk, and perhaps the officer who made the arrest. And if any Bridewell case was switched to a higher court, officers could still continue the action against the accused, as when the 'counterfeite incorrigible rogue' Thomas Phillips was locked up in Bridewell for the third time in 1622, and handed 'over to the marshall to present the law against him for fellonie'.[112] The same process of arrest and prosecution is evident in most other victimless offences, and not just in the capital city. A few cases from quarter sessions in the London area will set the scene for what follows. A beadle was instructed to 'prosecute' Alice Priestman who in show stumbled and fell to the ground one day, 'and lefte a new born child' on the street. One marshalman was asked to take the lead and prosecute an adultery case. A constable turned up in court to 'prosecute bills of

[111] BHC 8, fo. 239v.   [112] BHC 6, fo. 266.

inditement' against a gang who jumped on him as he tried to arrest a suspect and wrestled him from his grip. While another constable 'prefered' an indictment against Henry Haynes for 'abusinge' him as he tried to do his duty.[113] The City waged law against its rogue and lax officers: one watch order, passed in 1643, warned wards to pick a pair of 'honest and able men' to oversee watches each night, and to follow through on any negligence by going to court to 'give evidence and prosecute the law by way of indightment at the sessions of the peace' (1643); these 'overseers' were promised half of each fine six months later.[114]

Not enough notice has been taken so far of how parishes, wards, and guilds prepared and prosecuted cases. Wardmotes, made up of men 'of good name and fame', rooted out vice and disorder deep into the seventeenth century, and their arrows were often aimed at sexual offences by 'comen woemen of their bodyes or harlottes' and 'whoremongers', along with eating and drinking places of 'comon resort' where such 'sorts' gathered.[115] 'Speciall sessyons' for 'harlots, bawds, and scolds' and other 'abuses and dysorders' were held in the sixteenth century, more often than not to cope with a backlog of cases. Some 'sessyons' were set up for named wards, 'Faringdon Extra' more than any other, needless to say.[116] A clause in Bridewell's 1579 orders called for monthly wardmotes for the year to come and quarterly meetings after that at a time when the unwelcome side-effects of growth were felt by all: vestries were asked to meet a week before wardmotes convened to prepare cases for the inquest. St Margaret Lothbury vestry was quick off the mark, drawing up presentments six months after the order was put in force.[117] Deputies had leading roles in wardmotes: running hearings and preparing cases for the Court of Aldermen if pests did not heed ward warnings. The

---

[113] LMA CQSF 104/48, 121/2; MJ/SBR/5, fo. 49; MJ/SR/806/145; CQSF 91/18.
[114] LMA Jour. 40, fos. 55v, 75–6.
[115] LMA Rep. 19, fo. 503; Letterbook K, fo. 63v. On this longer history of wards see Caroline M. Barron, 'Lay solidarities: the wards of Medieval London', in P. Stafford, J. Nelson, and J. Martindale, eds., *Law, Laity, and Solidarities: Essays in Honour of Susan Reynolds* (Manchester, 2001), pp. 218–33; Barron, *London in the Later Middle Ages*, pp. 121–7; Rexroth, *Deviance and Power*, pp. 48–50 and chap. 5.
[116] LMA Reps. 11, fos. 11, 42; 12, fos. 173v, 200, 218v, 273v, 524; 14, fo. 509; 15, fo. 30. Special sessions for 'harlots, bawds, and scolds' were held until late in the sixteenth century from the evidence of the Repertories of the Court of Aldermen. See also Martin Ingram, 'Regulating sex in pre-Reformation London', in G. W. Bernard and S. J. Gunn, eds., *Authority and Consent in Tudor England: Essays Presented to C. S. L. Davies* (Aldershot, 2002), pp. 79–95.
[117] LMA Jour. 20, fo. 501 (any matter outside the wardmotes' 'power' but within the 'power' of Bridewell's court was to be taken there by the wardmote: Jour. 20, fo. 501v); GL MS 4352/1, fo. 36. See also GL MS 2968/2, fo. 38v; LMA Reps. 21, fo. 132; 22, fo. 344v.

'comen trobler and dysquyeter' of his neighbours, 'evil' James Langerake, at long last ended up before aldermen after 'gentle admonycon' 'meny tymes' given had had no effect on him: he is neither 'sorye' nor 'reformed', ward leaders jadedly reflected.[118] Wardmotes had a range of responsibilities under the rubric of public regulation that were often updated to meet new challenges: making sure that streets were kept spick and span and well lit after dark, or checking prices and weights and measures. They had authority to act against offenders ranging from odious traitors to loudmouths or thoughtless people letting animals loose on streets.[119] Wards took many cases to the Court of Aldermen, Bridewell, and City Quarter Sessions: cases involving subversive speech, work-shy layabouts, unruly servants, 'comon barrators', drunks, 'evyll rule', 'whoredom', 'harlotts', bawds, boarding migrants, and high-priced candles, amongst other things.[120] Wardmotes warned and fined in the main, though as we have seen more serious and difficult cases could be passed to aldermen. The wardmote presentment process was streamlined in 1652, and the most pressing matter was a better way to 'put' presentments 'into a [smoother] course of prosecution'. Robert Guppey (barber-surgeon) was given the job of 'followe[ing] and prosecute[ing] to tryall' all offenders whose names appeared on wardmote lists, and pocketed any resulting fines. Business must have been brisk two years later when John Elliott (merchant taylor) teamed up with him to 'prosecute' pests on wardmote lists 'to tryall', and the pair were busy bringing prosecutions in the next year. One parish picked a prosecutor to take offences brought to wardmotes to City's courts in 1657.[121]

There were well-trodden public routes through prosecution processes all the way up to a guilty verdict. Guilds also took 'forrein' buyers and sellers before aldermen and the number of these cases climbed over time. The Goldsmiths took matters into their own hands in 1620 and picked two men to track down meddling 'strangers', not the first time they turned to a 'servant' to prosecute on their behalf. Thomas Edwards prosecuted another company curse, 'gold end women', who 'hawked' all day long on the streets, and he took seven hawkers to court in 1632 with warrants from the mayor and magistrates. The City offered 'one halfe' of each

---

[118] LMA Rep. 13ii, fo. 323v.
[119] LMA Letterbooks K, fo. 63v; R, fo. 58v; GL MS 2050/1, fo. 158. Wardmotes are discussed in Archer, *Pursuit of Stability*, chaps 3 and 6; Beattie, *Policing and Punishment*, chaps 2–3.
[120] LMA Reps. 11, fos. 164, 329; 12, fos. 51v-2; 13ii, fo. 369; 14, fo. 250; 15, fos. 303v, 516v; 16, fo. 441; 17, fo. 21; 19, fos. 39, 59; 20, fo. 139; 23, fo. 482v; CQSF 113/2, 113/69, 113/75; GL MSS 3018/1, fos. 9, 66v; 9680, fo. 80; 4992/1, fo. 37.
[121] LMA Reps. 61, fo. 36; 62, fo. 51; 63, fos. 100v, 246, 247v; GL MS 1431/2, fo. 249.

'forfeiture' to 'prosecutors of offenders' in the next decade as a spur to stop the swarms of street-sellers.[122] Informers also hounded 'strangers' working in 'handicrafts' without a guild's blessing, as we have already noticed. The City helped out, hiring informers to go deep into the labyrinthine suburbs. Samuel Pordage (grocer and future marshal) got rich rewards 'for his diligent and honest service in the discoverye and prosecuting malefactors of all sortes to his great cost' in 1619. Other City moles prosecuted sabbath-day breaches or 'sutes by the waye of information' to stop greedy landlords 'devyding' houses, for example.[123]

If records are accurate, parishes spent more time and money prosecuting inmates and their landlords than any other offenders. One wrote down its three options for prosecution in 1637: it could take the case to a justice, the Mayor's Court, or Star Chamber.[124] St James Garlickhithe 'treated with an informer' to weed out inmates in 1651. Another parish forked out £2 to hire people to prosecute 'inmates [for] ye yeare'. And one other chose 'honest and able' men to take landlords to court at its own cost. St Benet Paul's Wharf vestry wanted to set an example by prosecuting ten 'bad' landlords at each sessions in 1663. St Botolph Billingsgate pledged that it would prosecute inmates and landlords 'from sessions to sessions' until they turned over new leaves or left London for good.[125] Other vestry actions triggered prosecutions; warned landlords to get rid of sponging inmates by 'faire meanes' or else face court; or looked for a 'course' to act against inmates, sometimes with the help of legal counsel.[126] Prosecution was not the only option. Parishes also made 'landlords of alleys' sign recognizances to make sure that no lodgers would seek hand-outs or beg on streets.[127] Westminster vestries waged law against builders of cottages on wasteland, people digging up gravel on the 'comon', thieves who stole church plate, hard-up inmates, lax constables, troublemakers at funerals, churchwardens who cooked the books, and other offences.[128] The prosecuting parish often crops up in churchwardens' accounts that list costs for warrants, recognizances, expert legal guidance, going to court, and sending delegates to courts or to building commissioners. Costs could run quite high: St Bartholomew-by-the-Exchange

[122] GCL company minute books P2, fos. 224v, 227v; O3, fo. 438; R2, fo. 87v; LMA Jour. 40, fos. 189v-90. See also GL MS 4655/1, fo. 57; GCL company minute books O2, fo. 255; Q, fos. 14v-16, 69; S1, fo. 191.
[123] LMA Reps. 34, fo. 131; 33, fos. 321, 328; 23, fo. 128. [124] GL MS 3908/1, fo. 62.
[125] GL MSS 4813/1, fo. 93; 1431/2, fo. 165; 4352/1, fo. 89; 877/1, fo. 214; 943/1, fo. 61; 4352/1, fo. 79.
[126] GL MSS 959/1, fo. 221; 818/1, fo. 150v; 819/1, fo. 69; 1431/2, fo. 89; 3570/2, fo. 160; 3908/1, fo. 95v; 978/1, fo. 71; 4216/1, fo. 121; 4813/1, fo. 78; 3570/2, fo. 67; 4352/1, fo. 92.
[127] LMA Reps. 17, fos. 427v-8, 432, 444, 446, 448, 452v; 18, fo. 7.
[128] WAC F2002, fos. 164, 280, 306; F2003, fos. 22, 136, 213, 314; E2416, fo. 279.

spent £1 6s when it took action to close down 'Millards Howse at the Cock'.[129]

Without victims the onus to prosecute fell on parishes and children were once again in the spotlight, pulling on purse-strings. Parish heads called at both Bridewell and Newgate to grill women about children left somewhere 'privily'. And if parents did come to light, the next cost was often for warrants and/or indictments to prosecute them or fix financial agreements for the upkeep of the child.[130] Parishes also went to court for warrants to get rid of wandering pregnant women before they gave birth. Others were prosecuted for taking pregnant women into their houses to hush up births, or for leading pregnant women into parishes.[131] The sudden appearance of an abandoned child was awful news for cash-strapped parishes, learning fathers' names was the key to this financial pickle. The next step to get warrants and indictments soon followed if fathers did not agree to pay towards the upkeep of their child.[132]

These custodial/paternity cases came before courts on a regular basis, and could drag on and drain finances. Money matters were not the only concern, however, morals also mattered in a case when St Martin Orgar still prosecuted the mother of a dead 'bastard child' at quarter sessions.[133] Parishes went to law about noise, violence, dirt, rubbish, and other troubles that almost always crop up when living space is at a premium. They took neighbourly tiffs all the way to court, as well as domestic spats, 'disorderly' houses, unlicensed alehouses, and lackadaisical people who treated plague rules carelessly. A parish paid for a warrant 'for an old woman supposed to be deade'. Others prosecuted women drying clothes in the churchyard, offensive libellers, 'coffeewomen', forgers of fake licences, and fiddlers playing on streets.[134] Religion was the core of parish

---

[129] GL MS 4383/1, fo. 422. See also GL MSS 6552/1, fo. 248; 3146/1, fo. 88v; 4524/1, fo. 322; 878/1, fos. 57v, 361; 577/1, fo. 67; 5714/1, fo. 105v; 4241/1, fo. 281; 4180/1, fo. 217v; 818/1, fos. 88v, 154, 187v; 4457/2, fos. 212, 258; 7673/1, fo. 89; 4071/2, fo. 65v; 2088/1, 1629–30, 1639–40; 593/4, 1640–1; 1432/4, 1638–9; 959/1, fos. 156v, 221; 662/1, fos. 40v, 106v, 142.

[130] For example, GL MSS 6552/1, fo. 72v; 3146/1, fo. 112v; 4383/1, fo. 304; 1176/1, 1603; 4385/1, fo. 106v; 590/1, fo. 241; 1046/1, fos. 38, 139v; 5090/2, fo. 177; 6574, fo. 176; 3907/1, 1651; 2593/1, 1621, fo. 6; 951/1, fo. 102; 4071/2, fo. 199; 2895/2, 1637–8; 593/4, 1640–1; 4570/2, fo. 317; 959/1, fo. 151v; 4051/1, fo. 53; 4409/2, 1650–1; 1303/1, 1628–9.

[131] See above, pp. 55–60.

[132] For example, GL MSS 2968/2, fo. 28v; 942/1, fo. 158v; 878/1, fo. 293; 5090/2, fo. 260; 5714/1, fos. 88–9v; 5018/1, fo. 41v; 1124/1, fo. 211; 2088/1, 1628–9; 1002/1, fo. 515v; 1432/3, fo. 164; 818/1, fos. 20, 24; 3146/1, fo. 123; 4385/1, fo. 134; 3556/1, fo. 155v.

[133] GL MS 959/1, fo. 215.

[134] GL MSS 1432/4, 1666–7; 3146/1, fos. 19, 89v; 4524/1, fo. 218v; 4423/1, fo. 187v; 4180/1, fo. 192; 818/1, fos. 129, 139v; 2088/1, 1642–3; 878/1, fo. 361; 5714/1, fo. 127; 4524/1, fos 58, 137v; 6836, fo. 106; 1432/4, 1666–7; 4457/2, fo. 213.

life, and Sunday work and drinking were always sore points. Sunday tipplers, like Marie Sollaway of St Ethelburga Bishopgate, only made matters worse if they turned up at church drunk, unable to string a single sentence together.[135] Parishes also prosecuted 'papists and recusants' who turned their backs on the true faith. One took legal action against its curate who refused to read 'an order from the Lords of ye Parliament' in 1642 (not the only time that ministers found themselves on the end of prosecutions from their own parishioners). Another took 'brownists' to City quarter sessions. St Mary Magdalene Milk Street dragged a few 'ranters' to court, and St Mary Aldermanbury spent twelve shillings to put a quaker on trial 'for working in ye church' in 1660. Other parishes prosecuted people who did not pay tithes on time. And if secular courts were not the best place to take a case, parishes could also turn to church courts to get wayward parishioners to toe the line.[136]

Parishes and guilds also took thieves to court. St Botolph-without-Bishopgate followed a thief who swiped lead from the vestry house all the way to the noose at the end of the line: first filing 'an action of felony' (eightpence), paying an officer to take the thief 'before a justis to be examyned' (twelvepence), covering the costs to draw up a recognizance and indictment (sixteenpence), and hiring 'the carr when the execution was done upon hym who stole the leade' (sixpence).[137] Parishes also spent money on warrants to search 'theefes howses', and there were cases when people made off with parish property: service books, bells, or lead from a porch or roof.[138] Warrants commonly cost somewhere between one and three shillings to search suspected places and make arrests, or to send someone suspicious to a lock-up, though a recognizance was sometimes all that was needed to put an end to the matter.[139] Parishes also spent money to stop cases erupting into full-blown trials. Having spent several shillings on a warrant and indictment for Mr Talboyes in 1637, St Margaret New Fish Street fixed a meeting

---

[135] GL MSS 4241/1, fo. 275; 878/1, fo. 87v; 9080/4, 1654; 9080/7, 1658; 4423/1, fo. 143.
[136] GL MSS 5090/2, fo. 261v; 4180/2, fo. 173v; 4071/2, fo. 140; 9237, fo. 87; 2596/1, fo. 124; 3556/2, 1660 (catholics and radicals); 942/1, fo. 119; 3146/1, fo. 36 (tithes); 4524/1, fo. 243v; 2593/1, 1606–7; 5090/2, fo. 13; 7673/1, fo. 106; 2088/1, 1632–3; 4241/1, fo. 357; 2895/2, 1638–9; 1016/1, fo. 37; 645/1, fo. 92; 2968/1, fo. 515; 4180/1, fo. 196v; WAC E2416, fo. 39; E12/1620; E15/1626; E18/1632 (church courts).
[137] GL MS 4524/1, fo. 2v.
[138] GL MSS 9235/2, fo. 168; 3146/1, fo. 15v; 4524/1, fo. 73v; 593/2, fo. 144v.
[139] GL MSS 2968/1, fo. 514; 4241/1, fo. 186; 4956/2, fo. 346v; 9235/1, fo. 240; 9235/2, fo. 466v; 2593/1, 1605–6, 1610; 951/1, fo. 173; 590/1, fo 208; 5090/2, fo. 246v; 5714/1, fo. 54; 4180/2, fo. 26; 2596/2, fo. 90 (search or arrest); GL MSS 6552/1, fo. 131; 3146/1, fos. 77, 113; 878/1, fo. 150v; 4241/1, fo. 370; 3907/1, 1616–17, 1619–20; 4051/1, fo. 131 (committals); GL MSS 1176/1, 1655; 590/1, fo. 100v; 9235/1, fos 5–5v; 959/1, fo. 157 (recognizances).

with him at 'The Sonn' to smooth things over, spending 5/8d on food and drink, but he did not turn up, so the choice on the table was whether to go ahead with the case or not.[140] Nor did costs always end with warrants and indictments. Legal counsel was needed in tricky cases,[141] and parish purses were also opened on the day of the trial for food and drink for parish officials going to court and any witnesses who went along with them. St Mary Aldermary spent twenty-one shillings 'for a dynner when Mr Watson was indicted' in 1618. Another parish spent 18/6d on witnesses at the White Lion and after at the Sun Tavern one court day in 1658. Holy Trinity the Less treated witnesses to 'a morninges draught' when they went to The Old Bailey for Mary Hobbert's trial in 1659 (4/6d). Other parishes were more stingy. St Katherine Coleman Street spent only 1/6d on witnesses at the trial of a 'madman' in 1659.[142] Witnesses were also compensated for losing a day's work or more. A carpenter was given two shillings by St Lawrence Jewry after he 'lost a dayes worke and halfe' by witnessing on its side against Mary Cottrell. While three witnesses received 7/8d for three days 'dynner' and 'for three dayes and a halfe worke' when they gave evidence 'agaynst the theefes' for St Botolph Aldgate.[143]

The scale and scope of public prosecution grew with London. An account of prosecution from public/petty crime angles invalidates nothing written so far about prosecuting felony. But it does give us more complicated impressions of the balance between prosecuting all forms of crime. It is no longer possible to see the early modern period as a gap between the late-medieval and modern periods when public prosecution was the rule of thumb.[144] Public prosecution there was in the sixteenth and seventeenth centuries, and plenty of it. And one last background for the boom in public prosecution is the amount of public information and knowledge about crime at this time. Another aspect of policing that has been taken too lightly to date, and is the subject of the next chapter.

---

[140] GL MS 1176/1, 1637.
[141] For example, GL MSS 951/1, fo. 102; 4385/1, fo. 135v; 5909/2, fo. 256; 4071/2, fo. 151v; 2088/1, 1584–5, 1640–1; 1002/1, fo. 515; 4180/1, fo. 200; 4180/2, fo. 164; 4409/1, fo. 261; 593/2, fo. 121v; 818/1, fo. 191v. St Michael le Querne paid a 'councellor' to plead at quarter sessions in 1659–60: GL MS 2895/2, 1659–60.
[142] GL MSS 6574, fo. 105; 1432/4, 1658–9; 4385/1, fo. 284v; 1124/1, fo. 189v. See also GL MS 1568, fo. 480 (dinner costing 4/10d).
[143] GL MSS 2593/1, 1608; 9235/2, fo. 129v.
[144] Cf. Klerman, 'Settlement and the decline of private prosecution', 5–8.

## 11  Policing: knowledge

### Active archives

We count crime endlessly, unpicking patterns on neat graphs, but hardly ever ask what the people who produced these records did with them four centuries ago. They did not build archives for us. What is now our raw data was an active archive back then. Records were retrieved, consulted, and put to use again and again to help make policy or to gather evidence for court cases. Archives were working places, one reason why London's leaders liked to keep records safe and close at hand. When he was bringing Stow's *Survey* up to date, John Strype found it 'very difficult to obtain' access to the City's archives, and it was only with the help of 'friends of quality and good account' that he was able to sit down one day in the bookhouse with a clerk hovering close by to copy 'very considerable notes' from them. Not just anyone could drop in to read records, and magistrates were very concerned that Strype might 'alter or prejudice the custom' of the city.[1] Then as now records were political, conveying policy explanations that were open to dispute or twisting in the wrong hands.

Records were brought along to the City courts if guidance was needed on a prickly matter, or if it was necessary to trace the development of a particular policy over time. Aldermen liked to have them at their fingertips, or in 'a place att hand for storage of them'.[2] Quite apart from the secrecy of their debates, this convenience explains why the passage of records to and from the Guildhall bookhouse was closely screened, not even the remembrancer could take 'books of the cittie' home with him in 1571 to speed up 'kalendar[ing]' them. Mayor's Court officials were given authority to 'commit' people who strayed into the bookhouse without consent to a 'compter'.[3] Thinking of 'bookes and records' as active archives also explains why the aldermen's patience snapped when they found out that the journals and repertories of City government were

---

[1] Strype, *Survey* vol. I, pp. i, iii, v.   [2] LMA Rep. 34, fos. 348v-9, 522.
[3] LMA Rep. 17, fo. 177; Letterbook Y, fo. 271v.

jumbled up in a 'disorderly' mess in 1633. 'Oftentymes' when clerks went to get books and records from shelves they found them missing and information was 'not to be had upon occasion of use thereof'.[4] 'Use' is a keyword here, letting us know that magistrates in sixteenth- and seventeenth-century London worked with numbers, case-histories, and information that streamed into the Guildhall from parishes, wards, or guilds across the length and breadth of the city.

Bridewell also had active archives that were off limits to anyone outside the governors' circles. The clerk brought the books to court and took notes of daily business that were 'openly read' at the next meeting.[5] These are the records that we use today, and they were used day in and day out by the court to pin crimes on people and check anything from the date of a lease to the amount of bread in the sick diet. Nor was this data chase limited to Bridewell's own records. Records from other courts were sometimes consulted to seal cases or to check on one of Bridewell's entitlements to land, for example. Different courts swapped information about crimes and criminals, and there was always a core group of Bridewell governors who were aldermen, justices, deputies, and guild officers, who were a natural source of information linking Bridewell to the Guildhall, the Old Bailey, and wards, parishes, and guilds. Knowledge in Bridewell's books was commonly conveyed through languages of recidivism; suspects were 'ancient', 'comon', 'known', 'notorious', or 'old' offenders. Data accumulated each time a recidivist turned up in court, as more came to light about offenders and the circumstances of their offending. One form of knowledge was jotted down on paper; another was lodged in the minds of magistrates and officers who encountered and experienced crime in courts and on streets all the time. And this sort of first-hand knowledge was even more extensive when recidivism rates soared at Bridewell after 1620. We have not yet fully grasped the extent to which knowledge of crimes and criminals helped to contain disorder at this time. This sort of information was used over and over again to capture, prosecute, and even deter offenders. A starting-point for containing crime was to know about the habits and haunts of offenders, and to make this knowledge count for policing and prosecution. We will see later on how tip-offs about seedy alehouses, cutpurse rings, or alleys with bad names helped to crack court cases.

---

[4] LMA Rep. 47, fos. 292-2v, 303. See also LMA Rep. 20, fos. 31, 133v. Cf. State archives in Sean Kelsey, *Inventing a Republic: the Political Culture of the English Commonwealth, 1649–1653* (Stanford, CA, 1997), pp. 14–17.
[5] BHC 7, fo. 243v.

We nearly always evaluate policing in the sixteenth and seventeenth centuries through contemporary characterizations or comments on the quality of constables or their office, or by counting with the help of carefully prepared tables of arrests or prosecutions. Missing here are the active archives that supplied magistrates and courts with updated information about problems. Their effectiveness cannot be measured with mathematical precision, although their existence and value can be described. Much of this activity was ironically off the record and we catch it in snatches when someone mentions their usefulness in achieving something. There are conversations that we will never know about, meetings in hidden 'corners' between officers and moles when important information was passed on, and records of surveillance, quantification, and planning that are now lost for good. Information grapevines in early modern London existed outside the courtroom and committal process and are rarely recorded on paper, although it is still possible to give some impressions of them and the uses to which they were put. This is the simple aim of this chapter. But before turning directly to crime control, I want to spend some time describing the broader cultures and systems of data gathering that expanded in these times of growth and linked aldermen in the Guildhall to the smallest vestry room. This will establish the larger climate of surveillance in which officials at all levels were encouraged to improve record management and information gathering, and to fine tune their numerical skills. Like weaving biographies, the larger aim was to understand the roots of problems and their sizes and shapes, and the common thread was always knowledge.

### Numbering Londoners

London's rulers once believed that the names of all vagrants rambling through their city could be written down in a single book. Aldermen 'provyded' a book in 1540 'wheryn the names of all vagabonds' and all laws 'made ageynsts them' were to be written down. This 'boke of recorde' was put in the safe keeping of the clerk of their court.[6] What became of it is not known, but the clerk might well have given up in despair, quickly realizing that it was a pipe-dream to think that the full extent of vagrancy could be captured between the same covers. A century later any headcount of vagrants or lodgers could have only been done on a ward-by-ward basis with returns reaching the Guildhall to be added up for grand totals. The scale and scope of counting soared after 1540. But

---

[6] LMA Rep. 10, fo. 287. City government established 'a separate register for the punishment of sturdy beggars' in the late fourteenth century: see Rexroth, *Deviance and Power*, p. 277.

this was not the first time that information was collated and people – good or bad – were counted for government purposes. The 'Domesday Book', after all, was only the most spectacular case of counting before 1500. But the amount of counting from the mid-sixteenth century on is striking. Paupers were added up in wards and parishes, and not many weeks went by without a 'search' or 'survey' to map and gauge the scale of problems, like the glut of 'alien' artisans or 'excessive number' of alehouses. And luckily for London, the ability to count and understand figures was also growing at the same time.[7] Widespread quantification was another response to speedy growth, and one that became more established through constant duplication.

Pipelines stretched from the Guildhall to all of the wards and parishes, and information flowed in both directions. They also went west to Whitehall, from where regular requests for information about the state of the city shaped Crown policies that were already affected by proximity to London. A letter from the Privy Council often sent aldermen scampering to their wards to start house-to-house inquiries for hidden catholics, for example, or, as in 1637, to produce a 'perfect and exact survey' of houses that had been built or divided since 1630.[8] It is certainly possible to talk about information cultures and systems at this time, if by that we mean a central government that processed data that was collected from metropolitan, municipal, or regional authorities to help run the state. Peter Burke calls the early modern state a 'paper state', meaning that for the first time 'the regular and systematic collection of information' became part and parcel of day-to-day administration of national affairs.[9] Anthony Giddens argues that the Crown only collected tax-lists and demographic data at this time, but it is clear that the Crown and City organized information about people and problems for crime-control, amongst other things, and that they worked hand in hand to gather and apply this data.[10] Recent work on the points of contact between the state

---

[7] Deborah E. Harkness, *The Jewel House: Elizabethan London and the Scientific Revolution* (New Haven, CT, and London, 2007), chap. 3; Keith Thomas, 'Numeracy in early modern England', *Transactions of the Royal Historical Society*, 5th series, 37 (1987), 103–32; David Glimp and Michelle R. Warren, eds., *Arts of Calculation: Numerical Thought in Early Modern Europe* (Basingstoke, 2004).

[8] LMA Remembrancia Book 8, fos 102-2v.

[9] Peter Burke, *A Social History of Knowledge From Gutenberg to Diderot* (Oxford, 2000), pp. 117–19 (quoting p. 118).

[10] Cf. Anthony Giddens, *The Nation-State and Violence: Volume Two of a Contemporary Critique of Historical Materialism* (Berkeley and Los Angeles, CA, 1985), pp. 48–9, 179. In *When Information Came of Age: Technologies of Knowledge in the Age of Reason and Revolution, 1700–1850* (Oxford and New York, 2000), Daniel R. Headrick wrongly writes that 'what was new in the Age of Reason and Revolution was the idea that numbers could be used to analyze something other than money, such as population,

and localities zooms in on articles of inquiry sent out from Westminster to all corners of the land to shape social policies, the Poor Law above all else, which was quintessentially an act of collaboration between Westminster and each one of the country's 10,000 plus parishes to accomplish common aims.[11] It is difficult to disagree with Darnton when he writes that 'every age was an age of information' in 'its own way', and that the dissemination of information has always 'shaped events' from the first day that data was gathered and stored.[12] So, apart from new technological possibilities, there are few aspects of surveillance familiar today that were entirely absent four centuries ago.

London's leaders knew that the best way to start tackling troubles like rowdy alehouses was to count them first, to cut 'the multitude of them to a reasonable stint and proportion'. The privy council wrote to the City in 1634 to order a count of licensed alehouses inside twenty days, all 'distinguished' by place and parish, so that magistrates could get down to the job of waging law against unlicensed alehouse keepers who brushed laws aside. Information was sorted by name and address, and a note was made of any signed sureties or recognizances.[13] Royal ministers asked City magistrates to count all alehouses in their patch more often after 1630, and such 'searches' turned up twenty-four in Covent Garden (1639, mostly run by chandlers), 127 in Middlesex (1633), while 211 alehouses

health, and illness, nature, or even divine providence' (quoting p. 60). While in his 'The rise of the information state: the development of central state surveillance of the citizen in England, 1500–2000', *Journal of Historical Sociology*, 14 (2001), 175–97, Edward Higgs writes that 'when the central state attempted to record information on its subjects directly in the early modern period it was mainly for political or military purposes. Here one might include the oaths of allegiance and test oaths' (178). In Higgs, *The Information State in England: the Central Collection of Information on Citizens Since 1500* (Basingstoke, 2004), chap. 2 – 'State information gathering in early modern England' – begins promisingly with the statement that 'what surveillance of the population took place (and there was a lot of it in early modern England), took place at the level of locality' (quoting p. 35), but gives us little understanding of these processes at work, describing laws and powers in the main, albeit with a brief mention of Norwich's Census of the Poor (p. 41).

[11] Braddick, *State Formation*, chaps 3–4; Hindle, *State and Social Change*, chaps 5–6; Hindle, *On the Parish?*; Slack, *From Reformation to Improvement*, esp. chap. 3; Slack, *Poverty and Policy*, esp. chaps 6–7; Henrik Langeluddecke, 'Law and order in seventeenth-century England: the organization of local administration during the personal rule of Charles I', *Law and History Review*, 15 (1997), 49–76.

[12] Robert Darnton, 'An early information society: news and the media in eighteenth-century Paris', *American Historical Review* (2000), 1–35, quoting 1–2. Although some scholars still follow a Whig line of historical development, and locate the roots of today's information cultures in the 'Age of Reason' and enlightened despotism. See, for example, Headrick, *When Information Came of Age*, pp. 70, 217–18.

[13] APC 1613–14, p. 601; LMA Remembrancia Book 8, fo. 92.

were counted in the city and its liberties a little later on.[14] The 'multitude of alehouses' is 'increasing dayly' and they are now 'growen' 'dangerous and ruinous', Common Council was told in 1618, and so another count was set up. An earlier one in 1579 had been sparked by 'the excessive number and disorder of alehouses' that let in 'wicked people' and caused 'much thefte, pilferinge, and incontinent life', along with an 'increase of harlots and consequently bastards'.[15] The City did not need to be told to count alehouses (or anything else for that matter). Aldermen ordered wards to carry out weekly 'searche[s]' for alehouses in the 1550s, and similar counts took place all through the next 100 years to limit 'unnecessarye' alehouses by coming up with a 'fit' number of 'good standing' set down in 'true certificates', and to stamp out disorders that went on all night in some of them.[16] Some parishes kept 'books' of alehouses and updated lists or 'certificates' of their numbers.[17] Tobacco sellers were also counted along with 'bowlinge alleyes', 'dysinge houses', 'tabling houses', 'schooles of fence', and 'schooles of daunsinge'. Common Council sent round strict orders to the wards in 1602 for 'a verie perfecte and exacte certificate' of all alehouses, 'tablinge howses, bowlinge alleyes, brothell howses and all others knowne or suspected of ill resorte', where gamblers, gluttons, beer guzzlers, and other good-for-nothings committed 'vicious accons' all day long, wasting time and family budgets. The hope, as usual, was that counting and comprehending the size of the problem would lead to a 'speedie remedie', and that the details of names, addresses, 'condicons', and trades of tobacco sellers or alehouse keepers would be a first step towards a 'reformaccon'.[18]

Getting numerical descriptions/definitions of 'evils' like 'unnecessary' alehouses, the dimensions of which had been only faintly glimpsed before, was a vital start, and from now on City policies were grounded in some knowledge of geography and numbers. The nature and pace of growth was a subject of endless debate inside the Guildhall and vestry rooms, and it sometimes seemed mammoth and beyond counting. Growth was said to be 'excessive' or another description of panic proportions that made it seem hard to imagine, although London's parts and people continued to be counted. The size of the city and its population

---

[14] TNA SP16/420/4, 16/231/17, 16/250/22. See also TNA SP16/226/77, 16/244/11, 16/249/91.
[15] LMA Jours. 30, fo. 293; 20, fo. 502.
[16] For example, LMA Reps. 21 fo. 162; 22, fo. 134; Jours. 27, fo. 380; 28, fo. 323; 31, fos. 68, 324; 34, fo. 295; 35, fo. 343v; 36, fo. 137; 37, fo. 340; 38, fo. 228v; 39, fo. 193.
[17] GL MSS 4524/1, fo. 115; 2968/2, fo. 172.
[18] LMA Jours. 26, fo. 12v; 32, fo. 51v; 18, fo. 390v; 20, fo. 324; 28, fos. 228v, 323; 30, fo. 129.

spawned continuous speculation, and London was drawn, mapped, and counted like never before. Headcounts gave clear impressions of growth, although their prime purpose was often more specific, like keeping tabs on 'aliens' or listing household heads one-by-one for muster rolls or tax registers. But counts grew in number from the first bursts of growth. Beadles kept lists of 'the names and surnames of all howsholders' in 1540, and one of their duties (listed in the Articles of the Charter and Liberties) was to keep up-to-date registers of movement in and out of their wards.[19] Counts became more necessary when the new Poor Law placed added burdens on parishes (1598, 1601). A scrivener was paid 2/6d by St Benet Gracechurch in 1600 for 'going from howse to howse' and 'wrighting all the names iii tymes'. Payments were logged in columns in parish and precinct accounts for 'wrytinge a booke of all the inhabitants'; a note was also made of 'sojurners' in St Katherine-by-the-Tower in 1599. Books of names had been kept to manage parish affairs long before the Poor Law. The City had a scheme of compulsory contributions to poor rates up and running half a century before the state, and paupers were added up all the way through Elizabeth's long reign. But more of these 'booke[s] of inhabitants' were needed with the passage of the Poor Law.[20] A census was commonly conducted in times of trouble and was followed by policies rooted in first-hand experience and observation. The names of all 'aged, decayed, and impotent poore people' were put on paper in 1572. Aldermen warned wards to draw up 'surveys and registers' of the poor and to keep a record of 'things' that ought to go before wardmote meetings in 1579, just one outcome of a far-reaching fifty-three clause Common Council Act that tackled poverty, health matters, and crime on many fronts, and included an article requiring vestries to note down the 'defalts' of paupers in books.[21]

The day-to-day administration of poverty produced a small mountain of paper as it could only run smoothly if parishes kept good up-to-date registers of their 'penconers', ratepayers, and hand-outs. Parish accounts in London refer to 'the poores booke', 'the leager booke for the poore',

---

[19] GL MS 2050/1, fo. 54; LMA COL/AC/08/1, fo. 14.
[20] GL MSS 1568, fo. 380; 9080/3; 9680, fos 2, 10–14. See also GL MSS 4071/1, fo. 104; 4180/1, fo. 204v; 4385/1, fo. 101; 4457/2, fo. 178v; 7673/1, fo. 47; 4409/1, fo. 72; Archer, *Pursuit of Stability*, chap. 5.
[21] LMA Jour. 20, 15v; Rep. 19, fo. 502v; Jour. 20, fo. 501v. For counting see my 'Inhabitants', in Carole Rawcliffe and Richard Wilson, eds., *Norwich Since 1550* (2004), pp. 63–88 (text) and pp. 490–7 (footnotes), an essay given a new title without my knowledge, the original title gives a better sense of its subject: 'Numbering Norvicians: information, institutions, identities'; Pelling, *Common Lot*, p. 101; Burke, *Social History of Knowledge*, p. 117; Slack, *Poverty and Policy*, pp. 49–55; Slack, *From Reformation to Improvement*, p. 154.

'the collectors greate booke', 'the poores rowle', or the 'booke of assessm[en]t'. The records of St Botolph-without-Bishopgate mention 'eight bookes for the poore' in a single year.[22] 'Bookes of the poore' were used by parishes to check entitlements for hand-outs and to list the names of paupers who could and could not work. The precinct of St Katherine-by-the-Tower compiled a 'booke' of 'the numberinge of all the poore' who received hand-outs in 1603, after getting guidelines from the lord chief justice.[23] Constables and churchwardens went from house-to-house in parishes and precincts to 'view' or 'survey' the poor, and after the counting was complete they often headed for an alehouse to eat and drink at the parish's expense; a meal that might have a little ritual or symbolic meaning as a commemoration of worthy parish efforts to help its own. St Botolph-without-Bishopgate spent 9/3d at The White Hart 'when ye churchwardens and constables went to take ye poores names of ye parishe' in 1626. Another parish spent £2 2s 2d on the end-of-count feast.[24]

Names were collected for particular purposes almost routinely, but also rather more generally 'for the better preservacon' of peace and 'prevencion of future daungers', as when the City, after an elbow from the Crown, instructed wards to draw up a 'roll of the names, surnames, dwelling places, professions, and trades' of all inhabitants in 1605. Magistrates wanted to be able to locate people in precincts and asked that 'the place' of residence 'be especiallie noted by streete, lane, alley, and signe or other speciall note easiest to be knowne'.[25] While not quite a city-wide census on the lines of smaller Norwich, these ward and precinct counts and lists were substantial and convenient compilations of information for the aldermen's table when social policies were on the day's agenda. But the City also tracked growth by counting migrants and all the new buildings that were suddenly springing up both inside and outside the walls. It might seem unlikely that such rapid movement and change could be pinned down on paper, but this did not stop London's leaders from counting 'aliens', inmates, vagrants, or street-sellers. They asked wards to count 'straungers' almost as soon as they started to turn up in waves. Lists of the 'hole number of straungers' living in each ward were

---

[22] For example, GL MSS 4524/1, fo. 69; 6552/1, fo. 92v; 590/1, fo. 208; 878/1, fo. 326; 3146/1, fo. 123; 4524/1, fo. 253v; 2968/1, fo. 466v; 942/1, fo. 186v; 559/1, fo. 47; 4423/1, fo. 168; 4241/1 fo. 429; 4956/3, fo. 15v; 9235/1, fo. 125; 1002/1, fo. 310; 5714/1, fo. 190; 4071/2, fo. 89; 1432/4, 1657–8; 9680, fo. 21v; LMA Jours. 29, fo. 328; 33, fo. 219v; 39, fos 79, 186v, 295.
[23] GL MS 9680, fo. 12. See also TNA SP12/120/50; LMA Jour. 35, fo. 278; GL MS 12806/3, fo. 64v; WAC F2002, fos. 47, 266; F2003, fo. 97.
[24] GL MSS 4524/1, fo. 237v; 3146/1, fo. 53. See also WAC F2003, fos. 100, 116, 149, 205.
[25] LMA Jour. 27, fos. 1, 93v-4; Letterbook S, fos 60v-1; Jours. 18, fo. 234v; 37, fo. 330v; 39, fo. 136; GL MS 3556/1, fo. 184v.

the statistical side of campaigns to limit their movement after dark in 1545, and to ask them, 'in gentle maner', to hand over their weapons.[26]

Regular counts of London's 'straungers' followed not long after, as the number of migrants from overseas kept climbing, and it became quite typical to get information about their names, numbers, nationalities, addresses, jobs, and the length of time spent in the city.[27] These 'inquiries', 'inquisicions', or 'searches' were acts of discovery that were also motivated by sharp political concerns, real scares about scarce work, and scrimping and saving on costs. It was hoped that they would soften concerns stemming from wild exaggerations about locust flocks of 'aliens'. The Crown called for a count of 'aliens' and a careful account of their 'trade and manner of lyving' in 1583 after a libel zipped through London 'againste straungers' that singled out the harm caused by foreign 'handicrafts men' stealing jobs in already squeezed labour markets. The Crown asked for other polls of 'straungers', and some were triggered by Walsingham's fears that foreign agents had slipped into the country under cover of 'honest' hard-working artisans on the run from religious repression.[28] Other counts were linked with efforts to better policing, like longer watches or curfews. And as prejudices about 'aliens' mingled with concerns about making ends meet when wages slumped, 'straungers' were investigated as 'inmates', 'pester[ing]' the city 'with multytudes of familyes and howsehouldes' squashed into one house.[29] Counts and character commentaries went back and forth between the Guildhall and Whitehall: '2 faire books made of the straungers' were dropped off at Whitehall in 1579.[30] Parishes prepared 'bocke[s] for the strayngers names', and one gave Mr Johnson two shillings in 1585 'for gooinge ii

---

[26] LMA Letterbook K, fo. 141v.
[27] For example, LMA Letterbooks R, fo. 310; S, fos. 60v-1; V, fo. 232v; Reps. 12, fo. 497; 13ii, fo. 581; 14, fo. 520v; 15, fo. 487; 16, fo. 449v; 19, fo. 477v; 21, fo. 132v; Jours. 17, fo. 332; 18, fo. 361; 19, fo. 406v; 20, fos. 113, 497v; 21, fo. 426v; 22, fo. 411v; 23, fo. 308v; GCL company minute books O3, fo. 388; P2, fo. 277v. Lien Bich Luu has found twenty-four surviving 'stranger' 'returns' from 1561–93, nine alone from 1567–8 when 'popular unrest' against 'aliens' was rising: '"Taking the bread out of our mouths": xenophobia in early modern London', *Immigrants and Minorities*, 19 (2000), 1–22, esp. 7. There are two good later editions of 'straunger' surveys: Richard E. G. Kirk and Ernest F. Kirk eds., *Returns of Aliens Dwelling in the City and Suburbs of London During the Reign of Henry VIII to that of James I*, 4 vols., Huguenot Society of London Publications, 10 (Aberdeen, 1900–8); and Irene Scouloudi, ed., *Returns of Strangers in the Metropolis 1593, 1627, 1635, 1639: a Study of an Active Minority*, Huguenot Society of London Publications, 57 (1985).
[28] LMA Remembrancia Book 1, fo. 247; TNA SP12/27/19; 12/47/19; 12/47/72; 12/67/28; 12/84/1–2; 12/160/27; 12/195/81.
[29] LMA Rep. 21, fo. 135v.   [30] LMA Rep. 19, fos. 481, 485v.

dayes about wth constables to take the strangers names'.[31] Orders to count came from the City, Crown, and Bishop of London, and they produced packets of paper. So much paper that it piled up without decent organization or order, so a proposal for an Office of Register of Strangers was put together in 1590 to catalogue papers. Sir Walter Chute was a 'suitor' at the Privy Council table two decades later to get their blessing for 'a register of all strangers coming to the kingdom' that would be kept up to date by his staff, although there is no further mention of his bureau after the idea was referred to a committee.[32]

But counting still continued out in London's wards and parishes, the City government asked for 'perfect and exact' counts of strangers long after 1600. Wards were instructed to take 'speciall care both for the truth and certentie of yor certificate' when 'an exact note' of 'aliens and strangers' was needed in 1610 to sort out 'greate inconveniences' in job markets. Exactness was a rule of thumb. The Crown sent orders for 'exact searches and surveys' over and over again. Each ward picked three 'principal' men in 1618 to take 'a particular account' of the number and 'conditions' of all 'aliens' inside its borders. The value of counting for getting at least partial understandings of urban ulcers like in-migration was never once questioned. These data flows made it possible to imagine London in series of numbers. The Crown saw only good in knowing which ward had the largest pockets of 'aliens', and where exactly they clustered on London's edges.[33] Jobs quickly became a leading concern, and privy councillors said in a tone that sounds weary that they were 'daily importuned by pitiful petitions' from native workers in 1636, who said that they were no longer able to put food on the table for their hungry families because there was not enough work to go round. In 1623, as in many other years, the City picked 'fit and able persons' to walk through each parish 'to take [a] particular and exact note of [the] number, condition, and trades' of all strangers, and their children and servants.[34]

In fact magistrates requested counts of migrants from other counties more often than immigrants from other countries, but both symbolized growth and the harm it could bring. Wards and parishes were ordered to

---

[31] GL MSS 4524/1, fos. 58, 92; 2968/1, fo. 249v; 4071/1, fo. 71; 942/1, fo. 87v; 559/1, fo. 29; 4385/1, fo. 143; 5714/1, fo. 29; 1568, fo. 503; 1016/1, fo. 183; 2596/1, fo. 143.

[32] Luu, '"Taking the bread out of our mouths"', 8; APC 1613–14, p. 268.

[33] LMA Jours. 30, fo. 129; 26, fo. 293v; 28, fo. 155v; 29, fos. 5v, 50v; 30, fo. 381v; 38, fo. 223v; Rep. 53, fo. 133v; APC 1617–19, p. 249; LMA Remembrancia Book 7, fos. 117–18, 175–8; TNA SP14/99/22–4; 14/99/42–4; 14/99/46–7; 14/121/163; 16/41/96–7; 16/44/13; 16/294/11; 16/300/75; 16/303/36–42; 16/305/11i-xx; 16/305/104; CSPV 1636–9, p. 512.

[34] TNA PC2/45/30; APC 1621–3, p. 458; TNA PC2/45/126; GCL company minute book P2, fo. 277v.

count inmates and to keep records of their names and last living places, along with the names and addresses of their landlords and the length of time they had spent in the city. 'Good, perfite and suer serches, surveys and viewes' tried to keep track of inmates in numerical atlases showing their dispersal. Questions were often asked about numbers of newly arrived inmates. And like 'strangers', the number of house-to-house 'surveighs' of inmates grew with London.[35] Inmates were monitored in counts of 'new allies' and divided houses to stop the 'filling and pestering of houses' and rising living costs.[36] Wards and parishes kept 'bokes' and 'noates' of 'names and qualities' of lodgers and landlords. St Katherine-by-the-Tower had a 'perfect booke of entry' of people arriving from elsewhere. Portsoken kept 'a boke for out landlords' and 'inmates booke'. Other parishes kept 'a booke for the inmates' or 'books of inmats and alehouses'. John Turner earned a shilling 'going about' St Andrew-by-the-Wardrobe in 1637 to take down 'the names of those that live in devyded houses'. St Dunstan-in-the-West forked out 26/6d 'for a dinner' after a count of 'new buildings and inmats' in 1614.[37] Inmates were hounded out of 'haunts', and hospitals fixed leases to ban people who might fall on the parish one day. Beadles toured Bridewell precinct to list tenants who rented rooms. Weekly rotas for house-to-house 'enquiries' were drawn up in 1638, though they were later cut back to monthly rounds. Tenants who took no notice of warnings were kicked out of their homes and risked prosecution. The other hospitals also kept count of landlords and lodgers and warned tenants about costs, contagion, and crime, slipping in threats of prosecution when necessary.[38]

There are stories of sloppy counting and careless beadles who did not list inmates as asked, but they are few in number.[39] There were still attempts to count vagrants, but people on the move could easily slip through the net. The City tried to round up and count beggars in the 1550s,[40] but counting was mainly valued for shaping understanding of

---

[35] LMA Jours. 19, fo. 164v; 26, fo. 266v; 30, fo. 129; Reps. 16, fo. 40v; 17, fos. 131v, 153, 425, 452v; 18, fos. 7, 130v; 19. fo. 251; 20, fos. 294v, 323, 366v; 21, fo. 45; 30, fo. 41v.
[36] LMA Jours. 19, fos. 216v-17; 29, fo. 328. See also LMA Jours. 28, fo. 228; 29, fos. 20, 188; 30, fo. 369; 32, fo. 241v; 33, fo. 219v; 37, fos. 344v-5.
[37] GL MSS 9680, fo. 92; 9237, fos. 70v, 73; 1176/1, 1624; 4524/1, fo. 115; 2968/2, fo. 100v; 2088/1, 1637-8. See also GL MSS 4216/1, fo. 46; 3016/2, fo. 468; 9234/1, fo. 33v; 9680, fo. 32; 819/1, fo. 99; 4813/1, fo. 82; 4956/3, fo. 31v; 457/2, fo. 288; 5090/2, fo. 284v; 5714/1, fo. 105; 7673/1, fo. 100v; 4956/2, fo. 133v; 4180/1, fo. 190; WAC F2002, fo. 17; F2003, fos. 192-3.
[38] BHC 8, fo. 153v; 9, fo. 873; 5, fos. 300v, 318; 7, fo. 299; 8, fos. 107v, 174, 258; 9, fo. 219; GL MS 33013, fo. 22; SBHA Governors' Journals 3, fo. 120; 4, fo. 67; LMA H1/ST/A1/4, fo. 101.
[39] For example, WAC F2003, fos. 189, 203.    [40] LMA Jour. 16, fo. 100.

the dimensions of vagrancy. The 1598 Poor Law made another impact here, parish account books mention steps taken to note vagrants that year. St Dunstan-in-the-West spent eighteenpence on 'a paper booke' to list 'vagrant people'. St John Walbrook paid for 'a paper booke to regester the rogues that were punished'. While St Martin-in-the-Fields kept a book in the 'round house' to list all vagrants who were 'passed away', which was brought along to vestry meetings 'every three weekes'.[41] Bridewell's clerk kept a 'register of rogues and vagrants' in a book from 1612, something else that is now lost. Each marshal wrote down the name of every vagrant he brought to Bridewell in a 'book' from 1619 on, and his record was checked for reliability against a 'book' kept up to date by the porter of all vagrants coming in and out of Bridewell.[42] Bridewell worked with books and numbers all the time. The steward was told to 'kepe a trewe note [of] howe manye prisoners are in the house from tyme to tyme' in 1579. Apprentices were listed one-by-one in register books, and careful 'notes' were made 'of the names of the boyes and wenches' who were sent overseas to Virginia in 1619 and after. It became common practice to send 'certificates' of annual tallies of vagrants punished, apprentices currently in service, and inmates 'working' in the 'house' to the Court of Aldermen for its information.[43]

Street-sellers were also counted more often after 1600, as they troubled markets and morals in greater numbers. 'So many' fishwives, Common Council noted with some alarm in 1607, that they cannot 'bee aney longer endured'. Herbwives, milkwives, and fruitsellers were noted in lists, although fishwives were counted more than any other hawker (regular counts were also taken of street 'badgers, kidders, and drovers' over the border in Middlesex[44]). Counting was the only way to put City ceilings on numbers of street-sellers into effect. Bridewell's clerk kept a 'register' of women who 'carrie and crie fishe and other things'. These headcounts were not enough on their own, however, and information was also gathered on the names, addresses, 'behaviors, qualities, yeares, [and] condicions' of street-sellers.[45] Like the ebb and flow of vagrants, these counts gave impressions of the scale of movement across the city over

---

[41] GL MSS 2968/1, fo. 435; 577/1, fo. 9; WAC F2003, fos. 192–3. See also GL MSS 4383/1, fo. 33; 1568, fo. 374; 4457/2, fo. 52.
[42] LMA Reps. 31(1), fo. 26; 34, fos. 125v-7. See also LMA Rep. 40, fo. 71.
[43] BHC 3, fo. 422; 5, fo. 158v; 6, fo. 101; 7, fo. 299v; 8, fos. 236v, 375v; 9, fos. 29, 190, 486.
[44] LMA Jour. 27, fo. 205; MJ/SBR/1, fos. 63–5, 125–6, 131, 195–8, 258, 310–11, 381, 441, 521, 560–2, 608; MJ/SBR/2, fos. 17–18, 67, 121–2, 303–4, 413–14.
[45] LMA Jours. 26, fo. 19; 27, fo. 205; 28, fos. 250, 300v, 303v, 309; 29, fo. 187; 22, fo. 380; Rep. 30, fo. 175. A Westminster parish reported, in 1603, that 'we have . . . ii oyster wives or cryers of fishe': WAC F6039, fo. 3v.

time. Counting was almost a reflex reaction by now if something was amiss. 'Papist priests lurke[ing] in secret manner', jesuits, and 'seminaries' were also counted at regular intervals. Rewards were offered for a job well done.[46] Parishes appointed 'inquisitors' and 'viewers' to catch and count catholics. St Alban Wood Street picked seven 'viewers' to note down the name and address of all jesuits, priests, and their 'helpers' in a 'certificate' in 1591. Another parish made fortnightly lists of resident recusants. Middlesex Quarter Sessions also counted catholics in columns: twenty-two on one day in 1608 (fourteen men/eight women), and thirty-three on another day three years later (twenty-one men/twelve women).[47]

It was hoped that numbers would reveal and constrain at one and the same time, not leaving anything to guesswork. Nor were these counts one-off reckonings quickly stored somewhere and left to gather dust out of sight and mind. The presentation of information was handled in ways that made it always accessible in handy books. Registers covered most situations and contained information that was put to use again and again: parish registers, of course (kept from as long back as 1538), as well as registers of disease, disorder, taxpayers, and local officials, amongst other things. The City began to keep a register of brokers around 1600, to try and put a stop to receiving and pawning stolen goods. This registry, backed strongly by City Acts and royal decrees, was imagined on a grand scale, and Parliamentary bills were tabled in 1610 and again in 1614 to set up 'a registry of all bargains, contracts, and pawns made by suspected persons such as brokers', although both ended up in Parliament's wastebasket. Keeping track of brokers and their bargains created a pile of paperwork, however. A City Act in 1623 bound brokers to keep 'a true and perfect entry in writing in two sheets of paper or more if nede bee in the nature of a duplicate' of each 'bargaine, contract, or pawne' that crossed their palms, but its flaws were evident in 'continuall experience at Newgate', the Goldsmiths' company pointed out gloomily not long after.[48] Almost anything was counted at one time or another: names and numbers of catechumens, 'commemoracons', 'communicants',

---

[46] For example, LMA Jours. 26, fo. 316v; 29, fo. 188v; 31, fo. 295; 33, fo. 199; 34, fo. 251v; 39, fo. 363; Reps. 20, fo. 416; 35, fo. 114v; TNA SP12/192/35; 12/176/16; 12/206/60; 14/61/44; 16/229/31; APC 1619–21, p. 353; 1628–9, p. 253.

[47] GL MSS 1264/1, fo. 8; 1016/1, fo. 86; See also GL MSS 4165/1, fo. 85; 594/1, fo. 20; 4524/1, fo. 322; 2968/2, to. 340v; 4385/1, fo. 28v; LMA MJ/SBR/1, fos. 67, 256–7, 367, 439.

[48] G. R. Elton, *Policy and Police: the Enforcement of the Reformation in the Age of Thomas Cromwell* (Cambridge, 1972), pp. 259–60; SRPC (134), pp. 276–8; HOL MP 26-4-1610, 9-5-1614; LMA Jour. 32, fos. 224v-5; GCL company minute book Q2, fo. 162v. See also LMA Rep. 13ii, fo. 472v; GCL company minute book Q2, fos. 161, 163.

constables, freemen, jurymen, meal recipients, men of quality living in London outside term-time, mustermen, parish apprentices and orphans, plague victims (and officers running from the plague to the countryside), people taking the 'protestacon' oath, preachers, sailors, Scotsmen, taxpayers, and watchmen.[49] There are books on almost anything everywhere we look: books mapping 'parish bounds', 'bread bookes', 'colebookes', 'tithe books', a 'booke of wills', and even 'a booke to register persons for the king's evill'.[50] A stationer got in touch with aldermen in 1607 with an offer to keep 'a register booke' of all people without a service, though this was the proverbial needle in a haystack.[51] Bridewell, Middlesex House of Correction, and the compters all kept 'books'.[52] Churchwardens and scavengers kept 'books' of office.[53] And when plague ripped through parishes, weekly and monthly 'reporte[s] of the dead' were gathered in overall mortality tallies published in Bills.[54] So many books to write that it is no wonder that parishes spent largish sums each year to buy paper, pens, inks, quills, and wax.[55]

When not filling up their own books, parishes copied City by-laws into books that were always on hand if clarification was needed on some policy. St Dunstan-in-the-West spent 4/4d 'for a booke to enter the precepts' in 1598. Parishes paid a few pence for copies of precepts to paste or write into books; one spent sixpence 'for the bookes of orders of

---

[49] For example, GL MSS 4071/2, fo. 103v; 4241/1, fo. 25 (catechumens); 9235/2, fos. 454, 501 ('commemoracons'); 3146/1, fo. 151; 4457/2, fo. 155v; 1432/3, fo. 59; 959/1, fo. 156v; 524/1, fo. 20 (communicants); 2593/1, 1636, fo. 5; LMA Jours. 26, fo. 352; (constables); 18, fo. 327v. (freemen); 37, fo. 116 (jurymen); GL MS 2089/1, 1631–2 (meal recipients); LMA Jours. 37, fo. 32 (men of quality); 18, fo. 234v; 33, fo. 245v; TNA SP12/58/13–14; GL MSS 9680, fo. 10v; 1002/1, fo. 475; 2968/2, fo. 333; 5090/2, fo. 285v; 2895/1, fo. 253v; 4409/1, fo. 124 (mustermen); WAC F2002, fos. 47, 77, 206 (apprentices and orphans); LMA Jour. 33, fo. 130; Remembrancia Book 1, fo. 227; GL MSS 9237, fo. 70v; 2088/1, 1630–1 (plague); 6574/1, fo. 173v; 3556/2, 1642; 662/1, fo. 112 (oathtakers); 9235/2, fo. 353v; 942/1, fo. 110v; 4241/1, fo. 458; 645/1, fo. 30; 593/2, fo. 154; 662/1, fo. 159 (preachers); LMA Jours. 17, fo. 67; 18, fo. 120 (sailors); 38, fo. 267v (Scotsman); 26, fo. 170; 27, fo. 342; TNA SP16/310/17; GL MSS 4524/1, fo. 124; 2968/1, fo. 538v; 2968/2, fos. 295v-6; 5714/1, fo. 28v; 7673/2, fo. 9; 4241/1, fo. 336; (taxpayers); LMA Jour. 28, fo. 155v; Rep. 54, fos. 271v-2 (watchmen).
[50] GL MSS 1146/1, fo. 6v; 4956/3, fo. 123; 4457/2, fos. 128v, 162v, 200v, 360v; 3556/1, fo. 106; 4596/3, fo. 28; 1176/1, 1621; 1303/1, 1684.
[51] LMA Rep. 28, fo. 99.    [52] GL MSS 5090/2, fo. 214v; 9680, fo. 30v; 2596/2, fo. 25.
[53] GL MSS 4457/2, fo. 55; 4524/1, fo. 252v; 942/1, fo. 184v; 6386, fo. 134; 4457/2, fo. 360v; 5714/1, fo. 202; 5090/2, fo. 280; 7673/2, fo. 69v; 4214/1, fo. 215; WAC F2002, fo. 258.
[54] LMA Jour. 35, fo. 262; GL MSS 9235/2, fo. 413v; 6836, fo. 80v; 4180/1, fos. 44v, 48v, 53, 61, 69v, 73; 2968/1, fo. 272; J. C., Robertson, 'Reckoning with London: interpreting the *Bills of Mortality* before John Graunt', *Urban History*, 23 (1996), 325–50; Paul Slack, *The Impact of Plague in Tudor and Stuart England* (1985), pp. 145–51, 240–53.
[55] GL MSS 9235/1, fo. 151; 9235/2, fo. 34; 878/1, fo. 334v.

414    Control

the city' in 1588.[56] These books of orders covered all pressing concerns at one time or another: split tenements and inmates, poverty and paupers, vagrants and beggars, plague and fire, and recusants and sabbath-breakers.[57] The paper-chain between the Guildhall and wards and parishes reached far and wide, and copies of statutes can also be found lining vestry shelves. Parishes bought 'bookes of statutes' to follow the latest turns in policy at Westminster and Whitehall. There was a scramble for the sweeping new Poor Laws in 1598 and 1601. St Christopher-le-Stocks spent two shillings on 'a booke of the last statutes and acts of Parliamente' in 1601. Parishes also bought copies of the Act 'touching bastards' (1624), for example, and 'the act of marriage' (1653).[58] But poverty produced more paper than any other single thing. One parish spent twelvepence on 'the booke of 4 statuts for ye poore' in 1624–5.[59] Others paid for a 'booke of orders' when dearth or plague loomed over the horizon.[60]

Parishes also sought information about particular people, property, legal cases, welfare measures, or wills. They paid fees to look through Exchequer, Chancery, and Court of Augmentation books, hiring boats to go to Whitehall, or to sail east to look at royal records stored in the Tower. St Dunstan-in-the-West paid twenty-three shillings to search and copy 'records of the Tower' in 1630. Central government picked up substantial sums when parishes copied bills and orders that had a direct bearing on their current concerns.[61] There was also a fee to hunt through records in the Guildhall 'bookhouse'. Hospitals also let parishes check charters, leases, tithes, and building plans when they had good reason to do so. St Benet Gracechurch sent someone to read through the Court of Aldermen repertories to see what was exactly said in an order for

---

[56] GL MSS 2968/1, fo. 425; 5090/2, fo. 85v.
[57] GL MSS 878/1, fo. 246; 6836, fo. 61; 2088/1, 1599–1600; 4596/2, fo. 198v; 662/1, fo. 94v (split tenements/inmates); 6836, fo. 63v; 4241/1, fo. 161v; 645/1, fo. 170; 4956/2, fo. 186v; 4570/2, fo. 183; 2968/1, fo. 443; 3016/1, fo. 108 (paupers); 2596/2, fo. 57; 2968/2, fo. 356v; 3570/1, fo. 2; 1431/2, fo. 98 (vagrants/beggars); 3146/1, fo. 43v; 878/1, fo. 293; 6836, fo. 82; 2596/1, fo. 192; 3570/1, fo. 29v (recusants/sabbath-breakers); 2968/2, fo. 246v; 942/1, fo. 79v; 1002/1, fo. 520; 3016/1, fo. 110; 943/1, fo. 52v; 4415/1, fo.9 (plague/fire).
[58] GL MSS 4524/1, fo. 112v; 942/1, fo. 164v; 4423/1, fo. 192; 951/1, fo. 21; 4385/1, fo. 110v; 5090/2, fo. 174; 4241/1, fo. 199; 2596/1, fo. 216; 2968/1, fo. 435. For Poor Laws: GL MSS 4423/1, fo. 64v; 7673/1, fo. 40; 2596/1, fo. 226; 4071/1, 1597–8; 2593/1, 1598–9. And for other Acts: GL MSS 577/1, fo. 71; 7673/2, fo. 39; 6552/1, fo. 227v; 593/2, fo. 108v.
[59] GL MS 4241/1, fo. 281.
[60] GL MSS 2593/1, 1631, fo. 5; 1636, fo. 5; 5714/1, fo. 104v; 662/1, fo. 94; 7674, fo. 18v; 4570/2, fo. 265; 3907/1, 1636–7; 1432/4, 1637–8; 4423/1, fo. 146v; WAC E14, 1624–5.
[61] GL MSS 2968/2, fo. 214v; 1176/1, 1620; 2593/1, 1611; 4423/1, fo. 28v; 4409/1, fo. 124; 818/1, fo. 54; 662/1, fo. 120; 559/1, fo. 9; 951/1, fo. 50; 2088/1, 1602–3; 4051/1, fo. 4.

'buylding' sheds 'by the churchside wher the yerbwifes sell theyr hearbs'.[62] Wills could cause storms when parishes quibbled crossly about bequests. St Margaret New Fish Street was not alone in taking the very sensible step of keeping a 'booke of wills', and some parishes sent clerks to the Prerogative Court to check the details of wills.[63] Money was most in mind when parishes searched through one another's registers for the names of fathers who had left children to their care; the ages of children to see if he/she was now old enough to go into service; or marriage certificates to see if they would bear out the claims of couples whose statements about their marriage seemed somewhat suspicious. St Sepulchre (Middlesex Division) paid St Thomas Apostle's parish clerk to copy 'a certificate of the marriage of John Preston and Joane his wife (nowe in the hospitall) whose child is left to the parrish'.[64]

All this checking and cross-referencing shows how much administration at all levels in London came increasingly to rely on records for their growing responsibilities. The vestry culture in parishes was a culture of books, records, letters, and numbers. Along with the records of City and central government, parishes worked with judicial papers to chase criminal cases or reduce the cost of financial burdens like abandoned children. All Hallows Lombard Street spent £4 10s 7d to look through all the 'records concerninge the naked boye and for charges of law' in 1618.[65] More often parishes paid for copies of 'examinacons' and 'confessions' in legal cases when mothers and midwives spoke about the births of children and the names of fathers. St John Zachary opened the parish purse for 'examinacons of the midwife and others about Wheelers childe'. Another parish gave money 'to Sr Nicholas Raintons clerke for a coppy of the weomens examinacons about St Gregoryes child' in 1640.[66] The unlucky limbo of children and pregnant women caught between parishes squabbling about costs led to a great deal of paperwork, as parishes turned to court records – a 'womans confession' – to try and find the ruling or golden piece of information that got them off the hook.[67] Children were not the only drain on parish purses that resulted in spats. All sorts of people might show up out of the blue one day to plunge parishes into a

---

[62] GL MS 1568, fo. 160. See also GL MSS 3356/2, 1639; 2089/1, 1638–9; 593/2, fo. 107v; 1303/1, 1664; 2895/2, 1648–9; 6574, fo. 102; 2088/1, 1628–9, 1632–3, 1655; 4383/1, fo. 436.
[63] GL MSS 4180/2, fo. 34v; 2968/2, fo. 214v; 4423/1, fo. 99; 951/1, fo. 48; 4385/1, fo. 292v; 1124/1, fo. 119; 3907/1, 1637–8; 4180/1, fo. 194; 4409/1, fo. 272v; 593/2, fo. 108v; 1432/4, 1645–6; 3356/2, 1639; 959/1, fo. 80; 4051/1, fo. 4; 662/1, fo. 101.
[64] GL MS 9080/4, 1654. See also GL MSS 9235/2, fos. 115, 200; 942/1, fo. 91v; 878/1, fo. 267; 590/1, fo. 100v; 7673/2, fo. 4v; 2895/2, 1605–6; 593/2, fo. 120; 593/4, 1640–1.
[65] GL MS 4051/1, fo. 17.   [66] GL MSS 590/1, fo. 149v; 7706, fo. 8v.
[67] GL MSS 2968/1, fo. 378v; 577/1, fo. 98; 4385/1, fo. 155; 2895/2, 1660; 818/1, fo. 98.

financial panic, leading to the kind of action that caused St Brides to pay to 'serche 2 bookes for an order about Blind Robin' in 1651.[68] Keeping track of people was costly. St Stephen Coleman Street paid for a copy of an order that explained why their charge Nicholson was still locked up in Newgate. Another parish paid Bridewell's clerk to comb through books to trace Susan Wallie's 'first comeing to Bridewell'. These examples only scratch the surface of a more bureaucratic mindset in London.[69]

The forms in which information was presented also catches the eye. Some clerks calendared and indexed books so that people could flick through them quickly to find a particular case or order. There is a handy index at the back of the accounts of St Benet Paul's Wharf's that lists actions and orders by page number. 'A table of the accomptes of church-wardens, branches of wills and orders' guided people through St Katherine Coleman Street's receipts and payments. A goldsmith drew up 'a callender' of names to lead readers through St Peter Westcheap's accounts in 1607. While the readers guide to St Alphage London Wall's ledgers included a 'table of the accompts', a chronological list of all churchwardens, and directions for finding inventories.[70] The vestry books of St Margaret's Westminster were clearly meant for daily use. They have a handy alphabetical index linked to page numbers for speedy searches: running heads included 'buryall cloth for children', 'poore children', 'letter to St Marts vestry', 'widdowes to Mr Hills almeshows', 'perambulation', 'records', 'ticketts for poore people', 'register', 'vagrants', and 'workehous'.[71] This all backs up Burke's belief that the alphabet was used more often at this time to put materials in simple sequence. Issac Bothomley compiled an 'alphabeticall book' of benefactors for St Martin-in-the-Fields in 1623; the same parish drew up alphabetical lists of pensioners and orphans (with payments next to names) in 1654, 1659, and 1673.[72] An A-Z list of offenders was written at the front of Bridewell's books from 1600 on to track recidivists. Pages were also numbered, and later on in this chapter we will follow Bridewell's clerks as they look through courtbooks to refer to particular pages for evidence.

---

[68] GL MS 6552/1, fo. 212.
[69] GL MSS 4457/2, fo. 57; 1432/4, 1663–4. See also GL MSS 559/1, fo. 5; 878/1, fo. 266; 4457/2, fo. 75; 7673/1, fo. 108v; 3907/1, 1638–9; 818/1, fos. 98v, 118; 6552/1, fo. 86v.
[70] GL MSS 878/1, back of book; 1124/1, front of book; 645/1; 1432/3, back of book.
[71] WAC E2416; E2419. St Martin-in-the-Fields vestry book for 1651–6 is indexed by main subject matters like policies and taxes, and by names of churchwardens: WAC F2003. An earlier book has a list of contents of books of orders from 1573–93, other orders are listed with page numbers next to them: WAC F2001, fo. 14v. 'A register of the writings belonging to the parrish and poor of the parrish of St Martin-in-the-Fields' begins in 1685, but indexes orders and documents from 1607 on: WAC F2062.
[72] Burke, *Social History of Knowledge*, pp. 184–7; WAC F2001, fo. 163v; F348–50.

Numbers, tables, letters, abstracts, indexes, and inventories all eased access to records when something was needed. Material London was set down on paper in orderly manner, even in hum-drum inventories of church goods.[73] Information was rarely scribbled down sloppily, but put in columns or rows with spaces in-between entries to follow from top to bottom in natural motions, and principal points were sometimes summed up in 'abstracts' that could be taken on board inside a minute.[74] The organization of pages mattered for meaning and presentation. Signatures or seals were marks of authority, embellishing pages with characters, colours, or squiggles.[75] The formulaic appearance of accounts reflects what must have been widespread understanding of the best way to order information. And even if handwriting was sometimes an untidy scrawl, the layout of the page was often the same, with columns still visible under the mess. At best this reveals an able awareness of how to use spaces, borders, and margins to convey data in clear ways. Spaces on the page divided deliberations, cases, and court days. Margins were rarely empty, a keyword or painted pointing finger guided readers with shorthand tables of contents often running down the sides. Offenders' names were listed in margins in Bridewell courtbooks and Court of Aldermen repertories (and other books), and policy matters were also summed up in a short word or two. Reading in the margins made data more easy to access in books that have all the appearance and arrangement of active archives, ready to be opened, as when one parish clerk brought along 'ye register booke of marriages, christenings and buryalls' to a vestry 'sitting' to check a few facts.[76]

Laws, names, and numbers were also hung up on walls in rooms where administrators and magistrates met to settle policy directions and hear cases, and also in tables on church walls that listed the ten commandments for all to follow.[77] Tables of 'penall statutes' covered vestry walls, along with guidelines for particular problems: St Dunstan-in-the-West hung up three 'tables' of 'orders for the sicknesses'.[78] Royal decrees were

---

[73] GL MSS 9235/2, fos. 165v, 372, 376v; 3146/1, fo. 15; 4071/1, fos. 41, 75; 7673/1, fo. 425v; 3556/1, fo. 165v; 5090/2, fo. 21; 4409/1, fo. 40v; 7674, fo. 63v.

[74] GL MS 4071/2, fo. 35.

[75] Tom Cummins and Joanne Rappaport, 'The reconfiguration of civic and sacred space: architecture, image, and writing in the colonial northern Andes', *Latin American Literary Review*, 26 (1998), 174–200, esp. 178; Brian Street, *Literacy in Theory and Practice* (Cambridge, 1984), chap. 4; M. T. Clanchy, *From Memory to Written Record: England 1066–1307* (Oxford, 1993), esp. pp. 308–17.

[76] WAC E2416, fo. 70.

[77] GL MSS 4180/1, fo. 238v; 4409/1, fos. 48, 75; 7673/1, fos. 30v, 425v; WAC F2002, fo. 88.

[78] GL MSS 2968/2, fo. 248v; 4383/1, fo. 314; 4385/1, fo. 233v; 5714/1, fo. 159v; 645/1, fo. 79v; 645/2, fo. 85v.

418    Control

also pinned on boards in 'publique places' in streets and churches, like billboards today, but with a rather different message.[79] Taxpayers were listed one-by-one on 'a waynskott table' in St James Garlickhithe, with amounts next to each name.[80] Other tables hanging on 'hookes' and 'eyes' listed orders for burials, marriages, carmen, 'orfantes', the right weight of coalsacks, and the duties of vestrymen, clerks, churchwardens, and sextons.[81] Tables informed like this, but they also helped to keep tabs on parishioners; to check who was absent from church, for example. Parishioners' names were carved on tables (sometimes with pew-places) like an attendance register. All Hallows the Great spent six shillings in 1622 on 'a great table of the names of all the parishe for presenting such as are absent from churche'.[82] All Hallows London Wall put up 'a bord' listing households 'that should send their servants to be catechized', to make sure that no one skipped class.[83] These 'bords' and 'tables' encouraged people to think in more arithmetical, alphabetical, and tabular ways. Significant, too, was their place in an optic order that regulated the visual through the display of information and images. Like any sign, 'boords' were meant to be seen and understood in particular ways. Some people drew their own impressions from the information that was put around by the authorities. Others wrote their own books to turn the tables on those above them. A Ludgate prisoner wrote down his jailor's 'abuses and disorders' in a 'booke', which he passed on to the Court of Aldermen in 1589, seeking to get him sacked.[84]

People, places, and problems were written down in a census, court-book, or tax-roll. The visuality of writing, the ways in which letters on pages call images to mind, is a good representation of the intuitive connections between seeing, writing, and listening. Eyes and ears picked up information all the time. Information was written and read on the page, and it was spoken out loud for people to hear or see if put across in an image. London was a 'paper city' in a 'paper state', described in maps, censuses, and many more written records. Not enough has been said so far about paper and police at this time. Yet there was no aspect of law and

---

[79] WAC F2003, fo. 63; GL MSS 7673/1, fos. 88v, 295v; 2895/2, 1638–9; 1016/1, fo. 86; 4180/2, fo. 34v; 4071/1, 1599–1600; 3907/1, 1590–1; 1002/1, fo. 528.
[80] GL MS 4180/1, fo. 48v.
[81] For example, GL MSS 3146/1, fo. 115v; 4956/2, fo. 228; 1002/1, fo. 388v; 4383/1, fo. 242; 9235/2, fos. 207v; 2968/2, fo. 28v; 4956/3, fo. 60; 4423/1, fo. 89; 4956/2, fo. 300.
[82] GL MS 818/1, fo. 28. See also GL MSS 4423/1, fo. 63v; 1016/1, fo. 159; 1002/1, fo. 189; 4051/1, fo. 23; 4956/3, fo. 28; LMA Jour. 19, fo. 106. In 1565 the curate of St Helen Bishopgate was asked to 'make a perfecte booke of all the names of the howseholders of this parishe wth their wife, children, and servants viz suche as shalbe of the age of xvi yeres or above', and 'delyver' it – or a 'true coppie' – to the churchwardens: GL MS 6836, fo. 270.
[83] GL MS 5090/2, fo. 195.    [84] LMA Rep. 21, fos. 121, 121v.

## Paper and police

It was still possible to know most of London's nooks and crannies around 1600. Constables could still go along to courtrooms with intimate knowledge about a criminal, a crime, or an alehouse that was friendly to thieves. There they could also outwit suspects with their superior knowledge and know-how, picked up in post or before in conversation. Thomas Harvey and Morris Powell turned up at Bridewell 'to bayle' John Clark in 1607: 'he is an honest boy', they said, fresh out of the country, just trying to get himself some work like everybody else. But a constable knew better: he is 'a comon cutpurse', he informed the bench, and I myself have 'taken him three severall tymes for pickpursinge'.[85] I am not for one minute suggesting that all constables were as careful and sharp-witted as Clark's accuser, but enough of them were to suggest that we must create a place for information in histories of policing the capital city four centuries ago. Data-gathering suggests smatterings of sophistication and science, but how often is it said that constables were fudging amateurs with no talent for the job in hand? How could a life-long leatherseller become a capable constable almost overnight? Such arguments seem tedious and nit-picking now, especially if they are based on the shortness of one-year terms constables are said to have served, counting off days like a prison sentence. We might think instead of a pool of middling men, many of whom saw their turn in office as an obligation of rank and status, also knowing that someone would stand in for them if something stopped them filling the post, someone who might have hired himself out year-after-year, getting worthwhile experience. Information was passed around by word of mouth and on paper. Constables contributed to this verbal flow, and anyone with a stake in running communities built up considerable knowledge of problems and policies. This knowledge was brought to court and put on paper for later use if circumstances or characters cropped up again. Memories did not need to stretch for long when a court met as often as the one inside Bridewell. Some offenders attended more meetings than many men sitting on the bench, notching up twenty-five appearances or more.

---

[85] BHC 5, fo. 175.

There was nearly always one or more recidivists in the courtroom each day, living breathing data with no chance to melt into the background. Governors and staff knew many of the suspects brought before them by 'fame' and name, and picked up useful information about the circumstances of crime at the same time. It is possible to track information flows through the Bridewell process (and elsewhere) and the forms that they took as they were first spoken, repeated, mulled over, and put down on paper. Records begin when officers bring offenders before the court: the bench questions, listens to answers, and evaluates; clerks scribble notes and update courtbooks, adding yet more names to handy alphabetical lists of offenders.

This circulation of information also involved marshals, beadles, warders, and other officers, many of whom were not raw recruits, and had good working knowledge of seedy people and places in their patches. Martha Scarle and Jane Kibble were drinking 'at unseasonable houres' in an alehouse in 1632 when the watch burst in through the door and rounded up the late drinkers for a night in Bridewell; the ward beadle said in court the next day that he had 'often' spotted Kibble out 'late in the streetes', a hammer-blow for her hopes to get a sympathetic hearing. Another beadle knew that a vagrant waterman standing in Bridewell's dock was 'a very lewd' thief and 'a daungerous person'. He was in a good position to know, as beadles were supposed to give their ward alderman accounts of the thieves, hucksters, brothels, and women 'of evil and noisome life' in their area every fifteen days.[86] Beadles, bellmen, constables, deputies, marshals, and warders all went along to Bridewell with important pieces of information about vagrants, 'lewd women', bawds, nightwalkers, 'notorious' pickpockets, 'comon pilferers', 'comon receiver[s]' of whores and knaves', and 'comon bayle[s]'.[87] On their daily laps of the city, marshals were well placed to learn about criminals and their habits and haunts. Marshal Bestney clinched the case against the 'spy to bawds and butterfoysts', Anne Foster, in 1628, when he passed on word to the court that she 'allwaies of late' lodged in 'a bawdy house'. Another marshal could say from his own intelligence that William Ashberry 'went from one cooke to another and cozened a hundred persons'. And again it was a marshal who made sure that Jane Frederick was locked up when she stood 'stiflye upon her honestye' and tried to talk Bridewell's bench into

---

[86] BHC 7, fo. 258v; 6, fo. 137v; LMA COL/AC/08/1, fo. 16.
[87] BHC 6, fos. 394v, 432v; 7, fo. 68v; 8, fo. 150 (beadles); 8, fos. 239v, 289 (bellmen); 5, fo. 355v; 6, fos. 206v, 363v; 7, fo. 258v; 8, fos. 161, 239v, 340 (constables); 2, fo. 125; 5, fo. 437; 8, fo. 238 (deputies); 7, fos. 43, 68, 84, 106, 165v; 8, fos. 8v, 42v, 157v (marshals); 6, fo. 1v; 8, fo. 130 (warders). Frank Rexroth calls beadles in late medieval London 'archive[s] of secrecy' and 'walking archive[s]': *Deviance and Power*, pp. 191, 197.

believing that 'she liveth by sewinge and her worke' in 1619: no, he said, 'shee is a comon haunter of tavernes' and leads a very 'suspitious' 'course of lyfe'. Many cases were comfortably cleared up with such front-line knowledge. Warder Gray of Bishopgate could speak with authority when charging that Elizabeth Jones was 'a comon nightwalker' in 1637: I 'hath taken her twice with drunken men', he said, and she 'purloyned from them both their hatts'.[88]

Most impressively, officers countered claims of innocence or mix-ups by suspects in the dock, hitting back with their own ammunition from their time policing London's streets. Anthony Mullens stood before Bridewell's bench one day in 1574, pledging with all his heart, 'as God is his soule', that it had never once entered his mind to plot to arrest John Goodfellow without good cause. It was not his lucky day, however, as a deputy had a different story to tell from the neighbourhood: he is 'a very roge', he said, with 'a very evell tonge', and someone who breeds 'discention' amongst neighbours. Nicholas Symons told the court that he was a good-natured drover in 1619, who had just popped into the city to sell his cattle. Far from it, a marshal said: 'he is a carrier of news to prisoners in Newgate and a daungerous fellowe'. George Cordell also tried to outfox the court: I am 'a pore man and of a poore trade', he said in 1608, and I do my best to scrape by. This is a pack of lies, a deputy said when he had finished: he is a 'vild vicious fellowe', who gives nothing to his family for them to live on, but spends his money on 'lewde women'.[89] Information was also obtained from suspects who hoped to get softer treatment if they spilled the beans on partners in crime. Some walked free after promising to get information about bigger catches, as happened to John Griffin in 1628 after he 'promise[d] to reveale the cutpurses and shew the marshalls how they shalbe taken'. John Barnes, a 'notorious pilfering boy and shopcreep', was let out of Bridewell in 1621 'to find his companions'.[90] Some promises were broken,[91] but some people came back with very helpful information. Governors also led examinations, trying to get to the bottom of cases. Petty offenders were not stretched on racks, but they did give up information under pressure, even though they risked danger if news of their treachery leaked out. George Smerken gave evidence about a string of bawdy houses in 1577, and said 'that if it should be knowne that hee hathe bewrayed this evill rule, he should be ill

---

[88] BHC 7, fos. 86, 212; 6, fo. 138v; 8, fo. 101. See also BHC 5, fo. 253v; 6, fo. 160v; 8, fo. 159.
[89] BHC 2, fo. 15v; 6, fo. 140v; 5, fo. 310v; LMA D/L/C 219, fo. 182. See also BHC 5, fo. 385v; 6, fo. 219v; 7, fo. 332; 8, fo. 239.
[90] BHC 7, fo. 79; 6, fo. 261v.   [91] For example, BHC 6, fo. 19v.

used as thrust in with a dagger or corrsed in the face with a dagger'. Pimp Henry Boyer dreaded what might happen next after he turned stool-pigeon, saying that 'he feareth that the gentlemen' and others whose 'lewd liffe' he 'opened' 'will seke his death and kill him as he goeth in the streete except God defend him'.[92]

Perhaps fed up now with their old 'lewd courses' or more likely seeking to save their own skins, some suspects turned their backs on former friends, some hoping to start all over again with a clean slate, they said. Agnes Hall was locked up in Bridewell by recorder's warrant in 1599 'for suspicion of felony', but she was soon on her way back home after she 'revealed many notorious whores' to the bench, and seemed 'very penitent for her faults'.[93] There were plenty of twists and turns in Bridewell as prisoners did their level best to get their charges dropped. Some of the most striking tip-offs over Bridewell's first century came in the course of the crackdown on prostitution in winter 1576–7, when rare deep knowledge of the 'bawdy' worlds emerged from stories told by turncoat pimps and prostitutes, worlds where the strong survived through sly double-dealing. Brothel keepers should never have counted on their friends.[94] Information was also tapped about other sex-crimes. Illegitimacy was one situation where the father's name was needed quickly to cover costs, and if questioning did not get the much needed name, courts had the option of asking midwives to squeeze the name out of the mother as she struggled and sweated in childbed. There was even a chorus of female opinion in the Bridewell cells – 'the singlewomen of the house', the 'women of the house', or 'the lewde women of this house' – that passed on information about other 'lewd' women in custody waiting for an appearance in court. Millicent Queryet was said to be 'knowen of theym to be a comon harlot' in 1559. While a group of 'comon harlots' 'disclosed some persons of lewd life and behavyor' in 1560. Other women were similarly exposed by 'the women of the house', who were all 'whores' or 'harlots' themselves and spent each day mixing with Queryet and other inmates in workrooms and cells, keeping an ear open for something to use against them for profit. Two women gave Bridewell's bench the name of the father of an illegitimate child in 1601 after the mother whispered it to them one day.[95] Prisoners snooped on others, just like neighbours in the world outside, and perhaps the bench asked them to keep their eyes and ears open, although it is more

---

[92] BHC 3, fos. 188v, 241v.  [93] BRHA BHC 4, fo. 108. See also ibid., fos. 335-5v.
[94] BHC 1, fos. 23, 24v, 25, 27, 211; 3, fos. 4-4v, 7v, 8, 10v-11, 180v. See also Archer, *Pursuit of Stability*, pp. 231–3; Paul Griffiths, 'The structure of prostitution in Elizabethan London', *Continuity and Change*, 8 (1993), 39–63.
[95] BHC 1, fos. 62, 84; BRHA BHC 4, fo. 220. See also BHC 1, fos. 17v, 62, 97, 151, 217v.

likely that they were trying to curry favour. Evidence from Bridewell's early books also suggests that a gang of 'senior' long-stay or regular recidivists ruled the roost in the women's wing, and that the threat to reveal harmful knowledge was one way of keeping the upper hand.

One Bridewell prisoner 'disclosed' a 'past murder',[96] but most tip-offs were rather less dramatic than that, and helped to break prostitution rackets before 1600, or to sort out paternity tangles. After 1600, as Bridewell took the lead in hearing cases spawned by urban growth, the brunt of attention turned towards theft-rings. There were certainly double-dealing thieves before 1600 who would turn their friends in if they stood to get something out of it. 'Picker' and 'briber' John Henry came clean about his past in a 'bill' in 1559 that listed the names of other 'very thieves and comon pickers'. 'Pickpurse' Anne Bayly (alias Middleton) named five other 'pickpursses', including her late husband, two years later.[97] But many more thieves were turned in by their companions after 1600. Ellis Barrett, a Bridewell apprentice who led a double-life as a cutpurse, named four other cutpurses who rented rooms at the Green Dragon 'in the upper end of Southwark' in 1598. Three decades later Richard Bullock, 'a confederate with cutpurses', was spared punishment for the moment after giving his word that he would work with the marshals to bring in cutpurses. Other thieves got off lightly after agreeing to help to track down fences and 'receivers of stolen goods'.[98] These informers were small fry in the main. But a crackdown on a gang of Dutch cutpurses around 1630 saw some of its leading lights promising 'to informe on others that are pickepocketts'. It seemed that there were moles everywhere in London and that no thief was safe. Poacher turned gamekeeper, Joan Leaver, combined forces with a beadle in 1652 'to find out persons uttering false money'.[99] Information about thieves and other offenders was put down on paper in Bridewell, judicial courts, and also in the Guildhall, and if this sort of information gathering and paper work is a sign of sound policing, then operations based on Bridewell were far from primitive.

Nobody saw as much of prisoners below stairs in Bridewell as the staff who were there with them when they worked, prayed, sat down to eat, and slept. The porter with his register of prisoners coming in and out through the gates should have had a sharply trained eye for recidivists. The matron spent the day keeping the 'women of the house' in check and she ought to have been able to pick out women who got on with work and others who

---

[96] BHC 1, fo. 131. [97] Ibid., fos. 12, 140.
[98] BRHA BHC 4, fo. 18; BHC 7, fo. 100; 6, fo. 342. See also BHC 5, fo. 377v; 6, fos. 215v, 261v; 7, fos. 27v, 45v, 79, 92v, 362.
[99] BHC 7, fos. 158v, 159v, 194v; 9, fo. 580. For the Dutch gang see above, pp. 162–3.

were slack and surly. Matrons were often called into court to give their opinions about women in the dock, and they sometimes added a few biographical scraps that helped the bench make up its mind. Marshal Bestney charged Dorothy Andrews with picking £20 from 'a gents pockett' in 1628, and the matron was able to add that she had recently been 'devorced from her husband' and had 'played the harlott' for a long while now. The matron also recognized two 'lewd' women in court in 1624, 'thone a whore, thother a bawde', and backed up a beadle at another time who charged 'lewde' and 'disordered' Mary Starkey with taking a 'gentleman into her lodging', making it clear to the court that she was 'knowne by [her and] some [others] in the house to be a comon whore'. Other pilferers, nightwalkers, receivers, or lewd and unruly women were identified by matrons in the courtroom.[100] Their knowledge of London's 'lewd' women was second to none, and their verbal and physical examinations of suspected women brought the facts of crime to life. Like others, they were able to pick out recidivists and a word to that effect in court could clinch cases. The bench watched the same people troop in and out of court week in and week out. The clerk flicked through courtbooks, making a note of previous prosecutions, jotting down 'here before', 'often here', 'here not long since', or 'latelie' or 'shortlie' here next to names. Sometimes old offenders were spotted straight away.[101] Margaret Forster (alias Taffety Meg), Anne Cave, and Elizabeth Rice were 'taken dawncing' and drinking at The Swan 'by the Spittle' with a bunch of drunk 'cavaleers' in 1601, and things looked bleaker for Forster and Rice because they had been in Bridewell before. Likewise, Edith David looked like a hardened offender in 1560 when 'taken in whoredome', and the clerk noted that she had 'led that lewd lyfe a longe tyme before', having 'bene sondry tymes admonyshed and yet nothing at all the better'.[102] Bridewell's books were calendars of bad reputations. Alice Sharpe was 'as badde as the best' in 1603. John Watkins and Henry Clitherowe were (respectively) 'a notorious shiftinge roague' 'famous for his villany', and 'an incorrigible roague and a famous infamous cheater and cozenor'.[103]

Many suspects were said to be 'comon' offenders already well known to courts or arresting officers.[104] Other words carried similar force. 'Defamed' described familiar faces at Middlesex quarter sessions. Galfridus Emmes

---

[100] BHC 7, fo. 59; 6, fo. 370; 7, fo. 67. See also BHC 7, fos. 30, 66, 117, 170, 276v; 8, fo. 319.
[101] BHC 1, fos. 6v, 16; 5, fos. 153, 316v; 6, fos. 120, 342, 408, 408v, 415; 8, fos. 130, 218v, 326v; BRHA BHC 4, fos. 129, 199, 213, 228v, 232, 253v, 322v, 323, 340v, 384.
[102] BRHA BHC 4, fo. 229; BHC 1, fo. 115v.   [103] BRHA BHC 4, fos. 342v, 347, 350.
[104] For example, BHC 5, fo. 230; 6, fos. 1v, 342; 8, fo. 326v; LMA MJ/SBR/1, fos. 266, 379, 477, 533, 645; MJ/SBR/2, fos. 70, 207, 477; MJ/SBR/3, fos. 142, 420.

from Cow Cross who picked £6 and forty shillings from two pockets was a 'defamed cutpurse'; while William Knight from Golding Lane was 'charged to be a common nightwalker' and 'defamed cutpurse'.[105] Back at Bridewell, Margaret Whalley was said to be 'an auncyent harlot', 'many tymes apprehended' 'for her lewde lyfe' in 1559 (she was back behind bars a fortnight later). 'Ancient' was still a live word in 1619, when Frances Fobber was called 'a cozenor and auncient professor in that wicked course'.[106] 'Guest' was another word for recidivist. Joanne Kendal and Anne Boswell, 'two vagrant idle rogues' who helped themselves to 'commyes and capons' in 1603, were 'knowen to be comen [Bridewell] guests'. Katherine Johnson and Mary Flender were picked out as 'vagrant daylie guests' in 1625. 'Guest' was also coupled with 'ancient' or 'old' to pick out old hands at crime.[107] Many suspects were 'notorious', 'notable', or 'noted' good-for-nothings. Margaret Henry (alias 'Tanyken') was 'comenlye noated to be a comen bawde' in 1579. Joan Craven was found in bed with George Bolton 'verye suspiciously [with] his hose down' and 'noted to be a coen dronckarde, a scold, and a bawde'. 'Noated' nicely implies writing as well as knowledge lodged in minds.[108] 'Notorious' or 'notable' also sum up long-term offending in handy words. There was no chance that the 'notorious cheater and cozenor', William Richardson, would escape with a soft sentence in 1624, as he had been 'a comon guest' at Bridewell for 'many yeares'. Mary Wood's odds of a light slap on the wrist were also low in 1603: she was 'a notorious harlot' who had been at Bridewell 'manie times' before.[109] 'Known' is one of the most commonly used adjectives in the courtbooks. Like officers, Bridewell's bench used knowledge of offenders' pasts to rebut made-up tales and lame excuses. John Goad said in 1600 that 'he came to London on Sunday last to gett worke and to enquire for his brother'. But the bench did not fall for this, noting 'that yt is well knowne to this court that he is a verie rogue'. Joan Butler was in court one week later and said that she came to London a week ago and was living with her cousin in Holborn and looking for work. Again, governors knew better: she is 'well knowne to be a comon wanderer about the citie', they said from memory, and 'a

---

[105] LMA MJ/SR/524/75, 524/34. See also MJ/SR/515/33, 524/38, 524/75.
[106] BHC 1, fos. 6v, 14; 6, fo. 90v. See also BHC 1, fo. 22; 5, fo. 92v.
[107] BRHA BHC 4, fo. 399v; BHC 6, fo. 400v. For examples from a small period covered in one courtbook, see BHC 6, fos. 2v, 15v, 17v, 21v, 22v, 25, 25v, 33.
[108] BHC 3, fos. 363, 337. See also WAC WCB2, fo. 37; LMA MJ/SBR/2, fo. 255; BHC 7, fo. 55v; 8, fo. 198v; 9, fo. 723.
[109] BHC 6, fo. 366; BRHA BHC 4, fo. 390. See also BHC 5, fos. 158, 230, 441; 6, fos. 1v, 17, 128, 135, 213, 261v, 358; 7, fo. 30; 8, fo. 35; BRHA BHC 4, fos. 347, 350; LMA MJ/SBR/1, fo. 645.

verie notable connynge and dissemblinge person'. John Robinson and Israel Andrews landed in court in 1627: Robinson was well 'knowne of old to be an ill liver and pilferer'; while Andrews was remembered to 'keepe a bawdy house' and to be 'long of ill name'.[110]

Other old offenders were 'knowen' to be 'daungerous', 'evil', 'lewd', or 'light', 'comon cosenors', 'whores', 'nightwalkers', 'harlots', and 'sluts', or 'notorious' thieves, vagrants, cutpurses, and pickpockets.[111] Old offenders were at a disadvantage from the second they walked into courtrooms because something was known about them that would do them no good at all. Knowing nothing about someone, on the other hand, was often reason enough for softer treatment from courts. Two vagrants – Richard Tunks and John Bash – were let off on the same day in 1622: Tunks for being 'no common customer here', Bash because he was 'no common person here'.[112] Knowledge about pasts and places could make or break cases. Four women 'of lewd conversacon' could not talk their way out of a sticky situation in 1627, when they were caught red-handed 'in a suspicious house' along Shoe Lane, that was 'noted to be a comon place for harboringe of lewd people'.[113] The addresses of alehouses were noted when they were counted, and the City asked for a list of 'howses verie infamous for incontinent rule out of our liberties and jurisdiction' in 1580. 'Notorious' and 'comon' houses turn up in Bridewell's casebooks all the time, and it was always a dark mark for any suspect if they were found in one. Margaret Walker was forced to face the music at the Bridewell court in 1602 after it became 'knowen to the court that the howse where she lieth is a howse of ill rule'. Other courts in the London area also picked up good knowledge about criminal worlds, even though they did not meet as often as the one inside Bridewell. A labourer's wife from White Cross Street got into trouble at Middlesex quarter sessions for running 'a lewd defamed howse'.[114]

Not too many recidivists slipped through Bridewell's net. Next to vagrant John Gurnet's name the clerk wrote down: 'borne at Henley upon Thames here 40 times'.[115] It did not take too long to piece together a biography from one of Bridewell's books, especially with handy name-indexes lining one side of each page. Hoping to look better in the eyes of the court after he was caught by the Queenhithe watch in 1609, vagrant

---

[110] BRHA BHC 4, fos. 162v, 165v; BHC 7, fos. 24, 133.
[111] For example, BHC 3, fo. 383; 5, fo. 63v; 7, fos. 21, 145, 248, 349; 8, fos. 3v, 73v, 101, 210v, 262; 9, fos. 735, 877; BRHA BHC 4, fos. 253v, 317, 363v, 368, 378v, 398v.
[112] BRHA BHC 4, fo. 323.   [113] BHC 6, fo. 442v.
[114] LMA Remembrancia Book 1, fo. 18v; BRHA BHC 4, fo. 299v; LMA MJ/SR/515/33. See also BHC 6, fo. 138v; LMA MJ/SBR/1, fos. 97, 525; MJ/SBR/2, fos. 84, 96.
[115] BRHA BHC 4, fo. 323v.

John Richardson said that he had once been the apprentice of a Bridewell pinner, the implication being that if he had done good once he could do so again. But the clerk looked for him 'in the booke' to see if he had indeed worked under a pinner in the 'house', and said that 'no such name is ther to be found' amongst the notes of apprentices. One year earlier the clerk 'searche[d in the book] for fyve yeares last past' to check if any 'proceedings' had been taken against Erasmus Percival to use against him now.[116] There were recidivists on almost all pages of the courtbooks. The bench was getting sick and tired of the sight of the 'comon roge, ronnegate, and naughtie vile whore' Katherine Elder in 1561, who was once 'againe brought into this house', they complained, and in the margins of the courtbook the clerk wrote '4 times'. A haberdasher's wife, who was grabbed 'creepyng through a gutter wyndowe' into a house 'in her pettycoate and barelegged' in 1560, was 'utterlye' adamant that she did no 'acte': 'a notorious harlot', the clerk noted in the book, 'and hath bene iii times befor'. As soon as the 'drabbe' Elizabeth Higgins stepped into the court in 1562 it was remembered that she had been there 'twise before for picking, pilferinge, idlenes, and begginge', while a quick check through the courtbook confirmed that John Stafford, a 'comon idle roge' and 'greate dissembler in begginge', had been 'twise whipped alredii' at Bridewell for 'dissembling'. Other offenders were followed for five or more appearances in the courtbooks, and this number was duly written down next to their names.[117]

In other cases the clerk wrote down how long it had been since someone last appeared in the courtroom, making his calculations from the books. Anne Usher (alias Gibbs) was charged with vagrancy in 1601, and straight away the clerk went looking for her in the courtbook: she was last here three years ago, he told the bench, '*as by the booke may appeare*', and since that time 'she hath gott her living with her needell', or at least that is what she says. Alice Wayneman dropped her accusation that Christian Erick had poisoned Mistress Randall in 1560, 'as in the 77 leafe doth appere', the clerk noted after going back to check the wording of the original entry.[118] Memories could stretch back much longer than a few months. A search was set up for Thomas Coo in 1627 who, it was remembered, had last been in Bridewell 'about fifteene yeares agoe'. Godfrey Lambright looked 'very giltye' in 1578, and a look in the books confirmed these hunches as the clerk carefully thumbed through the years

---

[116] BHC 5, fos. 377v, 295.
[117] BHC 1, fos. 175v, 97v, 208v; 2, fo. 72. See also BHC 1, fos. 6v, 14, 78v, 189v; 3, fo. 434; 5, fo. 191v; 6, fo. 398; 8, fos. 179v, 325, 350; BRHA BHC 4, fo. 262.
[118] BRHA BHC 4, fo. 260; 1, fo. 90v.

428     Control

to find that he had been in trouble 'five years sens for lewde life'. Another long trawl through the books confirmed that it had also been five years since the 'comen rogue and begger wth false lysenses', Edward Griffin, last turned up in the courtroom.[119] It was not uncommon for old offenders to return to the court after a handful of years, feeling sure that no one would remember them from so long ago, but then a word in the clerk's ear begins the pursuit through the papers. It was not difficult to dredge up the pasts of others: the 'old customer' Winifred Hand was 'taken' walking late in 1634 and the courtbooks said that she had been let out of Bridewell 'this day fortnight'; vagrant Alice Harvey was brought in only four days after she was last sent back home by the court; while the ink had hardly had enough time to dry when 'notorious nipp' William Reynolds walked into court in 1622, 'hee beinge discharged here last court day'.[120] And if a date or time did not spring to mind, the clerk referred to a season, festival, or mayoralty, as when the 'lewde' pair Dorothy Merry and Jane Browne were caught guzzling 'gallons of wyne' with 'many gents' in the Fountain Tavern on Fleet Street one night in 1619, and someone in court remembered that they had 'been in question here in the time of maioralty of Sr Thomas Middleton'.[121]

And the court could be even more precise, jotting down the exact date of a last appearance. Elizabeth Cooley was spotted walking along the streets one night in June 1638, although this was not the first time that she had been in hot water at Bridewell: 'hath bene often here', the clerk noted, on '25 of March last passed to Ware'. A 'common nightwalker' and 'rude person', Francis Wotten, stood in the dock on 23 June 1641 with no place to hide from her wayward past: 'here 2 June', the clerk noted next to this her latest lapse. Not for the first time Katherine Curtis was caught walking late at night in winter 1637: she 'was here the vi of September last', the clerk reported to the court, when a record was made that she was sent here from City quarter sessions for being a 'comon nightwalker'.[122]

Bridewell was not the only hospital court that worked with courtbooks to keep tabs on people. Orphans and patients were tracked down in the books of other hospitals, and Christ's had a particular need to note down the details of illegitimacy cases over its first few decades when it had jurisdiction in this area. One governor, William Norton, gave evidence at the Consistory Court in 1592 about a case that had come before

---

[119] BHC 7, fo. 24v; 3, fos. 346v, 384.
[120] BHC 8, fo. 6; 3, fo. 423v; 6, fo. 296v. See also BHC 1, fo. 18v; 3, fo. 366v; 8, fos. 87, 239, 284v, 372; BRHA BHC 4, fos. 40v, 81, 142.
[121] BHC 6, fo. 117.
[122] BHC 8, fos. 176v, 338; 6, fo. 117. See also BHC 8, fos. 260, 352, 371; BRHA BHC 4, fo. 341v.

Christ's court a decade or so earlier. He explained that Christ's clerk 'setteth down and keepeth a speciall booke and recorde', and that at the 'importunate entreatie' of Agnes Evans he (Norton) looked back through this book 'for the particuler proceedings and exa[m]i[n]acons' in 'a matter' from the past involving Evan Thomas and his servant Elizabeth Morris. Norton skimmed through the book as far back as 26 May 1582, where it was written down that Thomas admitted that 'he had the use of [Morris's] body'. Norton 'put his mark in the regester book', and 'caused a coppie of the wordes' to 'bee written owt of the recordes' for use a decade later to reach a verdict in a separate case.[123]

Such damaging evidence against suspects was portable, moving in the memories of magistrates who sat in more than one court, in the persons (and bodies in brands or 'markes') of offenders shunted between courts, and in the records of other courts that were made available to help the Bridewell bench (and other courts) build cases. One clause of the longwinded 1579 'Orders for Brydewell' instructed the governors to pick 'some mete persons to followe the causes at every sessions against such as shalbe comytted to prison'.[124] These 'mete' messengers doubtless brought word back to Bridewell about the fate of people who had been sent to sessions, and also any other offence or offender that caught their attention or stirred their memories. Bridewell officials also asked to see depositions and other documents that were drawn up somewhere else, either by paying for copies to be made and kept with the Bridewell files, or by going to read them at another court. Margery Thorne squared up to her master at Bridewell in 1577, telling the court that he was the only true father of her child: 'as her deposicon appeareth in that case taken in the Maiors Courte at Guildhall 4 Februar 1576[7]', the clerk duly noted by the side of this entry, having had the opportunity to read the original paperwork. The 'comon notorious pander', Henry Boyer, made yet another appearance at Bridewell in autumn of the same year and was immediately put in a tight spot after Anne Jervis's deposition, 'taken before my L[ord] Maior and Courte of Aldermen', was 'redde unto him', as in it she made a string of allegations against one of his friends. He also had some of his own 'confessions' read out to him from 'the booke of Bridewell folios 106, 117, 134' to check that these were the exact words that came from his mouth. The clerk also made copies of cases from the Bridewell books to help other courts and parishes sort out their quandaries. Stepney parish requested 'true coppies' of 'accusacions and other matters' in the Bridewell books about one of its parishioners – Daniel

---

[123] LMA D/L/C 214, fos. 160–1.  [124] LMA Jour. 20. fo. 501.

English – in 1603.[125] Bridewell's bench also thumbed through other records from the Guildhall or Westminster courts for information in a wide range of concerns. The clerk was instructed to go to Westminster in May 1600 to 'take out a coppy verbatim of Spillmans last patent out of Chauncery for gatheringe of ragges and bones', so that a Bridewell committee that was in the middle of an inquiry into street waste 'may see yt'. And Bridewell also kept an up-to-date archive of Court of Aldermen orders, each one copied by a Guildhall clerk not long after they were passed. Middlesex and Westminster quarter sessions also read through parish registers for confirmations of births and marriages to help make rulings in cases where paternity or provision for a small child was in the balance.[126]

As mentioned, there was always a clutch of aldermen and justices sitting on Bridewell's bench at any one time. We should imagine these magistrates as conduits, moving between courts, whose Newgate knowledge included data about previous prosecutions and prisoners, now stored up for use at Bridewell when a Newgate face stood in the dock. A governor told the rest of the bench in 1642 that John Gardener, who had been picked up the night before prowling around a warehouse, had 'come out of Newgate last day'. Newgate memories could stretch further back than this. It came to light that John Webb, who was in trouble for pilfering in 1622, 'had beene tried at Newgate for his life'. Other pilferers, burglars, vagrants, and nightwalkers on trial at Bridewell had also spent time in Newgate.[127] Some were skating on thin ice after getting a pardon. The clerk made a note that Marie Phillips, who was picked up vagrant in 1630, 'hath ben in Newegate and had her pardon'. Jane Mills and Jane Perrin were rounded up in 1633 and the court heard that they had both had 'their pardons 2 or 3 times at Newegate for their lives'. While John Page was in real danger of losing his life in 1634 when 'taken' lurking in Bartholomew Fair, as it turned out that he was 'a condemned person and had a pardon condicionally'. Although the 'notorious rogue and comon theefe' William Banks had a stroke of luck in 1623 when the court learned that he had 'been condempned to bee hanged and yet still persisteth in his vagrancy', but rather than send him along Fleet Street to Newgate and a likely second death sentence, the bench somewhat softly settled on

---

[125] BHC 3, fos. 180v, 240v, 242, 242v-3; BRHA BHC 4, fo. 412. See also BHC 5, fo. 395v; BRHA BHC 4, fos. 10, 67, 187, 262v, 331, 418, 445v, 451; WAC E15, 1627.
[126] BRHA BHC 4, fos. 160, 178, 249; LMA MJ/SBR/4, fo. 485; MJ/SBR/5, fo. 345; MJ/SP/1641/March sessions, 2; MJ/SP/1644/January sessions, 1; WJ/SP/1642/September sessions, 1. See also LMA MJ/SBR/1, fos 74–6; WAC WCB 1, fo. 280; WCB 2, fo. 121.
[127] BHC 8, fo. 382v; 6, fo. 281v. See also BHC 7, fo. 105; 8, fos. 35, 105v, 216, 382v; BRHA BHC 4, fos. 191v, 360.

whipping him and sending him home with a pass.[128] Other offenders were still at large, even though they ought to have been on board a boat bound for America. Lewis Rively was dragged from the Pope's Head tavern in Chancery Lane after 'a greate uproare at one of the clock at night', and his life was in the balance when word reached Bridewell that he was 'a condemned person' pardoned to go overseas, and he was soon on his way back to Newgate 'to be dealt withall'. Bridewell's bench needed no introduction to Frances Richardson in 1639, a 'comon nightwalker' who had chalked up a string of appearances. This time she claimed that she had not long left 'The White Lyon [prison in Southwark] upon l[ett]res of transportacon', but that 'her tyme' to set sail was 'not [yet] out': she was locked up until evidence arrived that she still had some time left to find a ship.[129]

In other cases the marks of a criminal past were singed on skin with sizzling irons. A 'marke' spelt trouble, and it was not easy to shake off a past that was stamped on skin, and hide a brand on a hand. Suspects were stripped and searched for marks on backs and shoulders. It was hard to give William Cole the benefit of the doubt after he was picked up with the princely sum of 40/4d in his pockets in 1631 and the court found that he had 'bene burned in the hand and in the shoulder'. John Skeggs had also had a lucky escape from the noose a short time ago, when he was brought to Bridewell from the streets in 1609 and word arrived that he had been 'burned on the hand last sessions for felony'. The 'comon', 'incorrigible', and 'notable nipp and cutpurse', Rice Wheeler, had already been 'burned in the back' in 1623.[130] Some bodies were covered in 'markes', although one was enough for a court to draw conclusions about the character of a large number of branded vagrants, thieves, cutpurses, and nightwalkers. Magistrates could point to paper and bodies for the piece of evidence that might bring a case to a successful conclusion.[131]

Whether character faults or past payments in a parish account book were at issue, something could be shown to be true because it 'appears by the booke'. Courts put a lot of trust in books and records.[132] Magistrates thought through numbers and words on the page, working with and between records. London was policed through paper. Even the monotonous listing of names, addresses, and jobs could say much in a culture in which certain jobs and districts had their own characters. Not many

---

[128] BHC 7, fos. 196, 351; 8, fo. 10.   [129] BHC 8, fos. 158v, 228v.
[130] Ibid., fo. 210v; BHC 5, fo. 353v; 6, fos. 352v, 350v.
[131] For example, BHC 5, fo. 433v; 6, fo. 389; 7, fos. 116, 231, 361; 8, fos. 44, 344v, 374v; LMA CQSF 91/10; MJ/SBR/4, fo. 406; MJ/SBR/6, fo. 450.
[132] GL MSS 4423/1, fos. 18v, 191, 192; 6836, fos. 95v, 97v; 951/1, fo. 56v; 1303/1, fo. 167; 7673/1, fo. 82v; 4071/2, fo. 83v; 4409/1, fo. 82.

aspects of life from the cradle to the grave were no longer put on paper, in chains that stretched across the London area. Apparent, also, is a sharpening concern for the secrecy and security of records in these troubled times. Paper was used more often to police; the noting of particular dates of previous visits to courts, for example, was more frequent in the second quarter of the seventeenth century. Counting and record-keeping may not yet have been sciences, but knowledge and information was in fluent circulation, at a time when the 'points of contact' linking Court, city, and country were growing in scope and scale.[133] We often think that more sophisticated surveillance societies came much later than this, perhaps by the eighteenth century, but most certainly by the one after.[134] That may be so if we always have in mind national head counts, cross-country communications, or snooping detectives with expert training. But if we leap back to the time around 1600, we are not in a backwater before numbers and information were taken seriously and put to use to tackle society's ills and lift its burdens. Far from it, collecting and counting data had become a matter of routine by this point.[135] No matter what else they said about London's crushing population boom and fading 'fame', magistrates had a lot of knowledge about their city 'nowadays' at their fingertips.

[133] G. R. Elton, 'Tudor government: the points of contact', reprinted in Elton, *Studies in Tudor and Stuart Politics and Government, Vol. III, Papers and Reviews 1973–1981* (Cambridge, 1983), pp. 3–57.

[134] See Higgs, *Information State in England*; Headrick, *When Information Came of Age*; Andrea A. Rusnock, *Vital Accounts; Quantifying Health and Population in Eighteenth-Century France and England* (Cambridge, 2002). Paul Slack takes another line in 'Government and information in seventeenth-century England', *Past and Present*, 184 (2004), 33–68.

[135] This is one argument of my next book on surveillance in sixteenth- and seventeenth-century England, to be called *Knowing England: Disciplining and Documenting Individuals, 1550–1700*.

# Conclusion

> There is a word in Arabic that I heard uttered over and over in the city; *ghamidh*, meaning 'mysterious' or 'ambiguous'. If Baghdad's soul is loss, its mood always seemed to be *ghamidh*. Through that word, I began, at first in a woefully superficial way, to understand the panorama of attitudes that is Baghdad. Communicating that shifting truth has been a challenge.
> Anthony Shadid, *Night Draws Near: Iraq's People in the Shadow of America's War* (New York, 2005), p. 10

> Such massive physical change has destroyed the mental map that made the old Tibetan culture possible. Lhasa is no longer Lhasa.
> Patrick French, *Tibet, Tibet: A Personal History of a Lost Land* (2003), p. 155

Make no mistake, London cannot be called stable on any day covered by this book. 'The city's sure in progresse', Thomas Freeman noted nervously in 1614. 'Shee swarmes', Donald Lupton wrote, choosing a vivid verb for effect that lets us feel what it was like to sit fretting in a Guildhall hot-seat or with Lupton at his desk in 1632, pen poised, anxieties spinning.[1] By now there was no going back to a time that no one could exactly date or define when things seemed stable and settled. Mind-boggling growth was the reality, that sometimes left people lost for words. Like Lhasa, London was no longer London. It had become 'the size of half the world', Venice's ambassador wrote in 1620, in the sort of embroidered rhetoric that was quite typical for these times.[2]

The Venetian was not right in his sums: London was nowhere near being 50 per cent of the world's extent, not in terms of size, riches, or influence (another ambassador was closer to the mark when guessing that

---

[1] Freeman is quoted in Manley, *Literature and Culture in Early Modern London* (Cambridge, 1995), p. 427; Donald Lupton, *London and the Country Carbonadoed and Quartered Into Severall Characters*, 1632, The English Experience, 879 (Amsterdam and Norwood, NJ, 1977), p. 1.
[2] CSPV 1619–21, p. 233.

over 300,000 'souls' filled the city in 1607).[3] But he put an impression or perception in words with a grain of truth for him, standing on the spot in London, digging for the latest news and gossip, riding round the city in coaches with eyes glued to the whirl of the world outside, hearing it with cocked ears. Continuous noise from dawn to dusk, choked streets, higgledy-piggledy buildings, columns of vagrants, crowded markets, stately edifices, loaded ships queuing up for the next berth on a quay, confident wealth sometimes sitting a stone's throw away from ugly poverty. Venice's diplomat could be both unkind and flattering to his host city, indulging in flights of fancy, waxing lyrical in long passages on London's trade, its retail bonanza, and dapper merchants, and then suddenly, in the same letter, turning darkly realistic, writing about a chilly city, one where drama seemed like a day-long addiction. Ambivalence; London existed as ambivalence or ambiguity (*ghamidh*), in the mind at any rate.[4] Contemporary rhetorics and perceptions cloud matters for us, saying first one thing and then something else that seems contradictory on the surface. But the best way to get to the bottom of this conundrum is to accept it; to accept that London with all its 'small worlds' has many histories, that for this reason (and others) rhetorics were a blend of ambivalences, and that they were used for effect, to make a point, persuade, or simply to urge officers to do better jobs. London 'always seemed to be *ghamidh*'. The city was this and it was that, but everyone could agree that 'shee swarmes', and no one ever said that London was safe, stable, quiet, or trouble free.

James Howell called the mayor London's 'pilot and master', an apt description for a city perched on a river, but also in one that always needed its magistrates to steer steady courses to pick a way through choppy waters.[5] Like Lupton, London's leaders used 'swarm' as a verb and noun to capture the pace and scale of vagrancy. They knew that they were living through topsy-turvy times, they said so continually in their perceptions of the state of their city. One can acknowledge the idea that a great deal of their talk of doom and gloom was tinged with exaggeration, but not at the cost of losing the sense that London was a city in flux and strife. There is no paradox here, since magistrates are always prone to hyperbole to try and squeeze each last drop of diligence and resilience from officers and citizens. The city was a whirl of continuous movement.

---

[3] CSPV 1603–7, p. 739.
[4] Cf. Lynda Nead, *Victorian Babylon: People, Streets, and Images in Nineteenth-Century London* (New Haven, CT, and London, 2000), p. 3.
[5] James Howell, *Londinopolis: An Historical Discourse or Perlustration of the City of London, the Imperial Chamber and the Chief Emporium of Great Britain* (1657), p. 38.

Magistrates came to accept this. But they wanted all movement to have a useful purpose, for the benefit of trade, provision, policing, and, ultimately, the city. They tried to build mental fences between citizens and criminals, in the hope that crime would seem something unclean and unbecoming for all 'decent' Londoners. They also tried to capture crime in a cage of chosen words, confining shifty people inside labels (and perhaps one day inside Bridewell), knowing now that they had good grounds to describe and prosecute them. And on top of this constant campaign to contain crime (and 'criminals') through classification, magistrates also tried to learn about the contours of crime, seeking better understandings of growth and its unwanted side-effects.

There was never a time when they did not feel that they were losing the city that had once seemed so familiar. But the dawning change was a gradual, grudging acceptance of this. There seemed no point now in trying to reverse growth. In effect, magistrates came to accept that London would always 'swarm', but this did not stop them from trying to keep their teeming city under control. 'Experience' and 'observation' taught them to put up with instability, not the sort that Rappaport describes as a riotous polar opposite to stability, but the hum-drum urban cadence of vagrancy, theft, or incessant 'night battles'. This gradual accommodation to growth cannot be called surrender or resignation. It was instead a pragmatic shift after decades of revelation and clarification about the scale and scope of troubles. Magistrates did not like much of what they saw in their midst, and if anything rhetorics heated up around 1625 when women and the environment became focal points for perceptions of crime, and concern about surrounding suburbs peaked when the City refused to fall in with the Crown's plan to put authority over the walls in the hands of 'a well disposed body under one command' (within a brand-new Incorporation).[6] This proposal raised storms, though it shows that both City and Court were seeking ways to limit growth, not turn it back. A tacit fatalism spread through the corridors of power. Vagrancy was now a lasting curse, not something that might disappear one day. And brighter perspectives on growth that made London a bigger and therefore better city became more pronounced now that Londoners realized they must make the best out of a tough situation. Howell's *Londinopolis* (1657) basks in London's size as a

---

[6] LMA Rep. 17, fo. 186. See also LMA Rep. 18, fo. 362v. For the Incorporation see Valerie Pearl, *London and the Outbreak of the Puritan Revolution: City Government and National Politics* (Oxford, 1961), 33–7; Robert Ashton, *The City and the Court, 1603–1643* (Cambridge, 1979), pp. 163–7; Norman G. Brett-James, *The Growth of Stuart London* (1935), chap. 9.

cultural mark of pride, and in an earlier letter he bragged that Amsterdam was 'far inferior to London for populousness'. Graunt and Petty calculated London's growth in columns and tables that were sources of power and pleasure in a budding imperial age.[7]

Like so much else in 'swarming' London, however, attitudes towards growth were ambiguous. 'Populous' was also an ambivalently affirmative term in Petty's time, as it had been for a long while.[8] One positive outcome of these 'helter skelter' decades, however,[9] was a deep appreciation of the need to find ways and means to boost policing. The opening of Bridewell was a landmark. Linked with growth from the start, it was quickly in the thick of crackdowns on vice and vagrancy, but before long most time and effort was spent on cleaning up crimes arising from growth. Strategies focused first on reversing growth and later keeping it in check with the backing of most Londoners, after decades of dire warnings about London's tumors. There was less opposition to policing reforms now that they were imagined first and foremost in terms of curbing 'sare' changes that added up to more vagrants, 'foreigners', robberies, expense, and hardship. In any event, bad blood towards Bridewell peters out (in records) after 1600. Nor was there much grumbling about funding policing (for a time at any rate). Nervy concern about growth far surpassed any lingering bad feelings about Bridewell or policing by-laws, and this was mainly due to the insistent pitter-patter of rhetorics of control and growth, sinking in after a while. It was not the nice prospect of social mobility somewhere down the line that stopped outbreaks of instability severe enough to bring London to its knees, or regular charity that left grateful paupers languidly deferential, or the creation of some sort of metropolitan identity based on guild brotherhoods. Londoners joined forces out of concern for the freedom's 'little worth', which for breadwinners boiled down to hanging on to jobs. Holding back growth was a rallying call that few could ignore. Rhetorics had effect in the long run,

---

[7] James Howell, *Familiar Letters or Epistolae Ho-Elianae*, 3 vols. (1903), vol. I, p. 16. See also Paul Slack, 'Perceptions of the metropolis in seventeenth-century England', in Peter Burke, Brian Harrison, and Slack, eds., *Civil Histories: Essays Presented to Sir Keith Thomas* (Oxford, 2000), pp. 161–80, esp. pp. 165–70.

[8] 'The London Journal of Alessandro Magno 1562', eds. Caroline Barron, Christopher Coleman, and Claire Gobb, *London Journal*, 9 (1983), 136–52, quoting 141 ('London is a very beautiful city, rich and populous'); John Jones, *The Arte and Science of Preserving Bodie and Soule in Healthe, Wisdome, and Catholike Religion* (1579), p. 37; John Ogilvy and William Morgan, *London Survey'd: Or an Explanation of the Large Map of London* (1677), n.p.; William Petty, *Two Essays in Political Arithmetick Concerning the People, Housing, Hospitals, etc, of London and Paris* (1687), p. 12; Petty, *Observations upon the Cities of London & Rome* (1687), pp. 2–4; Petty, *Five Essays in Political Arithmetick* (1687), p. 41; John Owen, *Britannia Depicta. Or Ogilvy Improv'd* (1720), p. 41.

[9] Manley, *Literature and Culture*, p. 427.

then, convincing enough citizens that they were living in deeply troubled times, while eulogizing their city's 'fame' and reminding them what they stood to lose if nothing was done to contain growth. Clever rhetorics, a developing system of law and order that was more effective and skillful than most existing accounts have led us to believe, a civic spirit that could at its strongest bind together governing bodies and some neighbours to stand up for their city (and their own interests), and administrative processes that showed a capacity to adapt to cope with stresses and strains: all of these had a hand in helping London to muddle through one of the stormiest patches in its lengthy history.[10]

It helps to know the city better if we imagine it as 'emotional states' or 'moods', now frozen in perceptions written down in records. Only then can we start to absorb what London meant for people at the time, each with their unique perspectives from their own surroundings and ties. All told, these perceptions gave physical, material London its deep and varied cultural significances, and show the terms on which magistrates came to understand sudden changes that often left them wondering what might lie around the next corner. They did not dwell on loss for too long. There was too much work to be done. Many magistrates, after all, had trading interests that taught them to plan ahead and forecast which way things might turn. The City looked forwards and backwards, thinking about its future appearance, economy, and society. But more time was spent on simply getting from one day to the next. Senses of loss never led to waves of overwhelming nostalgia and numbing lethargy, but resulted instead in more focused surveillance and attempts to clean up the city and crime. Loss and threat galvanized City leaders. London was continually reimagined by politicians, pamphleteers, poets, and playwrights, and also by anyone else in or out of government who spent any amount of time thinking about changes in the past few years or decades, usually mingling old and new, seeking to stabilize and understand larger London in outlines that soon became dated. Lost Londons indeed, but a resourceful city for all that, even with its roaming 'bands' of thieves and many more outstretched pauper hands. *Ghamidh.*

---

[10] Cf. A couple of recent important interpretations that focus on policy and process in keeping the metropolitan area as stable as possible: Ian W. Archer, *The Pursuit of Stability: Social Relations in Elizabethan London* (Cambridge, 1991); and more recently J. F. Merritt, *The Social World of Early Modern Westminster: Abbey, Court, and Community, 1525–1640* (Manchester, 2005).

# Appendix

The tables and maps that follow provide backing for my main arguments about perceptions of crime, prosecution strategies, the 'public' nature of committal processes and follow-up prosecutions, and geographies of offending and/or arrest. There is a lot of information: 35,399 cases shedding light on prosecution strategies and Bridewell's caseload after 1604 (resulting prosecution profiles and timelines can be read in tandem with Archer's findings for the Elizabethan court[1]), 50,277 times when suspects were depicted in labels, 39,516 cases when we know who brought someone to Bridewell's court, 1,106 Bridewell inmates who were ordered to cross the ocean to begin life all over again, and 820 more who also went overseas but this time to fight wars.

For better or for worse tables tend to represent the past, however messy it might have been, in neat columns of bare statistics collected and put into order by scholars using today's terms, tools, and techniques. This can create problems, needless to say, but at its level best quantification reveals patterns that can make the past seem suddenly more understandable. The advantages and disadvantages of numerical measurements have been mulled over for a long time now. But I don't want to spend time going through this little library of work at the moment, although I do think it is helpful to point out problems in the counting and categorization from which my tables and maps have taken shape. They show some strong swings in perceptions, policing, and prosecution, for instance, but underneath there is some fuzzy sorting of terms and types that needs clearing up, to make sure that nobody comes away from this book with any inaccurate impressions.

Tables 1a–6a group information about cases heard at Bridewell in the half century or so before 1657 (there is a gap in coverage from 1610–17) under five overall subject categories: domestic disorders, immorality and religion, public order, street disorders, and theft and cozening. These are broken down into prosecutions of particular offences with figures for each one in five-year clusters. There is no easy way to make these neat splits and almost inevitably there are overlaps and some strange bedfellows. The other four categories surely concern public order, street disorders contain large doses of morality, much theft takes place in domestic settings, and so on. Some offences belong in two or three or more categories, but they need to be placed somewhere. Building offences are not quite domestic disorders, but they clearly have links to the ordering of households,

---

[1] Ian W. Archer, *The Pursuit of Stability: Social Relations in Elizabethan London* (Cambridge, 1991), p. 239, Table 6.1.

Appendix

more than ever when authorities stepped in to stop house owners dividing their tenements to cram in more poor lodgers for a profit. The grounds for listing hospital offences under domestic disorders is the habit of calling hospitals houses in an effort to set paternal tones for relations inside their walls. Lewd appears under sexual offences, although it did not need to have sexual connotations to set concerns racing. Like vagrancy, lewd was a character stain, something suspicious and at odds with ruling cultures. Vagrancy is catalogued under illicit movement, but it was also quite clearly thought of as an alternative lifestyle, like begging or theft, and arguably has a place in all five subject headings. So, some hard choices needed to be made, unsurprisingly given the scope and scale of my samples. When all is said and done, the character of offences was summed up for clarity in ways that sometimes stretched points. Quibbles about some designations aside, however, the ultimate justification for grouping offences within slippery subject categories was to show beyond any shadow of a doubt how the nature of crime prosecuted at Bridewell changed significantly in the century or so after it first opened its doors. Something that is made clear in Table 6a and Chapter 5 of this book. The main aim of Tables 7a–7c is to show changing perceptions of crime by charting the course of labelling in the Bridewell court from its first nine courtbooks. In all 109 labels are tracked through these books, although one of them, recidivist, was not used at the time, but was thought to be a convenient way to bring the fourteen terms/labels used by the court to pinpoint returning suspects under one fold.[2] Separate totals are given for men and women so that the principal change in perceptions stands out loud and clear: the greater feminization of criminality in London from around 1625 on.

All courtbooks, needless to say, are subject to changing contemporary conventions, conceptualizations, or clerks. Bridewell had a string of clerks over its first century and we can suppose that each one was schooled in procedure in his first days in office, but that he might also have brought a few new methods or even quirks to his time in the post. Some things stay the same: the handy listing of names of offenders in the margins of courtbooks, for example, or lists of governors who came along to court. But some things also changed, including the appearance of the courtbooks, handwriting, not surprisingly, but also entries which get shorter as more and more suspects were squeezed into single hearings of the court. Descriptions of some offences also changed as time passed,[3] along with the ways in which committals were jotted down by clerks, something that has a particular bearing on the remaining tables and maps that cover policing and how suspects ended up at Bridewell's court. Some of these were adjustments if new officers or institutions arrived on the scene. Marshals and warders start to make their presences felt after 1600. Middlesex house of correction made a spurt

---

[2] The fourteen terms with total number of usages were as follows: 'ancient guest' (19), 'comon' (3,533), 'comon customer' (21), 'comon guest' (355), 'continual guest' (1), 'dailie guest' (1), 'frequent guest' (6), 'here before' (324), 'notable' (86), 'notorious' (400), 'old' (61), 'old customer' (705), 'old guest' (412), and, lastly, 'ordinary guest' (4). A note of explanation is also in order for the chronological headings of 7a–9c. There are overlaps – for example, 1626–34 and 1634–43 – because the basis for quantification is the period covered by each one of Bridewell's courtbooks.
[3] See chap. 5.

of committals to Bridewell in its first few years but they soon dried up. Trading companies sent in a handful of people once they began business, and the Corporation of the Poor joined them later on, although not in numbers that made any impression on overall trends.

There are no entries in the courtbooks that tell us in helpful detail how clerks were asked to note down the circumstances of committals in different ways. For that reason it is sometimes tricky to tell whether what we see on the page when the number of committals from a particular class of officers goes up or down is an administrative intervention or a part of policing procedure, refined outside Bridewell on London's streets. Is the big drop in committals attributed to the night-watch from the mid-1620s on, for example, a sign that watches were less active or that it became standard practice for them to hand over anyone they caught out late to a constable, deputy, or marshal to bring to a lock-up, or, if a suspect was first taken to a justice, only the justice signing the warrant is named in the books? The watch made the arrest; but it was left to someone else to make the committal. We read that vagrant and 'comon roge' Anne Godfrey was led to Bridewell by 'Sr Xpofer Drapers beadle' in 1579, after she was found walking suspiciously after dark by watchmen. The alleged 'comon harlot' Alice Maddocks was picked up vagrant by the watch late one night in the same week but was 'sent' to Bridewell by Deputy Gonnell. Similarly, three women 'taken vagrant at Kynsington Midd[lesex]' in the same year were sent to Bridewell by 'Mr recorder'.[4] This invites a question about each one of the 39,516 times when the clerk wrote down the name and/or office of someone responsible for sending someone to Bridewell: these are committals but who made arrests? It is quite clear in 25,147 cases when only 'public' officers like constables, night-watchmen, or marshals appear in entries that they are doing both. But how did a nightwalker or thief end up in the hands of the Court of Aldermen, the mayor alone, or a justice? This is all to say that these tables have complicated things to say about bringing London's low life to court if a magistrate or City official is credited with a committal. To make things knottier still, some big-wigs had double or treble identities: Sir Lionel Ducket, Sir Alexander Avenon, and Sir James Hawes each made a fair number of committals to Bridewell in the 1570s, but in what capacity is not always clear as they were all aldermen, justices, and Bridewell governors, and can only be given a single status on each occasion.

Luckily, none of this detracts from an overwhelming characteristic of Bridewell committals that is at odds with how the lion's share of scholarship understands the nature of policing and prosecution four centuries ago: the massive majority were made by 'public' officers or officials.[5] In matter of fact the involvement of 'public' officers in policing London is seriously understated in Bridewell's records. Time after time the clerk jots down that large groups of vagrants were brought to court from off the streets but there is no mention of an arresting officer: twelve 'comen vagrant roges were taken in the stretes' at one time in 1579 and we have no clue how they ended up in Bridewell.[6] But one thing is sure, none of them walked there on their own. A Bridewell cell was the last place that they wanted to be. Officers rounded up these vagrants, and at other times in similar situations this is duly

---

[4] BHC 3, fos. 420v, 385v.   [5] See chap. 10.   [6] BHC 3, fo. 352v.

Appendix 441

noted. A moment of forgetfulness might explain all occasions when no note was made. But even more likely from around 1600 on when batches of forty or more vagrants show up with no hint of how they got from the street to the court, is that these round-ups by officers were so routine by now that it really made no difference whether their role was put down on paper. Little difference back then, perhaps, but not now if we want to know all there is to know about processes and profiles of arrests and committals by which vagrants and others landed up in Bridewell. In addition, officers also dropped off suspects with justices or other City officials, meaning that at those times too their work at the point of arrest is not noticed. So, the role of 'public' officers is larger than the already heavy involvement shown in these tables, and because at various points in time magistrates asked marshals to hand over vagrants to the nearest constable, or deputies or constables were sometimes mentioned alone when they brought in suspects caught by the night-watch, the number of arrests by particular officers was either higher or lower than words on paper would lead us to believe. Clearly watchmen had a bigger role to play at the moment of arrest, and deputies seem busier in that drama because they often took charge of suspects from arresting officers for the trip to Bridewell. But, again, although there is some confusion about exact sources of arrest in these tables, it is still within the overall compass of policing by public officers. Almost incidentally, this same confusion adds force to arguments about chains of command or linking lines that made policing London in the century after 1560 more effective than we have thought up to now.[7]

While there is more that could be said about each one of these tables, I want to end with a question about what we see on maps of arrests. These maps plot arrests by wards to let us see quite quickly where most suspects were picked up across the city. I use them to pinpoint London's troublespots, always aware that Bridewell's location just over the city's west walls might have an influence on what we see, but not, I think, a distorting one.[8] A question that leaps to mind is whether we are mapping locations of arrests or offences; did suspects steal somewhere else before slipping over ward borders to make a getaway? Well over three-quarters of offenders who were put in Bridewell by 'public' officers were vagrants, nightwalkers, beggars, people drinking late, others with no job or evident means to get by, or people who had got on the wrong side of their neighbours for too long, offenders in other words who were picked up on the spot or caught red-handed, and unlikely to be on the run from chasing officers or victims. Consequently, in many cases both their arrest and offence can be locked in one place. Also worthy of mention is the tendency, heavily disapproved of by London's leaders at the time, for officers not to cross into next-door wards when they were running after suspects. There is a clear geography of crime and policing in these maps, the two Farringdon wards stand out, and strong supporting evidence from elsewhere suggests that this is an accurate picture and one that people at the time would have taken to heart.

There are nearly always issues of categorization in tables and maps drawn from such large numbers of cases and crimes. Overlaps are inevitable, not least in a culture that drew little or no distinction between sin and crime, where just about

---

[7] See chap. 8.  [8] See chap. 3.

every crime carried a moral stain and public order was broadly construed in terms that ranged all the way from domestic disorders to anti-social character flaws like idleness or lewdness. This all said, however, these tables and maps show some striking situations in London in the century or so after 1550: the 'public' nature of much policing and prosecution, for example, a greater gendering of criminality, and the growing prominence of environmental conceptions of crime around 1600 that were linked to London's quick growth and 'sare' changes.

## Prisons, Hospitals, and Markets

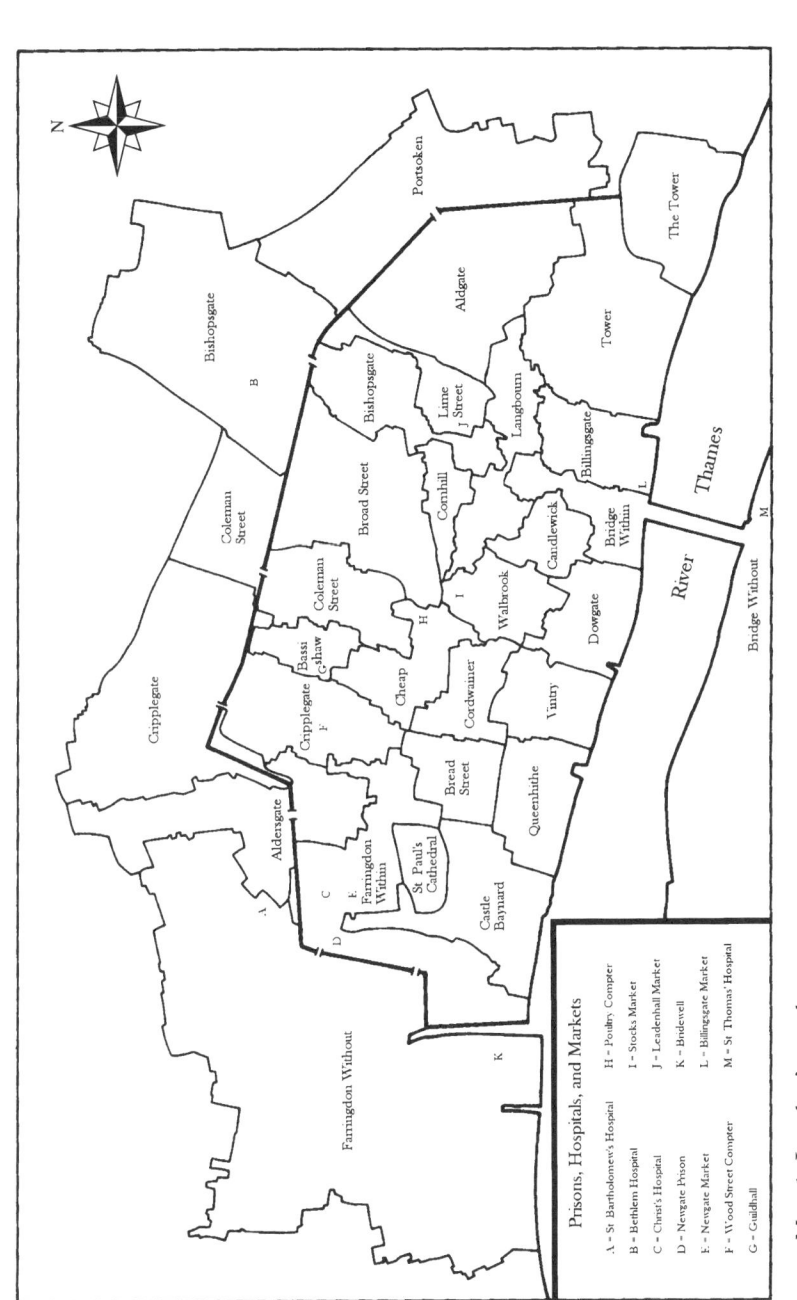

A – St Bartholomew's Hospital
B – Bethlem Hospital
C – Christ's Hospital
D – Newgate Prison
E – Newgate Market
F – Wood Street Compter
G – Guildhall
H – Poultry Compter
I – Stocks Market
J – Leadenhall Market
K – Bridewell
L – Billingsgate Market
M – St Thomas' Hospital

Map 1: London's wards

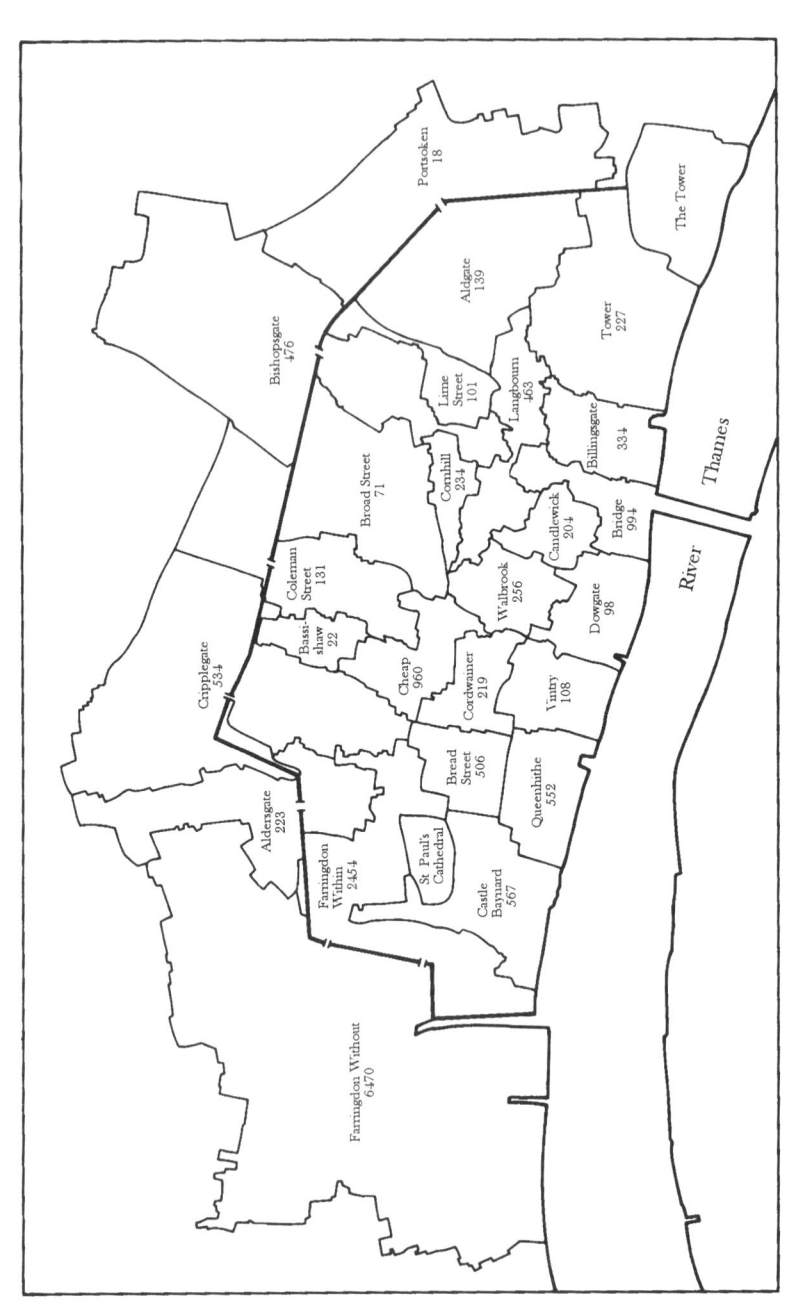

Map 2: Locations of arrests by 'public' officers by ward, 1604–1658

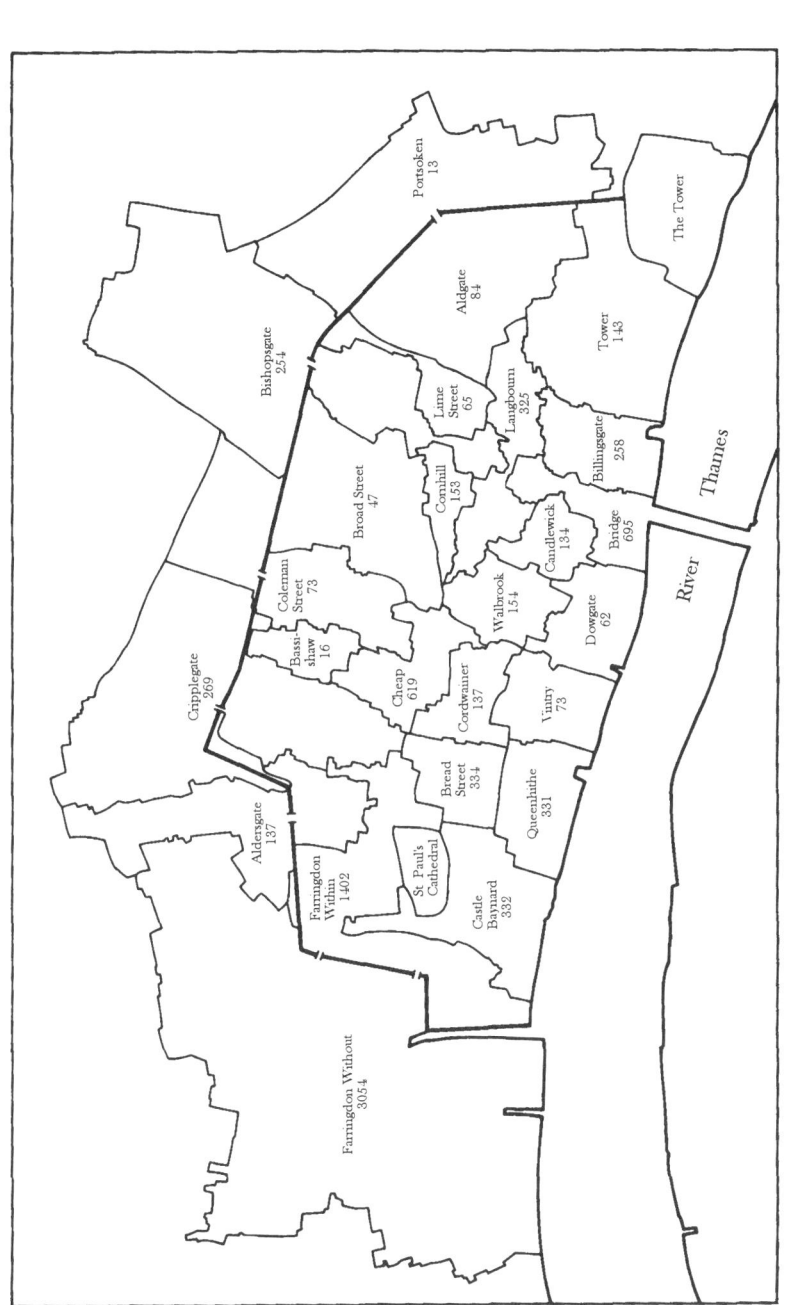

Map 3: Locations of arrests of vagrants by ward, 1604–1658

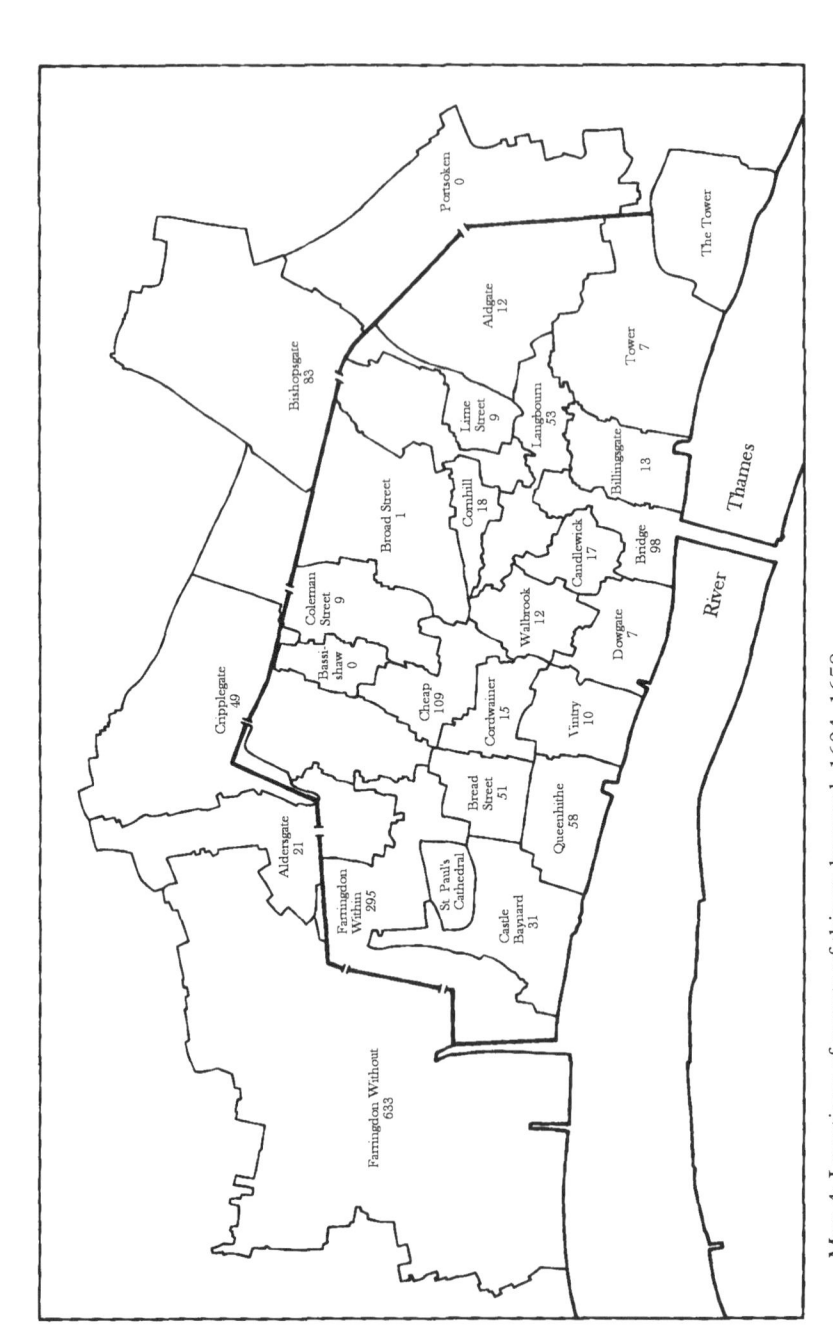

Map 4: Locations of arrests of thieves by ward, 1604–1658

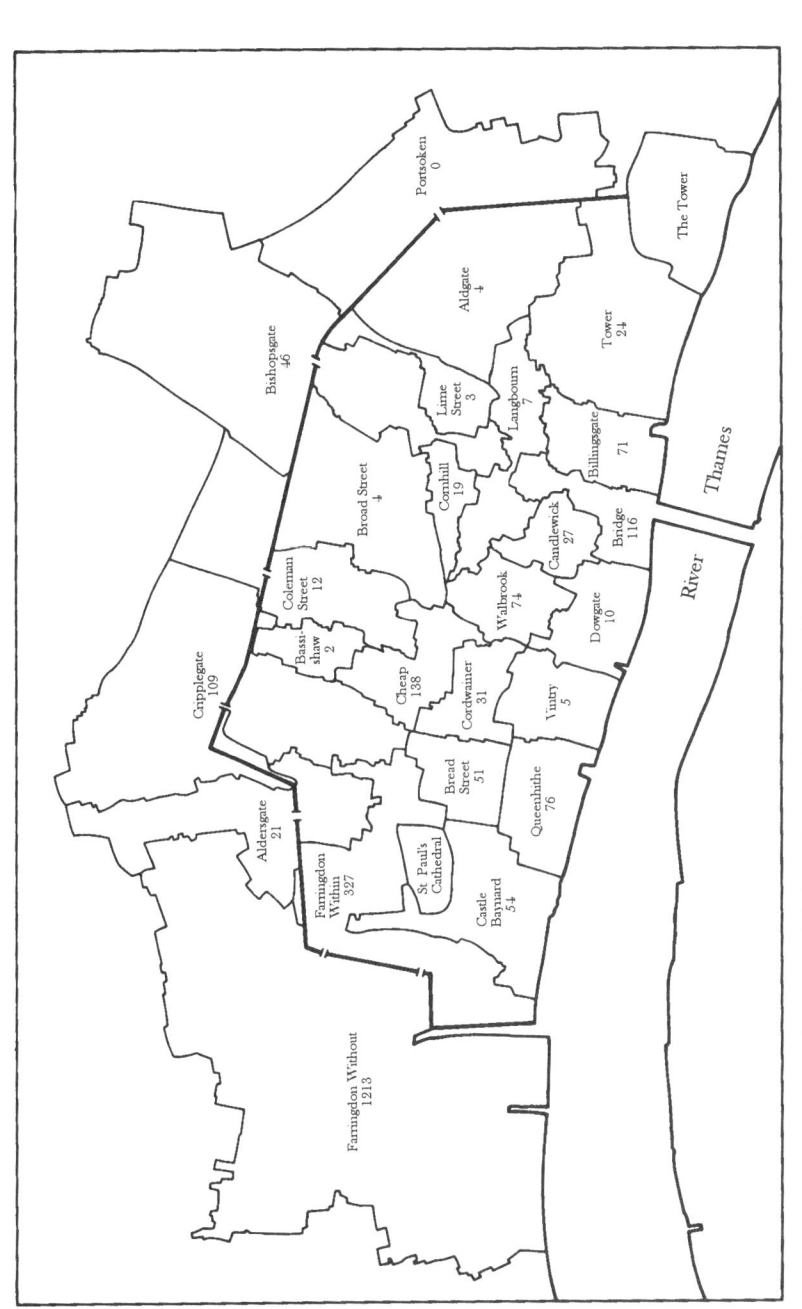

Map 5: Locations of arrests of nightwalkers and people walking late by ward, 1604–1658

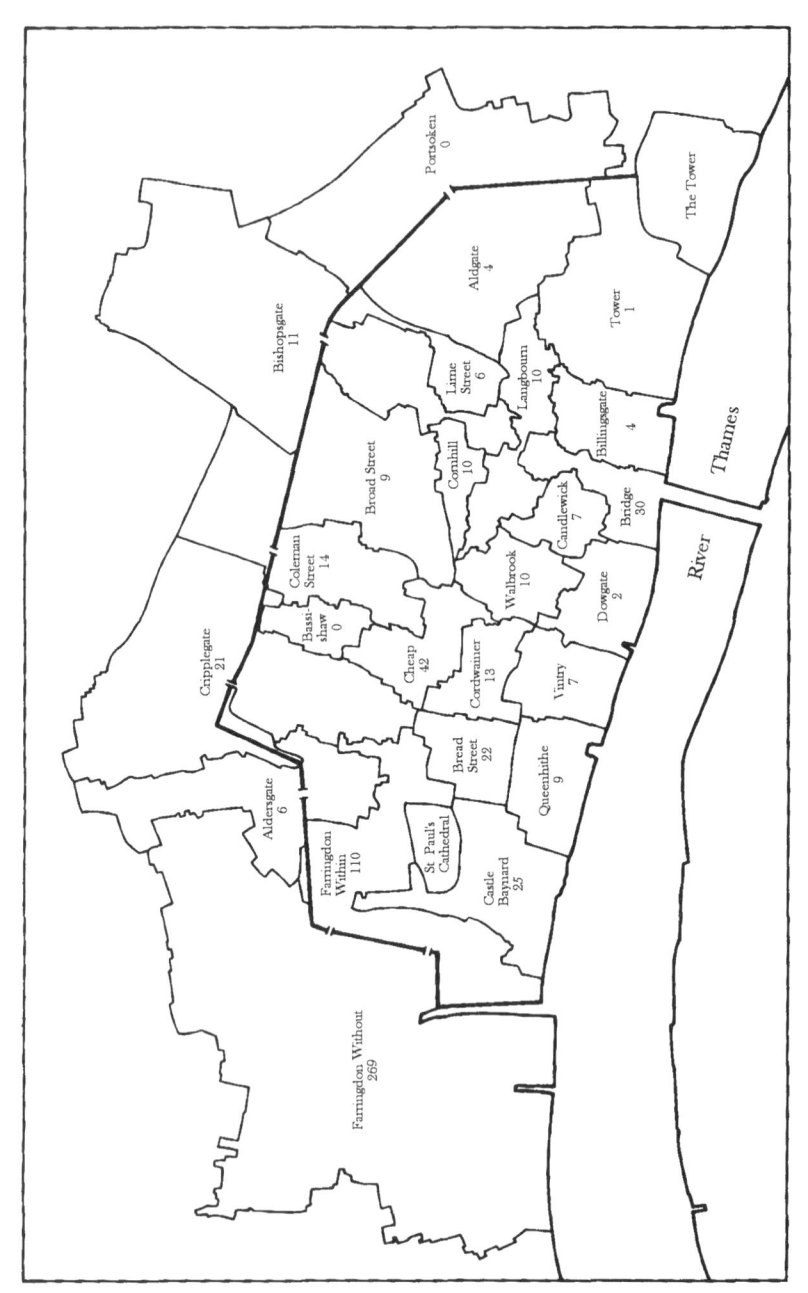

Map 6: Locations of arrests of beggars by ward, 1604–1658

Tables 1a–1b: *Domestic disorders prosecuted at Bridewell, 1605–1657*

Table 1a: *Household offences prosecuted at Bridewell, 1605–1657*

| | 1605–9 | 1618–22 | 1623–7 | 1628–32 | 1633–7 | 1638–42 | 1643–7 | 1648–52 | 1653–7 | Totals |
|---|---|---|---|---|---|---|---|---|---|---|
| Abandoning children | 17 | 20 | 24 | 46 | 38 | 34 | 12 | 6 | 11 | 208 |
| Building offences | 0 | 0 | 0 | 0 | 1 | 0 | 0 | 0 | 0 | 1 |
| Children disorders | 19 | 10 | 4 | 15 | 8 | 6 | 5 | 4 | 2 | 73 |
| Family neglect | 3 | 1 | 5 | 6 | 9 | 6 | 2 | 2 | 3 | 37 |
| Husband-wife disorders | 10 | 2 | 7 | 4 | 4 | 8 | 2 | 1 | 0 | 38 |
| Inmate | 12 | 0 | 0 | 0 | 0 | 0 | 0 | 0 | 0 | 12 |
| Lodging inmates | 5 | 1 | 2 | 0 | 0 | 0 | 0 | 0 | 0 | 8 |
| Lodging suspect people | 17 | 2 | 0 | 9 | 3 | 3 | 0 | 0 | 0 | 34 |
| Orphan conveying | 0 | 0 | 0 | 1 | 0 | 0 | 0 | 0 | 0 | 1 |
| Running from master | 172 | 102 | 65 | 110 | 65 | 103 | 13 | 15 | 37 | 682 |
| Running from parents | 10 | 4 | 4 | 2 | 1 | 3 | 0 | 0 | 0 | 24 |
| Servant disorders | 120 | 65 | 44 | 90 | 92 | 60 | 15 | 11 | 11 | 508 |
| Totals | 385 | 207 | 155 | 283 | 221 | 223 | 49 | 39 | 64 | 1626 |

Table 1b: *Hospital offences prosecuted at Bridewell, 1605–1657*

| | 1605–9 | 1618–22 | 1623–7 | 1628–32 | 1633–7 | 1638–42 | 1643–7 | 1648–52 | 1653–7 | Totals |
|---|---|---|---|---|---|---|---|---|---|---|
| Abusing B'well governors | 0 | 0 | 2 | 1 | 0 | 0 | 0 | 0 | 0 | 3 |
| Bailing B'well prisoners | 0 | 0 | 3 | 2 | 0 | 0 | 0 | 0 | 0 | 5 |
| B'well artmasters abuses | 0 | 0 | 0 | 1 | 0 | 0 | 0 | 0 | 0 | 1 |
| B'well prisoners disorders | 7 | 18 | 9 | 27 | 25 | 2 | 0 | 0 | 0 | 88 |
| B'well tenants disorders | 8 | 0 | 0 | 0 | 0 | 0 | 0 | 0 | 0 | 8 |
| Hospitals, patient disorders | 4 | 2 | 1 | 2 | 0 | 0 | 1 | 1 | 0 | 11 |
| Newgate, disorders | 0 | 1 | 0 | 0 | 0 | 0 | 0 | 0 | 3 | 4 |
| Totals | 19 | 21 | 15 | 33 | 25 | 2 | 1 | 1 | 3 | 120 |

*Tables 2a–2c: Immorality and religious offences prosecuted at Bridewell 1605–1657*

*Table 2a: Sexual offences prosecuted at Bridewell, 1605–1657*

| | 1605–9 | 1618–22 | 1623–7 | 1628–32 | 1633–7 | 1638–42 | 1643–7 | 1648–52 | 1653–7 | Totals |
|---|---|---|---|---|---|---|---|---|---|---|
| Bawd | 5 | 11 | 13 | 17 | 0 | 0 | 0 | 0 | 0 | 46 |
| Bawdy house keeping | 10 | 11 | 17 | 8 | 3 | 1 | 5 | 1 | 0 | 56 |
| Bawdy house taken in | 6 | 17 | 24 | 21 | 0 | 2 | 0 | 3 | 0 | 73 |
| Bigamy | 2 | 0 | 1 | 0 | 0 | 0 | 1 | 0 | 1 | 5 |
| Cross dressing | 0 | 3 | 1 | 4 | 0 | 0 | 1 | 0 | 0 | 9 |
| Fornication | 262 | 90 | 48 | 50 | 37 | 33 | 16 | 18 | 11 | 565 |
| Ill company taken in | 4 | 0 | 1 | 2 | 0 | 0 | 0 | 0 | 0 | 7 |
| Ill house keeping | 4 | 1 | 2 | 1 | 1 | 0 | 0 | 0 | 0 | 9 |
| Ill house taken in | 11 | 1 | 2 | 18 | 12 | 10 | 19 | 9 | 1 | 83 |
| Illegitimacy | 246 | 69 | 30 | 47 | 41 | 40 | 9 | 8 | 5 | 495 |
| Incest | 0 | 0 | 1 | 0 | 0 | 0 | 0 | 0 | 0 | 1 |
| Incontinent living | 9 | 47 | 37 | 14 | 8 | 6 | 3 | 1 | 0 | 125 |
| Infanticide | 0 | 0 | 0 | 0 | 1 | 0 | 0 | 0 | 0 | 1 |
| Keeping company | 27 | 47 | 24 | 94 | 86 | 48 | 27 | 22 | 27 | 402 |
| Lewd | 19 | 80 | 53 | 54 | 11 | 3 | 22 | 38 | 54 | 334 |
| Light | 1 | 0 | 1 | 1 | 0 | 0 | 0 | 0 | 0 | 3 |
| Lodging lewd people | 0 | 4 | 4 | 1 | 0 | 0 | 1 | 0 | 1 | 11 |
| Paternity false accusation | 4 | 4 | 2 | 6 | 2 | 4 | 0 | 0 | 0 | 22 |
| Pimp/procurer | 4 | 0 | 2 | 0 | 0 | 2 | 0 | 0 | 0 | 8 |
| Pregnant women carrying | 0 | 2 | 2 | 1 | 3 | 1 | 0 | 0 | 0 | 9 |
| Pregnant women lodging | 0 | 2 | 2 | 0 | 0 | 0 | 0 | 0 | 2 | 6 |
| Queen | 1 | 11 | 4 | 0 | 0 | 0 | 0 | 0 | 0 | 16 |
| Rape/sexual assault | 3 | 4 | 0 | 4 | 8 | 3 | 1 | 0 | 0 | 23 |
| Sex enticing others | 4 | 0 | 3 | 16 | 6 | 4 | 2 | 4 | 10 | 49 |
| Sodomy | 0 | 1 | 0 | 1 | 0 | 0 | 0 | 0 | 0 | 2 |
| Strumpet | 0 | 3 | 1 | 0 | 0 | 0 | 0 | 0 | 0 | 4 |
| Whore | 15 | 13 | 5 | 8 | 0 | 0 | 1 | 1 | 2 | 45 |
| Whoremonger | 2 | 0 | 0 | 0 | 0 | 0 | 0 | 0 | 0 | 2 |
| Totals | 639 | 421 | 280 | 368 | 219 | 157 | 108 | 105 | 114 | 2,411 |

Table 2b: *Alehouse disorders prosecuted at Bridewell, 1605–1657*

|  | 1605–9 | 1618–22 | 1623–7 | 1628–32 | 1633–7 | 1638–42 | 1643–7 | 1648–52 | 1653–7 | Totals |
|---|---|---|---|---|---|---|---|---|---|---|
| Alehouse haunting | 8 | 2 | 0 | 0 | 0 | 0 | 0 | 0 | 0 | 10 |
| Alehouse unlicensed | 0 | 0 | 0 | 0 | 0 | 0 | 0 | 0 | 1 | 1 |
| Drunk/drinking | 101 | 78 | 88 | 90 | 41 | 31 | 28 | 7 | 3 | 467 |
| Unlawful games | 4 | 2 | 0 | 0 | 0 | 0 | 0 | 0 | 0 | 6 |
| Totals | 113 | 82 | 88 | 90 | 41 | 31 | 28 | 7 | 4 | 484 |

Table 2c: *Religious offences prosecuted at Bridewell, 1605–1657*

|  | 1605–9 | 1618–22 | 1623–7 | 1628–32 | 1633–7 | 1638–42 | 1643–7 | 1648–52 | 1653–7 | Totals |
|---|---|---|---|---|---|---|---|---|---|---|
| Blasphemy | 1 | 8 | 1 | 1 | 0 | 0 | 0 | 0 | 0 | 11 |
| Divine service disrupting | 3 | 0 | 1 | 0 | 0 | 0 | 0 | 0 | 0 | 4 |
| Heresy | 0 | 2 | 2 | 0 | 0 | 0 | 0 | 0 | 0 | 4 |
| Minister abusing | 0 | 0 | 0 | 2 | 0 | 0 | 0 | 1 | 0 | 3 |
| Preaching unlicensed | 0 | 1 | 0 | 0 | 0 | 0 | 0 | 0 | 0 | 1 |
| Prophecies | 1 | 0 | 0 | 0 | 0 | 0 | 0 | 2 | 0 | 3 |
| Recusancy | 10 | 0 | 0 | 1 | 0 | 0 | 0 | 0 | 0 | 11 |
| Religious radicalism | 1 | 0 | 0 | 0 | 0 | 0 | 0 | 1 | 0 | 2 |
| Sunday drinking/working | 4 | 0 | 1 | 5 | 1 | 2 | 2 | 0 | 0 | 15 |
| Totals | 20 | 11 | 5 | 9 | 1 | 2 | 2 | 4 | 0 | 54 |

Tables 3a–3c: *Public order offences prosecuted at Bridewell 1605–1657*
Table 3a: *Violence and abuse cases prosecuted at Bridewell, 1605–1657*

|  | 1605–9 | 1618–22 | 1623–7 | 1628–32 | 1633–7 | 1638–42 | 1643–7 | 1648–52 | 1653–7 | Totals |
|---|---|---|---|---|---|---|---|---|---|---|
| Abusing people | 1 | 5 | 5 | 1 | 0 | 0 | 2 | 0 | 0 | 14 |
| Arson | 1 | 1 | 2 | 2 | 2 | 2 | 3 | 2 | 5 | 20 |
| Barratry | 0 | 0 | 0 | 1 | 0 | 0 | 0 | 0 | 0 | 1 |
| Misdemeanours | 29 | 3 | 5 | 3 | 1 | 3 | 1 | 6 | 3 | 54 |
| Murder/attempted murder | 2 | 0 | 0 | 9 | 0 | 0 | 0 | 2 | 0 | 13 |
| Neighbours abusing | 3 | 1 | 1 | 6 | 2 | 8 | 4 | 1 | 2 | 28 |
| Rayling words | 13 | 20 | 4 | 4 | 6 | 5 | 5 | 2 | 0 | 59 |
| Scolding | 3 | 0 | 1 | 3 | 0 | 0 | 4 | 0 | 0 | 11 |
| Seditious words | 0 | 2 | 1 | 0 | 3 | 9 | 11 | 0 | 0 | 26 |
| Suicide attempted | 1 | 0 | 2 | 1 | 0 | 0 | 0 | 0 | 0 | 4 |
| Tumult | 3 | 19 | 10 | 15 | 12 | 14 | 3 | 1 | 4 | 81 |
| Unruly | 3 | 3 | 2 | 3 | 0 | 0 | 2 | 0 | 0 | 13 |
| Vandalism | 1 | 3 | 3 | 2 | 1 | 1 | 1 | 1 | 1 | 14 |
| Violence | 36 | 11 | 26 | 54 | 33 | 31 | 5 | 2 | 2 | 200 |
| Totals | 96 | 68 | 62 | 104 | 60 | 73 | 41 | 17 | 17 | 538 |

Table 3b: Lifestyle and character offences prosecuted at Bridewell, 1605–1657

| | 1605–9 | 1618–22 | 1623–7 | 1628–32 | 1633–7 | 1638–42 | 1643–7 | 1648–52 | 1653–7 | Totals |
|---|---|---|---|---|---|---|---|---|---|---|
| At own hand | 0 | 0 | 0 | 0 | 0 | 1 | 0 | 0 | 0 | 1 |
| Bad | 0 | 0 | 1 | 0 | 0 | 0 | 0 | 0 | 0 | 1 |
| Dangerous | 0 | 6 | 0 | 3 | 0 | 0 | 19 | 3 | 11 | 42 |
| Disorderly | 17 | 2 | 3 | 1 | 2 | 1 | 9 | 6 | 19 | 60 |
| Dissolute | 0 | 0 | 0 | 0 | 0 | 0 | 0 | 1 | 0 | 1 |
| Evil/Evil life | 3 | 1 | 1 | 0 | 1 | 0 | 5 | 4 | 24 | 39 |
| Idle | 14 | 15 | 20 | 20 | 22 | 15 | 38 | 28 | 60 | 232 |
| Ill life | 0 | 4 | 2 | 4 | 2 | 0 | 3 | 0 | 8 | 23 |
| Incorrigible | 0 | 0 | 0 | 0 | 0 | 0 | 0 | 0 | 1 | 1 |
| Loose living | 5 | 8 | 6 | 1 | 0 | 0 | 2 | 1 | 0 | 23 |
| Mad/distracted | 9 | 10 | 5 | 9 | 0 | 6 | 2 | 5 | 7 | 53 |
| Masterless | 62 | 2 | 1 | 0 | 0 | 0 | 0 | 0 | 0 | 65 |
| Nasty | 0 | 0 | 0 | 0 | 0 | 0 | 0 | 1 | 0 | 1 |
| No account of living | 6 | 4 | 2 | 1 | 5 | 7 | 0 | 2 | 1 | 28 |
| Out of service | 9 | 16 | 21 | 19 | 8 | 24 | 13 | 0 | 1 | 111 |
| Suspicious | 2 | 4 | 8 | 6 | 11 | 3 | 11 | 5 | 28 | 78 |
| Vile | 0 | 0 | 0 | 0 | 0 | 0 | 0 | 0 | 1 | 1 |
| Work neglecting | 0 | 1 | 0 | 0 | 0 | 0 | 0 | 0 | 0 | 1 |
| Working unfree | 0 | 1 | 0 | 0 | 0 | 0 | 0 | 0 | 0 | 1 |
| Totals | 127 | 74 | 70 | 64 | 51 | 57 | 102 | 56 | 161 | 762 |

Table 3c: Officer abuse and political offences prosecuted at Bridewell, 1605–1657

|  | 1605–9 | 1618–22 | 1623–7 | 1628–32 | 1633–7 | 1638–42 | 1643–7 | 1648–52 | 1653–7 | Totals |
|---|---|---|---|---|---|---|---|---|---|---|
| Abusing officers | 32 | 14 | 13 | 16 | 6 | 11 | 11 | 1 | 0 | 104 |
| Abusing mayors | 0 | 1 | 0 | 0 | 0 | 0 | 0 | 0 | 0 | 1 |
| Abusing military men | 0 | 0 | 0 | 0 | 0 | 0 | 2 | 0 | 0 | 2 |
| Officers abuses | 3 | 2 | 2 | 0 | 0 | 0 | 0 | 0 | 0 | 7 |
| Spy | 0 | 0 | 0 | 0 | 0 | 0 | 4 | 0 | 0 | 4 |
| Treason | 0 | 0 | 0 | 0 | 0 | 0 | 45 | 0 | 0 | 45 |
| Totals | 35 | 17 | 15 | 16 | 6 | 11 | 62 | 1 | 0 | 163 |

Tables 4a–4b: *Street disorders prosecuted at Bridewell 1605–57*
Table 4a: *Illicit movement prosecuted at Bridewell, 1605–57*

|  | 1605–9 | 1618–22 | 1623–7 | 1628–32 | 1633–7 | 1638–42 | 1643–7 | 1648–52 | 1653–7 | Totals |
|---|---|---|---|---|---|---|---|---|---|---|
| Begging | 54 | 252 | 196 | 463 | 118 | 88 | 92 | 394 | 253 | 1,910 |
| Counterfeit pass | 5 | 2 | 3 | 3 | 2 | 1 | 5 | 0 | 0 | 21 |
| Counterfeiting madness | 0 | 1 | 1 | 0 | 0 | 0 | 0 | 0 | 0 | 2 |
| Deserting | 2 | 1 | 9 | 15 | 2 | 19 | 119 | 0 | 0 | 167 |
| Juggler | 0 | 1 | 0 | 0 | 0 | 0 | 0 | 0 | 0 | 1 |
| Linkcarrier | 0 | 2 | 0 | 0 | 0 | 0 | 0 | 0 | 0 | 2 |
| Markets haunting | 0 | 1 | 0 | 0 | 0 | 0 | 0 | 0 | 0 | 1 |
| Nightwalking | 161 | 298 | 205 | 224 | 290 | 397 | 238 | 190 | 140 | 2,143 |
| Rogue | 10 | 46 | 59 | 8 | 1 | 2 | 0 | 1 | 0 | 127 |
| Spirits | 0 | 0 | 0 | 0 | 0 | 2 | 10 | 2 | 7 | 21 |
| Streetwalking | 0 | 0 | 0 | 3 | 0 | 0 | 0 | 0 | 0 | 3 |
| Transportee escaping | 0 | 0 | 1 | 0 | 0 | 0 | 0 | 0 | 0 | 1 |
| Vagrant | 3,283 | 4,300 | 3,556 | 3,512 | 1,050 | 416 | 313 | 812 | 541 | 17,783 |
| Wandering | 23 | 1 | 11 | 6 | 22 | 26 | 16 | 6 | 4 | 115 |
| Watch taken in | 206 | 345 | 218 | 171 | 188 | 298 | 71 | 17 | 19 | 1,533 |
| Totals | 3,744 | 5,250 | 4,259 | 4,405 | 1,673 | 1,249 | 864 | 1,422 | 964 | 23,830 |

Table 4b: *Traffic and street-selling offences prosecuted at Bridewell, 1605–1657*

| | 1605–9 | 1618–22 | 1623–7 | 1628–32 | 1633–7 | 1638–42 | 1643–7 | 1648–52 | 1653–7 | Totals |
|---|---|---|---|---|---|---|---|---|---|---|
| Ballads singing and selling | 0 | 2 | 0 | 1 | 0 | 1 | 0 | 0 | 0 | 4 |
| Carmen disorders | 0 | 1 | 2 | 2 | 4 | 0 | 0 | 0 | 0 | 9 |
| Horses unregulated | 0 | 0 | 1 | 0 | 0 | 0 | 0 | 0 | 0 | 1 |
| Pamphlets selling | 1 | 0 | 0 | 0 | 0 | 3 | 4 | 5 | 1 | 14 |
| Porters disorders | 0 | 0 | 0 | 3 | 1 | 0 | 0 | 0 | 0 | 4 |
| Porters unlicensed | 3 | 2 | 10 | 2 | 9 | 2 | 0 | 0 | 0 | 28 |
| Streets blocking | 0 | 0 | 0 | 1 | 0 | 0 | 0 | 0 | 1 | 2 |
| Street selling | 8 | 0 | 0 | 0 | 0 | 1 | 1 | 0 | 0 | 9 |
| Watermen disorders | 0 | 0 | 0 | 0 | 0 | 0 | 0 | 0 | 0 | 1 |
| Totals | 12 | 5 | 13 | 9 | 14 | 7 | 5 | 5 | 2 | 72 |

Table 5a: *Theft and cozening prosecuted at Bridewell, 1605–1657*

| | 1605–9 | 1618–22 | 1623–7 | 1628–32 | 1633–7 | 1638–42 | 1643–7 | 1648–52 | 1653–7 | Totals |
|---|---|---|---|---|---|---|---|---|---|---|
| Children stealing away | 1 | 0 | 0 | 4 | 0 | 0 | 0 | 0 | 0 | 5 |
| Coining | 0 | 0 | 0 | 1 | 0 | 0 | 0 | 0 | 1 | 2 |
| Counterfeit letter | 0 | 0 | 0 | 1 | 1 | 0 | 0 | 0 | 11 | 13 |
| Cozening/cheating | 52 | 67 | 47 | 32 | 26 | 10 | 9 | 14 | 0 | 257 |
| Enticing to pilfer | 2 | 3 | 3 | 9 | 4 | 1 | 0 | 0 | 0 | 22 |
| Felony* | 6 | 1 | 2 | 1 | 4 | 7 | 2 | 6 | 0 | 29 |
| Lodging thieves | 0 | 1 | 4 | 2 | 0 | 0 | 0 | 0 | 0 | 7 |
| Pilfering | 397 | 726 | 871 | 1,157 | 568 | 528 | 218 | 300 | 187 | 4,952 |
| Receiving stolen goods | 4 | 3 | 5 | 21 | 7 | 2 | 1 | 0 | 0 | 43 |
| Unlawful selling | 3 | 0 | 1 | 1 | 2 | 0 | 2 | 0 | 0 | 9 |
| Totals | 465 | 801 | 933 | 1,229 | 612 | 548 | 232 | 320 | 199 | 5,339 |

*Note:*
*Although there is not a clear statement of offence I have counted these cases under Theft because most prosecuted felony was theft.

Appendix

Table 6a: *Number of prosecuted offences in overall categories, 1605–1657*

|  | Domestic Disorders No. (%) | Morality & Religion No. (%) | Public Order No. (%) | Street Disorders No. (%) | Theft & Cozening No. (%) | Totals |
|---|---|---|---|---|---|---|
| 1605–09 | 404 (7.14) | 772 (13.65) | 258 (4.56) | 3,756 (66.42) | 465 (8.22) | 5,655 |
| 1618–22 | 228 (3.28) | 514 (7.39) | 159 (2.28) | 5,255 (75.53) | 801 (11.51) | 6,957 |
| 1623–27 | 170 (2.88) | 373 (6.33) | 147 (2.49) | 4,272 (72.47) | 933 (15.83) | 5,895 |
| 1628–32 | 316 (4.78) | 467 (7.06) | 184 (2.78) | 4,414 (66.77) | 1,229 (18.59) | 6,610 |
| 1633–37 | 246 (8.42) | 261 (8.93) | 117 (4.00) | 1,687 (57.71) | 612 (20.94) | 2,923 |
| 1638–42 | 225 (9.53) | 190 (8.05) | 141 (5.97) | 1,256 (53.22) | 548 (23.22) | 2,360 |
| 1643–47 | 50 (3.35) | 138 (9.23) | 205 (13.72) | 869 (58.16) | 232 (15.53) | 1,494 |
| 1648–52 | 40 (2.02) | 116 (5.87) | 74 (3.74) | 1,427 (72.18) | 320 (16.19) | 1,977 |
| 1653–7 | 67 (4.38) | 118 (7.72) | 178 (11.65) | 966 (63.22) | 199 (13.02) | 1,528 |
| 1605–57 | 1,746 (4.93) | 2,949 (8.33) | 1,463 (4.13) | 23,902 (67.52) | 5,339 (15.08) | 35,399 |

Table 7a: Labels recorded in Bridewell's courtbooks by gender, 1559–1657

| | 1559–62 m–w | 1574–6 m–w | 1576–9 m–w | 1598–1604 m–w | 1604–10 m–w | 1617–26 m–w | 1626–34 m–w | 1634–42 m–w | 1642–58 m–w | Totals m–w |
|---|---|---|---|---|---|---|---|---|---|---|
| Abhominable | 2–2 | 0–1 | 0–0 | 0–0 | 0–0 | 0–0 | 0–0 | 0–0 | 0–0 | 2–3 |
| Arrogant(ly) | 3–1 | 0–0 | 0–0 | 0–0 | 0–0 | 0–0 | 0–0 | 0–0 | 0–0 | 3–1 |
| At own hand | 0–0 | 0–0 | 0–0 | 0–0 | 0–0 | 0–2 | 0–0 | 0–1 | 0–0 | 0–3 |
| Audacious | 0–0 | 0–0 | 0–0 | 0–1 | 0–0 | 0–0 | 0–0 | 0–0 | 0–0 | 0–1 |
| Bad | 0–0 | 0–0 | 0–0 | 7–3 | 1–1 | 0–1 | 0–0 | 2–0 | 0–0 | 10–5 |
| Barbarous | 0–0 | 0–0 | 0–0 | 0–0 | 2–0 | 0–0 | 0–0 | 0–0 | 0–0 | 2–0 |
| Base | 0–0 | 0–0 | 0–0 | 0–0 | 0–0 | 0–0 | 0–0 | 0–0 | 0–3 | 0–3 |
| Bawd | 13–73 | 4–5 | 55–85 | 2–27 | 1–4 | 0–0 | 0–0 | 0–0 | 0–0 | 75–194 |
| Beast(ly) | 3–1 | 0–0 | 0–1 | 0–0 | 0–0 | 0–0 | 0–0 | 0–0 | 0–0 | 3–2 |
| Beggar | 31–19 | 20–8 | 33–7 | 99–71 | 38–29 | 215–204 | 354–196 | 93–33 | 460–264 | 1,343–831 |
| Brave | 0–0 | 0–0 | 0–2 | 0–0 | 0–0 | 0–0 | 0–0 | 0–0 | 0–0 | 0–2 |
| Briber | 28–7 | 0–0 | 0–0 | 0–0 | 0–0 | 0–0 | 0–0 | 0–0 | 0–0 | 28–7 |
| Contentious | 0–0 | 0–0 | 0–0 | 0–0 | 0–0 | 0–0 | 1–2 | 0–0 | 0–0 | 1–2 |
| Cozener/cheat | 0–0 | 23–6 | 52–11 | 39–24 | 48–22 | 80–34 | 25–17 | 16–13 | 13–16 | 296–143 |
| Cutpurse | 9–8 | 28–2 | 20–1 | 34–1 | 36–2 | 81–10 | 60–11 | 2–1 | 5–1 | 275–37 |
| Dangerous | 0–0 | 0–0 | 0–0 | 14–0 | 3–0 | 71–4 | 22–0 | 19–1 | 77–5 | 206–10 |
| Desolate | 0–0 | 0–0 | 0–0 | 0–0 | 0–0 | 0–0 | 0–0 | 0–0 | 0–1 | 0–1 |
| Desperate | 2–1 | 0–0 | 0–0 | 0–0 | 1–0 | 0–0 | 0–0 | 3–0 | 1–2 | 7–3 |
| Detestable | 0–0 | 0–0 | 0–0 | 0–0 | 0–0 | 0–0 | 0–0 | 0–0 | 0–0 | 0–1 |
| Disorderly | 0–1 | 0–0 | 0–0 | 5–1 | 34–5 | 14–2 | 15–14 | 34–40 | 67–67 | 169–130 |
| Dissolute | 0–0 | 0–0 | 0–0 | 1–0 | 2–0 | 6–0 | 1–2 | 0–0 | 7–7 | 17–9 |
| Distempered | 0–0 | 0–0 | 0–0 | 0–0 | 0–1 | 0–1 | 0–0 | 0–0 | 0–0 | 0–1 |
| Drab | 0–9 | 0–0 | 0–0 | 0–0 | 0–2 | 0–0 | 0–0 | 0–0 | 0–0 | 0–11 |
| Drunkard | 7–1 | 18–8 | 18–14 | 31–4 | 46–6 | 33–12 | 0–0 | 0–0 | 0–0 | 153–45 |
| Evil | 12–22 | 23–12 | 10–20 | 4–20 | 4–2 | 0–0 | 0–1 | 4–3 | 21–27 | 78–107 |

Table 7a: (cont.)

| | 1559–62 m–w | 1574–6 m–w | 1576–9 m–w | 1598–1604 m–w | 1604–10 m–w | 1617–26 m–w | 1626–34 m–w | 1634–42 m–w | 1642–58 m–w | Totals m–w |
|---|---|---|---|---|---|---|---|---|---|---|
| Filcher | 12–1 | 9–3 | 15–11 | 39–24 | 8–0 | 2–0 | 0–0 | 0–0 | 0–0 | 85–39 |
| Filthy | 5–4 | 0–0 | 0–0 | 1–10 | 0–0 | 0–0 | 0–0 | 0–0 | 0–0 | 6–14 |
| Fine | 0–0 | 0–0 | 0–1 | 0–0 | 0–0 | 0–0 | 0–0 | 0–0 | 0–0 | 0–1 |
| Forward | 2–0 | 0–0 | 0–0 | 0–0 | 0–0 | 0–0 | 0–0 | 0–0 | 0–0 | 2–0 |
| Gadder | 1–14 | 0–0 | 0–0 | 0–0 | 0–0 | 0–0 | 0–0 | 0–0 | 0–0 | 1–14 |
| Haker | 0–0 | 0–0 | 0–1 | 1–0 | 0–0 | 0–0 | 0–0 | 0–0 | 0–0 | 1–0 |
| Hedgeharlot | 0–0 | 0–0 | 0–1 | 0–0 | 0–0 | 0–0 | 0–0 | 0–0 | 0–0 | 0–1 |
| Hedgehaunter | 0–0 | 0–0 | 1–0 | 0–0 | 0–0 | 0–0 | 0–0 | 0–0 | 0–0 | 1–0 |
| Hooker | 0–0 | 0–0 | 0–0 | 1–0 | 0–0 | 0–0 | 0–0 | 0–0 | 0–0 | 1–0 |
| Horrible | 0–1 | 0–0 | 0–0 | 0–0 | 0–0 | 0–0 | 0–0 | 0–0 | 0–0 | 0–1 |
| Idle | 98–29 | 73–30 | 29–7 | 71–17 | 46–25 | 158–72 | 87–69 | 108–72 | 190–182 | 860–503 |
| Ill | 0–0 | 0–0 | 5–4 | 0–4 | 6–4 | 1–6 | 5–21 | 4–7 | 3–15 | 24–61 |
| Impudent | 0–0 | 0–0 | 0–0 | 0–0 | 0–0 | 0–0 | 0–0 | 0–0 | 0–2 | 0–2 |
| Incorrigible | 0–0 | 0–0 | 0–0 | 10–0 | 10–0 | 18–3 | 5–0 | 4–2 | 4–2 | 51–7 |
| Inhumane | 0–0 | 0–0 | 0–0 | 0–0 | 1–0 | 0–0 | 0–0 | 0–0 | 0–0 | 1–0 |
| Intolerable | 0–0 | 0–0 | 0–0 | 0–0 | 0–0 | 1–0 | 0–0 | 0–0 | 0–0 | 1–0 |
| Lascivious | 0–0 | 0–0 | 0–0 | 0–0 | 2–2 | 0–0 | 0–2 | 0–0 | 0–0 | 2–4 |
| Lecher | 1–0 | 0–0 | 0–0 | 0–0 | 0–0 | 0–0 | 0–0 | 0–0 | 0–0 | 1–0 |
| Lewd | 68–88 | 13–1 | 70–30 | 53–77 | 42–51 | 162–264 | 12–214 | 38–64 | 81–237 | 539–1,026 |
| Lifter | 0–0 | 0–0 | 0–0 | 0–0 | 14–4 | 15–8 | 1–2 | 0–0 | 0–0 | 30–14 |
| Light | 0–0 | 0–0 | 0–0 | 0–4 | 0–26 | 0–5 | 0–2 | 0–0 | 0–0 | 0–37 |
| Lingerer | 0–0 | 0–0 | 0–0 | 0–0 | 0–0 | 2–0 | 0–0 | 0–0 | 0–0 | 2–0 |
| Loathsome | 0–0 | 0–0 | 0–0 | 0–0 | 1–0 | 0–0 | 0–0 | 0–0 | 0–0 | 1–0 |
| Lodger | 0–0 | 0–0 | 0–0 | 0–0 | 1–2 | 0–0 | 0–0 | 0–0 | 0–0 | 1–2 |
| Loiterer | 36–20 | 2–0 | 5–0 | 2–3 | 1–0 | 36–0 | 0–0 | 0–0 | 0–0 | 82–23 |
| Loose | 0–0 | 0–0 | 0–0 | 7–3 | 8–17 | 10–30 | 1–6 | 12–5 | 3–17 | 41–78 |
| Lurker | 0–0 | 0–0 | 0–0 | 0–0 | 0–0 | 4–0 | 0–0 | 0–0 | 0–0 | 4–0 |

Table 7a: (cont.)

| | 1559–62 m–w | 1574–6 m–w | 1576–9 m–w | 1598–1604 m–w | 1604–10 m–w | 1617–26 m–w | 1626–34 m–w | 1634–42 m–w | 1642–58 m–w | Totals m–w |
|---|---|---|---|---|---|---|---|---|---|---|
| Lusty | 1–0 | 0–0 | 0–0 | 1–0 | 0–0 | 25–0 | 4–0 | 3–0 | 1–0 | 35–0 |
| Malicious | 0–0 | 0–1 | 0–0 | 0–0 | 0–0 | 0–0 | 0–0 | 0–0 | 0–0 | 0–1 |
| Masterless | 40–0 | 5–0 | 16–3 | 8–0 | 88–4 | 26–1 | 1–0 | 0–0 | 0–0 | 184–8 |
| Micher | 3–1 | 0–0 | 0–0 | 0–0 | 0–0 | 0–0 | 0–0 | 0–0 | 0–0 | 3–1 |
| Monstrous | 0–0 | 0–0 | 2–1 | 0–0 | 1–0 | 0–0 | 0–0 | 0–0 | 0–0 | 3–1 |
| Nasty | 0–0 | 0–0 | 0–0 | 0–0 | 1–0 | 0–0 | 0–0 | 0–0 | 0–0 | 1–0 |
| Naughty | 72–72 | 6–0 | 0–10 | 0–1 | 0–0 | 0–0 | 0–0 | 0–0 | 0–0 | 78–83 |
| Nighthunter | 0–1 | 0–0 | 0–0 | 0–0 | 0–0 | 0–0 | 0–0 | 0–0 | 0–0 | 0–1 |
| Nightwalker | 0–0 | 1–68 | 0–21 | 7–108 | 2–195 | 73–414 | 7–316 | 7–589 | 0–577 | 97–2,288 |
| Ninner | 0–0 | 0–0 | 0–0 | 1–0 | 13–0 | 1–0 | 0–0 | 1–0 | 0–0 | 16–0 |
| Nip | 0–0 | 0–0 | 0–0 | 1–3 | 10–0 | 178–43 | 1–0 | 0–0 | 0–0 | 190–46 |
| No account of life | 0–0 | 2–0 | 0–0 | 7–17 | 9–2 | 30–14 | 43–34 | 79–67 | 69–67 | 239–201 |
| Obstinate | 0–0 | 0–0 | 0–0 | 2–0 | 0–0 | 0–0 | 0–0 | 0–0 | 0–0 | 2–0 |
| Out of service | 1–0 | 0–0 | 0–1 | 3–13 | 1–6 | 8–27 | 2–25 | 14–30 | 3–12 | 32–114 |
| Pack | 0–20 | 0–0 | 0–0 | 0–1 | 0–0 | 0–0 | 0–0 | 0–0 | 0–0 | 0–21 |
| Picker | 99–52 | 6–3 | 1–0 | 4–1 | 2–1 | 0–0 | 0–0 | 0–0 | 0–0 | 112–57 |
| Picklock | 0–0 | 0–0 | 0–0 | 1–0 | 0–1 | 1–0 | 0–0 | 0–0 | 0–0 | 2–1 |
| Pickpocket | 0–0 | 0–0 | 0–2 | 10–3 | 7–11 | 104–68 | 104–78 | 44–53 | 21–35 | 290–250 |
| Pickpurse | 20–7 | 1–1 | 0–0 | 3–2 | 1–0 | 1–4 | 0–0 | 0–0 | 0–0 | 26–14 |
| Picksack | 0–0 | 0–0 | 0–0 | 1–0 | 0–0 | 0–0 | 0–0 | 0–0 | 0–0 | 1–0 |
| Pilferer | 114–26 | 104–38 | 65–15 | 55–39 | 290–125 | 783–307 | 734–570 | 488–347 | 356–359 | 2,989–1,826 |
| Ranger | 0–0 | 0–0 | 0–0 | 0–2 | 0–0 | 0–0 | 0–0 | 0–0 | 0–0 | 0–2 |
| Receiver | 18–5 | 9–4 | 5–4 | 3–5 | 1–4 | 5–10 | 8–21 | 2–3 | 0–1 | 51–57 |
| Recidivist* | 110–250 | 201–185 | 266–179 | 165–151 | 262–205 | 598–450 | 426–664 | 174–768 | 195–679 | 2,397–3,531 |
| Rogue | 11–18 | 152–38 | 395–134 | 121–6 | 36–1 | 270–19 | 21–2 | 16–5 | 4–2 | 1,026–225 |

Table 7a: (cont.)

| | 1559–62 m–w | 1574–6 m–w | 1576–9 m–w | 1598–1604 m–w | 1604–10 m–w | 1617–26 m–w | 1626–34 m–w | 1634–42 m–w | 1642–58 m–w | Totals m–w |
|---|---|---|---|---|---|---|---|---|---|---|
| Rover/roving | 0–2 | 0–0 | 0–0 | 0–0 | 0–0 | 0–0 | 0–0 | 0–0 | 0–0 | 0–2 |
| Rude | 0–0 | 0–0 | 0–0 | 5–1 | 0–0 | 0–0 | 0–0 | 0–0 | 0–3 | 5–4 |
| Ruffian(ly) | 2–0 | 0–0 | 0–0 | 0–0 | 0–0 | 0–0 | 0–0 | 0–0 | 0–0 | 2–0 |
| Shameless | 3–2 | 0–0 | 0–0 | 0–0 | 0–0 | 0–0 | 0–0 | 0–0 | 0–0 | 3–2 |
| Shifter | 0–0 | 0–0 | 0–0 | 9–1 | 2–0 | 0–1 | 0–0 | 0–0 | 0–0 | 11–2 |
| Shopcreep | 0–0 | 0–0 | 0–0 | 0–0 | 0–0 | 1–0 | 0–0 | 0–0 | 0–0 | 1–0 |
| Shoplift | 0–0 | 0–0 | 0–0 | 0–0 | 0–0 | 0–0 | 0–1 | 0–0 | 0–0 | 0–1 |
| Slut | 0–1 | 0–0 | 0–0 | 0–0 | 0–0 | 0–0 | 0–0 | 0–0 | 0–0 | 0–1 |
| Stark | 0–0 | 0–0 | 1–0 | 0–0 | 0–0 | 0–0 | 0–0 | 0–0 | 0–0 | 1–0 |
| Stout | 3–0 | 13–2 | 4–0 | 0–0 | 0–0 | 0–0 | 0–0 | 0–0 | 0–0 | 20–2 |
| Straggler | 7–17 | 0–0 | 0–0 | 0–0 | 0–0 | 0–1 | 0–0 | 0–0 | 0–0 | 7–18 |
| Streetwalker | 0–0 | 0–0 | 0–3 | 0–0 | 0–0 | 0–0 | 0–3 | 0–0 | 0–0 | 0–6 |
| Stubborn | 25–1 | 0–0 | 0–0 | 3–1 | 0–0 | 0–0 | 0–0 | 0–0 | 0–0 | 28–2 |
| Sturdy | 4–0 | 0–0 | 0–0 | 21–6 | 29–2 | 20–1 | 6–1 | 2–1 | 7–0 | 89–11 |
| Suspicious | 25–15 | 15–17 | 12–17 | 3–9 | 28–17 | 56–12 | 24–26 | 27–20 | 65–39 | 255–172 |
| Swaggerer | 0–0 | 0–0 | 0–0 | 0–0 | 3–1 | 0–0 | 0–0 | 0–0 | 0–0 | 3–1 |
| Troublesome | 0–0 | 0–0 | 0–0 | 0–0 | 0–0 | 0–0 | 0–3 | 0–0 | 0–0 | 0–3 |
| Turbulent | 0–0 | 0–0 | 0–0 | 0–0 | 0–0 | 6–3 | 0–2 | 0–0 | 0–0 | 6–5 |
| Uncivil | 0–0 | 0–0 | 0–0 | 0–0 | 0–0 | 0–0 | 0–0 | 0–0 | 0–1 | 0–1 |
| Ungodly | 1–0 | 0–0 | 0–0 | 0–0 | 0–0 | 0–0 | 0–0 | 0–0 | 0–0 | 1–0 |
| Unhonest | 0–0 | 0–0 | 0–1 | 0–1 | 0–0 | 0–0 | 0–0 | 0–0 | 0–0 | 0–2 |
| Unorderly | 0–0 | 0–0 | 1–1 | 0–0 | 0–0 | 0–0 | 0–0 | 0–0 | 0–0 | 1–1 |
| Unruly | 4–0 | 1–8 | 0–1 | 3–1 | 18–5 | 90–33 | 29–37 | 3–5 | 2–1 | 150–91 |
| Vagabond | 164–1 | 30–3 | 24–9 | 0–0 | 0–0 | 0–0 | 0–0 | 0–0 | 0–0 | 218–13 |
| Vagrant | 0–0 | 0–0 | 201–57 | 3,366–1,506 | 2,913–1,013 | 5,328–2,608 | 2,714–1,564 | 640–415 | 976–753 | 16,138–7,916 |
| Valiant | 1–0 | 0–0 | 0–1 | 0–0 | 0–0 | 0–0 | 0–0 | 0–0 | 0–0 | 1–1 |

Table 7a: (cont.)

|  | 1559–62 m–w | 1574–6 m–w | 1576–9 m–w | 1598–1604 m–w | 1604–10 m–w | 1617–26 m–w | 1626–34 m–w | 1634–42 m–w | 1642–58 m–w | Totals m–w |
|---|---|---|---|---|---|---|---|---|---|---|
| Vicious | 1–0 | 0–0 | 0–0 | 0–0 | 1–0 | 0–0 | 0–0 | 1–0 | 0–0 | 3–0 |
| Vile | 35–12 | 0–0 | 0–0 | 0–0 | 0–0 | 0–0 | 0–0 | 0–0 | 0–1 | 35–13 |
| Wanderer | 9–10 | 0–0 | 2–0 | 85–56 | 29–13 | 26–16 | 22–19 | 120–125 | 65–77 | 358–316 |
| Wicked | 0–1 | 9–6 | 0–0 | 5–9 | 0–0 | 0–2 | 0–0 | 0–0 | 0–1 | 14–19 |
| Wild | 0–0 | 0–0 | 29–4 | 0–1 | 1–3 | 0–0 | 0–0 | 0–0 | 0–1 | 30–9 |
| Witch | 0–1 | 0–0 | 0–0 | 0–0 | 0–0 | 0–0 | 0–0 | 0–0 | 0–0 | 0–1 |

Note:
*Recidivist is not the court's term. It is one that I am using to cover a multiplicity of terms that were used by the court to mean a returning recidivist in 5,928 cases. They are (with total number of usages in brackets) 'ancient guest' (4 men/15 women), 'comon' (1,254 men/2,279 women), 'comon customer' (6 men/15 women), 'comon guest' (184 men/171 women), 'continual guest' (1 man), 'dailie guest' (1 man), 'frequent guest' (4 men/2 women), 'here before' (83 men/241 women), 'notable' (53 men/33 women), 'notorious' (264 men/136 women), 'old' (45 men/16 women), 'old customer' (252 men/453 women), 'old guest' (245 men/167 women), and, lastly, 'ordinary guest' (1 man/3 women).

Table 7b: *Labels recorded in Bridewell's courtbooks by individual volume*

|  | Men | Women | Totals |
| --- | --- | --- | --- |
| (1) 1559–62 | 1,106 | 816 | 1,922 |
| (2) 1574–76 | 768 | 450 | 1,218 |
| (3) 1576–79 | 1,337 | 660 | 1,997 |
| (4) 1598–1604 | 4,314 | 2,238 | 6,552 |
| (5) 1604–10 | 4,103 | 1,811 | 5,914 |
| (6) 1617–26 | 8,539 | 4,692 | 13,231 |
| (7) 1626–34 | 4,735 | 3,925 | 8,660 |
| (8) 1634–42 | 1,960 | 2,670 | 4,630 |
| (9) 1642–58 | 2,696 | 3,457 | 6,153 |
| Totals | 29,558 | 20,719 | 50,277 |

Table 7c: *Selected labels revealing rising female labelling*

| | 1559–62 m–w | 1574–6 m–w | 1576–9 m–w | 1598–1604 m–w | 1604–10 m–w | 1617–26 m–w | 1626–34 m–w | 1634–42 m–w | 1642–58 m–w | Totals m–w |
|---|---|---|---|---|---|---|---|---|---|---|
| Ancient guest | 0–2 | 0–0 | 0–0 | 0–0 | 0–0 | 0–1 | 0–2 | 4–10 | 0–0 | 4–15 |
| Beggar | 31–19 | 20–8 | 33–7 | 99–71 | 38–29 | 215–204 | 354–196 | 93–33 | 460–264 | 1,343–831 |
| Comon | 82–218 | 201–184 | 248–161 | 46–59 | 70–77 | 152–161 | 154–265 | 111–482 | 190–672 | 1,254–2,279 |
| Comon customer | 0–0 | 0–0 | 0–0 | 1–3 | 10–17 | 172–148 | 0–3 | 1–0 | 0–0 | 184–171 |
| Cozener/cheat | 0–0 | 23–6 | 52–11 | 39–24 | 48–22 | 80–34 | 25–17 | 16–13 | 13–16 | 296–143 |
| Disorderly | 0–1 | 0–0 | 0–0 | 5–1 | 34–5 | 14–2 | 15–14 | 34–40 | 67–67 | 169–130 |
| Evil | 12–22 | 23–12 | 10–20 | 4–20 | 4–2 | 0–0 | 0–1 | 4–3 | 21–27 | 78–107 |
| Here before | 20–24 | 0–0 | 7–6 | 24–22 | 7–2 | 0–0 | 0–0 | 25–184 | 0–3 | 83–241 |
| Idle | 98–29 | 73–30 | 29–7 | 71–17 | 46–25 | 158–72 | 87–69 | 108–72 | 190–182 | 860–503 |
| Ill | 0–0 | 0–0 | 5–4 | 0–4 | 6–4 | 1–6 | 5–21 | 4–7 | 3–15 | 24–61 |
| Lewd | 68–88 | 13–1 | 70–30 | 53–77 | 42–51 | 162–264 | 12–214 | 38–64 | 81–237 | 539–1026 |
| Loose | 0–0 | 0–0 | 0–0 | 7–3 | 8–17 | 10–30 | 1–6 | 12–5 | 3–17 | 41–78 |
| Nightwalker | 0–0 | 1–68 | 0–21 | 7–108 | 2–195 | 73–414 | 7–316 | 7–589 | 0–577 | 97–2,288 |
| No account of life | 0–0 | 2–0 | 0–0 | 7–17 | 9–2 | 30–14 | 43–34 | 79–67 | 69–67 | 239–201 |
| Old customer | 0–0 | 0–0 | 0–0 | 0–0 | 0–0 | 0–0 | 223–369 | 29–82 | 0–2 | 252–453 |
| Out of service | 1–0 | 0–0 | 0–1 | 3–13 | 1–6 | 8–27 | 2–25 | 14–30 | 3–12 | 32–114 |
| Pickpocket | 0–0 | 0–0 | 0–2 | 10–3 | 7–11 | 104–68 | 104–78 | 44–53 | 21–35 | 290–250 |
| Pilferer | 114–26 | 104–38 | 65–15 | 55–39 | 290–125 | 783–307 | 734–570 | 488–347 | 356–359 | 2,989–1,826 |
| Receiver | 18–5 | 9–4 | 5–4 | 3–5 | 1–4 | 5–10 | 8–21 | 2–3 | 0–1 | 51–57 |
| Streetwalker | 0–0 | 0–0 | 0–3 | 0–0 | 0–0 | 0–0 | 0–3 | 0–0 | 0–0 | 0–6 |
| Unruly | 4–0 | 1–8 | 0–1 | 3–1 | 18–5 | 90–33 | 29–37 | 3–5 | 2–1 | 150–91 |
| Vagrant | 0–0 | 0–0 | 201–57 | 3,366–1,506 | 2,913–1,013 | 5,328–2,608 | 2714–1,564 | 640–415 | 976–753 | 16,138–7,916 |
| Wanderer | 9–10 | 0–0 | 2–0 | 85–56 | 29–13 | 26–16 | 22–19 | 120–125 | 65–77 | 358–316 |
| Totals | 457–444 | 470–161 | 526–350 | 522–543 | 670–612 | 2,083–1,811 | 1,825–2,280 | 1,236–2,214 | 1,544–2,631 | |
| Percentages | 50.72–40.28 | 74.48–25.52 | 60.04–39.96 | 49.01–50.99 | 52.26–47.74 | 53.49–46.51 | 44.46–55.54 | 35.83–64.17 | 36.98–63.02 | |

Table 8a: *Bridewell committals by categories, 1559–1658*

| | 1559-62 | 1574-6 | 1576-9 | 1604-10 | 1617-26 | 1626-34 | 1634-42 | 1642-58 | Totals |
|---|---|---|---|---|---|---|---|---|---|
| Bridewell officers/warrant | 28 | 72 | 64 | 18 | 203 | 413 | 474 | 502 | 1,774 |
| City Government/ officials | 129 | 83 | 65 | 293 | 727 | 329 | 260 | 1,684 | 3,570 |
| Corporation of the Poor | 0 | 0 | 0 | 0 | 0 | 0 | 0 | 3 | 3 |
| Dutch Church | 0 | 0 | 0 | 2 | 0 | 0 | 0 | 0 | 2 |
| Guilds | 2 | 1 | 0 | 2 | 0 | 2 | 1 | 0 | 8 |
| Hospitals | 28 | 25 | 45 | 24 | 22 | 4 | 3 | 17 | 168 |
| Individuals | 12 | 4 | 10 | 8 | 8 | 45 | 4 | 1 | 92 |
| Justice | 13 | 28 | 119 | 1,468 | 2,057 | 1,525 | 1,107 | 318 | 6,635 |
| Master/parent/relative | 39 | 6 | 27 | 10 | 7 | 7 | 1 | 0 | 97 |
| Military | 0 | 0 | 0 | 0 | 2 | 17 | 0 | 161 | 180 |
| Parliament | 0 | 0 | 0 | 0 | 1 | 0 | 16 | 113 | 130 |
| Parish/ward | 1 | 7 | 12 | 10 | 6 | 2 | 0 | 1 | 39 |
| Prisons/houses of correction | 0 | 16 | 31 | 0 | 283 | 13 | 0 | 2 | 345 |
| 'Public officers' | 352 | 376 | 383 | 2,700 | 10,990 | 5,678 | 2,262 | 2,406 | 25,147 |
| Quarter Sessions | 0 | 0 | 8 | 58 | 137 | 170 | 102 | 330 | 805 |
| Religious authorities | 11 | 1 | 9 | 12 | 15 | 5 | 9 | 0 | 62 |
| Royal officials | 11 | 1 | 10 | 36 | 138 | 157 | 98 | 0 | 451 |
| Trading company | 0 | 0 | 0 | 0 | 3 | 0 | 0 | 0 | 3 |
| Victim | 0 | 0 | 0 | 0 | 0 | 0 | 3 | 0 | 3 |
| 'Voluntarily' came in | 0 | 0 | 1 | 0 | 1 | 0 | 0 | 0 | 2 |
| | 626 | 620 | 784 | 4,641 | 14,600 | 8,367 | 4,340 | 5,538 | 39,516 |

Table 8b: *Leading sources of Bridewell committals, percentage changes*

| | 1559–62 | 1574–6 | 1576–9 | 1604–10 | 1617–26 | 1626–34 | 1634–42 | 1642–58 | Totals |
|---|---|---|---|---|---|---|---|---|---|
| Bridewell officers/ warrant | 4.47 | 11.61 | 8.16 | 0.38 | 1.39 | 4.94 | 10.92 | 9.06 | 4.49 |
| City Government/ officials | 20.61 | 13.39 | 8.29 | 6.31 | 4.98 | 3.93 | 5.99 | 30.41 | 9.03 |
| Hospitals | 4.47 | 4.03 | 5.74 | 0.52 | 0.15 | 0.05 | 0.07 | 0.31 | 0.42 |
| Individuals | 1.91 | 0.64 | 1.27 | 0.17 | 0.05 | 0.54 | 0.09 | 0.02 | 0.23 |
| Justice | 2.08 | 4.52 | 15.18 | 31.63 | 14.09 | 18.23 | 25.51 | 5.74 | 16.79 |
| Master/parent/relative | 6.23 | 0.97 | 3.44 | 0.37 | 0.06 | 0.08 | 0.02 | 0.00 | 0.24 |
| Military | 0.00 | 0.00 | 0.00 | 0.00 | 0.01 | 0.20 | 0.00 | 2.91 | 0.45 |
| Parliament | 0.00 | 0.00 | 0.00 | 0.00 | 0.01 | 0.00 | 0.37 | 2.04 | 0.33 |
| Parish/ward | 0.16 | 1.13 | 1.53 | 0.21 | 0.04 | 0.02 | 0.00 | 0.02 | 0.10 |
| Prisons/houses of correction | 0.00 | 2.58 | 3.95 | 0.00 | 1.94 | 0.15 | 0.00 | 0.04 | 0.87 |
| 'Public officers' | 56.23 | 60.64 | 48.85 | 58.18 | 75.27 | 67.86 | 52.12 | 43.44 | 63.64 |
| Quarter Sessions | 0.00 | 0.00 | 1.02 | 1.25 | 0.94 | 2.03 | 2.35 | 5.96 | 2.04 |
| Religious authorities | 1.76 | 0.16 | 1.15 | 0.26 | 0.10 | 0.05 | 0.21 | 0.00 | 0.16 |
| Royal officials | 1.76 | 0.16 | 1.27 | 0.77 | 0.94 | 1.88 | 2.26 | 0.00 | 1.14 |

Table 8c: Committals to Bridewell by 'public' officers, 1559–1658

| | 1559–62 No. (%) | 1574–6 No. (%) | 1576–9 No. (%) | 1604–10 No. (%) | 1617–26 No. (%) | 1626–34 No. (%) | 1634–42 No. (%) | 1642–58 No. (%) | Totals No. (%) |
|---|---|---|---|---|---|---|---|---|---|
| Bailiff | 11 (3.12) | 0 (0.00) | 0 (0.00) | 0 (0.00) | 0 (0.00) | 0 (0.00) | 0 (0.00) | 0 (0.00) | 11 (0.04) |
| Beadle | 78 (22.16) | 11 (2.92) | 16 (4.18) | 299 (11.07) | 402 (3.66) | 13 (0.23) | 15 (0.66) | 3 (0.12) | 837 (3.33) |
| Bellman | 0 (0.00) | 0 (0.00) | 0 (0.00) | 6 (0.22) | 3 (0.03) | 0 (0.00) | 0 (0.00) | 0 (0.00) | 9 (0.03) |
| Constable | 32 (9.09) | 68 (18.08) | 86 (22.45) | 1,269 (47.0) | 6,876 (62.56) | 3,337 (58.77) | 1,838 (81.25) | 811 (33.71) | 14,317 (56.93) |
| Deputy (ward) | 222 (63.07) | 279 (74.20) | 225 (58.75) | 269 (9.96) | 624 (5.68) | 133 (2.34) | 51 (2.25) | 18 (0.75) | 1821 (7.24) |
| Marshal/marshalman | 0 (0.00) | 0 (0.00) | 0 (0.00) | 39 (1.44) | 1,802 (16.40) | 2,130 (37.51) | 358 (15.83) | 1,532 (63.67) | 5,861 (23.31) |
| Warder | 0 (0.00) | 0 (0.00) | 0 (0.00) | 213 (7.88) | 339 (3.08) | 6 (0.10) | 0 (0.00) | 21 (0.87) | 579 (2.30) |
| Watch | 9 (2.56) | 18 (4.79) | 56 (14.62) | 605 (22.41) | 944 (8.59) | 59 (1.04) | 0 (0.00) | 21 (0.87) | 1,712 (6.81) |
| Totals | 352 | 376 | 383 | 2,700 | 10,990 | 5,678 | 2,262 | 2,406 | 25,147 |

470  Appendix

Table 8d: *All sources of Bridewell committals, 1604–1658*

|  | 1604–10 | 1617–26 | 1626–34 | 1634–42 | 1642–58 | Totals |
|---|---|---|---|---|---|---|
| Alderman | 3 | 47 | 28 | 60 | 925 | 1,063 |
| Archbishop | 7 | 3 | 3 | 1 | 0 | 14 |
| Attorney General | 0 | 0 | 2 | 0 | 0 | 2 |
| Aunt | 0 | 1 | 0 | 0 | 0 | 1 |
| Beadle | 299 | 402 | 13 | 15 | 3 | 732 |
| Bellman | 6 | 3 | 0 | 0 | 0 | 9 |
| Bridewell warrant | 3 | 0 | 0 | 0 | 0 | 3 |
| Captain | 0 | 0 | 4 | 0 | 0 | 4 |
| Chamberlain | 11 | 24 | 7 | 2 | 9 | 53 |
| Christ's Hospital | 9 | 4 | 3 | 1 | 0 | 17 |
| Compter | 0 | 0 | 2 | 0 | 2 | 4 |
| Comptroller (royal) | 0 | 0 | 25 | 0 | 0 | 25 |
| Constable | 1,269 | 6,876 | 3,337 | 1,838 | 811 | 14,131 |
| Corporation of the Poor | 0 | 0 | 0 | 0 | 3 | 3 |
| Court of Aldermen | 6 | 11 | 6 | 7 | 0 | 30 |
| Dean Westminster Abbey | 1 | 0 | 0 | 0 | 0 | 1 |
| Deputy (ward) | 269 | 624 | 133 | 51 | 18 | 1,095 |
| Dutch Church | 2 | 0 | 0 | 0 | 0 | 2 |
| East India Company | 0 | 1 | 0 | 0 | 0 | 1 |
| Gentlemen | 4 | 8 | 45 | 4 | 1 | 62 |
| Governor (Bridewell) | 3 | 24 | 76 | 16 | 9 | 128 |
| Greencloth (royal) | 9 | 0 | 63 | 55 | 0 | 127 |
| Guilds | 2 | 0 | 2 | 1 | 0 | 5 |
| High Commission | 4 | 12 | 2 | 8 | 0 | 26 |
| Husband | 0 | 0 | 1 | 0 | 0 | 1 |
| Individuals | 4 | 0 | 0 | 0 | 0 | 4 |
| Justice | 1,468 | 2,057 | 1,525 | 1,107 | 318 | 6,475 |
| Knight Marshal (royal) | 0 | 48 | 25 | 17 | 0 | 90 |
| Lieutenant | 0 | 0 | 13 | 0 | 0 | 13 |
| Lord Admiral | 1 | 0 | 0 | 0 | 0 | 1 |
| Lord Chamberlain | 1 | 0 | 0 | 0 | 0 | 1 |
| Lord Chief Justice | 9 | 59 | 24 | 15 | 0 | 107 |
| Lord High Treasurer | 2 | 0 | 0 | 0 | 0 | 2 |
| Marshal | 39 | 1,799 | 2,125 | 358 | 1,528 | 5,849 |
| Marshalman | 0 | 3 | 2 | 0 | 4 | 9 |
| Master/Mistress | 6 | 4 | 5 | 0 | 0 | 15 |
| Matron (Bridewell) | 0 | 1 | 1 | 1 | 0 | 3 |
| Mayor | 155 | 399 | 272 | 136 | 660 | 1,622 |
| Middlesex House of Correction | 0 | 283 | 11 | 0 | 0 | 294 |
| Military | 0 | 2 | 0 | 0 | 161 | 163 |
| Parents | 4 | 2 | 1 | 1 | 0 | 8 |
| Parish | 5 | 6 | 2 | 0 | 1 | 14 |
| Parliament | 0 | 1 | 0 | 16 | 113 | 130 |
| Porter (Bridewell) | 6 | 30 | 19 | 14 | 23 | 92 |

Appendix 471

Table 8d: *(cont.)*

|  | 1604–10 | 1617–26 | 1626–34 | 1634–42 | 1642–58 | Totals |
|---|---|---|---|---|---|---|
| President (Bridewell) | 0 | 0 | 23 | 414 | 455 | 892 |
| Privy Council | 13 | 27 | 1 | 8 | 0 | 49 |
| Provost Marshal | 0 | 0 | 3 | 0 | 0 | 3 |
| Recorder | 101 | 243 | 15 | 51 | 89 | 499 |
| St Bartholomew's Hospital | 12 | 6 | 0 | 0 | 9 | 27 |
| St Thomas's Hospital | 3 | 12 | 1 | 2 | 8 | 26 |
| Quarter Sessions[*] | 58 | 137 | 170 | 102 | 330 | 793 |
| Sheriff | 17 | 3 | 1 | 4 | 1 | 26 |
| Star Chamber | 0 | 0 | 7 | 3 | 0 | 10 |
| Steward (Bridewell) | 0 | 0 | 1 | 0 | 0 | 1 |
| Temple | 1 | 4 | 0 | 0 | 0 | 5 |
| Treasurer (Bridewell) | 6 | 148 | 293 | 29 | 15 | 491 |
| Treasurer (royal) | 0 | 0 | 10 | 0 | 0 | 10 |
| Victim | 0 | 0 | 0 | 3 | 0 | 3 |
| Virginia Company | 0 | 2 | 0 | 0 | 0 | 2 |
| 'Voluntarily' came in | 0 | 1 | 0 | 0 | 0 | 1 |
| Warder | 213 | 339 | 6 | 0 | 21 | 579 |
| Wardmote | 5 | 0 | 0 | 0 | 0 | 5 |
| Watch | 605 | 944 | 59 | 0 | 21 | 1,629 |
|  | 4,641 | 14,600 | 8,367 | 4,340 | 5,538 | 37,486 |

*Note:*
[*] Quarter Sessions includes referrals from City, Westminster, and Middlesex Sessions, and also prisoners sent from Newgate with, I assume, a committal order from justices either in or out of formal sessions.

Table 9a: *Offences of Bridewell prisoners ordered to be transported, 1604–1658*

| | 1617–26 | 1626–34 | 1634–42 | 1642–58 | Totals |
|---|---|---|---|---|---|
| Arson threat | 0 | 0 | 0 | 1 | 1 |
| Ballad singer | 0 | 0 | 1 | 0 | 1 |
| Begging | 0 | 0 | 5 | 40 | 45 |
| Bridewell order | 22 | 11 | 11 | 89 | 133 |
| City magistrates (committal by) | 28 | 4 | 1 | 6 | 39 |
| Cozening | 0 | 0 | 5 | 0 | 5 |
| Deserting | 0 | 0 | 0 | 1 | 1 |
| Disorderly | 0 | 0 | 0 | 1 | 1 |
| Drunk | 0 | 1 | 0 | 0 | 1 |
| Evil/lewd/ill/suspicious | 0 | 1 | 0 | 9 | 10 |
| Family disorders | 2 | 2 | 1 | 3 | 8 |
| Greencloth Court (committal by) | 0 | 3 | 2 | 0 | 5 |
| Hospitals (committals from) | 2 | 0 | 0 | 0 | 2 |
| Idle | 0 | 0 | 1 | 4 | 5 |
| Incontinent living | 1 | 0 | 0 | 0 | 1 |
| Justice (committals by) | 9 | 5 | 13 | 35 | 62 |
| Keeping company | 1 | 0 | 1 | 2 | 4 |
| Lodging lewd people | 0 | 0 | 2 | 0 | 2 |
| Lord Chief Justice (committals by) | 1 | 0 | 0 | 0 | 1 |
| Middlesex House of Correction | 7 | 0 | 0 | 0 | 7 |
| Misdemeanours | 0 | 0 | 0 | 1 | 1 |
| Newgate (committals from) | 4 | 0 | 0 | 0 | 4 |
| Night taken late | 12 | 1 | 18 | 10 | 41 |
| Nightwalking | 0 | 2 | 13 | 11 | 26 |
| Nightwalking/pilfering | 0 | 0 | 2 | 0 | 2 |
| No account of life | 0 | 0 | 1 | 0 | 1 |
| Officers (committals by) | 96 | 34 | 21 | 8 | 159 |
| Out of service | 0 | 0 | 4 | 1 | 5 |
| Parish (committals by) | 1 | 0 | 0 | 0 | 1 |
| Pickpocket/nip | 1 | 0 | 4 | 2 | 7 |
| Pilfering | 0 | 10 | 23 | 18 | 51 |
| Servant disorders | 1 | 6 | 8 | 6 | 21 |
| Spirit | 0 | 0 | 0 | 2 | 2 |
| Vagrant | 194 | 61 | 62 | 72 | 389 |
| Vagrant pilferer | 4 | 6 | 9 | 16 | 35 |
| Virginia Company (committal by) | 2 | 0 | 0 | 0 | 2 |
| 'Voluntary' came in | 0 | 1 | 0 | 0 | 1 |
| Wandering | 0 | 0 | 3 | 1 | 4 |
| Whoredom | 0 | 0 | 0 | 1 | 1 |
| No offence recorded | 0 | 8 | 4 | 7 | 19 |
| Totals | 388 | 156 | 215 | 347 | 1,106 |

Table 9b: *Destinations of Bridewell prisoners ordered to be transported*

|  | 1617–26 | 1626–34 | 1634–42 | 1642–58 | Totals |
|---|---|---|---|---|---|
| Bermuda | 7 | 31 | 0 | 0 | 38 |
| Barbados | 0 | 5 | 21 | 1 | 27 |
| East Indies | 0 | 0 | 1 | 0 | 1 |
| New England | 0 | 0 | 0 | 5 | 5 |
| New Islands | 0 | 2 | 0 | 0 | 2 |
| St Christopher Isles | 0 | 13 | 6 | 0 | 19 |
| Smerna | 0 | 0 | 0 | 1 | 1 |
| Summer Islands | 0 | 4 | 0 | 0 | 4 |
| Virginia | 381 | 86 | 73 | 0 | 540 |
| Overseas (no destination noted) | 0 | 15 | 114 | 340 | 469 |
| Totals | 388 | 156 | 215 | 347 | 1,106 |

474    Appendix

Table 9c: *Offences of Bridewell prisoners pressed into armies, 1604–1658*

|  | 1604–10 | 1617–26 | 1626–34 | 1634–42 | 1642–58 | Totals |
|---|---|---|---|---|---|---|
| Alehouse/drinking/drunk | 3 | 2 | 2 | 1 | 0 | 8 |
| Begging | 0 | 0 | 8 | 4 | 0 | 12 |
| Bowling alley (taken in) | 0 | 0 | 4 | 0 | 0 | 4 |
| Bridewell order | 0 | 22 | 14 | 1 | 2 | 39 |
| Children disorderly | 1 | 0 | 0 | 0 | 0 | 1 |
| Counterfeiting madness | 0 | 1 | 0 | 0 | 0 | 1 |
| Counterfeiting passport | 1 | 0 | 0 | 0 | 0 | 1 |
| Cozening | 0 | 2 | 1 | 0 | 0 | 3 |
| Cutpurse | 1 | 4 | 8 | 2 | 0 | 15 |
| Dangerous/turbulent | 0 | 3 | 0 | 0 | 2 | 5 |
| Deserting/mutiny | 0 | 0 | 5 | 0 | 0 | 5 |
| Felony (suspicion of) | 0 | 1 | 0 | 0 | 0 | 1 |
| Idle | 1 | 1 | 1 | 0 | 2 | 5 |
| Justice (committed by) | 0 | 9 | 9 | 3 | 0 | 21 |
| Keeping company | 0 | 1 | 0 | 0 | 0 | 1 |
| Knight marshal (committal by) | 0 | 5 | 0 | 0 | 0 | 5 |
| Masterless | 13 | 0 | 0 | 0 | 0 | 13 |
| Mayor (committal by) | 0 | 8 | 6 | 2 | 4 | 20 |
| Misdemeanours | 1 | 0 | 0 | 0 | 0 | 1 |
| Newgate (committal from) | 3 | 3 | 6 | 0 | 0 | 12 |
| Night (taken late) | 1 | 8 | 4 | 2 | 0 | 15 |
| Officers (committals by) | 2 | 69 | 66 | 11 | 2 | 150 |
| Officers abused | 0 | 0 | 1 | 0 | 0 | 1 |
| Pickpocket | 1 | 1 | 0 | 2 | 0 | 4 |
| Pilfering | 0 | 13 | 20 | 2 | 0 | 35 |
| Porter disorders | 0 | 1 | 1 | 0 | 0 | 2 |
| Recorder (committal by) | 0 | 5 | 0 | 0 | 0 | 5 |
| Seafarer | 0 | 2 | 0 | 0 | 0 | 2 |
| Servant disorders | 1 | 0 | 4 | 0 | 0 | 5 |
| Suspected house taken in | 0 | 0 | 1 | 0 | 0 | 1 |
| Tinker | 0 | 0 | 0 | 1 | 0 | 1 |
| Vagrant/rogue | 127 | 86 | 40 | 4 | 0 | 257 |
| Vagrant pilferer | 3 | 10 | 4 | 2 | 0 | 19 |
| No offence recorded | 143 | 2 | 5 | 0 | 0 | 150 |
| Totals | 302 | 259 | 210 | 37 | 12 | 820 |

# Bibliography

## MANUSCRIPT SOURCES

BETHLEM ROYAL HOSPITAL ARCHIVES AND MUSEUM

BHC 4 Bridewell and Bethlem Hospital courtbook, 1598–1604

BRITISH LIBRARY

Additional Manuscript 48019
TT E38(12) *Brief Collections Out of Magna Charta: Or, the Knowne Good Old Lawes of England* (1643).

DORSET RECORD OFFICE

DC/DOB/8/1 Dorchester Offenders Book, 1629–37

ESSEX RECORD OFFICE, COLCHESTER BRANCH

D/B5/SB1/4 Colchester Sessions of Peace Justices Book, 1630–64
D/B5/SB4/3 Colchester Quarter Sessions Book, 1700–14

GOLDSMITHS' COMPANY LIBRARY

Company Minute Books O2-W (1599–1645)

GUILDHALL LIBRARY, LONDON

6 'Memoires Historicall Relating to the 5 Principall Hospitals in London'
9384 *A Brief Treatise or Discourse of Ye Validity, Strength, and Extent of the Charter of Bridewell and How Far Repugnant Both in Matter, Sense, and Meaninge to the Great Charter of England. Worthily Composed by Mr Searjant Fleetwood, Sometymes Seirjant at Lawe.*

### Ecclesiastical records
      9057/1 Archdeaconry of London, General Examination and Deposition Book, 1632–8

9064/14–21 'Acta Quoad Correctionem Delinquentium', 1593–1631
25175 Articles and presentments of St Paul's College of the petty canons to Bishop of London

**Hospital records**
Bridewell and Bethlem Hospital Courtbooks (consulted on microfilm)
The eight Bridewell and Bethlem courtbooks (one more, the fourth, was read in manuscript at Bethlem Royal Hospital Archive and Museum) have recently been given manuscript numbers (in brackets after each one). I, however, cite them through abbreviated title and number.
BHC1–9 (33011/1–9)
33011/1 Bridewell Hospital Courtbook, 1559–62
33011/2 Bridewell Hospital Courtbook, 1574–6
33011/3 Bridewell Hospital Courtbook, 1576–9
33011/5 Bridewell Hospital Courtbook, 1604–10
33011/6 Bridewell Hospital Courtbook, 1617–26
33011/7 Bridewell Hospital Courtbook, 1626–34
33011/8 Bridewell Hospital Courtbook, 1634–42
33011/9 Bridewell Hospital Courtbook, 1642–58
33001 Transcript and translation of Bridewell charter
33003 Charters of Bridewell and Bethlem
33009 Duties of Bridewell's officers and servants – undated (1770s?)
33013 Extracts from Bridewell court minutes, 1567–1709
33015 Rough book of extracts from court Minutes, 1559–1841, compiled by A. J. Copeland (1902)
33063/1 Bridewell Treasurer's Accounts, 1643–48
33126 Lists of Bridewell Presidents 1557–1912, with brief historical notes
33137/1 Prisoners admission/discharge orders, 1691–5
MS 'Case Whether Magistrates Can Commit Offenders to Bridewell For More Than Three Months' (1845).
'Legal Cases and Opinions Concerning the Mayor's Powers to City Magistrates to Commit Offenders to Bridewell' (1842).
12806/1 Christ's Hospital, Court Minutes, 1556–1563
12806/2 Christ's Hospital Court Minutes, 1562–92
12806/3 Christ's Hospital Court Minutes, 1592–1632
12806/4 Christ's Hospital Court Minutes, 1632–49
12819/2 Christ's Hospital Treasurers' Accounts, 1561–1608
12819/3 Christ's Hospital Treasurers' Accounts, 1608–16

**Livery Company records**
4097/1 Carmens' Company Minute Book, 1668–1800
4655/1, Weavers' Company Minute Book, 1610–42

55701/1 Fishmongers' Company Minute Book, 1592–1610
8200/1 Apothecaries' Company Minute Book, 1617–51
11588/1 Grocers' Company Minute Book, 1556–91

**Parish records**

524/1 St Michael Wood Street Churchwardens' Accounts, 1619–1718
559/1 St Swithin London Stone Churchwardens' Accounts, 1602–1725
577/1 St John Walbrook Churchwardens' Accounts, 1595–1679
590/1 St John Zachary Churchwardens' Accounts, 1591–1682
593/2 St Stephen Walbrook Churchwardens' Accounts, 1549–1637
593/4 St Stephen Walbrook Churchwardens' Accounts, 1637–1748
645/1 St Peter Westcheap Churchwardens' Accounts, 1435–1601
645/2 St Peter Westcheap Churchwardens' Accounts, 1601–1702
662/1 St Thomas Apostle Churchwardens' Accounts, 1612–1729
818/1 All Hallows the Great Churchwardens' Accounts, 1616–1708
878/1 St Benet Pauls Wharf Churchwardens' Accounts, 1605–57
942/1 St Botolph Billingsgate Churchwardens' Accounts, 1603–74
951/1 St George Botolph Lane Churchwardens' Accounts, 1590–1676
959/1 St Martin Orgar Churchwardens' Accounts, 1574–1707
1002/1 St Mary Woolnoth Churchwardens' Accounts, 1539–1641
1016/1 St Matthew Friday Street Churchwardens' Accounts, 1547–1678
1046/1 St Antholin Budge Row Churchwardens' Accounts, 1574–1708
1124/1 St Katherine Coleman Street Churchwardens' Accounts, 1609–71
1176/1 St Margaret New Fish Street Churchwardens' Accounts, 1576–1678
1181/1 St Michael Crooked Lane Churchwarden's Accounts, 1617–93
1279/2 St Andrew Hubbard Churchwardens' Accounts, 1525–1621
1303/1 St Benet Fink Churchwardens' Accounts, 1610–99
1432/3 St Alphage London Wall Churchwardens' Accounts, 1580–1631
1432/4 St Alphage London Wall Churchwardens' Accounts, 1631–77
1568 St Benet Gracechurch Churchwardens' Accounts, 1538–1724
2088/1 St Andrew-by-the-Wardrobe Churchwardens' Accounts, 1570–1688
2593/1 St Lawrence Jewry Churchwardens' Accounts, 1579–1640
2596/1 St Mary Magdalen Milk Street Churchwardens' Accounts, 1518–1606
2596/2 St Mary Magdalen Milk Street Churchwardens' Accounts, 1606–67
2601/1 St Michael Bassishaw Churchwardens' Accounts, 1617–1716

2895/1 St Michael le Querne Churchwardens' Accounts, 1515–1604
2895/2 St Michael le Querne Churchwardens' Accounts, 1605–1717
2968/1 St Dunstan-in-the-West Churchwardens' Accounts, 1516–1608
2968/2 St Dunstan-in-the-West Churchwardens' Accounts, 1608–28
3146/1 St Sepulchre (Holborn)-without-Newgate Churchwardens' Accounts, 1648–64
3556/1 St Mary Aldermanbury Churchwardens' Accounts, 1569–92
3556/2 St Mary Aldermanbury Churchwardens' Accounts, 1631–77
3907/1 St Lawrence Pountney Churchwardens' Accounts, 1530–1681
4051/1 All Hallows Lombard Street Churchwardens' Accounts, 1614–84
4071/1 St Michael Cornhill Churchwardens' Accounts, 1455–1608
4071/2 St Michael Cornhill Churchwardens' Accounts, 1608–1702
4180/1 St James Garlickhithe Churchwardens' Accounts, 1555–1627
4180/2 St James Garlickhithe Churchwardens' Accounts, 1627–99
4241/1 St Ethelburga Bishopgate Churchwardens' Accounts, 1569–1681
4383/1 St Bartholomew-by-the-Exchange Churchwardens' Accounts, 1598–1698
4385/1 Holy Trinity the Less Churchwardens' Accounts, 1582–1662
4409/1 St Olave Jewry Churchwardens' Accounts, 1586–1643
4409/2 St Olave Jewry Churchwardens' Accounts, 1643–1705
4423/1 St Christopher-le-Stocks Churchwardens' Accounts, 1575–1660
4457/2 St Stephen Coleman Street Churchwardens' Accounts, 1586–1640
4457/3 St Stephen Coleman Street Churchwardens' Accounts, 1656–85
4524/1 St Botolph-without-Bishopgate Churchwardens' Accounts, 1567–1632
4570/2 St Margaret Pattens Churchwardens' Accounts, 1558–1653
4956/2 All Hallows Staining Churchwardens' Accounts, 1533–1628
4956/3 All Hallows Staining Churchwardens' Accounts, 1645–1706
5018/1 St Pancras Soper Lane Churchwardens' Accounts, 1616–1740
5090/2 All Hallows London Wall Churchwardens' Accounts, 1566–1681
5714/1 St Mary Somerset Churchwardens' Accounts, 1614–1701
6386 St Helen Bishopgate Churchwardens' Accounts, 1565–1654
6552/1 St Brides Fleet Street Churchwardens' Accounts, 1639–78
6574 St Mary Aldermary Churchwardens' Accounts, 1597–1665
6836 St Helen Bishopgate Churchwardens' Accounts, 1565–1654
7673/1 St Alban Wood Street Churchwardens' Accounts, 1584–1639
7673/2 St Alban Wood Street Churchwardens' Accounts, 1637–1675
9080/1–8 St Sepulchre (Middlesex Division) Churchwardens' Accounts
9163 Christchurch Newgate Street Memoranda, 1574–1698

9235/1 St Botolph Aldgate Churchwardens' Accounts, 1547–85
9235/2 St Botolph Aldgate Churchwardens' Accounts, 1586–1691
9237 Portsoken Churchwardens' Accounts, 1622–78

9680 St Katherine-by-the-Tower Constables' Accounts, 1598–1706

2089/1 St Andrew-by-the-Wardrobe Poor Accounts, 1613–68
2999/1 St Dunstan-in-the-West Overseers' Account Book, 1633–87
7674 St Alban Wood Street Overseers' Accounts, 1627–75
7706 St Katherine Creechurch Overseers' Accounts, 1638–42

594/1 St Stephen Walbrook Vestry Minutes, 1587–1614
819/1 All Hallows the Great Vestry Minutes, 1574–1684
877/1 St Benet Paul's Wharf Vestry Minutes, 1579–1674
943/1 St Botolph Billingsgate Vestry Minutes, 1592–1673
952/1 St George Botolph Lane Vestry Minutes, 1600–85
959/1 St Martin Orgar Vestry Minutes, 1555–1643
978/1 St Clement Eastcheap Vestry Minutes, 1640–1759
1145/1 St Katherine Coleman Street Poor Rate Book 1608–27
1175/1 St Margaret New Fish Street Vestry Minutes, 1578–1789
1311/1 St Martin Ludgate Vestry Minutes, 1568–1715
1240/1 St Mary-at-the-Hill Vestry Minutes, 1609–1752
1264/1 St Alban Wood Street Vestry Minutes, 1583–1676
1431/1 St Alphage London Wall Vestry Minutes, 1593–1608
1431/2 St Alphage London Wall Vestry Minutes, 1608–1711
1453/1 St Botolph Aldersgate Vestry Minutes, 1601–57
2597 St Mary Magdalene Milk Street Vestry Minutes, 1619–68
3016/1 St Dunstan-in-the-West Vestry Minutes, 1588–1663
3570/1 St Mary Aldermanbury Vestry Minutes, 1569–1609
3570/2 St Mary Aldermanbury Vestry Minutes, 1610–1763
3579/1 St Matthew Friday Street Vestry Minutes, 1576–1743
3908/1 St Lawrence Pountney Vestry Minutes, 1617–73
4049/1 All Hallows Lombard Street Vestry Minutes, 1618–53
4060/1 St Nicholas Accons Vestry Minutes, 1619–1738
4072/1 St Michael Cornhill Vestry Minutes, 1463–1697
4165/1 St Peter Cornhill Vestry Minutes, 1570–1717
4214/1 St Benet Gracechurch Vestry Minutes, 1607–1758
4216/1 St Dionis Backchurch Vestry Minutes, 1647–73
4251/1 St Andrew Holborn Vestry Minutes, 1624–1714
4352/1 St Margaret Lothbury Vestry Minutes, 1571–1677

480　Bibliography

  4384/1 St Bartholomew-by-the-Exchange Vestry Minutes, 1567–1643
  4415/1 St Olave Jewry Vestry Minutes, 1574–1680
  4425/1 St Christopher-le-Stocks Vestry Minutes, 1593–1731
  4487/1 St Dunstan-in-the-East Vestry Minutes, 1537–1651
  4526/1 St Botolph-without-Bishopgate Vestry Minutes, 1616–90
  4813/1 St James Garlickhithe Vestry Minutes, 1615–93
  5019/1 St Pancras Soper Lane Vestry Minutes, 1626–99
  6554/1 St Brides Fleet Street Vestry Minutes, 1644–65
  9234/1-8 Parish Clerk's Memoranda Books, 1583–1625
  9236 St Botolph Aldgate Vestry Minutes and Memoranda Book, 1583–1640

**Ward records**
  68 Vintry Wardmote Inquest Book, 1687–1774
  473 Candlewick Wardmote Inquest Book, 1676–1802
  1169/1 Lime Street Wardmote Inquest Book, 1654–1779
  1499 St Botolph Aldersgate 'verdict' of wardmote inquest 1510
  1509/2, 7-8 Aldersgate Ward Precepts
  2050/1 Aldersgate Wardmote Inquest Book, 1467–1801
  2505/1 Bassishaw Wardmote Inquest Book, 1655–1752
  3018/1 St Dunstan-in-the-West Wardmote Inquest Book, 1558–1823
  4069/1 Cornhill Wardmote Inquest Book, 1571–1651
  4069/2 Cornhill Wardmote Inquest Book, 1652–1733
  4992/1 William Chaffers, ed., 'Records of Cordwainer and Bread Street Wards in the City of London' (1889).
  9234/1-5 St Botolph Aldersgate Memoranda Books

Broadsides 24.40, *The Humble Petition of Thomas Stanley . . . (On Behalf of Christ's Hospital, St. Thomas's Hospital, and Bridewell)* (1621?).

HOUSE OF LORDS RECORD OFFICE

House of Lords Main Papers

LONDON METROPOLITAN ARCHIVES

**City records**

The following City records are currently deposited at the London Metropolitan Archives, although I consulted them when they were still held at the old Corporation of London Record Office. These records are due to be transferred to the Guildhall Library in 2008 or 2009.
  Journals of Common Council, 11–41, 1507–1661
  Repertories of the Court of Aldermen, 9–67, 1533–1661

Bibliography 481

Remembrancia Books, 1–8, 1580–1640
City Letterbooks, N-X, 1515–75
City Cashbooks, 1–2
City of London Quarter Sessions Files, 71–135, 1616–57
Lord Mayor's Waiting Book, 1626–36
City of London Police Annual Report, 2000–1
CLRO/05/389/001 Southwark Leet Juries, Verdicts and Presentments MS 331-2-1
COL/AC/08/1 Articles of the Charter and Liberties of London: including Tower Ward Presentments.
COL/WD/03/044 'List of the Severall Wards in London With the Divisions and Precincts Within the Ward'

**Ecclesiastical records**
D/L/C 214–18 Diocese of London, Consistory Court Deposition Books,
1591–1608

**Hospital records**
H1/ST/A1/1 St Thomas's Hospital Governors Court Minutes, 1556–64
H1/ST/A1/2 St Thomas's Hospital Governors Court Minutes, 1564–68
H1/ST/A1/3 St Thomas's Hospital Governors Court Minutes, 1568–80
H1/ST/A1/4 St Thomas's Hospital Governors Court Minutes, 1580–1608
H1/ST/A1/5 St Thomas's Hospital Governors Court Minutes, 1619–77

**Middlesex Quarter Sessions records**
MJ/SP Middlesex Quarter Sessions Papers
MJ/SR Middlesex Quarter Sessions Rolls
MJ/SBR/1 Middlesex Sessions of the Peace Registers, 1608–13
MJ/SBR/2 Middlesex Sessions of the Peace Registers, 1613–18
MJ/SBR/3 Middlesex Sessions of the Peace Registers, 1618–23
MJ/SBR/4 Middlesex Sessions of the Peace Registers, 1623–9
MJ/SBR/5 Middlesex Sessions of the Peace Registers, 1629–33
MJ/SBR/6 Middlesex Sessions of the Peace Registers, 1634–9
MJ/SBR/7 Middlesex Sessions of the Peace Registers, 1639–41

**Southwark Quarter Sessions**
CLA/046/01/001 Southwark Quarter Sessions Book, 1667–8

**Westminster Quarter Sessions**
WJ/SP Westminster Quarter Sessions Papers
WJ/SR/NS29–50 Westminster Quarter Sessions Rolls, 1630–7

THE NATIONAL ARCHIVES

CSPV Calendar of State Papers Venetian
PC2/ Privy Council Registers
SP12 State Papers Domestic, Elizabeth 1
SP14 State Papers Domestic, James 1
SP16 State Papers Domestic, Charles 1
STAC5 Star Chamber Proceedings, Elizabeth 1
STAC8 Star Chamber Proceedings, James 1

NORTHAMPTONSHIRE RECORD OFFICE

Northamptonshire Quarter Sessions Minute Books 2–4, 1679–1727

NORWICH AND NORFOLK RECORD OFFICE

Norwich City Quarter Sessions Book, 1629–36
Norwich City Quarter Sessions Book, 1630–8
Norwich City Quarter Sessions Book, 1637–64
Norwich City Quarter Sessions Book, 1639–54
Y/C/19/5 Great Yarmouth Assembly Book, 1598–1625

NOTTINGHAMSHIRE RECORD OFFICE

DD4P/68 Duke of Portland's Papers: copy of Bridewell's royal letters patent

OXFORDSHIRE RECORD OFFICE

C/FC/1/A1/O2–4 Oxford Council Act Books B-D, 1591–1701
QS/C/A1/O1–2 Oxford City Quarter Sessions Minute Books, 1687–1711
QSM1/1/II Oxfordshire Quarter Sessions Book, 1693–7
QSM1/1/IV Oxfordshire Quarter Sessions Book, 1704–9

ST BARTHOLOMEW'S HOSPITAL ARCHIVE

Governors' Journal 1, 1549–61
Governors' Journal 2, 1567–86
Governors' Journal 3, 1586–1607
Governors' Journal 4, 1607–47
Governors' Journal 5, 1647–65
'The Ordre of the Hospitall of St Bartholomewes in West Smythfield in London' (1552)

STATIONERS' COMPANY HALL

Company Minute Books C-E, 1602–83

SUFFOLK RECORD OFFICE, IPSWICH BRANCH
B/105/2/1 Suffolk Quarter Sessions Order Book, 1639–51

WESTMINSTER ARCHIVES CENTRE
WCB1 Westminster Court of Burgesses Courtbook, 1610–13
WCB2 Westminster Court of Burgesses Courtbook, 1613–16

**Parish records**
  E5-39 St Margaret's Westminster, Churchwardens' Accounts, 1570–1659
  F2062 'A Register of the Writings Belonging to the Parrish and Poor of the Parrish of St Martin-in-the-Fields, (1685)
  E2413 St Margaret's Westminster, Vestry Minutes, 1591–1662
  E2416 St Margaret's Westminster, Vestry Minutes, 1674–93
  E2419 St Margaret's Westminster, Orders of the Vestry, 1591–1718
  F301-313 St Martin-in-the-Fields, Overseers' Accounts, 1574–87
  F2001 St Martin in-the-Fields, Vestry Minute Book, 1574–1640
  F2002 St Martin-in-the-Fields, Vestry Minute Book, 1623–52
  F2003 St Martin-in-the-Fields, Vestry Minute Book, 1651–6
  F3348-50 St Martin-in-the-Fields, 'Pentioners and Orphans Given in Charge to the Overseers of the Poore' (1654, 1659, 1673)
  F6039 St Martin-in-the-Fields, Answer to High Constable's Warrant (1603)

WILTSHIRE RECORD OFFICE
G22/1/205/2 Marlborough General Account Book, 1572–1727
G23/1/3 Salisbury Ledger Book, 1571–1640

## EARLY PRINTED BOOKS

Adams, Thomas, *The White Devil, Or the Hypocrite Uncased* (1613).
*A Letter to the President of the Royal Hospitals of Bridewell and Bethlem upon the Original Designs and Present Pursuits of one of these Ancient Foundations of Mercy . . . . From a Governor* (1830).
Allen, Robert, *A Treatise of Christian Beneficience* (1600).
*The Ancient Customes and Approved Usages of the Honourable City of London* (1639?).
*The Arraignement and Burning of Margaret Fern-seede, for the Murther of Her Late Husband Anthony Fern-Seede* (1609).
Atterbury, Francis, *The Power of Charity to Cover Sin: A Sermon Preach'd Before the President and Governors of the Hospitals of Bridewell and Bethlem, in Bridewell Chapel, August 16 1694* (1708).
*The Boke for a Justice of Peace* (1544).

Bowen, Thomas, *Extracts From the Records and Courtbooks of Bridewell Hospital* (1798).
Breton, Nicholas, *The Good and Badde: Or Descriptions of the Worthies and Unworthies of this Age* (1616).
Bridges, John, *A Sermon Preached at Paules Crosse on the Monday in Whitsun Weeke Anno Domini, 1571* (1571).
Bullein, William, *A Dialogue Both Pleasaunte and Pietifull Against the Fever Pestilence* (1564).
Bush, Rice, *The Poor Mans Friend, or Narrative of What Progresse Many Worthy Citizens of London Have Made in that Godly Work of Providing for the Poor* (1649).
*The Thirty-Second Report of the Charity Commissioners of England and Wales*, Per Acts 38 Geo.3.c.91 and Geo.3.c.81, part IV, 1840 (219), xix.
Chettle, Henry, *Kind-Hartes Dreame* (1592).
Coke, Edward, *The Second Part of the Institutes of the Lawes of England* (1644).
Dalton, Michael, *The Country Justice* (1661 edn).
Defoe, Daniel, *Augusta Triumphaus: Or, the Way to Make London the Most Flourishing City in the Universe* (1729).
Dekker, Thomas, *The Wonderful Year* (1600).
Denison, Stephen, *The White Wolfe: Or, a Sermon Preached at Pauls Crosse, Feb. 11 ... 1627* (1627).
Earle, John, *Micro-cosmographie, Or, A Peece of the World Discovered in Essays and Characters*, 5th edition (1629).
*An Ease for Overseers of the Poore* (1601).
Evelyn, John, *A Character of England*, 1651, reprinted in *The Miscellaneous Writings of John Evelyn*, ed. William Upcott (1825).
  *An Account of Architects and Architecture* (1707 edition).
*The Execution of Justice in England and for Maintenance of Publique and Christian Peace* (1583).
Fealty, Robert, *The Tree of Life Springing Out of the Grave*, in his *Clavis Mystica: a Key Opening Divers Difficult and Mysterious Texts of Holy Scripture, Handled in Seventy Sermons* (1636).
Fish, Simon, *A Supplicacyon for the Beggers* (1524).
Fletcher, Anthony, *Certaine Very Notable, Profitable, and Comfortable Similies* (1595).
Freart, Roland, *A Parallel of the Antient Architecture With the Modern*, trans. John Evelyn, 2nd edition (1707).
Fuller, William, *Mr W. F.'s Trip to Bridewell With a True Account of His Barbarous Usage in the Pillory ... Written by His Own Hand* (1703).
Gee, John, *The Foot Out of the Snare; With a Detection of Sundry Late Practices and Impostures of the Priests and Jesuits in England* (1624).
Godwin, Paul, *Historie des Larrons, Or the History of Thieves. Written in French and Translated Out of the Original by Paul Godwin* (1638).
Goodcole, Henry, *Heaven's Speedie Hue and Cry Sent After Lust and Murder Manifested upon the Suddaine Apprehending of Thomas Sherwood and Elizabeth Evans* (1635).
Gough, William, *Londinium Triumphaus* (1682).

Grafton, Richard, *A Chronicle at Large and Meere History of the Affayres of Englande* (1569).
Graunt, John, *Natural and Political Observations . . . Made Upon the Bills of Mortality* (1662).
H. I., *The House of Correction: Or, Certayne Satyricall Epigrams* (1619).
Hall, Joseph, *The Righteous Mammon: An Hospitall Sermon Preached in the Solemne Assembly of the City on Monday in Easter Weeke . . . 1618* (1618).
Heron, Edward, *Physicke for Body and Soule* (1621).
Heylyn, Peter, *Cosmographie* (1652).
Hill, Adam, *The Crie of England. A Sermon Preached at Paules Crosse, . . . September 1593* (1595).
Hitchcock, Robert, *Hitchcockes New Yeres Gift to Englande. A Pollitique Platt for the Honour of the Prince, the Greate Profite of the Publique State, Relief to the Poore, Preservation of the Riche, Reformation of Roges and Idle Persones, and the Wealthe of Thousandes that Knowes not Howe to Live* (1580).
Hodges, Nathaniel, *Loimolgia: Or, an Historical Account of the Plague in London in 1665*, 3rd edition (1721).
Howell, James, *Londinopolis: an Historical Discourse or Perlustration of the City of London, the Imperial Chamber and the Chief Emporium of Great Britain* (1657).
Howes, Edmund, *Annales, Or, A Generall Chronicle of England Begun by John Stow: Continued and Augmented With Matters Forraigne and Domestique, Ancient and Moderne, Unto the End of the Present Year, 1631* (1631).
Jackson, Thomas, *Londons New-Yeeres Gift, Or the Uncovering of the Foxe* (1609).
Jenison, Robert, *The Cities Safetie. Or a Fruitfull Treatise (and Usefull for These Dangerous Times)* (1630).
Johnson, Richard, *The Pleasant Walkes of Moore-fields* (1607).
Jones, John, *The Arte and Science of Preserving Bodie and Soule in Healthe, Wisdome, and Catholike Religion* (1579).
King, John, *A Sermon at Paules Crosse on behalfe of Paules Church, March 26 1620* (1620).
Lawrence, John, *A Golden Trumpet to Rowse up a Drowsie Magistrate: Or, a Patterne for a Governors Practise Drawne From Christs Comming to, Beholding of, and Weeping Over Hierusalem. As it was Sounded at Pauls Crosse the 11 of Aprill, 1624* (1624).
Lever, Thomas, *A Serman Preached at Paul's Crosse the xiii Daie of December* (1550).
*London College of Physicians. Certain Necessary Directions, As Well for Cure of the Plague as for Preventing the Infection* (1636).
*London's Cry: Ascended to God and Entered Into the Hearts and Eares of Men for Revenge of Bloodsheddes, Burglaiers and Vagabonds* (1620).
Maitland, William, *The History of London From Its Foundations by the Romans to the Present Time* (1739).
*The Manner of Crying Things in London* (1599?).
Mill, Humphrey, *A Night's Search Discovering the Nature and Condition of All Sorts of Nightwalkers With Their Associates* (1640).
Milles, Robert, *Abraham's Suite for Sodom: a Sermon Preached at Paules Crosse the 25th of August 1611* (1612).

Moss, Robert, *A Sermon Preach'd Before the Right Honourable the Lord Mayor of London, the Court of Aldermen, and the Governors of the Several Hospitals of the City, at the Parish Church of St Sepulchre ... in Easter Week* (1709).

Munday, Anthony, *A Briefe Chronicle of the Succese of Times from the Creation of the World to This Instant* (1611).

*The Survey of London Written in the Yeere 1598 by John Stow ... Since Then Continued and Much Englarged ... by Anthony Munday* (1618).

Mynshul, Geoffrey, *Characters of Prisons and Prisoners* (1638).

Ogilvy, John, and Morgan, William, *London Survey'd: Or An Explanation of the Large Map of London* (1677).

Owen, John, *Britannia Depicta. Or Ogilvy Improv'd* (1720).

Peacham, Henry, *A Discourse Between the Crosse in Cheap and Charring Crosse* (1641).

Petty, William, *Another Essay in Political Arithmetick Concerning the Growth of the City of London* (1683).

*Five Essays in Political Arithmetick* (1687).

*Observations upon the Cities of London and Rome* (1687).

*Two Essays in Political Arithmetick Concerning the People, Housing, Hospitals, etc, of London and Paris* (1687).

Procter, Thomas, *A Worthy Worke Profitable to this Kingdom Concerning the Mending of all High-waies, as Also for Waters and Ironworkes* (1607).

Purchas, Samuel, *The Kings Towre and Triumphant Arch of London. A Sermon Preached at Paules Crosse, August 5, 1622* (1623).

R. F., *A Collection of English Proverbs* (Cambridge, 1670).

Ridley, Gloucester, *The Life of Dr Nicholas Ridley, Sometime Bishop of London Shewing the Plan and Progress of the Reformation* (1763).

Shelford, Richard, *Lectures or Readings Upon the 6 Verse of the 22 Chapter of Proverbs Concerning the Vertuous Education of Youth* (1606).

*The Shutting Up Infected Houses as it is Practised in England, Soberly Debated* (1665).

*The Humble Petition of Thomas Stanley ... (On Behalf of Christs Hospital, St Thomas's Hospital, and Bridewell)* (1621?).

Strype, John, *A Survey of the Cities of London and Westminster: Containing the Original, Antiquity, Increase, Modern Estate and Government of Those Cities, Written at First in the Year MDXCVIII by John Stow ... Corrected, Improved, and Very Much Enlarged: and the Survey and History Brought Down from the Year 1633*, 5 books in 2 vols. (1720).

Taylor, John, *The Carriers Cosmographie. Or a Briefe Relation of the Innes, Ordinaries, Hoste[l]ries, and Other Lodgings in and Neere London* (1637).

W. A., *A Fruitfull and Godly Sermon, Preached at Paules Crosse* (1592).

Waddington, William, *Considerations on the Original and Proper Objects of the Royal Hospital of Bridewell Addressed to the Governors* (1798).

*A Warning for House-Keepers, Or, A Discovery of All Sorts of Thieves and Robbers* (1676).

Webbe, George, *Gods Controversie with England. Or a Description of the Fearefull and Lamentable Estate which this land at this Present is in ... Preached at Pauls Crosse upon Trinitie Sunday ... 1609* (1609).

West, Richard, *A Sermon Preached Before the Right Honourable the Lord Mayor and the Honourable Court of Aldermen and Governors of the Several Hospitals of the City of London ... Being One of the Anniversary Spittal Sermons* (1711).

Willis, Richard, *A Sermon Preach'd Before the Right Honourable The Lord Mayor of London and the Honourable Court of Aldermen and Governours of the Several Hospitals of the City ... on Easter Tuesday, 1702* (1702).

## EDITIONS OF EARLY BOOKS AND MANUSCRIPTS

*Amanda, Or the Reformed Whore*, 1635, ed., F. Ouvry (1869).

Archer, Ian, Barron, Caroline, and Harding Vanessa, eds., *Hugh Alley's Caveat: The Markets of London in 1598*, London Topographical Society, 137 (1988).

Awdeley, John, *The Fraternity of Vagabonds*, 1561, reprinted in Arthur Kinney ed., *Rogues, Vagabonds, and Sturdy Beggars: A New Gallery of Tudor and Early Stuart Rogue Literature* (Amherst, MA, 1990).

Bacon, Francis, *A Brief Discourse upon the Commission of Bridewell*, in *The Works of Francis Bacon*, eds. J. Spedding *et al.*, 14 vols. (1857–74), vol. VII.

Bolton, Edmund, *The Cities Advocate*, 1629, The English Experience, 715 (Amsterdam and Norwood, NJ, 1975).

Burnet, Gilbert, *The History of the Reformation of the Church of England*, 1679, ed., Nicholas Pocock (Oxford, 1865).

*The Letters of John Chamberlain*, ed., Norman Egbert McClure, 2 vols., The American Philosophical Society (Philadelphia, PA, 1939).

Chappell, W., ed., *The Roxburghe Ballads*, 14 vols., Ballad Society (1869–95).

Chapman, G. *et al.*, *Eastward Ho*, 1605, Tudor Facsimile Texts (New York, 1970).

Cockburn, J. S., ed., *Calendar of Assize Records: Hertfordshire Indictments: Elizabeth I* (1975).

Crompton, Richard, *Star-Chamber Cases, Shewing What Cases Properly Belong to the Recognizance of that Court. Collected for the Most Part Out of Mr Crompton, His Booke, Entituled The Jurisdiction of Divers Courts*, 1630, The English Experience, 723 (Amsterdam and Norwood, NJ, 1975).

Dasent, J. R., *et al.*, eds., *Acts of the Privy Council*, 46 vols. (1890–1964).

*The Private Diary of Dr John Dee*, ed., J. O. Halliwell, Camden Society publications, 19 (1842).

Dekker, Thomas, *The Seven Deadly Sinnes of London*, 1606, reprinted in A. B. Grosart, ed., *Non-Dramatic Works of Thomas Dekker*, 5 vols. (1884–6).

*The Honest Whore, Part 1*, in Thomas Bowers, ed., *The Dramatic Works of Thomas Dekker*, 4 vols. (Cambridge, 1955–61), vol. II.

*The Honest Whore, Part 2*, in Bowers, ed., *Dramatic Works*, vol. II.

(with John Webster) *Northward Ho*, in Bowers, ed., *Dramatic Works*, vol. II.

(with John Webster) *Westward Ho*, in Bowers, ed., *Dramatic Works*, vol. II.

*Lanthorne and Candle-light*, 1608, The English Experience, 585 (Amsterdam and New York, 1973).

*The Journals of All the Parliaments During the Reign of Queen Elizabeth Collected by Sir Simonds D'Ewes*, 1682, rev. O. Bowes (Shannon, 1973).

Dingley, Robert, *Proposals for Establishing a Public Place of Reception for Penitent Prostitutes*, 1758, reprinted in Randolph Trumbach, ed., *Prostitution Reform: Four Documents*, Garland Series, Marriage, Sex, and the Family in England, 1660–1800, 22 (1985).

*The Notebook of Robert Doughty, 1662–1665*, ed., James M. Rosenheim, Norfolk Record Society, 54 (1989).
Dunton, John, *The Night-Walker: Or, Evening Rambles in Search of Lewd Women*, 1696, ed., Randolph Trumbach, Garland Series, Marriage, Sex, and the Family in England, 1660–1800, 19 (1985).
*The History of the Life of Thomas Ellwood*, ed., C. G. Crump (1900).
Evelyn, John, *A Character of England*, in *Miscellaneous Writings of John Evelyn*, 1651, ed., William Upcott, 3rd edition (1825).
*The Diary of John Evelyn*, ed., E. S. De Beer, 6 vols. (Oxford, 1955).
Freshfield, E. ed., *Minutes of the Vestry Meeting and Other Records of the Parish of St Christopher le Stocks in the Parish of London* (1886).
   ed., *The Vestry Minute Book of the Parish of St Margaret Lothbury in the City of London, 1571–1677* (1887).
*Letters of Philip Gaudy of West Harling, Norfolk, and of London, to Various Members of his Family, 1579–1616*, ed., Issac Herbert Jeayes (1906).
Greene, Robert, *A Disputation Between a He-Cony-Catcher and a She-Cony-Catcher*, 1592, reprinted in A. V. Judges, ed., *The Elizabethan Underworld*, 2nd edition (1965).
   *The Second Part of Cony-Catching*, in A. V. Judges, ed., *The Elizabethan Underworld*, 2nd edition (1965).
   *A Notable Discovery of Cozenage*, 1591, reprinted in Arthur Kinney, ed., *Rogues, Vagabonds, and Sturdy Beggars: a New Gallery of Tudor and Early Stuart Rogue Literature* (Amherst, MA, 1990).
[Gwillim, John], *The London Bawd With Her Character and Life*, 4th edition, 1711, ed., Randolph Trumbach, Garland Series, Marriage, Sex, and the Family in England, 1660–1800, 17 (1986).
Harman, Thomas, *A Caveat for Common Cursitors, Vulgarly Called Vagabonds*, 1566, reprinted in Arthur Kinney, ed., *Rogues, Vagabonds, and Sturdy Beggars: a New Gallery of Tudor and Early Stuart Rogue Literature* (Amherst, MA, 1990).
Hartley, T. E., ed., *Proceedings in the Parliaments of Elizabeth I, Volume III, 1593–1601* (1995).
Howell, James, *Familiar Letters or Epistolae Ho-Elianae*, 3 vols. (1903).
*John Howes' MS, 1582, Being A Brief Note of the Order and Manner of the Proceedings in the First Erection of the Three Royal Hospitals of Christ, Bridewell, and St Thomas the Apostle*, ed., William Lampiere (1904).
Hughes, P. L. and Larkin, J. F., eds., *Tudor Royal Proclamations, 1588–1603* (Yale, 1969).
Josselin, Ralph, *The Diary of Ralph Josselin, 1616–1683*, ed. Alan Macfarlane, British Academy Records of Economic and Social History, New Series, III (1976).
Judges, A. V., ed., *The Elizabethan Underworld*, 2nd edition (1965).
Kinney, Arthur, ed., *Rogues, Vagabonds, and Sturdy Beggars: A New Gallery of Tudor and Early Stuart Rogue Literature* (Amherst, MA, 1990).
Kirk, Richard E. G. and Kirk, Ernest F., eds., *Returns of Aliens Dwelling in the City and Suburbs of London During the Reign of Henry VIII to that of James I*, 4 vols., Huguenot Society of London Publications, 10 (Aberdeen, 1900–8).

Larkin, J. F., ed., *Stuart Royal Proclamations, Volume II: Proclamations of King Charles I, 1625–1646* (Oxford, 1983).
Larkin, J. F. and Hughes, P. L., eds., *Stuart Royal Proclamations, Volume 1: Royal Proclamations of King James I, 1603–25* (Oxford, 1973).
Lupton, Donald, *London and the Country Carbonadoed and Quartered Into Severall Characters*, 1632, The English Experience, 879 (Amsterdam and Norwood, NJ, 1977).
*The Diary of Henry Machyn Citizen and Merchant-Taylor of London From A.D. 1550 to A.D. 1563*, ed. John Gough Nichols, Camden Society (1848).
'The London Journal of Alessandro Magno 1562', eds., Caroline Barron, Christopher Coleman, and Claire Gobb, *London Journal*, 9 (1983), 136–52.
Manley, Lawrence, ed., *London in the Age of Shakespeare: an Anthology* (University Park, PA and London, 1986).
Massinger, Philip, *The City Madam*, in Philip Edwards and Colin Gibson, eds., *The Plays and Poems of Philip Massinger*, 4 vols. (Oxford, 1976).
Nashe, Thomas, *The Terrors of the Night, or a Discourse of Apparitions*, 1594, in *The Works of Thomas Nashe Edited from the Original Texts*, ed., R. B. McKerrow, 5 vols. (1910), vol. I.
 *Christ's Tears Over Jerusalem*, 1593, Scolar Press Facsimile (Menston, 1970).
*The Diary of Samuel Pepys*, eds., Robert Latham and William Matthews, 11 vols. (1970–83).
Pilkington, James, *The Burning of St Paul's Church: Confutation of an Addition*, 1563, in *The Works of James Pilkington, B. D., Lord Bishop of Durham*, ed., James Schofield, Parker Society (1842).
Prockter, Adrian and Taylor, Robert, compiled, *The A–Z of Elizabethan London*, intro. John Fisher, London Topographical Society, 122 (1979).
Ridley, Nicholas, *A Treatise or Letter Written by Dr Ridley Instead of His Last Farewell to All His True and Faithfull Friends in God; With a Sharp Admonition Withal Unto the Papists*, in *The Acts and Monuments of John Foxe*, ed., S. R. Cattley, 8 vols. (1841).
Scouloudi, Irene, ed., *Returns of Strangers in the Metropolis 1593, 1627, 1635, 1639: a Study of an Active Minority*, Huguenot Society of London Publications, 57 (1985).
Shakespeare, William, *King Lear*, ed., R. A. Foakes, The Arden Shakespeare, 3rd series (1997).
 *Measure for Measure*, in *The Norton Shakespeare Based on the Oxford Edition*, eds., Stephen Greenblatt et al. (New York and London, 1997).
 *Much Ado About Nothing*, in *The Norton Shakespeare Based on the Oxford Edition*, eds., Stephen Greenblatt et al. (New York and London, 1997).
Stow, John, *The Survey of London*, 1598, ed., H. B. Wheatley, revised edition (1986).
Tawney, R. H. and Power, E., eds., *Tudor Economic Documents*, 3 vols. (1924).
Taylor, John, *A Bawd, a Vertuous Bawd, a Modest Bawd: As Shee Deserves, Reprove, or Else Applaud*, in *All the Works of John Taylor the Water Poet*, 1630, Scolar Press facsimile (1973).
'A journey through England & Scotland made by Lupold von Wedel in the years 1584 & 1585', ed., G. von Bulow, *Transactions of the Royal Historical Society*, new series, 9 (1895), 223–70.

*The Wandering Whore in Six Parts*, 1660, ed., Randolph Trumbach, Garland Series, Marriage, Sex, and the Family in England, 1660–1800, 17 (1986).

Welch, Saunders, *A Proposal to Render Effectual a Plan to Remove the Nuisance of Common Prostitutes From the Streets of the Metropolis*, 1758, reprinted in Randolph Trumbach, ed., *Prostitution Reform: Four Documents*, Garland Series, Marriage, Sex, and the Family in England, 1660–1800, 22, (1985).

'Whipping Cheer', in H. E. Rollins, ed., *A Pepysian Garland: Black-Letter Broadside Ballads of the Years 1595–1639, Chiefly From the Collection of Samuel Pepys* (Cambridge, 1922).

*The Life and Letters of Sir Henry Wotton*, ed., L. P. Smith, 2 vols. (Oxford, 1907).

Wright, T., ed., *Queen Elizabeth and her Times*, 2 vols. (1838).

## SECONDARY WORKS

Adair, Richard, *Courtship, Illegitimacy, and Marriage in Early Modern England* (Manchester, 1996).

Allerston, Patricia, 'Clothing and early modern Venetian society', *Continuity and Change*, 15 (2000), 367–90.

Andrew, Donna T., *Philanthropy and Police: London Charity in the Eighteenth Century* (Princeton, NJ, 1989).

'The press and public apologies in eighteenth-century London', in Norma Landau, ed., *Law, Crime, and English Society, 1660–1830* (Cambridge, 2002), pp. 208–29.

Andrew, Donna T., and McGowen, Randall, *The Perreaus and Mrs. Rudd: Forgery and Betrayal in Eighteenth-Century London* (Berkeley, CA, 2001).

Andrews, Jonathan, 'Identifying and providing for the mentally disabled in early modern London', in David Wright and Anne Digby, eds., *From Idiocy to Mental Deficiency: Historical Perspectives on People With Learning Disabilities* (1996), pp. 65–92.

Andrews, Jonathan et al., *The History of Bethlem* (1997).

Archer, Ian W., *The Pursuit of Stability: Social Relations in Elizabethan London* (Cambridge, 1991).

'The nostalgia of John Stow', in David L. Smith, Richard Strier, and David Bevington, eds., *The Theatrical City: Culture, Theatre, and Politics in London, 1576–1649* (Cambridge, 1995), pp. 17–34.

'The 1590s: apotheosis or nemesis of the Elizabethan regime?', in A. Briggs and D. Snowman, eds., *Fins de Siècle: How Centuries End, 1400–2000* (London and New Haven, CT, 1996), pp. 65–97.

'Material Londoners?', in Lena Cowen Orlin, ed., *Material London, ca. 1600* (Philadelphia, PA, 2000), pp. 174–92.

'Popular politics in the sixteenth and early seventeenth centuries', in Paul Griffiths and Mark S. R. Jenner, eds., *Londinopolis: Essays in the Cultural and Social History of Early Modern London* (Manchester, 2000), pp. 26–46.

'Government in early modern London: the challenge of the suburbs', in Peter Clark and Raymond Gillespie, eds., *Two Capitals: London and Dublin, 1500–1840*, Proceedings of the British Academy, 107 (Oxford and London, 2001), pp. 133–47.

'Social networks in Restoration London: the evidence of Samuel Pepys' diary', in Alexandra Shepard and Philip Withington, eds., *Communities in Early Modern England: Networks, Place, Rhetoric* (Manchester, 2000), pp. 76–94.

'The arts and acts of memorialization in early modern London', in J. F. Merritt, ed., *Imagining Early Modern London: Perceptions and Portrayals of the City from Stow to Strype, 1598–1720* (Cambridge, 2001), pp. 89–113.

'The government of London, 1500–1650', *London Journal*, 26 (2001), 19–28.

'The charity of early modern Londoners', *Transactions of the Royal Historical Society*, 6th series, 12 (2002), 223–44.

Arrizabalaga, J. et al., *The Great Pox: the French Disease in Renaissance Europe* (London and New Haven, CT, 1997).

Ashton, Robert, *The City and the Court, 1603–1643* (Cambridge, 1979).

Ayledotte, F., *Elizabethan Rogues and Vagabonds* (Oxford, 1913).

Bailey, Victor, 'The fabrication of deviance: "dangerous classes" and "criminal classes" in Victorian England', in Robert Malcolmson and John Rule, eds., *Protest and Survival: the Historical Experience: Essays for E. P. Thompson* (1993), pp. 221–56.

Bannister, Scott, *Names and Naming Patterns in England, 1538–1700* (Oxford, 1997).

Barnes, T. G., 'The prerogative court and environmental control of London building in the early seventeenth century', *California Law Review*, 58 (1970), 1332–63.

Barrell, John, *The Spirit of Despotism: Invasions of Privacy in the 1790s* (Oxford, 2006).

Barron, Caroline, 'Lay solidarities: the wards of Medieval London', in P. Stafford, J. Nelson, and J. Martindale, eds., *Law, Laity, and Solidarities: Essays in Honour of Susan Reynolds* (Manchester, 2001), pp. 218–33.

*London in the Later Middle Ages: Government and People, 1200–1500* (Oxford, 2004).

Barry, Jonathan, 'Introduction', in Barry and Christopher Brooks eds., *The Middling Sort of People: Culture, Society, and Politics in England 1550–1800* (Basingstoke, 1994), pp. 1–27.

Barthes, Roland, *On Racine*, trans. Richard Howard (New York, 1981).

Barton, Ann, 'London comedy and the ethos of the city', *London Journal*, 4 (1978), 158–80.

Beattie, J. M., *Crime and the Courts in England, 1660–1800* (Oxford and Princeton, NJ, 1986).

*Policing and Punishment in London 1660–1750: Urban Crime and the Limits of Terror* (Oxford, 2001).

Beier, A. L., *Masterless Men: the Vagrancy Problem in England, 1560–1640* (1985).

'Social problems in Elizabethan London', in Jonathan Barry, ed., *The Tudor and Stuart Town: a Reader in English Urban History, 1530–1688* (Harlow, 1990), pp. 121–38.

'Anti-language or jargon? Canting in the English underworld in the sixteenth and seventeenth centuries', in Peter Burke and Roy Porter, eds., *Languages and Jargons: Contributions to a Social History of Language* (Cambridge, 1995), pp. 64–101.

'Foucault *Redux*?: The roles of humanism, protestantism, and an urban elite in creating the London Bridewell, 1500–1560', *Criminal Justice History*, 17 (2002), 33–60.

'New historicism, historical context, and the literature of roguery: the case of Thomas Harman reopened', in Craig Dionne and Steve Mentz, eds., *Rogues and Early Modern English Culture* (Ann Arbor, MI, 2004), pp. 98–119.

Beik, William, *Urban Protest in Seventeenth-Century France: the Culture of Retribution* (Cambridge, 1997).

Bellany, Alastair, *The Politics of Court Scandal in Early Modern England: News Culture and the Overbury Affair, 1603–1660* (Cambridge, 2002).

Bembow, M., 'The Court of Aldermen and the Assizes: the policy of price control in Elizabethan London', *Guildhall Studies in London History*, 4 (1980), 93–118.

Beresford, M. W., 'The common informer, the penal statutes, and economic regulation', *Economic History Review*, 2nd series, 10 (1957), 221–38.

Berlin, Michael, 'Civic ceremony in early modern London', *Urban History Yearbook*, 13 (1986), 15–27.

Berlin, Norman, *The Base-String: the Underworld in Elizabethan Drama* (1968).

Borsay, Peter, *The English Urban Renaissance: Culture and Society in the Provincial Town, 1660–1770* (Oxford, 1989).

'The London connection: cultural diffusion and the eighteenth-century provincial town', *London Journal*, 19 (1994), 21–35.

'London, 1660–1800: a distinctive culture?', in Peter Clark and Raymond Gillespie, eds., *Two Capitals: London and Dublin, 1500–1840*, Proceedings of the British Academy, 107 (Oxford and London, 2001), pp. 167–84.

Boulton, Jeremy, *Neighbourhood and Society: a London Suburb in the Seventeenth Century* (Cambridge, 1987).

'Food prices and the standard of living in the "century of revolution", 1580–1700', *Economic History Review*, 53 (2000), 455–92.

'London, 1540–1700', in Peter Clark, ed., *The Cambridge Urban History of Britain: Volume II, 1540–1840* (Cambridge, 2000), pp. 315–46.

'The poor among the rich: paupers and the parish in the West End, 1600–1724', in Paul Griffiths and Mark S. R. Jenner, eds., *Londinopolis: Essays in the Cultural and Social History of Early Modern London* (Manchester, 2000), pp. 197–225.

Braddick, M. J., *State Formation in Early Modern England, c.1550–1700* (Cambridge, 2000).

Braddick, M. J. and Walter, John, 'Introduction: grids of power: order, hierarchy, and subordination in early modern society', in Braddick and Walter eds., *Negotiating Power in Early Modern Society: Order, Hierarchy, and Subordination in Britain and Ireland* (Cambridge, 2001), pp. 1–42.

Brenner, Robert, *Merchants and Revolution: Commercial Change, Political Conflict, and London's Overseas Traders, 1550–1653* (Cambridge, 1993).

Brett-James, Norman G., *The Growth of Stuart London* (1935).

Brigden, Susan, *London and the Reformation* (Oxford, 1989).

Brodsky, Vivien, 'Singlewomen in the London marriage market', in R. B. Outhwaite, ed., *Marriage and Society: Studies in the Social History of Marriage* (1981), pp. 81–100.

'Widows in late Elizabethan London: economic opportunity and family orientations', in Lloyd Bonfield, Richard M. Smith, and Keith Wrightson, eds., *The World We Have Gained: Histories of Population and Social Structure. Essays Presented to Peter Laslett on his Seventieth Birthday* (Oxford, 1986), pp. 122–54.

Burgess, Clive, 'London parishioners in times of change: St Andrew Hubbard, Eastcheap, c.1450–1570', *Journal of Ecclesiastical History*, 53 (2002), 38–63.

Burke, Peter, 'Popular culture in seventeenth-century London', in Barry Reay, ed., *Popular Culture in Seventeenth-Century England* (1985), 31–58.

'Perceiving a counter-culture', in Burke, *The Historical Anthropology of Early Modern Italy: Essays on Perception and Communication* (Cambridge, 1987), pp. 63–75.

*A Social History of Knowledge From Gutenberg to Diderot* (Oxford, 2000).

Cain, P., 'Robert Smith and the reform of the archives of the city of London, 1580–1623', *London Journal*, 13 (1987–8), 3–16.

Capp, Bernard, *The World of John Taylor the Water-Poet, 1578–1653* (Oxford, 1994).

'Long Meg of Westminster: a mystery solved', *Notes and Queries*, 45 (1998), 302–4.

'The double standard revisited: plebeian women and sexual reputation in early modern England', *Past and Present*, 162 (1999), 70–100.

'Arson, threats of arson, and incivility in early modern England', in Peter Burke, Brian Harrison, and Paul Slack eds., *Civil Histories: Essays Presented to Sir Keith Thomas* (Oxford, 2000), pp. 197–213.

*When Gossips Meet: Women, Family, and Neighbourhood in Early Modern England* (Oxford, 2003).

Carroll, William C., *Fat King, Lean Beggar: Representations of Poverty in the Age of Shakespeare* (Ithaca, NY, 1996).

Chandler, F. W., *The Literature of Roguery* (New York, 1907).

Clanchy, M. T., *From Memory to Written Record: England 1066–1307* (Oxford, 1993).

Clark, Peter, *The English Alehouse: a Social History, 1200–1830* (1983).

'A crisis contained? The condition of English towns in the 1590s', in Clark, ed., *The European Crisis of the 1590s* (1985), pp. 44–66.

'Migrants in the city: the process of social adaptation in English towns, 1500–1800', in Clark and David Souden, eds., *Migration and Society in Early Modern England* (1987), pp. 267–91.

*British Clubs and Societies 1580–1800: the Origins of an Associational World* (Oxford, 2000).

Clark, Stuart, *Vanities of the Eye: Vision in Early Modern European Culture* (Oxford, 2007).

Coates, Ben, 'Poor relief in London during the English Revolution revisited', *London Journal*, 25 (2000), 40–58.

*The Impact of the English Civil War on the Economy of London, 1642–1650* (Aldershot, 2004).

Cockayne, Emily, *Hubbub: Filth, Noise, and Stench in England* (New Haven, CT, and London, 2007).

Cody, Lisa Foreman, '"Every lane teems with instruction, and every alley is big with erudition": graffiti in eighteenth-century London', in Tim Hitchcock

and Heather Shore, eds., *The Streets of London From the Great Fire to the Great Stink* (2003), pp. 82–100.
Cohen, Esther, 'The animated pain of the body', *American Historical Review*, 105 (2000), 36–68.
Coleman, Julie, *A History of Cant and Slang Dictionaries, Volume I, 1567–1785* (Oxford, 2004).
Collinson, Patrick, 'John Stow and nostalgic antiquarianism', in J. F. Merritt, ed., *Imagining Early Modern London: Perceptions and Portrayals of the City from Stow to Strype, 1598–1720* (Cambridge, 2001), pp. 27–51.
Copeland, A. J., *Bridewell Royal Hospital and King Edward Schools* (1912).
Coquillette, Daniel R., *Francis Bacon* (Stanford, CA, 1992).
Corbin, Alain, *The Foul and the Fragrant: Odour and the Social Imagination*, trans. Miriam L. Kochan with Roy Porter and Christopher Prendergast (Leamington Spa, 1994).
Cowie, L. W., 'Bridewell', *History Today*, 23 (1973), 350–8.
Crawford, Patricia, 'The construction and experience of maternity in seventeenth-century England', in her *Blood, Bodies, and Families in Early Modern England* (Harlow, 2004), pp. 79–112.
Cummins, Tom and Rappaport, Joanne, 'The reconfiguration of civic and sacred space: architecture, image, and writing in the colonial northern Andes', *Latin American Literary Review*, 26 (1998), 174–200.
Dabhoiwala, Faramerz, 'Sex, social relations, and the law in seventeenth- and eighteenth-century London', in Michael J. Braddick and John Walter, eds., *Negotiating Power in Early Modern Society: Order, Hierarchy, and Subordination in Britain and Ireland* (Cambridge, 2001), pp. 85–101.
'Summary justice in early modern London', *English Historical Review*, 121 (2006), 796–822.
'Sex and societies for moral reform, 1688–1800', *Journal of British Studies*, 46 (2007), 290–319.
Damousi, Joy, *Depraved and Disorderly: Female Convicts, Sexuality, and Gender in Colonial Australia* (Cambridge, 1997).
Darnton, Robert, 'An early information society: news and the media in eighteenth-century Paris', *American Historical Review*, 105 (2000), 1–35.
Davies, M. G., *The Enforcement of English Apprenticeship, 1563–1642: a Study in Applied Mercantilism* (Cambridge, MA, 1956).
Davies, W. K. D. and Herbert, D. T., *Communities within Cities: an Urban Social Geography* (1993).
Davis, Jennifer, 'Prosecutions and their context: the use of the criminal law in later nineteenth-century London', in Douglas Hay and Francis Snyder, eds., *Policing and Prosecution in Britain, 1750–1850* (Oxford, 1989), pp. 398–426.
Davis, Natalie Zemon, *The Return of Martin Guerre* (Cambridge, MA, 1983).
*The Gift in Sixteenth-Century France* (Madison, WI, 2000).
Dawson, Anthony B. and Yachnin, Paul, *The Culture of Playgoing in Shakespeare's England* (Cambridge, 2001).
Dean, David, *Law-Making and Society in Late Elizabethan England: the Parliament of England, 1584–1601* (Cambridge, 1996).

De Beer, E. S., 'The early history of London street lighting', *History*, 25 (1940-1), 311-24.
De Certeau, Michel, *The Practice of Everyday Life*, trans. Steven Randall (Berkeley, CA, 1984).
Dionne, Craig, 'Fashioning outlaws: the early modern rogue and urban culture', in Dionne and Steve Mentz, eds., *Rogues and Early Modern English Culture* (Ann Arbor, MI, 2004), pp. 33-61.
Dionne, Craig and Mentz, Steve, eds., *Rogues and Early Modern English Culture* (Ann Arbor, MI, 2004).
Douglas, Mary, *Purity and Danger: an Analysis of the Concepts of Pollution and Taboo* (1966).
Dunn, P. N., *Spanish Picaresque Fiction: a New Literary History* (Ithaca, NY, 1993).
Earle, Peter, 'The female labour market in London in the late seventeenth and early eighteenth centuries', *Economic History Review*, 2nd series, 42 (1989), 328-53.
Egmond, Florike, *Underworlds: Organized Crime in the Netherlands, 1650-1800* (Oxford, 1993).
Ekirch, A. R., *At Day's Close: Night in Times Past* (New York, 2005).
Elton, G. R., 'Informing for profit: a sidelight on Tudor methods of law enforcement', *Historical Journal*, 11 (1954), 149-67.
  *Policy and Police: the Enforcement of the Reformation in the Age of Thomas Cromwell* (Cambridge, 1972).
  'Tudor government: the points of contact', reprinted in Elton, *Studies in Tudor and Stuart Politics and Government, Vol. III, Papers and Reviews 1973-1981* (Cambridge, 1983), pp. 3-57.
  *The Parliament of England, 1559-1581* (Cambridge, 1986).
Emsley, Clive, *Crime and Society in England, 1750-1900*, 2nd edition (Harlow, 1996).
  *The English Police: a Political and Social History*, 2nd edition (Harlow, 1996).
Estabrook, Carl B., *Urbane and Rustic England: Cultural Ties and Social Spheres in the Provinces, 1660-1780* (Manchester, 1998).
Evans, H. C., 'Comic constables – fictional and historical', *Shakespeare Quarterly*, 20 (1969), 427-33.
Evans, Nesta, 'The descent of dissenters in the Chiltern Hundreds', in Margaret Spufford, ed., *The World of Rural Dissenters, 1520-1725* (Cambridge, 1995), pp. 288-308.
Evans, Tanya, *'Unfortunate Objects': Lone Mothers in Eighteenth-Century London* (Basingstoke, 2005).
Evenden, Doreen, *The Midwives of Seventeenth-Century London* (Cambridge, 2000).
Falkus, Malcolm, 'Lighting in the dark ages of English economic history: town streets before the Industrial Revolution', in D. C. Coleman and A. H. John, eds., *Trade, Government and Economy in Pre-Industrial England: Essays Presented to F. J. Fisher* (1976), pp. 248-73.
Faller, Lincoln B., *Turned to Account: the Forms and Functions of Criminal Biography in Late Seventeenth- and Early Eighteenth-Century England* (Cambridge, 1987).
Farge, Arlette, *Fragile Lives: Violence, Power, and Solidarity in Eighteenth-Century Paris*, trans. Carol Shelton (Oxford, 1993).
Farmer, Sharon, *Surviving Poverty in Medieval Paris: Gender, Ideology, and the Daily Lives of the Poor* (Ithaca, NY, 2002).

Farr, James R., *Hands of Honour: Artisans and their World in Dijon, 1500–1650* (Ithaca, NY, 1988).
Fildes, Valerie, 'Maternal feelings re-assessed: child abandonment and neglect in London and Westminster, 1550–1800', in Fildes, ed., *Women as Mothers in Pre-Industrial England: Essays in Memory of Dorothy McLaren* (1990), pp. 139–78.
Finlay, Roger, *Population and Metropolis: the Demography of London, 1580–1650* (Cambridge, 1981).
Finlay, Roger and Shearer, Beatrice, 'Population growth and suburban expansion', in A. L. Beier and Finlay, eds., *The Making of the Metropolis: London 1500–1700* (Harlow, 1986), pp. 37–59.
Fisher, F. J., 'The development of the London food market, 1560–1640', *Economic History Review*, 5 (1934–5), 46–64.
Fisher, W., 'The Renaissance beard: masculinity in early modern England', *Renaissance Quarterly*, 54 (2001), 155–87.
  'Staging the beard: masculinity in early modern English culture', in Jonathan Gil Harris and Natasha Korda, eds., *Staged Properties in Early Modern English Drama* (Cambridge, 2002), pp. 230–57.
Fissell, Mary E., *Patients, Power, and the Poor in Eighteenth-Century Bristol* (Cambridge, 1991).
  *Vernacular Bodies: the Politics of Reproduction in Early Modern England* (Oxford, 2004).
Fletcher, Anthony, *Reform in the Provinces: the Government of Stuart England* (London and New Haven, CT, 1986).
Foster, F. F., *The Politics of Stability: a Portrait of the Rulers of Elizabethan London* (1977).
Foucault, Michel, *Discipline and Punish: the Birth of the Prison* (Harmondsworth, 1977).
Fox, Adam, *Oral and Literate Culture in England, 1500–1700* (Oxford, 2000).
Freist, Dagmar, *Governed by Opinion: Politics, Religion and the Dynamics of Communication in Stuart London, 1637–1645* (London and New York, 1997).
French, H. R., 'Social status, localism, and the "middle sort of people" in England, 1620–1750', *Past and Present*, 166 (2000), 66–99.
Friedrichs, Christopher, *The Early Modern City, 1450–1750* (Harlow, 1995).
Froide, Amy, M., 'Marital status as a category of difference: singlewomen and widows in early modern England', in Judith M. Bennett and Froide, eds., *Singlewomen in the European Past, 1250–1800* (Philadelphia, PA, 1999), pp. 236–69.
Fumerton, Patricia, 'London's vagrant economy: making space for "low" subjectivity', in L. C. Orlin, ed., *Material London, ca. 1600* (Philadelphia, PA, 2000), pp. 206–25.
  'Making vagrancy (in)visible: the economies of disguise in early modern rogue pamphlets', in Craig Dionne and Steve Mentz eds., *Rogues and Early Modern English Culture* (Ann Arbor, MI, 2004), pp. 193–210.
  *Unsettled: the Culture of Mobility and the Working Poor in Early Modern England* (Chicago, IL, 2006).
Gadd, Derek and Dyson, Tony, 'Bridewell Palace: excavations at 9–11 Bridewell Place and 1–3 Tudor Street, City of London, 1978', *Post-Medieval Archaeology*, 15 (1981), 1–79.

Gadd, Ian Anders, 'Early modern printed histories of the London livery companies', in Gadd and Patrick Wallis, eds., *Guilds, Society, and Economy in London, 1450–1800* (2002), pp. 29–50.
Gadd, Ian Anders and Wallis, Patrick, eds., *Guilds, Society, and Economy in London, 1450–1800* (2002).
Garrioch, David, *Neighbourhood and Community in Paris, 1740–1790* (Cambridge, 1986).
Gaskill, Malcolm, 'The displacement of providence: policing and prosecution in seventeenth- and eighteenth-century England', *Continuity and Change*, 11 (1996), 341–74.
  'Reporting murder: fiction in the archives in early modern England', *Social History*, 23 (1998), 1–30.
  *Crime and Mentalities in Early Modern England* (Cambridge, 2000).
Gatrell, V. A. C., 'Crime, authority, and the policeman-state', in F. M. L. Thompson, ed., *The Cambridge Social History of Britain 1750–1950: Volume III, Social Agencies and Institutions* (Cambridge, 1990), pp. 243–310.
  *City of Laughter: Sex and Satire in Eighteenth-Century London* (New York, 2006).
Geremek, Bronislaw, *The Margins of Society in Late Medieval Paris*, trans. Jean Birrell (Cambridge, 1987).
Giddens, Anthony, *The Nation-State and Violence: Volume Two of a Contemporary Critique of Historical Materialism* (Berkeley and Los Angeles, CA, 1985).
Ginzburg, Carlo, *The Night Battles: Witchcraft and Agrarian Cults in the Sixteenth and Seventeenth Centuries*, trans. John and Anne Tedeschi (Baltimore, MD, 1992).
Gladfelder, Hal, *Criminality and Narrative in Eighteenth-Century England: Beyond the Law* (Baltimore, MD, 2001).
Glass, D. V., 'Notes on the demography of London at the end of the seventeenth century', in Glass and R. Revelle, eds., *Population and Social Change* (1972), pp. 275–85.
Glimp, David and Warren, Michelle R., eds., *Arts of Calculation: Numerical Thought in Early Modern Europe* (Basingstoke, 2004).
Goldberg, P. J. P., *Women, Work, and Life-Cycle in a Medieval Economy: Women in York and Yorkshire, c.1300–1520* (Oxford, 1992).
  'Pigs and prostitutes: streetwalking in comparative perspective', in Katherine J. Lewis, Noel James Menuge, and Kim M. Phillips, eds., *Young Medieval Women* (Sutton, 1999), pp. 173–93.
Goldie, Mark, 'The unacknowledged republic: officeholding in early modern England', in Tim Harris, ed., *The Politics of the Excluded, c.1500–1850* (Basingstoke, 2001), pp. 153–94.
Gordon, Andrew, 'Performing London: the map and the city in ceremony', in Gordon and Bernhard Klein, eds., *Literature, Mapping and the Politics of Space in Early Modern Britain* (Cambridge, 2001), pp. 69–88.
Gowing, Laura, *Domestic Dangers: Women, Words, and Sex in Early Modern London* (Oxford, 1996).
  'Secret births and infanticide in seventeenth-century England', *Past and Present*, 156 (1997), 87–115.
  '"The freedom of the streets": women and social space, 1560–1640', in Paul Griffiths and Mark S. R. Jenner, eds., *Londinopolis: Essays in the

*Cultural and Social History of Early Modern London* (Manchester, 2000), pp. 130–51.
'Ordering the body: illegitimacy and female authority in seventeenth-century England', in Michael J. Braddick and John Walter, eds., *Negotiating Power in Early Modern Society: Order, Hierarchy, and Subordination in Britain and Ireland* (Cambridge, 2001), pp. 43–62.
*Common Bodies: Women, Touch, and Power in Seventeenth-Century England* (London and New Haven, CT, 2003).
Greenblatt, Stephen, *Will in the World: How Shakespeare Became Shakespeare* (New York, 2004).
Griffiths, Paul, 'The structure of prostitution in Elizabethan London', *Continuity and Change*, 8 (1993), 39–63.
'Masterless young people in Norwich, 1560–1645', in Griffiths, Adam Fox, and Steve Hindle, eds., *The Experience of Authority in Early Modern England* (Basingstoke, 1996), pp. 146–86.
*Youth and Authority: Formative Experiences in England, 1560–1640* (Oxford, 1996).
'Secrecy and authority in late sixteenth- and seventeenth-century London', *The Historical Journal*, 40 (1997), 925–51.
'Meanings of nightwalking in early modern England', *The Seventeenth Century*, 13 (1998), 212–38.
'Overlapping circles: imagining criminal communities in early modern London', in Alexandra Shepard and Phil Withington, eds., *Communities in Early Modern England* (Manchester, 2000), pp. 115–33.
'Politics made visible: order, residence, and uniformity in Cheapside, 1600–1645', in Griffiths and Mark S. R. Jenner, eds., *Londinopolis: Essays in the Cultural and Social History of Early Modern London* (Manchester, 2000), pp. 176–96.
'Contesting London Bridewell, 1576–1580', *Journal of British Studies*, 42 (2003), 283–315.
'Bodies and souls in Norwich: punishing petty crime, 1540–1700', in Simon Devereaux and Griffiths, eds., *Penal Practice and Culture, 1500–1900: Punishing the English* (Basingstoke, 2004), pp. 85–120.
'Inhabitants', in Carole Rawcliffe and Richard Wilson, eds., *Norwich Since 1550* (2004), pp. 63–88 (text) and pp. 490–7 (footnotes).
'Introduction: punishing the English', in Simon Devereaux and Griffiths eds., *Penal Practice and Culture, 1500–1900: Punishing the English* (Basingstoke, 2004), pp. 1–35.
'Building Bridewell: London's self-images, 1550–1640', in Norman L. Jones and Daniel Woolf, eds., *Local Identities in Late Medieval and Early Modern England* (Basingstoke, 2007), pp. 228–48.
Griffiths, Paul, Landers, J., Pelling, M., and Tyson, R., 'Population and disease, estrangement and belonging 1540–1700', in Peter Clark, ed., *The Cambridge Urban History of Britain: Volume II, 1540–1840* (Cambridge, 2000), pp. 195–233.
Gurr, Andrew, *Playgoing in Shakespeare's London*, 2nd edition (Cambridge, 1996).

Hanawalt, Barbara A., *Crime and Conflict in English Communities, 1300–1348* (Cambridge, MA, 1979).
 *'Of Good and Ill Repute': Gender and Social Control in Medieval England* (Oxford and New York, 1998).
Hansen, Adam, 'Sin city and the "urban condom": rogues, writing, and the early modern urban environment', in Craig Dionne and Steve Mentz, eds., *Rogues and Early Modern English Culture* (Ann Arbor, MI, 2004), pp. 213–29.
Hanson, Elizabeth, *Discovering the Subject in Renaissance England* (Cambridge, 1998).
Harding, Vanessa, 'The population of London, 1550–1700: a review of the published evidence', *London Journal*, 15 (1990), 111–28.
 'Mortality and the mental map of London: Richard Smyth's Obituary', in Robin Myers and Michael Harris, eds., *Medicine, Mortality, and the Book Trade* (Folkstone and Newcastle, DE, 1998), pp. 49–71.
 'Reformation and culture, 1540–1700', in Peter Clark, ed., *The Cambridge Urban History of Britain: Volume II, 1540–1840* (Cambridge, 2000), pp. 263–88.
 'City, capital, and metropolis: the changing shape of seventeenth-century London', in J. F. Merritt, ed., *Imagining Early Modern London: Perceptions and Portrayals of the City from Stow to Strype, 1598–1720* (Cambridge, 2001), pp. 117–43.
 'Controlling a complex metropolis, 1650–1750: politics, parishes, and powers', *London Journal*, 26 (2001), 29–37.
 *The Dead and the Living in Paris and London, 1500–1670* (Cambridge, 2002).
Harkness, Deborah E., *The Jewel House: Elizabethan London and the Scientific Revolution* (New Haven, CT, and London, 2007).
Harris, A. T., *Policing the City: Crime and Legal Authority in London, 1780–1840* (Columbus, OH, 2005).
Harris, P. R., 'The reports of William Udall, informer, 1605–1612', *Recusant History*, 8 (1965), 252–84.
Harris, Tim, *London Crowds in the Reign of Charles II: Propaganda and Politics from the Restoration until the Exclusion Crisis* (Cambridge, 1987).
Hartley, J. B., *The New Nature of Maps: Essays in the History of Cartography*, ed., Paul Laxton (Baltimore, MD, 2001).
Hay, Douglas, 'Controlling the English prosecutor', *Osgoode Law Journal*, 21 (1983), 167–80.
 'The criminal prosecution in England and its historians', *The Modern Law Review*, 47 (1984), 1–29.
 'Prosecution and power: malicious prosecution in the English courts, 1750–1850', in Hay and Francis Snyder, eds., *Policing and Prosecution in Britain, 1750–1850* (Oxford, 1989), pp. 343–95.
 'War, dearth, and theft in the eighteenth century: the record of the English courts', *Past and Present*, 95 (1992), 117–60.
Hay, Douglas and Snyder, Francis, 'Using the criminal law, 1750–1850: policing, private prosecution and the state', in Hay and Snyder, eds., *Policing and Prosecution in Britain, 1750–1850* (Oxford, 1989), pp. 3–52.

Headrick, D. R., *When Information Came of Age: Technologies of Knowledge in the Age of Reason and Revolution, 1700–1850* (Oxford and New York, 2000).
Healy, Margaret, *Fictions of Disease in Early Modern England: Bodies, Plagues and Politics* (Basingstoke, 2001).
Heidensohn, Frances, *Crime and Society* (Basingstoke, 1989).
Henderson, Tony, *Disorderly Women in Eighteenth-Century London: Prostitution and Control in the Metropolis, 1730–1830* (Harlow, 1999).
Herlan, R. W., 'Poor relief in the London parish of Antholin's Budge Row, 1638–1664', *Guildhall Studies in London History*, 2 (1977), 179–99.
 'Poor relief in the London parish of Dunstan in the West during the English Revolution', *Guildhall Studies in London History*, 2 (1977), 13–36.
 'Social articulation and the configuration of parochial poverty in London on the eve of the Restoration', *Guildhall Studies in London History*, 2 (1976), 43–53.
Herrup, Cynthia, *The Common Peace: Participation and the Criminal Law in Seventeenth-Century England* (Cambridge, 1987).
Hickman, David, 'Religious belief and pious practice among London's Elizabethan elite', *Historical Journal*, 42 (1999), 941–60.
Higgs, Edward, 'The rise of the information state: the development of central state surveillance of the citizen in England, 1500–2000', *Journal of Historical Sociology*, 14, (2001), 175–97.
 *The Information State in England: the Central Collection of Information on Citizens Since 1500* (Basingstoke, 2004).
Higgs, Laquita M., *Godliness and Governance in Tudor Colchester* (Ann Arbor, MI, 1998).
Hindle, Steve, *The State and Social Change in Early Modern England, c.1550–1640* (Basingstoke, 2000).
 'The keeping of the public peace', in Paul Griffiths, Adam Fox, and Hindle, eds., *The Experience of Authority in Early Modern England* (Basingstoke, 1996), pp. 213–48.
 *On the Parish? The Micro-Politics of Poor Relief in Rural England, c.1550–1750* (Oxford, 2004).
Hitchcock, Tim, 'The publicity of poverty in early eighteenth-century London', in J. F. Merritt, ed., *Imagining Early Modern London: Perceptions and Portrayals of the City from Stow to Strype, 1598–1720* (Cambridge, 2001), pp. 166–84.
 *Down and Out in Eighteenth-Century London* (2004).
Houston, R. A., *Social Change in the Age of Enlightenment: Edinburgh, 1660–1760* (Oxford, 1997).
 *Madness and Society in Eighteenth-Century Scotland* (Oxford, 2000).
Howard, Jean E., *Theater of a City: the Places of London Comedy, 1598–1642* (Philadelphia, PA, 2007).
Howard, Sharon, 'Investigating responses to theft in early modern Wales: communities, thieves, and the courts', *Continuity and Change*, 19 (2004), 409–30.
Hunter, Judith, 'English inns, taverns, alehouses, and brandy shops: the legislative framework, 1495–1797', in Beat A. Kumin and Ann B. Lusty, eds., *The World of the Tavern: Public Houses in Early Modern Europe* (Aldershot, 2002), pp. 65–82.
Hurl-Eamon, Jennine, *Gender and Petty Violence in London, 1680–1720* (Columbus, OH, 2005).

Ingram, Martin, 'Ridings, rough music, and mocking rhymes in early modern England', in Barry Reay, ed., *Popular Culture in Seventeenth-Century England* (1985), pp. 166–97.

'"Scolding women cucked or washed": a crisis in gender relations in early modern England?', in Jenny Kermode and Garthine Walker, eds., *Women, Crime, and the Courts in Early Modern England* (1994), pp. 48–80.

'Reforming manners in early modern England', in Paul Griffiths, Adam Fox, and Steve Hindle, eds., *The Experience of Authority in Early Modern England* (Basingstoke, 1996), pp. 47–88.

'Juridical folklore in England illustrated by rough music' in Christopher Brooks and Michael Lobban, eds., *Communities and Courts in Britain, 1150–1900* (1997), pp. 61–82.

'Law, litigants, and the construction of "honour": slander suits in early modern England', in Peter Coss, ed., *The Moral World of the Law* (Cambridge, 2000), pp. 134–60.

'Sexual manners: the other face of civility in early modern England', in Peter Burke, Brian Harrison, and Paul Slack, eds., *Civil Histories: Essays Presented to Sir Keith Thomas* (Oxford, 2000), pp. 87–109.

'Child sexual abuse in early modern England', in Michael J. Braddick and John Walter, eds., *Negotiating Power in Early Modern Society: Order, Hierarchy, and Subordination in Britain and Ireland* (Cambridge, 2001), pp. 63–84.

'Regulating sex in pre-Reformation London', in G. W. Bernard and S. J. Gunn, eds., *Authority and Consent in Tudor England: Essays Presented to C. S. L. Davies* (Aldershot, 2002), pp. 79–95.

'Shame and pain: themes and variations in Tudor punishments', in Simon Devereaux and Paul Griffiths, eds., *Penal Practice and Culture, 1500–1900: Punishing the English* (Basingstoke, 2004), pp. 36–62.

Innes, Joanna, 'Prisons for the poor: English bridewells 1555–1800', in Francis Snyder and Douglas Hay, eds., *Labour, Law, and Crime: a Historical Perspective* (Oxford, 1987), pp. 42–122.

'The role of transportation in seventeenth- and eighteenth-century English penal practice', in Carl Bridge, ed., *New Perspectives in Australian History* (1990), pp. 1–24.

James, Mervyn, 'Ritual, drama, and the social body in the late medieval town', in James, *Society, Politics, and Culture: Studies in Early Modern England* (Cambridge, 1986), pp. 16–47.

Jenner, Mark S. R., 'The politics of London air: John Evelyn's *Fumifugum* and the Restoration', *Historical Journal*, 38 (1995), 535–51.

'From conduit community to commercial network? Water in London, 1500–1725', in Paul Griffiths and Jenner eds., *Londinopolis: Essays in the Cultural and Social History of Early Modern London* (Manchester, 2000), pp. 250–72.

'Circulation and disorder: London streets and hackney coaches, c. 1640-c.1740', in Tim Hitchcock and Heather Shore eds., *The Streets of London From the Great Fire to the Great Stink* (2003), pp. 40–53.

Jenner, Mark and Griffiths, Paul, 'Introduction', in Jenner and Griffiths, eds., *Londinopolis: Essays in the Cultural and Social History of Early Modern London* (Manchester, 2000), pp. 1–23.

Johnson, R. C., 'The transportation of vagrant children from London to Virginia, 1618–1622', in Howard S. Reinmuth, ed., *Early Stuart Studies: Essays in Honour of David Harris* (Minneapolis, MN, 1970), pp. 137–51.

Johnston, Alexandra F. and Tittler, Robert, '"To catch a thief" in Jacobean London', in E. B. DeWindt, ed., *The Salt of Common Life* (Kalamazoo, MI, 1995), pp. 233–69.

Jones, Ann Rosalind and Stallybrass, Peter, *Renaissance Clothing and the Materials of Memory* (Cambridge, 2000).

Jones, Colin, *Charity and Bienfaisance: the Treatment of the Poor in the Montpellier Region, 1740–1815* (Cambridge, 1982).

Judges, A. V., ed., *The Elizabethan Underworld*, 2nd edition (1965).

Jutte, Robert, *Poverty and Deviance in Early Modern Europe* (Cambridge, 1994).

Karras, Ruth Mazo, 'The regulation of brothels in later medieval England', *Signs*, 14 (1989), 399–433.

*Common Women: Prostitution and Sexuality in Medieval England* (Oxford, 1996).

'Sex and the singlewoman', in Judith M. Bennett and Amy M. Froide, eds., *Singlewomen in the European Past, 1250–1800* (Philadelphia, PA, 1999), pp. 127–44.

Kazmierczak Manzione, Carol, *Christ's Hospital of London, 1552–1598: 'A Passing Deed of Pity'* (Selinsgrove, 1995).

'Sex in Tudor London: abusing their bodies with each other', in J. Murray and K. Eisenbichler, eds., *Desire and Discipline: Sex and Sexuality in the Premodern West* (Toronto, 1996), pp. 87–100.

Keene, Derek, 'Material London in time and space', in Lena Cowen Orlin, ed., *Material London, ca. 1600* (Philadelphia, PA, 2000), pp. 55–74.

Kelsey, Sean, *Inventing a Republic: the Political Culture of the English Commonwealth, 1649–1653* (Stanford, CA, 1997).

Kent, D. V., and Kent, F. W., *Neighbours and Neighbourhood in Renaissance Florence: the District of the Red Lion in the Fifteenth Century* (New York, 1982).

Kent, Joan, 'The English village constable 1580–1642: the nature and dilemmas of the office', *Journal of British Studies*, 20 (1981), 26–49.

*The English Village Constable 1580–1642: a Social and Administrative Study* (Oxford, 1986).

'The rural "middling sort" in early modern England, circa 1640–1740: some economic, political, and socio-cultural characteristics', *Rural History*, 10 (1999), 19–54.

Kesselring, K. J., *Mercy and Authority in the Tudor State* (Cambridge, 2003).

King, Peter, 'The rise of juvenile delinquency in England, 1740–1840: changing patterns of perception and prosecution', *Past and Present*, 160 (1998), 116–66.

*Crime, Justice, and Discretion: Law and Social Relations in England, 1740–1820* (Oxford, 2000).

'The summary courts and social relations in eighteenth-century England', *Past and Present*, 183 (2004), 125–72.

*Crime and Law in England 1750–1840: Remaking Justice from the Margins* (Cambridge, 2006).

Klerman, Daniel, 'Settlement and the decline of private prosecution in thirteenth-century England', *Law and History Review*, 19 (2001), 1–65.

Knowles, James, 'The spectacle of the realm: civic consciousness, rhetoric and ritual in early modern London', in J. R. Mulryne and Margaret Shewring, eds., *Theatre and Government under the Stuarts* (Cambridge, 1993), pp. 157–89.

Koslofsky, Craig, 'Court culture and street lighting in seventeenth-century Europe', *Journal of Urban History*, 28 (2002), 743–68.

Kostof, Spiro, *The City Shaped: Urban Patterns and Meanings through History* (Boston, 1991).

Lake, Peter, 'The Laudian style: order, uniformity, and the pursuit of the beauty of holiness in the 1630s', in Kenneth Fincham, ed., *The Early Stuart Church, 1603–42* (Basingstoke, 1993), pp. 161–85.

Lang, R. G., 'Social origins and social aspirations of Jacobean London merchants', *Economic History Review*, 2nd series, 27 (1974), 28–47.

Langbein, John H., *Prosecuting Crime in the Renaissance: England, Germany, France* (Cambridge, MA, 1974).

*Torture and the Law of Proof: Europe and England in the Ancien Regime* (Chicago, IL, 1976).

*The Origins of Adversary Criminal Trial* (Oxford, 2003).

Langeluddecke, Henrik, 'Law and order in seventeenth-century England: the organization of local administration during the personal rule of Charles I', *Law and History Review*, 15 (1997), 49–76.

Laquer, Thomas, 'Crowds, carnivals and the state in English executions, 1604–1868', in A. L. Beier et al., eds., *The First Modern Society: Essays in English History in Honour of Lawrence Stone* (Cambridge, 1989), pp. 305–55.

Lawson, P. G., 'Property crime and hard times in England, 1559–1624', *Law and History Review*, 4 (1986), 95–127.

Leinwald, T. B., 'London triumphing: the Jacobean Lord Mayor's Show', *Clio*, 11 (1982), 137–53.

Lemire, Beverly, 'Peddling fashion: salesmen, pawnbrokers, tailors, thieves, and the second-hand clothes trade in England, c.1700–1800', *Textile History*, 22 (1991), 67–82.

*Dress, Culture, and Commerce: the English Clothing Trade Before the Factory, 1660–1800* (1997).

Lidington, D. R., 'Parliament and the enforcement of the penal statutes: the history of the Act "In Restraint of Common Promoters" (18 Eliz I, c.5)', *Parliamentary History*, 8 (1989), 309–28.

Lindley, Keith, 'Riot prevention and control in early Stuart London', *Transactions of the Royal Historical Society*, 5th series, 33 (1983), 109–26.

Lis, Catharina and Soly, Hugo, *Disordered Lives: Eighteenth-Century Families and their Unruly Relatives*, trans. Alexander Brown (Oxford, 1996).

Littleton, Charles, 'Social interactions of aliens in late Elizabethan London: evidence from the 1593 return and the French Church consistory "actes"', *Proceedings of the Huguenot Society of Great Britain and Ireland*, 26 (1995), 147–59.

Luu, Lien Bich, 'Assimilation or segregation: colonies of alien craftsmen in Elizabethan London', *Proceedings of the Huguenot Society of Great Britain and Ireland*, 26 (1995), 160–72.

'"Taking the bread out of our mouths": xenophobia in early modern London', *Immigrants & Minorities*, 19 (2000), 1–22.

'Natural-born versus stranger-born subjects: aliens and their status in Elizabethan London', in Nigel Goose and Luu, eds., *Immigrants in Tudor and Early Stuart England* (Brighton and Portland, OR, 2005), pp. 57–75.

Macdonald, Michael and Murphy, Terence R., *Sleepless Souls: Suicide in Early Modern England* (Oxford, 1990).

Macculloch, Dairmaid, *The Boy King: Edward VI and the Protestant Reformation* (New York, 2001).

Mackenny, Richard, *Traders and Tradesmen* (Beckenham, 1987).

Manley, Lawrence, *Literature and Culture in Early Modern London* (Cambridge, 1995).

Manning, Roger, *Village Revolts: Social Protest and Popular Disturbances in England, 1509–1640* (Oxford, 1988).

Markus, Thomas A., *Buildings and Power: Freedom and Control in the Origin of Modern Building Types* (1993).

McCampbell, A. E., 'The London parish and the London precinct, 1640–1660', *Guildhall Studies in London History*, 2 (1976), 107–24.

McGowen, Randall, 'The Bank of England and the policing of forgery 1797–1821', *Past and Present*, 186 (2005), 81–116.

McIntosh, Marjorie Keniston, *Controlling Misbehaviour in England, 1370–1600* (Cambridge, 1998).

McKenzie, Andrea, 'Making crime pay: motives, marketing strategies, and the printed literature of crime in England, 1660–1770', in Greg T. Smith, Allyson May, and Simon Devereaux, eds., *Criminal Justice in the Old World and New: Essays in Honour of J. M. Beattie* (Toronto, 1998), pp. 235–69.

*Tyburn's Martyrs: Execution in England, 1675–1775* (2007).

McMullan, John L., *The Canting Crew: London's Criminal Underworld, 1550–1700* (New Brunswick, NJ, 1984).

McRae, Andrew, *God Speed the Plough: the Representation of Rural England, 1500–1660* (Cambridge, 1996).

'"On the famous voyage": Ben Jonson and civic space', in Andrew Gordon and Bernhard Klein, eds., *Literature, Mapping and the Politics of Space in Early Modern Britain* (Cambridge, 2001), pp. 181–203.

McSheffrey, Shannon, *Marriage, Sex, and Civic Culture in Late Medieval London* (Philadelphia, PA, 2006).

McStay Adams, Thomas, *Bureaucrats and Beggars: French Social Policy in the Age of Enlightenment* (Oxford, 1990).

Meldrum, Tim, 'London domestic servants from depositional evidence, 1660–1750: servant-employer sexuality in the patriarchal household', in Tim Hitchcock, Peter King, and Pamela Sharpe, eds., *Chronicling Poverty: the Voices and Strategies of the English Poor, 1640–1840* (Basingstoke, 1997), pp. 47–69.

*Domestic Service and Gender, 1660–1750: Life and Work in the London Household* (Harlow, 2000).

Mendelson, Sara and Crawford, Patricia, *Women in Early Modern England, 1550–1720* (Oxford, 1998).

Merritt, J. F., 'Puritans, Laudians, and the phenomenon of church building in Jacobean London', *Historical Journal*, 41 (1998), 935–60.

'Introduction: perceptions and portrayals of London, 1598–1720', in Merritt, ed., *Imagining Early Modern London: Perceptions and Portrayals of the City from Stow to Strype, 1598–1720* (Cambridge, 2001), pp. 1–24.

'The reshaping of Stow's *Survey*: Munday, Strype, and the Protestant city', in Merritt, ed., *Imagining Early Modern London: Perceptions and Portrayals of the City from Stow to Strype, 1598–1720* (Cambridge, 2001), pp. 52–88.

*The Social World of Early Modern Westminster: Abbey, Court, and Community, 1525–1640* (Manchester, 2005).

Midelfort, H. C. Erik, *A History of Madness in Sixteenth-Century Germany* (Stanford, CA, 1999).

Mikalachki, Jodi, 'Women's networks and the female vagrant: a hard case', in Susan Frye and Karen Robertson, eds., *Maids and Mistresses, Cousins and Queens: Women's Alliances in Early Modern England* (Oxford, 1999), pp. 52–69.

Mills, Helen, 'Mapping the early modern city', *Urban History*, 23 (1996), 145–70.

Morgan, Gwenda and Rushton, Peter, *Rogues, Thieves, and the Rule of Law: the Problem of Law Enforcement in North-East England, 1718–1800* (1998).

Morris, Lydia, *Dangerous Classes: the Underclass and Social Citizenship* (1994).

Muldrew, Craig, *The Economy of Obligation: the Culture of Credit and Social Relations in Early Modern England* (Basingstoke, 1998).

Multhalf, L. S., 'The light of lamp-lanterns: street lighting in seventeenth-century Amsterdam', *Technology and Culture*, 26 (1985), 236–52.

Munro, Ian, *The Figure of the Crowd in Early Modern London: the City and its Double* (Basingstoke, 2005).

Musson, A. J., *Public Order and Law Enforcement: the Local Administration of Criminal Justice, 1294–1350* (Woodbridge, 1996).

'Turning King's evidence: the prosecution of crime in late medieval England', *Oxford Journal of Legal Studies*, 19 (1999), 467–79.

Mylne, R. S., 'Old Bridewell', *Transactions of the London and Middlesex Archaeological Society*, new series, 2 (1910–13), 86–110.

Nead, Lynda, *Victorian Babylon: People, Streets, and Images in Nineteenth-Century London* (New Haven, CT, and London, 2000).

Neely, Carol Thomas, *Distracted Subjects: Madness and Gender in Shakespeare and Early Modern Culture* (Ithaca, NY, 2004).

Newman, J., 'Inigo Jones and the politics of architecture', in Kevin Sharpe and Peter Lake, eds., *Culture and Politics in Early Stuart England* (Basingstoke, 1994), pp. 231–45.

O'Donoghue, E. G., *Bridewell Hospital, Palace, Prison, and School, From the Death of Elizabeth to Modern Times* 2 vols. (1923, 1929).

Orlin, Lena Cowen, 'Boundary disputes in early modern London', in Orlin, ed., *Material London, ca. 1600* (Philadelphia, PA, 2000), pp. 345–76.

*Oxford Dictionary of National Biography*, eds., H. C. G. Matthew and Brian Harrison, 60 vols. (Oxford, 2004).

Paley, Ruth, '"An imperfect, inadequate, and wretched system"? Policing London before Peel', *Criminal Justice History*, 10 (1989), 95–130.

'Thief-takers in London in the age of the McDaniel gang, c. 1745–1754', in Douglas Hay and Francis Snyder, eds., *Policing and Prosecution in Britain, 1750–1850* (Oxford, 1989), pp. 301–41.

Palk, Deidrie, 'Private crime in public and private places: pickpockets and shoplifters in London, 1780–1823', in Tim Hitchcock and Heather Shore, eds., *The Streets of London From the Great Fire to the Great Stink* (2003), pp. 135–50.

Pearl, Valerie, *London and the Outbreak of the Puritan Revolution: City Government and National Politics* (Oxford, 1961).

'Change and stability in seventeenth-century London', in Jonathan Barry, ed., *The Tudor and Stuart Town: a Reader in English Urban History, 1530–1688* (Harlow, 1990), pp. 139–65, first published in *London Journal*, 5 (1979), 3–34.

'Puritans and poor relief: the London workhouse 1649–1660', in Donald Pennington and Keith Thomas, eds., *Puritans and Revolutionaries: Essays in Seventeenth-Century History Presented to Christopher Hill* (Oxford, 1978), pp. 206–32.

'Social policy in early modern London', in H. Lloyd-Jones, Blair Worden, and Pearl, eds., *History and Imagination: Essays in Honour of H. R. Trevor-Roper* (1979), pp. 115–31.

Peck, Linda Levy, *Consuming Splendor: Society and Culture in Seventeenth-Century England* (Cambridge, 2005).

Pelling, Margaret, *The Common Lot: Sickness, Medical Occupations, and the Urban Poor in Early Modern England* (Harlow, 1998).

'Defensive tactics: networking by female medical practitioners in early modern London' in Alexandra Shepard and Phil Withington, eds., *Communities in Early Modern England: Networks, Place, Rhetoric* (Manchester, 2000), pp. 38–53.

'Skirting the city? Disease, social change, and divided households in the seventeenth century', in Paul Griffiths and Mark S. R. Jenner, eds., *Londinopolis: Essays in the Cultural and Social History of Early Modern London* (Manchester, 2000), pp. 154–75.

*Medical Conflicts in Early Modern London: Patronage, Physicians, and Irregular Practitioners 1550–1640* (Oxford, 2003).

Perlman, Janice, *The Myth of Marginality: Urban Poverty and Politics in Rio de Janeiro* (Berkeley, CA, 1976).

Perry, Mary Elizabeth, *Crime and Society in Early Modern Seville* (New England, 1980).

Pettigree, Andrew, *Foreign Protestant Communities in Sixteenth-Century London* (Oxford, 1986).

Phillips, H. E., 'The last years of the Court of Star Chamber, 1630–1641', *Transactions of the Royal Historical Society*, 4th series, 21 (1939), 103–31.

Phythian-Adams, Charles, 'Ceremony and the citizen: the communal year at Coventry, 1450–1550', in Peter Clark and Paul Slack, eds., *Crisis and Order in English Towns, 1550–1750* (Toronto, 1972), pp. 57–85.

Pollock, Linda, 'Living on the stage of the world: the concept of privacy among the elite of early modern England', in Adrian Wilson, ed., *Rethinking Social History: English Society and its Interpretation, 1570–1920* (Manchester, 1993), pp. 78–96.

Porter, Stephen, 'The economic and social impact of the Civil War upon London', in Porter, ed., *London and the Civil War* (Basingstoke, 1996), pp. 175–204.

Postles, David, *Talking 'Ballocs': Nicknames and English Medieval Social Linguistics* (Leicester, 2003).
*Social Proprieties: Social Relations in Early-Modern England, 1500–1680* (Washington, DC, 2006).
'Surviving lone motherhood in early modern England', *The Seventeenth Century*, 21 (2006), 160–83.
Powell, Edward, *Kingship, Law and Society: Criminal Justice in the Reign of Henry V* (1989).
Power, M. J., 'Shadwell: the development of a London suburban community in the seventeenth century', *London Journal*, 4 (1978), 29–46.
'London and the control of the "crisis" of the 1590s', *History*, 70 (1985), 371–85.
'A "crisis" reconsidered: social and demographic dislocation in London in the 1590s', *London Journal*, 12 (1986), 134–45.
'The social topography of Restoration London', in A. L. Beier and Roger Finlay, eds., *London 1500–1700: the Making of the Metropolis* (Harlow, 1986), pp. 199–223.
'The east London working community in the seventeenth century', in Penelope J. Corfield and Derek Keene, eds., *Work in Towns, 850–1850* (Leicester, 1990), pp. 103–20.
Quetel, Claude, *The History of Syphilis*, trans. Judith Braddock and Brian Pike (Baltimore, MD, 1990).
Radzinowicz, Leon and Hood, Roger, *A History of English Criminal Law and its Administration from 1750*, 5 vols. (1948–86).
Rappaport, Steve, 'Social structure and mobility in sixteenth-century London: part I', *London Journal*, 9 (1983), 107–35.
'Social structure and mobility in sixteenth-century London: part II', *London Journal*, 10 (1984), 107–34.
*Worlds Within Worlds: Structures of Life in Sixteenth-Century London* (Cambridge, 1989).
Rawcliffe, Carole, *Medicine for the Soul: the Life, Death and Resurrection of an English Medieval Hospital* (Stroud, 1999).
Rawlings, Philip, *Drunks, Whores, and Idle Apprentices: Criminal Biographies of the Eighteenth Century* (1992).
Reid, Donald, *Paris Sewers and Sewermen: Realities and Representations* (Cambridge, MA, 1991).
Reid, Douglas, 'Weddings, weekdays, work, and leisure in urban England, 1791–1911', *Past and Present*, 153 (1996), 135–63.
Rexroth, Frank, *Deviance and Power in Late Medieval London* (Cambridge, 2007).
Reynolds, Bryan, *Becoming Criminal: Transversal Performance and Cultural Dissidence in Early Modern England* (Baltimore, MD, 2002).
Reynolds, Elaine A., *Before the Bobbies: the Night Watch and Police Reform in Metropolitan London, 1720–1830* (Basingstoke, 1998).
Roberts, Michael, 'Women and work in sixteenth-century English towns', in Penelope J. Corfield and Derek Keene, eds., *Work in Towns, 850–1850* (Leicester, 1990), pp. 86–102.
Roberts, Peter, 'Elizabethan players and minstrels and the legislation of 1572 against retainers and vagabonds', in Anthony Fletcher and Roberts, eds.,

*Religion, Culture, and Society in Early Modern Britain: Essays in Honour of Patrick Collinson* (Cambridge, 1994), pp. 29–55.

Robertson, J. C., 'Reckoning with London: interpreting the *Bills of Mortality* before John Graunt', *Urban History*, 23 (1996), 325–50.

'Stuart London and the idea of a royal capital city', *Renaissance Studies*, 15 (2001), 37–58.

'The adventures of Dick Whittington and the social construction of Elizabethan London', in Ian Anders Gadd and Patrick Wallis, eds., *Guilds, Society, and Economy in London, 1450–1800* (2002), pp. 51–66.

Rogers, Nicholas, 'Policing the poor in eighteenth-century London: the vagrancy laws and their administration', *Social History*, 24 (1991), 127–47.

'The politics of war and dearth, 1756–1757', in his *Crowds, Culture, and Politics in Georgian Britain* (Oxford, 1998), pp. 58–84.

Rublack, Ulinka, *The Crimes of Women in Early Modern Germany* (Oxford, 1999).

Ruff, Julius, R., *Violence in Early Modern Europe, 1500–1800* (Cambridge, 2001).

Rushton, Peter, 'Idiocy, the family and the community in early modern north-east England', in David Wright and Anne Digby, eds., *From Idiocy to Mental Deficiency: Historical Perspectives on People With Learning Disabilities* (1996), pp. 44–64.

Rusnock, Andrea, *Vital Accounts; Quantifying Health and Population in Eighteenth-Century France and England* (Cambridge, 2002).

Sabean, David Warren, *Power in the Blood: Popular Culture and Village Discourse in Early Modern Germany* (Cambridge, 1984).

Sacks, David Harris, 'London's dominion: the metropolis, the market economy, and the state', in Lena Cowen Orlin, ed., *Material London, ca. 1600* (Philadelphia, PA, 2000), pp. 20–54.

Salgado, Gamini, *The Elizabethan Underworld* (Stroud, 1977).

Samaha, Joel, *Law and Order in Historical Perspective: The Case of Elizabethan Essex* (New York and London, 1974).

Sanford, Rhonda Lemke, *Maps and Memory in Early Modern England: a Sense of Place* (Basingstoke, 2002).

Schen, Claire, *Charity and Lay Piety in Reformation London, 1500–1620* (Aldershot, 2002).

'Greeks and "Grecians" in London: the "other" strangers', in Charles Littleton and Randolph Vigne, eds., *From Strangers to Citizens: the Integration of Immigrant Communities in Britain, Ireland, and Colonial America* (Brighton and Portland, OR, 2001), pp. 268–75.

Schindler, Norbert, *Rebellion, Community and Custom in Early Modern Germany*, trans. Pamela E. Selwyn (Cambridge, 2002).

Seaver, Paul S., *The Puritan Lectureships: the Politics of Religious Dissent, 1560–1662* (Stanford, CA, 1970).

Shapin, Steven, *A Social History of Truth: Civility and Science in Seventeenth-Century England* (Chicago, IL, 1994).

Shapiro, Barbara J., *A Culture of Fact: England, 1550–1720* (Ithaca, NY, 2000).

Sharpe, J. A., 'Enforcing the law in the seventeenth-century English village', in V. A. C. Gatrell *et al.*, eds., *Crime and the Law: the Social History of Crime in Western Europe Since 1500* (1980), pp. 97–119.

'"Such disagreement betwyx neighbours": litigation and human relations in early modern England', in John Bossy, ed., *Disputes and Settlements: Law and Human Relations in the West* (Cambridge, 1983), pp. 167–87.

'"Last dying speeches": religion, ideology and public executions in seventeenth-century England', *Past and Present*, 107 (1985), 144–67.

'The people and the law', in Barry Reay ed., *Popular Culture in Seventeenth-Century England* (1985), pp. 244–70.

Sharpe, J. A., *Crime in Early Modern England, 1550–1750*, 2nd edition (Harlow, 1999).

Sharpe, Kevin, *The Personal Rule of Charles I* (New Haven, CT, and London, 1992).

Shaw, Diane, 'The construction of the private in medieval London', *Journal of Medieval and Early Modern Studies*, 26 (1996), 447–66.

Shesgreen, Sean, *Images of the Outcast: the Urban Poor in the Cries of London* (New Brunswick, NJ, 2002).

Shoemaker, Robert, *Prosecution and Punishment: Petty Crime and the Law in London and Rural Middlesex, c.1660–1725* (Cambridge, 1991).

'The decline of public insult in London, 1660–1800', *Past and Present*, 169 (2000), 97–131.

*The London Mob: Violence and Disorder in Eighteenth-Century England* (2004).

'Streets of shame?: The crowd and public punishments in London, 1700–1820', in Simon Devereaux and Paul Griffiths, eds., *Penal Practice and Culture, 1500–1900: Punishing the English* (Basingstoke, 2004), pp. 232–57.

Shore, Heather, 'Cross coves, buzzers, and general sorts of prigs: juvenile crime and the "criminal underworld" in the early nineteenth century', *British Journal of Criminology*, 39 (1999), 10–24.

'Mean streets: criminality, immorality and the street in early nineteenth-century London', in Tim Hitchcock and Shore, eds., *The Streets of London From the Great Fire to the Great Stink* (2003), pp. 151–64.

Sibley, David, *Geographies of Exclusion: Society and Difference in the West* (1995).

Siena, Kevin P., *Venereal Disease, Hospitals, and the Urban Poor: London's 'Foul Wards', 1600–1800* (Rochester, NY, 2004).

Slack, Paul, 'Vagrants and vagrancy in England, 1598–1664', *Economic History Review*, 2nd series, 27 (1974), 360–79.

'Books of orders: the making of English social policy, 1577–1631', *Transactions of the Royal Historical Society*, 5th series, 30 (1980), 1–22.

'Social policy and the constraints of government, 1547–1558', in Jennifer Loach and Robert Tittler, eds., *The Mid-Tudor Polity, c.1540–1560* (Basingstoke, 1980), pp. 94–115.

*The Impact of Plague in Tudor and Stuart England* (1985).

*Poverty and Policy in Tudor and Stuart England* (Harlow, 1988).

'Hospitals, workhouses, and the relief of the poor in early modern London', in Ole Peter Grell and Andrew Cunningham, eds., *Health Care and Poor Relief in Protestant Europe, 1500–1700* (London, 1997), pp. 234–51.

*From Reformation to Improvement: Public Welfare in Early Modern England* (Oxford, 1999).

'Great and good towns', in Peter Clark, ed., *The Cambridge Urban History of Britain: Volume II, 1540–1840* (Cambridge, 2000), pp. 347–76.

'Perceptions of the metropolis in seventeenth-century England', in Peter Burke, Brian Harrison, and Slack, eds., *Civil Histories: Essays Presented to Sir Keith Thomas* (Oxford, 2000), pp. 161–80.

'Government and information in seventeenth-century England', *Past and Present*, 184 (2004), 33–68.

Smail, Daniel Lord, *Imaginary Cartographies: Possession and Identity in Late Medieval Marseille* (Ithaca, NY, 1999).

Smith, A. E., *Colonists in Bondage: White Servitude and Convict Labour in America, 1607–1776* (Chapel Hill, NC, 1947).

Smith, D. L., 'The fourth earl of Dorset and the personal rule of Charles I'. *Journal of British Studies*, 30 (1991), 257–87.

'The 4th earl of Dorset and the politics of the sixteen-twenties'. *Historical Research*, 65 (1992), 37–53.

Smith Greg T., 'Civilized people don't want to see that kind of thing: the decline of public physical punishment in London, 1760–1840', in Carolyn Strange, ed., *Qualities of Mercy: Justice, Punishment, and Discretion* (1996), pp. 21–51.

Smuts, Malcolm, *Court Culture and the Origins of a Royalist Tradition in Early Stuart England* (Philadelphia, PA, 1987).

Souden, David, 'Migrants and the population structure of late seventeenth-century provincial cities and market towns', in Peter Clark, ed., *The Transformation of English Provincial Towns, 1660–1800* (1984), pp. 133–68.

Spierenburg, Pieter, 'Introduction', in Spierenburg, ed., *The Emergence of Carcereal Institutions: Prisons, Galleys, and Lunatic Asylums, 1550–1900* (Rotterdam, 1984), pp. 2–8.

*The Prison Experience: Disciplinary Institutions and their Inmates in Early Modern Europe* (New Brunswick, NJ, and London, 1991).

Street, Brian, *Literacy in Theory and Practice* (Cambridge, 1984).

Stuart, Kathy, *Defiled Trades and Social Outcasts: Honour and Ritual Pollution in Early Modern Germany* (Cambridge, 1999).

Sumner, Colin, *The Sociology of Deviance: an Obituary* (Buckingham, 1994).

Taylor, David, *Crime, Policing, and Punishment in England, 1750–1914* (Basingstoke, 1998).

Thomas, Keith, 'Numeracy in early modern England', *Transactions of the Royal Historical Society*, 5th series, 37 (1987), 103–32.

Thompson, E. P., 'Time, work-discipline, and industrial capitalism', *Past and Present*, 38 (1967), 56–97.

Thurley, Simon, *The Royal Palaces of Tudor England: Architecture and Court Life, 1460–1547* (New Haven, CT, and London, 1993).

Tittler, Robert, 'The emergence of urban policy, 1536–1558', in Jennifer Loach and Tittler, eds., *The Mid-Tudor Polity, c. 1540–1560* (Basingstoke, 1980), pp. 94–115.

*Architecture and Power: the Town Hall and the English Urban Community, c. 1500–1640* (Oxford, 1991).

*The Reformation and the Towns in England: Politics and Political Culture, c. 1540–1640* (Oxford, 1998).

'Swaddon the swindler and Pulman the "thief-taker": crime and variations in the great metropolis', in Tittler, *Townspeople and Nation: English Urban Experiences, 1540–1640* (Stanford, CA, 2001), pp. 156–76.

Todd, Barbara J., 'The remarrying widow: a stereotype reconsidered', in Mary Prior, ed., *Women in English Society, 1500–1800* (1985), 54–92.
Turner, David, *Fashioning Adultery: Gender, Sex, and Civility in England, 1660–1740* (Cambridge, 2002).
Twyning, John, *London Dispossessed: Literature and Social Space in the Early Modern City* (Basingstoke, 1998).
Ungerer, Gustav, 'Mary Frith, alias Moll Cutpurse, in life and literature', *Shakespeare Studies*, 18 (2000), 42–84.
  'Prostitution in late Elizabethan London: the case of Mary Newborough', *Medieval and Renaissance Drama in England*, 15 (2003), 138–223.
Van Elk, Martine, 'The counterfeit vagrant: the dynamic of deviance in the Bridewell court records and the literature of roguery', in Craig Dionne and Steve Mentz, eds., *Rogues and Early Modern English Culture* (Ann Arbor, MI, 2004), pp. 120–39.
Vanja, Christina, 'Madhouses, children's wards and clinics: the development of insane asylums in Germany', in Norbert Finzsch and Robert Jutte, eds., *Institutions of Confinement: Hospitals, Asylums, and Prisons in Western Europe and North America, 1500–1950* (Cambridge, 1996), pp. 117–32.
Vigarello, Georges, *Concepts of Cleanliness: Changing Attitudes in France since the Middle Ages*, trans. Jean Birrell (Cambridge, 1988).
Vogel, Morris J., 'The transformation of the American hospital', in Norbert Finzsch and Robert Jutte, eds., *Institutions of Confinement: Hospitals, Asylums and Prisons in Western Europe and America, 1500–1950* (Cambridge, 1996), pp. 39–54.
Voth, Hans-Joachim, *Time and Work in England, 1750–1830* (Oxford, 2000).
Wales, Tim, 'Thief-takers and their clients in later Stuart London', in Paul Griffiths and Mark S. R. Jenner, eds., *Londinopolis: Essays in the Cultural and Social History of Early Modern London* (Manchester, 2000), pp. 67–84.
Walker, Garthine, *Crime, Gender, and Social Order in Early Modern England* (Cambridge, 2003).
Walkowitz, Judith, *City of Dreadful Delight: Narratives of Sexual Danger in Late Victorian London* (1992).
Wall, Cynthia, *The Literary and Cultural Spaces of Restoration London* (Cambridge, 1998).
  '"At Sheakesper's Head, over-against Catharine-Street in the Strand": forms of address in London streets', in Tim Hitchcock and Heather Shore, eds., *The Streets of London from the Great Fire to the Great Stink* (2003), pp. 10–26.
Wallis, Patrick, 'Competition and cooperation in the early modern medical economy', in Mark S. R. Jenner and Wallis, eds., *Medicine and the Market in England and its Colonies, c. 1450–c. 1850* (Basingstoke, 2007), pp. 47–68.
Walsham, Alexandra, *Providence in Early Modern England* (Oxford, 1999).
Walter, John, *Understanding Popular Violence in the English Revolution: The Colchester Plunderers* (Cambridge, 1999).
Walvin, James, *Black and White: the Negro and English Society 1555–1945* (1973).
Ward, Joseph P., *Metropolitan Communities: Trade Guilds, Identity, and Change in Early Modern London* (Stanford, CA, 1997).
Wareing, John, 'Preventive and punitive regulation in seventeenth-century social policy: conflicts of interest and the failure to make "stealing and transporting

children and other persons" a felony, 1645–1673', *Social History*, 27 (2002), 288–308.
Weatherill, Lorna, *Consumer Behaviour and Material Culture in Britain, 1660–1760* (1988).
Webb, Sidney and Webb, Beatrice, *English Local Government . . . the Parish and the County* (1906).
Wernham, R. B., 'The public records in the sixteenth and seventeenth centuries', in L. Fox, ed., *English Historical Scholarship in the Sixteenth and Seventeenth Centuries* (Oxford, 1956), pp. 11–30.
White, J. G., *A Short History of the Royal Hospitals of Bridewell and Bethlem* (1899).
White, Paul Whitfied and Westfall, Suzanne R., eds., *Shakespeare and Theatrical Patronage in Early Modern England* (Cambridge, 2002).
Whitney, Charles, '"Usually in the werking daies": playgoing, journeymen, apprentices, and servants in guild records, 1582–92', *Shakespeare Quarterly*, 50 (1999), 433–58.
Wiener, Carol Z., 'The beleaguered isle: a study of Elizabethan and early Jacobean anti-catholicism', *Past and Present*, 51 (1971), 27–62.
Wiesner, Merry E., *Women and Gender in Early Modern Europe*, 2nd edition (Cambridge, 2000).
Williams, Laura, '"To recreate and refresh their dulled spirites in the sweet and wholesome ayre": green space and the growth of the city', in J. F. Merritt, ed., *Imagining Early Modern London: Perceptions and Portrayals of the City from Stow to Strype, 1598–1720* (Cambridge, 2001), pp. 185–213.
Wilson, Adrian, 'The ceremony of childbirth and its interpretation', in Valerie Fildes, ed., *Women as Mothers in Pre-Industrial England* (1990), pp. 68–107.
'Illegitimacy and its implications in mid-eighteenth-century London: the evidence of the foundling hospital', *Continuity and Change*, 4, (1989), 103–64.
Wilson, Eric, 'Plagues, fairs, and street cries: sounding out society and space in early modern London', *Modern Language Studies*, 25 (1995), 1–42.
Withington, Phil, *The Politics of Commonwealth: Citizens and Freemen in Early Modern England* (Cambridge, 2005).
Woodbridge, Linda, *Vagrancy, Homelessness, and English Renaissance Literature* (Urbana and Chicago, IL, 1996).
'Imposters, monsters, and spies: what rogue literature can tell us about early modern subjectivity', *Early Modern Literary Studies*, 9 (2002), 1–11.
'The peddler and the pawn: why did Tudor England consider peddlers to be rogues?', in Craig Dionne and Steve Mentz, eds., *Rogues and Early Modern English Culture* (Ann Arbor, MI, 2004), pp. 143–70.
Wrightson, Keith, 'Two concepts of order: justices, constables and jurymen in seventeenth-century England', in John Brewer and John Styles, eds., *An Ungovernable People: the English and their Law in the Seventeenth and Eighteenth Centuries* (1980), pp. 21–46.
*English Society, 1580–1680* (1982).
'Estates, degrees, and sorts: changing perceptions of the social order in Tudor and Stuart England', in Penelope Corfield, ed., *Language, History, and Class* (Oxford, 1991), pp. 30–52.

'"Sorts of people" in Tudor and Stuart England', in Jonathan Barry and Christopher Brooks, eds., *The Middling Sort of People: Culture, Society and Politics in England, 1500–1800* (Basingstoke, 1994), pp. 28–51.

'The politics of the parish', in Paul Griffiths, Adam Fox, and Steve Hindle, eds., *The Experience of Authority in Early Modern England* (Basingstoke, 1996), pp. 10–46.

Wrightson, Keith and Levine, David, *Poverty and Piety in an English Village: Terling 1525–1700* (Oxford, 1995).

Wrigley, E. A., 'A simple model of London's importance in changing English society and economy, 1650–1750', *Past and Present*, 37 (1967), 44–70.

Young, Iris Marion, *Justice and the Politics of Difference* (Princeton, NJ, 1990).

DISSERTATIONS AND UNPUBLISHED WORK

Archer, Ian, W., 'Governors and governed in late sixteenth-century London, c. 1560–1603: studies in the achievement of stability', DPhil thesis, University of Oxford (1988).

Brodsky, Vivien, 'Mobility and marriage in pre-industrial England: a demographic and social structural analysis of marriage, 1570–1690, with particular reference to London and general reference to Middlesex, Kent, Essex, and Hertfordshire', PhD thesis, University of Cambridge (1978).

Coates, Ben, 'The impact of the English Civil War on the economy of London, 1642–1650', PhD thesis, University of Leicester (1997).

Cockayne, E. J., 'A cultural history of sound in England, 1560–1760', PhD thesis, University of Cambridge (2000).

Daly, Christopher Thomas, 'The hospitals of London: administration, refoundation, and benefaction, c.1500–1572', DPhil thesis, University of Oxford (1994).

Dingle, A. M., 'The role of the householder in early Stuart London', MPhil thesis, University of London (1975).

Epstein, Alan J., 'The social function of the alehouse in early modern London', PhD thesis, New York University (1976).

Hardin, William, 'Spectacular constructions: ceremonial representations of city and society in early Stuart London', PhD thesis, University of North Carolina, Chapel Hill (1995).

Hickman, David J., 'The religious allegiance of London's ruling elite, 1520–1603', PhD thesis, University of London (1995).

Jenner, Mark S. R., 'Early modern English conceptions of "cleanliness" and "dirt" as reflected in the environmental regulation of London, c. 1530–c.1700', DPhil thesis, University of Oxford (1991).

Pennell, Sara, 'The material culture of food in early modern England, c.1650–1750', DPhil thesis, University of Oxford (1997).

Postles, Dave, 'The politics of naming and address in early modern England'.

Price, Lynda Ann, 'Parish constables: a study of administration and peacekeeping, Middlesex, 1603–1625', PhD thesis, University of London (1991).

Robertson, J. C., 'London 1580–1642: the view from Whitehall; the view from the Guildhall', PhD thesis, Washington University (1993).

Spraggs, G. M., 'Rogues and vagabonds in English literature, 1552–1642', PhD thesis, University of Cambridge (1980).

# Index

abandoning children 61–5, 66, 87, 91, 94, 124, 143, 145, 156, 182, 188, 208, 239, 255, 257, 262, 271, 272, 309, 313, 314, 327, 379–82, 384, 387, 393, 397, 415
  locations 62–4
  parishes policing 62
  rise in cases 61–2
  *see also* charity; maidservants; women
Abbot, Maurice 173
Abell, Bridget 279
Abraham, Andrew 122
Adair, Richard 65
Adams, Elizabeth 245
Adams, Mayhem 274
Adams, Nicholas 166
Addingsell, Grizelle 248
Addis, Robert 283
Aden, Rebecca 115
Agar, Dorothy 390
Alden, John 339
Aldersley, William 216, 218
alehouses 37, 38, 39, 40, 46, 59, 77, 104, 111, 119, 121, 147, 149, 158, 162, 164, 167, 169, 176, 208, 216, 221, 229, 235, 248, 254, 272, 282, 294, 297, 313, 316, 320, 322, 335, 338, 340–2, 348, 352, 355, 357, 372, 374, 375, 376, 379, 382, 383, 392, 397, 401, 407, 410, 419, 420, 421, 426
  disorders 95–6, 187
  receivers 163–4, 165, 166
  *see also* censuses/counts/'surveys'
Alexander, Judith 325
aliases 184, 185–6
Aliborne, Andrew 282
Allan, Anne 214
Allen, Edward 340
Allen, Henry 148
Allen, Mildred 392
Allen, Robert 112
Alley, Hugh 128, 309

alleys 21, 39, 54, 59, 64, 85, 109, 133, 208, 234, 293, 301, 305, 306, 345, 354, 387, 396, 401, 407
  Bell Yard 346
  Blackhorse Alley 346
  Charterhouse Yard 64
  Cock and Key Alley 111
  Codpiece Row 77, 153
  Crump Alley 177
  Garden Alley 150
  Harper Alley 52, 64
  Harrow Alley 374
  Jelly Alley 308
  Leg Alley 165
  Northumberland Alley 150
  Pepper Alley 161
  Priests Alley 143
  Ram Alley 364
  Scolding Alley 77
  Whore Alley 77, 153
  *see also* censuses/counts/'surveys'
almshouses 416
America 431
Amsterdam 9, 16, 436
Ancotts, Francis 283
Anderton, John 255, 256
Andrews, Dorothy 424
Andrews, Israel 426
Andrews, John 123
Angel, James 340
Angel, Joanne 278
apothecaries 261
Appelly, Christian 262
Appleby, John 115
Appleton, Katherine 183
applewife 125, 126, 132, 134
Appleyard, Ann 185
Appleyard, Richard 184–5
apprentices/apprenticeship 2, 47, 220, 264, 265, 283, 285, 286, 287, 288, 319, 336, 338, 341, 348, 371, 384
  apprentice literatures 30

# Index

apprentices/apprenticeship (cont.)
  disorders 127, 239, 242
  prostitutes 152, 172
  theft 165
  *see also* Bridewell, work; censuses/counts/ 'surveys'
Appryce, Griffin 43
Aproberte, Howell 106
Archer, Ian 4, 9, 20, 21, 29, 32, 33, 65, 202, 203, 207, 290, 292, 367, 402, 438
Arden, John 197
Armenia/Armenians 72
Arnold, Solomon 378
Artors, Agnes 111, 180
Arundel, Earl of 42, 63
Ashberry, John 174, 370
Ashberry, William 420
Ashemore, Alice 69
Ashley, Lawrence 374
Ashley, Margaret 197
Aspinall, Robert 289
at their own hands, living 134
Atkinson, Robert 264
Atterbury, Francis 15
Austin, Mary 278
Austin, Thomas 383
Avenon, Sir Alexander 440
Awdeley, John, *Fraternity of Vagabonds* 158

Bacon, Francis 225–7, 228
badging 42, 128, 129, 130
Badham, Mary 95, 207
Bagles, Elizabeth 343
Bagley, Anne 60
Baker, Frances 152
Baker, Joan 390
Baker, John 102
Ball, William 388
ballad-sellers/singers 21, 107, 168, 286, 318
  transported 286
Banks, John 373
Banks, William 430
Barbados 285, 287
Barber, John 319
Barbor, Marie 272
Barbor, Mary 272
Barker, Elizabeth 120
Barker, John 145, 377
Barker, Mary 321
Barlow, John 365
Barlow, Robert 163
Barnaby, Luce 374
Barnard, Thomas 180
Barnes, John 421
Barnfield, John 122

Baron, John 162
barrators 395
Barrett, Ellis 423
Barry, Lo, *Ram Alley* 78
Barthes, Roland 28
Barter, Margaret 325
Bartfield, Anne 244
Bartholomew Fair 86, 351, 430
  *see also* cutpurses; pickpockets; theft/thieves; vagrants
Bash, John 426
basketwomen 125
Bate, Anthony 217–19, 222, 223–4, 226, 227, 228, 230, 238, 256
Bath 302
Bath, Henry 81
Batris, John 108
Bayly, Anne 167, 423
Baynton, Sir Edward 150
Beades, Hugh 318
beadles 42, 52, 57, 64, 117, 131, 172, 214, 231, 237, 257, 260, 267, 297, 298, 303, 304, 308, 312–13, 324, 326, 331, 341, 344, 354, 377, 378, 379, 380, 381, 382, 384, 387, 390, 393, 406, 410, 423, 424, 440
  Willard 302
  abuses against 123, 189, 321, 323, 356–7
  abuses by 174, 175, 327, 330, 410
  arrests by 300, 388
  bonuses/top-up payments 301, 302
  loans/gifts 302
  salaries 300, 313
  sued 320
  time in office 298
  *see also* Bridewell, committals; informers/information
Beadley, Thomas 170
beards 256, 257
beasts/beastly, attitudes 143–4
Beattie, John 295, 361
Bedford, Ellen 55, 278
Beeston, Elizabeth 370
beggars/begging 14, 21, 22, 35, 38, 39, 41, 43, 79, 82, 85, 89, 93, 104, 112–23, 131, 140, 144, 184, 187, 189, 190, 200, 204, 222, 236, 240, 242, 262, 264, 266, 271, 280, 286, 306, 308, 313, 365, 367, 388, 389, 391, 414, 427, 439, 441
  ages 114
  career beggars 115–16, 148
  children 118–19
  churches 117, 145, 308

516  Index

beggars/begging (cont.)
  coaches 116
  coaching 190
  counterfeiting sickness/disability 119
  disorders 121–3
  gender 114
  markets 90
  Royal Exchange 94
  sex-ratio 205
  sick/disabled 115
  social status 114
  statutory ban 112, 114
  tactics 116–20
  takings 115, 119, 120
  teamwork 120
  Temple 94
  transported 286
  see also censuses/counts/'surveys';
    counterfeiting; France/Frenchmen;
    funerals; labels/labelling; London,
    outlying Places; St Paul's cathedral
Beier, Lee 32
Belfeld, William 320
Bellamy, John 168
Bell, Alice 388
Bell, Joanne 63
Bell, Simon 133
bellmen 304, 347, 348, 357, 359
  see also informers/information
Benjamin, Alice 235
Bennet, Cicely 266
Bentley, Edward 321
Bentley, Joseph 147
Bermuda 287
Bethlem/Bedlam 3, 12, 23, 119–20, 121,
    190, 214, 234, 237, 258–9, 262, 315
Bett, William 141
Bible, Robert 165
Bickerton, Edward 170
bigamy 238, 241, 245, 246
Biggs, Robert 164
bills of mortality 36–7, 41, 76, 191
Bingham, John 254
Birch, Ann 356
Bird, John 321
birders 127
Bishop of Carlisle 97, 160
Bishop of London 238, 306, 409
Bishops' Wars 46, 281
Black Luce 149, 151, 189
blackamores 73–4
Blackwell Hall 173, 346
Bliss, William 171
Bloke, Margaret 392
Blower, George 173

Blower, Michael 176–7
Blount, Nicholas 140
boarding/lodging houses 125, 208, 251, 266,
    267, 272, 282, 379, 382, 395, 420
  maids 208
  pregnant vagrants 59–61, 397
  vagrants 315
  see also theft/thieves; vagrants
Bohemia/Bohemians 72
Bolton, George 425
book of orders 41, 53, 305, 414
Bostock, Gertrude 272
Boswell, Anne 425
Boswell, Christopher 121
Bothomley, Issac 416
Bourne, Dennis 103
Bowen, Katherine 121
bowling alleys 282, 312, 352
  see also censuses/counts/'surveys'
Bowner, James 168
Bowyer, Lodowick 279
Bowyer, Martin 287
Box, John 296
Boyer, Henry 149, 152, 153, 215, 220, 223,
    248, 422, 429
Boyes, John 249
Bradley, Elizabeth 43, 231
Bradley, Grizelle, 258
Bradley, John 329
Bradshaw, Cicely 174
Bradshaw, Nan 160
Bragg, William 287
Braithwaite, Richard 286
branding 42, 156, 241, 255, 259, 282, 289,
    389, 431
Breame, Thomasine 151, 152, 153, 219,
    223, 224
Breame, Walter 162
Breech, William 251
Brett, William 184
Brian, Elizabeth 241
Bridewell 3, 11, 23, 47, 61, 82–4, 87, 104,
    115, 118, 122, 124, 194, 203, 267,
    268, 269, 306–7, 312, 315, 319, 359,
    366, 372, 384, 394, 395, 397, 401,
    411, 413, 436, 441
  attitudes towards 3, 213–32, 252, 436
  charity (inmates/vagrants) 260
  charter 213, 221, 225, 226–30, 251
  citizens, relations 217
  corruption/extortion/scandals 220–1, 243
  fishwives, regulating 129, 130
  foundation 11–13
  functions 11, 12, 15–19
  granaries 17

Index

Bridewell (cont.)
  jurisdiction 16, 194, 224–5, 226, 227, 229, 384
    challenged 218, 224–30, 252
    ecclesiastical courts 237–8
    punishment 225
  lodging inmates 54
  Marian backlash 13–14
  titles 17
  *see also* Parliament, bills
Bridewell, Court 154, 203, 208, 213–52, 424
  arrests, locations 85–9
  caseloads 19, 20, 82, 201–2, 204, 232, 438
  caseloads, changing complexion 201–2
  committals 236–7, 367, 440–1
    beadles 236, 385
    Bridewell bench/warrant 236, 385
    City 383, 385
    constables 236, 385–6, 386, 440
    Corporation of the Poor 385, 440
    crown 237
    deputies 236, 385
    fall 384, 385, 386
    guilds 384
    hospitals 265
    households 366, 393
    justices 230, 236–7, 383, 385
    malicious 237
    marshals 236, 386, 440
    parishes 384
    Parliament 237
    'private' 367
    'public' officers 236, 307, 383, 384–5, 393, 440, 441
    recorder 440
    victims 384, 393
    'voluntary' 384
    warders 386
    wards 384
    watches 236, 357, 386, 440
  confessions 249, 251
  courtbooks 19, 20–2, 194, 197, 201, 202, 233, 242, 244, 251, 290, 308, 383, 384, 386, 401, 416, 417, 424, 425, 426–8, 429, 439, 440
    deficiencies 20–1, 367
    security 222
  defendants strategies 250
  disorders 235
  election days 207, 233
  examinations 180–92, 243–4
    resistance 189–91
  felons/felonies 240–1

  legal mindedness 233, 243–51, 286
  leniency/sympathy 257, 259
  meetings, frequency 19–20, 21, 419
  process, questioned 218–20, 224
  process, secrecy 221–2
  proof 244–7, 251
  protocol 235
Bridewell, governors 177, 186, 195, 196, 198, 206–7, 217, 222–3, 223, 227, 230, 233, 236, 238, 240, 244, 247, 251, 254, 267, 327, 387, 391, 393, 420, 421, 422, 425–6, 427, 430–1, 440
  Clark 219
  Gardener 243
  Tito 172
  Winch 218–20, 223–4
    abuses against 122, 133, 216, 219, 222, 329
    abuses by 278
    bribes 220
    City committees 234–5, 305
    composition/numbers 233–4
  *see also* Gouge, William; informers/information
Bridewell, inmates 411
  'close' 254
  confinement, length 279–81
  escapes 155, 156, 162
  hygiene 253
  marriage 167
  mutiny 163
  numbers 17–18
  transfers to/from Christs 262
  *see also* registers
Bridewell, medical provision
  matrons 260
  sick diet 260
  sick ward 260
  sickness/conditions 263, 265
  surgeons 231, 253, 259, 260, 263, 268
  transferring inmates to and from other hospitals 260, 264–5
Bridewell, officers/officials
  beadles 18, 172, 173, 176, 221, 235, 243, 303, 380, 393
    abuses against 235
    bonuses/top-up payments 302
    salaries 300, 301
  clerks 19, 20, 179, 188, 189, 195, 197, 219, 221, 222, 228, 229, 231, 233, 235, 237, 244, 245, 249, 267, 279, 280, 281, 286, 287, 289, 382, 383, 393, 401, 411, 416, 424, 426, 427–8, 429, 430, 439, 440

Bridewell, officers/officials (cont.)
  matrons 174, 176, 206, 221, 235, 244, 270, 273, 391, 392, 393
    Kennell, Dorothy 175
    Millet, Alice 220–1
    abuses by 277
    pregnancy 'searches' 156
  matron's maid, abuses by 175
  porter 156, 221, 235, 239, 388
    abuses by 243
  president 236, 268
  stewards 411
    abuses by 220
  treasurer 179, 218, 219, 221, 229, 236, 243, 264, 391
    Warfield, Roger 223
  see also informers/information
Bridewell, religion 14, 277
  catechizing 277
  chapel 277
  minister 167, 231, 278
  reforming inmates 277–8
  repentance 249, 278, 280
Bridewell, work 18, 253, 277
  apprentices 20, 144, 367, 411, 427
  artmasters 18–19
Bridewell Bridge 84
Bridewell Precinct 84, 359, 410
Bridges, John 369
Bridgewater, Countess of 104
Briggs, Nicholas 122
Bright, William 341
Bristol 75, 191, 273
British Library 225
Brittain, Sir Henry 93
brokers 145, 164–5, 311, 323
  see also Parliament, bills; registers
Brolvin, Richard 118
Brookbank, Martha 271
Brooke, Agnes 373
Brooke, Anne 273
Brooks, Randal 371
Broughton, Mary 274
Brown, Thomas 374
Browne, Ellen 166
Browne, Jane 428
Browne, Richard 92
Browne, Robert 158, 239
Browne, Thomas 52
Browne, William 325
Browning, Thomas 249
Brunt, Mawdelyn 333
Brush, Elizabeth 391
brushwenches 125
Buck, Anne 390

Buckhurst, Lord 83
Buckingham, Duke of 34, 46, 103, 104
Buckinghamshire 184
Buckmaster, Thomas 169
Budde, Thomas 236
Buffet, Michael 236
buildings 2, 38, 39, 40, 41, 42, 45, 48, 145, 202, 235, 338, 382, 434, 438
  commissioners 396
  subdivisions 38, 40, 48, 49, 50, 51, 52, 54, 80, 309, 396, 414, 439
  see also censuses/counts/'surveys'; nobility; Parliament, bills
Bull, Elizabeth 338
Bull, John 117
Bullein, William 1
Bullock, Richard 423
Bullyvant, Christopher 123
Burchall, John 113
Burges, Thomas 318
Burke, Peter 403, 416
Burkill, John 61
Burnet, Gilbert, *History of the Reformation* 15, 364
Burrow, Elizabeth 267
Burrowes, Patient 197
Burwood, Alice 45
Bush, Rice 119
Busley, Thomas 287
Butler, Alice 323
Butler, Elizabeth 62, 63, 64
Butler, Joan 425
Butler, Marmaduke 377–8
Butler, Robert 114
Butler, Toby 235
Byllyard, John 163

cages 57, 182, 237, 261, 306, 313
Calcutta 32
Cambridge 103, 153, 171
Camel, Richard 122
Campion, William 157
Candy, William 106
Cannon, Jane 270
Cannon, Owen 96, 160, 184
cant 139, 140, 166, 170, 186, 197, 199
Canterbury 120
Carey, George, Sir 149
Carey, Susan 149
Caribbean 285
Carie, Elizabeth 90
Carlyle, Cuthbert 340
Carlyle, Robert 255
carmen 98, 320, 418
  disorders 99, 241

# Index

Carpenter, Henry 15, 364
Carr, Anne 257
carriers 38, 61, 69, 106, 149, 248, 273
   Daventry 106
   Portsmouth 106
   Wales 106
Carter, Anne 239, 245, 372
Carter, Francis 148
Carter, Marjery 134
Carthis, Mary 62
carting 239
carts 84, 98, 127, 309, 313
   numbers, limiting 98–100
Case, Agnes 188
Castle, Elizabeth 246
catechizing 418
   *see also* Bridewell, religion
catholics 39, 40, 158, 235, 308, 310, 316, 391, 398, 414
   anti-catholicism 34
   Jesuits 39, 144, 310
   plots by 46
   priests 39, 143, 144, 146, 255, 256, 308, 310
   *see also* censuses/counts/'surveys'
Cavandigoe, Peter 74
Cave, Anne 78, 424
Cawsey, Clare 124
Caxton, William 285
censuses/counts/'surveys' 39, 191, 305, 308, 313, 402–19
   alehouses 403, 404–5
   alleys 410
   apprentices 413
   beggars 410
   bowling alleys 405
   brothels 405
   buildings/houses 407
   catechumens 412
   catholics 403, 412
   communicants 412
   constables 412
   dancing schools 405
   dicing houses 405
   fencing schools 405
   fishwives 129, 411
   foreigners 403, 406, 407–9, 410, 420
   freemen 413
   fruitsellers 411
   herbwives 411
   inhabitants 314, 406, 407
   inmates/lodgers 53, 314, 406, 408, 410
   Jesuits 412
   jurymen 413
   landlords 410
   migrants 23
   milkwives 411
   mustermen 413
   orphans 413
   paupers 403, 406–7
   plague victims 413
   preachers 413
   priests 412
   protestation oath 413
   sailors 413
   Scotsmen 413
   street-sellers 411
   'tablinge houses' 405
   taxpayers 413
   tobacco sellers 405
   vagrants 402, 410–11
   watchmen 413
Chadborne, Brian 45
Chamberlain, Dominic 115, 148
Chambers, Ellen 131, 132
Chambers, Samuel 160, 259
Chapman, Godfrey 240
Chapman, William 239
charity 29, 114, 142, 436
   'fools'/'idiots' 258
   foreigners 72–3
   foundlings 182–3
   ministers 114
   mothers abandoning children 62, 63
   soldiers 114
   transportation costs 284–5
   vagrants 56, 61, 108, 190, 191, 258, 261
   *see also* Bridewell
Charles I 83
Charnley, William 117
Chelmsford 121
Chester 284
Chester, Rody 312
Chettle, Henry 79
Chickley, Frances 312
Child, Elsie 392
chimney sweeps 47
Christmas 40
Christ's Hospital 11, 12, 15, 23, 64, 65, 86, 106, 188, 219, 231, 253, 262, 267, 268–9, 270, 302, 306, 379, 428–9
   admissions 62, 106, 260
   attitudes 215
   beadles 64, 144, 381
   financial drain 216, 269
   inmates, numbers 261–2
   porter 64
   transfers to and from other hospitals 262
   *see also* Bridewell, inmates

## Index

churches 77, 109, 117
　disorders 95
　seating plans 294, 418
　*see also* beggars/begging; cutpurses; pickpockets; street-sellers; theft/thieves
churching 176
churchwardens 63, 293, 407, 413, 416, 418
　abuses against 321
　abuses by 396
churchyards 313, 346, 380
　vagrants 108, 109
Chute, Sir Henry 409
citizenship 31, 142–3
City, freedom, sinking 2, 5, 6, 80, 209, 232, 436
City government/officials/officers 9, 233, 236, 394, 441
　aldermen 2, 7, 42, 49, 83, 85, 95, 105, 111, 115, 118, 119, 127, 128, 129, 130, 131, 132, 134, 174, 176, 187, 203, 218, 219, 226, 227, 228, 229, 234, 236, 239, 240, 262, 267, 268, 296, 302, 305, 307, 308, 313, 315, 320, 324, 326, 330, 339, 351, 354, 358, 374, 377, 382, 384, 400, 401, 402, 403, 405, 406, 407, 413, 420, 430, 440
　　Bond 172
　　Bowes 306
　　Dixie 172
　　Gore 109
　　Hawton 267
　　Pype 172
　　Ramsey 387
　　River 172
　　Ryder 239
　　Starkey 172
　　abuses against 44, 175, 329
　cashbooks 23
　chamberlain's court 242
　charter 82
　committees 129, 234–5, 359
　common council 36, 39, 40, 46, 54, 98, 122, 124, 129, 130, 133, 179, 200, 208, 227, 295, 296, 297, 306–7, 308, 320, 331, 343, 345, 347, 354, 405, 406, 411
　　journals of common council 23, 226, 227, 228, 400
　'common crier' 378, 383
　court of aldermen 36, 50, 52, 83, 87, 225, 227, 233, 234, 242, 306, 315, 329, 383, 391, 394, 395, 411, 414, 418, 429, 430, 440

　　abused 43–4
　　repertories of court of aldermen 23, 228, 275, 400, 417
　court of orphans 15, 43–4
　letterbooks 23
　lobbying crown 49, 50, 51, 79, 86, 216, 218
　mayor 41, 63, 81, 93, 105, 121, 172, 208, 215, 226, 228, 231, 234, 236, 239, 243, 256, 267, 280, 296, 306, 320, 335, 351, 355, 356, 434, 440
　　abused 43, 47, 74, 123, 258, 328
　mayor's court 396, 400, 429
　mayor's officers 133
　recorder 49, 52, 227, 229, 234, 240
　remambrancer 4, 400
　remembrancia books 23
　rhetorics 8–10, 11
　sheriff's sergeants/yeomen
　　abuses against 323
　　abuses by 173, 174, 328–9
　sheriffs 43, 81, 163, 172, 222–3, 234, 355–7, 377
　　abuses against 323
　solicitor 320
　waterbailiff 129, 169
　yeomen of the waterside 129
　*see also* Bridewell, committals
civic ceremonies 5, 77
　funerals 5, 11
　mayor's inauguration 3, 5, 302, 303
Clapham, William 107
Clark, John 419
Clark, Peter 32
Clarke, Ellen 240
Clarke, Robert 288
Clarkealter, Roger 324
Clasey, John 364
Clay, William 259
Cleyton, Dorothy 391
Cliff, Cassandra 44
Clifford, Lady 172
Clifton, Dorothy 356
Clitherowe, Henry 424
Cloth Fair 318
clothing 31, 254, 256, 257
Clowes, William 266
coaches 39, 84, 98, 99, 116, 127, 336
　*see also* beggars/begging
coal/fuel 17, 235, 301, 311, 313, 418
　*see also* registers
Cobham, Elizabeth 266
Cock, Joseph 287
Cockley, John 248
coffee-houses 335

# Index

coffeewomen 125, 397
coiners/clippers 363
Coke, Edward 194, 199
Colchester 5, 367
Cole, Thomas 263
Cole, William 431
Colebrooke, Ezechias 355
Coleraine 120
collectors of the poor 293, 315
Collins, Justice 44
'comon fame' 197, 371–3
Compe, Elizabeth 153
compters 154, 327, 330, 386, 392, 400, 413
  Poultry 87, 88
  Wood Street 87, 88
  admissions/offences 87
  clerks 172
conduct books 273
conduits 47, 64, 77, 98, 109, 143, 171, 302, 334, 346
  *see also* London, streets, Cheapside
constables 58, 63, 76, 88, 132, 134, 156, 162, 172, 208, 236, 243, 291, 292, 293, 294–5, 296, 297, 298, 299, 302–3, 304, 306, 307, 308, 311, 312, 315, 318, 324, 327–8, 335, 341, 352, 353, 354, 356, 357, 358, 362, 368–9, 375, 376, 377, 391, 393–4, 407, 409, 419, 440, 441
  Allen 299
  Bradford 299
  Carter 299
  Clayton 299
  Collins 326
  Cook 299
  Creecher 299
  Davies 300
  Dicher 299
  Foster 299
  Hemmings 300
  Lodwin 300
  Mould 299
  Nash 299
  Parkinson 299
  Statfield 299
  Walker 299
  Waller 299
  abuses against 3, 122, 155, 217, 242, 283, 318, 319, 321, 321–2, 323, 344, 345, 394
  abuses by 51, 173, 174, 175–6, 177, 316, 325–7, 328, 329, 331, 387, 396
  arrests by 299–300, 388, 389–90, 392, 393
  assistance, people refusing 320
  bonuses/top-up payments 301
  bribes 176
  hired substitutes 294, 295
  numbers 303–4
  rescuing prisoners from 185
  salaries 300
  social status 296–7
  staffs 302
  sued 40, 320
  *see also* Bridewell, committalls; censuses/counts/'surveys'; informers/information; London, wards/precincts
Constantine, Peter 170
conventicles 46
Convex Light Company 343
Convey, William 236
Conway, Elizabeth 270
conycatching 169–70
Coo, Thomas 427
Cook, William 161
Cooke, Thomas 159
Cooke, William 166
Cooley, Ann 272
Cooley, Elizabeth 428
Cooper, Mary 243
Cope, Anne 62
Copeland, Robert
  *High-way to the Spital-house* 138
Copinger, Mabel 118
Copley, William 345
Coquillette, Daniel 225
Cordell, George 421
Cordell, Helen 248
corn 235, 267
Cornelius, Daniel 356
coroner 242
Coteene, Edward 288
Cotton, John 111
Cottrell, Mary 399
Coumgton, John 364
counterfeiting 14, 241, 259, 362
  begging licenses 121, 397, 428
  coin 90
  keys 168–9, 250
  passports 112, 242, 383
court moot 296
court of arches 296
court of augmentation 414
Court of Chancery 93, 296, 414, 430
Court of Common Pleas 296, 320
Court of Exchequer 94, 102, 414
  *see also* cutpurses
Courthop, Edward 342
Cowper, Mary 109

Cowper, Ralfe 179
Cox, Dorothy 273
cozeners/cheaters 40, 155, 157, 158, 159, 161, 163, 170, 185, 241, 242, 264, 266, 286, 333, 426, 438
  cards 140, 169–70
  dice 87, 140, 169–70
  press (army) 282
  sex-ratio 204
  transported 286
  *see also* labels/labelling
Craven, Joan 425
Creed, Thomas 372
*Cries* (1599) 4
crime/criminals
  collective/group 86
  defining in terms of citizenship/work 140
  defining in terms of dirt/filth 200
  defining in terms of movement 144
  'environmental crime' 35, 66, 199–204, 232, 435, 442
  feminized perceptions/female crime 66, 124, 180, 204–9, 384, 435, 439, 442
Croft, George 119
Crosby, Anne 282
cross dressing 186, 238, 245, 371
Crossdall, Matthew 143
Crosse, Humphrey 310
Crosshaw, John 258
crown/royal officials 2, 48–50, 51, 310, 311, 316, 352, 374, 404, 407, 408–9, 435
  attorney general 14, 43, 363
  capital city, improvements 6–7
  court 94
    vagrants 110
  Greenwich Palace 94, 110
  lord chancellor 43, 116, 216
  lord chief justice 82, 116, 254, 296–7, 358, 407
    Popham 228
  lord keeper 328, 329
  monarch 41, 43, 351
  privy council 23, 41, 42, 43, 49, 50, 53, 73, 99, 107, 116, 133, 295, 296, 305, 356, 403, 404–5, 409
  royal proclamations 23, 48–9
  state papers 23
  Whitehall 6, 7, 8, 41, 51, 94, 347, 403, 414
  *see also* Bridewell, committals
Crowshawe, John 390
Crutch, William 44
Crutchley, Richard 55
*Cryes of London* 4
cucking/ducking stool 131, 301

Cuffe, Katherine 238
Cumberland 114
cunning folk/diviners 364
Cunningham, Anne 371
curfew 242, 344, 347, 348
  breaches, walking late 89, 155, 156, 180, 248, 272, 441
  transported 286
Curtis, Katherine 428
Custom House 110
Cutpurse, Moll 84, 137, 187, 312, 378
cutpurses 35, 39, 75, 82, 92, 97, 141, 157, 158, 159–63, 167, 170, 184, 186, 187, 188, 190, 220, 302, 311, 325, 388, 389, 391, 401, 419, 421, 423, 425, 426, 431
  Bartholomew Fair 86
  bridge 90
  churches 207
  Exchequer 94
  markets 121
  playhouses 96
  press (army) 282, 283
  quarter sessions 94
  Spital 162
  Star Chamber 94
  takings 154
  teachers 166
  tools 168
  *see also* Holland/Dutchmen; labels/labelling

Dabhoiwala, Faramerz 20, 21, 367
Dade, John 240
Dagger, James 377–8
Dale, Francis 115
Dall, Pockey-Faced 78
Dalton, James 329
Dane, Mary 74
Daniel, John 377
Darby, Margaret 119
Darke, Anne 280
Darnton, Robert 404
Dartnell, Alice 392
Daunce, Thomas 107
Davey, Charles 264
David, Elizabeth 424
Davies, Ellen 94
Davies, Hugh 170
Davies, John 105, 168
Davies, Richard 175
Davis, Martha 108
Dawson, John 120, 251
Day, Richard 170
Deacon, Elizabeth 159
Deane, Mary 248

Deane, Richard 325
dearth 414
Death, Elinor 181
debtors 189
Defoe, Daniel 357
Dekker, Thomas 4, 36, 42, 78, 98, 166
   *Eastward Ho* 276
   *Honest Whore, Part II* 11, 152, 360
   *Lanthorne and Candle-Light* 180
   *Westward Ho* 161
Delabew, Abraham 241
Delight, Peter 259
Denison, Stephen 36
Denmark 283
Denny, James 120
deputy (ward) 44, 63, 105, 168, 172, 227, 234, 243, 253, 295, 297, 298, 299, 304, 308, 314–15, 327, 372, 376, 377, 378, 383, 391, 394, 401, 440, 441
   Gonnell 391, 440
   Grafton 315, 391
   Hickman 300
   Hodgson 248
   Stanguish 300
   Vinton 81
   Westwood 391
   Whitwell 300
   abuses against 321, 322, 323, 329
   arrests by 300, 390–1
   time in office 298
   *see also* Bridewell, committals; informers/information
Derborne, Thomas 122
Derman, Francis 142
Derrick, Henry 162
deserters (army) 186, 237, 264, 283–4
Devil 258
Devon 260
Devonshire, Countess of 43
Dey, Jane 376
dicing houses 341, 352
   *see also* censuses/counts/'surveys'
Dickinson, Joanne 355
Differy, Magdalene 333
dilapidation 10, 21, 35, 45, 305
Dionne, Craig 143
dirt/filth 7, 21, 38, 39, 45, 100–1, 200, 305, 343, 370, 397
discretion/decision-making 230–1
disease 35, 80, 200
disguise 184–5
Dissell, Henry 271–5
distraining 322
ditches 18, 334
   Fleet Ditch 83

Tower Ditch 18
   vagrants 108
Dixler, Nicholas 372
Dixon, Ellis 357
docks 109, 128, 129, 131, 133, 173
domestic disorders 143–4, 373, 439, 442
   wife-beating 14, 87, 143, 373–4
Donache, Lawrence 115
Donnolly, Marie 152, 218, 250, 251
Doomsday Book 403
Dorchester 16, 319
Dorley, Elizabeth 273
Dorset, Earl of 83
Dorte, Edward 371
Douglas, Mary 141, 182
Dowell, Thomas 122
Downes, Marie 141
Doyson, Elizabeth 388
Drake, Sir Francis 43
dreams 107, 258
drunkards/drunkenness 133, 134, 174, 185, 239, 271, 278, 280, 286, 340, 341, 355, 395
   press (army) 282
   transported 286
Du Tilh, Arnold 185
Duckett, Insham 250
Duckett, John 171
Duckett, Sir Lionel 440
Duffill, Ned 169
Duke of York 303
Duncan, Thomas 347
Dunn, Catherine 115
Dunning, Joan 279
Dunton, John 150, 151
Dunway, Simon 390
Durecke, Robert 165
Durrant, Margaret 377–8
Dye, Edward 167

Earle, John 292, 308
earthquake 37
East, Gilbert 148, 151, 152, 177, 218
East, Margaret 148, 250
East Anglia 113
East India Company 283
East Indies 286
Easton, Alice 61
eavesdropping 71, 339
ecclesiastical courts 70, 198, 202, 398, 428
   female litigants 207
   jurisdictional spats with Bridewell 14
   records 22
   *see also* Bridewell
Eddis, Margaret 77

Edmunds, Richard 319
Edward, John 149
Edward VI 12, 14, 17, 216, 226
Edwards, Philip 122
Edwards, Robert 343
Edwards, Thomas 265, 395
Elder, Katherine 427
Elder, William 311
elderly, leniency 257–8
Eliffe, Anne 274
Elizabeth I 46
Elliott, John 133, 395
Elliott, Margery 181
Elliott, Priscilla 251
Ellis, Anne 215, 223
Ellis, Margaret 92
Ellwood, Thomas 233
Emmes, Galfridus 154, 424
English, Daniel 429
environmental crime *see* crime/criminals
Erasmus 193, 276
Erick, Christian 427
Essex 75, 102, 335
Evans, Agnes 429
Evans, Alice 273
Evans, Bridget 272
Evans, Elizabeth 149, 186, 377
Evans, John 112, 319
Evans, Margaret 312
Evans, Thomas 101
Evelyn, John 16, 99, 101
'evil May-day' 33
Ewen, William 375

Faircloth, Sara 333
Fairfax, General 104, 356
Fareclowe, James 227
Farewell, Alice 151
Farrer, Jeremy 95
Faulkner, Elias 175
Fea, James 122
Fellows, Elizabeth 270
female crime *see* crime/criminals; violence, female
Fernando, Diega 190
Ferris, Anthony 278
Fetherton, Edward 259
Field, Henry 256, 257
Fielding, Henry 70
Fielding, Lord 335, 358
fields 92–3, 97, 109, 155, 167
Finch, Ellen 336
fire 71, 76, 120, 121, 301, 304, 333, 370, 414
  engines 313
  theft 147–8, 351

Fish, Grissel 371
Fisher, Agnes 278
Fisher, Bernard 341
Fisher, George 120
Fisher, Joan 148
Fisher, John 249
Fisher, Margaret 321
Fisher, Richard 248
Fisher, William 167
fishwives 21, 38, 39, 42, 124–5, 132, 133, 266, 307, 338
  attitudes towards 126
  insults 124
  policing/regulating 128–30
  pox 132
  *see also* Bridewell; censuses/counts/'surveys'; London, wards/precincts; registers
Fleet Prison 223
Fleet River 83, 84
Fleetwood, Sir George 283
Fleetwood, William 86, 160, 170, 225–7, 228, 311, 352
Flemming, Anne 180
Flender, Mary 425
Flood, William 240
floods 37
Flower, John 169
Fobber, Frances 425
Foldes, Elizabeth 152
Folfare, Alexander 120
Folliott, Abraham 170
football 314
Forbesse, John 170
foreign ambassadors 173, 274, 310, 433
  Portuguese 92, 152
  Spanish 117, 296
  Venetian 33, 45, 98, 104, 433, 434
foreigners 2, 31, 38, 39, 41, 72–3, 124, 130, 132, 200, 235, 295, 304, 308, 309, 310, 313, 351, 395–6, 436
  charity 191
  office-holding 296
  press (army) 281
  unrest against 33, 34, 46, 72
  *see also* censuses/counts/'surveys'; charity; registers
Forest of Dean 248
forgers/forgery 363
fornication 74, 154, 186, 187, 202, 244, 250, 273, 282, 344, 345, 395
Forster, Margaret 187, 424
fortune tellers 107, 170, 184
Foster, Anne 160, 420

# Index

Foster, Cuthbert 340
Foster, Frank 29, 33
Foucault, Michel 140, 276
foundlings/orphans 182–3, 260, 267
    baptisms 61
    *see also* charity
Fowler, Davy 173, 177
Fowles, Ely 150
Fowles, Thomas 150
Fox, Mary 270
France/Frenchmen 72, 188, 190
    beggars 122
    vagrants 106, 114
Frank, Thomas 237
Frank, William 124
Freart Roland 37, 48, 79
Frederick, Jane 420
Frederick, William 189
Free, Peter 327
Freeman, Thomas 433
French, Margaret 272
French, Stephen 153
fruitsellers 126–7, 131
Fryddy, Agnes 373
Fuller, Jane 150, 151
Fuller, Katherine 69, 149
Fuller, William 11
funerals, begging 117
Furres, Alice 357

Gallyard, Rebecca 180
gallows 33, 43, 138–9, 153, 157, 240, 284, 285
    'last dying words' 139, 276
gambling 169–70
Gannaway, Anne 159
Gardener, Edward 355
Gardener, John 430
Gardener, Margery 187
Gardener, Susan 59
Gardener, Thomas 148
Gardener, William 334
Gardiner, Bishop 14
Garford, William 289
Garrett, John 255
Garroll, Joan 154–5, 319
Gaskill, Malcolm 362
gates (city) 314, 348–9, 350, 351
Gatrell, Vic 201
Gently, Thomas 163
Geremek, Bronislaw 147, 177
German lands 137
Gerrard, John 186
Gibbs, Bridget 167
Gibbs, Elizabeth 59

Giddens, Anthony 403
Gilbert, Alice 103
Giles, Elizabeth 387
Giles, George 287
Gilman, Ezekiel 123
Gilman, James 324
Gilnor, Elinor 144
Gittens, James 107
Gittoe, William 122
Gladwell, Richard 281
Gloucestershire 256
Goad, John 425
Godden, Thomas 370
Godfrey, Anne 440
Goff, Nicholas 239
Gold, Jane 247
Gold, John 170
Gold, William 218
Goldsmith, Susan 266
Good, Alice 371
Goodcole, Henry 144, 330
Goodfellow, John 421
Goodier/Lambe, Anne 155–6
Goodson, Peter 238
Goodwin, Agnes 106
Goomer, Henry 371
Gouge, William 95, 207, 391
    *Domesticall Duties* 391
Gough, William 10
Governor, William 175
Gower, Mabel 239
Gowing, Laura 207
Grace, Nathaniel 43
graffiti 85
Granger, Anne 303
Graunt, John 9, 36, 436
Gray, Mabel, 364
Great Yarmouth 16
Greece/Grecians 72, 191
Green, John 115
Greene, Anne 118
Greene, Elizabeth 118, 235
Greene, George 219
Greene, John 376
Greene, Margery 148
Greene, Robert 138
Greenwood, Margery 222
Greet, Margaret 254
Gregory, Alice 86, 166
Gresham, Sir Thomas 47
Grey, Agnes 336
Grey, Margaret 389
Griffen, Humphrey 120
Griffin, Edward 120, 121, 327, 428
Griffin, Elizabeth 245

Griffin, John 318, 421
Griffin, Mary 184
Griffin, Robert 105
Groom, William 144
Gryse, Elizabeth 248, 336
Guerre, Martin 185
Guildhall Library 225
guilds 3, 4, 30, 32, 64, 80, 142, 231, 233, 234, 239, 242, 308, 309, 394, 395, 398, 401, 436
  Apothecaries 47
  Drapers 269
  Fishmongers 239
  Goldsmiths 164, 395, 412
  Grocers 47
  Mercers 314
  inmates 54
  printed histories 4
  records 23, 31
  social discrimination 32
  *see also* Bridewell, committals
Gunpowder Plot 255, 350
Gunter, Thomas 321
Gunwell, Thomas 112
Guppey, Robert 395
Gurnet, John 426
Guy, Sara 47, 143
Guy, William 227
Gwyllimas, John 312
Gwyn, Elizabeth 372
Gwynne, John 254
gypsies 106–7

Haddington, Josiah 105
haglers 125, 128
Haines, John 119
hair 254, 256
Hall, Agnes 422
Hall, Elizabeth 181
Hall, Ellen 102
Hall, John 111
Hall, Mary 382
Hall, Richard 188
Hall, Thomas 249
Hambeldon, Bridget 167
Hammond, John 114
Hammond, Margaret 160
Hampshire 61, 102, 103
Hampton, George 250
Hanawalt, Barbara 362
Hancock, Agnes 61
Hancock, John 154
Hand, Winifred 428
Handley, Rebecca 371
Handrey, John 191

hangman 172
  abuses by 174
Harbert, Thomas 167
hard labour 281, 288
Harding, Isabella 169
Harding, Margaret 357
Harley, Anthony 282
'harlots' 39, 87, 92, 111, 132, 161, 177, 185, 186, 188, 217, 219, 220, 229, 239, 245, 249, 251, 257, 258, 264, 266, 278, 294, 388, 390, 392, 394, 395, 405, 422, 426
Harman, Thomas 139, 140, 167
  *Caveat for Common Cursetors* 138, 158
Harris, Alice 59
Harris, Katherine 356
Harris, Peter 200
Harris, Thomas 115
Harrison, Richard 249
Harrison, Thomas 147
Hart, Martin 260
Hart, Will 312
Hartley, William 116
harvest failures 33
Harvey, Alice 428
Harvey, Elizabeth 336
Harvey, Thomas 419
Harwood, George 92
Harwood, William 322, 373
Hasseldon, Oliver 371
Hassels, Francis 336
Havering, Thomas 123
Hawes, Sir James 440
hawkers 39, 125, 126, 309, 313, 395
Hawkins, Rebecca 108
Hawkins, William 303
Hayes, Thomas 108
Hayesley, Thomas 184
Haynes, Alice 266
Haynes, Henry 394
Haynes, Walter 248
Hayward, Henry 383
Head, Margaret 374
Head, Richard, *The English Rogue* 70
Hedrick, Daniel 403
healers 85, 213, 259, 260, 261
Healey, Agnes 273
Healy, Margaret 193
Hedger, Richard 284
Helinge, Elizabeth 249
Hellick, William 288
Helliker, Joan 92
Henley-on-Thames 426
Henry V 362

# Index

Henry, John 423
Henry, Margaret 425
herbwives 98, 125, 126, 127, 128, 131, 415
　see also censuses/counts/'surveys'
Herefordshire 180
Herne, Justice 44
Hertford 381
Hewetson, Anthony 373
Hewson, Christopher 163
Heyden, James 340
Heylyn, Peter 36
Heywood, Thomas 41
Hicks, John 391
Hicks, Sir Baptist 63
Hicks Hall 7
Higgins, Agnes 343
Higgins, Elizabeth 427
Higgs, Edward 404
high commission 231, 238
Highgate Hospital 120
highway robbery 18, 365
Hill, Adam 37
Hill, Agnes 319
Hill, Anthony 75
Hilton, Jane 214
Hindle, Steve 368
Hippie, Joan 118
Hitchcock, Humphrey 172
Hitchcock, Robert 28
Hitchin, John 243
Hitter, Christopher 310
Hoare, Elizabeth 264
Hobbert, Mary 399
Hodges, William 119
Hodgkins, Anne 160, 249
Hoggard, Rachel 270
Holcroft, Thomas 90
Holden, William 156
Holderness, Edward 388
Holland/Dutchmen 72, 191, 272, 296, 301, 371, 423
　cutpurse gang 154, 162–3
　Rotterdam 162
Holland, Earl of 42
Holland, Ellen 280
Holland, Grace 167
Holland, Lodowick 283
Holland, William, 170
Holloway, Anne 131
Holmes, John 330
Holt, Joan 392
Holt, Michael 352
Hope, Elizabeth 245, 250
Hopkins, Margaret 122
Hopkins, Thomas 103

Hore, John 86
Horley, Thomas 132
Horsey, Joanne 132
hospitals 11, 23, 40, 64, 73, 77, 132, 219, 228, 231, 262–9, 304, 305, 306, 307, 312, 313, 346, 379, 410, 414, 439
　beadles 300, 303, 380
　inmates, lodging 54
　pecking order/tensions 216, 267–9
　religion 14–15
　see also Bridewell, committals; medical grid; Parliament, bills
House of Lords 23, 328, 329
householder
　status 142
houses of corrections/bridewells 16, 38, 193, 194, 277, 279, 367
　Acle 277
　Middlesex 38, 384, 413, 439
　Westminster 384
Howard, Matthew 114
Howard, William 159
Howe, Anne 186
Howell, James 10, 30, 79, 92, 292, 358, 434
　*Londinopolis* 10, 435
Howell, John 119
Howes, John 13, 14, 203, 219, 228, 238, 362
Hoxton, Sir Owen 172
hucksters 123, 127, 128, 311, 420
Hudrix, Marseles 162
Hudson, Clare 245
Hudson, William 189
hue and cry 240, 320, 326
Huff, Henry 95
Huffum, Fagg 342
Hughes, Katherine 223
Hundson, Lord 220
Hungary/Hungarians 72
Hunt, John 283
Hunt, Thomas 159
Hunter, John 54
Huntington Library 225
Hurst, William 254
Hussey, William 320
Hussy, Margaret 184
Hutchinson, Elizabeth 272
Hyame, Robert 345
Hyde, Margaret 374

Ichenor, Mary 274
illegitimacy 65, 150, 154, 156, 174, 180, 186, 202, 238, 241, 242, 262, 270, 272, 366, 377, 383, 405, 422, 428

incest 238, 373
incorporation (suburbs) 317, 435
infanticide 241, 271
inflation 33, 304
informers/information 53, 304, 309–11,
    312, 326, 381, 396
  abuses by 310
  Bridewell officers 423
    bench 424
    clerks 424
    matrons 423–4
    porters 423
  Bridewell prisoners 163, 190, 278, 421–3
  moles 364, 423
  'public officers'
    beadles 420
    bellmen 420
    constables 419, 420
    deputies 420, 421
    marshals 420, 420–1, 421
    warders 420, 421
Ingram, Martin 202, 365
inmates 21, 38, 39, 40, 49, 51–2, 66,
    145, 200, 202, 204, 235, 300,
    305, 306, 308, 309, 313, 384,
    391, 396, 414
  definition 52–3
  sickness, causing 51–5
  St Bartholomew's Hospital 70
  see also Bridewell; Christ's Hospital;
    guilds; hospitals; sickness;
Inns of Court 64, 81–2, 173, 184
  Inner Temple 238
  Lincoln's Inn 81, 296
  Staple Inn 81
  see also censuses/counts/'surveys'
insults 92, 142, 144, 200–1, 310
Ireland/Irish 74–6, 123, 166, 187, 190, 191
  vagrants 73, 74–5, 106, 114
Ireland, Rebecca 159
Irish Rebellion 75
Isle of Rhe 172, 297
Isle of Wight 73, 289
Italy 137

Jackson, Martha 279
Jackson, Peternella 273, 378
Jackson, Thomas 7, 36
Jackson, William 105
Jacob, Elizabeth 335
James, John 391
Jefferson, Alice 171
Jefferson, Frances 274
Jeffrey, John 168
Jenning, Mary 241

Jennison, Robert 27
Jervis, Ann 151, 429
Johns, Elizabeth 108
Johnson, Alexandra 311
Johnson, Avery 185
Johnson, Dorothy 239
Johnson, Francis 170
Johnson, James 287
Johnson, Katherine 425
Johnson, Lawrence 142
Johnson, Nicholas 115
Johnson, Richard 5, 92
  *Pleasant Walkes of Moore-fields*
    15, 16
Johnson, William 247
Jones, Alice 118
Jones, Andrew 95
Jones, Christopher 81
Jones, Daniel 169
Jones, Elizabeth 166, 258, 421
Jones, Henry 168
Jones, Hugh 318
Jones, John 36, 37
Jones, Katherine 152
Jones, Margaret 118
Jones, Thomas 214
Jonson, Ben 3
  *Bartholomew Fair* 153
juries 226
jurymen 293
Justice, Martha 123
justices of the peace 19, 225, 228, 229–30,
    234, 236, 240, 241, 243, 311, 317,
    359, 363, 366, 372, 377, 396, 398,
    401, 430, 440, 441
  abused 44, 200, 328
  neighbouring counties 307, 352
  shortages 38
  warrants 228, 229–30, 236
  see also Bridewell, committals; Middlesex

Kempsall, Richard 318
Kendal, Joanne 425
Kendal/Locke, Susan 156–7, 159
Kenny, Anne 118
Kent 102, 112, 120
Kent, Joan 291
Kerdesse, Roger 190
Ketteridge, Margaret 387
Kibble, Jane 341, 420
Kinder, Anne 185
Kinder, Tom 184–5
King, Gabriel 245
King, Robert 259
King's Bench 173

# Index

King's Bench Prison 186, 302
king's evil 109, 260, 265
  *see also* registers
Klerman, Daniel 363
Knight, William 425
Knott, Frances 279
Kyne, Elyn 125

labels/labelling 11, 192–9, 204–5, 206, 435, 439
  'accompt' of living 205
  beggar 196
  briber 196
  cozener 196
  cutpurse 196, 198, 205
  dangerous 205
  disorderly 198, 205
  filcher 197
  idle 194, 196, 198
  ill 205
  incorrigible 205
  lewd 196, 198, 205, 207, 439
  lifter 197
  loose 205
  lusty 205
  masterless 205
  nightwalker 194, 196, 198, 207
  ninner 197, 205
  nip 197, 205
  out of service 196, 205
  picker 197
  pickpocket 197
  pickpurse 196, 198
  pilferer 196
  receiver 196
  rogue 194, 196, 199, 205
  stout 205
  stubborn 205
  sturdy 205
  suspicious 196
  unruly 196, 205
  vagabond 196, 199, 205
  vagrant 193, 194, 195, 196, 198
  'whore' 193
  numbers 194
  sex-ratio 205
Laman, Bridget 271
Lambe, Dr John 328
Lambe, Henry 155
Lambeth Palace 34
Lambright, Godfrey 427
Lancaster, Sarah 214
Landes, Richard 143

landlords (inmates) 21, 53, 54, 369, 396
  occupations 54
  *see also* censuses/counts/'surveys'
Lane, John 251
Langbein, John 253, 363
Langerake, James 395
Langley, George 357
Langton, Jane 134
Laud, Archbishop 46
Launcelott, Edward 255
Laurence, Elizabeth 321
Lawrence, John 10, 36, 37, 78, 333, 337, 349
lazarhouses 261, 262
Lea, Lucretia 289
Leake, Joseph 389
Leake, Michael. 54
Leaver, John 423
Lee, Andrew 94
Lee, John 183
Lee, Katherine 125
Lee, Margaret 102, 107
Lee, Richard 326
Lee, Robert 240
Leech, John 279
Leicester, Earl of 50, 217
Leicester, Eliza 255
Leicester, Lord 42
Leicester, William 287
Leman, Elizabeth 119
Lene, William 108
Lent 280
*lettres de cachet* 19, 366
Lever, Thomas 12
Lewes, Raffe 338
Lewis, Anne 186, 373
Lewis, Margaret 321
Lewis, Mary 153
Lewis, Thomas 99
Lhasa 433
libels 46–7, 145, 339, 397, 408
liberties 81–2
  Barmoodes 81
  Tower 81
Libie, William 249
Light, Joseph 338
lightermen, disorders 160
lighting (night) 202, 305, 308, 314, 316, 342–9, 395
  neglect/abuses 344–5
Lilburne, John 214
Lincoln, Earl of 169
Lincolnshire 337
linkcarriers 347
Lister, Mary 92
Little, Mary 390

530  Index

Llewellyn, Margery 248
Llewellyn, Thomas 248
Lloyd, Catherine 125
Lloyd, Griffin 143
Loader, Joanne 62, 63, 64
Locke, Henry 156
Locke, Joseph 370
Loggin, William 289
Loggins, William 161, 166
Loggyn, Thomas 249
London,
  anonymity? 69–70
  growth 1, 9, 36–40, 80
  houses per acre 70–1
  perceptions 9
  population turnover 70, 293
  sex-ratio 69
  stability/instability, debate 28–35
London Bridge 245, 345
  crime 90–1, 113, 167, 388
  selling 123
  watch 90
  *see also* cutpurses; theft/thieves; vagrants
London, outlying places
  Bermondsey 274
  Clerkenwell 69, 79, 104, 111, 149, 150, 155, 161, 177, 310, 376
  Covent Garden 50, 341, 356, 404
  Cow Cross 111, 161, 330, 353, 425
  Croydon 113
  East Smithfield 72, 161, 266
  Finsbury 150, 176
  Gravesend 91, 113, 285, 289
  Grays 91
  Hackney 77
  Hampstead 113
  Harrow-on-the-Hill 113
  Highgate 113
  Hornsey 274
  Hyde Park 62, 326
  Islington 57, 92, 113, 375
  Kensington 440
  Kingston 113
  Lambeth 61, 113, 160, 266, 381
    riots (1640) 90
  Limehouse 341
  Newington 57
  Paris Garden 280
  Peckham 381
  Ratcliffe 57, 113, 165
  Shoreditch 79, 121, 150, 161, 236, 382
  Southwark 16, 70, 72, 80, 91, 106, 115, 132, 155, 161, 168, 171, 228, 262, 315, 330, 334, 336, 355, 364, 376, 381, 423, 431
  vagrants, beggars, nightwalkers 90–1, 113, 115
  Stepney 79, 113, 161, 429
  Wapping 59, 79, 310, 319
  Whitechapel 61, 72, 77, 79, 113, 142, 150, 153, 182, 321, 323, 374
  Woolwich 118
London, parishes
  All Hallows Lombard Street 415
  All Hallows London Wall 183, 300, 418
  All Hallows Staining 285
  All Hallows the Great 57, 376, 418
  Holy Trinity the Less 399
  Little St Bartholomew 296
  St Alban Wood Street 412
  St Alphage London Wall 416
  St Andrew-by-the-Wardrobe 110, 410
  St Andrew Holborn 134, 161
  St Andrew Undershaft 392, 393
  St Antholin Budge Row 338
  St Bartholomew-by-the-Exchange 182, 396
  St Benet Fink 73, 381
  St Benet Gracechurch 57, 406, 414
  St Benet Paul's Wharf 296, 382, 396, 416
  St Botolph Aldersgate 379
  St Botolph Aldgate 117, 126, 315, 399
  St Botolph Billingsgate 346, 396
  St Botolph Bishopsgate 113, 182, 183, 200, 375, 381, 398, 407
  St Brides Fleet Street 83, 84, 294, 416
  St Christopher-le-Stocks 346, 414
  St Clement Eastcheap 126
  St Dionis Backchurch 53
  St Ethelburga Bishopsgate 398
  St Giles Cripplegate 113, 176, 357
  St Giles-in-the-Fields 113, 115
  St Helen Bishopsgate 109, 285, 382
  St James Garlickhithe 285, 396, 418
  St John Walbrook 53, 411
  St John Zachary 53, 346, 382, 415
  St Katherine Coleman Street 399, 416
  St Katherine Kreechurch 75
  St Laurence Pountney 53
  St Lawrence Jewry 399
  St Margaret Lothbury 394
  St Margaret New Fish Street 53, 398, 415
  St Martin Orgar 58, 182, 397
  St Mary-at-Hill 161
  St Mary Aldermanbury 398
  St Mary Aldermary 382, 399
  St Mary Magdalene Street 398
  St Mary Woolnoth 101, 297
  St Michael Cornhill 109, 345, 346, 348, 381

Index 531

London, parishes (cont.)
  St Michael Crooked Lane 57
  St Michael le Querne 183
  St Michael Wood Street 182
  St Peter Cornhill 117, 345, 379
  St Peter Westcheap 77, 382, 416
  St Sepulchre 64, 85, 86, 111, 113, 117, 155, 172, 293, 339, 357, 375, 377
  St Sepulchre (Middlesex Division) 57, 310, 320, 415
  St Stephen Coleman Street 58, 59, 416
  St Stephen Walbrook 62, 380, 381
  St Thomas Apostle 415
London, places
  Alsatia slum 81
  Barbican 392
  Blackfriars 62, 82, 83, 84, 113, 156, 299, 379, 391
  Charing Cross 100, 166, 214, 236, 267
  Christchurch 64
  Custom House Quay 113
  Eastcheap 341
  Holborn 86, 147, 155, 177, 339, 356, 372, 425
  Leadenhall 282, 390
  Lincolns Inn Fields 50, 100
  Ludgate 134
  Moorfields 7, 57, 58, 75, 77, 92–3, 153, 155, 309, 315, 438
  Moorgate 350, 356, 359
  Newgate 77, 87, 155, 334, 350
  Old Bailey 151, 172, 355
  Paul's Wharf 61
  Smithfield 61, 86, 89, 113, 125, 152, 160, 161, 197, 264, 268, 319, 365, 438, 439
  Snow Hill 57
  St Lawrence 150
  St Magnus Corner 88
  Temple Bar 50, 54, 64, 101, 359
  Tower Hill 103, 108, 149, 284, 359
  Whitefriars 81, 82, 113, 336
London (and nearby areas), streets
  Aldersgate Street 213, 274
  Birchin Lane 64
  Bishopgate Street 64, 88, 150, 171, 255, 272, 378
  Botolph Lane 346
  Bridewell Lane 24, 84
  Broad Street 127, 147
  Candlewick Street 89
  Carter Lane 272
  Chancery Lane 373, 431
  Charterhouse Lane 61

Cheapside 42, 44, 57, 63, 64, 87, 88, 89, 98, 118, 121, 125, 153, 155, 216, 219, 247, 275, 339, 378, 390, 391
  Cheapside Conduit 47, 64, 105
  Cheapside Cross 47, 98
Chick Lane 103, 111, 148, 155, 174
Clifford Inn Lane 126
Coleman Street 89
Cornhill 89
Cow Lane 341
Creed Lane 99
Crooked Lane 346
Distaff Lane 341
Elbow Lane 334
Fenchurch Street 88
Fetter Lane 338
Field Lane 342
Fleet Street 64, 83, 84–5, 100, 108, 125, 142, 155, 161, 164, 241, 246, 260, 270, 295, 298, 299, 319, 342, 428, 430
Foster Lane 121
Golding Lane 125, 175, 425
Gracechurch Street 88, 126
Gracious Street 169, 171
Grays Inn Lane 283
Gutter Lane 392
Ivy Lane 81
Kent Street 327
Kentish Street 237
King Street 121, 150
Lombard Street 64, 88, 89
London Stone 89
Long Acre 356
Long Lane 118, 121, 190, 246
Lothbury 89, 239
Ludgate 88
New Fish Street 126, 215
Old Street 114
Paternoster Row 219
Poultry 89
Pudding Lane 346
Seacoal Lane 272
Seocle Lane 160
Shoe Lane 372, 392, 426
Silver Street 271
Soper Lane 346
St John Street 60, 99, 111, 151, 340, 353
St Katherine's Lane 378
Strand 320
Suffolk Lane 245
Thames Street 88, 89, 150, 161
Thieving Lane 77
Threadneedle Street 89
Turnagain Lane 111

London (and nearby areas), streets (cont.)
  Turnmill Street 77–8, 104, 111, 121, 124, 148, 151, 157, 161, 175, 310
  Tuttle Street 340
  Warwick Lane 160, 215
  Water Street 100
  Watling Street 89
  Whitecross Street 59, 161, 175, 426
  Wood Street 180, 371, 392
London, wards/precincts 30, 50
  Aldersgate 85, 155, 334, 372
    arrests in 89
  Aldgate 7, 78, 150, 248, 322, 332, 352, 382, 389
  Bassishaw 304, 314, 350
    arrests in 88, 89
  Billingsgate 88, 131, 132, 166
    arrests in 88, 89
  Bishopgate 88, 156, 181, 337, 350, 353, 354, 391, 421
    arrests in 88, 89
  Bread Street 298, 346
    arrests in 88, 299
  Bridge 85, 88, 90, 156, 298–9, 304
    arrests in 88, 299, 300
    fishwives, numbers 128
  Broad Street 89
    arrests in 88
  Castle Baynard 296, 299, 314
    arrests in 88
  Cheap 105, 155, 156, 298, 299, 314, 393
    arrests in 88, 89, 299
  Coleman Street 89, 314
  Cordwainer 89, 298
    arrests in 89, 299
  Cornhill 54, 64, 105, 123, 124, 125, 126, 133, 172, 202, 301, 339, 344, 345, 350, 352, 369
  Cripplegate 54, 155, 156, 298, 314, 350
    arrests in 88, 299
  Dowgate 89, 113
    arrests in 88, 299
  Farringdon Within 72, 85, 87, 155, 298, 300, 304, 314, 441
    arrests in 87, 299
  Farringdon Without 72, 84–6, 298, 300, 304, 314, 350, 356, 394, 441
    arrests in 85, 86, 299
    constables, numbers 85
    fishwives, numbers 128
    special sessions 85
    troublespot 85
  Langbourn 88
    arrests in 88, 89
  Lime Street 89, 304, 350
    arrests in 88
  Portsoken 54, 263, 410
    arrests in 88
  Queenhithe 47, 89, 91, 113, 298, 299, 355, 426
    arrests in 88, 300
  St Dunstan-in-the-West 54, 61, 84, 100, 126, 202, 293, 337, 340, 410, 411, 413, 414, 417
  St Katherine-by-the-Tower 77, 79, 149, 150, 151, 161, 271, 288, 301, 406, 407, 410
  Tower 340
    arrests in 88, 300
  Vintry 62, 89
    arrests in 89
  Walbrook 89, 298, 318
    arrests in 299
Lord, Mary 172
Low Countries 40, 72, 282, 283
Lowde, Goodman 57
Lowe, Phyllis 165
Lowe, Ralph 245
Lubeck 73
Ludgate Prison 418
Lumley, Sir Martin 63
Lupton, Donald 1, 2, 67, 76, 124, 433, 434
Lusher, Christopher 89, 148
Luther, Martin 15
Lynte, Thomas 164
Lyster, Mary 257

Mabbes, Daniel 353
Machyn, Henry 217
madness 184, 185–6, 199, 258–9, 301, 399
Magna Carta 226
Magno, Alexander 10, 93, 333
Maidenhead 180
maidservants 273, 379
  abandoning children 65
  theft 165, 190, 247
  vulnerability 69
Malen, John 339
Malmes, Arthur 331
Mammoth, Martha 356
Manby, Ann 197
Manori, Agnes 278
Manster, Yarrin 162
maps 4, 76
March, Robert 246
markets 88–90, 109, 146, 208, 316, 318, 346, 366, 378, 389, 411, 434
  Billingsgate 47, 91, 124, 129, 130, 309, 321, 338
  Cheapside 127, 128

# Index

markets (cont.)
  Cornhill 128
  Leadenhall 88, 89, 90, 127
  Newgate 87, 127, 131, 215, 288, 298, 300
  Stocks 88, 89, 387
  forestallers 124, 126, 129, 309, 338
  orders 185
  regrators 126, 128
  *see also* cutpurses; pickpockets; theft/thieves; Westminster
Markham, Griffin 255
Marlborough 16, 364
Marlow 180
marriage 278, 284, 415, 430
  *see also* Parliament, statutes
Marshal, Agnes 61
Marshal, Ann 257
Marshal, James 64
marshalmen 303, 329, 393
  Copestake 328
  abuses against 319, 324, 325
  abuses by 173, 174, 175, 283, 328, 330
  bonuses/top-up payments 301, 302
  bribes 162
marshals 77, 96, 107, 122, 234, 236, 240, 274, 297, 304, 307, 308, 314, 315–16, 326, 327, 393, 411, 421, 423, 439, 440, 441
  Bestney 302, 325, 328, 329, 392, 420, 424
  Davis 172, 297, 300, 302, 315, 325, 327, 328
  Fitch 155, 157, 300, 327, 328, 330, 392
  Parker 302, 328
  Pordage 297, 302, 325, 396
  Read 324
  Simpson 324
  Walrond 173–4, 297, 315, 326
    abuses against 318, 319, 320, 324–5
    abuses by 173, 327–8, 329
    bonuses/top-up payments 301, 302
    bribes 155
    costs 316
    pensions/loans 302
    salaries 300–1
    social standing 315
    sued 320
  *see also* Bridewell, committals; informers/information
Marten, Thomas 295
martial law 104, 316–17
Martin, John 73
Martyn, Ralph 242
martyrs 14
Mary I 13, 120

Maryne, John 96
Mason, John 112
Mason, Oliver 249
masques 339
Massie, Richard 180
masterless 14, 45, 362
Matfield, Nicholas 389
Matthew, Elizabeth 250
Matthews, Diana 318
Matthews, John 265
May, Susan 372
May Eve 351
Mayfield, John 255
McMullan, John 70, 81, 82, 139
Medcalfe, George 242
medical grid 260–9
  parishes/hospitals/medical fees 260–1
Medley, Richard 374
Mekens, William 218, 220
Mekins, John 240
Meme, John 165
merchants 94, 126, 288–9, 296, 297, 434
Meredith, John 263
Merrell, William 47
Merrick, Bridget 330
Merrick, Meredith 116
Merrick, Thomas 61
Merry, Dorothy 428
Mess, William 326
Middlesex 16, 50, 85, 104, 113, 158, 292, 311, 326, 352–3, 404, 411
  justices 50, 78, 81
  *see also* houses of corrections/bridewells
Middleton, Sir Thomas 314, 428
middling sort 293–4, 304, 377, 419
midwives 58, 59, 64, 77, 176, 191, 245, 269–70, 271, 336, 337, 379, 415, 422
  *see also* censuses/counts/'surveys'
migrants 27–8, 71–2, 80
  *see also* censuses/counts/'surveys'; women
milkwomen/maids 130, 131
Mill, Humphrey 182, 343
Miller, Alice 148
Mills, Jane 430
Mills, William 247
ministers 234, 276, 285, 335
  abuses against 259
  abuses by 388
  *see also* Bridewell, religion; censuses/counts/'surveys'; charity
Minnie, Myles 248
minstrels 107, 339
Mitchell, William 115, 133

Molineux, Abraham 370
Monday, Mary 287
Monday, William 159
Moody, Edward 341
Moore, Katherine 74, 161
Moore, Michael 322
Moore, Margaret 372
Moore, Susan 213
Mopine, Edward 105
Morgan, Henry 279
Morgan, Thomas 146
Morley, William 115, 148
Morrece, James 168
Morris, Elizabeth 429
Morton, Dorothy 392
Moss, John 163
Moss, Richard 273
Mosse, Joan 16, 364
Mosten, William 283
Mott, Elizabeth 247
Moulden, Joan 186, 266
Mountain, Thomas 14
Moxen, Margaret 272
Muffin, Edward 375
Mugg, Thomas 297
Muggleton, Lodowick 280
Mullens, Anthony 421
Munch, John 107, 258
Munday, Anthony 3, 7
murder 365, 423
musicians 340, 341, 397
  *see also* vagrants
Musklett, Justice 44
muster lists/rolls 313, 406
  *see also* censuses/counts/'surveys'
Mynshul, Geoffrey 280, 348
Myou, Helenor 74
Mytton, Dorothy 335

Nabokov, Vladimir 137
naming (offenders) 181–91
Nashe, Thomas 79, 151, 161, 332, 333, 338, 343
Naylor, Henry 337
Needham, Elizabeth 64
neighbourliness 21, 30, 70, 71, 369–71
neighbours
  policing 236, 362, 372–8
Nelson, Phillipa 116
Neville, Jane 222–3
New England 286
New Exchange 6, 7
New Prison 312
Newborough, Mary 163, 278

Newgate Prison 38, 86, 143, 155, 167, 173, 174, 175, 180, 234, 236, 240, 241, 254, 255, 259, 267, 282, 284, 285, 289, 311, 329, 348, 349, 351, 374, 384, 397, 412, 416, 421, 424, 430, 431
  ordinary 144, 330
Newington, Arlington 195
Newman, Abigail 183
Newman, Henry 392
Newman, Richard 287
Newsam, John 240
Nicholl, Richard 112
Nicholls, Elizabeth 264
nicknames 186–9
night 332–60
  attitudes/dangers 332–3
  conviviality/sociability 340–2
  noise 338, 339–40, 370, 397
  sleep 337–8
nightwalkers/nightwalking 21, 39, 59, 78, 82, 86, 87, 89, 91, 93, 154, 155, 156, 159, 167, 179, 185, 189, 195, 199, 204, 208, 235, 241, 246, 247, 257, 264, 271, 278, 279, 280, 286, 333–4, 343, 351, 355, 356–7, 390, 391, 393, 420, 425, 426, 430, 431, 440, 441
  Royal Exchange 94
  sex-ratio 205
  transported 286, 287
  *see also* labels/labelling; London, outlying places
nightworkers 334
  'gongfarmer' 334
  'nightmen' 334
nips 21, 141, 158, 168, 170, 186, 187, 240, 264, 311
  transported 287
nobility
  abused 43, 46
  building houses 50
Noble, Margaret 251
Norfolk 121
Norman, Angellet 388
North, John 246
North, Margery 382
Northampton 16
Northumberland 121
Norton, Ann 337
Norton, Thomas 4
Norton, William 428
Norwich 364, 407
  mayor's court 19, 366
Nowell, Margery 375

## Index

nurses 380, 381, 382
Nys, Daniel 101

oath of allegiance 288
office-holding 29, 31, 32, 293
  fining 295, 296
  privilege, claiming 295–6
  refusals to serve 294–5
officers
  abuses against 189, 318, 319, 321, 322, 323, 441
  abuses by 328, 394
  arrests by 383–93
  corruption 329–31
  numbers 304
  rescuing prisoners from 319
  *see also* Parliament, bills
Old, Sybil 358
Old Bailey 38, 158, 174, 229, 399, 401
Oliver, Thomas 116
optic order 41–2, 418
Orton, Barbara 169
orphans 418, 428
  *see also* registers
Ostend 283
Ouncestead, Elizabeth 270
out of service 134, 208, 272, 273, 274, 308, 379
  *see also* labels/labelling; registers
Overall, William 102
Overberry, Elizabeth 163, 248
overseers of the poor 63, 293
Owen, Anne 332
Owen, Margaret 189
Owen, Rose 245
Oxford 16, 112, 121
Oxford, Lord 153
oysterwenches/women 125, 132

Packwood, Andrew 111
Page, John 86, 430
Palatinate 281
Paler, Richard 288
Pallas, William 160
Palmer, Anne 118
Palmer, Elizabeth 245
Palmer, Joan 159
Palmer, Margaret 122
Palsted, Elizabeth 249
Pangman, Katherine 343
Panton, Zachery 265
pardons 430, 431
Pare, Hugh 169
Parfield, Ann 378
Paris 9, 344

Paris, Mary 356
parishes 182, 233, 240, 263, 292, 293, 295, 309, 312, 314, 320, 325, 353, 362, 378, 379, 394, 401, 403–18
  accounts 22, 31, 53, 56, 61, 100, 182, 183, 191, 313, 379, 396, 406, 411, 416, 417, 431
  clerks 63, 172, 369, 415, 417, 418
  investigations/prosecutions 367, 368, 379–83, 396–9
  registers 186, 191, 412, 415, 417, 430
  *see also* Bridewell, committals; medical grid
Park, Robert 287
Parker, Isabel 339
Parker, Millicent 118
Parker, Robert 69
Parkinson, Thomas 321
Parliament 34, 40, 79, 91, 104, 165, 189, 203, 221, 225, 279, 343, 350, 398, 414
  bills
    Bridewell/hospitals 227–9
    brokers registry 412
    building 49, 55
    corruption by officers 329
    prostitution 203
  statutes 414, 417
    bail/committal (1554, 1555) 363
    houses of correction (1610) 194, 198, 367
    infanticide (1624) 209, 414
    marriage (1653) 414
    metropolitan police (1829) 14, 361, 363
    pickpockets (1567) 157, 158, 198
    poor laws (1598, 1601) 234, 369, 404, 406, 411, 414
    vagrancy/houses of correction (1744) 367
    vagrancy/poor relief (1572) 158, 198, 199, 305
    work-stocks and houses of correction (1576) 198
  *see also* Bridewell, committals
Parnott, George 240
Parris, Philidelfia 257
Parry, Agnes 150
Parson, Elizabeth 274
Passmore, John 52
Pastell, John 166
Paston, Roger 323
Paul's Cross 3, 12, 37, 46, 216, 369
Pavenla, Alviza 278
paving 6, 100–1
pawning/pawnshops 164–5, 412
Payne, Margaret 340

Peacham, Henry 98
Peacock, John 158
Pearl, Valerie 32, 33, 34
Peel, Alice 258
Pellam, Christian 59
Pembroke, Earl of 364
Pennyfeather, Elizabeth 278
Pepper, Roger 377–8
Pepys, Samuel 90, 92, 332, 333, 335–6, 339, 340, 347, 348, 349, 358
perambulations 416
Percival, Erasmus 427
Percy, Anne 266
Percy, Thomas 255
Perkins, John 103
Perlman, Janice 144
Perrin, Jane 430
Perringie, Peter 73
Perryman, Grace 45
pesthouses 262, 301
Peter, Mary 74
Peters, Mary 78
Petre, Maurice 142
Petty, William 36, 37, 436
petty chapmen 124
Pewter, Edward 118
Phillips, Anne 323
Phillips, Joan 118
Phillips, John 378
Phillips, Mary 430
Phillips, Susan 272
Phillips, Thomas 240, 393
Philmore, John 310
physical descriptions (suspects) 255–7
Pickering, John 121
Pickering, William 268
pickpockets 47, 75, 82, 98, 145, 153, 154, 155, 156, 157, 158, 159, 160, 162–3, 167, 170, 187, 188, 243, 248, 264, 280, 289, 312, 364, 388, 391, 420, 423, 426, 427
   Bartholomew Fair 86, 162
   Bridge 90
   churches 163
   fairs 153, 163
   markets 89–90, 148, 163
   playhouses 96
   press (army) 282
   Royal Exchange 94
   sex-ratio 204
   Spital 95, 162
   takings 154
   teachers 166
   tools 168
   transported 286, 287
   Westminster Abbey 95
   *see also* labels/labelling; Parliament, statutes
Pierce, John 302
Pilkington, Bishop 14
pillory 44, 118, 121, 284, 330
Pinckerney, Joanne 59
Pink, Edward 168
pirates 73
Pitman, Thomas 54
Pitts, Mary 325
plague 19, 37, 38, 42, 45, 52, 101, 133, 147, 176, 200, 233, 235, 242, 257, 262, 269, 301, 302, 314, 316, 336, 338, 358, 397, 413, 414, 417
   *see also* street-sellers
players 107
plays/playhouses 39, 84, 158, 335, 336
   Blackfriars 347
   Cockpit 100
   Fortune 96
   *see also* censuses/counts/'surveys'; cutpurses; pickpockets; prostitution
Plocket, Nicholas 142
Pogmore, Gervase 189
Poland 137
Poley, Katherine, 372
policing 8, 11, 305, 307–8, 435, 436
   information 401–2
   organization 304–17
   'professionalization' 362
   *see also* hue and cry; neighbours; Parliament, statutes; records
poor relief 306
   *see also* Parliament, statutes
Porter, Joan 189
Porter, Margaret 238
porters 38, 44, 45, 57, 58, 310, 369–71
Portsmouth 103
Portugal/Portuguese 72, 191
Potter, Alice 240
poverty 12, 35, 414, 437
Powell, Edward 160, 188
Powell, Maurice 419
Powell, Stacey 282
Powell, Thomas 389
Powell, William 347
Powesse, John 389
pox 91, 132, 155, 156, 188, 208, 255, 263, 265–7, 269
   *see also* fishwives; St Thomas's Hospital
Pratin, William 288
preaching 85
pregnancy, 'searches' 269–71
prerogative court 415

# Index

press (army) 6, 162, 191, 234, 281–4, 352
  'voluntary' 283
  *see also* cozeners/cheaters; cutpurses; drunkards/drunkenness; foreigners; pickpockets; rogues; theft/thieves; tinkers; vagrants
Prest, Alice 91
Preston, John 415
Price, Alice 132
Price, John 377
Price, Lynda Ann 292
Price, Margaret 180
price controls 309, 395
Prick, John 162
Pride, Colonel 279, 281
Priestmen, Alice 393
printing presses 38, 46, 78, 146
prisoners of war 234, 264
prisons 305
  escapes 154, 241, 256, 282, 348, 351
privacy 71
privies 108, 109
Proctor, Joanne 124
Proctor, Thomas 98
Proff, Abraham 319
Proof, John 170
prosecution
  private 361–8
  public 362–8
prostitution 21, 199, 202, 203, 235, 422, 423
  bawds 106, 157, 160, 185, 187, 188, 201, 219, 241, 244, 246, 250, 251, 254, 257, 258, 388, 394, 395, 420, 425
  brothels 78, 85, 93, 142, 148–9, 150, 157, 159, 163, 175, 176, 188, 217, 218, 220, 221, 223, 245, 248, 257, 266, 272, 322, 330, 347, 372, 374, 389, 392, 420, 421, 422, 426
  career/living by 148–9, 150
  clients 151, 172–3, 201, 251
  families 167
  fees 152–3
  pimps 77, 93, 149, 151, 158, 163, 176, 201, 214, 218, 219, 220, 223, 251, 267, 422, 429
  playhouses 97
  prostitutes 201, 217, 219, 220, 249, 250, 267, 355, 367, 422
    clothes 152, 217
    stealing from clients 72–3, 153
    rents 151
    takings 150, 151–2
    theft 153–4
  *see also* censuses/counts/'surveys'; Parliament, bills

protestant dissenters 304
proverbs 257
providence 41
provost marshals 304, 316–17
  Heath 325
Prue, Prudence 372
public penance 238
Pugh, Humphrey 93
Pulman, John 311
Pulman, Nicholas 141
punishment 275–90, 305
puritans 219
Purvis, Margaret 122
Pynfold, David 376
Pynnots, Martin 366

quarter sessions 38, 94, 125, 202, 234, 244, 281, 285, 287, 296, 384, 393, 394, 396, 397
  City sessions 22, 240, 281, 311, 395, 398, 428, 429, 431
  Middlesex sessions 22, 162, 175, 281, 364, 365, 412, 424, 426, 430
  Westminster sessions 22, 312, 369, 430
  *see also* cutpurses; London, wards/precincts; theft/thieves
Queryet, Millicent 422
Quince, John 263

Racine, Jean 28
rag gatherers 124, 131, 200, 258, 430
  crime 131–2, 165
Railton, Robert 339
rakers 83
  abuses by 316
Ramsden, Bartholomew 185
rape/sexual abuse 241, 242, 250, 251, 271, 373, 391
Rappaport, Steve 31, 33, 34, 35, 435
Rash, John 184
Ratcliffe, Andrew 114
Ratcliffe, Katherine 342
Rathborne, Elizabeth 258
Rawlins, John 122
Raynton, George 167
Reade, James 220
rebellions 12, 316
  Kett 314, 316, 350, 353
  Wyatt 350
recidivism 74, 198, 242, 244, 247, 275, 281, 401, 416, 420, 423, 424, 425, 426, 427, 439
sex-ratio 206
records 416, 418, 420
  indexing/calendaring 416–17

records (cont.)
  margins 417
  policing, information 381, 401, 414–16, 429–30
  *see also* guilds
Reeve, John 280
registers 412, 416
  bread 413
  Bridewell prisoners 423
  brokers 412
  coal 413
  disease 412
  fishwives 411
  king's evil 413
  orphans 416
  paupers 416
  people out of service 413
  strangers 409
  taxpayers 412
  tithes 413
  vagrants 411
  wills 413, 415
religious radicals 237, 385
  brownists 398
  quakers 398
  ranters 398
religious refugees 72, 280
Rennaunt, Ellyn 388
Restoration comedy 78
Revolution/Civil War 350, 359, 384, 385
rewards 309, 311–12
Reynolds, David 162
Reynolds, Elizabeth 151, 273
Reynolds, Frances 258
Reynolds, Pheba 153
Reynolds, Richard 186
Reynolds, William 428
Rice, Elizabeth 424
Rich, Constantine 324
Rich, Thomas 294
Richard, Austen 143
Richards, Evan 246
Richardson, Frances 154, 278, 289, 389, 431
Richardson, John 219, 427
Richardson, Nicholas 120
Richardson, Thomas 265
Richardson, William 425
Ridley, Bishop 13, 14, 361
Ridley, Oliver 123
Rio de Janeiro 177
riots 33–4, 173, 294, 363, 379
  enclosure riots 350
  *see also* London, outlying places
Rively, Lewis 431

roaring boys 338, 342
Roberts, Frances 321
Roberts, Ginkins 43
Roberts, Katherine 151
Robinson, Edward 373
Robinson, John 426
Robinson, Lawrence 147
Robinson, Margaret 122
Robinson, Ursula 64
Rodes, Elizabeth 249
Roe, Christian 167
Rogers, Alice 319
Rogers, Michael 112
rogue literature 4, 137, 157, 158, 170–1, 197, 199
rogues 239, 241, 313
  press (army) 282
  sex-ratio 205
  *see also* labels/labelling
Rolles, Richard 151, 153, 176–7, 223, 224, 267
Rome 49, 108
Rose, Elizabeth 357
Rowe, Thomas 44
Rowse, Helen 271
Rowse, Winifred 115, 148
Royal Exchange 7, 44, 47, 64, 94, 97, 126, 156, 208, 243, 311, 344, 345, 346
  disorders 94–5
  thieves 140
  *see also* beggars/begging; nightwalkers/nightwalking; pickpockets; street-sellers; theft/thieves; 'whores'
Ruddy, Christopher 173
rumours 45–6, 145, 379, 390
Russell, Patrick 119
Russell, Phyllis 223

sabbath 235, 271, 310, 314, 396, 398, 414
  street selling 127, 131, 309
Sackville, Sir Edward 289
Sad, Mary 77
Sadler, John 334
Sadler, Margaret 132
Saffron Walden 155
sailors 38, 43, 79, 86, 103–4, 311, 314, 316, 345
  *see also* censuses/counts/'surveys'
Salisbury 16, 115, 272
Salisbury, Richard 111
Salisbury House 83
Sampson, Morgan 315
Sanderford, Edward 279
Sandwich 112, 335

Saunders, Anne 322
Savage, Thomas 103
Savoy Hospital 161, 308
scavengers 100, 293, 413
    abuses by 316
Schofield, George 168
scolding 133, 279, 301, 339, 341, 394, 425
Scotland/Scottish 188, 248, 283, 301
    vagrants 73, 114
    *see also* censuses/counts/'surveys'
Scott, Anne 148
Seaman, John 287
Searle, Martha 420
searches 146, 255, 307, 308, 347, 351–2, 379–83, 398, 427
    resisted 322, 323
second-hand markets 164
Selby, Robert 364
Semprey, John 190
servants 16, 250, 348, 364, 372, 377, 418
    disorders 127, 241, 250, 278, 279, 286, 395
    running away 92, 186, 262, 264, 265, 279
    theft 132, 165–6
service 415
servingman 180
sewers 18
sextons 380, 381, 418
sexual crime, prosecutions falling 201–2, 203
Shakespeare, William
    *Comedy of Errors* 184, 185–6
    *King Lear* 119, 179
    *Measure for Measure* 291, 377
    *Much Ado About Nothing* 291, 367
Sharpe, Alice 149, 424
Shambrooke, William 52
Shaw, John 148, 150, 151, 163
Shaw, Robert 160
Shawe, Ellen 255
Shepard, Richard 174
Sherborne, John 319
Shereman, William 113
Shigwell, William 324
Shoemaker, Robert 365
Shrewsbury 120
Shropshire 102, 107
Shrove Tuesday 33, 316, 323
sickness 21, 39
    'green woman' 182
    inmates, causing 51–5
    *see also* Bridewell, medical provision; vagrants
Siena, Kevin 261
Simpson, John 340
Simpson, Richard 289
Sims, Joan 43

Skeggs, John 431
Skinner, John 245
Skinner, Thomas 123
Skull, John 345
Slack, Paul 6, 10
slaves/slavery 73
Slingsby, Lady 42
Slugger, Susan 132
Sly, Clement 255
Sly, William 171
smells/stench 21, 83, 100–1, 111, 369, 370
Smerken, George 421
Smith, Agnes 151
Smith, Anne 251
Smith, Elizabeth 43
Smith, Jasper 104
Smith, Joan 246
Smith, Mary 246, 265
Smith, Robert 167
Smith, Stephen 167
Smith, William 285
Smithwick, Richard 160, 166
smog 71, 101
smugglers 363
Snape, James 54
Snape, Justice 45
Snow, John 102
Soame, Sir Stephen 79
social mobility 30, 31, 436
Sodom 37
sodomy 95
soldiers 38, 40, 103–4, 282, 301, 314, 316
    imitating 120
    *see also* charity
Solloway, Marie 398
Somerset 114, 121
Somerset, Duke of 350
songs 107
Spain/Spaniards 73, 137, 188, 301
Spaniard, William 54
Spanish match 46
'special officers' 308–9
Spedding, J., 225
Speerne, Anthony 108
Spencer, Sir John 63
Spierenburg, Peter 289
spirits 241, 288–9
Spital 123, 150, 187, 424
    sermons 5, 11, 268
    theft 95
    *see also* cutpurses; pickpockets
St Bartholomew's Hospital 11, 12, 23, 64, 115, 125, 254, 260, 262, 263, 264, 265, 266, 268, 269, 306
    attitudes towards 215

St Bartholomew's Hospital (cont.)
  beadles 266
    salaries 300
  'foul wards' 266
  governors 142, 370
  hospitiler 265
  lodging inmates 54
  patients, numbers 261
  sisters 266
St Christopher's Island 289
St James Fair 330
St Paul's Cathedral 6, 41, 47, 81, 87, 104, 107, 173, 188, 219, 339, 359
  beggars 117, 120, 200
  Paul's Churchyard 110, 208, 299, 353
  Paul's Gate 164, 176
  theft 95, 140, 166
  vagrants 110
  see also theft/thieves
St Thomas's Hospital 11, 12, 23, 97, 161, 231, 254, 260, 262, 263, 264–5, 266, 267, 268, 269
  attitudes towards 215
  beadles, salaries 300
  lock 115
  patients, numbers 261
  pox 155, 156
stables 108
Stadborne, John 318
Stafford, John 427
Staffordshire 363
standards of living 33
Stanhope, John 245
Stanley, Agnes 171
Stanley, Gervase 255
Stanley, Thomas 221
Stansby, Margaret 374
Stapleton, John 264
star chamber 23, 50, 88, 94, 142, 143, 217–18, 222–4, 230, 231, 236, 293, 295, 330, 337, 342, 363, 370, 396
  see also cutpurses
Starkey, Mary 424
Steele, John 121, 324
Stephen, John 168
Stephenson, Alice 197
Stephenson, John 141
Stephenson, Monger 119
Stevens, Dorothy 312
Stevens, Mary 131
Stewart, Alan 225
Steyre, Sybil 120
stocks 93, 98, 128, 253, 306
Stone, Francis 336
Stonehill, Robert 108

Stoole, John 184
Stow, John 2, 3, 5, 7, 10, 36
  *Survey of London* 2, 3, 4, 76, 303, 400
Strafford, Earl of 33, 350
Strange, Mary 168
Street, John 105, 318
Streetly, Hannah 378
street-sellers 39, 46, 77, 123–34, 208, 235, 307, 308, 313, 316, 396
  books/pamphlets/news 126
  churches 125–6
  disorders 126–7, 131–3
  numbers growing 124
  plague 133
  preventive polices 127–31
  Royal Exchange 126–7
  theft 131–2
  see also censuses/counts/'surveys'; sabbath; women
streets 100–1
  cleaning 18, 100, 101, 305, 395
  poor condition 84
Strone, John 356
Strype, John 400
Styles, Walter 105
Styles, William 105
Styring, Anne 134
subsidy book/rolls 296, 313, 314, 322
subsidymen, status 142
suburbs 2, 29, 78–80, 160, 164–5, 317, 409, 435
suicide 258
summary justice 20, 204, 363, 365, 367, 384, 385
surgeons 261, 262, 266, 267, 269
surveillance 11, 41, 50, 191, 400–32, 437
Sutton's Hospital 7
Swaine, Walter, 373
Sweden 281
Symon, Bartholomew 119
Symons, Nicholas 421

tables 417–18
Tailor, Joan 250
Tailor, Richard 356
Tailor, Thomas 169, 195
Tankered, John 121
Tannenbaum, Frank 179
Tawney, R. H. 102
tax lists/rolls 191, 406, 418
Tayleford, Henry 222
Taylor, Agnes 375
Taylor, Alice 124
Taylor, Anne 121
Taylor, Francis 278

# Index

Taylor, George 47
Taylor, John 99
   *The Carriers Cosmographie* 106
Taylor, Mary 273–4, 355
Taylor, Richard 169
Temple 94, 296, 319, 372
   *see also* beggars/begging; theft/thieves
Tench, Samuel 265
Thames 83, 232, 258, 284
   accidents 91, 383
   dredging 18
   riverside, crime 91, 113
   riverside, policing 91, 314, 350
theft/thieves 21, 22, 35, 39, 40, 43, 45, 75, 79, 81, 82, 87, 89, 101, 106, 140, 143, 144, 145, 146, 147, 150, 154, 156, 158, 159, 185, 186, 187, 188, 189, 191, 196–7, 201, 204, 207, 229, 241, 242, 244, 251, 257, 264, 265, 266, 271, 272, 279, 280, 281, 301, 330, 332, 333, 343, 347, 350, 351, 352, 355, 358, 364, 365, 366, 372, 389, 396, 398, 399, 405, 419, 420, 423, 424, 426, 427, 430, 431, 435, 436, 437, 438, 439, 440–1
   Bartholomew Fair 86
   bridge 90, 91
   career/living by 148
   churches 95
   families 166–7
   fields 92
   lodging houses 160–2, 167
   markets 90, 147
   press (army) 283
   quarter sessions 94
   rackets in stolen goods 163, 311–12
   receivers 97, 132, 153, 163–6, 221, 236, 241, 423, 424
      sex-ratio 204
   Royal Exchange 94
   sex-ratio 204
   St Paul's 95
   teachers 166–7, 170
   Temple 94
   transported 286
   tricks/techniques/tools 167–9, 248
   *see also* fire; labels/labelling; maidservants; prostitution; Royal Exchange; servants; Spital; St Paul's cathedral; street-sellers; Westminster Abbey
thief-takers 311, 312
Thomas, Evan 429
Thomas, John 231, 347
Thompson, Elizabeth 248
Thompson, John 248
Thompson, Judith 238
Thompson, William 120
Thorne, Margery 429
Thorowgood, John 121
Thorpe, Richard 102
Tiffin, Anthony 236, 254
Timbs, John 10
tinkers 123
   press (army) 282
tithes 398
   *see also* registers
Tittler, Robert 311
tobacco 119, 271, 282, 355
   *see also* censuses/counts/'surveys'
Todd, Edward 115
torture 243, 249, 253
Tosser, Thomas 144
Totley, Joanne 249
Tower (of London) 173, 297, 414
   *see also* liberties
trading, illegal 39, 40
traffic 38, 39, 71, 98–100
trained bands 93, 104, 304, 315, 316
transportation 155, 284–9, 431, 438
   destinations 286
   escaping 289
   numbers 285
   parents'/masters' consent 287
   'voluntary' 286
   *see also* ballad-sellers/singers; beggars/ begging; charity; cozeners/cheaters; curfew; drunkards/drunkenness; nightwalkers/nightwalking; nips; pickpockets; theft/thieves; vagrants
Transylvania/Transylvanians 72
treasury 363
Trenitt, John 284
Tribe, Elizabeth 42
Triffe, Issac 90
Trinity College, Cambridge 171
tripewives 125
Tristram, William 186
Trosse, Jane 153, 176, 267
Trumball, Philip 285
Tunks, Richard 426
Turkey/Turks 73, 190, 265, 301
   vagrants 114
Turner, John 38
Turner, Mary 246
Turner, Richard 318
Turner, Walter 147
Turrell, Hugh 325
Tuss, Mary 388
Tyburn 139, 155, 235, 241, 273, 276, 302

# 542  Index

Udall, Gawen 256
underworlds 137, 138, 139, 140–1
unemployment 33
Uppley, Bridget 373
Usher, Anne 427

vagrants 7, 8, 11, 12, 13, 14, 16, 21, 22, 28, 35, 38, 39, 40, 41, 42, 43, 49, 51, 79, 82, 84, 86, 87, 89, 91, 94, 101, 102–12, 131, 132, 133, 141, 145, 146, 154, 155, 156, 171–2, 185, 187, 189, 195, 199, 201, 203, 214, 219, 231, 234, 238, 241, 248, 251, 257, 260, 262, 264, 266, 271, 272, 279, 280, 281, 282, 288, 297, 298, 301, 303, 304–5, 307, 308, 309, 311, 312, 314, 315, 316, 317, 319, 321, 324, 326–8, 334, 343, 347, 350, 351, 353, 357, 358, 362–8, 372, 375, 379, 384, 386, 389, 390, 391, 393, 411, 414, 416, 420, 425, 426, 427, 430, 431, 434, 435, 436, 439, 440–1, 441
  abusing officers and magistrates 104–5
  abusing passers-by 105
  attitudes towards 143
  Bartholomew Fair 86
  bridge 91
  children 105–6
  defined 142, 388
  dropping dead 92, 109
  gangs 110
  giving birth 92, 109–10
  jugglers 107
  lodging places 111
  musicians 107
  passports, numbers 305
  pregnant 21, 55–60, 66, 124, 208, 314, 397
  press (army) 282, 283, 283–4
  prosecutions rising 203–4
  'sad' and 'silly' 107–9
  sex-ratio 69, 204–5
  sickness 109
  stench/filth 200, 253
  transported 286, 287
  *see also* boarding/lodging houses; censuses/counts/'surveys'; charity; churchyards; crown/royal officials; ditches; France/Frenchmen; Ireland/Irish; labels/labelling; London, outlying places; Parliament, statutes; registers; Scotland/Scottish; St Paul's Cathedral; Turkey/Turks; Wales
Varrante, Judith 251

Vaughan, Elizabeth 237
Vaughan, Katherine 118, 190
Vaughan, Owen 154, 161
Veasey, Simon 59, 60
Venables, David 120
Venables, Thomas 235, 254
vestries 30, 32, 171, 234, 293, 294, 295, 296, 297, 304, 327, 345, 348, 376, 394, 396, 402, 406, 411, 414, 415, 417, 418
  social discrimination 32
  vestry books 22, 53, 369, 416
victimless crimes 366–7
victuallers, unlicensed 310
Viner, William 170
violence, female 189
Virginia 89, 148, 156, 285–9, 315, 411
Virginia Company 284
virginity 'searches'/'tryals' 271–5
Volmer, Agnes 132
Von Wedel, Lupold 11

Wade, Sir William 236
Wadley, Edward 186
Waffoll, Richard 187
Wales 187, 245, 248, 374
  vagrants 113, 114
Walker, Anne 62
Walker, Elizabeth 186, 249
Walker, Margaret 426
Walker, James 287
Walker, Thomas 235
Wall, Maudley 376
Waller, Henry 154, 162
Waller, Katherine 90
Wallie, Susan 416
Wallinger, Gillian 283
Wallins, Thomas 286
walls 235
Walsh, Elizabeth 78
Walsingham, Sir Francis 408
wanderers, sex-ratio 205
Ward, Joseph 80
Ward, Justice 44
Ward, Richard 264
warders 93, 297, 298, 303, 304, 308, 313–14, 326, 380, 381, 439
  Slater 300
  abuses against 93, 318, 323
  abuses by 316, 327
  arrests by 300
  bonuses/top-up payments 302
  salaries 300
  *see also* Bridewell, committals; informers/information

# Index

wards/wardmotes 3, 23, 67, 111, 127, 202, 233, 234, 240, 282, 292, 295, 296, 303–4, 306, 308, 312, 313, 314, 325, 344, 345–6, 353, 369, 377, 378, 379, 391, 394, 394–5, 401
  books 23
  *see also* Bridewell, committals
Ware 428
Warren, Margaret 152
watch/watchmen 42, 57, 58, 85, 86, 88, 91, 104, 107, 142, 147, 156, 184, 202, 254, 303, 305, 308, 313, 315, 332, 333, 334, 335, 336, 336–7, 340, 342, 347, 349–59, 378, 380, 394, 420, 426, 440, 441
  abuses against 319, 323
  abuses by 174, 231, 353–7
  bonuses/top-up payments 301
  Midsummer Watch 351
  numbers 304, 350
  poor quality 354
  privilege, claiming 354
  salaries 301
  *see also* Bridewell, committals; censuses/counts/'surveys'; London Bridge
watch-houses 359
water supply 6, 7, 235
waterbearers 47
Waterman, Julian 159
watermen 44
  disorders 91, 113, 144, 160, 281
Watford 190, 383
Watkins, John 424
Watson, Charles 172
Watson, Katherine 143
Watson, William 255, 257
Wattwood, Richard 148, 151, 152, 163, 177
Wayneman, Alice 427
Webb, Anne 77
Webb, John 376, 430
Webb, Richard 286
Webb, Simon 184
Webb, William 60
Webbe, George 37
Weed, Nicholas 258
Welch, Elizabeth 63
wells 370
Wells, Dorothy 208
West, Humphrey 282
West Country 113
Westminster 50, 59, 60, 61, 80, 101, 115, 120, 134, 160, 174, 312, 322, 334, 340, 364, 369, 396

Abbey
  theft 95
  *see also* pickpockets
court of burgesses 22, 80
markets 128
St James Fair 214
waits 340
  *see also* house of corrections/bridewells
Westminster, parishes
  St Clement Danes 111, 161, 326, 340, 376
  St Martin-in-the-Fields 38, 50, 55, 117, 326, 411, 416
  St Margaret's 16, 38, 126, 401–2, 416
Weston, Jane 148, 164
Wetherall, Joanne 134
Wetton, Isabel 125
Wetton, William 259
Whalley, Margaret 425
Wheeler, Helen 257
Wheeler, Rice 431
Whelpston, Elizabeth 286
Whetson, John 168
Whetstone 103
whipping 42, 47, 64, 111, 112, 115, 118, 120, 181, 184, 189, 216, 222, 223, 231, 233, 239, 247, 248, 249, 253, 262, 265, 274, 275–6, 277, 279, 287, 289–90, 301, 306, 326, 427, 430
whipping post 275, 306
Whitacre, Anne 274
White, Agnes 148
White, Elizabeth 132, 187
White, James 381
White, John 166
White, Thomas 158
White Lion Prison 431
Whitehorn, Jane 392
Whitsun ales 327
Whittington, Dick 4, 30, 31, 65
whoremongers/whoremasters 201, 203, 217, 255, 256, 266, 394
'whores' 104, 133, 149, 151, 159, 160, 187, 195, 203, 214, 217, 255, 266, 272, 301, 422, 426
  Royal Exchange 94
  *see also* labels/labelling
Wickham, Alice 254
widows 68
Wilbrome, Robert 108, 259
Wilcock, Robert 171
Wild, Jonathan 312
Wildiung, Patrick 72
Wiles, William 115, 148
Wilkes, Anne 150

Wilkinson, Anne 63
Wilkinson, Jane 124
Wilkinson, Robert 168
William, Christopher 132
Williams, Agnes 219
Williams, Alice 59
Williams, Anne 146
Williams, Hugh 310
Williams, John 108
Williams, Katherine 152
Williams, Margaret 254
Williams, Walter 169
Williamson, John 121
Williamson, Robert 296
wills 415, 416
  *see also* registers
Wilmott, George 168
Wilson, Adrian 65
Wilson, Agnes 323
Wilson, Elizabeth 319
Wilson, James 158
Wilson, Katherine 123
Wilson, Richard 95, 159
Wilson, William 70
Wilton, Anne 288
Wilton, John 286
Wiltshire 121
Winter, Richard 141
Wise, Dorothy 151
Wise, Thomas 43, 177, 218, 223–4
witches/witchcraft 195, 364, 365, 375
Wither, John 264
Withers, Frances 172
Withers, Sir William 172
Wolfe, William 371
women 31, 235
  conveying away pregnant vagrants 57–9, 380
  helping pregnant vagrants 59, 60
  independence, suspicions 134
  metropolitan women 67–9, 124, 207–9
  migrants 134, 207–8
  reporting domestic disorders/sexual crimes 373
  searches for abandoned children 380
  street-selling 98, 124
  urban growth 67–9, 206–9
Wood, Dennis 171
Wood, Mary 425
Wood, Nicholas 184
Wood, Thomas 374
Woodbridge, Linda 139
Woodward, Dorothy 174
Wootten, Frances 254
Worcester, Earl of 217
workhouse 416
Worrall, William 120
Wotten, Francis 428
Wray, Anne 118
Wray, Mary 121
Wrey, Jasper 218
Wright, Jeremy 169
Wright, Thomas 167, 310
Wright, William 263
Wyatt, Henry 282
Wylye, Joan 63
Wynch, Robert 364
Wynott, Emme 266

Yarner, Joseph 278
yarnwives 125, 127
Yeomans, Jane 254
Yorkshire 134, 185, 190
Young, Agnes 43
Young, Joanne 330
Young, John 373
young people 31, 42, 95
  leniency 257

Zeager, Elizabeth 159